PEARSON

ALWAYS LEARNING

J. Michael Hogan • Patricia Hayes Andrews •
James R. Andrews • Glen Williams

Public Speaking and Civic Engagement
with Additional Materials
by Mary E. Triece

Third Custom Edition for the University of Akron

D1302473

Taken from:
Public Speaking and Civic Engagement, Third Edition
by J. Michael Hogan, Patricia Hayes Andrews,
James R. Andrews, and Glen Williams

Pearson Learning Solutions, 501 Boylston Street, Suite 900, Boston, MA 02116
A Pearson Education Company
www.pearsoned.com

Printed in the United States of America

1 2 3 4 5 6 7 8 9 10 V354 17 16 15 14 13

000200010271765580

MC

ISBN 10: 1-269-32457-8
ISBN 13: 978-1-269-32457-1

BRIEF CONTENTS

CONTENTS

PART II Developing Your Speech

PART III   Presenting Your Speech

PREFACE

Alot has happened since we published the first edition of *Public Speaking and Civic Engagement* in 2008. In some ways, the world has changed dramatically. We elected the first African-American president in U.S. history. We have endured the worst economic downturn since the Great Depression. New technologies and social networking sites have changed how we communicate, do business, and participate in civic life. There are now many different ways to be a "good citizen" because new patterns of communication and civic engagement have replaced "politics as usual." Today, more and more young people are "getting involved" in ways unimaginable just a few years ago, both in their own communities and as part of national or even international political or social movements.

Of course, some things never seem to change. Even as we bring an end to the long war in Afghanistan, we see ominous new threats on the horizon—in Syria, Iran, and elsewhere around the world. Signs of economic recovery have been evident in recent years, yet a growing European debt crisis threatens to throw our economy back into recession. Meanwhile, we continue to debate health care reform, educational policy, environmental protection, immigration, and countless other contentious issues. At times, our political debates seem so heated and polarized that we cannot imagine them ending in agreement and compromise. Yet somehow our democracy survives the most vigorous, even passionate debates. Indeed, robust debate is necessary to maintain the health of our deliberative democracy.

As citizens, we have a responsibility to participate in debate and deliberation over issues of public importance. And that requires that we learn how to *communicate* with others—how to share our insights and ideas, how to listen carefully and critically, and how to deliberate with our fellow citizens. This book can help you become a better communicator *and* a better citizen. It will help you understand both the principles of public speaking and your rights and responsibilities as a citizen in a democracy.

WHAT'S NEW IN THE THIRD EDITION?

The third edition of *Public Speaking and Civic Engagement* retains the most popular features of the first two editions, but we have added several new features and updates, and we continue to strive for a more concise, accessible style throughout the book. Although the basic principles of effective speaking remain the same, we have revised and expanded our coverage of several important topics, including communication apprehension and critical listening. We have also updated examples, statistics, and other types of information throughout the book, and we have included still more material from actual student speeches. At the same time, we cut less useful or outdated material and eliminated some redundancies in earlier editions. The result is a somewhat shorter book, yet one still packed with practical guidance and the latest information about the political, cultural, and technological developments that affect public speaking.

The most noticeable change may be that this new edition has one fewer chapter. In response to reviewer suggestions, we have eliminated the overlap in the first two chapters by combining them into one. The ethics of speech remains a central concern of the book, however, and we have added a number of new features and examples. In addition, we have clarified and emphasized more the learning objectives in each chapter. Users of earlier editions will notice other changes as well, including the following revisions:

Chapter 1:

- A more concise introduction to the role of public speaking in a democratic society, combining material previously in the first two chapters of the book
- A more upbeat discussion of the role of young people in American politics, taking note of a variety of different ways that young people "get involved" in their communities
- Updated examples from the presidency of Barack Obama, the 2012 Republican primaries, and other recent events
- A continued emphasis on the ethics of public speaking, with more concise discussions of ghostwriting, plagiarism, and other ethical issues

Chapter 2:

- A completely revised chapter integrating the basic principles of speaking and listening
- Increased emphasis on how to listen critically
- A new *Focus on Civic Engagement* feature about building a climate for peace through better listening
- A new article by former congressman Lee Hamilton on how to listen to politicians

Chapter 3:

- A new, more in-depth discussion of communication apprehension and speaking with confidence
- An expanded discussion of how communication apprehension can adversely impact academic and job performance, and an expanded treatment of factors that contribute to communication apprehension
- A new *Highlighting Communication Apprehension* feature describing college programs that help students manage their communication apprehension
- A new bulleted list of physiological reactions associated with speaking anxiety
- A new list of key questions speakers should ask about their audience and the occasion as they prepare to speak

Chapter 4:

- An expanded discussion of economic status as a consideration in audience analysis
- A new *Highlighting Religion and Politics* feature focusing on Mitt Romney's Mormon religion
- A new *Highlighting Audience Demographics* feature reflecting on what it means to be "rich" in America
- A new *Focus on Civic Engagement* feature about the role of group membership—specifically, union membership—in motivating people to get involved in politics

Chapter 5:

- An expanded discussion of the speaker's ethical obligations in choosing a topic

Chapter 6:

- Updated coverage of online searches and how to search more efficiently
- A revised discussion of utilizing library resources, particularly subscription databases
- New coverage of how to use online networks and social media for information gathering

Chapter 7:

- A new *Highlighting Specific Examples* feature, quoting a speech by Senator Richard Lugar on the need to ratify the "Law of the Seas" convention
- A new *Focus on Civic Engagement* feature, looking at the use of contrast in a story about the differences among candidates in the GOP presidential primaries

Chapter 8:

- Expanded examples illustrating how to promote clarity in organizing ideas
- A new example illustrating the categorical pattern of organization
- New examples of transitions and introductory devices, including previews, summaries, visualizing the future, and the use of quotations

Chapter 9:

- An expanded discussion of different types of outlines
- Clarification of the relationship between formal and keyword outlines
- Fresh information and statistics in all sample outlines

Chapter 10:

- A new feature, *Highlighting Active and Interesting Language*, showing how an advocate for the homeless made effective use of language to make his argument more emotionally compelling

Chapter 11:

- A new feature, *Highlighting Eye Contact,* about cultural differences relating to eye contact and gaze
- A new table listing patterns of eye contact that should be avoided
- A new table listing nonverbal behaviors to avoid when speaking
- Fresh new examples illustrating key principles of delivery

Chapter 12:

- A new *Highlighting* feature on *Prezi,* an increasingly popular alternative to PowerPoint
- New material comparing different methods of delivery and new advice on how to handle the question-and-answer period following your speech

Chapter 13:

- A new outline illustrating the spatial pattern of organization
- An expanded discussion of devices for capturing and maintaining your audience's attention
- A new annotated speech illustrating the principles of informative speaking, "Preparing Students for Community Involvement"

Chapter 14:

- New examples from the 2012 State of the Union address, the Republican presidential primaries, the shooting of Representative Gabrielle Giffords, and other recent news events
- An updated *Focus on Civic Engagement* feature on the efforts of former presidents Bush and Clinton to promote civil discourse

Chapter 15:

- Clearer definitions and updated references to online sources on reasoning and fallacies

Chapter 16:

- New examples of vivid language and rhythmic phrasing in famous ceremonial speeches

Chapter 17:

- A new *Focus on Civic Engagement* feature on *A Crucible Moment,* a report from the U.S. Department of Education calling for a national effort to improve "civic learning" in colleges and universities
- An expanded and updated discussion of study circles and town hall meetings
- A new feature, *Highlighting Leadership,* with practical tips for running more efficient and productive meetings
- A new list of the various "task" and "building and maintenance" roles that group members might enact as members of a committee or other deliberative group

OUR APPROACH AND THEMES

Three convictions continue to guide our approach to *Public Speaking and Civic Engagement*:

- We believe that public speaking is not just a valuable personal skill but also an important part of engaged citizenship in a democracy. You will deliver many speeches in your life, but the most important will be those you deliver as a citizen.
- We approach public speaking as a collaborative partnership between the speaker and the audience. No speaker can succeed alone—the audience is crucial to the planning, delivery, and outcome of the speech.
- We view public speaking as more than a set of performance skills. Truly successful speakers have ideas or information worth communicating. They think critically and reason soundly, and they are not just effective speakers, but also careful and critical listeners, engaged citizens, and ethical human beings.

The Speaker as Citizen

Preparing a classroom speech should be no different from planning a speech for a business conference or a town hall meeting. The classroom is a public space, and your fellow students are citizens. You should treat a speech to your classmates as seriously as you would a speech to any other group of co-workers or citizens.

In treating public speaking as a type of civic engagement, this book encourages you to develop an ethic of active participation. It urges you to read widely and reflectively, and it holds you responsible for becoming well informed about your topic. As you begin to seek out opportunities to speak in public, you will learn to listen critically yet also to respond in a spirit of mutual respect and cooperation. You will learn to speak persuasively, but you also will be encouraged to join *with* your fellow citizens in a spirit of inquiry and common cause. As you work with others to find solutions to our common problems, you will come to understand what it means to deliberate "in good faith."

The emphasis on civic engagement makes this book different from many public speaking books. Some books treat public speaking as a tool of personal success—a skill that you need to "beat the competition" or climb the ladder of success. We approach public speaking as something more than that. Emphasizing ethical and civic concerns, we view public speaking as an essential tool of democratic citizenship. Protected by the First Amendment to our Constitution, our right to free speech distinguishes us from citizens in totalitarian states and empowers us to govern ourselves. In this book, speech is treated as a means for defining our purposes and identity as a nation, discussing the choices we face, and resolving the differences and disagreements among us. Even ceremonial speeches are treated as important expressions of our democratic culture and traditions. Your course in public speaking will contribute to your personal and professional success. But the best reason to study public speaking is that it will help you become a better citizen. By becoming a better speaker, you will be better prepared to participate in civic life.

The Speaker-Audience Partnership

This book does not treat the audience as something to be changed or manipulated, but rather as an active partner in the communicative process. From the earliest stages of planning a speech to the question-and-answer period that may follow, your listeners will be important to your success. You need to consider your listeners' needs and interests in tandem with your own. You need to ask these questions: What are my listeners' priorities and concerns? How can I persuasively advance my own ideas while still respecting their values and beliefs? Am I open to being influenced by my audience even as I try to persuade them? What can I do to promote a genuine spirit of democratic deliberation in which my audience and I have a shared interest in finding common ground?

When considering your audience, it is important to recognize that our society is now more diverse than ever before. Your audience may consist of people of all genders, races, and religions. It may even include people from other parts of the world. At the very least, your audience will have widely varying interests and values and hold differing political or religious opinions. Respecting this diversity is crucial to connecting with your audience. In this book, we recognize the challenges of communicating in an increasingly diverse society, yet we also stress the need for people to come together in a spirit of dialogue and collaboration. If we hope to find solutions to our common problems, we need to communicate effectively and work together to realize our shared goals.

Respecting the speaker-listener partnership is more than a practical necessity; it is an ethical obligation. Ethical speakers keep in touch with the audience's needs, concerns, and welfare, even as they pursue their own purposes in speaking. In *Public Speaking and Civic Engagement*, we treat the speaker-listener partnership as both a practical necessity and an ethical responsibility.

The Citizen-Critic

By studying public speaking, you will become not only a better speaker but also a more careful and engaged listener—one who pays close attention when other people speak and thinks carefully about what they are saying. In our mass-mediated society, we can point to any number of speakers who try to fool the public with a "slick" delivery or deceptive, even manipulative speeches. As a student of public speaking, you will learn to recognize and resist the techniques of these demagogues and propagandists. You will learn to be a more critical consumer in the "marketplace of ideas."

Our democracy rests on the assumption that ordinary citizens are smart enough to govern themselves. Yet it is not always easy to distinguish between sound, well-reasoned arguments and speeches carefully designed to distract or mislead us. Part of your responsibility as a citizen is to learn *how* to distinguish between good and bad arguments, between speeches that contribute something valuable to public discussion and those that serve only the selfish interests of the speaker. By studying public speaking, you will learn to listen carefully and think critically about the speeches you hear. You will learn how to evaluate the quality of a speaker's evidence and reasoning. You will study ethical principles that have been part of the study of speech for centuries, and you will become familiar with famous speeches in history that both promoted and violated those principles. In short, you will become a "citizen-critic"—a careful and informed listener who holds all who speak in public to high intellectual and ethical standards.

SPECIAL FEATURES

Public Speaking and Civic Engagement offers a number of distinguishing features designed to make the book an engaging teaching and learning tool.

A Unique Approach

A strong introductory chapter establishes the unique framework of the book by highlighting the connections between public speaking and democratic citizenship. From the start, you will be encouraged to think of public speaking not just as a tool of personal success, but also as a way to serve others in a democratic society. The introductory chapter also sets a strong ethical tone for the book, introducing the theme that public speaking entails certain responsibilities beyond your personal interests: the responsibility to become well informed on your topic, for example, and to respect those who sincerely disagree with your views. The book includes chapters on all the topics typically addressed in a public speaking textbook, including communication apprehension, audience analysis, organization, and style. Yet throughout the book, the focus on civic engagement is sustained by an emphasis on the ethics as well as the techniques of public speaking and by historical and contemporary examples of both responsible and irresponsible speakers.

Among the unique chapters of the book are those discussing the various *types* of public speaking. Distinguishing persuasive from informative speaking in terms of the situations that "invite" persuasion, the book defines *public controversy* and discusses a speaker's *burden of proof* in various situations. It also discusses different ways to prove your claims and to make reasonable arguments based on sound evidence and reasoning. At the same time, it sustains a strong emphasis on the ethics of persuasion, distinguishing between responsible persuasion and the manipulative and deceptive techniques of the propagandist or demagogue. The book also offers the first serious treatment of ceremonial speaking as a mode of civic engagement and community building, and its chapter on communicating in groups focuses on town hall meetings and other deliberative forums. In these chapters and throughout the book, the emphasis is not only on how to prepare an effective speech but also on the importance of being a committed and responsible speaker. That is what makes this book unique: it combines sound instruction in the techniques of public speaking with a sustained emphasis on the ethics of speech and the importance of public speaking and civic engagement in our democratic society.

Focus on Civic Engagement

Most chapters include boxed special features showcasing real-world examples of politicians, celebrities, students, and ordinary citizens who have made a difference by speaking out or otherwise getting involved in the civic life of their community or their nation. These stories about real people—young and old, famous and not so famous—are designed both to illustrate course concepts and to inspire students to get involved themselves.

> **FOCUS ON CIVIC ENGAGEMENT | "Granny D" Gets Involved**
>
> In 1995, a newly proposed law regulating campaign financing, the McCain-Feingold bill, failed to win congressional approval. In New Hampshire, 85-year-old Doris Haddock decided to do something about it. Incensed that some congressional leaders had stated that the American public didn't care about the issue, Haddock—or "Granny D," as she became known—decided on a dramatic gesture to attract attention to the issue and gain support for reform.
>
> After getting into shape by taking long walks around her hometown of Dublin, New Hampshire, Granny D set out to walk across the country to rally support for campaign finance reform. On January 1, 1999, she began her walk in Pasadena, California. By the time she arrived in Washington, DC, on February 29, 2000, she was 90 years old and had walked 3,200 miles. In Arizona, she was hospitalized for dehydration and pneumonia. Near the end of her journey, she faced heavy snows and had to cross-country ski for 100 miles between Cumberland, Maryland, and Washington.
>
> All along the way, Granny D gave speeches and urged public support for campaign finance reform. When she reached the nation's capital, she was met by more than 2,000 people, including representatives of various reform groups and several members of Congress. Many of these supporters walked the final miles with her.
>
> Granny D is widely credited with helping to push the final bill into law. Al Gore, in adopting a finance reform plank in his campaign platform during the
>
>
>
> Doris Haddock, better known as "Granny D," talks about campaign finance at the State House in Concord, New Hampshire, on April 20, 2000. Haddock, of Dublin, New Hampshire, walked from California to Washington, DC, to promote campaign finance reform.

Highlighting Key Concepts

Extended examples of key concepts such as ethos, visual literacy, critical listening, fallacies, and cultural diversity are illustrated through special "highlighting" features throughout the book.

> **HIGHLIGHTING LISTENING AND LEADERSHIP**
>
> Listening has been linked to effective leadership in the business and professional world as well as in the public arena.
>
> - Leadership experts, such as Ronald Heifetz of Harvard University, point out that the foundation of good listening is "curiosity and empathy." Excellent listeners are able to look *beyond* the speaker's verbal and nonverbal messages and uncover the underlying argument beneath the disagreement or conflict.
> - Former Chrysler CEO, Lee Iacocca (credited with saving Chrysler from bankruptcy in the 1980s), emphasizes the strong link between motivating employees to give their best efforts and listening to their ideas, questions, and concerns. Even if the "system" labels someone as "average or mediocre," they may truly excel simply because someone has "listened to [their] problems and helped [them] solve them."
>
> well as local government officials as they talked with her about "their concerns and aspirations for the families and communities."
> - Col. Eric Kail, the course director of military leadership at the U.S. Military Academy at West Point, argues that a good leader is empathetic—he or she connects with others by listening carefully to what they have to say and resists the temptation simply to wait for them to pause to speak.
> - In 2009, President Obama traveled to London for the first time during his presidency. He expressed a balanced commitment to advancing ideas and listening thoughtfully and responsively. He had come, he said, "to listen and not to lecture."
>
> *Sources:* From Andrew D. Wolvin, "Listening Leadership, *International Journal of Listening* 19. Copyright © 2005 by *International Journal of Listening;* from Eric Kail, "Leadership Character: The Role of Empathy," http://www.washingtonpost.com/blogs/guest-insights/post/leadership-character-the-role-

Annotated Speeches

Nearly half of the book's chapters conclude with an annotated speech that offers critical commentary and analysis. Each speech deals with a substantive issue and provides a real-world illustration of civic engagement. The speakers include political figures, celebrities, students, and ordinary citizens, and the speeches cover a range of issues such as global climate change, health care reform, and the role of young people in politics.

> **NOTRE DAME COMMENCEMENT SPEECH**
>
> President Barack Obama
>
> *Sunday, May 17, 2009, Notre Dame, Indiana*
>
> When President Obama was invited to speak at the University of Notre Dame, critics of his stand on abortion, among them some students, a number of Catholic bishops, and outside anti-abortion groups, staged protests on the campus and spoke out on the national news. Their contention was that a Catholic university should not honor a leader who held views contrary to official Catholic doctrine. The university and a large majority of students, however, approved of the president's visit. This controversy formed the backdrop against which the speech was given.
>
> Thank you, Father Jenkins, for that generous introduction. You are doing an outstanding job as president of this fine institution, and your continued and courageous commitment to honest, thoughtful dialogue is an inspiration to us all.
>
> Good afternoon, Father Hesburgh, Notre Dame trustees, faculty, family, friends, and the class of 2009. I am honored to be here today, and grateful to all of you for allowing me to be part of your graduation.
>
> THE PRESIDENT BEGINS WITH AN OBLIQUE REFERENCE TO FATHER JENKINS'S REFUSAL TO BOW TO PRESSURE TO WITHDRAW THE INVITATION, LABELING IT COURAGEOUS AND SUPPORTIVE OF THOUGHT-

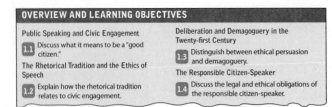

OVERVIEW AND LEARNING OBJECTIVES

Public Speaking and Civic Engagement

1.1 Discuss what it means to be a "good citizen."

The Rhetorical Tradition and the Ethics of Speech

1.2 Explain how the rhetorical tradition relates to civic engagement.

Deliberation and Demagoguery in the Twenty-first Century

1.3 Distinguish between ethical persuasion and demagoguery.

The Responsible Citizen-Speaker

1.4 Discuss the legal and ethical obligations of the responsible citizen-speaker.

Pedagogical Features in Each Chapter

Within the text, we provide a variety of pedagogical features that clarify and reinforce the material or summarize key points. Specifically, each chapter contains:

- An *Overview* and numbered Learning Objectives to emphasize key topics addressed in the chapter
- *Previews* to give readers a map of the material in each section of the chapter
- *Real-world examples* to illustrate, highlight, and clarify principles discussed
- A *Summary* to reiterate the chapter's core concepts
- *Questions for Review and Reflection* to help students review the ideas presented in each chapter and to assist them in test preparation

At the end of the book, a Glossary defines key terms and technical language appearing throughout the book. Another useful pedagogical tool, Questions for Application and Analysis, can be found in the Instructor's Resource Manual.

Instructor and Student Resources

Key instructor resources include the following:

- Instructor's Manual and Test Bank (available at www.pearsonhighered.com/irc; instructor login required) ISBN: 0205931448
- PowerPoint Presentation Package (available at www.pearsonhighered.com/irc; instructor login required) ISBN: 0205931456
- Teacher Training Video
- MyTest online test generating software (available at www.pearsonmytest.com; instructor login required) ISBN: 0205931464
- Pearson Public Speaking Video Library

For a complete listing of the instructor and student resources available with this text, please visit our online catalog at www.pearsonhighered.com/communication.

Service-Learning Resources

For those interested in approaching the course from a service-learning perspective, the Instructor's Manual includes a sample syllabus for a service-learning approach to public speaking. The manual also suggests activities and assignments for a service-learning approach to the course and provides a list of organizations, Web sites, and other resources on service learning.

MyCommunicationLab®

www.mycommunicationlab.com

Our MyLab products have been designed and refined with a single purpose in mind—to help educators create that moment of understanding with their students.

MyCommunicationLab is an online homework, tutorial, and assessment program that truly engages students in learning. It helps students better prepare for class, quizzes, and exams—resulting in better performance in the course—and provides educators a dynamic set of tools for gauging individual and class progress. And, MyCommunicationLab comes from Pearson, your partner in providing the best digital learning experiences.

MyCommunicationLab Highlights:

- **MediaShare:** This comprehensive file upload tool allows students to post speeches, outlines, visual aids, video assignments, role plays, group projects, and more in a variety of file formats. Uploaded files are available for viewing, commenting, and grading by instructors and class members in face-to-face and online course settings. Integrated video capture functionality allows students to record video directly from a webcam and allows instructors to record videos via webcam, in class or in a lab, and attach them directly to a specific student and/or assignment. The MediaShare app is available via iTunes at no additional charge for those who have purchased MediaShare or MyCommunicationLab access.

- **The Pearson eText:** Identical in content and design to the printed text, the Pearson eText lets students access their textbook anytime, anywhere, and any way they want—including downloading to an iPad. Students can take notes and highlight, just like a traditional text.

- **Videos and Video Quizzes:** Videos provide students with the opportunity to watch and evaluate chapter-related multimedia. Many videos include automatically graded quiz questions.

- **Personality Profile:** PersonalityProfile is Pearson's online library for self-assessment and analysis. Online resources provide students with opportunities to evaluate their own and others' communication styles. Instructors can use these tools to show learning and growth over the duration of the course.

- **Study Tools:** A personalized study plan, chapter assessment, key term flashcards, an audio version of the text, and more provide a robust range of study tools to focus students on what they need to know, helping them succeed in the course and beyond.

- **Class Preparation Tool:** Finding, organizing, and presenting your instructor resources is fast and easy with Pearson's class preparation tool. This fully searchable database contains hundreds of resources such as lecture launchers, discussion topics, activities, assignments, and video clips. Instructors can search or browse by topic and sort the results by type. Personalized folders can be created to organize and store content or download resources, as well as upload your own content.

ACKNOWLEDGMENTS

We are indebted to many individuals who provided encouragement, support, and inspiration as we began this project and who helped make the first edition a success. We extend our special thanks to the undergraduates at Indiana University, Southeast Missouri State University, and Penn State University, whose enthusiasm for our approach to public speaking was unwavering, and to the graduate students at these schools, whose passion for critical pedagogy and civic engagement led to provocative discussions and, in some cases, to exciting new ideas.

We also wish to thank a number of friends, current or former students, and colleagues who contributed to either the first or the second edition of the book. Some have served as reviewers, others have supplied ideas or materials used in the book, and all have given us encouragement and inspiration. These include the following:

Rukhsana Ahmed, Ohio University
Kevin J. Ayotte, California State University, Fresno
Diane M. Badzinski, Bethel College
Kristin M. Barton, Dalton State College
Sean Beppler, Syracuse University
Jennifer A. Bieselin, Florida Gulf Coast University
Lynn Borich, Missouri State University
LeAnn M. Brazeal, Kansas State University
Kristine Bruss, University of Kansas
Nanci M. Burk, Glendale Community College
Martín Carcasson, Colorado State University
Ellen R. Cohn, University of Pittsburgh
Linda Czuba Brigance, State University of New York at Fredonia
Donnette Dennis-Austin, Broward College
Cynthia Duquette Smith, Indiana University
Michael Eaves, Valdosta State University
Lyn J. Freymiller, Penn State University
Cory Geraths, Penn State University
Grace Giorgio, University of Illinois
John Gore, Ivy Tech State College
Kathryn Gromowski, Penn State University
Debra Hawhee, Penn State University
Gary Hiebsch, College of the Ozarks
Patricia S. Hill, University of Akron
Tracey Holden, University of Delaware
Mark E. Huglen, University of Minnesota, Crookston
Daisy L. Johnson, Heartland Community College
Hillary Jones, Penn State University
Una Kimokeo-Goes, Willamette University
Stephen A. King, Delta State University
Rick Lindner, Georgia Perimeter College
Steve E. Martin, Ripon College

Rick Maxson, Drury University
Mark May, Clayton State University
Richard McGrath, Central College
Sara Ann Mehltretter Drury, Wabash College
Lisa M. Orick-Martinez, Central New Mexico Community College
Matthew J. Olsen, Southeast Missouri State University
Dean A. Pape, Ripon College
Shawn J. Parry-Giles, University of Maryland
Barry C. Poyner, Truman State University
Claire H. Procopio, Baton Rouge Community College
Kimberly Rosenfeld, Cerritos College
Jody M. Roy, Ripon College
Claudia Ruediger, Southeast Missouri State University
Shawn Spano, San Jose State University
Sanda Tomuletiu, Duquesne University
Mary E. Triece, University of Akron
Esin C. Turk, Mississippi Valley State University
Jill Weber, Hollins University
Katerina Katsarka Whitley, Appalachian State University
Alaina M. Winters, Heartland Community College

We also are grateful for those who were our inspiration and mentors: the late Gayle Compton, Donald Zacharias, Lloyd Bitzer, Stephen E. Lucas, the late J. Jeffery Auer, and the late Robert G. Gunderson—all gifted and caring teachers and engaged citizens of their communities. Through actions and words, they taught us about the importance of communication and what it means to be a good citizen in a democracy.

Finally, we want to thank the staff at Pearson, especially Karon Bowers, our editor-in-chief, who has supported our project, listened to our concerns, challenged our thinking, and made suggestions that improved our work. Others who played an instrumental role in this third edition are editors Corey Kahn and Stephanie Chaisson, and project manager Hema Latha at Integra.

In 1952, William Norwood Brigance, a professor of speech at Wabash College, published his ground-breaking text, *Speech: Its Techniques and Disciplines in a Free Society*. In it, he wrote:

Democracy and the system of speechmaking were born together. Since that early day we have never had a successful democracy unless a large part, a very large part, of its citizens were effective, intelligent, and responsible speakers. Today, as twenty-three centuries ago, a system of speechmaking is imperative for preserving democracy.

Brigance's philosophy inspired our writing of *Public Speaking and Civic Engagement*, and it is to his memory that we again dedicate this book.

MIKE HOGAN
PATTY ANDREWS
JIM ANDREWS
GLEN WILLIAMS

Democratic Citizenship and the Ethics of Public Speaking

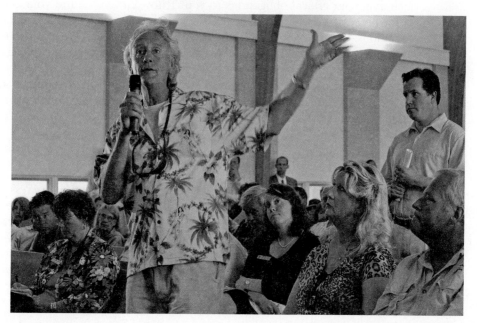

OVERVIEW AND LEARNING OBJECTIVES

Public Speaking and Civic Engagement

1.1 Discuss what it means to be a "good citizen."

The Rhetorical Tradition and the Ethics of Speech

1.2 Explain how the rhetorical tradition relates to civic engagement.

Deliberation and Demagoguery in the Twenty-first Century

1.3 Distinguish between ethical persuasion and demagoguery.

The Responsible Citizen-Speaker

1.4 Discuss the legal and ethical obligations of the responsible citizen-speaker.

What does it mean to be a "good citizen"? For some, it means voting in elections, donating money to political candidates, or making "statements" about their political views by displaying bumper stickers or yard signs. For others, citizenship means getting involved in their local community, perhaps raising money for a worthy cause or joining with neighbors to clean up a local park. Whatever citizenship means to you, it involves sharing ideas with others and talking about important issues and controversies. In other words, being a citizen means *communicating* with others. Throughout history, the ability to communicate effectively has been not only the mark of great leaders but also an important skill for ordinary citizens.

This book is dedicated to helping you become a better speaker—*and* a better citizen. It offers practical advice about preparing and delivering speeches in a variety of public settings. Beyond that, it discusses the responsibilities of citizenship, including your ethical obligations to your fellow citizens and to your community. In the process, we will introduce you to a number of people—both famous and not so famous—who have made a difference by "speaking out." We will also teach you how to recognize and resist the techniques of demagogues and propagandists—those who use the power of speech to manipulate and deceive others. When you complete your course in public speaking, you will have the confidence and skills necessary to participate fully in civic life. More than that, you will have a better understanding of what it means to be a "good citizen."

PUBLIC SPEAKING AND CIVIC ENGAGEMENT

1.1 Discuss what it means to be a "good citizen."

Preview.   *As you read this, you may be a full-time student, a business major, or a student who hasn't yet decided on a major. You are many other things as well. You are a daughter or a son; you may be a single parent, a United Methodist, a part-time employee, a movie buff, a sports fan, or a camp counselor. We all play many different roles in life, but we all have one thing in common: we are citizens in a democracy. Our country's future depends on how well we perform that role. As citizens, we have a responsibility to get involved in the civic life of our communities, and we need public speaking skills to do that effectively.*

In Foxborough, Massachusetts, a local resident named Phillip Henderson organized a group of neighbors to fight plans by a fast-food chain to build a new franchise on an environmentally sensitive site. Henderson's group, the Quality of Life Committee, fought for seven years to stop the development, and the disputed land is now part of a 19-acre protected wetland and wildlife preserve.[1] In Washington State, Pete Knutson, the owner of a small family fishing operation, organized an unlikely alliance of working-class fishermen, middle-class environmentalists, and Native Americans to protect salmon fisheries in the Pacific Northwest. Standing up against powerful special interests, Knutson's alliance pushed for cleaner streams, enforcement of the Endangered Species Act, and an increased flow of water over regional dams to help boost salmon runs.[2]

"Getting involved" is not something just older Americans do. All across America, college and even high school students have been making a difference by participating in politics or other sorts of civic or service activities. In one survey, two-thirds of the respondents between ages 18 and 30 said that they had volunteered their time, joined a civic or service organization, or advocated some public cause in the past three years.[3] In 2002, the Center for Information and Research on Civic Learning and Engagement (CIRCLE) found that more than 40 percent of young people surveyed had participated in a charitable event, and more than half had boycotted some product "because of the conditions under which it was made."[4] In its 2006 survey, CIRCLE again found young people "involved in many forms of political and civic activity," including voting, grassroots organizing, or volunteer work. More than 70 percent of the young people surveyed said they "followed what's going on" in government and public affairs, and more than a third said they had volunteered or participated in "political discussions."[5]

The Challenges of Democratic Citizenship

Unfortunately, not all Americans feel the need to "get involved." Over the past half century, barely half of all eligible Americans have bothered to vote in presidential elections,[6] and the United States continues to trail most of the world's democracies in voter turnout.[7] Young people historically have been especially apathetic about voting. After the 26th Amendment lowered the voting age from 21 to 18 in 1971, turnout among Americans aged 18–24 steadily declined over the next two decades, from 52 percent in 1972 to only 36 percent in 2000.[8] Other indicators of civic engagement have also declined over the past half century because fewer people have been paying attention to the news, attending public meetings, working for political causes, signing petitions, writing to their elected representatives or local newspapers, or speaking at political meetings and rallies.[9] By the mid-1990s, 32 million fewer Americans were involved in these sorts of activities than was the case just two decades earlier.[10]

A crowd of young people participate in a get-out-the-vote rally. The rally reflected the increased participation of young voters in the 2004 and 2008 elections.

Yet there are hopeful signs of civic renewal in America. As scholar Robert Putnam has observed, the terrorist attacks of September 11, 2001, at least "interrupted" the downward trend in "political consciousness and engagement," increasing the public's interest in political affairs to levels "not seen in at least three decades."[11] This spike in political awareness was evident in the 2004 elections, when Americans voted at the highest rate since 1968.[12] In 2008, voters again turned out in record numbers, with 131 million Americans going to the polls to elect the first African-American president in U.S. history. That represented 61.6 percent of the nation's eligible voters, according to George Mason University political scientist Michael McDonald—a level of civic engagement not seen since the 1960s.[13] Still more evidence of a revival in civic engagement is evident in recent surveys of incoming college freshmen that reveal the highest level of political interest since the 1960s.[14] Today's young people not only vote more than young people 20 or 30 years ago,[15] but according to some political scientists, they also have embraced new norms of "engaged citizenship" that are more inclusive and more deeply rooted in democratic ideals than the duty-oriented norms of their parents or grandparents.[16]

Young people are making a difference all across America by working for political causes or by "getting involved in civic activities or volunteer work in their local communities. Some college students even give up their spring breaks to help others. According to Break Away, a nonprofit group that organizes "alternative" spring breaks, nearly 65,000 students from across the country spent their spring vacations in 2009 building homes, tutoring migrant farmworkers or inner-city kids, working with homeless people, or participating in other sorts of volunteer or community service.[17]

Some of the credit for these positive trends must go to the many schools, charitable foundations, and civic groups that have launched new initiatives to promote engaged citizenship, particularly among young people. For example, the Saguaro Seminar, which is an ongoing initiative of the John F. Kennedy School of Government at Harvard University, is working to develop "far-reaching, actionable ideas to significantly increase Americans' connectedness to one another and to community institutions."[18] At the University of Texas, the Annette Strauss Institute for Civic Participation has a similar mission: "(1) to conduct cutting-edge research on how civic participation, community understanding, and communication are undermined or sustained and (2) to develop new programs for increasing democratic understanding among citizens."[19] Another initiative, Project Pericles, provides funding to colleges across the nation to improve their community-service efforts and to "make civic engagement a part of the curriculum in every department."[20] And at the more than 1,100 colleges and universities affiliated with Campus Compact, millions of students have been involved over the past 20 years in a variety of civic and community-service projects.[21]

By volunteering to help others, you can have an immediate, tangible impact. Perhaps that explains why so many young people prefer community service over more "traditional" political activities, such as supporting political candidates or signing petitions. According to CIRCLE, many of today's college students are "turned off" by the "spin" and "polarized debate" of electoral politics, and they seek more "open and authentic" ways to participate in civic affairs. In comparison to Generation X, today's so-called Millennials are more politically active and aware. Yet many are tired of the "competitive and confrontational atmosphere" of electoral politics and are finding new ways to "get involved."[22] Still, if you really hope to make a difference, you can't ignore traditional politics. Many of the problems we face today—including the problems that most concern young people, like the high cost of a college education—are, in the final analysis, *political* problems.

The Engaged Citizen

So we come back to our original question: what does it mean to be a "good citizen"? And what can *you* do to help make the world better? We've already suggested part of the answer: *get involved*, whether that means voting in the next

Watch the Video
"Grant Proposal
Presentations" at
MyCommunicationLab

presidential election, speaking out at a local town hall forum, or volunteering to help others in your community. In recent years, more and more young people are voting, and there are indications that at least some young people are turning to the Internet more frequently for political news and information.[23] But there is more to being a "good citizen" than just voting or being well informed. If you really hope to "make a difference," you need to *communicate* with others, and you need to understand what it means to communicate *responsibly*.

"Getting involved" in politics does *not* mean that you must be loud or combative, like some of the political activists and commentators we see on TV. As political scientist Morris P. Fiorina has suggested, those people seem "completely certain of their views; they are right and their opponents are wrong." They view all who disagree not just as misguided or misinformed, but as "corrupt, stupid, evil, or all three."[24] Most of us are not so sure of ourselves, and we take more moderate, middle-of-the-road positions on complex issues. For most of us, politics is not about scoring points or defeating some enemy; it is about finding solutions to difficult problems. It is about working together to advance the "common good." This is not to say that we should ignore or silence those who feel passionately about some issues—those whom sociologist Eric Hoffer once called "true believers."[25] But while "true believers" have played an important role in American history, giving voice to the powerless and calling attention to injustices that were being ignored, our system of government ultimately depends on accommodating a diversity of voices and finding compromises on tough political issues. As Fiorina concludes, the "less intense and less extreme" voices in politics should be given *at least* as much weight as those of the passionate activists. Not only would that "lower the decibel level of American politics," but it also would focus attention on more "mainstream concerns."[26]

Of course, some people might engage politics or other civic activities just to advance their own selfish interests. It looks good on a résumé or a college or job application to be "involved" in one's community. But civic engagement is about more than career advancement. It is also a commitment to some cause greater than yourself. Wherever you get involved—in your school, at your place of work, in your town, or in a broader national or even international arena—you contribute to the *common* good. Everyone is better off when you get involved. *Somebody* has to take the lead in making our world better. Why not you?

Even busy college students can make a big difference. At Penn State University, for example, the largest student-run charitable organization in the world raises money to fight childhood cancer with an annual dance marathon. "THON," as it is popularly called, involves thousands of students in a variety of activities, from planning the event to the care and feeding of the dancers themselves. THON even has a communications committee for "Penn State students with a passion for spreading the word." To date, this group of involved students has raised more than $78 million to combat pediatric cancer. In 2012 alone, THON raised more than $10.6 million.[27]

The good citizen not only helps others but also strives to be well informed and thoughtful. In a democracy, you have a right to your opinion. At the same time, you have an *ethical* obligation to speak honestly, to know what you're talking about, and to remain open to changing your own mind. Good citizens keep up with current events, and they recognize the difference between an informed opinion and one grounded in ignorance or prejudice. They take advantage of opportunities to

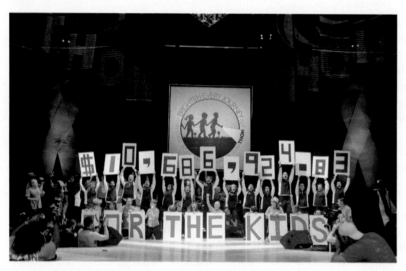

Participants in the 2012 Penn State Dance Marathon hold up signs bearing the grand total of money raised for fighting childhood cancer at that year's "THON": $10,686,924.83.

learn more about the issues, and they carefully weigh all the arguments before forming their own opinions. They may feel strongly about their views, but they respect the opinions of others. Good citizens—people of good will—can and will disagree, sometimes passionately. But they remain committed to free and open debate and to resolving their differences through democratic processes.

Perhaps by speaking out you will someday influence the decision of your local school board or city council. Or by discussing political issues with your neighbors, maybe you will help change public opinion or influence the outcome of an election. You do not have to be a famous politician or a celebrity to make a difference. In the mid-1990s, Doris Haddock, an 85-year-old great-grandmother from New Hampshire, took it upon herself to improve the political process by campaigning for campaign finance reform. Testing both her public speaking skills and her physical endurance, "Granny D" (as her supporters and admirers called her) literally walked across America, speaking to thousands of her fellow citizens—a feat recalled in the following Focus on Civic Engagement. Whatever the results of your *own* ways of participating, it is important—both to you and our democracy—that you get involved. Before you do, however, you should first develop the knowledge and skills you need to "speak out" effectively and responsibly. The principles of effective and ethical speaking date back to ancient times, and they have been handed down to us in what scholars call the *rhetorical tradition*.

THE RHETORICAL TRADITION AND THE ETHICS OF SPEECH

1.2 Explain how the rhetorical tradition relates to civic engagement.

Preview. *Rhetoric is an ancient discipline concerned with the techniques and ethics of speech. The three traditions of scholarship and teaching in rhetoric focus on the knowledge and skills necessary for democratic citizenship:*

- The tradition of rhetorical theory that dates back to ancient Greece and Rome
- The tradition of rhetorical criticism, which emphasizes the critical analysis of public discourse in all its various forms
- The tradition of historical studies in public address, which focuses on the lessons we may learn from the speakers, speeches, social movements, and persuasive campaigns of the past

Each of these traditions helps to define the ethics of speech in a democratic society, and those ethical rules must be kept in mind at every stage of the speech-making process.

The scholarly traditions of rhetorical theory and criticism have something important to teach us. In recognizing rhetoric as one of the oldest scholarly traditions,

---

▶ FOCUS ON CIVIC ENGAGEMENT | "Granny D" Gets Involved

In 1995, a newly proposed law regulating campaign financing, the McCain-Feingold bill, failed to win congressional approval. In New Hampshire, 85-year-old Doris Haddock decided to do something about it. Incensed that some congressional leaders had stated that the American public didn't care about the issue, Haddock—or "Granny D," as she became known—decided on a dramatic gesture to attract attention to the issue and gain support for reform.

After getting into shape by taking long walks around her hometown of Dublin, New Hampshire, Granny D set out to walk across the country to rally support for campaign finance reform. On January 1, 1999, she began her walk in Pasadena, California. By the time she arrived in Washington, DC, on February 29, 2000, she was 90 years old and had walked 3,200 miles. In Arizona, she was hospitalized for dehydration and pneumonia. Near the end of her journey, she faced heavy snows and had to cross-country ski for 100 miles between Cumberland, Maryland, and Washington.

All along the way, Granny D gave speeches and urged public support for campaign finance reform. When she reached the nation's capital, she was met by more than 2,000 people, including representatives of various reform groups and several members of Congress. Many of these supporters walked the final miles with her.

Granny D is widely credited with helping to push the final bill into law. Al Gore, in adopting a finance reform plank in his campaign platform during the 2000 presidential election, credited Senator John McCain, former senator Bill Bradley, and Granny D.

Granny D passed away on March 9, 2010 at the age of 100. In her final years, she remained politically active. In 2003, she launched a drive to register more working women to vote, and in 2004, she ran for the

Doris Haddock, better known as "Granny D," walked from California to Washington, DC, to promote campaign finance reform. She went on to become a popular speaker around the country, and in 2004 she even ran for the U.S. Senate.

U.S. Senate herself. She may not have defeated New Hampshire's incumbent senator, but she did win a respectable 34 percent of the vote.

Source: "In Memory of Granny D Political Activist and Senior Citizen," www.grannyd.com/ (accessed January 16, 2012). ▶

we realize that the ability to communicate in public has long been considered an important part of democratic citizenship. By learning to speak in public and by developing a clear understanding of the *ethics* of speech, we develop what the ancient rhetoricians called civic virtue.

Watch the Video "President Bush's Address to the Nation" at **MyCommunicationLab**

Speaking Responsibly

The study of speech dates back to ancient times, with some of the great Greek and Roman thinkers, including Aristotle and Cicero, counted among the earliest rhetorical theorists. In the classical tradition, personal ethics and civic virtue, or devotion to one's community and the common good, were the cornerstones of rhetorical education. For example, Isocrates, a Greek orator and teacher of rhetoric who lived from 436 to 338 BC, viewed the study of rhetoric not only as preparation for life and leadership in Athenian politics but also as a tool for creating unity out of diversity and defining the "public good." For Isocrates, rhetoric was more than a collection of techniques for persuading an audience. It was a source of the communal values and the moral standards that made democracy itself possible.[28] Similarly, the Roman rhetorician Quintilian described the ideal orator as "a good man skilled in speaking"—with the emphasis on the "good man."[29] Quintilian's ideal orator was more than an effective speaker. He was, first and foremost, a good citizen—a civic leader, a lover of wisdom and truth, a sincere advocate of worthy causes, and a servant of the community. For both Isocrates and Quintilian, responsible orators promoted the best interests of the whole community, not just their own selfish interests.

We must acknowledge the greater challenges of public speaking in the modern world. Unlike the ancients, we live in a diverse, multicultural society, and we must take account of changing social values, new information technologies, and the realities of the consumer age. But that does not mean we cannot still strive to be good citizens and ethical speakers—that is, people who assume the responsibilities of leadership, tell the truth, believe sincerely in our causes, and engage in reasoned and ethical speech. In today's world, it is more important than ever that we rise above our own selfish interests and think about the larger public good. If we hope to resolve the difficult problems we face, we must learn to deliberate *together* and find common ground.

The classical rhetorical tradition still has something important to teach us: that public speaking in a democratic society must be grounded in a strong code of ethics and a commitment to the public good. The classical tradition suggests an approach to public speaking that emphasizes not the techniques of manipulation, but rather the character of the speaker and the shared interests of speakers and listeners. Now more than ever, we need citizens with civic virtue, citizens who know how to deliberate with their fellow citizens. That requires that

"Don't worry too much about math, science, or history — just make sure you get good marks in *rhetoric.*"

Source: Reprinted by permission from www.cartoonstock.com.

we embrace the ideals of Isocrates and the virtues of Quintilian's ideal orator and *demand* that all who speak in public do so responsibly. And that is where the second tradition of scholarship and teaching in rhetoric comes in—the tradition of rhetorical criticism.

Thinking Critically

Today, citizens must be more than skilled speakers. They must also have the skills necessary to critically evaluate the messages of others. In the economic marketplace, we have consumer watchdogs who warn us against false advertising and defective products. But in the "marketplace of ideas," we must learn to protect ourselves against those who may seek to manipulate or deceive us. We must learn how to recognize and resist illogical arguments, misleading or irrelevant evidence, and appeals to our emotions that short-circuit our thinking.

When should we believe that presidential candidate who promises change or that lawyer who publicly declares his client innocent? How do we decide who is speaking ethically—or who has some conflict of interest that might lead to deceptive or manipulative speech? By doing some research, we can often distinguish between advocates who are speaking sincerely and truthfully and those who are not. But often we must render judgments on the spot, without the benefit of research or time for reflection. In the day-to-day world of democratic life, we all must be citizen-critics,[30] ready and able to make our own judgments about who deserves to be believed—and why.

By studying public speaking, you are not only developing your ability to communicate effectively but also learning how to recognize misleading arguments, faulty reasoning, or inadequate evidence in other people's speeches. Demagogues, or speakers who employ "highly suspect means in pursuit of equally suspect ends,"[31] abound in our media-saturated world. So it is important that we, as citizens, recognize and resist their attempts to mislead us. Should we believe that speaker who insists that the U.S. government is actually behind some recent terrorist attack? What about that politician who claims he knew nothing about those illegal campaign contributions? And should we listen to that preacher who insists that all "good Christians" must vote for a particular candidate? Studying the principles and methods of public speaking can help you decide how to respond to such appeals. It can also help you distinguish between a reasonable argument and an attempt to manipulate or deceive.

Obviously, not everything you read or hear is true, so you need to learn how to evaluate competing claims and arguments. Consider, for example, the debate over a national sales tax. Proponents argue that this tax would simplify the tax structure and impose exactly the same burden on all citizens. Those opposed to such a tax insist that it is grossly unfair, placing the greatest burden on those who can least afford to pay. How would you go about sorting out the competing claims of advocates on both sides of this debate? How would you evaluate all the contradictory testimony, statistics, and other forms of evidence? In short, whom should you believe? Students of public speaking learn to take nothing at face value. Becoming a citizen-critic means learning how to evaluate claims, weigh all the evidence, and come to reasoned conclusions based on a careful examination of the arguments on all sides of an issue.

In a democracy, it is not enough that we ourselves speak responsibly; we must also demand that *all* who speak in public live up to high ethical standards. Critical listening and thinking are no less central to the rhetorical tradition than the skills of preparing and delivering a speech. If democratic deliberation is to lead to sound collective judgments, we all must learn to be more critical consumers in the "marketplace of ideas."

Lessons of the Past

Watch the Video "Harry S. Truman's Decision to Drop the Bomb" at **MyCommunicationLab**

Finally, a healthy democracy requires a common store of historical and political knowledge. It requires appreciation for the well-crafted argument and the eloquent speech, as well as an understanding of the American rhetorical tradition and our unique history as a deliberative democracy. In short, it requires some measure of historical and civic literacy. Unfortunately, as Bruce Cole, former chairman of the National Endowment for the Humanities, has noted, Americans have forgotten much of their own country's history, and that historical "amnesia" clouds our vision of the future. "We cannot see clearly ahead if we are blind to history," Cole argues, because "a nation that does not know why it exists, or what it stands for, cannot be expected to long endure." Urging more study of our history and political traditions, Cole concludes: "We must recover from the amnesia that shrouds our history in darkness, our principles in confusion, and our future in uncertainty."[32]

One of the best ways to learn about our past is by studying the great speakers and speeches of American history. The most basic principles of our government were forged by speakers who assumed the responsibilities of leadership and put the public good ahead of their own personal opinions and interests. During the Constitutional Convention, for example, Benjamin Franklin admitted that he had reservations about the proposed U.S. Constitution. Nevertheless, he consented to ratification "because I expect no better, and because I am not sure that it is not the best. The opinions I have had of its errors I sacrifice to the common good."[33] Similarly, Abraham Lincoln is remembered as a great president in part because of his lofty, high-minded speeches in the closing days of the Civil War. Putting that terrible tragedy in perspective and beginning a process of national healing, Lincoln used his second inaugural address to urge "malice toward none" and "charity for all." Pledging to "bind up the nation's wounds," Lincoln pointed the way to "a just and lasting peace among ourselves and among all nations."[34]

Many of the issues and controversies debated in the early years of our republic are still with us today. Past debates shape the way we think about our own times. The great controversy over slavery and the rights of freed slaves after the Civil War echo in today's debates over racial discrimination and affirmative action. In the nineteenth century, Susan B. Anthony's demand for women's suffrage laid the groundwork for today's debates over women's rights and gender equality. Debates over the Pure Food and Drug Act of 1906 foreshadowed today's arguments over genetically engineered foods, food additives, and labeling requirements. We may think we live in an unprecedented age of scientific and technological progress, yet many of the challenges we face today have roots deep in our past.

By studying the great speakers and speeches of the past, we learn not only about the origins of contemporary controversies but also about the principles of public advocacy and democratic deliberation. By examining the speeches of the great African-American abolitionist Frederick Douglass, for example, we can learn how appeals to "higher law" can motivate us to live up to our national ideals. By studying the inaugural addresses and fireside chats of Franklin Roosevelt, we can witness the power of speech to boost morale and promote sacrifice for the common good. By reflecting on how our ancestors debated controversies over America's role in the world or our economic and social policies, we can learn how to disagree while still working together toward common goals. American history is, in large measure, a history of people who made a difference by "speaking out." By studying those voices, we can both learn about our past and find inspiration and guidance for meeting today's challenges.

Watch the Video "Franklin D. Roosevelt's First Inaugural Address" at **MyCommunicationLab**

The Ethics of Speech

Throughout its history, America has seen its share of demagogues and propagandists. For every Lincoln or Roosevelt, we can point to a Joseph McCarthy—the 1950s anticommunist crusader known for his false accusations and character attacks. We can also think of hate groups like the Ku Klux Klan, and we can recall religious cults that have brainwashed people into blind obedience. We sense that all of these speakers, by deceiving and manipulating people, violated some ethical rules. But what *are* our ethical obligations as speakers? When do we have a responsibility to "speak out" in the first place? And what are our ethical responsibilities when we do choose to speak in public?

Explore the Exercise "Ethical Speaking" at **MyCommunicationLab**

Your most basic ethical obligation as a speaker is to tell the truth and take responsibility for what you say. You also have an ethical obligation to give credit where credit is due for ideas or language that you borrow from others. No doubt you recognize that principle from your other classes; you probably have been warned about plagiarism and told to cite your sources. Yet honesty and accountability are more than just academic requirements. They suggest a broader commitment to intellectual honesty and social responsibility—a commitment that we should demand of *all* who speak in public.

Explore the Exercise "Avoiding Plagiarism" at **MyCommunicationLab**

Plagiarism   In a survey of 4,500 high school students in 2002, some 75 percent admitted to cheating in school, with more than half admitting to plagiarizing work they found on the Internet. Even more troubling, some did not see anything wrong with cheating. "What's important is getting ahead," said one student at George Mason High School in Falls Church, Virginia. "In the real world, that's what's going to be going on."[35] Unfortunately, cheating already has become a way of life for this student, and she will probably continue to cheat—at least until she gets caught. Other students do not cheat intentionally but instead commit plagiarism "accidentally." Cheating results not only from the attitude that "getting ahead" is more important than honesty but also from simple carelessness or confusion over what constitutes academic dishonesty.

So what exactly *is* plagiarism? According to Northwestern University's "Principles Regarding Academic Integrity," plagiarism may be defined as "submitting material that in part or whole is not entirely one's own work without attributing those same portions to their correct source."[36] At first glance, this definition makes plagiarism a simple matter: you should never "borrow" all or even part of your speech from somebody else—at least not without acknowledging your sources. Yet the issue is complicated by gray areas in our definitions of plagiarism as well as by confusion over when and how to cite your sources in an *oral* presentation. Thus, it is important that you have a clear understanding not only of what constitutes plagiarism but also of how to avoid inadvertent plagiarism when preparing and delivering a speech.

Students sometimes take shortcuts in their speech class that constitute obvious and deliberate plagiarism. You are obviously guilty of plagiarism if you take your whole speech from a file at your fraternity house, for example, or if you buy your speech from an Internet site that sells ready-made papers and speeches. You are also guilty of plagiarism if you "cut and paste" all or part of your speech from Internet sources. But what if you "borrow" just a few quotations from that same source? Or what if you just paraphrase an article you read, borrowing some information and ideas but putting them into your own words? Does that constitute plagiarism? Here is where misunderstanding the rules may result in accidental plagiarism.

Paraphrasing refers to putting the ideas or insights of others into your own words. When paraphrasing, you should strive for language that differs significantly from the original. Yet that still doesn't excuse you from giving credit for ideas or insights that are not your own. You need not document your own unique insights or conclusions, nor do you need to cite sources for what can be considered common knowledge or generally accepted facts. Yet how do you know when you have a genuinely original idea? And what constitutes common knowledge? Here is a useful rule of thumb: when in doubt, cite your sources.

If you find yourself tempted to take your speech off the Internet, remember that new technologies not only have made it easier to cheat; they also have made it easier to *catch* cheaters. Many teachers now use Internet search engines, or Web sites such as Turnitin.com, in their fight against plagiarism. At Turnitin.com, papers are checked against several massive databases, including more than 10 billion Web sites; more than 70 million student papers already submitted to the site; and more than 10,000 major newspapers, magazines, and scholarly journals. Turnitin even checks papers against an electronic library of thousands of books, including many literary classics. Within seconds, Turnitin.com returns an "Originality Report" highlighting possible instances of plagiarism and linking those passages to their sources. Although Turnitin.com is used mostly by teachers to detect and deter plagiarism, students can also use the site to learn more about how to paraphrase and how to cite their sources properly.[37]

Plagiarism can cost you much more than a good grade on your speech. At most universities, penalties for plagiarism can range from warnings, grade penalties, or academic probation to expulsion from the university and even invalidation of a degree already granted. Beyond the classroom, plagiarism can have serious, real-world consequences. In 1988, for example, Vice President Joseph R. Biden, then a U.S. senator from Delaware, was forced to withdraw from the race for the Democratic presidential nomination when an opposing campaign released a videotape showing him repeating passages taken directly from a speech by British Labour Party leader Neil Kinnock.[38] More recently, Nevada's Republican governor Jim Gibbons, when he was a congressman, delivered a hard-hitting attack on liberals at a Lincoln Day dinner in Elko, Nevada, including this stinging shot at the music and film industries: "I say we [tell] those liberal, tree-hugging, Birkenstock-wearing, hippie, tie-dyed liberals to go make their movies and music and whine somewhere else." Unfortunately for Gibbons, it soon came out that he had stolen almost his entire speech from a copyrighted address delivered in 2003 by Alabama State Auditor Beth Chapman. "Not only is it a bad speech," commented one Democratic Party leader, "it's a bad, stolen speech."[39]

Among those whose reputations have been damaged by accusations of plagiarism are such well-known figures as the Reverend Martin Luther King Jr. and historians Stephen Ambrose and Doris Kearns Goodwin. In these cases, the plagiarism may have been unintentional, but the accusations nevertheless proved embarrassing. At other times, the plagiarism is clearly deliberate, as in the case of a young *New York Times* reporter named Jayson Blair. Blair's blatant use of stolen and fabricated stories led to his own resignation and to the resignations of two high-ranking editors at the *Times*.[40] Plagiarism is *not* just something that you worry about in college. In the "real world," the penalties for plagiarism are severe, and the consequences can be devastating.

Ghostwriting   Presenting somebody else's words or ideas as your own is not always unethical. Since ancient times, ghostwriters, or professional speechwriters, have helped others write their speeches. Although you should never deliver a speech written by somebody else in your speech class, ghostwriting is now considered an inevitable part of our political and corporate culture. Many political and business leaders are simply too busy to write their own speeches. The president of the United States employs a whole team of researchers and speechwriters. Generally, we do not consider this unethical, so long as the speaker takes full responsibility for his or her words.

The earliest ghostwriters actually helped make democracy possible. Assisting citizens as they prepared speeches for the deliberative and legal assemblies of the Greek city-state, the first ghostwriters also *taught* the art of public speaking. Subsequently, ghostwriting "proliferated through the ages," and today almost every speech by a major political, business, or academic leader is "written by someone else."[41] America's first president, George Washington, had a speechwriter:

Alexander Hamilton. So, too, have many other presidents, including some whom we consider among our greatest orators: Franklin Delano Roosevelt, for example, and John F. Kennedy.[42] President Ronald Reagan employed not only a ghostwriter but also a whole team of researchers and writers to help prepare his speeches. One of those writers, Peggy Noonan, wrote many of Reagan's most famous lines.[43] Still, we remember those famous words as the words of Ronald Reagan.

When does ghostwriting become unethical? According to Craig R. Smith, a former presidential speechwriter, ghostwriting becomes unethical when the use of a speechwriter is "hidden from the audience." According to Smith, if "someone who uses a ghostwriter denies it," then he or she is "lying and acting unethically." Beyond that, Smith holds ghostwriters to the same ethical standards to which he would hold any writer or speaker: if their speeches are "purposefully deceptive," then they are unethical. For Smith, as for most professional ghostwriters, speech writing is a noble profession dedicated only to ensuring that their clients' ideas get "fair play in the marketplace of ideas."[44]

Today, ghostwriters rarely hide their role in the speech-making process. To the contrary, some presidential speechwriters have become celebrities in their own right, writing best-selling memoirs or achieving fame in politics, journalism, or even popular entertainment.[45] Nowadays, the real ethical questions surrounding ghostwriting involve the role of research and new technologies in the speechwriting process. With polling and focus groups, speechwriting teams can now create what one scholar has described as "quantitatively safe" speeches,[46] or speeches scientifically designed to offend nobody. They can also test which arguments or evidence the public will find convincing or determine which emotional appeals will best move the public. Famous for such research, former Clinton adviser Dick Morris used polling data to position Clinton in the most politically advantageous positions, although he denies that he ever distorted the truth or manipulated public opinion.[47] Thus, the ethics of using polling data to help craft political messages remains a debatable issue. Some defend the practice, although others criticize politicians for pandering to public opinion.[48]

DELIBERATION AND DEMAGOGUERY IN THE TWENTY-FIRST CENTURY

1.3 Distinguish between ethical persuasion and demagoguery.

Preview. *Those who speak in public need not be objective, or free of all personal opinions and biases, but they do have an obligation to be well informed and fully prepared. In most respects, the rules of ethical speech have not changed since ancient times, although unethical speech, or demagoguery, has assumed new forms in the modern world.*

As the late U.S. senator Daniel Patrick Moynihan used to say, we are all entitled to our own opinions, but not to our own facts.[49] What Moynihan meant, of course, is that we should never twist the truth or invent "facts" just to win an argument. As public speakers, we have an ethical obligation to speak honestly and to gather reliable information about our topic. We also have an obligation to remain open to other points of view and to respect those who disagree with our opinions. Democratic deliberation is not about winning and losing. It is about joining with other citizens in a search for solutions to our common problems.

Deliberating in Good Faith

Perhaps you've heard the expression deliberating "in good faith." What does that mean? Does it mean that we must always strive to be objective? The answer is no. Nobody is completely objective. We all have personal experiences, religious beliefs, political biases, and social values that influence our opinions. As a speaker, nobody expects you to erase your past, nor do audiences demand that you deny your own beliefs and values, however controversial they may be. To the contrary, democratic deliberation is all about airing those differing opinions. It is about reconciling our disagreements through discussion and debate. Your fellow citizens do not expect you to be perfectly objective, but they do expect you to make good arguments in support of your opinions. That means providing sound reasoning and evidence to back up your views. It also means being open-minded enough to consider other people's views and perhaps even to change your opinion when confronted with compelling evidence.

Explore the Exercise "Persuasive Speech: S.A.D.D." at **MyCommunicationLab**

In many situations, you will be *expected* to take sides on a controversial issue. If, for example, you plan to speak on the health care crisis in America, your audience will expect you to criticize existing policies and advocate some alternative system for providing health care in America. Yet that does not mean that you will simply announce your proposal and wait for your audience to shout its approval. You must provide *reasons* for your opinion and *evidence* to back it up. Nor does taking a stand on a controversial issue mean that once you deliver your speech, you should close your mind to the possibility of changing your own opinion. Ethical speakers avoid allowing their existing opinions to blind them to new information, and they remain open to persuasion by advocates with different points of view. Once you have carefully researched your topic, you may be confident that your conclusions are thoughtful and fair. But down the road, you may need to reevaluate your opinion in light of new information or changing circumstances.

As a public speaker, you have an ethical obligation to be well informed and fully prepared. Speaking in public is not like casual conversation, in which you just "bounce a few ideas" off a friend. It is a *formal presentation*, often in a setting where people have gathered to discuss issues crucial to their own lives and communities. In such a setting, you owe it to your listeners to investigate your topic carefully and to provide information that is relevant, reliable, and up to date. More than that, you should organize and deliver that information in the most effective manner possible. Being fully prepared means more than developing an informed opinion—although that is a crucial first step. It also means carefully organizing your ideas, choosing the right language to express them, and supplying solid evidence to back up them up.

When you speak in public, you ask your fellow citizens not only for their time and attention but also for their trust. You therefore have an *ethical* obligation to contribute something useful to their deliberations—to deliver a speech "worth listening to," as William Norwood Brigance put it.[50] Perhaps you can contribute some fact that others have overlooked. Or maybe you have a unique way of looking at a problem or some new ideas for solving that problem. Whatever your contribution, you should investigate your topic thoroughly, consider all sides of the issue, and make sure that you have your facts straight. As we noted at the beginning of this section, you have a right to your own opinion but not to your own facts.

Demagoguery and the Ethics of Emotional Appeal

As Charles Lomas observed in *The Agitator in American Society*, demagoguery is a word that is loosely thrown around in American politics and is "difficult to define."[51] To the Greeks who invented the word, a "demagogue was simply a leader of the people." Yet even in ancient Greece the term implied deceit and manipulation, with Euripides describing the demagogue as "a man of loose tongue, intemperate, trusting to tumult, leading the populace to mischief with empty words."[52]

Today, we use the term *demagogue* to describe speakers who deceive or manipulate their audiences, usually by provoking strong emotional responses. In a widely cited study, for example, historian Reinhard Luthin defined the demagogue as a "mob-master" who, with "considerable histrionic variety and always noisily," seeks to "whip up and intensify the emotions, the prejudices and the passions, of the voting public." According to Luthin, the demagogue stirs up emotions but rarely offers much in the way of "public service and constructive thinking."[53]

Demagogues typically appeal to the darker emotions, such as fear, anger, or hatred. During the Great Depression, for example, Huey P. Long, a U.S. senator from Louisiana, exploited the fears and hopelessness of many Americans by offering a quick fix to America's economic woes: a vague, utopian plan to "share the wealth." Similarly, Senator Joseph McCarthy became a household name in the 1950s by exploiting fears of communism and the uncertainties of the Cold War era. McCarthy accused high-ranking government officials and even U.S. military leaders of disloyalty, but these reckless accusations later proved unfounded. But for a time he whipped the entire country into an anticommunist frenzy.

Of course, not all appeals to emotions are, in and of themselves, unethical. Emotions play an important role in all aspects of our lives. As speakers, we must recognize that people get excited, upset, or angry about issues that concern them. Emotions are also a powerful motivator. If you want your audience to *do* something, you simply cannot ignore the role of emotions in human behavior. Many speakers use emotional appeals to move people to do good—donate time or money to a charitable cause, for example, or fight for better schools in their community. Various charitable organizations use emotional appeals to persuade us to save starving children in Africa or neglected and abused animals in the United States. The Red Cross uses emotional appeals to solicit aid for victims of hurricanes and other natural disasters. The Veterans of

Senator Huey P. Long's flamboyant speaking style mesmerized audiences, yet many considered him a demagogue because of his emotional appeals and his utopian plan to "share the wealth." Long was assassinated at age 42 by the son-in-law of a political rival.

Foreign Wars appeal to our emotions when they call on us to "support our troops." Appeals to emotions take many forms, and they are not *all* bad. If your goals are ethical and you are honest in what you say, there is nothing inherently wrong with appealing to emotions.

Yet emotional appeals should never *substitute* for sound, well-supported arguments, and as speakers we need to give careful thought to when—and under what circumstances—emotional appeals may be appropriate. In addition, we need to recognize that *some* forms of emotional appeal are, almost by definition, unethical. Name-calling, for example, is a kind of emotional appeal that is always unacceptable. By calling people derogatory names rather than responding to their arguments, you demean, degrade, or even dehumanize others. In the hands of the demagogue, name-calling is *designed* to do just that—to short-circuit the reasoning process by demeaning those with different points of view. Thus, the demagogue may characterize all feminists as "man-haters" or all evangelical Christians as religious "fanatics." This sort of name-calling (what the Greek rhetoricians called *ad hominem*) is not only intellectually dishonest but it also silences others and undermines democratic debate.

Finally, scholars have identified a number of specific rhetorical techniques typically employed by the demagogue. According to J. Justin Gustainis, demagogues not only employ excessive emotional appeals and name-calling. They also focus attention on their own personalities rather than the issues, oversimplify complex matters, and make logically unsound arguments. Like emotional appeals, none of these tactics is *necessarily* demagogic. Political candidates, for example, may emphasize their personal qualifications for office, and speakers sometimes oversimplify complex issues for uninformed or uneducated audiences. Demagogues, however, *habitually* use such tactics, and they do so to promote their own selfish interests, not the public good. In other words, demagogues deceive and manipulate others to promote *themselves*, and in the process they rarely show "concern for the truth."[54]

However offensive they may be, even demagogues enjoy the protections of the First Amendment. Direct incitements to violence go beyond the bounds of free speech, but even the most offensive forms of name-calling and stereotyping are generally considered protected speech under our Constitution. In recent years, a number of colleges and universities have tried to ban so-called hate speech on campus, but these speech codes rarely stand up in court. Nor do libel and slander laws offer much protection against even the most vicious personal attacks on public figures. Perhaps that helps explain why there is so much "mudslinging" during our political campaigns. Inevitably, some will exploit our right to free speech to say unfair or even offensive things about others.

In an era of rapid technological and social change, the ethical questions surrounding public speaking have become increasingly complicated. Hate speech has found a new home on the Internet, where its sources can remain anonymous and not be held accountable. Meanwhile, our society grows more diverse every day, complicating our efforts to identify shared ethical standards. Yet the basic principles of ethical speech—honesty, accountability, good faith, and commitment to the larger "public good"—remain as relevant today as they were more than 2,000 years ago. It is up to all of us—each and every one of us—to speak out against demagoguery and contribute something positive and constructive to the public dialogue.

THE RESPONSIBLE CITIZEN-SPEAKER

1.4 Discuss the legal and ethical obligations of the responsible citizen-speaker.

Preview. *In a democracy, every speaker should be committed to communicating responsibly. Responsible speakers examine their own motives. They insist on accuracy and are concerned with the ways in which they acquire and present information. They see human communication as respectful dialogue and strive to live up to the legal and ethical standards of the larger community.*

As a speaker, you hope to influence your audience. As a citizen, however, you have larger obligations to go beyond media sound bites and spin and present information that is truthful, reliable, and complete. You want your audience to respond positively to what you say, but that does not mean that you should be willing to say *anything* to "win the day." Nor does it mean that you should shamelessly pander to your audience. You want to be an *effective* public speaker, but you also want to communicate *responsibly*. But what does that mean—to communicate "responsibly"? What are the *responsibilities* that go along with the *right* of free speech in America?

Watch the Video "Tobacco Ordinance Public Hearing (Shirley Sears and Andy Storms)" at **MyCommunicationLab**

Watch the Video "Tobacco Ordinance Public Hearing (Paul Hager, local citizen)" at **MyCommunicationLab**

Characteristics of the Responsible Citizen-Speaker

First, communicating responsibly means speaking honestly and truthfully, with a genuine concern for the well-being of your listeners. Responsible speakers also examine their own motives, and they do not slant the truth just to "win" an argument. Responsible speakers are committed to respectful dialogue; they honor the right of their listeners to raise questions, suggest alternatives, or even disagree. Responsible speakers carefully research their topics and present their findings accurately. Responsible speakers adapt to their audience's interests and needs, but they do not pander. They may compromise on some issues, but they do not abandon their core beliefs to win their audience's approval.

Responsible speakers also respect the diversity of their audiences. We live in a world where men and women of all ages, races, religions, and educational backgrounds must come together to resolve problems. During the 1980s, immigrants accounted for more than one-third of U.S. population growth, and our increasing cultural diversity can now be seen in all regions of the country.[55] An overwhelming 92 percent of Americans recognize that the United States is now made up of many different cultures.[56] No matter where you speak, you can no longer assume that all of your listeners will be like you, sharing the same values, beliefs, and experiences. Not all your listeners will view fraternities and sororities the same way. Not all will trust the police to protect them, and not everybody will define success in terms of how much money one makes. Some of your listeners may have a completely different understanding of "family values" than you do. Indeed, they may reject your most cherished principles and values. But that does not mean you should avoid talking about controversial public issues. In our diverse, multicultural society, it is more important than ever that we learn how to communicate both effectively and responsibly. We may be a more diverse nation today, but we still have common problems and shared aspirations, and we still need to work together for the common good.

Public deliberation is what democracy is all about; it is the mechanism through which we come together to talk about our common problems and to make collective decisions. We are not born with the habits and skills of democratic deliberation, however. For our democracy to work, we must *learn* how to deliberate, and we must agree upon some *rules* of deliberation. Some of those rules are actually written into law; others are more informal social norms.

Legal and Ethical Issues in Public Speaking

Watch the Video
"Shelley Lane" at
MyCommunicationLab

Imagine having to speak to an audience you know to be opposed to your ideas. How far will you go to win their agreement? Or imagine you are making a sales presentation to a group of potential customers. Are you willing to say *anything* in order to "close the deal"? Would you knowingly resort to misleading statements or attack the competition to make that sale?

Everyone who speaks in public must wrestle with these sorts of questions, and in recent years the lines between acceptable and unacceptable speech have become even more blurred. The news media nowadays seem most interested in voices from the extremes of the political spectrum: Ann Coulter on the right, for example, or Michael Moore on the left. Some public figures, such as Howard Stern, even push the boundaries of decency and good taste. Still others, such as white supremacist Matthew Hale, openly preach hate and advocate violence. So where do we draw the line? What are the limits of free speech in America? And who has the power to define the rules of acceptable speech? We have laws against slander and libel, of course, and the Supreme Court has ruled that speech that threatens public safety is outside the protections of the First Amendment. Yet controversies remain. To what extent, for example, should the Federal Communications Commission (FCC) be able to regulate what we see on television or hear on the radio? Should a city government be allowed to close an art exhibit that it deems obscene? Do "pro-life" activists have a First Amendment right to advocate violence against doctors who perform abortions? All of these questions point to difficult dilemmas for our free society.

Citizens have a right to free speech in America, including the right to protest. But along with those rights come a responsibility to respect certain legal and ethical standards.

Generally, we all recognize that there must be limits to free speech. By law, for example, we do *not* have a First Amendment right to slander or threaten others, nor do we have a right to incite mob violence. Beyond these legal limitations, however, there are few clear guidelines for acceptable speech. As a result, all public speakers must make choices. As a public advocate, will you resort to name-calling or exaggerated fear appeals to win an argument? Will you attempt to prevail by labeling your opponents "ignorant" or "radical" or by trying to scare your audience into agreeing with your position? Or will you show respect for your listeners by grounding your speech in the best available information, supporting it with sound evidence and reasoning, and acknowledging the legitimacy of opposing points of view?

Issues that matter to people should be explored in depth, not clouded by language that dismisses rather than engages the arguments of the opposition. In the heat of political battle, some speakers may be tempted to exaggerate their case, to state mere opinions as fact, or to make promises they cannot keep. Those who resort to such methods sometimes carry the day, but in the long run they likely will be denounced by their fellow citizens and discredited in history. You may think that it doesn't matter much what you talk about in your public speaking classroom, but the classroom *is* a public forum. What you say in the classroom does matter, and communicating responsibly *is* part of your assignment. As you prepare for your first public speaking assignment, don't forget: the truly successful citizen-speaker is both an effective advocate for his or her ideas *and* a good citizen.

HIGHLIGHTING ETHICAL COMMUNICATION

In 1999, the leading professional organization for scholars and teachers of communication, the National Communication Association, adopted the following Credo for Ethical Communication:

1. We advocate truthfulness, accuracy, honesty, and reason as essential to the integrity of communication.
2. We endorse freedom of expression, diversity of perspective, and tolerance of dissent to achieve the informed and responsible decision making fundamental to a civil society.
3. We strive to understand and respect other communicators before evaluating and responding to their messages.
4. We promote access to communication resources and opportunities as necessary to fulfill human potential and contribute to the well-being of families, communities, and society.
5. We promote communication climates of caring and mutual understanding that respect the unique needs and characteristics of individual communicators.
6. We condemn communication that degrades individuals and humanity through distortion, intimidation, coercion, and violence, and through the expression of intolerance and hatred.
7. We are committed to the courageous expression of personal convictions in pursuit of fairness and justice.
8. We advocate sharing information, opinions, and feelings when facing significant choices while also respecting privacy and confidentiality.
9. We accept responsibility for the short- and long-term consequences for our own communication and expect the same of others.

Source: Reprinted by permission from the National Communication Association. www.natcom.org.

Study and Review materials for this chapter are at **MyCommunicationLab**

SUMMARY

 Listen to the Audio Chapter Summary at **MyCommunicationLab**

Public Speaking and Civic Engagement

1.1 Discuss what it means to be a "good citizen."

- Democratic citizenship entails responsibilities as well as rights, including the responsibility to "get involved."
  - For some, getting involved may mean supporting political candidates, while for others it may mean volunteering to help others or simply "speaking out" on the issues.
  - The engaged citizen strives to be well informed and thoughtful when speaking out on matters of public concern.

The Rhetorical Tradition and the Ethics of Speech

1.2 Explain how the rhetorical tradition relates to civic engagement.

- The tradition of scholarship and teaching in rhetoric emphasizes the knowledge and skills necessary for democratic citizenship.
  - Theories of rhetoric dating back to ancient Greece and Rome have emphasized the ethics of speech and the concept of civic virtue.
  - Rhetorical criticism teaches us to be citizen-critics—that is, to carefully evaluate the arguments and evidence we hear in speeches or in the mass media.
  - By studying the great speakers and speeches of the past, we can learn about American history

and about the principles and traditions of democratic deliberation.
- The ethical speaker pursues worthy goals, is honest and accountable, avoids plagiarism, and takes full responsibility for words spoken in public.

Deliberation and Demagoguery in the Twenty-first Century

1.3 Distinguish between ethical persuasion and demagoguery.

- Although the basic rules of ethical speech have not changed since ancient times, demagoguery has assumed new forms, and the ethical issues relating to speech have been complicated by technological and social change.
  - The ethical speaker deliberates "in good faith" and is well informed and fully prepared.
  - The ethical speaker avoids the techniques of the demagogue and never substitutes appeals to the emotions for sound, well-supported arguments.

The Responsible Citizen-Speaker

1.4 Discuss the legal and ethical obligations of the responsible citizen-speaker.

- The responsible citizen-speaker is committed to honesty, respects the diversity of his or her audience, and understands the legal and ethical constraints on free speech in a democratic society.

QUESTIONS FOR REVIEW AND REFLECTION

Public Speaking and Civic Engagement

1.1 Discuss what it means to be a "good citizen."

1. How is public speaking related to "civic engagement"? What does it mean to "get involved" as a citizen, and what sorts of involvement are most satisfying or effective?
2. Do you believe that Americans are really less politically engaged or community spirited than they were in the past? Can you think of ways that citizens have become *more* engaged in recent years?
3. On your campus, what activities, clubs, or other special opportunities invite students to participate in civic affairs? Can you think of at least three examples?

The Rhetorical Tradition and the Ethics of Speech

1.2 Explain how the rhetorical tradition relates to civic engagement.

4. How is the rhetorical tradition related to civic engagement or good citizenship? What kinds of knowledge and skills do we learn by studying rhetoric?
5. What are the most important ethical concerns surrounding public speaking in a democracy? What does it mean to speak "ethically"? How, if at all, have the ethical considerations in public speaking changed over time?
6. How would you define *plagiarism*, and how might we distinguish between deliberate and "accidental" plagiarism?
7. What ethical concerns, if any, are raised by the practice of ghostwriting? Is ghostwriting always

unethical, or is it unethical only under certain circumstances? How might we distinguish ethical from unethical ghostwriting?

Deliberation and Demagoguery in the Twenty-first Century

1.3 Distinguish between ethical persuasion and demagoguery.

8. What does it mean to deliberate in "good faith"? Does deliberating in good faith mean being completely objective? Can you be passionate about your political views and still deliberate in good faith?
9. Define *demagoguery*. How does demagoguery relate to the use of emotional appeals? Is it always demagogic to appeal to your audience's emotions? How, if at all, would you distinguish between ethical and unethical emotional appeals? Beyond emotional appeals, what other appeals or techniques in public speaking might be considered demagogic?

The Responsible Citizen-Speaker

1.4 Discuss the legal and ethical obligations of the responsible citizen-speaker.

10. What are the characteristics of the responsible citizen-speaker? What are some of the legal and ethical considerations relating to public speaking in a democracy?

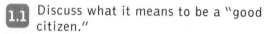 Study and Review the Flashcards at **MyCommunicationLab**

Secretary of State Hillary Clinton

The National Prayer Breakfast is an annual event in Washington, DC where prominent people—from Mother Teresa, to former British Prime Minister Tony Blair, to the humanitarian rock star Bono—are invited to reflect on the role of religious faith in their life and work. Every president since Dwight Eisenhower has attended the event, and it now attracts some 3,500 participants from more than 100 countries. Hosted by The Fellowship Foundation, a group of conservative Christians within Congress, the event provoked controversy in 2010 after reports linked the sponsoring group to efforts to pass anti-gay legislation in Uganda. Ignoring calls to boycott the event, Clinton instead used the breakfast as an opportunity to denounce intolerance and violence in the name of religion and to go on record as strongly opposed to such discriminatory legislation.

Thank you. Thank you very much. I have to begin by saying I'm not Bono. (Laughter.) Those of you who were here when he was, I apologize beforehand. (Laughter.) But it is a great pleasure to be with you and to be here with President and Mrs. Obama, to be with Vice President Biden, with Chairman Mullen, with certainly our host today, my former colleagues and friends, Senators Isakson and Amy Klobuchar. And to be with so many distinguished guests and visitors who have come from all over our country and indeed from all over the world.

I have attended this prayer breakfast every year since 1993, and I have always found it to be a gathering that inspires and motivates me. Now today, our minds are still filled with the images of the tragedy of Haiti, where faith is being tested daily in food lines and makeshift hospitals, in tent cities where there are not only so many suffering people, but so many vanished dreams.

When I think about the horrible catastrophe that has struck Haiti, I am both saddened but also spurred. This is a moment that has already been embraced by people of faith from everywhere. I thank Prime Minister Zapatero for his country's response and commitment. Because in the days since the earthquake, we have seen the world and the world's faithful spring into action on behalf of those suffering. President Obama has put our country on the leading edge of making sure that we do all we can to help alleviate not only the immediate suffering, but to assist in the rebuilding and recovery. So many countries have answered the call, and so many churches, synagogues, mosques, and temples have brought their own people together. And even modern technology through Facebook and telethons and text messages and Twitter, there's been an overwhelming global response. But, of course, there's so much more to be done.

When I think about being here with all of you today, there are so many subjects to talk about. You've already heard, both in prayer and in scripture reading and in Prime Minister Zapatero's remarks, a number of messages. But let me be both personal and speak from my unique perspective now as secretary of state. I've been here as a first lady. I've been here as a senator, and now I am here as a secretary of state. I have heard heartfelt descriptions of personal faith journeys. I've heard impassioned pleas for feeding the hungry and helping the poor, caring for the sick. I've heard speeches about promoting understanding among people of different faiths. I've met hundreds of visitors from countries across the globe. I've seen the

CLINTON OPENS ON A LIGHT NOTE, ESTABLISHING COMMON GROUND BY RECALLING THE ROCK STAR BONO'S HUMOROUS KEYNOTE ADDRESS THE PREVIOUS YEAR. SHE BUILDS HER OWN CREDIBILITY BY MENTIONING HER LONG ASSOCIATION WITH THE EVENT.

TURNING QUICKLY TO WORLD EVENTS, CLINTON DESCRIBES THE U.S. RESPONSE TO THE EARTHQUAKE IN HAITI AND THE IMPORTANT ROLE OF RELIGIOUS GROUPS IN THE RELIEF EFFORTS.

ADOPTING A PERSONAL TONE, CLINTON RECALLS BEING INSPIRED BY PREVIOUS NATIONAL PRAYER BREAKFASTS. IN THE PROCESS, SHE CRITIQUES THE "SMALLNESS, IRRELEVANCY, AND EVEN MEANNESS" OF OUR "POLITICAL CULTURE" AND RECALLS HOW HER OWN PERSONAL FAITH HAS BEEN STRENGTHENED BY HER CONNECTIONS TO PEOPLE WHO, POLITICALLY, WERE ON THE "OPPOSITE SIDE."

leaders of my own country come here amidst the crises of the time and, for at least a morning, put away political and ideological differences. And I've watched and I've listened to three presidents, each a man of faith, speak from their hearts, both sharing their own feelings about being in a position that has almost intolerably impossible burdens to bear, and appealing often, either explicitly or implicitly, for an end to the increasing smallness, irrelevancy, even meanness, of our own political culture. My own heart has been touched and occasionally pierced by the words I've heard, and often my spirit has been lifted by the musicians and the singers who have shared their gifts in praising the Lord with us. And during difficult and painful times, my faith has been strengthened by the personal connections that I have experienced with people who, by the calculus of politics, were on the opposite side of me on the basis of issues or partisanship.

After my very first prayer breakfast, a bipartisan group of women asked me to join them for lunch and told me that they were forming a prayer group. And these prayer partners prayed for me. They prayed for me during some very challenging times. They came to see me in the White House. They kept in touch with me and some still do today. And they gave me a handmade book with messages, quotes, and scripture, to sustain me. And of all the thousands of gifts that I received in the White House, I have a special affection for this one. Because in addition to the tangible gift of the book, it contained 12 intangible gifts, 12 gifts of discernment, peace, compassion, faith, fellowship, vision, forgiveness, grace, wisdom, love, joy, and courage. And I have had many occasions to pull out that book and to look at it and to try, Chairman Mullen, to figure out how to close the gap of what I am feeling and doing with what I know I should be feeling and doing. As a person of faith, it is a constant struggle, particularly in the political arena, to close that gap that each of us faces.

In February of 1994, the speaker here was Mother Teresa. She gave, as everyone who remembers that occasion will certainly recall, a strong address against abortion. And then she asked to see me. And I thought, "Oh, dear." (Laughter.) And after the breakfast, we went behind that curtain and we sat on folding chairs, and I remember being struck by how small she was and how powerful her hands were, despite her size, and that she was wearing sandals in February in Washington. (Laughter.)

We began to talk, and she told me that she knew that we had a shared conviction about adoption being vastly better as a choice for unplanned or unwanted babies. And she asked me—or more properly, she directed me—to work with her to create a home for such babies here in Washington. I know that we often picture, as we're growing up, God as a man with a white beard. But that day, I felt like I had been ordered, and that the message was coming not just through this diminutive woman but from someplace far beyond.

So I started to work. And it took a while because we had to cut through all the red tape. We had to get all the approvals. I thought it would be easier than it turned out to be. She proved herself to be the most relentless lobbyist I've ever encountered. (Laughter.) She could not get a job in your White House, Mr. President. (Laughter.) She never let up. She called me from India, she called me from Vietnam, she wrote me letters, and it was always: "When's the house gonna open? How much more can be done quickly?"

Finally, the moment came: June, 1995, and the Mother Teresa Home for Infant Children opened. She flew in from Kolkata to attend the opening, and like a happy child, she gripped my arm and led me around, looking at the bassinets and the pretty painted colors on the wall, and just beaming about what this meant for children and their futures.

A few years later, I attended her funeral in Kolkata, where I saw presidents and prime ministers, royalty and street beggars, pay her homage. And after the service, her successor, Sister Nirmala, the leader of the Missionaries of Charity, invited me to come to the Mother House. I was deeply touched. When I arrived, I realized I was one of only a very few outsiders. And I was directed into a whitewashed room where the casket had already arrived. And we stood around with the nuns, with the candles on the walls flickering, and prayed for this extraordinary woman. And then Sister Nirmala asked me to offer a prayer. I felt both inadequate and deeply honored, just as I do today. And in the tradition of prayer breakfast speakers, let me share a few matters that reflect how I came on my own faith journey, and how I think about the responsibilities that President Obama and his administration and our government face today.

As Amy said, I grew up in the Methodist Church. On both sides of my father's family, the Rodhams and the Joneses, they came from mining towns. And they claimed, going back many years, to have actually been converted by John and Charles Wesley. And, of course, Methodists were methodical. It was a particularly good religion for me. (Laughter.) And part of it is a commitment to living out your faith. We believe that faith without works may not be dead, but it's hard to discern from time to time.

And, of course, John Wesley had this simple rule which I carry around with me as I travel: Do all the good you can by all the means you can in all the ways you can in all the places you can at all the times you can to all the people you can, as long as ever you can. That's a tall order. And, of course, one of the interpretive problems with it is, who defines good? What are we actually called to do, and how do we stay humble enough, obedient enough, to ask ourselves, am I really doing what I'm called to do?

It was a good rule to be raised by and it was certainly a good rule for my mother and father to discipline us by. And I think it's a good rule to live by, with the appropriate dose of humility. Our world is an imperfect one filled with imperfect people, so we constantly struggle to meet our own spiritual goals. But John Wesley's teachings, and the teachings of my church, particularly during my childhood and teenage years, gave me the impetus to believe that I did have a responsibility. It meant not sitting on the sidelines, but being in the arena. And it meant constantly working to try to fulfill the lessons that I absorbed as a child. It's not easy. We're here today because we're all seekers, and we can all look around our own lives and the lives of those whom we know and see everyone falling so short.

And then, of course, as we look around the world, there are so many problems and challenges that people of faith are attempting to address or should be. We can recite those places where human beings are mired in the past—their hatreds, their differences—where governments refuse to speak to other governments, where the progress of entire nations is undermined because isolation and insularity seem less risky than cooperation and collaboration, where all too often it is religion that is the force that drives and sustains division rather than being the healing balm. These patterns persist despite the overwhelming evidence that more good will come from suspending old animosities and preconceptions from

TURNING TO HER OWN PERSONAL "FAITH JOURNEY," CLINTON DESCRIBES HERSELF AS A METHODIST, A FOLLOWER OF THE TEACHING OF JOHN WESLEY. IN THE PROCESS, SHE BUILDS HER OWN CREDIBILITY AS ONE WHOSE MISSION IN LIFE IS TO "DO GOOD."

CONSIDERING THE ROLE OF "PEOPLE OF FAITH" IN WORLD AFFAIRS, CLINTON LAMENTS THAT RELIGION TOO OFTEN DIVIDES RATHER THAN UNIFIES. SHE CITES NORTHERN IRELAND AS PROOF THAT IT IS POSSIBLE TO OVERCOME EVEN THE MOST DEEPLY ENTRENCHED RELIGIOUS DIFFERENCES.

engaging others in dialogue, from remembering the cardinal rules found in all of the world's major religions.

Last October, I visited Belfast once again, 11 years after the signing of the Good Friday Agreement, a place where being a Protestant or a Catholic determined where you lived, often where you worked, whether you were a friend or an enemy, a threat or a target. Yet over time, as the body count grew, the bonds of common humanity became more powerful than the differences fueled by ancient wrongs. So bullets have been traded for ballots.

As we meet this morning, both communities are attempting to hammer out a final agreement on the yet unresolved issues between them. And they are discovering anew what the scripture urges us: "Let us not become weary in doing good, for at the proper time we will reap a harvest if we don't give up." Even in places where God's presence and promise seems fleeting and unfulfilled or completely absent, the power of one person's faith and the determination to act can help lead a nation out of darkness.

Some of you may have seen the film Pray the Devil Back to Hell. It is the story of a Liberian woman who was tired of the conflict and the killing and the fear that had gripped her country for years. So she went to her church and she prayed for an end to the civil war. And she organized other women at her church, and then at other churches, then at the mosques. Soon thousands of women became a mass movement, rising up and praying for a peace, and working to bring it about that finally, finally ended the conflict.

TURNING TO ANOTHER TROUBLED PART OF THE WORLD, CLINTON IDENTIFIES TWO AFRICAN COUNTRIES WHICH HAVE SUFFERED GREATLY FROM VIOLENCE AND WARFARE: LIBERIA AND CONGO. IN BOTH, SHE SUGGESTS, PEOPLE OF FAITH—PARTICULARLY WOMEN—HAVE LED EFFORTS TO STOP THE VIOLENCE AND RESTORE PEACE AND HOPE.

And yet the devil must have left Liberia and taken up residence in Congo. When I was in the Democratic Republic of Congo this summer, the contrasts were so overwhelmingly tragic—a country the size of Western Europe, rich in minerals and natural resources, where 5.4 million people have been killed in the most deadly conflict since World War II, where 1,100 women and girls are raped every month, where the life expectancy is 46 and dropping, where poverty, starvation, and all of the ills that stalk the human race are in abundance.

When I traveled to Goma, I saw in a single day the best and the worst of humanity. I met with women who had been savaged and brutalized physically and emotionally, victims of gender and sexual-based violence in a place where law, custom, and even faith did little to protect them. But I also saw courageous women who, by faith, went back into the bush to find those who, like them, had been violently attacked. I saw the doctors and the nurses who were helping to heal the wounds, and I saw so many who were there because their faith led them to it.

As we look at the world today and we reflect on the overwhelming response of outpouring of generosity to what happened in Haiti, I'm reminded of the story of Elijah. After he goes to Mount Horeb, we read that he faced "a great wind, so strong that it was splitting mountains and breaking rocks in pieces before the Lord, but the Lord was not in the wind; and after the wind an earthquake, but the Lord was not in the earthquake; and after the earthquake a fire, but the Lord was not in the fire; and after the fire a sound of sheer silence—a still small voice." It was then that Elijah heard the voice of the Lord. It is often when we are only quiet enough to listen that we do as well. It's something we can do at any time, without a disaster or a catastrophe provoking it. It shouldn't take that.

CLINTON DEMONSTRATES HER COMMAND OF BIBLICAL TEXTS BY RELATING THE STORY OF ELIJAH. SHE THEN EXPOUNDS UPON THE ETHICAL COMMANDS COMMON TO ALL RELIGIONS: CARE FOR THE POOR AND SUFFERING, THE GOLDEN RULE, AND LOVE FOR ONE'S NEIGHBORS.

But the teachings of every religion call us to care for the poor, tell us to visit the orphans and widows, to be generous and charitable, to alleviate suffering. All religions have their version of the Golden Rule and direct us to love our neighbor and welcome the stranger and visit the prisoner. But how often in the midst of our own lives do we respond to that? All of these holy texts, all of this religious wisdom from these very different faiths act out of love.

In politics, we sometimes talk about message discipline—making sure everyone uses the same set of talking points. Well, whoever was in charge of message discipline on these issues for every religion certainly knew what they were doing. Regardless of our differences, we all got the same talking points and the same marching orders. So the charge is a personal one. Yet across the world, we see organized religion standing in the way of faith, perverting love, undermining that message.

Sometimes it's easier to see that far away than here at home. But religion, cloaked in naked power lust, is used to justify horrific violence, attacks on homes, markets, schools, volleyball games, churches, mosques, synagogues, and temples. From Iraq to Pakistan and Afghanistan to Nigeria and the Middle East, religion is used a club to deny the human rights of girls and women, from the Gulf to Africa to Asia, and to discriminate, even advocating the execution of gays and lesbians. Religion is used to enshrine in law intolerance of free expression and peaceful protest. Iran is now detaining and executing people under a new crime—waging war against God. It seems to be a rather dramatic identity crisis.

So in the Obama administration, we are working to bridge religious divides. We're taking on violations of human rights perpetrated in the name of religion. And we invite members of Congress and clergy and active citizens like all of you here to join us. Of course we're supporting the peace processes from Northern Ireland to the Middle East, and, of course, we are following up on the president's historic speech at Cairo with outreach efforts to Muslims and promoting interfaith dialogue, and, of course, we're condemning the repression in Iran.

But we are also standing up for girls and women, who too often in the name of religion, are denied their basic human rights. And we are standing up for gays and lesbians who deserve to be treated as full human beings. (Applause.) And we are also making it clear to countries and leaders that these are priorities of the United States. Every time I travel, I raise the plight of girls and women, and make it clear that we expect to see changes. And I recently called President Museveni, whom I have known through the prayer breakfast, and expressed the strongest concerns about a law being considered in the parliament of Uganda.

We are committed, not only to reaching out and speaking up about the perversion of religion, and in particularly the use of it to promote and justify terrorism, but also seeking to find common ground. We are working with Muslim nations to come up with an appropriate way of demonstrating criticism of religious intolerance without stepping over into the area of freedom of religion or non-religion and expression. So there is much to be done, and there is a lot of challenging opportunities for each of us as we leave this prayer breakfast, this 58th prayer breakfast.

In 1975, my husband and I, who had gotten married in October, and we were both teaching at the University of Arkansas Law School in beautiful Fayetteville, Arkansas—we got married on a Saturday and we went back to work on a Monday. So around Christmastime, we decided that we should go somewhere and celebrate, take a honeymoon. And my late father said, "Well, that's a great idea. We'll come, too." (Laughter.)

And indeed, Bill and I and my entire family—(laughter)—went to Acapulco. We had a great time, but it wasn't exactly a honeymoon. So when we got back, Bill was talking to one of his friends who was then working in Haiti, and his friend said, "Well, why don't you come see me? This is the most interesting country. Come and take some time." So, indeed, we did. So we were there over the New Year's holidays. And I remember visiting the cathedral in Port-au-Prince, in the midst, at that time, so much fear from the regime of the Duvaliers, and so much poverty, there was this cathedral that had stood there and served as a beacon of hope and faith.

After the earthquake, I was looking at some of our pictures from the disaster, and I saw the total destruction of the cathedral. It was just a heart-rending moment. And yet I also saw men and women helping one another, digging through the rubble, dancing and singing in the makeshift communities that they were building up. And I thought again that as the scripture reminds us, "Though the mountains be shaken and the hills be removed, yet my unfailing love for you will not be shaken nor my covenant of peace be removed."

As the memory of this crisis fades, as the news cameras move on to the next very dramatic incident, let us pray that we can sustain the force and the feeling that we find in our hearts and in our faith in the aftermath of such tragedies. Let us pray that we will all continue to be our brothers' and sisters' keepers. Let us pray that amid our differences, we can continue to see the power of faith not only to make us whole as individuals, to provide personal salvation, but to make us a greater whole and a greater force for good on behalf of all creation.

So let us do all the good we can, by all the means we can, in all the ways we can, in all the places we can, to all the people we can, as long as ever we can.

God bless you. (Applause.)

Source: From Hillary Rodham Clinton, "Keynote Address at the 58th National Prayer Breakfast, February 4, 2010." Published 2010 by U.S. Department of State.

Listening and Speaking in a Democratic Society

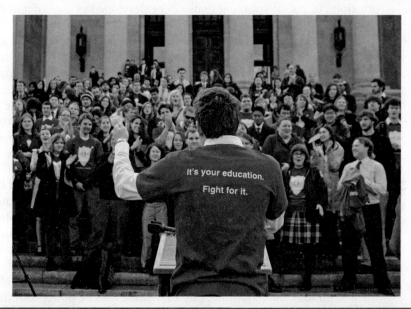

OVERVIEW AND LEARNING OBJECTIVES

The Speaker-Listener Partnership

2.1 Explain the nature and significance of the speaker-listener partnership.

The Engaged listener

2.2 Understand the meaning and benefits of engaged listening.

Barriers to Good Listening

2.3 Understand the barriers that prevent you from listening effectively.

Critical Listening

2.4 Describe what it means to practice active and critical listening.

Preparing Yourself to Speak

2.5 Understand your own interests, the needs and characteristics of your audience, and the requirements of the speaking situation.

Building and Delivering Your Speech

2.6 Know the basic principles involved in constructing and presenting an effective speech.

S ome view communication as a one-way street. If you get what you want, according to this view, your speech is effective. But that's only part of the picture. In a democratic society, the true value of a speech must be judged by the outcome for all parties involved: the speaker *and* the listeners. In addition, a speech should be judged by its larger contributions to society. Does it contribute something useful to public discussion? Does it help the community resolve important controversies, or does it motivate members of the community to do good things?

In this chapter, we will first examine the role of the critical listener as a fundamental part of the communication process. Then we will preview a few of the basic principles of public speaking that will be developed in more detail throughout the rest of this book.

To be an effective listener—in the classroom, in professional life, or in your community—you must listen attentively, respectfully, and critically. Listening carefully is not only an essential part of effective communication but also an important responsibility. When you listen carefully, you become a better-informed and more discerning consumer of information and ideas. You are also more likely to make good decisions about whom to vote for, what causes to support, and what courses of action to pursue. Of course, we do not listen in a vacuum. The good listener will make every effort to become as informed about the issues as possible so as to test the speaker's ideas and arguments against what he or she already knows. Keeping up with the major events and controversies of the day is part of your responsibilities as a good listener.

To be an effective speaker, you must respect your listeners' needs, sensitivities, and rights. You must know something about their beliefs, values, tastes, and prejudices. If you hope to get a response from your listeners, you need to consider what characteristics they share as a group and what qualities individual members bring to the situation. Seeing public speaking as a mutually beneficial experience for both speaker and listener means that taking advantage of an audience—getting them to do something harmful, buy something useless, or act in destructive ways—should never be your goal. Public speaking is a way of promoting the common good, and as such, it is governed by shared ethical principles.

THE SPEAKER-LISTENER PARTNERSHIP

2.1 Explain the nature and significance of the speaker-listener partnership.

Preview. *As a speaker, you hope to get a response from your audience. As a form of civic engagement, however, public speaking is listener-centered and assumes an equal, collaborative partnership between speakers and listeners. For a speech to be truly successful, the audience as well as the speaker should derive some benefit from the exchange.*

More than 40 years ago, communication scholar David Berlo, in his groundbreaking book *The Process of Communication*, argued that all communication, including public speaking, should be viewed as a process.[1] Later, Gerald Miller described that process as "transactional," or as an exchange between the "sender" and the "receiver."[2] In this model, communication is seen as a process in which speakers and listeners continuously exchange messages and negotiate meanings. As communications scholars Steve Duck and David McMahon put it, transactional communication is the process of constructing "shared messages or understandings between two or more individuals."[3]

In other words, the speaker should make adjustments based on the messages that come back from the audience. Listeners are not passive; they send information about their reactions to the speaker. Together, the speaker and the listener create a relationship in which they negotiate shared meanings and interpretations.

Figure 2.1 illustrates how a transactional model of communication differs from the idea of simply sending out a message to

CONTEXT

Speaker/Encoder
(Sender/Receiver)

Listeners/Decoders
(Receivers/Senders)

Noise

Noise

Message*

CHANNEL

Feedback*

Response/
Effect

*verbal and
nonverbal

FIGURE 2.1

A Transactional
Model of
Communication

an audience. As a speaker, you encode a message; that is, you take your ideas and you put them in a form to be sent though a channel (the speech). Your listeners then decode your message—that is, they interpret your message—and send verbal and nonverbal messages back to you, the speaker. As these messages go back and forth, there is the possibility of interference, or noise, that disrupts the communication process. Moreover, all of this occurs within a situation or context that can also influence the way messages are sent and received.

This transactional model of communication fits well with our view of public speaking as a form of civic engagement. When you speak in public, your goal should never be to manipulate your audience just to get your way. Rather, you should join *with* your fellow citizens in talking together about issues and problems of common concern. This transactional process—this exchange—presents a variety of challenges. Sometimes messages flow smoothly. At other times, "noise" may distort or interrupt the message flow, or the context may make it difficult to communicate. A hot, stuffy room might make it more difficult to communicate than a more comfortable setting. A captive audience, or one that is required to attend a presentation, is more likely to be preoccupied with other matters than an audience that has come specifically to hear you speak. As a speaker, you might even create distractions yourself by distributing too many handouts or by delivering your speech poorly. Any kind of interference, such as a squeaky microphone or a hostile audience member, might create "noise" in the system. Furthermore, all of us filter messages through our own beliefs and values. We understand, believe, or act based partly on our own experiences, the values we hold, our age or gender, or our cultural traditions. All of these factors will be discussed in greater detail in Chapter 4, where we consider how to analyze and adapt to your audience. For now, just remember that the situation in which you speak and the backgrounds and interests of your listeners can have a big effect on the way your message is received. A good speaker will anticipate and take account of these influences.

Speeches always take place in a context. If you are a student at Tulane University or the University of New Orleans, you might be more interested in the economic impact of hurricanes than a student at the University of Wisconsin. If you know a student who was robbed while walking across your campus, you might be more interested in personal safety on campus than other students in your class. If environmental activists have tried to stop logging in a nearby state forest by spiking trees or sabotaging equipment, students on your campus might be more aware of the debate over the tactics used by some radical environmental groups. In short, *where* and *when* you speak can make a big difference. Your speeches must be designed not only for a specific audience but also for a particular place and time.

Viewing public speaking as a process is important. Both speakers and listeners must be involved in the communication process, and both have larger responsibilities to the community. As a speaker, you have an obligation to address serious matters of public concern, and your listeners have a responsibility to listen and fairly evaluate your ideas and proposals. If you succeed as a speaker, both you and your listeners will benefit. As rhetorical scholar William Norwood Brigance once observed, you have a right to free speech, but you also have a responsibility to deliver *"useful goods to the listener."*[4]

THE ENGAGED LISTENER

2.2 Understand the meaning and benefits of engaged listening.

Preview. *Listening may serve various purposes, including enjoyment, gathering information, or the critical assessment of ideas. When you listen well, you experience an array of positive benefits, including increased knowledge and awareness of the world around you and a clearer sense of your own values. Your willingness to listen is crucial to your role as an engaged citizen. As a citizen, you have an obligation to listen to your fellow citizens and to give their views respectful consideration.*

Depending on your goals, you may approach listening differently in differing situations.[5] Sometimes you listen for enjoyment, as when you listen to good music. You do not expect to be analytical or critical; you are simply listening to be entertained or inspired. On other occasions, you may engage in empathic listening, or listening to show your support and understanding for the feelings of another person. As a citizen, however, you are most likely to engage in either informational or critical listening. In informational listening, you hope to learn or expand your knowledge of a particular subject. You want to understand and remember what you are hearing. In critical listening, you aim to analyze and evaluate a speaker's message. You make judgments about the relevance, accuracy, timeliness, and validity of the message. In many instances, informational listening serves as the foundation for critical listening; what you learn from listening can help you evaluate other messages you might encounter.

Positive Outcomes of Effective Listening

There are plenty of good reasons for becoming a better listener. In the classroom, better listening skills can improve your grades; good listening at work can lead to higher productivity and better workplace morale. In our communities, listening more carefully to one another can reduce conflict and help us solve problems.

Indeed, we all benefit when people become more careful and respectful listeners.[6] Here are just a few of the reasons we all should become better listeners:

- *Listening carefully helps you become better informed.* Many of our ideas come from listening to others. Whether you are participating in a group discussion, watching the news, or talking with a friend, listening better can help you make more informed decisions. Students who are good listeners usually perform better in their classes. Citizens who are good listeners become better-informed voters and tend to participate more actively in civic life.
- *Listening to others is part of your responsibility as a citizen.* When you listen closely to others' arguments, you show respect for their views and can respond more thoughtfully and intelligently. By listening carefully as others share their ideas, you also communicate a desire for dialogue and collaboration. By listening respectfully and attentively while others are speaking, you demonstrate your faith in the democratic process and your conviction that the views of every citizen deserve a respectful hearing.
- *Listening gives you a clearer sense of who we are and what we value.* Listening allows you to compare and contrast your own beliefs and values with those of your fellow citizens. By listening to others, you get a better sense of who you are and how your views compare to those of others. If you find that your views are out of the mainstream, you may want to ask, "What influences or life experiences have shaped my unique perspective on this issue?" or "Why might others have developed a different point of view?"
- *Good listening helps you develop and sustain better interpersonal relationships.* Listening to others shows that you care about them. Furthermore, good listening is often reciprocated. When you show that you care by listening carefully to the problems, perspectives, or ideas of others, they are more likely to give your views full and fair consideration.
- *By becoming a better listener, you can become a better speaker.* By carefully observing how others communicate, you can learn to communicate more effectively yourself. Moreover, listening carefully helps you better understand your audience when you speak. By listening to what your audience members say about themselves—by interacting with them before or after a speech—you can gather information that will help you frame your own ideas and arguments.

In short, effective listening is both a practical necessity and an ethical responsibility for citizens in a democracy.

Preparing for Critical Listening: Your Responsibility as a Citizen

If you are to listen effectively, you must possess sufficient information and knowledge to comprehend and assess the ideas of others. If you plan to attend a community forum on affordable housing, for example, you should know something about the topic in advance. How expensive is housing in our community? How does our community compare with surrounding communities? What might account for the high cost of housing in our area? What options do we have for creating more affordable housing? Who needs to be involved in addressing the problem? These are only a few of the questions that the thoughtful citizen might ask even *before* attending the forum.

HIGHLIGHTING LISTENING AND LEADERSHIP

Listening has been linked to effective leadership in the business and professional world as well as in the public arena.

- Leadership experts, such as Ronald Heifetz of Harvard University, point out that the foundation of good listening is "curiosity and empathy." Excellent listeners are able to look *beyond* the speaker's verbal and nonverbal messages and uncover the underlying argument beneath the disagreement or conflict.
- Former Chrysler CEO, Lee Iacocca (credited with saving Chrysler from bankruptcy in the 1980s), emphasizes the strong link between motivating employees to give their best efforts and listening to their ideas, questions, and concerns. Even if the "system" labels someone as "average or mediocre," they may truly excel simply because someone has "listened to [their] problems and helped [them] solve them."
- As Hillary Clinton prepared to run for the U.S. Senate in New York in 2000, she embarked on a "listening tour" that enabled her to obtain firsthand feedback from everyday Americans as

well as local government officials as they talked with her about "their concerns and aspirations for the families and communities."

- Col. Eric Kail, the course director of military leadership at the U.S. Military Academy at West Point, argues that a good leader is empathetic—he or she connects with others by listening carefully to what they have to say and resists the temptation simply to wait for them to pause to speak.
- In 2009, President Obama traveled to London for the first time during his presidency. He expressed a balanced commitment to advancing ideas and listening thoughtfully and responsively. He had come, he said, "to listen and not to lecture."

Sources: From Andrew D. Wolvin, "Listening Leadership, *International Journal of Listening* 19. Copyright © 2005 by *International Journal of Listening*; from Eric Kail, "Leadership Character: The Role of Empathy," http://www.washingtonpost.com/blogs/guest-insights/post/leadership-character-the-role-of-empathy/2011/04/04/gIQAQXVGQM_blog.html (accessed February 2, 2012); from Barack Obama, Joint Press Availability with President Barack Obama and Prime Minister Gordon Brown, April 1, 2009. Published 2009 by The White House, Office of the Press Secretary. ◤

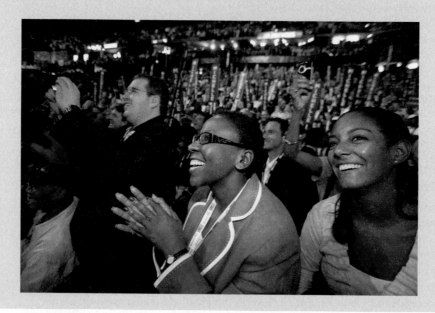

The National Issues Forums (NIF) is a network of educational institutions, civic groups, churches, and other organizations that convene gatherings where citizens can talk about public issues. They emphasize deliberation, not debate, using a structured approach that stresses "listening carefully to the views of others and talking through the conflicts that arise when people disagree." These forums occur throughout the country and focus on timely and critical topics, such as health care, immigration, and terrorism. The results are shared with local, state, and federal officials. Former Florida legislator Scott Clemens emphasizes the real benefit of having lawmakers attend a forum where they listen more than they speak. He points out that legislators don't have to play the role of "experts." Instead, they "have the chance to listen...to really focus on what people are saying." To read more about NIF, see Chapter 17.

Source: National Issues Forums Institute, "News," www.nifi.org/news. See in particular Bruce Feustel, "Connecting Citizens with Legislators" (accessed January 2, 2012).[7]

In your public speaking class, you may not know much about some of the topics your classmates will address. Even so, you should make an effort to be as well informed as possible. Get into the habit of regularly consulting reputable news sources—on the Internet, in newspapers and magazines, and on television. Make an effort to talk about important public issues with your classmates, family, and friends. By becoming more knowledgeable about a wide variety of local, state, national, and international issues, you can become a better listener and a more informed citizen.

As we become better informed, we are better able to distinguish fact from opinion, assess the quality of a speaker's ideas and arguments, and pose thoughtful questions. Listeners who are uninformed have difficulty distinguishing sound and useful information from that which is irrelevant, invalid, or unreliable. Sometimes poorly prepared listeners may not be able to grasp a speaker's arguments at all.

Clearly, there are both personal and social benefits to good listening. When speakers *and* listeners are well informed, democratic deliberation works better and the prospects for constructive problem solving are enhanced.

BARRIERS TO GOOD LISTENING

Preview. *Most of us underestimate the effort it takes to listen effectively. We want to listen well but often fail to recognize the barriers we need to overcome if we hope to become better listeners. Most of these barriers are grounded in our attitudes toward listening as well as in certain deficiencies in our listening behaviors. As we learn to identify and understand the barriers to good listening, we come to understand that good listening is an acquired skill.*

2.3 Understand the barriers that prevent you from listening effectively.

Passivity Syndrome

Many of us think listening is easy, at least for us! After all, we have been listening since we were born, and as students we listen for many hours every day. Perhaps we feel that we already know all there is to know about listening. Or maybe we feel that the primary responsibility for good listening rests with the speaker. This line of reasoning—known as the passivity syndrome—is rooted in a view of public speaking as a one-way street. The passivity syndrome fails to knowledge the transactional nature of communication—the fact that effective communication requires the active participation of both speakers and listeners.

Listening is an active process.[8] When we attend a public talk, we hope to learn, grow, be stimulated, or perhaps discover new strategies for solving a community problem. If we come away empty-handed, we must share some of the blame. If we hope to derive some benefit from listening, we must do our part. We must get actively involved in the communication process by listening more carefully.

Automatic Rejection

Listening is more difficult when a speaker challenges our existing beliefs or values. We prefer listening to speakers whose thinking is consistent with our own.[9] This is the case, for example, with TV viewers. A poll taken before the 2010 Congressional election showed that 78 percent of those who watched the conservative Fox News intended to vote Republican, while 58 percent of those who watched the more liberal MSNBC planned to vote Democratic.[10]

Sometimes we try to escape from distressing communication. Some will turn off the TV in disgust when a politician they dislike begins to speak. Others may utter disrespectful comments or otherwise "talk over" a speaker they do not want to hear. Even when attending an event in person, some listeners may pretend to listen to a speaker while thinking about something else. Still others will concentrate on refuting the speaker's ideas, losing the thread of the argument because they were too busy coming up with their own counterarguments. It is hardly surprising, then, that during question-and-answer periods, those who oppose the speaker's position often ask questions that reveal that they were not listening closely to the speech.

As an effective and ethical listener, you should allow the speaker to state his or her whole case before you jump to conclusions. You should give every speaker a fair and honest hearing before raising objections. It is perfectly acceptable to disagree with

FOCUS ON CIVIC ENGAGEMENT | Building a Climate for Peace through Critical Listening

In November of 2011, former secretary of state Madeleine Albright spoke to an audience of university students as part of a series on "Making War, Making Peace." She decried all the political bickering in the United States, which she argued was undermining America's role in inspiring and guiding other nations. She urged her audience to learn by listening to the views of others, especially those with whom they disagree. As in relations between countries, individuals need to hear and seek to understand views that are contrary to their own. She pointed out that there might be some personal satisfaction in "winning" an argument, but engaging in a dialogue in order to "stretch your mind" is more likely to lead to wisdom. And wisdom, according to Albright, is what will be needed to create a "climate for lasting peace."

Source: The Herald Times (Bloomington, Indiana), November 3, 2011, A3. ▲

points made by the speaker, but during the speech itself, you should just note those points and continue listening. After you have listened to the speaker's whole argument, you are in a better position to respond to those ideas with which you disagree.

Unfortunately, too many public advocates today simply refuse to listen to others. On political talk shows, for example, we frequently see speakers interrupt or shout down

those who disagree with their views, apparently thinking this is how you "win" a debate. Although these sorts of "debates" may be entertaining to some, they are hardly models of effective and constructive listening. If democratic deliberation is to lead to sound collective decisions, we need to listen to one another without becoming combative or defensive. Genuine listening means listening actively with an open mind and respect for those with whom you may disagree.[11]

Short Attention Span

How long can you listen to someone speak without starting to fidget or finding that your mind is wandering? Can you easily listen to your professor's 45-minute lecture and remain focused and attentive throughout? If you can, you have an excellent attention span.

Modern technology has significantly changed the way we listen and what we listen to. In the age of television and the Internet, we can hardly imagine listening to a series of seven political debates, each lasting three hours. Yet that is exactly what happened during the famous Lincoln-Douglas debates in 1858; the people of Illinois flocked to hear two candidates for the Senate engage in a "sustained public discussion" of the issues.[12] Accustomed to long speeches, sermons, and lectures, Americans of the nineteenth century were happy to listen to Daniel Webster speak for hours when commemorating the landing of the Pilgrims or debating the great issues of the day on the floor of the Senate.[13] The most famous preacher of that era, Henry Ward Beecher, would entertain huge crowds for hours with his provocative and entertaining lectures.[14]

Today, our attention spans are simply not as long as they used to be. We now demand shorter messages, sometimes losing interest after only a few minutes. Some experts advise teachers to break their lectures into small chunks, with no chunk lasting longer than fifteen minutes.[15] In political debates, candidates offer little more than "sound bites," or quick, nonspecific answers that can be easily remembered and quoted. According to experts, television has contributed to our shorter attention spans by breaking every ten or twelve minutes for commercials or station identification.[16] Not only television but also newspapers, video games, text messaging, tweets, and social networking sites have all conditioned us to expect our information in short bits—"sidebars" or "sound bites."

As listeners, we have a responsibility to overcome our own short attention spans. We need to accept that we will sometimes be asked to listen to talks that run 30 minutes or more, and we need to work at remaining attentive in such situations. If we find ourselves fading in and out during a speaker's presentation, we need to catch ourselves, refocus our attention, and practice some of the techniques of active listening discussed later in this chapter. Good listening does not just happen. We must make an effort to overcome our short attention spans and become better listeners.

Stereotyping

Watch the Video
"Morris Dees" at
MyCommunicationLab

In the early twenty-first century, we thankfully have left behind many sexual, cultural, racial, religious, and ethnic stereotypes. Even so, not all stereotypes have disappeared. Although racial and gender stereotypes have been discredited in recent years, even well-meaning people still sometimes stereotype older people, people with disabilities, or people from particular ethnic groups or geographical regions. Moreover, racism and sexism may have taken on new, more subtle forms, and some scholars believe they continue to be deeply embedded in our society.[17]

As early as 1922, journalist Walter Lippmann likened stereotypes to "pictures in the head," or mental reproductions of reality, and from there, the term gradually came to mean generalizations—or, quite often, overgeneralizations—about the members of a group.[18] The *Merriam-Webster Dictionary* defines *stereotype* as "a standardized mental picture that is held in common by members of a group and that represents an oversimplified opinion, prejudiced attitude, or uncritical judgment."[19] When stereotyping, we observe a few members of a particular category (African-American males, Asians, older women, homosexuals, and so forth) and draw conclusions about all others belonging to that same group. The difference between making a generalization about a group of individuals and stereotyping them is that, in stereotyping, we leave no room for individual differences. We believe that every individual fits the same mental mold we have created for the group. Stereotyping, then, often becomes a device for relegating an entire class of people to inferior status. This enables those in power to justify their dominance over the stereotyped group.

Stereotyping represents a problem in many realms of life. Scholars have linked stereotyping to prejudice and discrimination, as well as to lower self-esteem, adverse health outcomes, and impaired performance among the targets of racial and sexist stereotyping.[20] Stereotypes may be based on direct experience, family members' expressed views and attitudes, or various media portrayals, but whatever their source they can unfairly categorize and stigmatize people.

Stereotyping can greatly interfere with our ability to listen effectively. When we are preoccupied with a speaker's gender, race, age, or other characteristic, we are focusing on dimensions that may have little or nothing to do with his or her message. We are not focusing fully on the information and ideas being communicated. For example, suppose you were listening to a speech that addressed the problem of the glass ceiling, an invisible barrier of prejudices and discrimination

HIGHLIGHTING STEREOTYPES IN THE MEDIA

One of the main places that children and adults learn stereotypes is the mass media. Many studies have found that advertisements, television programs, movies, and other media are saturated with racial and gender stereotypes, as well as stereotypes about age, occupation, education, class, geographical location, or sexual orientation.

The sheer volume of advertising suggests that many people are exposed to stereotypes on a daily basis that may profoundly influence how people perceive and relate to one another. One study found that male interviewers who had watched sexist television commercials later judged a female job applicant as less competent, remembered less biographical information about her, and remembered more about her physical appearance than did interviewers who had not watched these kinds of commercials.

Beyond advertising, other media-based stereotypes wield considerable influence. For instance, research has shown the following:

■ White television viewers who watch a stereotyped comic portrayal of black people are later more likely to judge a black defendant guilty of an assault.

■ Males who view movie scenes objectifying women are later more likely to believe that a date rape victim experienced pleasure and "got what she wanted."

■ People who watch a music video objectifying women later rate a woman as more sexual and submissive when she returns a man's advances.

■ Heterosexual men who look at attractive women in magazine erotica later rate their romantic partners as less attractive.

These studies and many more document the negative influences of media stereotypes on social perception and behavior.

Source: Scott Plous, "The Psychology of Prejudice, Stereotyping, and Discrimination: An Overview," in *Understanding Prejudice and Discrimination*, ed. S. Plous (New York: McGraw-Hill, 2003), 3–48. ▲

that hampers women's ability to rise to the top of business and professional organizations. Would you listen to that speech carefully and with an open mind if you already had stereotyped the speaker as a radical feminist?

Stereotypes are invariably misleading. Everybody is unique, and nobody perfectly fits the stereotypes that may be applied to them. In all communication situations—and public speaking is no exception—we need to respect each person's individuality and resist falling for stereotypes.

Distractions

Sometimes we fail to listen effectively because of distractions in our surroundings. We may even use distractions as excuses for our own failure to listen. We sit in the last row and then complain about the speaker's voice not carrying very well. Or perhaps we sit by an open window and find ourselves distracted by a lawn mower, the shouts of children, or the beauty of the view. We tell ourselves that we had every intention of listening carefully but fell prey to distractions.

In addition, speakers themselves sometimes present distractions. Most public speakers are "on display" before they make their speeches. Seated at a luncheon table or on a speaker's platform, they can be viewed before speaking to the audience. Thus there is plenty of time for listeners to look at them and form early—and often misguided—impressions. Some listeners may be impressed by a speaker who appears in an Armani suit. They may suspend their critical faculties and believe what he says simply because he *looks* successful. If we allow ourselves to be distracted by first impressions, we have failed to fulfill our responsibilities as listeners. We should recognize the first impression for what it is—a *first* impression—and not allow it to determine our ultimate reactions to a speech.[21]

Nonverbal communication is important and cannot be ignored, of course, but what we observe with the eyes is only the beginning. We are there to *listen* to the speaker's complete presentation. Only then—on the basis of all that we have heard and observed—can we formulate a reasonable reaction to the speaker and the speech.

Finally, we need to recognize that visual images can sometimes distract us from listening closely. In some cases, visual images may function as powerful influences on our ideas and behaviors without our even being aware of their impact. The colors used in some images, for example, can elicit feelings or establish moods—and may influence the way we feel about what the speaker is saying.[22] In some cases, as communication scholar Kathleen Hall Jamieson has argued, visual images can even *substitute* for persuasive political arguments.[23] As discerning audience members, we must critically evaluate visual messages by asking ourselves how what we are *seeing* may influence our thoughts, feelings, and beliefs. We will return to the subject of visual images later in this book (Chapter 12).

Effective listening provides the foundation for critical and constructive thinking and is an important tool of civic engagement. Good listening is essential if citizens are going to exchange information and ideas and work together to solve problems through democratic deliberation.

CRITICAL LISTENING

2.4 Describe what it means to practice active and critical listening.

Watch the Video "Melissa Beall: Difference Between Listening and Hearing" at **MyCommunicationLab**

Preview. *Critical listening requires effort. As we work to improve our listening skills, we must remind ourselves of our ethical responsibility to take listening seriously and to listen to others attentively. However, it is also essential that we be good listeners by preparing ourselves to listen and by actively engaging the speaker's ideas.*

In an ideal world, all speakers would be well prepared, articulate, and knowledgeable. They would strive to engage us intellectually and emotionally. They would deliver their presentations with passion and conviction and present clear and forceful arguments. They would attempt to minimize distractions. They would structure their remarks logically and emphasize main ideas through their delivery, language, and the strategic use of presentational aids. They would listen carefully when their listeners asked questions after the speech, and they would respond thoughtfully and respectfully to each question.

Unfortunately, not all speakers live up to this ideal. As a result, we need to assume our own responsibilities as listeners and thoughtfully and analytically consider what the speaker has to say. This means that we have to come prepared to listen and to listen actively.

Preparing to Listen

As a listener, you have responsibilities that go beyond just trying to be attentive. If you want to listen fairly and critically, you must prepare yourself to do so.

Be informed   Before you attend a speech or community forum, read as widely as you can on the topic. It is almost impossible to analyze and evaluate a speaker's ideas and arguments if you are uninformed. Knowing something about the issues will help you identify potential areas of agreement or disagreement that you want to hear more about. With this information, you can formulate some tentative questions for the speaker.

Recognize your own biases   Commit yourself to listening with an open mind. Give some thought to your existing views and any potential biases you may have toward the speaker or topic. Who we are colors how we listen to and interact with speakers. Your background, your personal characteristics, and the roles you play in life all contribute to certain predispositions and biases that influence how you listen. No one can totally eliminate bias, but you can, through self-analysis, discover some of the forces at work in your own listening behaviors. Only by understanding yourself—what you bring to a speaking situation and who you are in relation to it—will you be able to listen in a critical yet fair-minded way.

Identify your goals   The speaker has a purpose in getting up to talk. As an audience member you, too, should have a purpose, whether that purpose is to learn, to evaluate, or to prepare for your own speech before the same audience. Do you want simply to gather information from a speech? Or do you hope to better understand an opposing point of view? Are you interested in relating the topic to your life or in preparing to speak out yourself on the topic the speaker is addressing? Your purposes may evolve as you listen. You may begin by thinking you just want information about a problem, such as global warming. But as you listen, you may decide that you want to get involved—to do something to address the problem. By listening purposefully, you can respond to the message on your own terms while still maintaining a healthy respect for the speaker's position and purpose.

Understand the circumstances and target audiences   The setting of a speech imposes certain restrictions and expectations on a speaker. A political candidate who buys 30 seconds of radio time is limited in what he or she can say. A speaker at an outdoor rally works under different constraints from one in a lecture hall. When you listen, be aware of how the particular setting may be affecting the speaker's efforts. If the speaker is given little time to speak, for instance, you may be less critical if his or her main points are not fully developed. If the speaker had no time to prepare, you may forgive minor errors or an unpolished style. The circumstances under which the speaker prepared and delivered the speech should always be taken into account.

Sometimes a speaker's words are aimed at more than one audience. For example, at a large state university, a series of racial incidents resulted in several protest demonstrations and rallies on campus. At these rallies, students spoke to an audience of their peers—their immediate audience. However, these students also knew that members of the press were present. Through the press, the speakers hoped to send messages to a wider audience on campus and in the community. The types of appeals speakers make, or the types of arguments they advance, may be puzzling to listeners who do not reflect enough on the target audience.

Consider the Speaker's Purpose Understanding what the speaker hopes to accomplish by speaking helps prepare us to listen effectively. Speakers do not always make their purposes clear, and some may even intend to mislead the audience. If a speech is poorly structured, it may not be easy to identify the speaker's goal or purpose. Knowing something about the setting, the speaker, and the general nature of the topic may help you identify the speaker's goal. Once you think you know the basic purpose of the speech, you are in a better position to make judgments about the quality of the speaker's ideas and information.

Active Listening

Becoming a critical listener means leaning to participate actively in the communication process. Here are some steps you need to take to become a more active listener.

Take notes as you listen Effective note taking can help you follow the speech and record critical information and ideas for later use.[24] Because note taking requires some action on your part, it also can help keep you engaged in active listening.[25]

HIGHLIGHTING NOTE TAKING

Here are some strategies that can make your note taking more effective:

1. *Write down the ideas and key points that are most important.* You cannot write down everything the speaker says. Focus instead on jotting down the thesis and main ideas.

2. *Use keywords to record main ideas.* Attempting to write down every word is inefficient and likely impossible. Routinely omit articles (*the, a, an*), many prepositions, and some verbs. Just make sure you retain the *sense* of the idea being communicated.

3. *Abbreviate and use symbols whenever possible.* Some of these may be unique to you. So long as you understand them, you will be fine. For example, in taking notes on a speech on civic engagement, you may simply write *CE* in place of *civic engagement. CA* may be used to designate *communication apprehension.* More common symbols may include *w* (for *with*), *w/o* (for

without), = (for *equal*), > (for *more than*), or < (for *less than*).

4. *Organize your notes as a rough outline of the speech.* Once you have identified major headings, you can also record substantiating material. Leave room in the left-hand margin and between items in your notes so that you can add things as the speaker presents them. Do not concern yourself with following a formal outlining format. Nearly any format will work, so long as you are able to distinguish main ideas from supporting (subordinate) material.

5. *Use your notes to help you evaluate the speech.* Your notes serve two purposes: recording the speaker's ideas and assessing their quality. If you feel a main idea is unsubstantiated, you may write "weak" in brackets next to the recorded idea. If you think of a specific question or concern, jot that down as well. ▲

In taking notes, you may want to jot down a basic outline of the speech as well as specific questions you will want to ask after the speech. You also may make note of any statistics, facts, or particular examples that you want to remember. Some researchers argue that it is not until *after* a speech is over that we typically process most of the ideas and information we gathered while listening. A good set of notes can help in this process of analysis and reflection.[26]

Evaluate the quality of the speaker's ideas and supporting material This is one of your most important tasks and is at the heart of critical listening. The speaker is seeking to get some specific response from you. To do that, she or he will present ideas and offer evidence to make those ideas understandable or believable. Your job is to ask how well those ideas further the speaker's purpose. If, for example, the speaker wants you to give money to a particular cause, you will listen for the ways that doing so will benefit your community or advance the values you hold. If a speaker asserts that a new building project is not environmentally friendly, you will want to listen for the opinions of experts or scientific evidence that supports such a claim. Much of what follows in this book will be directed toward helping you both construct sound arguments as a speaker and evaluate them as a listener. The principle to keep in mind is that you have the right to demand that speakers back up assertions. A healthy skepticism is fundamental to critical thinking and listening.

Be aware of the potential influence of the speaker's ethos Often when you listen to a speech, you have some initial perceptions of the speaker's credibility. You may find yourself overly influenced by *who* the person is rather than *what* he or she says in the speech. If, for example, you do not like the speaker, it may be that you just do not *want* to believe anything this speaker has to say. On the other hand, if you admire the speaker, you may not listen as critically as you should. If the matter is not of vital importance, it may not matter whether your judgment is biased by your opinion of the speaker. But suppose it is a serious matter that could affect your health or the well-being of your community. Separating your personal views of the speaker from your assessment of his or her message *can* be vital.

Offer Feedback

You can do this in two ways. First, you can *use* nonverbal communication to show the speaker that you are actively listening. When you look at the speaker or lean forward as he or she talks, you show your interest in the speech. You also may smile or nod your head in agreement to show the speaker that you are interested, are engaged, or even endorse his or her point of view. Through your facial expressions, you can show interest, agreement, confusion, or concern.[27] Second, you may have the opportunity to ask questions or make comments after the speech. Knowing that you might ask questions may help you focus your attention and listen carefully and critically. You will want to ask intelligent, perhaps even challenging questions after the speech, so it is important that you listen carefully as the speech is given.

As a listener, you play a crucial role in the communication process. Rather than listen passively, you should strive to be an active, critical participant in the process. As you practice engaged and critical listening, you will learn to evaluate what you hear, and you will find yourself becoming a better speaker as well. As an effective listener, you will also make better, more informed choices about what to believe—choices that will better serve both you and your community. As you learn to become a more active and critical listener, you will also become a more effective and engaging speaker.

PREPARING YOURSELF TO SPEAK

2.5 Under-stand your own interests, the needs and characteristics of your audi-ence, and the requirements of the speaking situation.

Preview. *In this section, we introduce some of the basic principles of public speaking that will be developed in greater detail throughout this book. These principles will guide you in selecting a topic, establishing credibility, and analyzing your audience.*

This book will help you acquire the skills you need to speak in public. But first, you must have some *reason* to speak. In your public speaking class, you may speak because you've been given an assignment to do so. In life outside the classroom, however, the need to speak goes deeper than that: it is part of your role as a citizen in a democracy. Our history is filled with examples of people who felt the need to speak out, including some who risked their lives by doing it. William Lloyd Garrison, the fiery nineteenth-century abolitionist, for example, spent much of his life speaking out against slavery, often facing hostile mobs and threats against his life. More than 30 years before the Civil War, Garrison described his determination to end slavery in the first issue of his famous abolitionist periodical, the *Liberator*: "I am in earnest—I will not equivocate—I will not excuse—I will not retreat a single inch; and I will be heard!"[28] Few of us are as passionately involved with a cause as William Lloyd Garrison. But as citizens in a democracy, we all have the right and the responsibility to speak out on matters of public concern.

Once you have made the decision to speak, you may think that the next step is to write your speech. But what about preparing *yourself* to speak? This is not just a trick of words. It is important to think about what *you* need to do to get ready to speak. Preparing yourself to speak means, first, making the decision to speak in public and then learning about the principles of effective and ethical public speaking.

Know Yourself

Explore the Profile "Self-Perceived Communication Competence Questionnaire" at **MyCommunicationLab**

You are your most important asset as a public speaker. Your own beliefs, abilities, knowledge, and potential are the foundation on which any speech is built. Yet few people have speeches in their heads just waiting to be delivered. Getting ready to give a speech is hard work; it involves study, research, reflection, and a desire to contribute to public discussion. It begins with what you know and care about. In Chapter 5, we will examine ways to develop significant topics. The key word here is *significant*. Your speeches ought to be about things that matter, things that are important on your campus or in your community, things that affect you and your audience locally, nationally, or globally.

Many students initially think they don't have anything to talk about. But there are no doubt many things that are important to you—such as the knowledge you gain as a student of literature or history or the concerns that motivated your decision to become a teacher, lawyer, computer specialist, or manager. What problems have you and your friends faced as you pursue your education? What does the future hold for you and your audience in a world filled with both opportunities and dangers? When you turn your attention to such questions, you begin to generate ideas for topics that you might address in your speeches.

Although you may first canvass your own interests and concerns in deciding what to talk about, you also need to think about another dimension of yourself: your credibility. Perhaps you've heard the expression, "If you could only see yourself as others see you." As a speaker, you need to do just that—try to see yourself as others do. We use the word *ethos*, a concept developed more than 2,000 years ago by the philosopher-rhetorician Aristotle, to describe how an audience perceives your character, intelligence, and motives as a speaker.

Some speakers have a well-established ethos related to their expertise or experiences. During the 2008 primary election, Barack Obama valued Senator Ted Kennedy's endorsement because the senator had strong ethos among many Democratic voters. In the Republican primaries of 2012, Newt Gingrich saw his lead in the polls disappear as a series of negative reports about his past undermined his ethos. The advantages or disadvantages of notoriety, however, are not afforded to most of us. What you do to prepare for your speech and what you do during the speech itself will most affect how your audience perceives you. Being well prepared lets the audience know that you take them and your topic seriously—and that you are in command of the facts. Being able to communicate directly and easily with your audience reassures them that you can be trusted. In short, you should consider how you will be perceived and what you might do to improve your own ethos as you prepare to speak.

Know Your Audience

Speeches are delivered to specific audiences, and you should consider your audience's needs, interests, beliefs, and knowledge. Your knowledge of yourself must be supplemented by knowledge about those who will be listening to what you have to say.

Knowing your audience makes it possible to adapt to their special needs or interests. If you wished to critique plans to reform Social Security, for example, you might emphasize different points, depending on the age of the audience. If talking to people about to retire, you might emphasize the immediate impact of the reform proposal on benefit payments. If, on the other hand, you are talking to an audience of college students, you might emphasize instead the long-term solvency of the system—whether Social Security will still be there for them when they retire in 40 or 50 years. This doesn't mean you would ignore the impact of the plan on age groups not represented in your audience, but only that the emphasis would change as you adapt to your listeners. Further, the United States encompasses people from many different cultures, not all of whom have the same priorities, values, or experiences.

It would be foolish to assume that everyone belonging to a particular demographic group, such as older people or college students, will react in exactly the same way to a message. But it is possible to make limited generalizations about listeners based on their group characteristics. We'll take this up in detail in Chapter 4, but the point here is simply that you must consider carefully the characteristics of the

Senator Margaret Chase Smith of Maine reminded her audience of basic values as she stood up against character assassination and reckless charges made by Senator Joseph McCarthy and his followers.

audience and take them into account when you speak.

Adapting to your audience does not mean pandering to what your listeners may *want* to hear. In the 1950s, for example, a Republican senator from Wisconsin, Joseph McCarthy, made vicious, unsubstantiated personal attacks on politicians, government officials, and other public figures, accusing them of Communist sympathies. In the anticommunist climate of the time, criticizing McCarthy's crusade was dangerous, possibly leading to the destruction of one's own career and personal life. It was in this atmosphere of fear that Senator Margaret Chase Smith of Maine rose in the Senate to introduce "A Declaration of Conscience." "I speak," she began, "as a Republican. I speak as a woman. I speak as a United States senator. I speak as an American." In spite of the risk of political backlash, she asserted that "those of us who shout the loudest about Americanism in making character assassinations are all too frequently those who, by our own words and acts, ignore some of the basic principles of Americanism: the right to criticize; the right to hold unpopular beliefs; the right to protest; the right of independent thought." The "exercise of these rights," she went on to say, "should not cost one single American citizen his reputation or his right to a livelihood nor should he be in danger of losing his reputation or livelihood merely because he happens to know someone who holds unpopular beliefs."[29] Senator Smith did not succeed in silencing Senator McCarthy and his supporters; it would be four more years before the Senate formally censured McCarthy for his campaign of character assassination. But in making her case, Smith reminded her audience of basic values that they shared and offered hope to those who objected to McCarthy's irresponsible accusations.

As a speaker, you never set out to deliberately alienate your audience. In speaking your mind, however, you will sometimes tell an audience something they don't want to hear. It is important, of course, that controversial ideas be presented respectfully and supported with convincing arguments and strong evidence. When you are presenting unpopular ideas, your persuasive challenge becomes greater.

Know the Situation

The setting for a speech can significantly influence how your audience responds. You may be speaking in a comfortable or an uncomfortable physical setting. Or you may be close to your audience or separated from them by an orchestra pit. You may be speaking directly to them or using a microphone. You may be talking to them first thing in the morning or right after lunch. Your audience may be there because they are interested in what you have to say or because their attendance is required. It is to your advantage to know in advance something about the setting in which you will be speaking so that you can anticipate potential problems and capitalize on any advantages that the setting may afford.

Shortly after his election in 1912, President Woodrow Wilson dramatically illustrated the importance of a speech's setting. What we now refer to as the State of the Union address was, at the time, called the "annual message." Since Thomas Jefferson's day, this message had been written out by the president and then sent to Congress, where it was read aloud by a clerk. It rarely generated much excitement. Wilson decided to break with precedent and appear in person before a joint session of Congress to deliver his annual message. Although some deplored the break with tradition, Wilson's speech captured national attention and generated so much excitement that every president since has followed his example.[30]

In addition to the setting, the temporal context of your speech will influence how it is received. Consider how much the events of September 11, 2001, changed the context for former president George W. Bush's speeches. After the terrorist attacks, political disagreements suddenly seemed petty, and some even thought it disrespectful or unpatriotic to criticize the commander in chief. President Bush's speeches, at least for a time, received more respectful attention and less partisan criticism. By 2008, however, the context had changed and both the Republican and Democratic candidates for president criticized Bush's policies. With the president's approval ratings dropping below 30 percent and the economy in a slump, Bush became a "lame duck" president and the target of more criticism.

On a smaller scale, you face the challenge of recognizing and adapting to what is going on in your listeners' world. As one student was preparing a class presentation on student financial aid programs, the student newspaper at her school published a story detailing proposed cuts in such programs. She needed to take account of the fact that her audience might be aware of that newspaper story, so she spoke specifically about those proposed cuts. Before you speak, you need to be aware of what is happening in your audience's immediate world that is relevant to your topic.

Aim for Audience Response

Think about the model of communication we presented earlier in the chapter. When you speak, your goal is to bring about some specific response from your audience. This principle is fundamental to everything else you will learn about public speaking, although it does *not* mean that you will resort to any means necessary to get that response. Still, knowing specifically what you want the audience to believe or do will help you determine what ideas to include in your speech. Do you want your audience simply to understand a concept or to take a specific action? For example, if you were giving an informative speech about solar energy, you could explain how it works and the types of equipment needed. If, however, you wished to give a persuasive speech, you might spend less time on such background information and focus more on the need to reduce our dependence on foreign oil and the environmental advantages of solar energy.

HIGHLIGHTING PREPARATION

Sound preparation is crucial to the success of your speech. Below is a checklist of questions that you should always ask as you begin thinking about a speech you will be delivering.

1. Does the audience expect me to address a particular topic or aspect of that topic?
2. Who will make up the audience for my speech?
   a. audience size
   b. age (range and distribution)
   c. sex (mixed or largely same sex)
   d. race/ethnicity
   e. values (religious, political, economic, etc.)
3. What will the speaking environment look like?
   a. size and arrangement of room
   b. availability of podium, blackboard, flip chart, microphone
   c. degree of formality
   d. location of building (Do I need to get a map?)
   e. parking issues?
4. Are there any time constraints?
5. Will questions follow the speech?
6. What is the anticipated length of the entire meeting? When should I arrive?
7. When should I arrive? Can I arrive early or check out the setting ahead of time? ▶

One of the first things you should do in preparing yourself to speak is to determine your specific purpose as precisely as possible because that will affect all your other choices. Your choice should be realistic, yet that does not mean you should never think big or take a long-range view. Elizabeth Cady Stanton, who organized the first women's rights convention in Seneca Falls, New York, in 1848, advocated that women should have the same rights as men, including the right to vote. It would be another 70 years before women could vote in national elections, but Stanton at least raised the issue in 1848 and started a national debate over women's rights.[31] There may be times when you will realize that your views are not widely accepted and that it is unrealistic to think you can change people's minds overnight. In such situations, you might aim for a more modest response—to get your listeners to admit that there is some problem that needs to be addressed, or to get them at least thinking about an issue that concerns you.

BUILDING AND DELIVERING YOUR SPEECH

2.6 Know the basic principles involved in constructing and presenting an effective speech.

Preview. *In this section, we introduce you to principles, to be elaborated in later chapters, that will guide you as you gather relevant material, construct sound arguments, organize your speech, and deliver it effectively.*

Gather Relevant Materials

As you begin to work on your speech, most likely you will have some information already in your head. You may be building on your knowledge of the stock market, the frustrations with the educational system that led your family to choose homeschooling, or your experiences when volunteering at a shelter for battered women. But even with this kind of experience or knowledge, you have to learn a great deal more to become a credible speaker. Once you have decided on the specific topic of your speech, you still need to explore other sources of information and find supporting material to back up your ideas. It is especially important to realize that in the process of learning more about your topic, you may even change your position. As you do research, you may find that some of your preconceptions are wrong. You should always be open to the possibility that your own views may change.

Gathering pertinent information might begin with reading about an issue in a general news magazine, such as *Time* or *Newsweek*. This will give you a broad overview and offer multiple perspectives. You also might search for materials on the Internet, although you need to be careful when using information from the Web. Because it is relatively easy to post material, many Web sites present highly biased or even totally false information, rumors, or unsubstantiated gossip. Even the names of Web sites can be misleading. If, for example, you were to come upon http://www.martinlutherking.org/, you might think you had found a good source of biographical information about the famous civil rights leader. In fact, that site is hosted by Stormfront, a white supremacist hate group. The Southern Poverty Law Center has described this site as "the first major hate site on the Internet…created by former Alabama Klan leader Don Black in 1995."[32] Unless you know an online source to be highly reliable (a government bureau, the *New York Times*, or a professional journal, for example), it is best to confirm information through other sources. Of course, you can always find reliable articles, books, and government publications in your campus or local public library. You may also want to interview experts, depending on the subject of your speech. Experts can be quoted as sources, and often they can direct you to additional resources. Whatever sources you use, they must be authoritative, reliable, and correctly cited, as we will discuss further in Chapters 6 and 7.

All speakers, no matter how knowledgeable, can benefit from learning more about their topic. Any topic of importance calls for research, and the process of research does not stop as you construct your speech.

Construct a Reasonable Argument

Watch the Video "U.S. Involvement in Iraq—Dawn Johnson" at **MyCommunicationLab**

After you decide what you hope to accomplish in your speech, you need to set about framing your ideas and finding materials that support those ideas. You should seek information that will connect your topic with your audience's feelings, needs, and emotions—what is often referred to as *pathos*—and that makes logical sense. Remember that public speaking is a process: your purpose may change as you gather more information. As you learn more, however, what you hope to accomplish will become clearer.

Consider the following example. You are about to cast a vote in a presidential election for the first time. As you try to sort out the issues and where the candidates stand, you realize that a lot of things going on in the campaign do not really encourage you to think for yourself. You would like to look at the issues and decide which person and/or party would provide the best leadership. There are a lot of irrelevant appeals for your vote, however, and a lot of misinformation has been disseminated. You may wonder, for example, why the endorsement of a rock star or a country music singer should matter in a presidential election. You see the media paying a lot of attention to personal accusations and to who is ahead in the latest polls. Much of what the candidates say about education or jobs is ignored by the media. You see 15- or 30-second television ads that offer slogans and assertions with nothing to back them up. Voting on the basis of celebrity endorsements or unsubstantiated personal attacks does not seem reasonable to you. Moreover, the tone of the campaign seems to you to trivialize the whole electoral process.

As you mull this over, you determine that you want to talk about presidential campaigns and, more specifically, about media coverage and advertising in presidential campaigns. Finally, you shape this into a specific purpose, describing the response you want from your audience: *I want my audience to look more critically at the political information presented to them during presidential campaigns.* You then ask yourself: Why do I believe this is so? Why should my audience agree with me? By answering these questions, you begin to form main ideas—ideas that will be convincing—such as the following:

- Celebrity endorsements can mislead voters.
- Campaign advertising is often misleading.
- Campaign news focuses too much on polls and other aspects of the "horse race."

As you then set about studying the topic, these ideas may be modified or new ones may emerge. As you conduct research, you will find specific data or relevant information that will help you make these ideas more convincing to your audience—that is, you will find good supporting material. For example, you might find information that does the following:

- Describes the lack of credentials and expertise among well-known celebrities who have been politically active
- Quotes from political experts on the content and effects of political ads
- Documents statistically how much news coverage is devoted to the "horse race" rather than issues

This process helps you build your argument. As you begin to find relevant supporting material, you will be able to refine your ideas and make those ideas more convincing to your audience. Consulting different kinds of sources and looking for differing perspectives will help you build the strongest, most compelling argument possible.

Give Your Message Structure

Well-organized speeches are easier for your audience to follow. They help your audience remember what has been said, and they tend to be more persuasive. If your audience perceives that you are disorganized—if they cannot follow your ideas—they will have trouble accepting your information and arguments and may doubt your credibility.

For an audience to follow your ideas, those ideas must relate to one another logically. Taken together, they must present a coherent case in support of your argument. You should introduce your speech by relating your topic to your audience, gaining their attention and interest, and establishing your own credibility. In your introduction, you should also state your thesis and preview your main arguments.

The body of your speech should then be built around those main ideas, bolstered by supporting materials, and you can help your listeners move from one idea to the next by utilizing strong transitions. Finally, your conclusion, as the last word of the speech, should repeat your thesis, summarize your main ideas, and leave your listeners with a memorable thought or a call to action.

Your main ideas should be organized in a logical pattern that is clear to your audience. Using a clear pattern of organization helps the audience take mental notes and remember what you have said. In Chapter 8, we will discuss various patterns of organization commonly used in speeches, including topical, chronological, and spatial patterns. For now, suffice it to say that a well-structured speech has several essential characteristics: a clear purpose, a short introduction that points out the importance of the topic and builds the speaker's ethos, clear transitions, well-developed and adequately supported main ideas, and a conclusion that raises thought-provoking questions or inspires listeners to act.

Speak Directly with Your Audience

How you present your speech can have a great impact on how your audience responds to your ideas. By choosing language suitable to the audience and the occasion, and by developing a conversational and direct speaking style, you will promote understanding and belief on the part of your audience. Suitable language is language that is precise, clear, interesting, and appropriate to both the audience and the situation. Beginning speakers sometimes believe that public speaking always demands formal language, and the result is a speech that sounds stiff and unnatural. Perhaps you've heard a friend describe a particular event or personal experience in a spontaneous and animated way and then later tell the same story less effectively in a formal speech.

It helps to think of public speaking as an enlarged conversation with friends. Speaking to an audience is not the same as a casual conversation. After all, you plan a speech in advance, and it is more carefully organized than casual remarks. In a speech, you should also avoid language that is *too* informal, including the "fillers" we sometimes use in casual conversation—the "likes" and "you knows" that clutter everyday speech. Yet the same conversational style that you use when talking with friends may be perfectly appropriate in most of your speeches. In addition, many of the personal experiences and stories you talk about with your friends may well work in your speech, depending on the topic.

Of course, not all situations call for the same style of delivery. On formal occasions, you may choose to speak from a written manuscript. At other times, you may be asked to speak impromptu, with little or no time for preparation. On rare occasions, you may be expected to memorize your entire speech. Most often, however, you will be speaking extemporaneously—that is, with careful preparation but with minimal notes and a less formal, more direct, and conversational style.

No matter how much work you put into preparing yourself to speak, what the audience finally sees and hears will determine their response. The best delivery does not call attention to itself; you don't want the audience to pay more attention to *how* you talk than to *what* you have to say. Good delivery, in most contexts, is conversational and relaxed. If the delivery is good, listeners can hear and understand what you say and will not find themselves distracted by mannerisms, inappropriate language, or an overly dramatic presentation.

The principles we have presented here will help you become an effective listener and speaker. They will also help you become a more engaged citizen. Although all of these principles will be discussed in more detail later in this book, it is important that you reflect on them from the start, as you first begin to think about speaking in public. They will influence how you *prepare* yourself to speak.

One other question should also be considered at the outset: Does the idea of getting up in front of an audience to speak make you nervous? If so, you are not alone; feeling apprehensive about speaking in public is normal. In the next chapter, we offer some practical advice on dealing with that nervousness.

 Study and Review materials for this chapter are at **MyCommunicationLab**

SUMMARY

 Listen to the Audio Chapter Summary at **MyCommunicationLab**

The Speaker-Listener Partnership

2.1 Explain the nature and significance of the speaker-listener partnership.

- The transactional model of communication emphasizes how speech is successful only if it benefits both speaker and audience.

The Engaged listener

2.2 Understand the meaning and benefits of engaged listening.

- Good listening leads to many positive outcomes, including better interpersonal relationships and healthier communities.

Barriers to Good Listening

2.3 Understand the barriers that prevent you from listening effectively.

- Good listeners overcome the barriers to communication by avoiding passivity, automatic rejection of speakers' ideas, inattention and stereotyping, while ignoring distractions.

Critical Listening

2.4 Describe what it means to practice active and critical listening.

- To practice critical listening, you must be prepared to listen and be an active listener. Prepare to listen by being informed, recognizing your own biases, listening with a purpose, understanding the circumstances, and considering the speaker's purpose. Become an active critical listener by evaluating the quality of the speaker's ideas and evidence, being aware of the potential influence of the speaker's ethos, offering feedback, and taking notes.

Preparing Yourself to Speak

2.5 Understand your own interests, the needs and characteristics of your audience, and the requirements of the speaking situation.

- When preparing to speak, you must take into account the ways in which the speaker, the audience, and the situation interact by examining your own knowledge, ability, beliefs, and potential, discovering the audience's needs, interests, beliefs, and knowledge, understanding how the setting and other outside factors may influence the speech, and devising a clear purpose that reflects the desired response.

Building and Delivering Your Speech

2.6 Know the basic principles involved in constructing and presenting an effective speech.

- As you build your speech, you will seek out relevant sources of information, construct a sound argument, and give your message structure.

QUESTIONS FOR REVIEW AND REFLECTION

The Speaker-Listener Partnership

2.1 Explain the nature and significance of the speaker-listener partnership.

1. Explain the significance of the speaker-listener partnership. Offer one example of how the speaker and listener are mutually interdependent.
2. Explain what is meant by a transactional communication model. What are the main components? Why is it important to think of communication in this way?

The Engaged listener

2.2 Understand the meaning and benefits of engaged listening.

3. What are the benefits of being an engaged listener? Can you think of instances in which you have benefited by being engaged?

Barriers to Good Listening

2.3 Understand the barriers that prevent you from listening effectively.

4. What are the barriers to effective listening? Have you experienced such barriers? How might you overcome them?

Critical Listening

2.4 Describe what it means to practice active and critical listening.

5. What does it mean to be a critical listener? Do you believe you would change any of your own listening behaviors to become an active critical listener? What are those behaviors?

Preparing Yourself to Speak

2.5 Understand your own interests, the needs and characteristics of your audience, and the requirements of the speaking situation.

6. As you begin to prepare a speech, how will you take into account the interactions between yourself, your audience, and the situation? What specific factors will you need to consider?

Building and Delivering Your Speech

2.6 Know the key principles involved in gathering relevant materials to build a sound, well-structured argument.

7. If you are to build a well-argued and well-organized speech, what are the most important steps you must take?
8. What are the most important factors that will help you successfully deliver your speech?
9. In your view, are any of the steps in preparing to speak more important than others? Why?
10. As you learn to give speeches, what do you imagine will be your greatest challenge? How might you begin to overcome that challenge?

✓ Study and Review the Flashcards at **MyCommunicationLab**

Speaking with Confidence

OVERVIEW AND LEARNING OBJECTIVES

Understanding Communication Apprehension

3.1 Define communication apprehension.

Factors That Contribute to Communication Apprehension

3.2 Describe underlying factors that contribute to communication apprehension.

Managing Communication Apprehension

3.3 Employ strategies for managing communication apprehension while preparing yourself to speak.

No one was more universally admired than our nation's first president, George Washington. Yet this heroic figure was extremely nervous when delivering his first inaugural address. One senator who attended the ceremony observed that this "great man was agitated and embarrassed more than ever he was by the leveled cannon or pointed musket."[1] His successor, the second president of the United States, was also terrified about delivering his inaugural address. After a sleepless night, John Adams felt ill and was afraid he might faint during his speech. He was so scared that he told his wife, Abigail, that he was "in great doubt whether to say anything" at all "besides repeating the oath."[2]

Nearly everyone is asked to speak in public at some time in their lives. For some of us, public speaking is central to our professions as managers, lawyers, salespersons, ministers, community organizers, nonprofit agency directors, or educators. As citizens in a democracy, each of us is presented with many opportunities to express our views on matters important to us and our communities. If you hope to have an impact in your community, you *must* be willing and able to share your views and ideas in public.

Yet, many fear public speaking. Some even avoid certain careers or turn down opportunities for promotion because they know they will have to speak in public. Students may avoid taking a public speaking class or pursuing particular majors to avoid a public speaking requirement. Others may attend community meetings but have no say in the decisions that are made because they could not bring themselves to speak out. Even strong, experienced leaders grapple with the fear of public speaking and decline opportunities to really take charge of a situation by speaking up.

UNDERSTANDING COMMUNICATION APPREHENSION

Preview. *The first step in learning to deal with communication apprehension is to understand what it is and how it may affect you and undermine your effectiveness as a speaker and citizen. Those experiencing high communication apprehension may perform less effectively in the classroom, on the job, and in the community. While most of us may not be affected by severe communication apprehension, we are all apt to suffer from it to some degree.*

A recent film, *The King's Speech*, tells the true story of King George VI, who suffered from such extreme communication apprehension that he was virtually paralyzed by stuttering whenever he tried to deliver a speech. After intense work with a speech therapist, he successfully delivered an inspirational radio address in 1939— as Europe was being overrun by Nazi armies—in which he proclaimed Britain's determination to prevail over Hitler's Germany. When even kings and national heroes suffer from communication apprehension, it is not surprising that the rest of us become nervous when asked to speak in public. In one famous survey, it was discovered that people are more afraid of public speaking than they are of dying.[3] Comedian Jerry Seinfeld joked about this finding:

> According to most studies, people's number one fear is public speaking. Number two is death. Death is number two. Does that seem right? That means to the average person, if you have to go to a funeral, you're better off in the casket than doing the eulogy.[4]

3.1 Define communication apprehension.

Explore the **Profile** "Personal Report of Public Speaking Anxiety (PRPSA)" at **MyCommunicationLab**

With great effort and practice, King George VI learned to manage his communication apprehension and deliver compelling and powerful speeches.

For many people, however, fear of speaking is no laughing matter. Doctors at Duke University Medical Center actually consider public speaking sufficiently stressful that they include it on a list of "mental stress tests." Physicians use these tests in identifying those most at risk for future heart problems.[5]

Communication scholar James McCroskey, who has studied communication apprehension for more than 40 years, defines it as "an individual's level of fear or anxiety associated with either real or anticipated communication with another person or persons."[6] Unlike stage fright, communication apprehension is not limited to acting or traditional public speaking situations but may also extend to anxiety about speaking up in meetings and other smaller, less public communication contexts. It is not the same as shyness, where an individual may be more reserved or less talkative than others even though he or she is not particularly apprehensive about communicating.[7]

Although most of us experience only occasional or moderate communication apprehension, research has shown that high communication apprehension is associated with a number of negative outcomes. For example, students who struggle with high communication apprehension tend to prefer large lecture classes over

HIGHLIGHTING COMMUNICATION APPREHENSION | How Universities Are Helping Students

- At Penn State University, a special class, "Speech Anxiety," has been offered since 1965. Today, three sections of the class are taught every semester, with enrollment restricted to 20 students in each. Students are screened carefully before being admitted. Once in the class, they have the chance to present their speeches in small groups, move on to speaking in front of the instructor, and finally, give their speech to the whole class.
- The University of Wyoming developed a special course to address communication apprehension seven years ago as part of a student retention

effort. There, public speaking is integrated into a course that also emphasizes social conversations and group communication.
- Other colleges (including Hamilton College, Randolph-Macon College, and Arizona State University) have opened speech labs where students can practice their speeches, receive feedback, and learn techniques for managing their apprehension.

Source: Rachel Aviv, "Don't Be Shy," *The New York Times,* www.nytimes.com/2007/11/04/education/edlife/reticence.html? (accessed February 4, 2012). ▲

smaller classes that encourage interaction, and often learn less and receive lower grades.[8] They are more likely to sit on the sides or in the back of the classroom where the instructor is less likely to call on them.[9] They are also less likely to seek the assistance of available tutors even when they feel they need help.[10] Of course, highly apprehensive students try to avoid taking public speaking classes. McCroskey tells the story of a straight-A engineering student who enrolled in a required public speaking class and dropped it twelve times![11] A number of colleges and universities have developed special sections of the basic public speaking course that are reserved for students with high apprehension.

In addition to problems with academic performance, researchers also report that individuals with high communication apprehension tend to perform less effectively in job interviews (and so are less likely to be hired), they seek jobs with low communication demands (and often, lower wages), and once in the workforce, they report less job satisfaction.[12] Equally important, they are less likely to be selected as friends or turned to as opinion leaders.[13] Not only can communication apprehension become a significant barrier to your personal and professional success, but it can also rob you of your voice as a citizen.[14] Indeed, if you are afraid to speak out, you *have* no voice in our democratic system.

FACTORS THAT CONTRIBUTE TO COMMUNICATION APPREHENSION

Preview. *Most speakers who have experienced communication apprehension would prefer to feel more confident when they speak. Often they don't really understand what it is they fear or why they feel anxious in some situations but remain calm and confident in others. Understanding the underlying causes of communication apprehension is the essential first step in learning to manage it effectively.*

3.2 Describe underlying factors that contribute to communication apprehension.

Watch the Video "Martin Cox: How to Relax Before Giving a Speech" at **MyCommunicationLab**

Poor Preparation

Sometimes speakers feel apprehensive about speaking in public because they know they are ill-prepared. Perhaps their ideas are poorly documented or their thoughts disorganized, or they may have failed to practice delivering their speech aloud from their notes. Unlike some other causes of communication apprehension, poor preparation is something you can easily address.

Trait Anxiety

Some speakers suffer from what McCroskey calls trait anxiety. They are generally apprehensive whenever they are called upon to speak.[15] If they are asked to share their thoughts in a meeting, introduce a speaker, or make a presentation of any kind, their hearts race. They may refuse requests to speak by saying, "I'm just not good at this kind of thing" or "I'll do anything but *that*!" Speakers with trait anxiety do all they can to avoid speaking in public, even if the "public" is a group of people they know from their church or neighborhood. Even informal speeches to small groups make these people nervous. They have speaking anxieties no matter what the context, topic, or audience.

> **FIGURE 3.1**
>
> ### Assessing Your Communication Apprehension
>
> Communication scholar James McCroskey developed the following instrument to help people identify their level of communication apprehension. Answer the statements, and then calculate your overall score and your sub-scores for each of the four communication contexts.
>
> #### Personal Report of Communication Apprehension (PRCA-24)
>
> DIRECTIONS: This instrument is composed of twenty-four statements concerning feelings about communicating with other people. Please indicate the degree to which each statement applies to you by marking whether you: **strongly agree (1-SA), agree (2-A), are undecided (3-U), disagree (4-D), or strongly disagree (5-SD)**. Work quickly; record your first impression.
>
> 1. I dislike participating in group discussions.
>
>   1 - SA   2 - A   3 - U   4 - D   5 - SD
>
> 2. Generally, I am comfortable while participating in group discussions.
>
>   1 - SA   2 - A   3 - U   4 - D   5 - SD
>
> 3. I am tense and nervous while participating in group discussions.
>
>   1 - SA   2 - A   3 - U   4 - D   5 - SD
>
> 4. I like to get involved in group discussions.
>
>   1 - SA   2 - A   3 - U   4 - D   5 - SD
>
> 5. Engaging in a group discussion with new people makes me tense and nervous.
>
>   1 - SA   2 - A   3 - U   4 - D   5 - SD
>
> 6. I am calm and relaxed while participating in group discussions.
>
>   1 - SA   2 - A   3 - U   4 - D   5 - SD
>
> 7. Generally, I am nervous when I have to participate in a meeting.
>
>   1 - SA   2 - A   3 - U   4 - D   5 - SD
>
> 8. Usually I am calm and relaxed while participating in meetings.
>
>   1 - SA   2 - A   3 - U   4 - D   5 - SD
>
> 9. I am very calm and relaxed when I am called upon to express an opinion at a meeting.
>
>   1 - SA   2 - A   3 - U   4 - D   5 - SD
>
> 10. I am afraid to express myself at meetings.
>
>   1 - SA   2 - A   3 - U   4 - D   5 - SD

FIGURE 3.1 (*Continued*)

11. Communicating at meetings usually makes me uncomfortable.

    1 - SA   2 - A   3 - U   4 - D   5 - SD

12. I am very relaxed when answering questions at a meeting.

    1 - SA   2 - A   3 - U   4 - D   5 - SD

13. While participating in a conversation with a new acquaintance, I feel very nervous.

    1 - SA   2 - A   3 - U   4 - D   5 - SD

14. I have no fear of speaking up in conversations.

    1 - SA   2 - A   3 - U   4 - D   5 - SD

15. Ordinarily I am very tense and nervous in conversations.

    1 - SA   2 - A   3 - U   4 - D   5 - SD

16. Ordinarily I am very calm and relaxed in conversations.

    1 - SA   2 - A   3 - U   4 - D   5 - SD

17. While conversing with a new acquaintance, I feel very relaxed.

    1 - SA   2 - A   3 - U   4 - D   5 - SD

18. I'm afraid to speak up in conversations.

    1 - SA   2 - A   3 - U   4 - D   5 - SD

19. I have no fear of giving a speech.

    1 - SA   2 - A   3 - U   4 - D   5 - SD

20. Certain parts of my body feel very tense and rigid while giving a speech.

    1 - SA   2 - A   3 - U   4 - D   5 - SD

21. I feel relaxed while giving a speech.

    1 - SA   2 - A   3 - U   4 - D   5 - SD

22. My thoughts become confused and jumbled when I am giving a speech.

    1 - SA   2 - A   3 - U   4 - D   5 - SD

23. I face the prospect of giving a speech with confidence.

    1 - SA   2 - A   3 - U   4 - D   5 - SD

24. While giving a speech, I get so nervous I forget facts I really know.

    1 - SA   2 - A   3 - U   4 - D   5 - SD

(Continued)

FIGURE 3.1 (*Continued*)

SCORING: Compute sub-scores for four communication contexts—group discussions, meetings, interpersonal conversations, and public speaking—and an *overall* communication apprehension score. To compute your sub-scores, merely add or subtract your scores as follows: Use 18 as the base score to which you add your scores on designated items (for example, items associated with communicating in meetings). Then subtract from that number your total score on the other times designated within that same context to get your sub-score. Repeat with each item for each communication context.

Sub-scores	Scoring Formula
Group discussion	18 + scores for items 2, 4, and 6; – scores for items 1, 3, and 5
Meetings	18 + scores for items 8, 9, and 12; – scores for items 7, 10, and 11
Interpersonal conversations	18 + scores for items 14, 16, and 17; – scores for items 13, 15, and 18
Public speaking	18 + scores for items 19, 21, and 23; – scores for items 20, 22, and 24

Scores on the four contexts (groups, meetings, interpersonal conversations, and public speaking) can range from a low of 6 to a high of 30. Any score above 18 indicates some degree of apprehension.

To determine your overall CA score, add together all four sub-scores.

Your score should range between 24 and 120. If your score is below 24 or above 120, you have made a mistake in computing the score.

Scores between **83 and 120** indicate a high level of communication apprehension. Scores between **55 and 83** indicate a moderate level of communication apprehension. Scores between **24 and 55** indicate a low level of communication apprehension.

Source: McCroskey, *An Introduction to Rhetorical Communication, Personal Report of Communication Apprehension (PRCA-24),* © 1982 by Pearson Education, Inc. Reproduced by permission of Pearson Education, Inc.

State Anxiety

Other speakers may suffer from state anxiety, which means that a particular set of circumstances triggers their communication apprehension. They may, for example, see a particular audience or speech setting as threatening. When confronted with giving a speech in a large auditorium for the first time, for example, an otherwise calm and confident speaker may suddenly feel anxious. Or a speaker might become anxious when asked to speak to an audience of important people or people who have higher status than the speaker. Professional contexts can also activate this anxiety trigger; some speakers understandably become nervous if they sense that their job or career might be on the line when they speak. Finally, most speakers feel more anxious if they anticipate a hostile or negative response from their listeners. This may be especially true if their topic is highly controversial or emotional, like gay marriage, abortion, or gun control.[16]

Self-Expectations

Some speakers have unrealistic self-expectations, hoping for perfection when they deliver a speech.[17] If they make the slightest mistake—stumbling over a word or dropping their notes—they feel like a failure. They are their own harshest judges.

Other speakers' self-expectations may be too low. Perhaps they had a disappointing speaking experience early in their lives and have avoided speaking in public ever since. Anticipating failure, they may even stop caring or preparing.

Fear of Evaluation

Sometimes, speakers fear evaluation by others. They may perceive that listeners will judge them critically and be quick to note flaws in their performance.[18] They don't realize that listeners typically want to see speakers succeed. Of course, you are evaluated when you give a speech in your public speaking class, but even there your instructor is hoping that you and your classmates will demonstrate learning and improvement and will perform well.

Fearing That Listeners Perceive Apprehension

Some speakers imagine that audience members know when they are feeling anxious. They are keenly aware of their racing hearts and trembling hands and assume that others will be quick to notice. Studies show, however, that listeners—including trained speech teachers—are typically poor judges of the level of a speaker's anxiety.[19] In general, listeners rate speakers as significantly *less* anxious than speakers rate themselves. In some cases, listeners may perceive an anxious speaker as calm and confident.

Fear of Failure

Even though most of us experience communication apprehension at some time in our lives, we may feel isolated or fear failure when we experience it. In classroom settings, for example, student speakers may perceive classmates as confident while *they* feel panicked.[20] They may also assume that confident speakers will be more effective. But history has taught us that outstanding pubic speakers often suffer from communication apprehension. The great Roman orator Cicero wrote, "I turn pale at the outset of a speech and quake in every limb and in all my soul."[21] Other excellent speakers who have reported feelings of speech anxiety include Winston Churchill, William Jennings Bryan, John F. Kennedy, Jerry Garcia, and Maria Shriver. Feeling anxious about speaking does not necessarily lead to failure.

Overreacting to the Body's Physiological Responses

When speakers become apprehensive, they may experience an array of physiological reactions. Some will have trembling hands, while others' mouths go dry. Figure 3.2 provides a list of the body's most common physiological reactions to communication

---

FIGURE 3.2

Physiological Reactions to Anxiety

- Parched mouth
- Frog in the throat
- Shortness of breath
- Butterflies in the stomach
- Trembling hands or legs
- Inability to gesture
- Distracting gestures
- Frozen facial expression
- Flushed cheeks
- Red blotches on neck
- Feelings of weakness or light-headedness
- Clinging to the podium
- Sudden urge to visit the restroom
- Darting eyes (looking everywhere but at the audience)
- Mind going blank—may lead to vocalized pauses ("um" or "uh") or repetition of fillers (such as "you know" or "okay")
- Shaking voice
- Clammy hands
- Loss of focus on speech
- Hot flashes
- Nervous pacing

---

apprehension. Overreacting to these physical symptoms at the start of your speech can aggravate your anxiety. If you can make it through the first few seconds, many of these reactions will soon subside, especially if you are talking about a topic that really matters to you personally.

Most of us experience only mild to moderate communication apprehension, but for some, speaking anxiety can be quite severe—so severe, in fact, that they may avoid speaking at all.[22] Fortunately, we can all learn strategies to help us better manage our fears of public speaking.

Watch the Video
"Informative Speech:
Fear of Public Speaking" at
MyCommunicationLab

3.3 Employ strategies for managing communication apprehension while preparing yourself to speak.

MANAGING COMMUNICATION APPREHENSION

Preview. *There are a number of useful strategies for managing communication apprehension. They have been used by students, politicians, business and professional speakers, and even U.S. presidents. Most important are careful preparation and a real commitment to the issue you are addressing. Other techniques range from doing your homework on the setting and audience for your speech to exercising for relaxation.*

Because all of us experience communication apprehension to some degree, we have to find ways to overcome it. Even great leaders have to find ways of conquering their fear of speaking, no matter how momentous the occasion or how high the stakes. In 1859, for example, Abraham Lincoln faced the biggest challenge of his young political career when he was invited to speak at the Cooper Union in New York City, a traditional proving ground for presidential candidates. Self-educated and with a "rough-and-tumble" style,[23] Lincoln was hardly known as a great orator. Yet now his whole future—indeed, the future of the nation—rested on this single speech. A successful speech would make him a leading candidate for president; a poorly received speech could doom his career. As his law partner, William H. Herndon, recalled, "No former effort in the line of speech-making had cost so much time and thought as this one."[24] In the end, that effort paid off. After putting off the sponsors long enough to carefully research and prepare his remarks, Lincoln delivered a tremendously successful speech—a speech that Harold Holtzer aptly characterized in the subtitle of his book *Lincoln at Cooper Union: The Speech That Made Abraham Lincoln President.*

Because of his painstaking speech preparation and deep conviction about the spread of slavery, Abraham Lincoln was able to deliver one of his most eloquent speeches at Cooper Union—a speech that served to establish his credibility as a candidate for president.

How did Lincoln do it? Part of the answer, of course, lies in the extra time he took to research and prepare his speech. But just as important was his firm conviction that he was *right* in taking the position he took: that the Republican Party should oppose the further spread of slavery in America. In other words, Lincoln was thoroughly prepared and firmly *believed* in what he said, and those are the most critical factors in dealing with communication apprehension. This leads to the two most fundamental principles in combating communication apprehension: addressing substantive issues to which you are committed and being well prepared.

Address Issues to Which You Are Committed

A genuine commitment to your topic can help you overcome the anxiety you may have about speaking in public. You are more likely to speak with confidence if you are addressing a topic that really matters to you and your audience. As part of a community forum on health care, for example, an emergency room doctor might speak out on the critical importance of finding ways to care for the uninsured—perhaps arguing that universal health insurance would ensure that everyone who needed health care would get it, thereby creating a more humane society. A student whose roommate has been attacked outside the school library might make an

Explore the Concept "Overcoming Nervousness" at **MyCommunicationLab**

FOCUS ON CIVIC ENGAGEMENT | The Ripon College Speakers Bureau

Successful speakers say that the best way to overcome communication apprehension is simply to gain experience, giving as many speeches as possible in a wide variety of settings. Taking a public speaking class may not be enough. One also needs experience in "real-world" situations, which vary widely in terms of the settings and the audiences for your speeches.

Ripon College, a small liberal arts school in Wisconsin, has a long and distinguished tradition of teaching speech and debate. In 2006, however, two faculty members at the college, Jody Roy and Steve Martin, decided that public speaking should be about more than speaking to other students in a classroom or competing for a trophy in a speech or debate contest. They envisioned students becoming engaged citizens and leaders in their communities, as emphasized in the classical and neoclassical rhetorical traditions. The result was the formation of the Ripon College Speakers Bureau, a co-curricular program that creates partnerships between student speakers and local and national nonprofit groups.

Since its inception in 2006, the Speakers Bureau has helped students at Ripon College put into practice what they learn in the classroom. Advocating on behalf of these local and national partners, the students have benefited both themselves and their communities. Currently, Ripon students serve as advocates for Students Against Violence Everywhere, a national nonprofit association promoting conflict management skills and good citizenship, as well as the Huntington's Disease Society of America, which promotes awareness of this devastating degenerative brain disorder. Ripon students also have assisted a number of local partners, including the Green Lake Area Animal Shelter and the Ripon Public Library.

The Speakers Bureau trains participating students and then sends them into the community, often to speak to middle school or high school students. Alyssa Paulsen, for example, has spoken to high school students in Sheboygan, Wisconsin, about how to discourage bullying and harassment. Sarah Hopkins spoke to 280 low-income middle-school students in Racine, Wisconsin, encouraging them to follow their dreams of attending college. Ryan Greene speaks to both college students and adult prison inmates about the causes and harms of domestic violence. And Shawn Karsten, who lost his father to suicide, shares his highly personal narrative with young people struggling with their own family tragedies. Since participating in the Speakers Bureau, Shawn has become a professional speaker, traveling around the country telling his story of life with a famous but tragically alcoholic father. Speaking to audiences at leadership conferences, at-risk youth programs, school assemblies, educational conferences, and addiction and grief-management programs, Shawn's most popular speeches include "From Pain to Purpose," which recounts how he found peace by reaching out to help others, and "This is What It Feels Like to be Your Kid," which is targeted at adults in alcohol and addiction recovery programs.

More and more students are getting involved with the Speakers Bureau at Ripon College, yet it has become so popular with its partner organizations that it has trouble filling all its requests for student speakers!

Source: Ripon College, "Bookings, Flight Schedules, and Network News Interviews: Speakers Bureau Scrambles to Keep Up with Demand," *The Proof: Department of Communication Newsletter* (Winter 2009).

impassioned plea to a group of campus administrators, asking them to fund more lighting, police patrols, and campus escort services. Because of the commitment of these speakers to their topics, any communication apprehension they might have felt at the start of their speeches would likely fade as they focused on their arguments and the importance of persuading their audiences.

Be Well Prepared

There is no better psychological defense for dealing with communication apprehension than honestly being able to say to yourself that you *are* well prepared. You have selected a topic of interest and value to you as well as your audience. You have done your homework, perhaps even conducting an audience survey. You have devoted significant time and effort to gathering information and to broadening your understanding of the subject. You have carefully organized your speech into a clear, coherent, and unified whole. You have practiced by going over your speech—aloud—several times, timing yourself and fine-tuning your ideas. You have asked friends for feedback. You feel confident that there is little more you could have done to prepare for your speech.

Reminding yourself of your careful preparation can be reassuring and even liberating as you grapple with feelings of anxiety. Your delivery will reflect your careful preparation, and the audience will sense that you have worked hard out of respect for their time and attention. Also remember that your audience *shares* responsibility for the success of your speech. Just as you have prepared well and met your responsibilities as a speaker, your audience, too, will fulfill its responsibility to listen carefully and constructively to what you have to say.

The best way to reduce speech anxiety is to address topics that genuinely concern you and to be well prepared for your presentation. In addition, you may employ a variety of other strategies for managing communication apprehension. As you give more speeches, you will no doubt find strategies that work especially well for you. For now, however, let's examine some of the specific strategies that experienced speakers have found helpful for dealing with communication apprehension.[25]

Develop a Positive Attitude

What do you think of when you imagine yourself making a speech? Do you picture yourself stumbling over your own words, dropping your note cards, or freezing as you attempt to respond to a listener's question? Research has clearly shown that

FOCUS ON CIVIC ENGAGEMENT | Speaking with Conviction

In 1993 a young man named Quay Hanna graduated from college, got on a bus, and traveled throughout the country. He had grown up in a small town where there was little diversity but a lot of suspicion of those who were different. Racism seemed to him to be just a reflection of reality. As is explained on his Web site, "Nine weeks, thirty-seven states, and twelve-thousand miles later, he got more than an incredible journey and hundreds of stories to tell. As he traveled, he was forced to confront his own racist and prejudiced beliefs, making him realize that he had more to offer the world than his lifelong hatred of others." So Quay set out to talk about his transformation from a self-proclaimed "redneck" to a passionate advocate for racial understanding. Speaking with conviction and passion to thousands of young people throughout the United States, Quay has helped his listeners examine their own prejudices and beliefs. Professor Jody Roy of Ripon College, who has done extensive research on hatred and prejudice, writes that "Quay's conviction, his complete commitment to his topic, is a critical part of his exceptional success."

Source: www.quayhanna.com

people with high speech anxiety tend to have more negative thoughts before the delivery of a speech than people who are comfortable speaking.[26] It stands to reason, then, that developing more positive thoughts may help in managing or reducing anxiety.

When you dread making a speech, when you think of it as a burden or something that you "have to do" for a class or for your job, you are more likely to develop severe communication apprehension. What if you learned to view it differently: as an opportunity to change minds, to share what you know, or to make a real difference in the community where you live? In other words, you should start telling yourself: "I want to give a speech because what I have to say may help my audience." The principle here is simple: speakers who anticipate success rather than failure suffer less apprehension about speaking.

Practice Your Speech

Ideally, you should practice over a period of a few days, not a few hours. It is always a mistake to put off rehearsing your speech until the last minute. Prepare your speech well in advance and give yourself ample time to practice. You may be able to get a friend or a few friends to listen to your speech. Practicing early and often is the key here. No one can tell you exactly how many times to practice or what techniques may work best for you. As you give more speeches over time, you will learn what approach works best for you.

Anticipate the Speech Situation

There are times in life when it is nice to be surprised, but before or during the delivery of a public speech is not one of them. As we have said before, effective speakers know their audiences. Gathering information about your audience and the speaking situation *before* you speak helps you focus on the audience right from the start. If, for example, you have decided to speak at the local school board or at a meeting of the city council, plan to attend one of their meetings beforehand so you can see how they conduct business and how other speakers present their views. Whenever someone invites you to make a speech, try to obtain as much information as you can. If the organization has a Web site, you will want to visit that, and you might also ask the person who invited you to speak to respond to a few questions before the speech. Figure 3.3 provides some basic questions that you may want to ask about your audience and the speech situation.

Practice Active Listening

Active listening can be a powerful tool for managing communication apprehension.[27] Rarely do you make a speech under circumstances in which you arrive, immediately stand up and talk, and then quickly depart. More likely, your speech will be part of a longer program, meeting, or banquet, and others will speak before you. Listening closely to those speakers will draw your attention away from your own anxieties and may even give you ideas about last-minute changes to your own speech. In community settings, listening carefully to others as they share their experiences may help you focus on the importance of the issue and enable you to relax a bit as you prepare to share your own. In your speech class, you will be listening

> **FIGURE 3.3**

Collecting Information before You Speak

DON'T make assumptions about the audience's knowledge by overestimating or underestimating what they know.

DO ask:

- Who *are* my listeners (classmates, board members, community leaders, government representatives, volunteers)?
- What do they already know about my topic?
- What would they like to learn or need to know about my topic?
- What is their likely range of attitudes toward my topic?

DON'T get lost or arrive late!

DO ask:

- What is the location of the building where I will speak?
- Where should I park?
- What are specific directions to the room where I will speak?
- How early should I arrive?
- Where are the restrooms?

DON'T make assumptions about the room in which you will speak.

DO ask:

- How large is the room?
- Where will I be seated before I speak (in the audience, on a stage, at a table)?
- How will the room be arranged (traditional rows of seats, chairs in a circle, cozy room, formal boardroom, classroom)?
- Will the equipment/items I need be available (podium, Internet access, microphone, glass of water)?

DON'T ignore time limits/constraints.

DO ask:

- How much time has been allotted for my speech?
- Will there be time for questions following my speech (expected time frame)?

DON'T violate other listener norms or expectations.

DO ask:

- Should I plan to be present for the entire meeting?
- Will other business, speakers, a lunch, or a reception precede or follow my presentation?
- What is the anticipated time frame for the entire meeting?
- What are the ways that groups interact and citizens present ideas in public meetings (these might differ from a traditional speaking setting)?

to other speakers before and after you make your speech. Instead of fretting over your notes, strive to listen carefully to those who speak before you. You may learn something, and you might also find yourself a bit more relaxed when it is your turn to speak. In addition, you may be able to refer to something in an earlier speech that complements your own speech in some way.

Exercise for Relaxation

If you feel tense and nervous before you speak, you can do some simple physical exercises to relax. One excellent way to relax is by breathing deeply. Deep breathing allows you to take in a large quantity of air, giving you a good supply of oxygen and the potential for enhanced vocal control. You will also want to breathe deeply before you speak and to continue breathing deeply and regularly while you are delivering your speech for better vocal support and ongoing relaxation.

Isometric exercise, which involves tensing and then relaxing specific muscles, can also be a useful relaxation technique. Try clenching and unclenching your fists, pressing your legs firmly together and then relaxing them, or squeezing the palms of your hands together as if you were trying to flatten a piece of clay. Alternatively, you can push your leg, arm, or foot against some immovable object, such as a wall, a table, or even the podium. After you have pressed firmly, release the muscle, relaxing it as completely as possible. These isometric exercises are subtle—you can do them without being noticed, even in the middle of your speech. They can also be used before and after the speech.

Finally, performing aerobic exercise before your speech can help reduce communication apprehension. Aerobic exercise, such as walking, jogging, running, or swimming, is not only good for your cardiovascular system and general well-being, but it also helps reduce tension and brings communication apprehension into a manageable range.

Acknowledge Potential Benefits of Moderate Communication Apprehension

Some people have serious problems with speech anxiety and are virtually incapacitated by their fear of speaking.[28] Most of us, however, can learn to manage our communication apprehension, and experienced speakers even find ways to channel their nervous energy in positive directions. They are able to do this, in part, because they have developed specific techniques that work for them. Some speakers, for example, begin their speaking day with meditation, prayer, a two-mile run, or a quiet walk. Everyone benefits from getting a good night's rest and eating a light, nutritious meal before making a speech. Wearing comfortable clothes that make you feel good about yourself also contributes to a positive mental attitude. What is important is to learn what helps *you* most in managing your feelings of anxiety.

In most speaking situations, a little anxiety can be a *good* thing because that little spurt of adrenaline can energize your mind and body, keep you alert, and perhaps even contribute to a more dynamic delivery. As you gain experience as a public speaker, you will become more comfortable and confident standing up before an audience, and eventually you may even come to anticipate and welcome that adrenaline rush that we all feel when we speak in public.

Maintain a Sense of Perspective

No matter how well you prepare for any speech, bad things can happen: the microphone may fail; the person who introduces you may mispronounce your name; or you may get something under your contact lens or drop one of your note cards. By preparing well, you can reduce the likelihood that something will go wrong, but you will never have complete control over the situation. Do not be intimidated by that fact. The unpredictability is what makes public speaking both challenging and interesting.

You need to maintain a sense of perspective. Prepare well, do your best, be flexible, and pay attention to feedback from your listeners. Even if, in your judgment, your entire speech goes badly—that is, *you* feel disappointed in your performance—you should view it as a learning experience. Concentrate on what you learned. Get ready to have another go at it. No matter how brilliantly or poorly you think you performed, it is important that you view each speech as a chance for personal growth. If you are truly committed to speaking out, you will have other opportunities to speak on the subject.

By employing any or all of these strategies for managing communication apprehension, you *can* become a more poised and confident speaker.

✓ Study and Review materials for this chapter are at **MyCommunicationLab**

SUMMARY

 Listen to the Audio Chapter Summary at **MyCommunicationLab**

Understanding Communication Apprehension

 3.1 Define communication apprehension.

- Nearly everyone experiences some level of communication apprehension.
  - Communication apprehension extends beyond public speaking situations to include speaking up in meetings and other more informal settings.
  - Experiencing *high* communication apprehension has been associated with mental stress, diminished academic performance, and speaking avoidance.

Factors That Contribute to Communication Apprehension

3.2 Describe underlying factors that contribute to communication apprehension.

- A number of factors contribute to communication apprehension. These include the following:
  - Poor preparation

- Trait anxiety (general apprehension across speaking situations)
- State anxiety (apprehension triggered by a particular set of circumstances)
- Self-expectations (either too high or too low)
- Fear of evaluation
- The fear that listeners perceive apprehension
- Fear of failure
- Overreacting to your body's physiological reactions

Managing Communication Apprehension

3.3 Employ strategies for managing communication apprehension while preparing yourself to speak.

- Commitment to your topic and thorough preparation are fundamental to managing communication apprehension and building your confidence as a speaker.

- Preparation and commitment may be supplemented with other techniques, including the following:
    - Develop a positive attitude.
    - Practice your speech.
    - Anticipate the speaking situation (collect information about the listeners and setting before you speak).

- Listen actively (as others conduct a business or community meeting or give their own speeches prior to your speech).
- Exercise for relaxation.
- Acknowledge the possible benefits of moderate apprehension.
- Maintain a sense of perspective.

QUESTIONS FOR REVIEW AND REFLECTION

Understanding Communication Apprehension

3.1 Define communication apprehension.

1. What is meant by communication apprehension?
2. How might high communication apprehension affect you as a student or in speaking situations beyond the classroom?

Factors That Contribute to Communication Apprehension

3.2 Describe underlying factors that contribute to communication apprehension.

3. Complete the communication apprehension self-assessment presented in Figure 3.1. What is your level of communication apprehension, based on this instrument?
4. The book lists several factors that may contribute to a speaker's communication apprehension. Which of these have you experienced? Elaborate.
5. Which, if any, of the physiological reactions associated with communication apprehension have you experienced?

Managing Communication Apprehension

3.3 Employ strategies for managing communication while preparing yourself to speak.

6. The book suggests that commitment and preparation are the most significant factors in reducing communication apprehension. Do you agree or disagree? Explain.
7. What are some additional useful strategies for managing communication apprehension discussed in the book? Have you tried any of these techniques in the past? Did they work for you?
8. Figure 3.3 lists the sorts of questions you might ask as you prepare to speak in a business or community setting. Which of these have you found most helpful in managing communication apprehension?
9. List other strategies you have tried to increase your speaking confidence. To what extent and in what ways have they been effective?

✓ Study and Review the Flashcards at **MyCommunicationLab**

Diverse Audiences in a Democratic Society

OVERVIEW AND LEARNING OBJECTIVES

Understanding Diverse Audiences

4.1 Describe the audience characteristics you need to consider as you prepare your speech.

Identifying Individual Listener Needs and Values

4.2 Identify individual needs and values relevant to your speech.

Identifying Communal Needs and Values

4.3 Identify communal needs and values that might impact your speech.

Gathering Information for Audience Adaptation

4.4 Know how to gather relevant information about an audience.

Ongoing Strategies for Audience Adaptation

4.5 Implement strategies for adapting to audiences as you deliver your speech.

Audiences come together to hear about matters of importance, although they may have different reasons for being concerned about an issue. A new interstate highway may not come anywhere near your property, but you still may be concerned about the possible impact of the highway on the environment or the economy. Others, such as real estate developers or construction workers, might have their own reasons for being interested in the issue. Some audience members may come to hear a speech simply to learn more about an issue; others who show up already have strong views. Sometimes an audience is even *required* to listen to a speech, as in your public speaking class or in a job-training program, for example.

As a responsible speaker and listener, you try to recognize your own biases and understand how they can affect your judgment. At the same time, you need to think about how the characteristics and biases of your audience may affect *their* reactions to your speech. Before you speak, you will want to gather all the information you can about your audience so you can adapt what you have to say to your listeners.

UNDERSTANDING DIVERSE AUDIENCES

4.1 Describe the audience characteristics you need to consider as you prepare your speech.

Explore the Concept
"Audience Analysis" at
MyCommunicationLab

Preview. *As a responsible speaker, you must think carefully about your listeners. You and the members of your audience form a partnership, and you need to frame and deliver your message with the characteristics of your audience in mind.*

Many factors go into making people who they are. These factors can influence the way people see events and how important an issue is to them, which in turn can mold their values, determine how attentive they will be to a speech, or suggest whether they will accept or reject change. Table 4.1 lists some audience demographics that every speaker must consider. These audience characteristics often shape listeners' values and beliefs. If you know a lot about your listeners, you will be in a better position to determine what might be relevant to them, to appeal to their interests and concerns, and to recognize how their assumptions and perspectives might differ from your own. Understanding demographics, along with the individual and community values that grow out of them, will form the basis of the strategies you will use to adapt to your audience.

The demographics of an audience may suggest certain *tendencies*, but you can never really predict human behavior. Advertisers study demographics carefully and try to promote their products in publications, on TV shows, and on Web sites that will reach a particular target audience. Yet not all teenage girls read *Seventeen*, and those who do will not all respond to an ad in the same way. Nor will every member of AARP (formerly the American Association of Retired Persons) be interested in long-term-care insurance. As we pointed out in Chapter 2, we cannot assume that all people within a particular demographic group are the same. Yet advertisers know better than to run ads for denture cleaners on MTV or ads for in-line skates on a show with older viewers. It would be foolish to disregard the tendencies of certain groups to share characteristics that may influence how they respond to your message.

> ## TABLE 4.1
>
> ### Audience Demographics
> - Age
> - Gender
> - Race and ethnicity
> - Intercultural factors
> - Religion
> - Geographic/cultural environment
> - Education
> - Occupation or profession
> - Economic status

Age and Values

The age of audience members will influence the way they receive messages. Some may argue that age is mostly a state of mind rather than a physical fact. Even so, our age influences the sorts of experiences we have had and the issues that most concern us.

Being "young" or "old" means, in part, living through different times. Although two people of exactly the same age can have widely divergent experiences, they also share certain experiences and memories that influence the way they perceive the world. Today's students may look back on World War II or the turbulent 1960s as ancient history. Their views have been shaped by the terrorist attacks of September 11, 2001, and the long wars in Iraq and Afghanistan, not by the Japanese attack on Pearl Harbor or the antiwar protests of the Vietnam era. By 2025, another generation of college students will come of age with no memory of planes crashing into the World Trade Center or the earthquake that devastated Japan in 2011. The point, of course, is that the shared experiences of a generation affect its outlook. That is just one reason that you, as a speaker, must consider the age of your audience.

Audience members who are over age 40 are more likely to be married, have children, and own homes than are audience members who are under age 20. Each generation will have danced to different music, watched different movies, admired different political leaders, and used different technologies during their formative years. As a result, different issues have different degrees of saliency, or personal relevance, for people of different ages. In debates over Social Security, for example, older people tend to be more suspicious of changes in the program, while younger people are more likely to support reform, probably because they think those reforms might benefit them in the long run.[1] To take another example, college students who graduated in 2012 might view a weak economy as diminishing their ability to get good jobs, whereas older Americans might worry more about the effects of the economic downturn on their retirement accounts.

Shared experiences, social mores, and personal concerns related to age all have an impact on one's values. Recent research demonstrates, for example, that

HIGHLIGHTING AGE AND VALUES | Dr. Bristow Speaks to the AMA

Well, without going so far as to even hint that any of us in this room today are "elderly," let me say that your support is critical. If you agree with me and America's physicians that the program now being considered by Congress is best for patients, best for the generations to follow, and, yes, best for doctors, too, then speak out.

If I've done my job of "selling it here," then help us sell it everywhere. Write. Call. FAX. Send e-mail. Whenever it's possible, actually visit your Senators and Representatives. Let them know you support the AMA's plan to transform Medicare. Tell them you want it for today, sure. But tell them that—even more important—you want it for tomorrow. For your children's sake. For your grandchildren's sake....

I'm reminded of something I saw last night when I was driving home—here at Rossmoor. I turned a corner and my headlights shined [*sic*] on three deer. A stag, a doe, and a fawn.

You know what their first instinct was? No. They didn't run. That was their second act. The first thing that the stag and the doe did was turn so that their bodies shielded the fawn from the approaching harm. And that's what every older generation does. We shield our young from harm. We protect the generation we're leaving behind. It's an instinct as primal as food and shelter and warmth.

And that's what is being asked of us today. We are like those deer.... We are harvesting the accumulated wisdom and knowledge of a lifetime and sharing it with those who have it in their power to enact change to help the generations to come. To protect the generations to come. It is our time.

Source: Reprinted by permission from Lonnie R. Bristow, "Dr. Bristow Speaks to the AMA." Copyright © 1995 by Lonnie Bristow.

a generation that has lived through hard economic times is more likely to value security and stability than a generation that has experienced few threats to their material well-being. Generally, older groups who value stability will tend to be more resistant to change, whereas younger people are usually more adventuresome and willing to take risks. Likewise, older people are more likely to value tradition and conformity than are younger people.[2]

In our *Highlighting Age and Values* feature, note how Lonnie Bristow, a former president of the American Medical Association, urged an older audience to accept the AMA's plan to reform Medicare—not so much because it would benefit them but for their children's and their grandchildren's sake.

Gender Roles and Stereotypes

Although anatomy defines our sex—whether we are male or female—gender identity is more complex. Differences and similarities in the way men and women behave, what they value, and what they believe are shaped in large measure by social norms and expectations that vary across cultures and change over time. There was a time in the nineteenth century, for example, when it was considered scandalous or even unnatural for a woman to speak in public or for a man to take care of children. In the twenty-first century, however, behaviors that society assigns to men and women are much more flexible, at least in Western societies. Although some parts of the world still have strict rules about what men and women should wear, how they should relate to each other, and even whether they should appear together in public, women in our culture have more freedom of choice. Still, it is important to remember that gender, along with many of the demographics discussed here, is socially constructed, which is to say that different cultures have different ideas about what roles, behaviors, or even modes of dress are appropriate for men and women.

As men and women challenge prescribed gender roles and as attitudes toward sexuality change, listeners will respond differently to gender-related issues. One can no longer assume that only women will want to hear a speech about fashion or that only men are interested in sports. Jokes that portray women as vain, silly, or nagging are not only in bad taste but also offensive, and references to men as insensitive, arrogant, and unfeeling seem outdated.[3]

Even though gender roles are more flexible now than in the past, the gender composition of your audience remains an important concern. Your listeners' gender still has an impact on their outlook and experiences. For example, single women and widows have more difficulty obtaining credit than do men. Furthermore, men's and women's tastes and interests still differ, and our popular culture reflects those differences. Movie producers target some films at female audiences (so-called "chick flicks") and others at males (war movies, for example). Listeners' sexual orientations also lead to different experiences and perspectives. Women and men with longtime same-sex partners, for example, still face greater barriers in adopting children and in obtaining housing than do male-female couples.

As with age, gender may influence how salient a particular topic may be. Certain health concerns are obviously of more concern to women, such as breast cancer, whereas men may be more concerned about prostate cancer. More women still tend to be caregivers than men and are thus likely to be more attentive to topics related to that subject. Thoughtful speakers give serious attention to how the issues they address or the plans they advocate may affect men and women differently.

Although all of this may be true, we need to constantly remind ourselves that no demographic category—whether age, race, or gender identity—automatically predetermines an individual listener's responses, interests, or life experiences. *Stereotypes*, or common assumptions about people of a particular group, often prove misguided. It is sometimes assumed, for example, that gays tend to work in certain industries, such as fashion or interior design. Yet a survey of more than 4,000 gay men and lesbians conducted by Overlooked Opinions, a Chicago market-research firm, reported that 40 percent more homosexuals are employed in the finance and insurance industries than in the entertainment and arts industries, and 10 times as many homosexuals are in the computer industry as in the fashion industry. There are also more homosexuals working in science and engineering than in social services.[4]

In addition, we should not assume that because an issue is sometimes labeled a "women's issue" that male listeners will not care about it. A *good* speaker should be able to persuade an audience of women *and* men to participate in a breast cancer walk. Similarly, a *good* speaker should strive to persuade both men and women to care about the problem of sexual assault on campus, perhaps even to take part in a "Take Back the Night" march.

Although the distinction between generalizing and stereotyping is sometimes hard to make, stereotyping is harmful. The feminist movement of the late twentieth century should have taught us all one truth: men and women may have concerns and experiences unique to their sex, but they also have aspirations, attitudes, and aptitudes that are common to all people. The advocate who hopes to inspire, engage, and motivate listeners must be sensitive to both differences and commonalities across genders.

Men, women, and people of different ages and races can be brought together to fight for common causes, as in this American Cancer Society Relay for Life.

Explore the Concept "Culture" at **MyCommunicationLab**

Race and Ethnicity

At one time, Americans were thought to be a relatively homogeneous people. The myth was that we arrived as immigrants, and then emerged from the "melting pot" of U.S. culture with a distinctively American character. Today, there still may be certain ways of looking at things that are especially or even uniquely American. In recent years, however, we have come to realize that the melting-pot concept can be misleading. Within our broader culture are a variety of subcultures that continue to differ. Although people who fall within these various groupings may share characteristics with the general U.S. culture, they also differ in ways that could affect their responses to your speech.

The color of one's skin is biologically determined based on genetic factors. The constellation of characteristics said to make up "race," however, is not determined by biological, genetic, or inherited factors but is the product of politics, social definitions, and personal preferences.[5] People may *define* themselves as members of a particular race and see the world through African-American, Asian-American, or Caucasian eyes.[6] It is important to understand how these racial identities may influence your listeners.

Over time, we have come to realize that just as each race has its own identity, each also has its own perceptions and problems. Recognizing these racial differences is not racism. Racism, or the belief in the superiority or inferiority of particular races, leads to prejudice, antagonism, fear, and oppression. It denies the essential humanity of those who are different and thus severely limits the potential for communicating successfully. Racism is often about power because dominant groups use racial differences to justify subordinating others. Historically, European colonial powers used race to justify dominating Africans and Asians politically and economically, and the United States excused some of its historical policies in the Philippines and elsewhere in the same way. The "ethnic cleansing" that we still witness in certain parts of the world likewise reflects efforts to keep particular racial groups or tribes in subordinate positions.

Those who appreciate the distinctions between people of different races are better equipped to talk effectively with diverse audiences. Speakers must understand that people of color and white Americans have different histories and cultural experiences. Communication between different races can be extremely complicated and, too often, fraught with distrust.[7] Some Americans, for example, may view affirmative action programs as reverse discrimination, while others consider such programs necessary to level the playing field. By the same token, some African Americans may be skeptical that the local police are really there to "serve and protect" them, either because they've had a bad experience with the police or because they believe that racism is systemic in America.

Despite these challenges, successful communication across races can and does occur every day.[8] For that to happen, however, speakers must be sensitive to the racial makeup of their audiences and reflect on how race may influence an audience's beliefs and attitudes on a particular issue.

The forebears of most Americans came from someplace else. With the exception of Native Americans, whose ancestors migrated to the North American continent in prehistoric times, most Americans can trace their ancestors to people who emigrated from other countries beginning in the seventeenth century, and new immigrants are still arriving each day. Depending on when they arrived, on their habits and tastes, and on where they settled, the outlook of these immigrants has been colored by their own national history, customs, and experiences. Because some listeners identify strongly with their ethnic heritage, you need to realize that they may be particularly sensitive to issues that involve their country of origin or their ethnic group. Cuban Americans, for example, may feel strongly about relations with the communist regime in Cuba, while an immigrant from Mexico may worry more about the effects of strict immigration legislation. A culture's particular viewpoints and values can influence even its transplanted citizens and their descendants. For example, different ethnic groups may have different expectations regarding care for their parents in their old age. As a study by AARP concluded, older Americans of Asian and Latino descent still expect their children to take care of them, whereas parents of European heritage are more likely to view living with their children as a sign of failure. European-Americans are more likely to expect a combination of family care and community services as they age.[9]

One of the most significant problems plaguing the world today is ethnocentrism, the belief that one's own ethnic heritage is superior to all others. The results of such feelings can range from discrimination and exclusion ("We don't associate with *those* people") to the outright warfare that has torn apart countries in the Balkans and that still plagues parts of Africa and the Middle East. It is important that speakers respect differences in customs, practices, and beliefs grounded in ethnic origins and take them into account when speaking to ethnically diverse audiences.

Cultural Differences

Beyond racial and ethnic differences, those who grew up in cultures outside the United States may hold values and exhibit behaviors that differ from those of other Americans. Scholars may not agree on the causes of those differences, yet most agree that the

Watch the Video
"Intercultural
Communication" at
MyCommunicationLab

differences are real. Some of the most recent studies have implications for the ways people communicate with each other, how they judge speaker credibility, and how they react to arguments opposed to their own views. In a recent study, for example, student subjects were asked to analyze a conflict between mothers and daughters. "American subjects quickly came down in favor of one side or the other. Chinese subjects were more likely to see merit in both sides, commenting, for example, 'Both the mothers and the daughters have failed to understand each other.'"[10] Many other examples demonstrate such cultural differences. While many Americans often seem in a hurry, viewing time as something not to be wasted, people from other cultures may prefer to move more slowly, spending time getting to know one another instead of "getting right down to business." Whereas Americans tend to be individualistic and value their privacy, cultures that are more group-oriented associate privacy with loneliness and isolation. Americans also tend to be future-oriented, while more traditional societies tend to honor the past. In cultures that value subtlety and indirection, Americans may seem blunt and insensitive when they are just trying to be open and direct.[11] These are just a few of the intercultural differences that may affect how we communicate.[12]

Watch the Video
"Successful Japanese—U.S.
Business Communication" at
MyCommunicationLab

You might see some of these differences emerge in your classroom if you have classmates who are international students. Students from other countries have different cultural and linguistic backgrounds and sometimes face problems adapting to American cultural practices. They may seem very shy when they are only showing deference. They may be more reluctant to disagree with ideas of others than would American students. And, of course, they are not likely to have the command of English that you have. Getting to know these students and their different ways of communicating will help you become aware of how diverse audiences can be and how different adaptive approaches can be effective. If you are an international student yourself, you know how puzzling American communicative practices can be. While struggling to master a language that is not native to you—with its peculiar idioms and unfamiliar slang—you have the added job of trying to absorb the American culture. This is not an easy task. Undertaking it means trying to get to know your American classmates, immersing yourself in the culture of the United States, and avoiding the temptation to spend all of your time only with students from your country. It also means taking special pains to overcome any reluctance you might have to ask questions—of your instructors and your American classmates. Don't forget that, coming from a different culture, you have much to add that will enrich your fellow American students' education.

Cultural differences, both within American subcultures and across international lines, affect all of our efforts to communicate—in the classroom and in the community—and we need to make strenuous and sincere efforts to bridge cultural divides and emphasize what we all have in common. It can be hard work to communicate effectively across cultural lines, but the effort is necessary if we hope to work together in our increasingly interdependent world.

Religion

Your listeners' religious beliefs—or lack of religious beliefs—can also influence how they evaluate and respond to your speech. On some issues, religious leaders have taken a clear political stand. Not all Catholics are opposed to legalized abortion, for example, but many do embrace their church's official opposition to abortion. Similarly, Jews tend to be strong advocates of U.S. support for Israel, and most Quakers are pacifists who oppose all war.

Religion can also influence your audience's general attitude toward political controversies. Some religions stress obedience and conformity, whereas others emphasize individualism and challenging state authority. Some religions stress personal salvation and rarely take strong stands on controversial political or social issues; others insist that all such issues are of concern to the church. Religious teachings can make a difference in the way people respond to a speech. Fundamentalists, for example, may be more open to messages that emphasize tradition, whereas those with more liberal religious views may respond positively to calls for social reform.[13]

Conventional wisdom once advised public speakers to avoid talking about religion. Some instructors even advise students not to choose religious speech topics because they are too personal or potentially explosive. Yet religious differences are reflected in many of the most important social and political controversies of our time, and we cannot simply ignore the role of religion in public life. If you *do* talk about a religious issue, it is important to recognize that not everybody in your audience may share your assumptions about what is "true" and what religious sources are "authoritative." The essential teachings of world religions have different sources—for Christians, the Bible; for Muslims, the Koran; for Jews, the Talmud—and even within these faith traditions, there are widely varying interpretations of sacred texts and their meaning in secular life. In Israel, for example, the role of women under Jewish law has generated intense controversy; in the United States, some fundamentalist Christians argue that the Bible explicitly condemns homosexuality, but liberal Christians draw very different conclusions from their understanding of the life and teachings of Jesus.

It is important to remember that your audience may hold fundamentally different religious beliefs. That does not mean we cannot communicate across religious differences. In our time, many bitter divisions over social issues, such as abortion, stem cell research, and gay marriage, grow from varying interpretations of religious doctrines and moral principles. That should not make it impossible, however, for those on different sides of religious controversies to talk with each other and seek common ground. The speech following this chapter, given by President Obama at the University of Notre Dame, is an example of a speaker's efforts to get beyond deep divisions rooted in religion while respecting different views on a controversial issue.

Geographical Environment

Where a listener lives can make a difference in how he or she reacts to a speech. Even though people may come from the same part of the country, their outlooks can differ depending on the kind of community in which they live. Newark, New Jersey, is not the same as Franklin, New Jersey; Chicago, Illinois, is not the same as Peoria, Illinois; and Dallas, Texas, is not to be confused with College Station, Texas.

People who have grown up in rural areas may develop different habits and lifestyles from those who grew up in the city. Muggings, commuting on unreliable

HIGHLIGHTING RELIGION AND POLITICS

Ideally, in a country where there is no religious test for elected office, religion should play no part in how one votes. But in the world of practical politics, religion can make a difference. In the 2012 Republican primaries, for example, Mitt Romney's Mormonism was believed to hurt him with evangelical Christians. In states with significant Mormon populations, however, it seemed to be a distinct advantage. In Nevada, for example, Mormons make up 25 percent of the GOP electorate and are very active in the caucuses; 95 percent of them voted for Romney. Given the particular circumstances, therefore, the religious demographic can be crucial.

Source: "Mitt Romney's Mormon Advantage," www .washingtonpost.com/blogs/the-fix/post/mitt-romneys-mormon-advantage/2012/02/02 (accessed February 2, 2012).

trains, or moving at a frantic pace may be unimaginable to the rural resident, whereas the city dweller imagines that rural life would be dreadfully boring. Each area has a different set of problems and concerns. To the urbanite, the following may be the most important questions: How do we reduce crime? How do we improve mass transit? How do we create more affordable housing? By contrast, the resident of a farming community may be more interested in these questions: How do we save the family farm? How can we reduce property taxes? What can be done to stabilize the prices paid to farmers for their produce?

Over time, different sections of the country have developed unique ways of looking at things. Easterners, Westerners, Southerners, Southwesterners, and Midwesterners have different ethnic mixes in their populations, different industries, different religious views, and different approaches to social and political problems. Westerners, for example, often boast of their rugged individualism; New Yorkers value their cultural and artistic sophistication; and many Sunbelt communities are proud of their climates and reputations as safe, comfortable places for older citizens to live. Further, people can also exhibit different communication behavior. A professor teaching in Louisiana told a colleague that native Louisianans among her students were often upset by the ways that students from the East asked questions or made comments. They saw as rude or aggressive the assertive communication patterns that the Easterners believed were normal and never suspected could be interpreted as disrespectful.

Education

Education provides us with specific knowledge, ways to solve problems rationally, awareness of the choices open to us, and ways of evaluating the best choices to make. To be truly engaged, you must be informed on issues of civic concern. Being an informed citizen is fundamental to being an effective speaker.

The educational level of listeners—their acquired knowledge—influences how they react to messages. You may be giving a speech on emergency preparedness to a junior high school assembly and a speech on the same topic to a college group. Yet what each group expects from your speech will differ, based on what they already know about the topic and their different experiences. Even first- and second-year college students differ in their levels of sophistication and knowledge, and both groups differ in these respects from college seniors.

How well audience members have been educated will determine not only whether they are familiar with your speech topic but also whether they can intelligently evaluate the message. One speaker may claim that a proposed health care plan would fail to meet the needs of low-income families. Another may claim that voting for a particular candidate will improve your economic situation. Educated listeners should be in a good position to evaluate such claims. They should have specific facts at their disposal and already know something about the topic.

Suppose, for example, that you hear someone argue that force must be used in response to a foreign-policy crisis. And suppose they back up that claim by comparing the current situation with the situation Americans faced in the 1940s when confronted by Nazi Germany. If, as an educated person, you take the time to think, you will not automatically accept the comparison just because you know Nazism was evil. You will ask questions about the legitimacy of the comparison. You will demand that the speaker *prove* that the situation before World War II was really similar to the present situation. You sometimes hear policy proposals criticized as "socialism." Socialism has specific political and economic characteristics that rarely apply to policies advanced by mainstream American politicians. As an educated person, you should not be automatically persuaded simply by someone's use of the "socialism" label—or any other label.

As you judge a speaker's argument, you should apply principles you have learned and the knowledge you have acquired to render an *informed* judgment. If you find the speaker unconvincing, or if you cannot fully test the argument by your own knowledge and experience, you should suspend judgment. You should wait and see—listen to other arguments, read more material, and assemble more facts—before you make a decision. That is what it means to have an *educated response* to a speech.

Occupation or Profession

Your job or profession can make a difference in the attitudes you hold and the ways in which you grasp specific information. When people hear a message, they sometimes ask themselves, "How is this going to affect me?" When discussing how to improve our schools, for example, a travel agent may be uneasy about a proposal to keep schools open all year because that may mean canceled vacations and less business. People who work at the school or who provide transportation for students, on the other hand, may be all for the idea.

The occupations we hold make us feel differently about the world around us. Teachers, doctors, construction workers, dancers, postal clerks, and lawyers all deal with specific sets of problems. The constant practice of these problem-solving skills is what establishes people as experts. When experts listen to a speech, they bring a whole set of competencies and attitudes with them to the speaking situation. An engineer, for example, will respond to technological information as a specialist, and the speaker must be aware of this. Professional experience also will affect responses to issues. Recently, an insurance company covering a large number of university employees informed its clients that anesthesiologists at the local hospital had

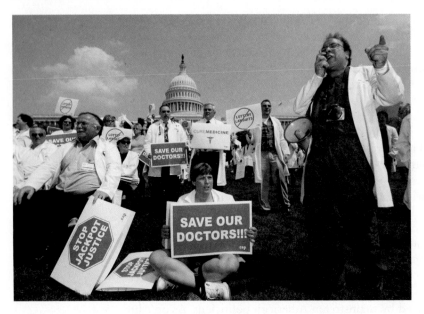

Sharing common occupations may cause listeners to see issues in a way especially related to their professional problems and interests.

withdrawn from the plan. Policyholders were asked to consider a medical center 50 miles away for elective surgery. Many policyholders initially saw this as a greedy move on the part of the doctors. A clinical psychologist with a private practice, however, noted that most health care providers were also unhappy with the insurance company. She sympathized with the anesthesiologists. In this case, health care providers viewed this issue from a perspective strongly influenced by their professions.

Finally, one's job or profession may affect one's perspective on what are the most important or relevant issues relating to a specific topic. Take the problem of health care, for example. Most people seem to agree that everyone should have some kind of coverage. Yet as Barack Obama learned when he tried to bring together the various stakeholders in the health care debate, those stakeholders have specific concerns that are sometimes difficult to reconcile. Large corporations want a plan that relieves them of the high cost of health care benefits, and small-business owners worry that providing health care benefits to just a few employees would be too costly. Insurance companies are concerned about losing business if the government assumes more responsibility for health care, and physicians object to plans that give insurance companies the power to decide which medical procedures may be appropriate. Consumers worry about having to pay higher premiums and absorb higher deductibles. As another example of perspective, advocates of so-called "Right to Work" laws tend to be associated with corporate interests that favor dismantling unions, while the most vocal opponents, quite naturally, tend to be union members. If a speaker fails to anticipate and prepare for responses stemming from these different occupational perspectives, even a good idea may be rejected.

Economic Status

The income of listeners may influence their response to a speech. Again, the extent to which this factor is important and the precise ways in which it may affect listener responses depend on the speaker's subject and purpose. The topic of a message may naturally interest some income groups and not others. A speech on tax shelters, for example, may have limited appeal to low-income listeners. By the same token, those with high incomes may not be interested in a speech on need-based tuition assistance.

How groups think their income level compares with that of others may have profound effects on the communication process. People in the middle-income group, for example, may see themselves as overburdened with taxes and yet excluded from the benefits of social welfare. Such people may look on social welfare programs with the jaundiced eye of those expected to foot the bill. In 2011, the "Occupy Wall Street" movement contrasted the richest "one percent" with the 99 percent of Americans who were not so well off. The movement's facts, tactics, and goals were all contested, but the issue of economic disparity became part of our national political debate. The president called for higher taxes on the wealthy, while the Republicans accused the president of stirring up "class warfare."[14] And during the Republican primaries, when Mitt Romney released his tax returns, economic status again emerged as an important issue with the potential to sway voters based on their economic status.

Professional persuaders, such as advertisers, go to great lengths to target their messages to particular income groups. They carefully choose a mailing list (such as American Express cardholders) that will put their material in the hands of those who can afford to buy their product. They carefully choose the magazines in which they advertise, the time slots for their television ads, and the radio stations that air their ads. They are concerned with many factors besides income, but it is crucial that they reach people who can afford to buy their products.

The financial resources available to listeners may determine their response to any idea or proposal involving money. A student urging other students to volunteer for a service project, for example, may need to consider whether his listeners could afford to work without pay for the summer or whether they could afford to participate in the project for only a few hours a week. The wise speaker tries to anticipate how listeners' income may influence their response to his or her message.

In addition to the specific characteristics that distinguish listeners, it is also important to remember that all of us—no matter who we are or what we do—have fundamental human needs that have to be met and common values that we all embrace.

HIGHLIGHTING AUDIENCE DEMOGRAPHICS

No single characteristic defines audiences, although sometimes one feature may overshadow others, depending on the context in which a speech is given. In the controversy over tax policy, for example, the fact that some millionaires pay at a rate of about 15 percent will be of singular importance to middle-class listeners who make considerably less money and yet pay at higher rates. But other demographics may interact to produce different listener profiles. When talking about the one percent who make the most money in the United States, geography will influence who should be counted. If you live in Manhattan, for example, you would have to earn $790,000 a year, or 12 times the national median income, to be counted in the top one percent of earners, whereas if you live in Macon, Georgia, earning $270,000—about six times the median income—would put you in the top one percent. Further, characteristics such as race or occupation can have a bearing on who is considered "rich." A good speaker will take into account the way in which demographics interact with one another.

Source: "Among the Wealthiest One Percent, Many Variations," *New York Times,* January 15, 2012, p. 20.

IDENTIFYING INDIVIDUAL LISTENER NEEDS AND VALUES

 4.2 Identify individual needs and values relevant to your speech.

Watch the Video "Citizens for Community Justice" at **MyCommunicationLab**

Preview.   *Like all people, audience members have fundamental needs. Maslow's hierarchy provides an excellent conceptual framework for understanding those shared needs—physical well-being, safety and security, love and belonging, esteem, and self-actualization.*

So far, we have considered the ways that audience members may differ and how you need to acknowledge those differences in analyzing your audience. Yet whatever differences listeners may bring to the speech situation, they still share certain universal human needs.

In a groundbreaking work, psychologist Abraham H. Maslow described basic human needs in terms that help us understand and develop tactics for listener involvement.[15] As illustrated in Figure 4.1, Maslow presented the needs in a hierarchy, noting that some needs are more basic than others.

Satisfying Basic Physiological Needs

People have physiological needs. Basic to all human life is the need to be physically secure. We all need food and drink, clothing, shelter, and sexual gratification if we want to feel comfortable and avoid the discomforts of pain, sickness, injury, and so on.

Most of the audiences you will talk with, however, have had their basic needs met. Freed from the preoccupation of satisfying those needs, most listeners will be more successfully engaged by appealing to their "higher" needs.

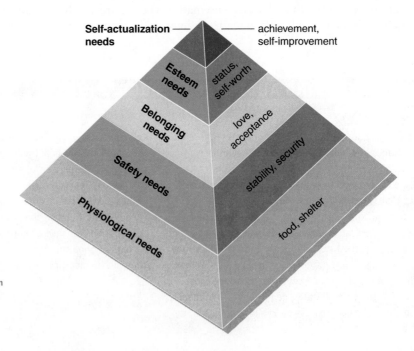

FIGURE 4.1

Maslow's Hierarchy

Source: Reprinted by permission form Maslow, A.H., *Motivation and Personality.* Copyright © 1987 by Pearson Education, Inc.

Ensuring Listeners' Personal Safety

We all desire a secure world. We all want to be protected from dangerous, surprising, or unfamiliar situations that threaten our safety. In any organized society, we have many people and groups—police, firefighters, military personnel—dedicated to ensuring our safety. We have government agencies, such as the Food and Drug Administration, that protect us from being poisoned. Despite all these efforts, of course, bridges still do collapse sometimes, and tainted foods still do escape detection and sicken or even kill people. Thus, we all still worry about our safety, and those concerns may influence how we respond to a speaker. The wise speaker will consider what ways, if any, listeners may find her proposal threatening or how it may make them feel safer.

Reinforcing Feelings of Love and a Sense of Belonging

Once safety needs are satisfied, people begin to think of other needs, such as belonging needs or the need to be loved by others. There is a distinct human need to be accepted, wanted, or welcomed into groups. People join clubs, maintain close family or ethnic ties, associate themselves strongly with a church or religious movement, or take great pride in their patriotic feelings toward their country. All these associations help them meet their need to be accepted and be part of a larger group. Individuals feel more powerful when acting as a part of a group that they feel represents or protects their interests. So, for example, unions from different parts of the country may raise money and provide other support for union members in states like Wisconsin or Indiana, where laws designed to undermine the strength of unions recently passed. At the same time, organizations like the Chamber of Commerce, which represents business interests, appealed to its members to support these efforts to restrict or eliminate the collective bargaining rights of unions.

Listeners are likely to be more emotionally involved when they believe that a speaker is advocating a proposal that will be of direct benefit to those whom they love, reduce their feelings of isolation, or promote the interests of the groups to which they belong.

Helping Listeners Feel Appreciated by Others

In addition to a sense of belonging, people want to feel that they have some worth and importance. People like to feel that they control their destiny, that they are not constantly under the thumb of other people, and that others recognize them as being good or important human beings. This need is frequently the basis of advertising that would have us believe that driving a particular type of car or wearing some fashionable style of shoes will help us acquire status. These kinds of appeals to status are aimed more at achieving the communicator's sales goals than genuinely benefiting the listener. On the other hand, a student describing her experiences as a volunteer helping to rebuild homes destroyed by Hurricane Katrina may legitimately emphasize all the expressions of gratitude from those she helped. Those expressions of gratitude demonstrate the importance of the volunteer's work and reveal what her listeners may hope to gain by volunteering for similar missions: the sense that they will make important contributions that others will appreciate.

Helping Listeners Realize Their Own Potential

When people know that others respect them, they can begin to think about self-ful-fillment. These self-actualization needs reflect that we all want to realize our own po-tential. Not everyone has the same goals or the same ambitions. For some, the highest ambition in life may be great material wealth; for others, realizing one's own potential may mean making a difference in the lives of his or her fellow citizens. At a town hall meeting in France in April 2009, as noted in our *Focus on Civic Engagement*, President Obama made the case for realizing one's own potential by serving others.

Most people strive to better themselves throughout life yet never achieve ev-erything they had hoped for. Nevertheless, the speaker who realizes that people *want* to realize their highest potential can appeal to that desire. In advocating more support for the arts and humanities, for example, a student might stress the impor-tance of a broad liberal education for one's "emotional intelligence," or the intel-ligence one needs for healthy everyday living and good relationships with others. By promoting "emotional intelligence," she might conclude, studying outside one's own professional field can lead to a richer and more satisfying life.[16]

Identifying Audience Values

When you analyze an audience by cataloging listener characteristics and identi-fying their needs, you are doing so, in part, to uncover audience values. You are looking for areas of agreement as well as potential conflict, and you will want to think about how listeners' values may shape the way you approach your speech. For certain audiences, patriotic values may be extremely important; for others, the desire to get ahead or to advance their education may take precedence.

All of us possess a network of interlocking values, some of which conflict with others. For example, Americans tend to admire individualism, yet we also recog-nize the need for teamwork.[17] We may profess the golden rule—do unto others as we would have them do unto us—while also valuing a competitive spirit. We hear of the "work ethic," the "business ethic," and the "Puritan ethic," all of which sug-gest different sets of values at work in our society. Your challenge as a speaker is to identify the values most relevant to the issue you are discussing.

Once you have considered your audience's values, you should reflect on how those values translate into specific attitudes and beliefs. For instance, you may de-termine that both you and your listeners value integrity and social responsibility. Yet in an election year, you may discover that your listeners distrust the political candidate you are supporting. Whereas you see the candidate as honest, experi-enced, and trustworthy, your listeners may see her as unqualified or dishonest or untrustworthy. In this case, you would not try to change listener values (which you share). Instead you would try to convince them that they have misjudged your candidate. Perhaps they believe that your candidate's background has not prepared her adequately for the office she seeks. Or maybe they do not like your candidate's record on environmental protection, which is a real priority for them. Whatever the nature of their objections, you need to understand those objections before you can adapt your speech to your audience. Perhaps you can establish common ground by emphasizing the values you share. Then you can try to change their beliefs and attitudes toward your candidate.

FOCUS ON CIVIC ENGAGEMENT | President Obama on Public Service

...I truly believe that there's nothing more noble than public service. Now, that doesn't mean that you have to run for President. (Applause.) You know, you might work for Doctors Without Borders, or you might...be somebody working for the United Nations, or you might be the mayor of Strasbourg. Right? (Applause.)...

But the point is that what I found at a very young age was that if you only think about yourself—how much money can I make, what can I buy, how nice is my house, what kind of fancy car do I have—that over the long term I think you get bored. (Applause.) I think...if you're only thinking about yourself, your life becomes diminished; and that the way to live a full life is to think about, what can I do for others? How can I be a part of this larger project of making a better world?

Now, that could be something as simple as...the joy of taking care of your family and watching your

children grow and succeed. But I think especially for the young people here, I hope you also consider other ways that you can serve, because the world has so many challenges right now, there's so many opportunities to make a difference, and it would be a tragedy if all of you who are so talented and energetic, if you let that go to waste; if you just stood back and watched the world pass you by.

Better to jump in, get involved. And it does mean that sometimes you'll get criticized and sometimes you'll fail and sometimes you'll be disappointed, but you'll have a great adventure, and at the end of your life hopefully you'll be able to look back and say, I made a difference.

Source: From "Remarks by President Obama at Strasbourg Town Hall." Published 2009 by The White House, Office of the Press Secretary.

IDENTIFYING COMMUNAL NEEDS AND VALUES

Preview. *Listeners are usually members of a variety of communities. The groups and organizations your listeners belong to and identify with will have an impact on their response to your speeches.*

4.3 Identify communal needs and values that might impact your speech.

As we mentioned earlier in the chapter, our sense of belonging is rooted in the nature of the groups with which we identify. But we typically belong to more than one group. You need to address a question regarding your audience: What group affiliations are uppermost in the minds of my listeners? A single listener may belong to the American Baptist Church, the Democratic Party, the Parent-Teacher Organization, the American Bar Association, and the executive board of the United Way. These affiliations will almost certainly influence how your listeners respond to your speech.

The Saliency of Key Group Memberships

Some memberships may be more important than others. When you attend a meeting of a particular group (a fraternity, a political club, the Boys and Girls Club, or the Future Farmers of America), the reasons for being in that organization may be important to you at that moment. You hear and respond to messages as a member of that group. At other times, and in other contexts, the goals of that group may seem less relevant.

No single group membership is foremost in all our decisions. Whether we are Democrats or Republicans hardly matters if we are considering the need for an extra crossing guard at a nearby elementary school. However, at times, a particular group membership may be so important that all other concerns pale in comparison.[18] Some devout Catholics and evangelical Christians, for example, vote against any candidate who favors legal abortions, while dedicated members of the National Rifle Association (NRA) may care only about a candidate's stand on gun control. These single-issue voters may completely ignore their disagreement with a candidate's positions on the economy, foreign affairs, or the environment; all that matters is their position on that one highly controversial issue. Democratic theory suggests that we should consider a variety of issues along with the personal qualifications of candidates in deciding how to vote. But as a speaker, we must realize that our listeners' salient group memberships can greatly influence their opinions.

Complicating the speaker's task is the fact that important issues sometimes force us to consider multiple group associations. Consider, for example, the issue of poverty. The latest statistics from the Census Bureau show how poverty relates to gender and age: poverty affects children under age 18 more than any other age group, and women typically have principal responsibility for children. Poverty is also a matter of race and ethnicity: 24.7 percent of blacks and 21.9 percent of Latinos live below the poverty line, whereas non-Latino whites represent only 8.6 percent of the poor population.[19] Furthermore, although the number of people living in poverty has decreased slightly in recent years, the number of people in *extreme* poverty (those with incomes at less than half the poverty level) has increased.[20] When you consider the effects that poverty can have on the cost of social programs, health care, and educational opportunities, one can easily imagine that this issue affects everybody. Yet, a good speaker still reflects on how poverty disproportionately affects certain groups and adapts his or her remarks accordingly.

> Membership in groups that are important to listeners will influence how they react to messages that are salient to those groups.

A further complication arises when our audience identifies with two groups whose goals conflict. In Florida, for example, the National Rifle Association supported a bill that would have made it a felony for an employer to prohibit employees from bringing guns to work. The bill was strongly opposed by the Chamber of Commerce, a leading association of businesspeople. A legislator who had received high ratings from both the chamber and the NRA admitted that "it's very awkward for me."[21] In such situations, a speaker needs to take the listeners' conflicting opinions into account, but in the end it may prove impossible to reconcile such incompatible goals.

It should be clear by now that it is important to design your speech for the specific audience you will

▶ FOCUS ON CIVIC ENGAGEMENT | Group Membership

Group memberships played a significant role in an effort to recall Governor Scott Walker of Wisconsin after he pushed for a law to curtail the collective bargaining rights of unions. Union members were galvanized into action. With the help of Democrats who had opposed the legislation, they collected over a million signatures, almost twice as many as the 540,208 needed. Among the supporters of the recall effort were people with many different levels of education, different religious affiliations, and many other differences. In this case, however, one's union membership was the most salient factor.

Source: "Wisconsin Recall Petition Gets Over 1 Million Signatures," *January 18, 2012,* Washingtonpost.com/politics/2012/01/18/gIQAD4sr8P_story.html (accessed February 15, 2012). ▶

address. As a good citizen, you hope to achieve your purposes as a speaker, but you also hope to serve the larger public interest and contribute something positive to your community. To connect your message with your listeners, you begin by analyzing the situation and the audience. To adapt your message to your audience, you need to gather as much information about your listeners as you can.

GATHERING INFORMATION FOR AUDIENCE ADAPTATION

Preview. *There are different ways of collecting information about your audience. Information can be gathered by conducting research on the Internet, through interviewing, or with an audience survey. You should continuously assess your audience before, during, and after your speech.*

Gathering information about your audience is extremely important. As we have emphasized throughout this chapter, you need to adapt your message to your specific listeners if you hope to achieve your goals as a speaker, and your listeners will also get more out of your speech if it is designed specifically to address their interests and needs. But how do you go about getting the information you need to adapt your speech to a particular audience?

Internet Research

You can learn much about an organization or group you will be addressing by conducting research on the Internet. Suppose you represent a group that wants to promote discussion of an important issue on campus, such as recent increases in tuition costs, how proposed immigration laws may affect international students, or new regulations on off-campus housing. If you wanted to find ways to engage other students, perhaps you might search your university's Web site for student organizations that may be interested in hosting a forum on such topics, or perhaps your university's student government could take up the issue. If you were to conduct such a search at Indiana University, for example, you might begin at the Union Board home page, where you would find contact persons for the Debates and Issues Committee, which organizes public forums, and the Lectures Committee, which engages outside speakers with special expertise.[22] Or, at Pennsylvania State

4.4 Know how to gather relevant information about an audience.

Watch the Video "The Process of Developing a Speech: Audience Analysis" at **MyCommunicationLab**

University, you might visit the Web site or even the Facebook page of the Student Programming Association (SPA), which promotes "outreach and collaboration" among a wide variety of student organizations, including a Distinguished Lecture Series and other public forums.[23]

Interviewing for Information

A good way to begin gathering information about an audience is to interview the person who asked you to speak. Usually, this contact person is a member of the group or organization that you will address and can tell you much about the audience. Your goal is to find out as much as you can about the audience—their experiences, level of knowledge, values, and interests—and the particular speaking situation.[24] Regardless of the specific topic, here are some of the questions you may want to ask:

- How many listeners will likely be present when I speak?
- How diverse is the audience in terms of age, gender, and other characteristics?
- Could you describe the room where I'll be speaking?
- How knowledgeable is the audience about my topic?
- What relevant experiences might audience members have had?
- How likely are they to be open to the sort of information I'm discussing or the proposal I'm making?
- Are there likely to be great differences of opinion or experience within the audience?
- How much time is available for my presentation?
- Will there be a question-and-answer period after the speech?

Of course, you will want to adapt this basic interviewing format to the specific situation.

You also may consider attending a meeting of the group that you will address to learn for yourself about their concerns, interests, and values. This strategy is practical only if you have the time and the opportunity. Your contact person should prove helpful in arranging this.

Administering an Audience Survey

With the permission of the group you will be addressing, you may also construct and administer an *audience survey*, which allows you to pursue questions about your listeners' characteristics, knowledge, and opinions in greater depth. This approach to gathering information is sometimes used in public speaking classes, where some instructors encourage students to design and administer a brief questionnaire to learn more about their fellow students. Even though you may not be able to administer such a survey in other settings, the survey suggests the kind of information that you should attempt to find out about any audience before you speak.

Although survey construction can be fairly complicated, you can learn to design a basic questionnaire that will serve as a valuable analytical tool.[25] Some principles to guide you as you design your audience survey include the following:

- *Use the survey to collect relevant demographic information about the audience.* For some topics, for instance, you may want to know the age or major of your audience. For others, you may want to know about their political affiliation or religion.

- *Allow your listeners to remain anonymous as they complete the survey.* They are more likely to respond with candor if they do not have to identify themselves.
- *Use different kinds of questions to gather the kind of information you need.*[26] Some questions may ask audience members to check the appropriate answer from among several choices. Others may ask them to write a few sentences.
- *Limit your audience survey to a few good questions that can be answered in a short period of time.* This way, respondents will be more willing to participate and are more likely to provide you with accurate and better-developed responses. If listeners take the questionnaire home, they will be more inclined to complete and return the survey if it is not too long and complicated. Better yet, get them to complete the survey on the spot, if at all possible.
- *Be sure to use the results of the survey as you craft your speech and adapt your message to your audience.* Administering an audience survey is not just an academic exercise. It is one of the most direct means available of finding out about your audience's knowledge, opinions, and values.

When you conduct an audience survey, you may choose to probe listener attitudes regarding a specific topic, or you may survey their beliefs and values more generally.

Devising Good Questions for an Audience Survey

Whether you are interviewing for information or constructing an audience questionnaire, you should include both closed and open questions (see Chapter 6). Closed questions yield limited information, whereas open questions may be hard to tabulate and are more time consuming to complete. The key is balance.[27]

There is no magic formula for constructing an audience survey, but here are some tips to guide you:

- *Begin the survey with closed, fixed-choice questions relevant to your topic to collect basic demographic and other factual information:*

  What is your class standing?
  Freshman _____ Sophomore _____ Junior _____ Senior _____
  Are you registered to vote?
  Yes _____ No _____ Not sure _____
  If you are registered to vote, are you registered as a(n):
  Democrat _____ Republican _____ Independent _____ Other _____
  Do you drive or would you consider driving an SUV?
  Yes _____ No _____ Maybe _____
  Do you like to walk?
  Frequently _____ Sometimes _____ Not much _____

Through these kinds of questions, you can collect "bottom-line" information quickly. However, the responses give you no insight into how strongly listeners identify with the choices they make. For example, one person may be registered as an independent but consistently vote for candidates from one party.

■ *Use scale questions to acquire more precise information from respondents or to understand how firmly committed they are to their opinions and beliefs:*

How many news broadcasts do you typically watch or listen to each week?
Seven or more _____ Five or six _____ Three or four _____
One or two _____ None _____

Indicate the extent to which you agree or disagree with the following statements:
I believe that a flat tax of 15 percent for everybody would be the fairest tax.
Strongly agree _____ Somewhat agree _____ Somewhat disagree _____
Strongly disagree _____ Not sure _____
I read a newspaper or newsmagazine, print or online.
All the time _____ Most of the time Rarely _____
Never _____ Not sure _____

Scale questions allow you to gather more precise information and to measure degrees of commitment.

■ *You will also want to include some open questions on your survey to provide greater depth of response:*

How do you feel about the proposal to make this campus pedestrian-only by the year 2015?

In your view, why do so few U.S. citizens vote in the presidential elections?

Through open questions, you give the audience the freedom to respond as they choose. By examining their responses, you may grow to better understand *why* they believe as they do and how they justify their actions and opinions. At the same time, you may find that some listeners will give you irrelevant information and some will simply refuse to write out a response. When used in combination with other questions, however, open questions should enrich your survey's results.

■ *Finally, avoid leading or loaded questions.* Make sure you phrase your questions with neutrality and objectivity so that you do not lead respondents to a particular answer. If you were giving a speech about drinking on campus, you might ask this question on your audience survey: "Describe your drinking habits." A leading version of the same question might read, "Describe the last time you drank excessively." The second version assumes that the respondent does, in fact, drink excessively. By contrast, the first version invites the respondent to describe an array of behaviors ranging from complete abstinence to extreme drinking. All survey questions should be written in the most neutral way possible.[28]

Table 4.2 is an example of an audience survey used by one public speaking student who was interested in giving a persuasive speech on vegetarianism. She

> **TABLE 4.2**

Sample Audience Survey on Vegetarianism

1. Please check the categories that most accurately describe you:
   Sex: Male _____ Female _____
   Major: Liberal arts _____ Business _____ Health care professions _____
   Music _____ Engineering _____ Other _____

2. How would you define vegetarianism?

3. Are you a vegetarian?
   Yes _____ No _____

4. Do you have a close friend or relative who is a vegetarian?
   Yes _____ No _____ Not sure _____

5. Do you agree or disagree with the following statement?
   Vegetarians can enjoy a nutritious and flavorful diet.
   Strongly agree _____ Somewhat agree _____ Undecided _____
   Somewhat disagree _____ Strongly disagree _____

6. If you are a vegetarian, please explain your reasons for becoming one.

7. In your view, what are the main reasons that people choose to become vegetarians?

initially hoped to get her audience to agree that vegetarianism was both ethically and morally preferable to eating meat.

After studying the following results of her survey, she decided to change her basic approach.

1. Definitions of vegetarianism varied widely among audience members. About one-third believed that a person is a vegetarian if he or she does not eat red meat. Two class members believed that vegetarians do not eat any animal products (such as milk or eggs). The speaker knew that she would have to take some time early in the speech to clarify her definition of vegetarianism.

2. Only two students (other than the speaker herself) out of a class of 24 students were vegetarians. In addition, six other students, or 25 percent of the class, said that they had a vegetarian friend or relative. The speaker realized that she could not count on much direct experience among the audience.

3. The reasons the two students gave for becoming vegetarians were primarily related to their own health rather than moral objections to consuming meat.

4. Sixty percent of the class did not believe that vegetarians could enjoy a healthy, flavorful diet.

5. Students tended to view vegetarians as having taken a rather extreme approach to a healthy diet. Some cited dangers. Out of the class, two or three seemed hostile toward vegetarians—one calling them "kooks" and another

referring to them as "granola." In general, men were more negative than women. Nearly 70 percent of the women discussed animal rights as one reason for vegetarianism. Students' majors seemed unrelated to their responses.

The speaker's own commitment to vegetarianism grew from a deep ethical conviction regarding animal rights. Based on the survey results, however, she felt that converting this particular audience to her point of view would be unrealistic, given their initial views and the short time available for persuading them. Instead, she decided to make them aware of the problems (for both animals and humans) associated with factory farms (with a specific focus on poultry farms). She would acknowledge inhumane killing, but she would go beyond that to discuss the dangerous working conditions and the low pay of the workforce, along with the unsanitary conditions under which the chickens are bred, fed, and killed—making them unsafe for consumers. As a result of her survey, then, she had devised a more modest but potentially attainable goal: her specific purpose was to get her audience to purchase only free-range chickens—for the welfare of the workers, the animals, and the consumers.

Had the speaker not conducted the audience survey and had she given her original speech, she surely would have been doomed to failure. As it was, her speech was extremely well received, and five or six students said that they were going to purchase only free-range chickens in the future.

The audience survey is an extremely helpful tool that enables a speaker to gather the kind of information he or she needs to adapt a message to the concerns, experiences, and priorities of an audience.

Thus, through various avenues—using the resources available to you through the Internet, the community, your contact person, and the group itself—you should be able to craft your speech with a clear sense of your audience.

ONGOING STRATEGIES FOR AUDIENCE ADAPTATION

4.5 Implement strategies for adapting to audiences as you deliver your speech.

Preview. *Sometimes we assume that audience analysis is done only before the day of the speech. Of course, much analysis will be done in advance. But a resourceful speaker can continue to assess and adapt to the audience immediately before, during, and even after a speech.*

Many speeches are delivered at conferences, public meetings, and other ongoing events. When you arrive at a conference or meeting room and begin to interact with the audience before your speech, you may learn a good deal about their interests and priorities. If you wish to be heard during the time allotted for public input at a city council meeting, attend one beforehand, or, if possible, watch a few meetings on your local community-access channel. Get to the meeting early and observe the audience. You may discover that the audience looks a little different from what you had imagined. They may be younger, they may sound more conservative, or they may express interests you had not anticipated in advance. Based on what you learn immediately before the speech, you may choose to make minor adjustments in your presentation.

It is even possible to adapt to your audience while you are speaking. If you sense that the audience is bored, you may cut some material and move on to the next point. You may, for example, have underestimated the audience's knowledge of the subject and realize that you can use less repetition and restatement than you had planned. Or if the audience seems puzzled, you may use additional examples to help clarify an idea. You may use more humor if the audience seems to enjoy it. If the setting is more informal than you anticipated, you could move closer to listeners if you sense that the podium is creating a barrier. Finally, based on your perceptions of how much you are "on target" with your planned remarks, you may choose to shorten your speech so that you can devote more time to the audience's questions after the speech.

Audience analysis and adaptation is an ongoing process. From the moment you learn you are scheduled to make a speech until the moment you stop interacting with listeners, you can continue to learn more about them and adjust your strategy, style, and responses. And from this experience, you may reflect on what you have learned and consider what you would do differently if you were to give your speech again. This kind of reflective analysis will help you deliver better speeches in the future.

 Study and Review materials for this chapter are at **MyCommunicationLab**

SUMMARY

 Listen to the Audio Chapter Summary at **MyCommunicationLab**

Understanding Diverse Audiences

4.1 Describe the audience characteristics you need to consider as you prepare your speech.

- A speaker-listener partnership with mutual benefits is central to the success of any public speaking venture.
- Consider the listeners' diversity of values, beliefs, and attitudes while remaining mindful of the needs and values they likely share.
- In analyzing your audience, you should avoid stereotyping while considering the relevance of such factors as the following:
  - Age
  - Gender
  - Race and ethnicity
  - Cultural factors
  - Religion
  - Geography
  - Education
  - Occupation
  - Economic status

Identifying Individual Listener Needs and Values

4.2 Identify individual needs and values relevant to your speech.

- Recognize that all listeners share some universal human needs: basic physiological needs, as well as the need for safety and security, love and belonging, esteem, and self-actualization.

Identifying Communal Needs and Values

4.3 Identify communal needs and values that might impact your speech.

- Consider the communal needs and values of audiences related to the groups with which they identify and the relevance of these associations to your topic.

Gathering Information for Audience Adaptation

4.4 Know how to gather relevant information about an audience.

- Gather specific information about your listeners by exploring the Internet, interviewing relevant people, observing the audience in their natural environment, or conducting an audience survey.

Ongoing Strategies for Audience Adaptation

4.5 Implement strategies for adapting to audiences as you deliver your speech.

- Because audience adaptation is an ongoing process, you can make adjustments immediately before and even during the speech, as you assess, watch, listen, and reflect on the communication experience.

QUESTIONS FOR REVIEW AND REFLECTION

Understanding Diverse Audiences

4.1 Describe the audience characteristics you need to consider as you prepare your speech.

1. What is your understanding of the meaning of *audience adaptation*?
2. What are the major stereotypes associated with the following groups: football players, sorority members, accountants, lawyers, and college professors? For each category, offer at least one example of someone you know who violates the stereotype.
3. What are the major audience characteristics you ought to consider when planning a speech? Why is each important? Think of one or two possible topics for your speech. How would audience demographics affect these topics?

Identifying Individual Listener Needs and Values

4.2 Identify individual needs and values relevant to your speech.

4. The following are some possible speech topics:
   a. Gun control
   b. The health care crisis
   c. Alternative energy sources
   d. Pain management
   e. Becoming a volunteer for the local animal shelter

   Of the needs described in Maslow's hierarchy, which ones would you probably want to consider

in speaking about each of these topics? Why would those needs be especially important?

Identifying Communal Needs and Values

4.3 Identify communal needs and values that might impact your speech.

5. Consider the list of topics in the preceding question. How would you appeal to the needs and values of your own student community when discussing each of these?

Gathering Information for Audience Adaptation

4.4 Know how to gather relevant information about an audience.

6. Consider a possible topic for your speech. Where would you begin to look for information about your audience? What kind of information about your audience would be most relevant to your topic? What would be the most crucial information you would want to collect from a survey of your classmates?

Ongoing Strategies for Audience Adaptation

4.5 Implement strategies for adapting to audiences as you deliver your speech.

7. What audience-adaptation methods do think will be most useful to you during and after you make a speech?

 Study and Review the Flashcards at **MyCommunicationLab**

NOTRE DAME COMMENCEMENT SPEECH

President Barack Obama

Sunday, May 17, 2009, Notre Dame, Indiana

> When President Obama was invited to speak at the University of Notre Dame, critics of his stand on abortion, among them some students, a number of Catholic bishops, and outside anti-abortion groups, staged protests on the campus and spoke out on the national news. Their contention was that a Catholic university should not honor a leader who held views contrary to official Catholic doctrine. The university and a large majority of students, however, approved of the president's visit. This controversy formed the backdrop against which the speech was given.

Thank you, Father Jenkins, for that generous introduction. You are doing an outstanding job as president of this fine institution, and your continued and courageous commitment to honest, thoughtful dialogue is an inspiration to us all.

Good afternoon, Father Hesburgh, Notre Dame trustees, faculty, family, friends, and the class of 2009. I am honored to be here today, and grateful to all of you for allowing me to be part of your graduation.

I want to thank you for this honorary degree. I know it has not been without controversy. I don't know if you're aware of this, but these honorary degrees are apparently pretty hard to come by. So far I'm only 1 for 2 as President. Father Hesburgh is 150 for 150. I guess that's better. Father Ted, after the ceremony, maybe you can give me some pointers on how to boost my average.

I also want to congratulate the class of 2009 for all your accomplishments. And since this is Notre Dame, I mean both in the classroom and in the competitive arena. We all know about this university's proud and storied football team, but I also hear that Notre Dame holds the largest outdoor 5-on-5 basketball tournament in the world—Bookstore Basketball.

Now this excites me. I want to congratulate the winners of this year's tournament, a team by the name of "Hallelujah Holla Back." Well done. Though I have to say, I am personally disappointed that the "Barack O'Ballers" didn't pull it out. Next year, if you need a 6′2″ forward with a decent jumper, you know where I live.

Every one of you should be proud of what you have achieved at this institution. One hundred and sixty-three classes of Notre Dame graduates have sat where you are today. Some were here during years that simply rolled into the next without much notice or fanfare—periods of relative peace and prosperity that required little by way of sacrifice or struggle.

You, however, are not getting off that easy. Your class has come of age at a moment of great consequence for our nation and the world—a rare inflection point in history where the size and scope of the challenges before us require that we remake our world to renew its promise; that we align our deepest values and commitments to the demands of a new age. It is a privilege and a responsibility afforded to few generations—and a task that you are now called to fulfill.

This is the generation that must find a path back to prosperity and decide how we respond to a global economy that left millions behind even before this crisis hit—an economy where greed and short-term thinking were too often rewarded at the expense of fairness, and diligence, and an honest day's work.

THE PRESIDENT BEGINS WITH AN OBLIQUE REFERENCE TO FATHER JENKINS'S REFUSAL TO BOW TO PRESSURE TO WITHDRAW THE INVITATION, LABELING IT COURAGEOUS AND SUPPORTIVE OF THOUGHTFUL DIALOGUE. THE NOTION OF THOUGHTFUL DIALOGUE IS AN UNDERLYING THEME OF THE SPEECH.

PRESIDENT OBAMA THEN ATTEMPTS TO ESTABLISH RAPPORT WITH THE AUDIENCE THROUGH REFERENCES TO FATHER HESBURGH, THE UNIVERSITY'S FORMER LONGTIME PRESIDENT. HE ALSO USES HUMOR TO RELATE TO LOCAL EVENTS WITH WHICH THE STUDENT AUDIENCE WILL BE FAMILIAR.

We must decide how to save God's creation from a changing climate that threatens to destroy it. We must seek peace at a time when there are those who will stop at nothing to do us harm, and when weapons in the hands of a few can destroy the many. And we must find a way to reconcile our ever-shrinking world with its ever-growing diversity—diversity of thought, of culture, and of belief.

In short, we must find a way to live together as one human family.

It is this last challenge that I'd like to talk about today. For the major threats we face in the 21st century—whether it's global recession or violent extremism; the spread of nuclear weapons or pandemic disease—do not discriminate. They do not recognize borders. They do not see color. They do not target specific ethnic groups.

THE PRESIDENT DESCRIBES THE MANY CHALLENGES FACING THE GRADUATES. HE SUGGESTS THAT THEY ALL ARE CONNECTED TO HIS FUNDAMENTAL PREMISE: FINDING COMMON GROUND IS ESSENTIAL TO RESOLVING DISPUTES.

Moreover, no one person, or religion, or nation can meet these challenges alone. Our very survival has never required greater cooperation and understanding among all people from all places than at this moment in history.

Unfortunately, finding that common ground—recognizing that our fates are tied up, as Dr. King said, in a "single garment of destiny"—is not easy. Part of the problem, of course, lies in the imperfections of man—our selfishness, our pride, our stubbornness, our acquisitiveness, our insecurities, our egos; all the cruelties large and small that those of us in the Christian tradition understand to be rooted in original sin. We too often seek advantage over others. We cling to outworn prejudice and fear those who are unfamiliar. Too many of us view life only through the lens of immediate self-interest and crass materialism; in which the world is necessarily a zero-sum game. The strong too often dominate the weak, and too many of those with wealth and with power find all manner of justification for their own privilege in the face of poverty and injustice. And so, for all our technology and scientific advances, we see around the globe violence and want and strife that would seem sadly familiar to those in ancient times.

We know these things; and hopefully one of the benefits of the wonderful education you have received is that you have had time to consider these wrongs in the world, and grown determined, each in your own way, to right them. And yet, one of the vexing things for those of us interested in promoting greater understanding and cooperation among people is the discovery that even bringing together persons of goodwill, men and women of principle and purpose, can be difficult.

HERE THE PRESIDENT OFFERS EXAMPLES OF COMMON GROUND THAT MAY BE FOUND BETWEEN OPPOSING SIDES OF A QUESTION.

The soldier and the lawyer may both love this country with equal passion, and yet reach very different conclusions on the specific steps needed to protect us from harm. The gay activist and the evangelical pastor may both deplore the ravages of HIV/AIDS, but find themselves unable to bridge the cultural divide that might unite their efforts. Those who speak out against stem cell research may be rooted in admirable conviction about the sacredness of life, but so are the parents of a child with juvenile diabetes who are convinced that their son's or daughter's hardships can be relieved.

The question, then, is how do we work through these conflicts? Is it possible for us to join hands in common effort? As citizens of a vibrant and varied democracy, how do we engage in vigorous debate? How does each of us remain firm in our principles, and fight for what we consider right, without demonizing those with just as strongly held convictions on the other side?

Nowhere do these questions come up more powerfully than on the issue of abortion.

As I considered the controversy surrounding my visit here, I was reminded of an encounter I had during my Senate campaign, one that I describe in a book I wrote called *The Audacity of Hope*. A few days after I won the Democratic nomination, I received an e-mail from a doctor who told me that while he voted for me in the primary, he had a serious concern that might prevent him from voting for me in the general election. He described himself as a Christian who was strongly pro-life, but that's not what was preventing him from voting for me.

What bothered the doctor was an entry that my campaign staff had posted on my website— an entry that said I would fight "right-wing ideologues who want to take away a woman's right to choose." The doctor said that he had assumed I was a reasonable person, but that if I truly believed that every pro-life individual was simply an ideologue who wanted to inflict suffering on women, then I was not very reasonable. He wrote, "I do not ask at this point that you oppose abortion, only that you speak about this issue in fair-minded words."

Fair-minded words.

After I read the doctor's letter, I wrote back to him and thanked him. I didn't change my position, but I did tell my staff to change the words on my website. And I said a prayer that night that I might extend the same presumption of good faith to others that the doctor had extended to me. Because when we do that—when we open our hearts and our minds to those who may not think like we do or believe what we do—that's when we discover at least the possibility of common ground.

That's when we begin to say, "Maybe we won't agree on abortion, but we can still agree that this is a heart-wrenching decision for any woman to make, with both moral and spiritual dimensions.

"So let's work together to reduce the number of women seeking abortions by reducing unintended pregnancies, and making adoption more available, and providing care and support for women who do carry their child to term. Let's honor the conscience of those who disagree with abortion, and draft a sensible conscience clause, and make sure that all of our health care policies are grounded in clear ethics and sound science, as well as respect for the equality of women."

Understand—I do not suggest that the debate surrounding abortion can or should go away. No matter how much we may want to fudge it—indeed, while we know that the views of most Americans on the subject are complex and even contradictory—the fact is that at some level, the views of the two camps are irreconcilable. Each side will continue to make its case to the public with passion and conviction. But surely we can do so without reducing those with differing views to caricature.

Open hearts. Open minds. Fair-minded words.

It's a way of life that has always been the Notre Dame tradition. Father Hesburgh has long spoken of this institution as both a lighthouse and a crossroads. The lighthouse that stands apart, shining with the wisdom of the Catholic tradition, while the crossroads is where "...differences of culture and religion and conviction can co-exist with friendship, civility, hospitality, and especially love." And I want to join him and Father Jenkins in saying how inspired I am by the maturity and responsibility with which this class has approached the debate surrounding today's ceremony.

This tradition of cooperation and understanding is one that I learned in my own life many years ago—also with the help of the Catholic Church.

I was not raised in a particularly religious household, but my mother instilled in me a sense of service and empathy that eventually led me to become a community organizer after I graduated college. A group of Catholic churches in Chicago helped fund an organization known as the Developing Communities Project, and we worked to lift up South Side neighborhoods that had been devastated when the local steel plant closed.

It was quite an eclectic crew. Catholic and Protestant churches. Jewish and African-American organizers. Working-class black and white and Hispanic residents. All of us with different experiences. All of us with different beliefs. But all of us learned to work side by side because all of us saw in these neighborhoods other human beings who needed our help—to find jobs and improve schools. We were bound together in the service of others.

And something else happened during the time I spent in those neighborhoods. Perhaps because the church folks I worked with were so welcoming and understanding; perhaps because they invited me to their services and sang with me from their hymnals; perhaps because I witnessed all of the good works their faith inspired them to perform, I found myself drawn—not just to work with the church, but to be in the church. It was through this service that I was brought to Christ.

At the time, Cardinal Joseph Bernardin was the Archbishop of Chicago. For those of you too young to have known him, he was a kind and good and wise man. A saintly man. I can still remember him speaking at one of the first organizing meetings I attended on the South Side. He stood as both a lighthouse and a crossroads—unafraid to speak his mind on moral issues ranging from poverty, AIDS, and abortion to the death penalty and nuclear war. And yet, he was congenial and gentle in his persuasion, always trying to bring people together; always trying to find common ground. Just before he died, a reporter asked Cardinal Bernardin about this approach to his ministry. And he said, "You can't really get on with preaching the Gospel until you've touched minds and hearts."

My heart and mind were touched by the words and deeds of the men and women I worked alongside with in Chicago. And I'd like to think that we touched the hearts and minds of the neighborhood families whose lives we helped change. For this, I believe, is our highest calling.

You are about to enter the next phase of your life at a time of great uncertainty. You will be called upon to help restore a free market that is also fair to all who are willing to work; to seek new sources of energy that can save our planet; to give future generations the same chance that you had to receive an extraordinary education. And whether as a person drawn to public service, or someone who simply insists on being an active citizen, you will be exposed to more opinions and ideas broadcast through more means of communications than have ever existed before. You will hear talking heads scream on cable, read blogs that claim definitive knowledge, and watch politicians pretend to know what they're talking about. Occasionally, you may also have the great fortune of seeing important issues debated by well-intentioned, brilliant minds. In fact, I suspect that many of you will be among those bright stars.

THE USE OF NOTRE DAME'S FORMER PRESIDENT, FATHER HESBURGH, A REVERED FIGURE, AND CARDINAL BERNARDIN, BOTH CREDIBLE SOURCES FOR THIS AUDIENCE, PROMOTES IDENTIFICATION AND ADDS TO THE PRESIDENT'S OWN CREDIBILITY. THE PERSONAL EXAMPLE OF OBAMA'S WORK WITH SEVERAL FAITH COMMUNITIES, INCLUDING CATHOLICS, FURTHER STRENGTHENS HIS ETHOS.

In this world of competing claims about what is right and what is true, have confidence in the values with which you've been raised and educated. Be unafraid to speak your mind when those values are at stake. Hold firm to your faith and allow it to guide you on your journey. Stand as a lighthouse.

But remember, too, that the ultimate irony of faith is that it necessarily admits doubt. It is the belief in things not seen. It is beyond our capacity as human beings to know with certainty what God has planned for us or what He asks of us, and those of us who believe must trust that His wisdom is greater than our own.

This doubt should not push us away from our faith. But it should humble us. It should temper our passions, and cause us to be wary of self-righteousness. It should compel us to remain open, and curious, and eager to continue the moral and spiritual debate that began for so many of you within the walls of Notre Dame. And within our vast democracy, this doubt should remind us to persuade through reason, through an appeal whenever we can to universal rather than parochial principles, and most of all through an abiding example of good works, charity, kindness, and service that moves hearts and minds.

For if there is one law that we can be most certain of, it is the law that binds people of all faiths and no faith together. It is no coincidence that it exists in Christianity and Judaism; in Islam and Hinduism; in Buddhism and humanism. It is, of course, the Golden Rule—the call to treat one another as we wish to be treated. The call to love. To serve. To do what we can to make a difference in the lives of those with whom we share the same brief moment on this Earth.

So many of you at Notre Dame—by the last count, upwards of 80 percent—have lived this law of love through the service you've performed at schools and hospitals; international relief agencies and local charities. That is incredibly impressive, and a powerful testament to this institution. Now you must carry the tradition forward. Make it a way of life. Because when you serve, it doesn't just improve your community, it makes you a part of your community. It breaks down walls. It fosters cooperation. And when that happens—when people set aside their differences to work in common effort toward a common good; when they struggle together, and sacrifice together, and learn from one another—all things are possible.

After all, I stand here today, as President and as an African-American, on the 55th anniversary of the day that the Supreme Court handed down the decision in *Brown v. the Board of Education. Brown* was of course the first major step in dismantling the "separate but equal" doctrine, but it would take a number of years and a nationwide movement to fully realize the dream of civil rights for all of God's children. There were freedom rides and lunch counters and billy clubs, and there was also a Civil Rights Commission appointed by President Eisenhower. It was the twelve resolutions recommended by this commission that would ultimately become law in the Civil Rights Act of 1964.

There were six members of the commission. It included five whites and one African-American; Democrats and Republicans; two Southern governors, the dean of a Southern law school, a Midwestern university president, and your own Father Ted Hesburgh, President of Notre Dame. They worked for two years, and at times, President Eisenhower had to intervene

IN COMMENTING ON THE LACK OF CIVIL DISCOURSE THAT OFTEN PREVAILS OVER CONTENTIOUS ISSUES, THE PRESIDENT COMPLIMENTS HIS AUDIENCE AS THOSE WHO WILL ENGAGE IN WELL-INTENTIONED DEBATE IN THE FUTURE. HE FOLLOWS THIS BY CONNECTING FAITH WITH THE NEED TO BE OPEN MINDED.

THE PRESIDENT OFFERS ANOTHER APPEAL TO COMMON GROUND THROUGH THE SHARED BELIEF IN THE GOLDEN RULE AND THE SHARED COMMITMENT OF ALL RELIGIONS TO SERVICE.

THE DISCUSSION OF FATHER HESBURGH'S WORK WITH CIVIL RIGHTS BOTH RESONATES WITH NOTRE DAME AND OFFERS A SPECIFIC EXAMPLE OF HOW PEOPLE WITH DIFFERENT POINTS OF VIEW, WORKING IN GOOD FAITH, CAN COME TOGETHER.

personally since no hotel or restaurant in the South would serve the black and white members of the commission together. Finally, when they reached an impasse in Louisiana, Father Ted flew them all to Notre Dame's retreat in Land O'Lakes, Wisconsin, where they eventually overcame their differences and hammered out a final deal.

Years later, President Eisenhower asked Father Ted how on Earth he was able to broker an agreement between men of such different backgrounds and beliefs. And Father Ted simply said that during their first dinner in Wisconsin, they discovered that they were all fishermen. And so he quickly readied a boat for a twilight trip out on the lake. They fished, and they talked, and they changed the course of history.

I will not pretend that the challenges we face will be easy, or that the answers will come quickly, or that all our differences and divisions will fade happily away. Life is not that simple. It never has been.

But as you leave here today, remember the lessons of Cardinal Bernardin, of Father Hesburgh, of movements for change both large and small. Remember that each of us, endowed with the dignity possessed by all children of God, has the grace to recognize ourselves in one another; to understand that we all seek the same love of family and the same fulfillment of a life well-lived. Remember that in the end, we are all fishermen.

If nothing else, that knowledge should give us faith that through our collective labor, and God's providence, and our willingness to shoulder each other's burdens, America will continue on its precious journey towards that more perfect union. Congratulations on your graduation, may God bless you, and may God bless the United States of America.

THE CONCLUSION OFFERS A CHALLENGE TO THE AUDIENCE, REMINDS THEM OF THE SUPPORT HE TAKES FROM TWO HIGHLY CREDIBLE FIGURES, AND ALLUDES TO THE BIBLICAL REFERENCE TO JESUS'S DISCIPLES AS FISHERS OF MEN.

Source: www.whitehouse.gov/the_press_office/Remarks-by-the-President-at-Notre-Dame-Commencement/ (accessed May 17, 2012). Published 2009 by The White House, Office of the Press Secretary.

Developing Significant Topics

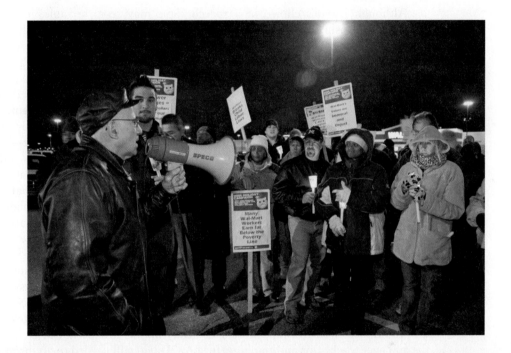

OVERVIEW AND LEARNING OBJECTIVES

Finding a Suitable Topic

5.1 Generate significant speech topics.

Narrowing the Topic

5.2 Revise and narrow your topic.

Ethical Obligations in Selecting a Topic

5.3 Determine how ethical considerations affect your choice of a topic.

General Purposes

5.4 Distinguish among the goals of informative, persuasive, and ceremonial speeches.

Crafting and Testing Specific Purposes

5.5 Devise a clear specific purpose that aims for an attainable audience response.

Constructing a Thesis Statement

5.6 Write a clear, concise thesis statement.

After giving a poor speech, a student went to talk to his instructor and told this story. Two weeks before he was scheduled to give a five- to seven-minute informative speech, David had not yet chosen a topic. He admitted that he was clueless. As he sat in his political science class, he had a bright idea. His professor was explaining how a president is elected in the United States. David had taken several pages of notes and read two chapters on the subject. That seemed to him to be a lot of information. Why not, David thought, just summarize his notes and develop a short speech? He felt great relief as he decided to speak about presidential elections.

Although David's choice of a speech topic may seem sensible, it was not. Randomly choosing a topic can prove disastrous. In David's case, the choice was inspired by convenience rather than the demands of the situation. For one thing, his topic was too broad to be covered in the available time. His information was also too technical for his listeners. In short, David had problems because he failed to take into account his audience's knowledge and interests. This "boiled-down" version of a lecture was not appropriate for his public speaking assignment.

To make matters worse, David had not taken the time to come up with a clear focus for his speech. He thought only about his general purpose—talking about presidential elections—instead of the specific ideas he wanted his audience to understand. Beginning with his own interests, coupled with important issues of the day, David should have asked himself, "What do I care about that would be significant and interesting to this audience?" Many worthy topics might have emerged from this kind of reflection. David might have chosen to speak about political action committees, campaign finance reform, or the evolution of the national party conventions. These topics might have grown out of what David already knew something about, but they also could have been fashioned to connect with the interests and needs of the audience. David forgot that his own interests are an especially good point of departure when thinking about a speech topic. Naturally, David would have to do additional research to address these topics intelligently. He would also need to think more specifically about how he hoped to influence the audience's behavior and thinking. In short, David still needed to go through the process of refining and narrowing his topic.

FINDING A SUITABLE TOPIC

5.1 Generate significant speech topics.

Watch the Video "Martin Cox Discusses Tips on Developing a Topic for a Speech" at **MyCommunicationLab**

Preview. *As you start thinking about a topic, first focus your attention on what you know and care about. Taking an inventory of your personal concerns and their relationship to community issues, your intellectual and educational interests, your career goals, and your leisure activities will help you come up with good speech topics. These interests represent a starting point for identifying matters of public concern that you are motivated to learn more about.*

Deciding what to talk about may or may not be one of your initial concerns as a speaker. In some situations, the topic of your speech will be predetermined. You may be invited to talk because of your expertise or experience, and the invitation determines the topic. If, for example, you have been active in an environmental group, you may be asked to speak at a service club about environmental problems in your community. Or perhaps the student association at your school distributes funds to campus organizations, and you have been chosen to speak as an advocate for your group. Sometimes the situation determines the topic, as when you attend a public meeting to speak for or against a specific proposal. Many times, however, you will be asked to determine your own topic. Your public speaking class is one such situation. In most cases, you will be assigned only a *type* of speech, but you will choose the topic. Your task, then, will be to find the right topic—one that is important, fits with your interests, meets the needs of the situation, and positively impacts your listeners.

Early in your public speaking class, you may be assigned a specific topic that does not require much preparation or specialized knowledge, just to help you get comfortable speaking before a group. You may be asked to give a short speech describing a person you admire, for example, or a speech introducing yourself or a classmate. Normally, however, you will have to choose your own topic, whether speaking in or outside your class. In most cases, neither circumstances nor setting nor audience demands will determine your specific topic. It will be up to you to choose the best topic.

Brainstorming Topics of Public Concern

Explore the Concept
"Visual Brainstorming" at
MyCommunicationLab

Keeping up with the news is one way to identify potential speech topics. Reading widely about the issues that affect your community, the nation, and the world can help you not only identify topics of public significance but also begin to form your own opinions and arguments.

Suppose, for example, you read an article online about the controversy surrounding the plan to build an oil pipeline from Canada to Texas. At the outset, you may have given little thought to this controversy, but you begin to see it as an important issue and a good topic for a speech. As you read further, you become more interested. You notice contradictory opinions. On the one hand, proponents argue that this project will reduce dependence on foreign oil and create more jobs. At the same time, you learn that the oil is to be shipped to Port Arthur, Texas, to be exported, thus having virtually no effect on domestic consumption. Opponents also raise questions about the environmental impact of building the pipeline. You begin to wonder whether we ought to be looking for other ways to reduce our dependence on foreign oil through alternate energy sources. As you gain more knowledge of the subject, you not only decide that this is a good topic for your speech but also begin to form your own opinions on the issue. By choosing a topic that you are interested in and know will be worthwhile for your listeners, you are set up to do your best work.[1]

However extensive your initial knowledge of the topic, you should always be willing to do additional research, consulting reference works, good newspapers (such as the *New York Times* or the *Wall Street Journal*), periodicals, books, and other library resources. Many of these resources are also available online.

In *Highlighting Sources for Identifying Topics of Public Concern*, we describe one university's online guide to library resources. Your own college or university may have a similar online guide that can help you identify and research topics of public concern.

What Matters to You?

Another good way to identify possible topics is by thinking about your own interests and experiences. Following your own interests is crucial. You will give a much better speech if you care about the topic you choose. The fundamental question is, "What do I already know and care about?" This does not mean, "What can I already give a speech about?" Do not try to find a ready-made speech in your head or limit yourself to topics on which you are already an expert. That kind of thinking could lead you to imagine that you can just give a speech "off the top of your head." In fact, giving a good speech takes a lot of work, and part of that work is learning more about your topic. Research is essential to support your personal knowledge, opinions, and experiences, but research also may lead you to change your initial topic or your opinions about that topic.

Conducting a Self-Inventory

By doing a self-inventory—taking a thoughtful look at what you really know and care about—you can come up with a list of potential topics. Think about issues that affect you and your community. Or do an inventory of your intellectual and educational interests, your career goals, and your leisure activities and interests. By doing a self-inventory, you can begin to generate possible topics that are both meaningful to you and significant issues for your audience.

Begin by brainstorming—writing down anything that comes to your mind under a particular category. At first, don't worry about whether the topic would be interesting to your audience, whether you will be able to get enough material, or anything else. Just put down all the possibilities that come to you. When you have come up with a number of ideas, you can then evaluate each topic, considering whether it may be a good topic for your speech.

Personal Concerns and Community Issues   The best place to begin your search for a topic is with issues and questions that are important to you *and* important to your community. Here are two major questions to start you thinking of topics in this category.

Watch the Video "Citizens for Community Justice" at **MyCommunicationLab**

- **What is going on in my life that bothers or concerns me?** All of us know of things that we would like to change. We have all been upset by certain people or events, and we all have values and ideals that we wish others would embrace. Begin a list of things that frustrate or upset you—things that you would like to see changed—and then consider the possible speech topics you might generate from such a list.

  One student began her self-inventory of personal concerns by reflecting on the difficulty she and her friends were having completing their degree requirements in four years. That suggested a speech arguing that the college ought to offer more courses during the summer, or perhaps a proposal to change the college's degree requirements. She also considered ways that the university might help students better balance work, study, and classes, leading to a proposal that the university offer workshops or support groups for students. She often worried about proposed cutbacks in student loans, suggesting a speech opposing such cuts or advocating more state support for students. Finally, she recalled that spring break was coming up soon, and she began to wonder if there was a better way to spend that time than lying on a beach. This led her to explore opportunities for getting involved in volunteer work over the break, such as through Habitat for Humanity's Collegiate Challenge. By looking at her own concerns, she had generated a number of possible topics to explore.

- **What is happening outside my immediate world that is unfair, unjust, or in need of reform?** What good things going on in the world deserve more support? As you read newspapers and newsmagazines, watch television news programs, and search the Internet, write down issues that capture your interest. Ask yourself what kinds of news stories concern you the most, and consider what topics may arise out of those concerns. Perhaps a story about a tragic death on campus will lead you to speak about the dangers of binge drinking. Or maybe a story about Congress passing a new "Bill of Rights" for credit card holders got you thinking about how easy it is for college students to get credit cards and go into debt. As you follow the news about the turmoil in the Middle East and the repercussions of the "Arab Spring," you may want to examine what role the United States should play when insurgents try to remove a dictatorial government. As you hear news about the development of nuclear weapons in Iran or North Korea, you may reflect on nuclear proliferation treaties and how well they work. The possibilities are limitless. Pay attention to what is happening in your community, your country, and the world and you will generate a long and varied list of possible speech topics.

Intellectual and Educational Interests   Your self-inventory can prod you to consider important topics that you would like to know more about. When considering your intellectual and educational interests, you may ask yourself these questions:

- **What do I like to read?** One student listed the books she had most enjoyed reading in the past year and asked herself what they had in common. Two books that she particularly liked, *Three Cups of Tea* and *A Thousand Splendid Suns*, dealt with cultural values in the Muslim world and how values are learned or imposed. This led her to consider a speech topic dealing with different cultural values, and then to a possible topic: the differences between Islamic values and traditional Western values. She was still a long way from a specific topic, but she had taken the first step.
- **What interesting things have I learned from television or movies?** Another student began by considering the television programs and movies he most enjoyed and came up with a list of sitcoms, dramas, reality shows, and nature films. As he thought about the significant issues that might emerge from the shows he watched, all sorts of possible topics arose. A fan of *The Daily Show* and *Saturday Night Live*, he began to consider the influence of comedy shows on politics. His favorite TV shows, such as *Body of Proof* and the *CSI* franchise, focused on forensic medicine. Thinking about this led him to consider the growing controversy over mandatory collection of DNA samples, legal in some states, versus constitutional protection against illegal searches. The movie *The Help* led him to think about race relations and how they have changed since the early days of the civil rights movement. His problem was not finding a topic, but selecting, narrowing, and developing one of the many topics that his brainstorming generated.
- **What specific courses, or issues covered in my courses, have particularly interested me?** Courses in your major field of study can also be a source of topics. Here are some examples of topics generated by students from their majors: a physics major spoke on the benefits of space exploration; an English major chose to talk about the ways literary works shape our view of the world; a psychology major explained how cognitive dissonance is experienced and its consequences in making important decisions; a business major decided to examine the tensions between the profit motive and ethics in large corporations. In each case, the topic grew from something the student had learned about in a course, and all addressed important issues.

Career Goals   Students usually have an ultimate career goal in mind; many may already be pursuing a career. The major question to start with here is, "What do I hope to do with my life?" Follow up on this question by brainstorming possible issues associated with that profession. One student who planned to be a lawyer brainstormed by asking these questions: Do lawyers have an obligation to work with any client who can afford to hire them? What if you think a potential client is guilty? Is it right to approach a potential client who has suffered a tragic loss? What do you do if your personal interests conflict with a client's best interests? What can be done about the widespread mistrust of lawyers? As he considered these questions, he soon realized that they all raised important questions about the ethical code that lawyers follow.

Other careers may suggest additional topics. A future teacher may speak about the role of teachers' unions in promoting quality education. A future engineer may address the dangers of our deteriorating infrastructure. If you plan to be an accountant, perhaps you would speak on the proposal for a flat tax to replace the graduated income tax. A future research chemist may speak about generic drugs and how they affect consumers. If you hope to become a marketing analyst, you may choose to address how wise consumers make choices among similar products. A future television producer may speak about how viewers can influence network programming. Giving a speech related to your future career has the added bonus of providing you with information you can use in the future. By thinking about your prospective career, you may not only discover a good speech topic but also learn more about the career you are considering.

Concern for problems, whether in the world, the country, or your community, will generate significant topics for speeches. These students, who are helping with clean up following a tornado in Southern Indiana, would have many compelling experiences on which to build a speech.

Leisure Activities and Interests   Things you do for pleasure or enjoyment may be a source of speech topics. Yet a word of caution is in order: speeches that some audiences may find useful or interesting may seem ordinary or trivial to others. For example, you may have experience teaching children how to string their own tennis rackets, but your college classmates would not likely respond well to a speech titled "How to String a Tennis Racket." Playing bridge, dancing, or watching football may be enjoyable for you, but do they suggest speech topics that your audience would consider substantive and important? Probably not.

Nevertheless, a sports enthusiast *could* come up with some significant topics. Among the hotly debated issues in the sports world today are the use of performance-enhancing drugs, the obligations of colleges and universities to support women's athletics, and the enormous salaries paid to some professional athletes. Similarly, a movie buff may decide to talk about how films help shape the rules of social interaction in our culture or the ways in which our history is manipulated in films to promote particular political beliefs or social values. Someone who sees a lot of movies may also address the topic of censorship or the controversy over how movies and other forms of entertainment are rated.

Conducting a self-inventory that surveys your intellectual and educational interests, career goals, personal and social concerns, and favorite leisure activities and interests will serve as a starting point as you search for your own topics. Of course, the broad topics you generate through brainstorming may need to be narrowed and focused. A consideration of the situation and the audience will help you do this.

NARROWING THE TOPIC

 Revise and narrow your topic.

Explore the Concept "Topic" at **MyCommunicationLab**

Watch the Video "Martin Cox Discusses Tips in Developing a Topic for a Speech" at **MyCommunicationLab**

Preview. *The potential speech topics that emerge from brainstorming are just that—potential topics. Once you have chosen a topic, you can then narrow and refine your choice by considering how the situation, time constraints, and audience will influence your speech.*

Any topic must be appropriate for the audience and the occasion. It must stretch listeners' present understanding or perception of your topic or add to their knowledge. As you refine the purpose of your speech, conduct research, develop arguments and supporting material, and organize your ideas, you will probably find that you need to fine-tune your topic. The first step is to consider your audience carefully and to decide more precisely what you hope to accomplish. In the previous chapter, we discussed audience analysis and adaptation. For now, let us review two guidelines that will help you focus and refine your topic.

Consider the Situation

- Does the topic I am considering relate to recent events that may be of concern to my listeners?
- Would I be able to convince my listeners to care as much about my potential topic as I do?
- Do I have sufficient time to cover the topic adequately?

Consider the Audience

- What does my audience already know?
- What common experiences has my audience had?
- What do my listeners and I have in common?
- How diverse is my audience?

Let us consider how to apply the guidelines in specific cases through an example.

Ruiz, a meteorology major, was interested in how weather systems developed. For him, situational factors proved decisive in narrowing his topic. When he asked himself if his audience would be familiar with any immediate events relevant to his topic, he thought of all the recent news stories about the devastation caused by weather disasters. Although they had all seen on television the flattened landscapes in "tornado ally" and the destructive power of major hurricanes, they did not live in an area that had been directly affected by such traumatic events. He wondered how he might encourage his listeners to be more concerned about weather disasters and therefore support investing in improved methods of weather forecasting. If his audience could understand how disasters caused by weather have consequences for *everyone*, he reasoned, they would find his speech more interesting and convincing. He also asked himself how much he could say in seven minutes, the time allotted for his speech. This kind of thinking helped him focus on how weather disasters, even in a distant part of the country, could affect his audience. This is how he began his speech:

> Everyone is aware of the devastating effects of Hurricane Katrina in 2005. That storm cost many lives, destroyed people's homes and businesses, and forced homeless victims to move to other parts of the country. We have all heard about the millions of dollars spent by the government to help people rebuild. We may even have relatives or friends from the affected areas. Schools and universities in our own state took in students, and people opened their homes to strangers displaced by the storm. Rebuilding still goes on today, years after the event. In just the last few years, we've seen the terrible effects of tsunamis in Asia, forest fires raging through dry woods, and tornados flattening people's homes in seconds. From a purely humanitarian point of view, that is probably sufficient for us to support efforts to improve weather forecasting in America.

> But there are also other, less dramatic ways that weather-related disasters directly impact us. After you watched scenes of that hurricane hit the Gulf Coast, I'm sure you noticed that the price of gasoline went up. The same thing happens to the price of bread and breakfast cereals when rivers in the wheat-producing states flood following heavy winter snows. It happens all the time: the terrible tsunami in Japan disrupts auto production, and the price of Japanese cars goes up. There's a drought in California, and all of a sudden iceberg lettuce costs twice as much. As Mark Twain once quipped, "Everybody talks about the weather, but nobody does anything about it." Yet today we have the scientific and technological knowledge to do a much better job predicting the weather, if only we are willing to commit the necessary resources to that effort. Specifically, we need to invest more in weather prediction technologies and early-warning systems that have the potential to save lives and property.

This student went from selecting possible topics though a self-inventory to narrowing the possibilities by considering his own interests. He then focused his speech on a topic that mattered to his audience and concerned the welfare of the broader community.

Considerations of situation and audience are just as important to speakers outside the classroom. A public health official, for example, may be asked to speak to a community group about the potential dangers of a new flu strain. Just as the student speaker did, this speaker needs to consider the situation. Is there a real threat of an epidemic? Had there been a lot of coverage of the issue in the local media? Are flu shots available? He also needs to ask questions about the audience. Do his listeners have much medical knowledge? Is there serious concern among the group that the flu will be widespread? Is the group made up of people who are more susceptible to the flu? Does the audience include parents who may be worried about their children? Based on such considerations, he may decide to narrow the topic to explain exactly what is known about the new strain and how it is transmitted. Or he may want to explain the symptoms of the flu, how to avoid contracting it, and what to do if one exhibits the symptoms. He may, instead, choose to assure his audience that there is no need to panic and focus on the reasons the flu is *not* likely to affect them. So, from the topic of flu, this speaker may narrow the topic in a number of ways to better suit the situation and audience.

ETHICAL OBLIGATIONS IN SELECTING A TOPIC

5.3 Determine how ethical considerations affect your choice of a topic.

Preview. *As you choose a topic, you should consider your ethical obligations to the audience. You should commit to becoming knowledgeable about your topic through careful research. Although you may have strong feelings about your topic, you also should strive to be fair-minded. And you will want to exercise good judgment in considering the audience's standards of taste.*

Ethics may be described as a set of behavioral standards. Some would argue that ethics are universal and unchanging, but others argue that they are relative to a particular culture or situation. In either case, such standards represent a behavioral code, and a person who lives by that code is considered ethical. If your listeners sense that you are ethical, they will find your speech more convincing.[2]

As a speaker, you will draw on your own ethical code in choosing a topic, as well as in deciding how to approach that topic. Ethical considerations cannot be taken up after you have finished your work, nor can they be dealt with and dismissed early on. As we pointed out in Chapter 1, the rhetorical tradition emphasizes the ethical underpinnings of public speaking. You will make many choices as you prepare yourself to speak: a good speaker integrates ethical concerns into every aspect of his or her speech.[3]

Some ethical choices should be obvious: it is clearly wrong to make up information and statistics or to distort or manufacture quoted material. Repeating as "true" some rumor or allegations for which there is no proof is also unethical. Although we may not always agree on what is ethical, you should take certain ethical considerations into account when you choose a topic—namely, your responsibility for accuracy, fair-mindedness, good taste, and sound judgment.

Accuracy

When searching for a topic, you would not reject a possibility because you did not know enough to speak about it without any preparation. As we pointed out earlier in the chapter, you should not expect to have a ready-made speech in your head. A major part of preparing to speak is learning more about your topic. You may not be an expert in a particular field, but you owe it to your audience to know as much as possible about your topic. What does this have to do with ethics?

Without careful research, you cannot come to a sound conclusion yourself. Speaking with the purpose of influencing people carries with it the ethical obligation to know what you are talking about and to believe in what you say. If you are not knowledgeable, you may inadvertently misinform, mislead, or even harm your audience. Suppose, for example, that you wanted to speak about the problem of obesity in America. If you were to give a speech based on just one article about dieting, you might suggest practices that would hurt rather than help your listeners. The article may be outdated, it may not have covered all the potential objections to a certain diet, it may have asserted as fact matters that are not yet scientifically verified, or it may have come from a biased source. Even if you are not trying to persuade an audience, you still have an ethical obligation to strive for accuracy. Any speech that contains misleading or untrue information is considered unethical.

Just as important as the quantity and quality of your information is the credibility of your sources. Would you want to try an amazing marshmallow diet touted by a supermarket tabloid? Or would you feel more comfortable taking advice based on a study reported in the *New England Journal of Medicine*? When you are giving a speech, you are the information resource for your audience. Citing reputable sources will not only make you more credible; doing so is also your obligation as an ethical speaker.

Urging people to take actions or to modify their behavior in ways that could have negative consequences is clearly unethical. The consequences need not be physical, such as endangering one's health. Misinformation or poorly developed ideas can also lead to bad decisions on economic, social, or political matters that affect people's lives. So, for example, faulty information or poorly thought-out arguments could mislead listeners into making poor economic investments, dangerous medical decisions, or voting against the best interests of their communities.

Objectivity versus Subjectivity

We rarely, if ever, achieve the ideal of perfect objectivity. None of us can be entirely neutral toward topics we know or care about. We cannot help having subjective reactions based on our experiences and the values we have learned. We have religious feelings, political biases, or expectations for social behavior that are a part of us whether we consciously recognize them or not. As a speaker, you cannot erase your past and approach any topic as if it had no relationship to your life. On the contrary, potential topics grow from such life experiences. Nor does an audience really expect such complete objectivity. What an audience *does* expect, however, is fair-mindedness—a willingness to suspend your own biases and to remain open to competing ideas.

Because you will select significant topics of public concern or from your particular areas of interest or expertise, you will likely have preexisting opinions, biases, or strong feelings about those topics. However, an ethical speaker approaches topic selection in a fair-minded way. You may be in favor of a comprehensive government health care plan modeled on Medicare, or you may prefer a plan that helps consumers obtain affordable health care through private insurance companies. Whatever position you take, you have the ethical obligation to be open to the possibility that your research may lead you to modify your initial point of view. Ethical speakers remain open to changing their minds and do not avoid or screen out information that may challenge their initial opinions. Once you have thoroughly researched your topic and come to a thoughtful and fair conclusion, you can be more confident in taking a strong, well-reasoned stand on an issue.

Taste and Judgment

Generally, you should avoid topics that audiences may find embarrassing or offensive. Putting listeners in such a position may be considered unethical. An audience-centered perspective is crucial here. *You* may find certain topics appealing, amusing, or of great importance. Thinking about how your audience will react to your topic, however, may put it in a different light.

Imagine a student in your public speaking class giving a speech that tried to convert you to his or her religion. Although the student has the right to hold particular beliefs, your classroom is likely made up of people whose beliefs differ and who may be offended by a speaker trying to convert them. The likelihood of offense increases when the audience is a captive one: listeners in a classroom have no choice but to hear that speech; they cannot simply get up and leave. Attempting to force one's beliefs on a captive audience will likely be viewed as a tasteless demonstration of poor judgment on the part of the speaker. Moreover, trying to change deeply held beliefs is not a practical goal in a single speech. In a public speaking class, you need to be wary of trying to radically change your listeners' views, especially on issues that arouse great passion or deeply divide your audience.

This does not mean that you should avoid controversial topics. Most issues of significant public concern stir up strong feelings and spirited debate. Being engaged will inevitably lead you to advocate positions that are contested. What is important is that you be sensitive to contrary opinions and aware of the limits imposed by those opinions. A speech simply explaining the beliefs of a particular religion may be appropriate—as long as you do not try to convert your listeners. In any case, different audiences may view the same topic in different ways. As an ethical speaker, you must consider each audience separately and try to understand its members' particular tastes and dispositions toward your topic.

Once you have selected a topic, you still need to hone in on the general and specific purposes of your speech.

GENERAL PURPOSES

5.4 Distinguish among the goals of informative, persuasive, and ceremonial speeches.

Watch the Video "Martin Cox Discusses Tips on Developing the Purpose of a Speech" at **MyCommunicationLab**

Preview. *Public speaking is always purposeful—that is, a speaker always aims to get responses from listeners. Sometimes the principal kind of response you want from an audience is understanding, so you give an informative speech. At other times, you want to influence the way listeners feel, what they believe, or how they act. In those cases, you give a persuasive speech. Finally, you may give a ceremonial speech when you want to reinforce values and engage in community building.*

Just as speakers contemplate the situation, their own interests, and those of the audience in selecting a topic, they use those same considerations to formulate their general and specific purposes. As you refine your topic, you try to translate it into a specific statement of the audience response you desire. Successful public communication rests on having a clear purpose. The first step in determining your purpose is to consider the general response you want from your audience. Sometimes you want your audience to simply understand some concept or process; on other occasions, you may hope to change their minds or motivate them to act.

In most classroom speeches, your general purpose will likely be part of the assignment. At work or when you speak in the community, however, your general purpose may not be determined in advance, and you will need to make choices based on the situation and the audience. Let us now consider the three general purposes that will account for most of the speeches you give.

Informative Purposes

When we talk about informing people, we naturally think about giving them new information. But as a speaker, what do you want *from* your audience when you give an informative speech? You want *understanding*; you give an informative speech to gain understanding from your listeners.

This is not just playing with words; an important concept is involved. Have you ever been in a class where the instructor gave a lecture with a lot of information that you did not understand? Have you gotten directions from someone but then found that you still could not reach your destination? Have you ever been given instructions on how to do a job, only to find that you still could not complete the task? If anything like this has happened to you, you have experienced the difference between just getting information and gaining understanding. In all of these cases, the person attempting to communicate with you failed to help you understand.

When you give an informative speech, your goal is to help your listeners understand something they did not understand before. After you have finished speaking, listeners will not just have *heard* something new; they will have *learned* something new. This focus on learning will lead you to avoid topics that are controversial, searching instead for topics that add to the listeners' knowledge. We discuss informative speaking in more detail in Chapter 13.

Persuasive Purposes

Persuasion surrounds us; it intrudes on almost every aspect of our lives. We are urged to give our time to worthy causes, to donate money to charity, to vote for particular politicians, or to protest a decision by the local school board. We are asked to embrace new beliefs or values, to accept new ideas, and to defer to the opinions of others. Like informative messages, persuasive messages aim to get something from us: agreement, empathy, or maybe even some change in our behavior. Persuasive speakers do not just want us to understand their point of view; they want to influence our beliefs, values, and actions.

Persuasion is more than telling listeners what they ought to do or believe. It is more than simply giving an audience facts or statistics. It is more than simply stating your opinion. It is more than asking, recommending, or demanding. We often hear advertisers, politicians, telemarketers, or salespeople give many reasons we should accept their arguments. But we do not always do what they would like us to do. We are not always persuaded.

Persuasion requires that we give our audience good reasons for accepting our claims. As a speaker, you want listeners to feel more strongly about an issue, to agree with you, or to take some definite action. We discuss the goals of persuasive speaking in more detail in Chapters 14 and 15.

Ceremonial Purposes

Watch the Video
"A Wedding Toast" at
MyCommunicationLab

Many speaking occasions offer the opportunity for community building. We may be called on to honor someone, celebrate an event of shared significance, or pay tribute to someone we have loved or lost. Ceremonial speaking uplifts us, comforts us, and reinforces our sense of community with others.[4]

In his commencement speech at Notre Dame, President Obama sought to blunt criticism by emphasizing common values.

In ceremonial speeches, we articulate and reinforce shared values. We ask questions such as these: What brought us together? What defines us as a community? Which of our accomplishments gives us the most pride? What are the principles *we* cherish? In some ceremonial speeches, we may honor our heroes—those who personify or illuminate our shared values. By holding them high, praising their accomplishments, and remembering how they lived their lives, we are reminding ourselves of the values we cherish. On other occasions, we may be presenting an award, honoring graduates, or trying to motivate our listeners to serve their communities. In doing so, we offer encouragement and inspiration to our listeners. We suggest how hard work, determination, and the desire to succeed will ultimately pay off. In the United States, we may celebrate values associated with our founders or some national holiday. In other cultures, different values may be celebrated.[5] But the general purpose of ceremonial speaking remains the same: to reaffirm and strengthen the shared values that define our communities and our cultures.

Ceremonial speeches may be given by anyone—political leaders, community leaders, citizens, or students speaking in a classroom. U.S. presidents give a variety of ceremonial speeches, such as inaugural addresses, commemorative speeches on national holidays, and commencement addresses. Sometimes they are even called on to comfort the nation in times of tragedy. Thus, for example, Ronald Reagan delivered a famous eulogy to the astronauts killed when the space shuttle *Challenger* exploded shortly after takeoff in 1986, referring to them as "seven heroes…who were daring and brave and [who] had that special grace."[6] More often, presidents are asked to mark special occasions or national holidays. On Memorial Day 2009, for example, President Barack Obama delivered a speech calling on all Americans to "pause in national unity" at three P.M., "ring a bell," and offer a "prayer" and a silent "thank you" to all who had died defending America. He then asked his listeners to "commit to give something back to this nation—something lasting—in their memory" and to "affirm in our own lives and advance around the world" those values that Memorial Day represents: those "enduring ideals of justice, equality, and opportunity for which they and so many generations of Americans have given that last full measure of devotion."[7]

In your speech class, you may not be called on to eulogize national heroes or memorialize those who have died in battle. But you may be asked to deliver a ceremonial speech marking a special occasion or paying tribute to an important person in your own life. One word of caution: be careful about choosing ceremonial topics that strongly affect you emotionally. Eulogizing a close friend or relative who has died recently, for example, can be difficult for some people.

We will discuss ceremonial speaking in greater detail in Chapter 16.

Your general purpose, then, points you in the direction you want to go. The next step is to refine that general purpose into a specific purpose statement that spells out precisely the response you want from your audience.

CRAFTING AND TESTING SPECIFIC PURPOSES

Preview. *Specific purpose statements describe the response you want from your audience. They are shaped by your goals as a speaker, the situation in which you speak, and the potential benefits to the audience. You can test your specific purpose by making sure that it aims for a specific response from the audience, reflects the realities of the situation, and is clear and ethical.*

Although speakers may hope to accomplish many things in a speech, the specific purpose is the ultimate response that the speaker hopes to achieve. Crafting the specific purpose statement carefully is a vital step in clearly focusing the speech.

5.5 Devise a clear specific purpose that aims for an attainable audience response.

Watch the Video "Genetic Cloning" at **MyCommunicationLab**

Purpose and Response

Successful speakers think carefully about the response they desire from their audience and never allow themselves to be vague or unclear about their specific purpose. Imagine, for example, a speaker who said, "My purpose is to talk about energy conservation." Such a statement identifies no specific purpose. It says something vague about the speaker's topic, but it does not specify an audience response. Furthermore, "energy conservation" is so broad that it says little about the speaker's specific goals. With the purpose stated this broadly, the speaker would have a difficult time choosing what to include and what not to include in the speech. If you want to give an informative speech, you should state specifically what you want your audience to understand. Returning to our example, you might say: *I want my listeners to understand ways in which each one of them can conserve energy in their daily lives.* If, on the other hand, you wished to give a persuasive speech, you might take a specific position on any number of controversies surrounding the best *ways* to conserve energy. You might, for example, state your purpose this way: *I want my audience to agree that the government should invest more in the development of solar and wind power.* Or you might decide to address a different controversy: *I want my audience to agree that the best way to end our dependence on fossil fuels is to build more nuclear power plants.* These potential purposes all relate to the topic of energy conservation, yet each represents a very different specific purpose.

Purpose and the Situation

The specific purpose of your speech should also be shaped by the demands of the situation. Recent events can suggest topics you can develop in different ways with different specific goals. Here are some examples:

- In the summer of 2011, a young woman student at a large Midwestern university went missing. After weeks of searching, she was not found (her disappearance was still unsolved as of spring of 2012). In such a situation, it was inevitable that campus safety became a widespread concern. Incoming students were addressed by speakers with a specific purpose: *I want my listeners to understand how to stay safe when going out at night on the campus and in town.* As well as this informative purpose, students gave persuasive speeches, such as the following: *I want my audience to agree that the university should institute safety workshops to be given in all the dorms,* or *I want my listeners to join the student volunteer escort service.*

- At a time when university trustees were considering tuition hikes, students were vitally concerned about the rising rates. One gave an informative speech with a specific purpose: *I want my audience to understand how the "529" plan—the prepaid college tuition savings plan—works.* Another gave a persuasive speech: *I want my audience to agree that tax increases should be enacted to lower tuition rates.* Yet another chose a specific purpose: *I want my audience to agree that the university should freeze tuition rates at the present level as other private schools have done.*

- In the spring of 2012, events in Syria prompted speeches with conflicting specific purposes from different speakers. Some supported the dissidents: *I want my audience to agree that the United States should give direct military aid to the Syrian dissidents.* Others took the opposite view: *I want my audience to agree that it is not in the best interest of the United States to intervene in Syria.* Whatever your specific purpose, it should reflect careful consideration of the situation about which you'll speak.

Purpose and Audience Benefits

In devising a specific purpose, you need to consider how you want listeners to respond and what you have to offer your listeners. The benefits to the audience should be apparent in the speech.

When you go to the grocery store, it helps to have a clear goal: you plan to buy food, and you probably have a list of specific items. You don't go to the store "just to shop." Shopping is a means to an end. In the same way, giving a speech is not just "talking about something." It, too, is a means to an end. When you speak, you want a specific reaction from your audience, and you hope to provide some benefit to them as well. If, for example, the topic is the school's "study abroad" program, a student who has studied abroad might generate different specific purposes depending on what would most benefit the audience. If a meeting has been called for the purpose of letting students who are interested in the program know how to participate, your purpose would likely be an informative one, such as *I want my audience to understand who is eligible and how to apply for the study abroad program.* If you achieve your purpose, your listeners will clearly benefit because they will know if they can apply and how to do it. Giving the speech in a class where many students have not thought about the program would call for a different speech with a different purpose, such as *I want my audience to agree that our university's study abroad program offers many opportunities to learn about different cultures while earning college credit.* In fact, such a purpose has several possible variations, all of which could be designed to help listeners see how the program would have direct benefits for them.

Testing Specific Purposes

Because your specific purpose is the foundation of your speech, we have devoted a great deal of space in this chapter to describing how to develop it. Let us consider some quick ways to test the specific purposes you develop. Basically, you can ask yourself four questions to determine whether you have a sound specific purpose statement.

A Good Specific Purpose Asks for an Audience Response Does your purpose statement call for a response from the audience? Here are some ideas that are *not* good specific purposes because they suggest no audience response:

- What to do about Syria?
- The humanitarian crisis in Syria
- Stability in the Middle East
- Our responsibility in the Middle East

These may be topics or titles, but they do not designate the response you want from the audience. Each of them has the potential to generate a variety of specific purposes—some of them even contradictory, for example: *I want my audience to agree that the United States should work through the United Nations to reach a negotiated settlement in the Syrian civil war; I want my audience to agree that the United States should consider direct military intervention in Syria;* or *I want my audience to agree that the United States and it allies should provide arms to the Syrian opposition.* All of these possibilities call for an audience response.

A Good Specific Purpose Is Realistic Does your specific purpose reflect the realities of the situation? Among the factors you should consider in crafting a realistic specific purpose are the amount of time you have to give a speech, the probability that your listeners can actually respond the way you want them to, whether the speech's goals have some reasonable expectation of success, and what kind of impact the setting or occasion may have on the outcome of the speech.

Consider the following specific purpose: *I want my audience to understand how Congress works.* This is an absurdly broad topic that could well be the subject of an entire course in political science. What can you accomplish in a short speech? If you are giving an informative speech, you may craft a more focused, achievable purpose in the time available to you, such as *I want my audience to understand how conference committees resolve differences between House and Senate versions of a bill.* If you are giving a persuasive speech, its purpose could be *I want my audience to agree that lobbyists have too much influence over congressional legislation.* Or, to take another example, suppose you were to offer as a specific purpose *I want my audience to agree with me that all federal elections should be publicly funded.* This is a correctly stated specific purpose, but you need to consider whether such a policy is feasible and realistic in the current political climate. The practicality of your purpose is an important consideration. To take another example, you are unlikely to succeed if you ask your fellow students to help organize a fund-raiser during final exam week.

A Good Specific Purpose Is Clear Is your specific purpose clear? An audience can be confused by a speech that grows out of a vague purpose. Communication is almost always unsuccessful when speakers are unclear about what they want to accomplish.

I want my audience to agree with me about immigration is not a clear statement of purpose. Although it sounds like a purpose statement, it shows that the speaker does not know precisely *what* he or she wants the audience to believe or do. Do you want to persuade your audience to agree that a specific policy should be supported? If so, your specific purpose might be the following: *I want my audience to agree that a guest worker program remains the best plan for controlling illegal immigration while allowing deserving immigrants a chance to become U.S. citizens.*

A Good Specific Purpose Is Ethical   So far, in discussing specific purposes, we have been concerned with issues of response, clarity, and realism. These are all important considerations, but they could all be fulfilled and still the purpose could be unethical.

As we pointed out previously in the chapter, ethical speakers pursue goals that are in the best interests of their listeners and their society. The following specific purpose, for example, is clearly not ethical: *I want my audience to understand how they can avoid paying taxes by hiding their cash in offshore accounts.* Cheating on your income tax not only is socially irresponsible, it is also illegal. Yet even if something *is* legal, we sometimes still face ethical questions, questions about right and wrong.[8] Suppose a speaker in your class wanted to give a speech with this purpose: *I want my audience to understand how to purchase term papers over the Internet.* You would not be sent to jail for buying your term papers online, but you would be guilty of academic dishonesty. This speaker would be advocating something that violates both the ethical norms and the specific regulations of every college and university in the country. Nor would it be ethical for a speaker to promote a fad diet that is seriously questioned by health professionals and may actually cause harm. Again, to knowingly advocate such a diet would be unethical.

Of course, ethical boundaries are not always clear. Conflicts of interest often occur in public debates over controversial issues. Take, for example, the issue of capping medical malpractice awards. On the one hand, we realize that large malpractice awards raise the cost of insurance for doctors and the cost of health care for everyone. On the other hand, we sympathize with the victim of malpractice who may have lost a limb or even his or her life because of the carelessness of a doctor. What is the ethical position to take in this controversy? Both sides in this controversy can make the case that they are advocating the more ethical policy and that their interests are the same as the public's interest.

Like other aspects of public speaking, our specific purposes often have ethical implications. As speakers, we need to think about who we are, who our listeners are, and what we have to gain or lose. As speakers, we have an ethical obligation to ask how our audience may benefit or be hurt or misled by the information that we are sharing with them or the actions we are urging them to pursue.

CONSTRUCTING A THESIS STATEMENT

5.6 Write a clear, concise thesis statement.

Preview.   *The thesis statement grows from your specific purpose. It is a clear, declarative statement that embodies the principal idea of your speech. It should be focused without being cluttered with too much detail.*

After you have determined your specific purpose, you need to formulate a declarative statement that sums up the thesis of your speech, sometimes called the central idea or thesis statement of the speech. You should think of this as your speech in a nutshell. A well-formulated thesis statement will help you focus your research and plan your speech. If you are successful, the thesis statement is what listeners will carry away with them—what they will remember as the heart of your speech.

Guidelines for Constructing a Thesis Statement

Keep three basic guidelines in mind when constructing a thesis statement.

1. The Thesis Statement Is a Single, Complete Declarative Sentence That Embodies the Idea That You Want the Audience to Understand or Accept in Order to Accomplish Your Specific Purpose. It is important to emphasize that the thesis is a *declarative* sentence—an idea you want to convey to your audience—not a question or a phrase that simply announces the topic. This is not a good thesis statement: *How can we improve our public schools?* A good thesis would answer that question and specify *how* you propose to improve public schools: *The real key to improving public schools is hiring more qualified teachers.*

The thesis statement grows from your specific purpose. In effect, it answers the question, "What do listeners have to understand or feel or believe or do if I am going to get the response I want?" Consider the following examples of specific purposes and the thesis statements that may grow out of them.

> **Specific purpose:** *I want my audience to understand how one qualifies for unemployment insurance.*
> **Thesis statement:** *Unemployment insurance is available for a limited time period and only for those who meet specific criteria.*

> **Specific purpose:** *I want my audience to agree that the "No Child Left Behind" policy failed to improve American education.*
> **Thesis statement:** *The "No Child Left Behind" policy employed unreliable measures of student progress and teaching effectiveness.*

> **Specific purpose:** *I want my audience to sign a petition supporting the extension of an interstate highway through our county.*
> **Thesis statement:** *A new interstate would mean economic growth in our county without threatening the environment.*

> **Specific purpose:** *I want my audience to agree that a flat tax should not replace the graduated income tax.*
> **Thesis statement:** *A flat tax would be unfair to low- and middle-income taxpayers, while the rich would benefit substantially.*

2. The Thesis Statement Should Be Clear and Specific without Being So Detailed as to Include All Your Main Ideas. The thesis statement is not a summary of all the main points in a speech. Instead, it should encompass all those ideas in a single thought. Consider these examples of a thesis statement for a persuasive speech:

A good thesis statement: *Paying our city employees a living wage is a moral and practical imperative.*

Now compare that to a thesis statement that tries to include all the points you hope to make and ends up as a kind of summary of the whole speech.

A poor thesis statement: *All city employees deserve a living wage because those who are inadequately compensated are more likely to suffer from stress, develop health problems, live in substandard housing, and have strained relationships that can lead to divorce, neighborhood tensions, and even violence.*

Now compare these two thesis statements:

A poor thesis statement: *A recent survey reported in the* New York Times *revealed that when individuals are inadequately compensated for their work, more than half of them develop problems with depression and low self-esteem.*

This is a poor thesis statement because it neglects the driving idea of the speech in favor of providing specific evidence that will be used later in the speech. Now consider a shorter, clearer thesis statement:

A good thesis statement: *Low wages can cause serious psychological damage.*

3. The Thesis Statement Should Be Focused and Limited in Scope. You want to be sure that you do not try to accomplish too much or too many different things in one speech. If you find yourself including more than one idea in your thesis statement, you are probably trying to do too much in a single speech. Consider, for example, the following statement:

A poor thesis statement: *A school voucher system will improve public education and should be coupled with national standardized tests to measure student achievement as well as with content examinations for teachers.*

This statement includes at least three ideas that could be separate speeches. The thesis statements for those speeches might look like this:

Good thesis statements:

■ *School vouchers will give parents the ability to choose the best schools for their children.*
■ *Standardized tests lead to greater accountability in public education.*
■ *The school board's plan to require periodic content examinations for teachers will improve the quality of classroom instruction.*

Avoiding Common Mistakes

As you develop your own thesis statements, you can avoid the most common mistakes by keeping certain principles in mind. A good thesis statement follows these principles:

■ It should *not* be written as a question or a topical phrase.
■ It should *not* be a preview of the speech.
■ It should *not* be too complex and hard to follow.

■ It should *not* present excessively detailed information.
■ It should *not* present too many ideas for a single speech.

The *Highlighting the Process* feature reviews and illustrates the process of moving from selecting a topic to devising a thesis statement.

HIGHLIGHTING THE PROCESS | From Topic to Purpose to Thesis

As a way of reviewing the procedure we have been describing, consider the process step by step.

1. *Select possible topics.* Consider the following list of possible topics generated from a self-inventory and through brainstorming public issues.
   ■ Student financial aid
   ■ Affordable housing for the working poor
   ■ Materialism in America
   ■ Nuclear proliferation
   ■ U.S. policy toward Iran

2. *Consider situational and audience factors.* Because there had been so many stories in the media lately about nuclear proliferation and the threat of a nuclear war, you decided that would be a timely topic.

3. *Pick your tentative topic.* Lots of possibilities are open to you as you narrow the topic, such as the nuclear proliferation treaty, the dangers of Iran getting the bomb, or the threat of terrorists obtaining nuclear weapons. Perhaps you decide that one serious problem does not get the attention that it should: the tension between India and Pakistan, two nuclear powers with a history of mutual hostility. So your tentative topic is the threat of nuclear war between India and Pakistan.

4. *Determine the general purpose.* If your assignment is to give a persuasive speech, you then plan a speech to gain agreement or to support a policy.

5. *Craft a specific purpose statement.* You need to determine exactly what response you want from your audience. After conducting and evaluating an audience survey, you discover that many of your listeners are only mildly aware of the antagonism between India and Pakistan. Because of their lack of awareness, they appear unconcerned about the potential seriousness of the problem. So you develop this specific purpose statement: *I want my audience to agree that the India-Pakistan conflict over Kashmir poses a serious threat to world peace.*

6. *Write a thesis statement.* Your purpose will still be somewhat tentative. You can modify it as you gather and organize material for the speech and then be ready to craft a thesis statement. In this case, that thesis statement might be the following: *The conflict between India and Pakistan over Kashmir could result in a nuclear war that could ultimately involve the United States.* ▲

✓ Study and Review materials for this chapter are at **MyCommunicationLab**

SUMMARY

 Listen to the Audio Chapter Summary at **MyCommunicationLab**

Finding a Suitable Topic

5.1 Generate significant speech topics.

■ Preparing yourself to speak begins with the choice of a topic.

■ Doing a self-inventory and/or brainstorming significant public issues when choosing a topic is a helpful first step.

Narrowing the Topic

5.2 Revise and narrow your topic.

- The next step is to narrow the topic so that it is manageable in the time limit, meets the expectations of the assignment or occasion, and can be made interesting to an audience.
- Because the audience is central to the development of your speech, you need to pay particular attention to how the topic will reflect the listeners' knowledge and experience.

Ethical Obligations in Selecting a Topic

5.3 Determine how ethical considerations affect your choice of a topic.

- In choosing a topic, you must also remember your ethical obligations to be accurate and fair-minded and to exercise good judgment in accommodating the tastes and standards of the audience.

General Purposes

5.4 Distinguish among the goals of informative, persuasive, and ceremonial speeches.

- Speeches aim at getting responses from audiences. The principal kinds of responses that speakers aim for in most cases—in the classroom, in the community, and in professional settings—are the general purposes: informative, persuasive, and ceremonial.

- The goal of informative speeches is to gain audience understanding.
- The goal of persuasive speeches is to influence beliefs, opinions, and actions relating to a public controversy.
- The goal of ceremonial speeches is to reinforce shared values as a vehicle of community building.

Crafting and Testing Specific Purposes

5.5 Devise a clear specific purpose that aims for an attainable audience response.

- Based on the topic you have chosen, you will be able to create a specific purpose that states precisely the response you want from your audience in a particular situation. A specific purpose is the foundation on which the thesis statement is built.

Constructing a Thesis Statement

5.6 Write a clear, concise thesis statement.

- The thesis statement—the guiding idea of the speech that you want your listeners to take away from it—should be carefully crafted to be precise and inclusive without being cluttered with too many details.

QUESTIONS FOR REVIEW AND REFLECTION

Finding a Suitable Topic

5.1 Generate significant speech topics.

1. What are the major things to consider when looking for a speech topic? Give a specific example of how each of these categories may relate to you personally.
2. What are some things you will do to make sure that you are exploring significant topics of public concern? Be specific.

Narrowing the Topic

5.2 Revise and narrow your topic.

3. Why is focusing and narrowing your topic important?
4. Here are some broad speech topics:
   - Adult literacy
   - Recycling
   - Domestic abuse
   - Student loans
   - Careers in health care

Choose one and narrow it to a more specific topic that could be given in an 8–10 minute speech.

Ethical Obligations in Selecting a Topic

5.3 Determine how ethical considerations affect your choice of a topic.

5. What are some of the ethical considerations involved in selecting a topic? Why are they important?

General Purposes

5.4 Distinguish among the goals of informative, persuasive, and ceremonial speeches.

6. What are the general purposes of public speaking? Define each.
7. How will determining a general purpose help you begin to formulate a specific purpose?

Crafting and Testing Specific Purposes

5.5 Devise a clear specific purpose that aims for an attainable audience response.

8. What is meant by a specific purpose? Why is it important for every public speaker to have a specific purpose?

9. What are the criteria you ought to use to evaluate your specific purpose?
10. Can a single speech have multiple purposes? Why or why not?
11. Suppose someone decides to give a speech with this specific purpose: *I want my audience to vote to repeal the state law that requires motorcyclists to wear safety helmets.* Using the criteria for evaluating purpose statements discussed in this chapter, is this an effective purpose statement? Why or why not?

Constructing a Thesis Statement

5.6 Write a clear, concise thesis statement.

12. What is a thesis statement, and why is it important for a speaker to develop one?
13. Following are three thesis statements. Which one is the best and why?
   - *Would you like to do something that is both fun and useful this summer?*
   - *Volunteering to work for Habitat for Humanity this summer will be a rewarding personal experience and will provide a useful public service.*
   - *If you volunteer to work for Habitat for Humanity, you will get good physical exercise, learn new skills, meet interesting people, get to work with kids your own age, provide homes for needy and deserving people, and earn the gratitude and respect of the people you help.*

 Study and Review the Flashcards at **MyCommunicationLab**

Responsible and Productive Research

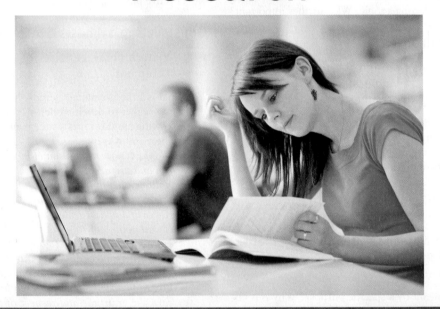

OVERVIEW AND LEARNING OBJECTIVES

A Productive Start

6.1 Establish a focus to guide your research.

The Creative Enterprise of Building a Speech

6.2 Take careful, thoughtful notes to develop insight and draft your speech.

Developing Information Literacy

6.3 Recognize the importance of information literacy and know its components.

Searching the Internet

6.4 Find quality information on the Internet more efficiently and productively.

Investigating Like a Professional: Using Library Resources

6.5 Utilize the library for obtaining materials and assistance.

Gathering Information through Interviews

6.6 Use effective interviewing techniques to gather information.

Gathering Information through E-mail and Online Networking

6.7 Use e-mail and online networking to gather information.

Citing Sources of Quoted and Paraphrased Material

6.8 Know how and when to cite sources in your speech.

After his six-year-old son, Adam, was abducted and brutally murdered, John Walsh made it his mission to help other victims of violent crime.[1] He recalls walking into Cornell University's library one morning and saying, "I'm the father of a little boy who was murdered. I don't go to classes here or anything, and I don't have a card, but I was wondering if I could use the library?"[2] They welcomed him and assisted his research. He discovered that more could be done—and done more quickly—to recover a missing racehorse or an automobile than to track down a missing child. Outraged, he became a man on a mission.[3]

When Walsh landed the opportunity to address legislators on Capitol Hill, he did more than recount his family's tragic ordeal; he came equipped with facts and figures. Walsh made a compelling case for "a centralized reporting system" and "a nationwide search system for missing children."[4] Well informed, professional, and articulate, he was someone to be taken seriously.

When the Missing Children Act was finally passed one year later, President Reagan invited Walsh and his wife to the signing ceremony. As he listened to the president commend their work, it dawned on him what they had accomplished— "that a heartbroken couple from Florida with no money and no lobby and no resources and nobody behind them except a bunch of caring, passionate people with no real power had actually helped get a federal bill passed."[5]

The Missing Children Act of 1982 was but the beginning of John Walsh's career as one of America's best known crime fighters. For more than 20 years, he has hosted television's *America's Most Wanted*—a program that has, to date, helped reunite hundreds of abducted children with their families and capture more than 1,165 fugitives.[6]

Walsh's story underscores the importance of informing yourself about your subject if you hope to become an effective advocate. Being knowledgeable allows you to formulate better ideas and have more confidence when you speak. You will also enhance your credibility. As you supply the information that informs your thinking, your audience will find you more believable and trustworthy. They will see that you have met your ethical obligation to be knowledgeable about your topic.

This chapter will help you become well informed. We focus on various possibilities for finding information, including print and electronic media as well as interviewing experts and others who have useful information and experience. First, however, we consider how you can effectively and efficiently conduct your investigation, providing suggestions for taking notes and beginning the construction of your speech. These tips can help make the process more manageable and satisfying. Finally, this chapter discusses the importance of identifying your sources during your presentation and shows you how to do so effectively and properly.

A PRODUCTIVE START

Preview. *You begin building a speech by identifying your purpose in speaking and narrowing your focus. Once you have established your focus, you can quickly survey material to determine its relevance, and you can better formulate the main ideas of your speech.*

As we pointed out in Chapter 5, you begin the process of crafting a speech by formulating a thesis statement—however tentative—to guide your investigation. The

6.1 Establish a focus to guide your research.

Watch the Video
"Childhood Obesity" at
MyCommunicationLab

thesis at this stage is a working thesis, an attempt to articulate the overall idea you are examining. For example, after reading predictions that a flu pandemic would likely "flood hospitals" with uninsured patients and further tax an "already over-burdened system,"[7] Michaela, a pre-med student, decided to explore the matter for a persuasive speech. She crafted the following basic idea (working thesis) to focus her research: *The flaws in our health care system could make a pandemic even more disastrous than it otherwise would be.* Her thesis mirrored her specific purpose—the response she wanted from her listeners: *I want my audience to accept the view that there are flaws in our current health system that would put us all at increased risk during a pandemic.* Michaela would now have a good focus to guide her research.

You may, like Michaela, need some initial investigation to arrive at a purpose and tentative thesis. Some probing may be necessary. For a concise look at how to begin your research, see *Highlighting How to Begin Your Investigation.*

▶ HIGHLIGHTING HOW TO BEGIN YOUR INVESTIGATION

Your choice of topic will dictate which of the following approaches will work best. Many people may, out of habit, begin with a Web search, but what your library has to offer (accessible from your computer via the Internet) often produces faster, superior results. We especially recommend using your library's reference materials and subscription databases.

■ *Access/visit the reference section of your library.* Various reference materials provide facts, data, and other information about your topic and how it has been discussed recently as well as in the past. Here are a few noteworthy examples of what is available, many in electronic form.
  ■ *Credo Reference.* This popular database contains more than 575 reference items, many previously available only in print form.[8]
  ■ *American Decades.* This collection discusses the major issues Americans have grappled with during a particular decade. Because many issues persist (e.g., violence in our public schools), this collection can provide an excellent overview and background information.
  ■ *Contemporary World Issues.* In this series, scholars and nonacademic experts examine international matters of controversy. These

book-length works are written for the general public.
  ■ *Encyclopaedia Britannica.* This award-winning encyclopedia, with peer-reviewed entries by leading authorities, offers excellent background information on historical and contemporary topics and issues. It also provides a list of authoritative works for further reading, making it a good place to launch an investigation.
  ■ *Facts on File: Issues and Controversies.* This collection offers objective, thorough coverage of the hottest issues of our time.
  ■ *Facts on File: World News Digest.* This compilation provides a week-by-week account of major news events, from 1940 to the present day, providing excellent background information and data for historical as well as contemporary issues and events.
■ *Discover what reliable news sources have provided.* Newspapers, newsmagazines, and radio and television news sources often provide background information as well as in-depth reporting. Their archives (often available and searchable on their official Web sites) transport us back in time, providing a good sense of what happened and how people felt about it. Simply be alert to any bias that may exist, because many news sources have political leanings.[9]

Finding Relevant Information: A High-Speed Pursuit

Once you have a clear focus, you can proceed quickly. Rather than painstakingly reading every article that has a promising title, skim through them to detect which ones contain relevant information and ideas. If an abstract (a brief summary) is available, use it to determine an article's usefulness. Scan the drop-down menus of a credible Web site and quickly explore (and bookmark) any links that seem on target. Evaluate a potentially relevant book by scanning its table of contents and index and then skimming pages that seem promising. This quick survey will help you locate the most valuable material.

Keep your mind free to focus on what you are skimming. Rather than try to keep a mental record of which sources are valuable and where you found what information, generate a working bibliography, adding quick notes regarding the

Finding material in newspapers and newsmagazines has never been easier. Several databases index and provide access to major U.S. newspapers, and some also index regional and international newspapers. For example, *NewsBank Access World News* provides information and perspectives from more than 600 U.S. and 500 international sources—a mix of newspapers, wire services, and news agencies, with many of the international sources translated into English. Other, similar databases include the following: *ProQuest Newsstand; LexisNexis Academic;* and *InfoTrac Newsstand.*

- *Explore government publications.* Federal, state, and local agencies collect and report data on every topic imaginable. For example, the U.S. Census Bureau (www.census.gov) provides a wealth of information about social, political, and economic conditions. You can learn, for instance, how many households in the United States have one or more computers and whether they have Internet access, and you can compare today's figures with those from previous years. You can also compare your state with other states.

- *See what has been discussed and acted on by policy makers.* Congressional hearings define the policy issue and bring together expert witnesses and other sources of testimony. *ProQuest Congressional* indexes and provides full text of these discussions as well as relevant documents, such as regulations. It also will keep you apprised of the status of a particular bill. You can obtain similar information and services from *CQ Researcher,* which provides in-depth reports and commentary on the major issues of the day, including various viewpoints. It also summarizes and analyzes proposed and existing legislation. You can even have daily updates e-mailed to you about a topic. You can also utilize thomas.loc. gov, an online service by the Library of Congress providing information about legislative activity and more.

- *Consult a nonpartisan fact tank.* The Pew Research Center (pewresearch.org) is a favorite source for journalists and citizens alike, reporting empirically based data about a wide range of issues at home and abroad.

- *Search a subscription database for relevant articles.* For how to do so, see the feature on *Highlighting Databases as a Research Tool* later in this chapter.

- *Conduct an online search for credible Web sites.* Use the strategies and resources we discuss in this chapter for a fruitful, efficient search.

usefulness of each source. Once you have identified which sources are valuable, you can read them more closely, carefully extracting information and ideas from them.

THE CREATIVE ENTERPRISE OF BUILDING A SPEECH

6.2 Take careful, thoughtful notes to develop insight and draft your speech.

Preview. *As you compile material for a speech, you can proceed most productively if you establish a method for gathering, recording, and organizing material. The manner in which you take notes can facilitate the discovery of ideas and aid in the process of constructing your speech.*

From the moment you begin contemplating your topic, you begin formulating ideas for your speech on the basis of what you already know or believe. You begin envisioning the areas you will discuss, material you will include, your purpose and thesis, and how to introduce and conclude your speech. This is not busywork; you have begun the process of preparing the speech and should log these thoughts so that none escape.

As you investigate, you gather information and ideas from a variety of sources and arrive at new insights of your own. Your speech will consist of each of these elements arranged into a coherent form and made more understandable and appealing through good oral style. Your mind will operate on all these levels as you sift through material and record thoughts and information that ultimately may or may not make it into the final draft of your speech.

While researching your topic, record more than information. You also need to note the idea the information suggests and contemplate where it should appear in your speech. Jot down other thoughts that come to you—possible sources to consult, modifications needed for your thesis, the design of a presentational aid, and so forth.

Once you have determined the best sources, take notes methodically to save time and maximize productivity.

This process of preparation is crucial. The quality of a speech is directly related to the quality of critical and creative thought that goes into its preparation.

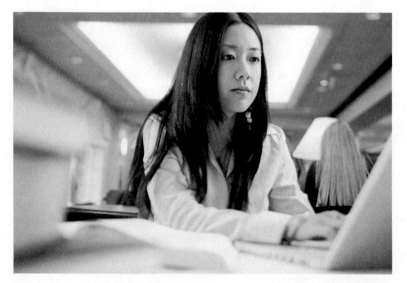

The Creative Process

Creative thought cannot be rushed; an early start is essential. Once you have a topic in mind, you will notice anything that is relevant, and these various stimuli will help you formulate ideas for your speech.[10] You will also have time for *reflection*—time to evaluate information, to test ideas, and to begin making sense of all you have found.[11]

If you are like most people, you will have good days when everything seems to make sense and fall into place and days when you struggle to get anywhere.[12] When your thinking is "stuck," you probably need a "time-out."[13] Once you are no longer fixated on the problem, your mind can operate quietly in the background, making associations and generating new ideas.[14] An early start allows time for these breaks.

A break can be time well spent. When you return to the task, you may experience a rush of ideas and a new, improved understanding of the subject and your goals for the speech. You do not have to be "on task" for these ideas to emerge. As cognitive psychologists explain, "The classic example of coming up with great ideas while taking a shower may simply reflect the importance of releasing oneself from fixated retrieval processes."[15] When these inspirations appear, jot them down as soon as possible to prevent them from escaping. Your energy can then be directed elsewhere, allowing your mind to continue working creatively.[16]

Along with quiet time, you may also benefit from some intensive thinking. For example, you might write down whatever pops into your head without stopping to analyze or critique it. Afterward, you will have something to review and evaluate.[17] You might try a particular brainstorming technique, such as mind mapping (see Figure 6.1) or concept mapping.[18] Both of these formalized techniques advocate the use of keywords and phrases and hand-drawn pictures to capture thoughts and discern relationships. Like other brainstorming strategies, these techniques have specific benefits:

- Allowing speedy recording for less-restricted flow of thought
- Promoting free association (rather than any restrictions a sentence may impose)
- Stimulating recall of related information, such as previous learning or experiences
- Generating new ideas and perspectives
- Promoting understanding of relationships
- Assisting organization via grouping/classifying
- Unleashing creativity, especially for visual learners

In addition to capturing thoughts on paper, try thinking aloud, perhaps with a friend. You may surprise yourself with the ideas that roll off your tongue,[19] and you may also receive valuable feedback from your listener. As with other inspirations, record these immediately!

Along with allowing time for your creative processes to work, you also need time for *incorporation*. Incorporation involves deciding if and where specific information and ideas belong in the speech. You will make these evaluations as you search for materials and continue to fine-tune the focus of your speech.

Productive Note Taking: Drafting as You Investigate Your Topic

To take notes productively, you'll want to keep track of where you got what information as well as how it contributes to your speech. To maximize efficiency and avoid frustration, devise a format for recording source information and for taking notes, and stick to it.

FIGURE 6.1

Mind mapping your thoughts can fuel creativity and assist organization. As with any brainstorming activity, some items will be discarded as you make your way forward.

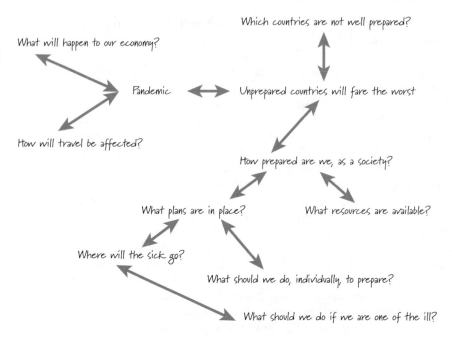

For Source Information The format should allow you to find, at a glance, whatever you are looking for—whether it is the page number for a quotation, the title of an article, or the publication date. Keeping good records allows you to cite your sources properly and to save time while taking notes.

- **Utilize bibliography-creation tools.** When using a library subscription database, use its built-in citation feature to create a bibliography. Once you know you are going to use an item, take a few seconds to grab the already-formatted bibliographic entry and paste it into a Works Cited page. A librarian can walk you through the process.
- **Follow the assigned style guide.** For nondatabase sources, record source information correctly, using the style guide (*MLA, APA,* or *The Chicago Manual of Style*) your instructor has approved for your formal bibliography.
- **Record source information completely.** Avoid having to retrace your steps to acquire missing information.
- **Assign each source a code.** The code can be the author's last name (or the last name of the first author listed). Coding each source saves you from having to repeat a full-blown bibliographic entry for each note you make from that source (see Figure 6.2). If you are typing your bibliography as you go, simply type the code you assign in bold at the front of each entry. You can delete the codes later when finalizing your formal bibliography.

For Taking Notes A variety of approaches, used alone or in combination, can serve you well.[20] You may enter notes electronically with a computer (perhaps even using a program such as Microsoft OneNote), by hand on note cards or a pad, or in the margins of material you've printed or photocopied. In any case,

> **Walsh, B. "How to Prepare for a Pandemic."** *Time*, May 18, 2009, 30–33.

FIGURE 6.2
Sample Source Entry

Record source information carefully and completely to avoid backtracking later.

you'll want to be able to easily navigate your notes and rearrange them as needed. In addition, you'll want to process material as you go, contemplating how it fits into your speech. Doing so will help spark your creativity.[21]

- **Limit each entry.** Restrict each entry to a single idea and the information on which that idea is based (see Figure 6.3). By confining each note to one idea and its basis, you will be able to arrange and rearrange entries and—as a result—easily organize your speech. Entries with more than one idea and bit of information would undermine your ability to arrange and organize.

  If you are typing your notes, confine each entry to a third of a page to ensure that entries are properly focused—limited to examining a single idea. If you're writing notes by hand, use 4×6 index cards or half sheets of paper. If you're writing in the margins of a copy or printout, you'll want to keep a running inventory of those ideas, placed perhaps into a working outline—a rough sketch of your speech in progress (see Chapter 9).

- **Coordinate notes with source entries to save time.** As noted earlier in the chapter, the codes you have assigned each source will eliminate what would amount to busywork because they save you from writing comprehensive source information over and over again for each new note from a source. A glance at the code tells you where you got what. (See Figures 6.2 and 6.3 to see an example of a note entry coordinated with a source entry.)

- **Format consistently.** Whether you're typing entries or writing by hand, use the same format. Record information in what would be the center of an index card, *placing quotation marks around any material you record word for word from the source.* Place the code you have assigned the source and the specific page number or numbers (if it is printed material) in parentheses in a bottom corner. Enter the idea suggested by the information as a heading in the upper-right (or left) corner. For notes entered on a printout or photocopy, coordinate entries with a working outline.

- **Create a meaningful heading.** The heading is more than a descriptor; it should relate the information to the goals of your speech. Rather than write something vague like "health care system," for example, you might enter "numerous uninsured = bigger outbreak," to capture the essence of the information. Obviously, you have some sense of why the information is valuable. Force yourself to write it down, even if you believe that it will be obvious later. Use a concise phrase to articulate the idea suggested by the information. You may often enter the information before writing the idea because you may not have fully determined the meaning and the best wording. Before moving on, though, articulate the idea, even if it is only an approximation. You can revise it later. The point is that you

---

[Idea]   Numerous uninsured = bigger outbreak

"But truly preparing the country for a pandemic means tackling the basic flaws at the heart of the health care system—starting with the some 50 million . . . who lack any health insurance. They're more likely to flood hospitals for care during a pandemic, further taxing what will be an overburdened system. . . . '[Like] the Typhoid Marys of the last century . . . they'll be spreading this disease in ways that are completely unpredictable.'" [Quoted material]

[Source]   Walsh, B., p. 33

FIGURE 6.3

Sample Note Entry (Coordinated with the Sample Source Entry)

Think about what you're recording in terms of what it means and where it belongs in your speech.

will want to think about the meaning and relevance of all the information you encounter, especially in terms of how it contributes to your speech.

Think of how inefficient it would be to operate otherwise. Rather than mindlessly taking notes and letting them accumulate into a large collection that you will have to sort through later, make sense of material as you go. Group the entries into categories, noting the areas that emerge. The ideas entered in the headings of your notes may become subpoints in your speech, which you can go ahead and plug into a working outline.

- **Clearly note your original thoughts.** Record your own, original thoughts in similar fashion, so that you can easily find and use them. You might jot down an idea for the introduction, for instance, or the basis for a good, illustrative example or analogy.

As you group and arrange the entries in your notes, create a rough sketch—a working outline—of your speech. Watch it grow and evolve as you continue to sort through your notes and arrange them, reflecting on whether the material belongs in the speech, where it belongs, and its implication for your overall idea—the thesis. You can begin this process at any point during your research, perhaps tackling one area of the speech at a time. For example, you might write about a problem before researching possible solutions.

Once you have created a rough outline, you will be able to evaluate what you have produced—retaining the good, modifying what needs to be rewritten, deleting faulty or extraneous material, and conducting any additional research that may be needed. This activity, called *revision*, is not an "autopsy"[22]; it does not merely occur after you have a complete first draft of your speech. Instead it occurs anytime you re-assess what you have done, whether it is a word, a sentence, or a title. No set formula exists for when and how often revision should occur, but it must occur from time to time throughout the drafting process if you expect to produce a quality message.

The key to good preparation is working through multiple drafts—something professional speechwriters recognize and do. For example, Peggy Noonan—one of President Reagan's speechwriters—would only begin to get comfortable with her progress "on about the fourth draft."[23] Noonan writes, "I'd see that I'd written three or four sentences I liked, and that would relax me...[and I'd think] 'there's something of worth here!'"[24] Other presidential speechwriters report similar experiences. Ray Price, one of President Nixon's speechwriters, recalls that, on average, major presidential addresses went through "14 drafts."[25] President George W. Bush's 2006 State of the Union Address reportedly went through about "two dozen drafts."[26]

President Obama also recognizes the need for careful revision and multiple drafts. In 2004, he "spent months writing the convention speech that would catapult him onto the national stage."[27] He continues to exercise such diligence; he prefers ample lead time for every speech—time to gather and refine his thoughts. According to *Time*, President Obama does some of his "best writing...late at night when he's all alone, scribbling on yellow legal pads. He then logs these thoughts into his laptop, editing as he goes along."[28] At other times, he thinks aloud, running his thoughts by his small team of advisers and writers. At some point, he involves them in the writing—exchanging a series of drafts but "exercising the final say."[29]

Whether you are a professional or a novice, the process is the same. As you contemplate your speech, there is a constant flow between information and ideas as you check them against each other.[30] Your investigation tests the tentative thesis you have constructed; you will refine your thesis (and main points) in light of what your investigation reveals. You develop and revise your speech as you evaluate content and arrangement, detect and repair weaknesses, recognize the need for more material, and try out the best phrasing for an idea. Preparing a speech, like any complex creative process, involves intense, multidimensional cognitive activity.[31]

Quintilian, an early teacher of speech, emphasized the importance of revision. Quintilian noted that "correction takes the form of addition, excision, and alteration" and that

> Revision is an important part of the writing process and can occur at any time.

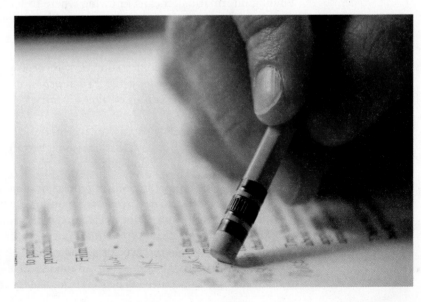

"erasure" is "as important a function of the pen as actual writing."[32] In other words, one has to learn to be critical of one's own work. Critical thinking is essential for evaluating your own work, and it is also essential as you gather materials, a topic to which we now turn.

DEVELOPING INFORMATION LITERACY

6.3 Recognize the importance of information literacy and know its components.

Explore the Concept "Research" at **MyCommunicationLab**

Preview. *Knowing how to find and evaluate relevant information has become increasingly important in our personal, professional, and public lives. Using information responsibly is also essential to reasoned deliberation and sound collective decision making.*

Among the most important skills we can learn as citizens in a democracy are those associated with locating and gathering reliable information. The same skills we use to research a speech topic will serve us well throughout college, in our careers, and in our role as informed, active citizens. These skills, termed information literacy, involve developing the ability to "recognize when information is needed" and to "locate, evaluate, and use effectively the needed information."[33] These abilities have become increasingly important in the information age; we are bombarded with information in "unfiltered formats," making it necessary that we ascertain its "authenticity, validity, and reliability."[34] As the Association of College and Research Libraries has noted, "the uncertain quality and expanding quantity of information pose large challenges for society. The sheer abundance of information will not in itself create a more informed citizenry without a complementary cluster of abilities necessary to use the information effectively."[35]

Let us examine more closely the skills that make up information literacy.

Finding Information

"Finding information" means knowing where to look for good information. A library provides access to reference materials, periodicals, and government documents and publications.

Reference Sources Reference sources with peer-reviewed entries by recognized authorities, such as *Encyclopaedia Britannica*, are more trusted than Wikipedia, which allows anyone to author or alter an entry.[36]

Periodicals Periodicals also vary in type and quality. Cornell University Library provides an excellent overview, distinguishing between scholarly, substantive news, popular, and sensational periodicals.[37]

- **Scholarly.** This type of periodical reports original research or experimentation by scholars or researchers respected within a particular scholarly community. Authors carefully and properly document all sources (e.g., *Public Opinion Quarterly, Rhetoric & Public Affairs*).
- **Substantive news.** In this type of periodical, the author's expertise varies, as does the degree to which sources are cited. Articles are written for an "educated audience" of "concerned citizens"[38] (e.g., *Newsweek, The Los Angeles Times*).

- **Popular.** Articles in this type of periodical are written by staff members or freelance authors, providing "generally little depth" and "rarely, if ever," citing sources. Their principal purpose is "to entertain the reader, to sell products...and/ or to promote a viewpoint"[39] (e.g., *People, Good Housekeeping*).
- **Sensational.** Written with simple language and "flashy headlines," this type of publication is "designed to astonish." Its main purpose "seems to be to arouse curiosity and to cater to popular superstitions," assuming "a certain gullibility in their audience"[40] (e.g., *The National Enquirer, The Star*).

As you may surmise, scholarly sources are generally trustworthy, whereas substantive news sources vary in quality. Popular sources should be scrutinized especially carefully. As for the sensational, need we even say?

Government Documents and Publications These are highly trusted sources. Topics range from *aquaculture* to *zero tillage*. The publications present census data and other statistical information. States, counties, and some cities also create documents, as do foreign governments and international bodies. These items are now often available online. You'll find the following sites well organized and well maintained.

- **USA.gov** (www.usa.gov). This site provides links to federal offices and agencies as well as a number of federally funded entities. It also provides a link to each state or territory's home page.
- *State and local government on the Net* (www.statelocalgov.net). As the name suggests, you will find links to each state or territory's official pages as well as to county and city pages. If a town has a Web site, you will be able to find it here.
- **C-SPAN** (www.c-span.org). You have likely watched the Cable-Satellite Public Affairs Network at some point and know of its mission to provide unfiltered access to legislative activity and various civic meetings and events. Its Web site provides links to governmental and nongovernmental sites, including blogs.

Evaluating Information

"Evaluating" entails assessing the credibility of a source and the information it offers so you will not be misled or mislead others. Penn State's Libraries advise us to consider the following factors (which we have adapted).[41]

Currency Does the date of publication meet your needs? Examine a book's copyright page, a periodical's publication date, or the date a Web page was created and/ or updated.

Authority Is the author an expert? Printed works, especially journals and books, provide an author's note that reveals the author's expertise and also commonly lists other works the author has written. Also consult biographical reference sources, such as *Contemporary Authors*. For Web sites, determine who has posted the pages and what the person or group's motivation may be. Also check to see whether the site lists experts or professional organizations that endorse the site.

Validity/Accuracy Is evidence provided for claims? Are sources cited? Is the information consistent with that provided by other sources? If the information is dated, is it still accurate?

Audience Who is the intended audience? Experts? The general public? Is the level of the content and wording appropriate for you and your needs?

Point of View (Bias) In light of what you know from other sources, is the information balanced or one-sided? Does it promote a particular viewpoint or seem to have an agenda? Does it acknowledge other viewpoints and represent them fairly? If any sponsor or sponsors are indicated, would they favor a particular view? One sure sign of potential bias or an agenda is advertising. Does the source feature ads for products or services or for a particular social or political cause?

Properly Using Information

Information literacy also requires one to use information responsibly. Guidelines for proper use include the following:

- Integrate information from a variety of sources.
- Acknowledge any biases or agenda a source may have.
- Cite sources properly and accurately within a speech and in a bibliography.
- Quote or paraphrase accurately.
- Respect others' intellectual property and adhere to all guidelines pertaining to copyrighted material and fair use.

Developing and exercising these abilities for finding, evaluating, and properly using information will serve you well. The same skills that employers find attractive will set you up for lifelong learning and active citizenship. You can begin developing these skills and reaping the rewards in your speech class.

SEARCHING THE INTERNET

6.4 Find quality information on the Internet more efficiently and productively.

Preview. *Computer applications have simplified the storage and exchange of information. The World Wide Web has become easier to navigate, but the questionable quality of much of what is posted online requires caution. Experts offer guidance for determining the quality of information encountered.*

Most of us take "the Web" for granted, but it is quite a phenomenon when you stop and think about it. Since it came on the scene around the early 1990s, the Internet has grown exponentially and beyond textual form to images, sound, and video.[42] It has increasingly influenced the way we conduct business and make decisions—personal and political.

Locating Information

Easy-to-use browsing software (such as Safari and Internet Explorer) and highly refined search technologies allow us to find information on the Web with relative ease. Continued innovations will make searches even simpler.[43]

To locate information, you can proceed in various ways:

keyword Search   Choose any popular search engine (e.g., Google, Yahoo!, or Bing) and search by keyword(s), much as you do with a database. (Consult each engine's directions for specific guidance.) Vary the keywords, proceeding through trial and error to determine which word or words yield the best results. For example, launching Google with "smoking and children" will produce results that are too broad if you want to find out how exposure to tobacco smoke affects children differently from adults. "Smoking and children and health" will yield better results; the returns will be more precise and more manageable in number. You may also try an "advanced" search if the engine offers one.

An "advanced" search can be smart. It allows a search to be confined, for example, to a particular domain. A regular Google search for "fracking" (or hydro-fracturing), for instance, primarily turns up items from advocacy groups who make a case for their side of the issue. In contrast, an advanced search that specifies .edu as the domain yields results where the topic is treated more comprehensively and documented more thoroughly. You could also compare your results with those of Google Scholar, which focuses on scholarly literature.

Be aware that each search engine uses different criteria for a search and will, as a result, generate a unique list. If you do not find what you want with one engine, try another one. Or try a metasearch engine—such as Dogpile or Mamma—which launches several engines for the search (see Table 6.1).

Subject Directory   In some instances, you may find it more effective to explore by subject heading. Most search engine sites offer this alternative, providing short-cuts to information sites for various common subjects. For example, Yahoo! News provides direct links to major media outlets. The News option is searchable, and it is also subdivided into categories such as science, technology, health, and politics. A subject directory can also help you establish a focus. If you are interested in alternative energy but are not sure what alternatives exist, a subject directory will provide an inventory and general information about each. You will also discover the key terms to use for a productive search.

Traveling Direct   Most Web addresses (*uniform resource locators*, or *URLs*) are kept simple so users can recall an address or easily guess it. The Environmental Protection Agency's site, for example, is at www.epa.gov. The Sierra Club, an

TABLE 6.1			
Popular Search Engines			
altavista.com	ask.com	bing.com	lycos.com
excite.com	google.com	yahoo.com	scholar.google.com
Popular Metasearch Engines			
dogpile.com	metacrawler.com	search.com	mamma.com

environmental group, is at www.sierraclub.org. To guess more accurately, be aware that the last three letters designate the organization's kind of Internet membership. The most common domains are as follows:

- **.com** (commercial companies)
- **.gov** (government agencies)
- **.edu** (educational institutions)
- **.org** (nonprofit organizations)

When you find a good site (regardless of how you found it), save its URL so you can return directly to it and have the information you need to cite it in your formal bibliography. To determine whether a site *is* a good one requires careful scrutiny, a matter we will now take up.

Evaluating Internet Resources

Watch the Video
"Credibility of
Online Sources" at
MyCommunicationLab

The Internet can be described as an endless expanse of "unorganized fragments" that are added to daily by "a myriad of cranks, sages, and persons with time on their hands who launch their unfiltered messages into cyberspace."[44] Anyone who has spent any time on the Web recognizes the truth in these words and knows not to take everything found on the Web at face value. Five critical questions can help us evaluate information on the Web:

1. *What is the source of this information?* You would certainly dismiss a story from a supermarket tabloid that told you aliens had landed in Denver. Although we may readily spot a tabloid as a sensational source, the Web presents a challenge because we do not have as clear an understanding of the source. The extensions offer some insight. As we've noted, sites ending in .edu indicate an educational institution as sponsor, and .gov is government sponsored. Sites ending in .org are usually sponsored by nonprofit organizations, many of them advocacy groups. Sites with .com usually are trying to market goods or services, although many reputable news sources (such as CBS and The Daily Beast) are in the .com domain. News from PBS and NPR resides in the .org domain.

    For many sites, we have to look beneath the surface to determine authorship. If a group sponsors the page, what do you know about it? Do not be fooled by the name. For example, in the summer of 2000, a group calling itself Citizens for Better Medicare posted "information" on the Web. Their name suggested an admirable goal, but the Web page did not disclose that the group had been formed by the drug industry to lobby against the Clinton administration's proposal to provide drug coverage for the elderly.[45] Conducting an online search of the name of the group may help you determine who they are, or the browser's View menu may have an option to identify an opened page's sponsor.

2. *What is the purpose of the page?* Some Web pages are designed to give information; others advocate certain policies or causes. It is not always easy to tell the difference because advocacy groups frequently try to give the impression that they are just giving you the facts. The purpose of the page is sometimes given as a mission statement or a "Who We Are" or "About Us" link. When

considering information provided by an advocacy group, remain aware of the source's agenda and use that information accordingly—checking other sources to verify accuracy. Information on sites sponsored by companies should also be investigated. If advertisements appear on the site, you can suspect that the content may be influenced.

3. *How balanced and accurate is the content?* Careful study of a Web page can illuminate bias. Are a variety of viewpoints acknowledged? Are the claims supported by good arguments and credible evidence? Are credible sources cited? What about the links to other pages—does this page send you to other sites that are credible? Is there any information presented that you know to be inaccurate or misleading? How do the information and claims hold up when considered against what you have learned from reputable sources?

    In short, judge a Web site the same way you would evaluate any attempt to persuade you to do or believe anything. In the chapters that follow, we will be specific about what makes a sound argument, how to detect fallacies, and what kind of evidence is both effective and ethical. You will want to apply all these tests to material you find on the Web. But for now, at least ask yourself if the content that is presented seems fair, if it is convincing to you, and why you find it so.

4. *How current is the site?* Check to see how recently the site was updated. Regular updating indicates that the site is still active. A page that has been left unchanged for a long time should be viewed with suspicion. If a site *is* maintained regularly, the information is more likely to be up-to-date, though one can never be certain what, specifically, has been updated.

5. *When was the site created?* The creation date lets you know the site has been around a while as opposed to having been newly erected. A longer history may suggest some integrity.

If you cannot answer most of these questions after close inspection of the site, that in itself should raise doubts in your mind about the site's credibility. Be skeptical of a source that does not identify itself or its purpose, that makes unsubstantiated claims, or that is out of date.

The thing to remember is that the Internet is not a one-stop research source. Information should be cross-checked with other sources. By all means, use the Internet in your research, but do not use it thoughtlessly and do not use it exclusively. Purdue University's Online Writing Lab provides a good summary of the attitude you should take toward Internet research: "Internet sources can be very timely and very useful, but they should not be your sole source of information."[46]

As authors, we certainly follow this advice. As the endnotes to our chapters reveal, we often have used the Web during our quest for information. We have spent most of our time, though, using library resources. Once you get a taste of what the library has to offer, chances are you, too, will see the wisdom of consulting its experts and using its vast array of easily navigated, high-quality materials, perhaps even beginning your search there.

INVESTIGATING LIKE A PROFESSIONAL: USING LIBRARY RESOURCES

6.5 Utilize the library for obtaining materials and assistance.

Preview. *Virtual and actual visits to a college or public library provide access to information sources you otherwise would not have. Librarians provide instruction and assistance to acquaint you with the best research tools and help you develop your skills in gathering and evaluating information.*

Librarians can be very helpful to the student or citizen doing research for a speech. Professional librarians are schooled in the latest information and communication technologies, and they use this knowledge and skill daily. They are adept at locating and retrieving information and also work cooperatively with other librarians in the academic, public, and private sectors to classify and organize information so that it is well managed and easily retrieved. Government officials, business leaders, academic researchers, and others rely on librarians for the information they need.[47] So, too, can you, as a student or an ordinary citizen, benefit from the expertise of your local librarian.

A library's staff of professionals can help you locate and retrieve current, reliable information about your topic. They can offer this assistance in person, of course, but you can also "talk" to librarians online. You probably will be best served by combining these two ways of interacting with librarians.

Given the abundance of information available on the Web, many people may think searching via Google or another popular search engine is the best way to locate and gather information for a speech or other assignment. In fact, *Newsweek* reports that "71% of middle and high school students use the Internet as their number one research venue."[48] According to the Online Computer Library Center (OCLC), this trend continues into college.[49] Certainly, a Web search can provide useful information (as discussed earlier in the chapter). But a library's online resources, once you master them, can produce superior and even quicker results.

Each library, of course, will vary in terms of its resources and services. Spend a few minutes perusing your library's home page to see what is available. Even though libraries differ, certain resources will be pretty much constant.

Subscription Databases Your school's library likely subscribes to several databases (e.g., ProQuest Research Library, Wilson OmniFile, EBSCOhost Academic Search Complete)—immense, searchable collections of indexes, abstracts, and full-text materials. Your status as a student allows you access, and you will certainly want to harness their power. As the American Library Association notes, "database searching has become a central tool in modern research."[50] The popularity of databases is understandable in light of the advantages they offer in terms of variety, timeliness, and efficiency.

- *Variety.* Databases index and include a variety of materials, allowing you to cast a wide net. Some index articles from newspapers and newsmagazines as well as scholarly journals, government documents, chapters in books, and broadcast news and commentary.
- *Timeliness.* Databases are updated frequently, indexing and providing access to materials recently produced. For example, EBSCOhost and LexisNexis

update their database collections continually, as do many other database companies that index and provide full-text articles from newspapers and other news sources.

- *Efficiency.* Databases are an efficient way to find relevant articles and other materials. An electronic database allows you to search a span of ten years or more, simultaneously, in multiple indexes, and you can combine two or more keywords to focus the search. Each database will differ in its search procedures. Consult its "help" feature for tips for searching so you can obtain the best results.

Catalogs   A library offers a wide variety of resources, including periodicals, books, and films. The library's online catalog simplifies finding materials, allowing users to search by subject, author, title, or keyword. The catalog will also indicate whether an item is available or on loan. Once you discover a relevant item, the catalog likely will allow you to search for similar items. For instance, you may be able to find books on the same subject as a book you have found by clicking on its call number. The catalog may also feature integrated shelving, allowing you to locate relevant items across media—books, films, government documents, reference books, and other holdings.

Access to Other Libraries' Collections   If your library has little available for a particular topic, it will still be able to help. Your library provides a gateway to other libraries' catalogs, allowing you to search their collections and easily request an interlibrary loan (especially because many libraries now belong to a consortium of libraries with regular courier service among the members). Your library is also most likely a member of the OCLC, a group of more than 53,000 libraries from around the world that cooperatively produce and maintain WorldCat, a supercatalog available online. WorldCat will help you discover what relevant items exist, sometimes providing an abstract or full text.

Assistance Searching the Internet   A library may also provide links to trusted sites on the Web, such as ipl2 (formerly known as the Internet Public Library, a well-organized, well-maintained directory that indexes thousands of popular and important issues. At ipl2 (www.ipl.org/), experts evaluate Web content and provide links only to sites they deem reliable and trustworthy, saving you from having to wade through lots of questionable sites while searching for information.[51] In addition to ipl2, librarians also recommend www.libraryspot.com, which provides links to expert-approved reference and library sites on a variety of subjects.

Assistance Evaluating Internet Resources   Libraries often provide pointers for evaluating sources and content found on the World Wide Web (akin to what we provide in this chapter). For example, the Cornell University library provides excellent pointers for evaluating Web content and searching the Web.[52]

Reference Materials   The library's site likely provides online access to reference materials, such as almanacs, encyclopedias, yearbooks, and dictionaries.

Customized Assistance   Libraries often provide online research guides (also called subject guides), customized for certain disciplines or classes. These, such as the one featured in Figure 6.4 (for public speaking), can greatly assist your research.

Personal Assistance Many libraries provide help by e-mail or messaging. They may also post the phone number for the reference desk—the area of the library staffed by librarians.

Visiting your library in person can also prove beneficial. You can more quickly develop your proficiency at locating and gathering quality information, and you will have access to some materials not available online. Get to know your library's layout and resources. Take a guided tour if one is offered. Knowing what is available and where it is located will allow you to be more efficient and productive. You will spend less time asking questions and more time on research.

When you do have questions, though, librarians can help. They can help you select and use the appropriate index or database for your search for articles, editorials, and other publications or transcripts. Once they understand the type of information you need, they can recommend appropriate resources and help you learn how to use them.

Being at the library also allows you to search its collections thoroughly. Once you have found an item in the catalog that seems relevant, scout the stacks. For

HIGHLIGHTING DATABASES AS A RESEARCH TOOL

Most academic and public libraries feature **subscription databases**—often your best and most efficient means of obtaining quality information. These pointers will assist you in your use of library databases:

1. *Determine the best search term(s).* Finding the right search terms made quite a difference when researching television's effects on the cognitive development of very young children. While searching EBSCOhost's Academic Search Complete, we entered "television" and "children," which yielded more than 4,130 entries, with most not on target. When we conducted the search using "television" and "toddlers," we got 25 entries, with nearly every one containing precisely the information we were seeking.

   Trickier searches include those for which the search terms may not be as obvious. For example, if you wished to research the social benefits of youth involvement in team sports, you would probably have to experiment with various keywords. Once a promising title appears, launch the search again using the search terms under which the item was indexed, or—if available—choose the option to "find other, similar items."

2. *Determine the best database.* Read the database description to see what material it indexes and search the ones most relevant [e.g., EBSCOhost's Consumer Health Complete, if researching the issue of vaccines for the human papillomavirus (HPV)]. If the results are lacking in one database, search another. You can search multiple databases at the same time, though doing so may or may not prove productive. One risk is that you will have too many entries to wade through. It may prove more effective to launch one database at a time, until you find one or two that produce the best results.

3. *Ask an expert.* If you experience problems using a database, visit the library in person and ask a librarian to assist you. Librarians are usually found at the reference desk during regular business hours. They may also be able to assist you through text messaging or e-mail. Check to see what your library offers.

4. *Select the best full-text option.* If you have a choice between HTML and PDF, choose PDF. It will provide the most comprehensive printing—including all tables and charts. HTML may also contain typographical errors and other mistakes. In addition, PDF will preserve the original pagination, allowing you to cite your sources more easily. ▶

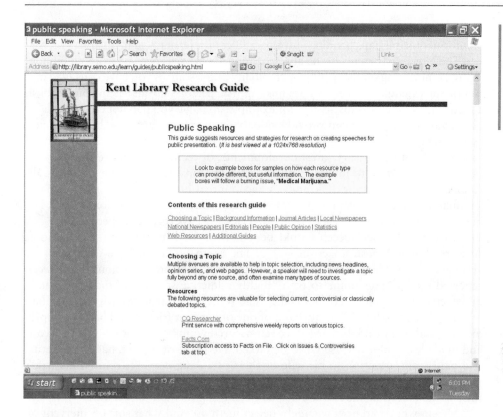

FIGURE 6.4
Research guides, such as this one at Southeast Missouri State University, can help you investigate your topic.

example, if you discover a book, scan the spines of neighboring books for titles that seem promising. Even if the book is on loan, you may wish to visit its location on the shelves to scout the area. You may also try a traditional method for locating relevant books—searching by Library of Congress (LC) subject headings. These foot searches can often turn up books that otherwise may be overlooked. A librarian can teach you this method in a matter of minutes.

Your research may take you to more than one library. Some campuses, especially large universities, have specialized libraries for particular disciplines (e.g., journalism) or special collections (e.g., the papers of a famous politician). Remember your local public library, too. It likely has many of the same databases and reference materials that academic libraries offer as well as librarians to assist you.

GATHERING INFORMATION THROUGH INTERVIEWS

6.6 Use effective interviewing techniques to gather information.

Preview. *Interviewing can provide valuable information for your speech. Determine whether people with expert knowledge or direct experience are available to help you. Prepare carefully by gathering the background information you need and generating good questions. Conduct the interview professionally and efficiently, and follow up appropriately.*

Interviewing for information can yield numerous benefits. Interviews can furnish information and a perspective that otherwise could be lacking—especially for local concerns. In addition to providing valuable information, an interview can lead you to additional resources. The person you interview may provide or suggest other sources of information, perhaps handing you a pamphlet or referring you to an article or Web site. The interviewee may also be able to critique your ideas or your working bibliography, commenting on the quality or credibility of the sources you have consulted and identifying essential sources that are missing. The person may also help you establish a focus for the speech—discussing, for example, an angle you had not considered.

A variety of people can provide valuable information and insights. Once you determine what you need to know, you can determine whom to consult. If you need to know about the history, latest developments, or technical issues related to your topic, you may want to interview an expert. Also consider laypeople who have direct experience with your topic and can recount real-life experiences. They help put a human face on a problem or illustrate the connection to the local community. For many topics, you would benefit from interviewing experts *and* laypeople.

Megan knew her speech would benefit from both expert and lay opinions. After reading a *Newsweek* cover story, "The Meth Epidemic," she decided to investigate the problem in her community and propose some solutions. *Newsweek* reported methamphetamine to be a "highly addictive stimulant" that often went undetected until users were hooked.[53] The report rang true for Megan; she had witnessed this firsthand. The husband of one of her best friends had become unpredictable and undependable. The once self-assured young professional grew nervous and made less and less sense when he talked. He had lost weight, had no appetite, and paid scant attention to his wife or their two daughters. He refused his wife's pleas to see a physician. It was only after his business folded and he defaulted on their home loan that she learned he had been using methamphetamine.

Megan wondered how we might detect meth use and what sort of intervention might be best. Her focus suggested assistance from experts, particularly a counselor who helped people overcome addictions and a professor from the criminal justice program on her campus (a member of a local drug task force) who could explain clues that signaled use of methamphetamine. Interviewing these local experts would give her speech greater meaning and authenticity than relying on media reports alone.

To derive the greatest benefit, you will want to prepare for an interview carefully, conduct it efficiently, and report it accurately.

Preparing the Interview

Determine What You Need to Know or Confirm   What is missing from existing reports/coverage? What needs further confirmation? Generate a set of specific questions that get at your curiosities.

Determine Who Might Supply the Answers   Experts? Laypeople? A combination?

Contact the Person to Schedule a Meeting   Briefly explain how you believe he or she may be able to help you. If the person feels unable to assist, she or he may suggest someone who can.

Devise and Provide Questions   Once you have scheduled a time to meet, you might request a fax number or e-mail address so you can provide a brief set of questions in advance so the person can consider his or her responses before talking with you.

Fine-Tune Your Questions

- Keep questions simple and to the point, as well as few in number.
- Ask a combination of closed and open questions. Closed questions ask for a simple "yes" or "no" response, whereas open questions ask the interviewee to express and explain a belief or opinion.
- Let the person you are interviewing see that you've done your homework and are sincere and thoughtful in your approach to the topic.
- Feel free to ask tough questions, but do so respectfully and diplomatically.

Megan followed these guidelines when devising the following questions for the person she knew on the drug task force. (She would alter or change questions for other people she interviewed.)

1. According to *Newsweek*, meth users often go undetected by friends and family. Is this true? Why?
2. What are some signs that someone is using meth?
3. Why do users find meth so attractive?
4. What should we do if we suspect a friend or family member is using meth?
5. What explains the high rate of recidivism for meth offenders reported in local news?
6. What measures may make a relapse less likely?

Megan did well crafting her questions. She encouraged elaboration by employing mostly open questions. She was also diplomatic. She did not ask the law enforcement official, "What explains your failure to rehabilitate meth users?" Instead, she posed the question more tactfully, using the term *recidivism*—a concept that law enforcement officials regularly discuss. The questions also revealed that Megan had done her homework. She did not ask basic, factual questions that she could have answered with other sources. Instead, she asked questions that showed she had prepared and that called for the expertise of the person she interviewed.

> Interviewing experts and laypersons can provide invaluable information and insights for your speech.

Conducting the Interview

No matter how well you prepare in terms of initial research and formulating questions, the actual act of conducting the interview will

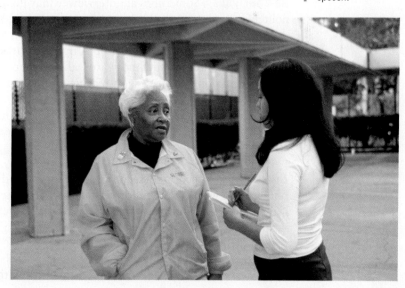

be a crucial point in the information-gathering process. A few simple pointers will help produce good results.

Be Professional Dressing appropriately and arriving on time, for example, create a positive impression, as does thanking the person as you begin and establishing a cordial and respectful tone.

Quickly Get Down to Business Remind the person of the purpose of your project and how you believe she or he can help you (e.g., "I'm trying to discover why meth is so attractive to its users and how we might better address a problem *Newsweek* calls an epidemic."). The person can then understand how to assist.

Let the Person See What You Know and Don't Know Mention some of the sources you have consulted and what they suggest (e.g., "Assistant U.S. Attorney Christopher Casey told *Newsweek* that meth has 'seduced whole families and turned them into zombies.'[54] Does this seem accurate?").

Be Genuinely Involved Focus on their responses, providing nonverbal feedback such as nods or smiles, whatever is appropriate. Quick comments, such as "Hmm…interesting" or "Really?" can convey how you are processing the message. Taking notes also signals that you find the remarks valuable or noteworthy.

Employ a Good System for Keeping Notes Enter your questions on one side of a page, reserving the other side for the interviewee's responses and for your reflections about those responses. Leave plenty of space between questions in case the person pursues an angle you had not considered. Be sure to obtain permission before using an electronic recording device.

Be Courteous Sometimes an interviewee may go off on a tangent. If this happens, politely steer the person back on topic when you get the opportunity.

Another tactic for keeping the interviewee on track and conducting the interview more efficiently is to make open questions less open. For example, instead of asking "What are the chief motivators that prompt people to try meth?" you might ask, "What is one of the biggest reasons that people decide to try meth?

Be Respectful Allow the person to have his or her say, even when you disagree with what is being said. You can question specific statements, but do so tactfully.

Be Accurate Accurately record statements made during the interview. Repeat key phrases you wish to quote, for verification, and likewise repeat paraphrased material to check your accuracy. The interviewee will welcome follow-up questions that begin, "If I understand correctly, what you're saying is…" These questions can also prompt helpful elaboration.

Also make sure you have the person's name and title entered correctly—perhaps request a business card. You will need the information for your bibliography.

Achieve Good Closure   Conclude on schedule—within the agreed-upon time. Convey your gratitude with a smile and by thanking the person for her or his time.

Rather than a face-to-face meeting, you may have to interview the person using some other means, such as telephone or e-mail (which we will discuss shortly). When interviewing by phone, follow the same general guidelines discussed earlier in the chapter, with these additional pointers.

Use a Three-Part Introduction   A three-part introduction consists of the following:

- Indicate the person you are calling.
- Identify yourself and your affiliation.
- Briefly explain why you are calling. For example, you might say, "May I speak with Officer Dunleavy? This is Megan Juarez, a student at Oklahoma State, and I'm seeking information about the methamphetamine problem in our region."

Be Considerate   When the person with whom you wish to speak comes on the line, quickly thank the person by name and repeat your purpose for calling. As a courtesy, ask if there is a better time to call.

Be Brief   People do not expect to be interviewed for an hour on the phone. Keep the number of questions reasonable so that the interview can be concluded within about ten minutes.

Be Well Prepared   Follow a set of questions as you would during a face-to-face interview. The questions will keep you on track and ensure that you cover all you wish to cover.

Convey a Positive Impression with Your Voice   Enunciate clearly. Speak fluently, avoiding vocalized pauses and verbal fillers. Also, be as attentive to your facial expressions as you would be if you were face-to-face; your manner will affect the tone of your voice.

Bring the Conversation to a Close   Begin signaling when you are nearly done asking questions by saying something like, "I have only two more quick questions." End by expressing your gratitude.

If You Must, Leave a Recorded Message   If voice mail picks up, use the same three-part introduction you would with a secretary. Request that the person return your call. Provide your number, stating it clearly. As a courtesy, repeat your number. Indicate when you are available. Be sure your voice creates a positive impression. Thank the person.

After the Interview

As soon as possible after the interview, review your notes to make sure you accurately recorded the person's statements. You will also be better able to fill in the details for anything that appears sketchy. Send a quick thank-you to the person interviewed to show your gratitude and to help keep open the line of communication.

GATHERING INFORMATION THROUGH E-MAIL AND ONLINE NETWORKING

6.7 Use e-mail and online networking to gather information.

Preview. *E-mail can be an effective and efficient means to gather information, offering several noteworthy advantages. A few pointers increase the likelihood of getting good results. Online networks may also prove beneficial as we seek relevant information, insights, and opinions.*

E-mail can assist your investigation in several ways. For one thing, you can send source citations and full-text materials to your e-mail account for safe storage and later use, taking full advantage of material already in electronic form. E-mail can also be a good way to request information. An expert on your subject may be too busy to meet you in person but happy to answer questions via e-mail. E-mail can also make long-distance inquiries feasible.

E-mail proved essential to Eva while she investigated her topic. Eva learned from a news report about a nearby city's regulations for barking dogs that addressed the problem 24 hours a day. Owners faced fines that increased incrementally with each disturbance. Eva's hometown addressed the problem only between 11 P.M. and 7 A.M. Eva thought her city's policy ignored the rights of people who had to work at night and should be able to sleep, undisturbed, during the day. It also failed to consider the rights of the ill, such as an elderly man she knew who received hospice care in his home. A neighbor's dogs barked continuously during the day, only a few yards from the bedroom where he tried to rest. The man's wife asked the neighbor to do something so the man could rest, but the dogs continued to bark.

Eva felt something had to be done. She contacted the nearby city via a link on its Web site and requested details about its new ordinance for barking dogs. Within 24 hours, the city e-mailed her a copy of the ordinance, which she appended to the written argument she had drafted for a revised disturbance ordinance. Eva was now ready to attend a city council meeting and request that her city adopt a similar policy.

E-mailing for information can pay off. Be mindful, though, that not all sites allow inquiries or are as prompt or helpful as the city Eva contacted. Continue your search for information elsewhere while awaiting a reply. Also, be sure that any request is not for information you can find with relative ease on that agency's Web pages or elsewhere.

To obtain the best results from e-mail communications, follow these guidelines.

Keep Inquiries Short, Simple, and to the Point   Because e-mail is used for convenience, receivers do not want to be burdened by lengthy messages or inquiries that require elaborate responses.

Format for a Quick Read and Quick Response   Keep paragraphs short, and leave a blank line between them. Keep sentences short and easy to process—and conversational yet professional. Use a bulleted or numbered list when you are making a series of points or asking a series of questions.

Be Careful with the Subject Line   Craft a subject line that clearly identifies you and your purpose and also reduces the risk of the message being deleted before it is opened (e.g., "citizen re: ordinance for dogs").

Disclose Your Objective in the First Line of the Message   Receivers do not want to guess what a message is about. Let them know immediately (e.g., "After seeing a report about your new ordinance for barking dogs, I hope to have my city adopt a similar policy.").

Keep the Look Simple and Professional   Leave out fancy fonts and colors, and—as a general rule—avoid using emoticons (such as smiley faces).

Remember That What You See May Not Be What They Get   Be mindful that formatting (e.g., italics, indentations) may appear differently on the recipient's monitor.

Critique and Proofread Before Sending   Check clarity, grammar, spelling, and punctuation. Mistakes can harm your credibility and have a negative impact on the response you will receive.

Never Say Anything in E-mail That You Would Not Say in Public   E-mail is not private communication; it can be easily forwarded and shared (intentionally or otherwise) with others.

Like e-mail, online networks, when used with discretion, can yield useful information and insights into a topic. For example, naturalnews.com discusses the safety of our food supply, problems with pharmaceuticals and medical procedures, and a wide range of other topics related to one's health and well-being. Many online networks also offer to send you "alerts" via e-mail, messaging, or Twitter. When seeking information from these networks, keep in mind that the information they provide often has not undergone the rigors of editorial review. You would do well to compare their coverage with sources that *have* undergone editorial review and are deemed reputable.

Belonging to an interest group on a social media site may also prove useful. For instance, a friend of ours serves on a city advisory board. A city official was to meet with the board to discuss what cyclists thought about the city's new bike lanes. Our friend posted an inquiry to a *Facebook* group for triathletes, knowing that the 160-plus members of that group could provide input he could use at the meeting. Within a few days, he had two pages of material.

CITING SOURCES OF QUOTED AND PARAPHRASED MATERIAL

Preview. *Once you have gathered information from a variety of sources and have integrated it into your speech, you will want to be sure to reveal those sources to your audience. You may also need to assemble a comprehensive bibliography for your formal outline, formatting it correctly.*

6.8 Know how and when to cite sources in your speech.

Although you probably have a great interest in your speech topic, you likely are not an expert. Even if you can be regarded as an expert, you still need to seek additional information and opinions, just as most experts do.

Watch the Video
"Living Wills" at
MyCommunicationLab

Guidelines for Incorporating Material

When you incorporate material into your speech, you may quote the source verbatim, or you may choose to paraphrase. In either instance, you will need to reveal the source *during* your presentation. As we discussed in Chapter 1, plagiarism is a serious matter. Be sure that material taken from another source is properly acknowledged and that the audience understands when you are quoting or paraphrasing material from an outside source.

Deciding whether to quote or paraphrase can be determined in light of a few simple guidelines. Quote information when one of the following applies:

- You want to bolster your own ethos by associating your ideas with that of a recognized authority.
- You are presenting information that is so startling or unusual that the audience will doubt its accuracy unless a respected source is cited.
- You support an unpopular position and wish to blunt its unpopularity by citing the opinion of a source whom the audience will respect.
- You cannot express the information any more clearly or any more eloquently than the original source.

Revealing sources during your presentation does more than safeguard against plagiarism; it fulfills one of your most important ethical obligations as a speaker. Ethical speakers openly acknowledge what others have contributed to their thinking.

Revealing sources is not only right, it is smart. As we will see in Chapters 7 and 14, speakers who cite quality sources during a presentation will bolster their ethos, and their audience will more likely accept their message.[55] As Professor William Norwood Brigance observed more than a half century ago, "One is known by the company he [or she] keeps; and when listeners find that you have been keeping company with eminent people of ideas and with expert collectors of information, they are impelled to accept you and your ideas."[56]

In short, by citing reputable sources, you will meet your ethical responsibility and you will impress your audience with how well you did your homework. The audience will see that you were well prepared to speak.

Guidelines for Citing Sources during Your Presentation

When you cite sources during your presentation, you need not provide complete bibliographic information. Avoid interrupting the flow of the speech with unnecessary detail. You need not, for instance, specify the page numbers of an article or volume number of a journal. Simply provide enough information to convince the audience of the credibility of the source and allow them to see that the information is up to task. For example, you could say:

"Time *magazine reported last month…*"

"*In a 2005 interview on ABC's 20/20, former secretary of state Colin Powell stated…*"

"*The Federal Aviation Administration's Web site currently specifies…*"

"*Dr. George Edwards, a distinguished professor of political science here at Texas A&M, told me in a recent interview…*"

In this last entry, notice how Dr. Edwards's expertise is revealed. Not only is the audience provided with his title, but they are also informed of his area of expertise so they will know why he should be considered credible. If you continue to draw on a particular source, let your listener know. For instance, you might say, "Professor Edwards also told me..." or "In that same interview, Powell made clear..." or "*Time* also identified..."

Establish that the information is current whenever the latest information is needed. When you're providing historical information, the date of publication may not be as important. If, for instance, you are discussing renewed interest in locally produced foods, you might mention the victory gardens of the 1940s and rely on sources from that era or any time since.[57] When discussing what we know now about the benefits of eating local foods, however, you would want to rely upon more recent ideas and data, such as that found in a major article on the subject in *The New York Times Magazine* in October 2008.[58]

Although source information in the speech can be abbreviated, you will need the full citation for every source you use. For one, your instructor will likely require complete bibliographic information in a list of sources at the end of your formal outline. You should also be able to provide complete source information to anyone who may ask about it after your presentation.

To ensure that you cite your sources orally during your presentation, cite them parenthetically in your speaking outline. If, for instance, you were making reference to Colin Powell in the manner described earlier in the chapter, you might place (Powell, *20/20*) in your speaking outline. In addition to referencing your sources orally during a presentation, you should also identify the source on any PowerPoint slides or other visual aids when the content is taken from a source. For the formal outline that you submit to your instructor, format in-text citations (as well as the bibliography of references/works cited) according to whichever style guide your instructor has approved. (*Note*: For examples of *Chicago Manual* style, see the endnotes after each chapter in this text.) For information about MLA or APA style, go to Purdue University's Online Writing Lab (http://owl.english.purdue.edu/).

 Study and Review materials for this chapter are at **MyCommunicationLab**

SUMMARY

 Listen to the Audio Chapter Summary at **MyCommunicationLab**

A Productive start

 6.1 Establish a focus to guide your research.

- Being well informed will allow you to do well in your speeches, and it will also be vital in your career and in your role as a citizen. When you are well informed, you will be better able to do the following:
  - Formulate well-founded ideas.
  - Provide quality support for your ideas.
  - Have confidence when you speak.
  - Enhance your credibility.
  - Meet your ethical responsibility.

- A working thesis can help focus your research, allowing you to discern whether information is relevant and which sources will likely prove most valuable.

The Creative Enterprise of Building a Speech

6.2 Take careful, thoughtful notes to develop insight and draft your speech.

- Taking notes methodically will provide a good record of where you got what information and will also help you think about your speech and begin writing it.

Developing Information Literacy

6.3 Recognize the importance of information literacy and know its components.

- Evaluating all that you encounter is part of using information responsibly and becoming a responsible speaker.
- Using various resources can help you become well informed.

Searching the Internet

6.4 Find quality information on the Internet more efficiently and productively.

- The World Wide Web, if used judiciously, can provide a wealth of information.

Investigating Like a Professional: Using Library Resources

6.5 Utilize the library for obtaining materials and assistance.

- Your school's library and many public libraries provide access to many informational resources and professional assistance.

Gathering Information through Interviews

6.6 Use effective interviewing techniques to gather information.

- Interviews with professionals and laypeople alike can provide good information and insights.

Gathering Information through E-mail and Online Networking

6.7 Use e-mail and online networking to gather information.

- Using various resources can help you become well informed.
- E-mail often can substitute for an interview as well as provide a means of efficiently managing information that is available in electronic form.

Citing Sources of Quoted and Paraphrased Material

6.8 Know how and when to cite sources in your speech.

- Citing sources responsibly not only is ethical but also can enhance credibility.

QUESTIONS FOR REVIEW AND REFLECTION

A Productive Start

6.1 Establish a focus to guide your research.

1. How will a working thesis statement help you formulate ideas and find relevant material?

The Creative Enterprise of Building a Speech

6.2 Take careful, thoughtful notes to develop insight and draft your speech.

2. Identify the various creative processes that are involved in crafting a speech.
3. What are the important do's and don'ts in recording information?
4. Why is revision so important in speech preparation?

Developing Information Literacy

6.3 Recognize the importance of information literacy and know its components.

5. What is information literacy? Why is it especially important today?

Searching the Internet

6.4 Find quality information on the Internet more efficiently and productively.

6. How would you go about finding information using the Internet?
7. How would you evaluate the integrity of a Web site?

Investigating Like a Professional: Using Library Resources

6.5 Utilize the library for obtaining materials and assistance.

8. Describe at least three important library resources and explain how they could be helpful to you in preparing a speech.

Gathering Information through Interviews

6.6 Use effective interviewing techniques to gather information.

9. What is the role of interviewing in speech preparation?
   a. How would you prepare for an interview?
   b. What are the guidelines for conducting an interview?
   c. How would you follow up an interview?

Gathering Information through E-mail and Online Networking

6.7 Use e-mail and online networking to gather information.

10. How can e-mail be useful to you when preparing a speech?

Citing Sources of Quoted and Paraphrased Material

6.8 Know how and when to cite sources in your speech.

11. Under what circumstances should you quote material in your speech?
12. How should you cite sources as you deliver a speech, and why is it important to do so?

✓ Study and Review the Flashcards at **MyCommunicationLab**

Supporting Your Ideas

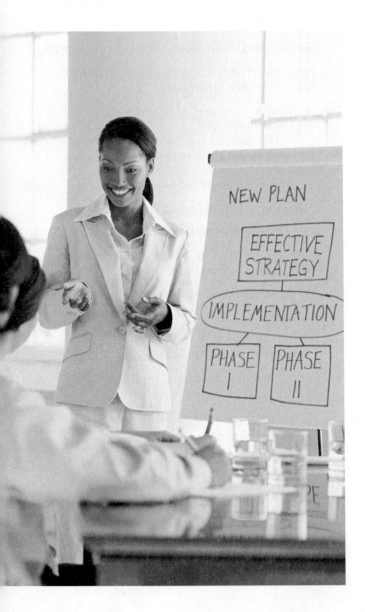

In daily conversations, we often assert our views while providing little, if any, evidence. We may refer to an article we read or a Web site we visited. We may cite an occasional statistic. But we rarely feel the need to support our assertions or opinions with extensive evidence. By contrast, when we prepare to make some *public* statement about an important issue, the expectations and norms change. As speakers, we should back up our statements with evidence from reputable sources. And as listeners, we should expect speakers to substantiate their opinions with supporting material.

The need to use evidence to support ideas varies with the situation, the audience (and our relationship to them), and the complexity of the idea. If you and your listeners agree on a topic, for example, you will not need much supporting material to make your ideas understandable and believable. Suppose, for example, that you are asking a group of listeners to vote for a political candidate who is running on a platform of educational reform. If your listeners already favor the reforms your candidate supports, then you may not need to use a great deal of supporting material to sway them. However, if you are asking for the support of a different group of listeners—a group that is worried about the cost and effectiveness of your candidate's reform platform—then you have to come armed with statistics, comparisons, and other forms of supporting material. In short, the nature and amount of proof you need to convince one audience may not be enough for another.

Of course, not all supporting material is of equal quality. As listeners, what should we make of the supporting material used by speakers? Does it strengthen or undermine the speakers' arguments? Does it enhance or hinder each one's credibility? What critical standards should we use to assess the quality of supporting material used by speakers in the classroom or the community?

One speaker may point out, "Police report that the problem of theft is growing on our campus—with more than 20 robberies reported this year so far. That is nearly *twice* as many as last year—and the school year is far from over!" A speaker talking about the problem of domestic violence may share this statistic: "According to the Middle Way House Web site, one woman is beaten every 15 seconds in this country."[1] Still another speaker may try to make his statistics more meaningful with a comparison like this one: "According to Dr. Richard A. DeVaul at Texas A&M University's College of Medicine, 100,000 people die annually in the United States from adverse drug reactions. This is the same as if a 727 airliner crashed every day, killing all aboard—approximately 274 individuals per day."[2] Yet another speaker might oppose the proposed location of a new homeless shelter by asserting: "Shop owners fear that a shelter in this location will hurt their businesses."

As listeners, what should we make of the supporting materials used by these speakers? Does each speaker support his or her arguments with sound evidence? How should we assess *both* the nature and quality of their supporting materials? Whether you are considering using a particular piece of evidence in your own speech or you are evaluating the evidence presented by another speaker, it is important that you develop a critical attitude toward supporting material and consider the quantity and quality, as well as the ethical implications, of those materials.

In this chapter, we will first discuss the various types of evidence, how you might incorporate them into your speeches, and the potential pitfalls to avoid when using them. We will next consider how comparison and contrast can be an

Watch the Video "Rathergate and Fallout over Unsubstantiated Claims" at **MyCommunicationLab**

effective form of support when used appropriately. Finally, we will consider criteria for critically examining or evaluating all types of supporting material.

SUPPORTING IDEAS WITH EVIDENCE

7.1 Identify and understand how to use the principal types of supporting evidence: facts, definitions, examples, statistics, and testimony.

Watch the Video "The Process of Developing a Speech: Generating Credibility" at **MyCommunicationLab**

Preview. *Good evidence can make ideas and arguments more understandable and convincing. Good speakers use a variety of evidence, including facts, definitions, examples, statistics, and testimony.*

Suppose you hoped to convince your fellow students in your public speaking class of the following assertion: "The minority recruitment program here at our university has been a complete failure." On the basis of that assertion alone, your audience would not know what to believe. You have not described the program, compared its success rate to other programs, or offered any other evidence of its failures. To strengthen your argument, you need to support it with evidence. Evidence is the body of fact and opinion that you present in support of your claims.

The kinds of evidence you use will depend on the purpose and topic of your speech. Some speeches, such as technical reports, rely heavily on statistical evidence, perhaps reinforced with charts or graphs. Other speeches may make more use of examples or the opinions of experts. Whatever kind of speech you deliver, it will be more interesting and convincing if you use a variety of good, credible evidence. And don't forget to cite the sources of your evidence; it is important that your audience knows that your evidence came from credible sources (see the guidelines for citing sources in Chapter 6).

Facts

Nearly every speaker will use facts as evidence. Facts are data that can be verified by observation. As facts are repeatedly verified by experts and other observers, they come to be thought of as "established" facts. Generally we judge factual information as simply true or false, correct or incorrect, verified or unverified. So, for example, a speaker may share the following facts:

- According to the U.S. Census Bureau, as of March 2012, the population of the United States is estimated at 313,181,790.
- In the state of Indiana, voter registration closes 30 days before the day of the election.
- The Thirteenth Amendment to the U.S. Constitution abolished slavery and involuntary servitude in the United States, except as punishment for certain crimes.

Each of these cases is likely to be considered by listeners as an established fact.

Speakers, however, often take facts and interpret them or try to color their meaning. A student who tried unsuccessfully to vote in Indiana, for example, might label the *fact* that voter registration closes 30 days before the election "unfair" or "discriminatory." Using this kind of interpretive language does not change the fact; it suggests a larger argument about the policy that would need to be supported with other forms of evidence. How, for example, do the voting rules in Indiana compare with those in other states? Are particular groups of people, such as college students, disadvantaged by this rule? How might a change in the rules affect voter turnout? What do voting experts say about the fairness or effects of the 30-day rule?

The language used to describe facts is often interpretive or even "loaded," so it's important that you critically evaluate *how* certain facts are labeled or described. It is an accepted fact, for example, that some alleged terrorists held at the U.S. detention facility at Guantanamo Bay, Cuba, were subjected to a procedure known as "waterboarding," which involves trying to get information from prisoners by simulating the experience of drowning. Describing waterboarding as an "enhanced interrogation technique," of course, casts it in a much more positive light than labeling it "torture."

To make sure your facts are sound, validate them by consulting multiple, credible sources. If you find inconsistencies, keep searching. Pay particular attention to the credibility of your sources. You should accept as fact only the observations of those who are genuinely trustworthy. With contemporary topics, make sure your sources are up-to-date. What looks like a factual discrepancy at first glance may simply reflect differences in when the data were collected or reported.

Definitions

Sometimes speakers need to define a word or concept used in their speeches. It is important to ensure a common understanding of key concepts, especially if a word or term can be understood in different ways. In general, you should provide definitions for any terms that may be unfamiliar, especially technical terms. A speaker explaining various options to a group of soon-to-be-retired workers commented that "after 10 years, your retirement funds are fully vested." Aware that some in his audience might not know the meaning of "vested," he went on to say, "That is, your retirement funds belong to you, and they cannot be taken away." Similarly, you should define any acronyms that may be unfamiliar. Not everyone may know that CORE is short for the Congress of Racial Equality or that CAP stands for Community Action Program.

Definitions can be persuasive as well as informative. A persuasive definition reflects your way of looking at a controversial subject. Others may define the same term or concept quite differently, but *yours* is the definition you want the audience to reflect on, and hopefully accept. Pulitzer Prize–winning author David Shipler uses this approach in defining *poverty* and *the poor* in his book *The Working Poor*. He writes, "'Poverty' is an unsatisfying term, for poverty is not a category that can be delineated by the government's dollar limits or annual income. In real life, it is an unmarked area along a continuum, a broader region of hardship than society usually recognizes. More people than those officially designated as 'poor' are, in fact, weighed down with the troubles associated with poverty. Therefore, I use 'poor' not as a statistician would. I use it imprecisely as it should be used, to suggest the lowest stratum of economic attainment, with all of its accompanying problems."[3]

Definitions, then, can be straightforward—meant only to clarify and provide uncontroversial information—or they can challenge the audience to think in new or creative ways. When new definitions are embraced, listeners may see problems in a different light or be inspired to think or act in different ways.

Watch the Video
"HIV/AIDS in America" at
MyCommunicationLab

Examples

One of the most difficult challenges you face as a public speaker is trying to make general principles or abstract notions interesting and meaningful to your audience. One way to do this is by using good examples. Examples provide concrete illustrations and can interject life and meaning into the ideas you are communicating.

When carefully selected, examples can function as compelling evidence. In a speech on genocide, for example, you may cite statistics on the number of people killed, but the true horrors of genocide are communicated best through specific examples. That is what makes Elie Wiesel's *Night* or *The Diary of Anne Frank* or *Hotel Rwanda* so powerful: their characters are people with whom we can identify; they provide concrete examples that make the statistics both more terrible and more real.

There are two principal kinds of examples that a speaker can use to support ideas: actual examples and hypothetical examples. Each kind may be brief or developed as a more extended narrative.

Actual Examples   An actual example deals with a real case; it is something that actually happened. Even a brief example, if well chosen, can make your point more vivid and memorable. In a speech delivered at Yale University, for example, J. Edward Hill, president of the American Medical Association, noted that "at any one time, six in ten Americans are overweight and about one in three are considered obese." After sharing this and related statistics suggesting that obesity had become a significant problem in America, he offered this concrete example: "Perhaps more telling [than the statistics] is a newspaper item I read last week, about the Batesville Casket Company, which last year launched its 'Dimensions' line of super-sized coffins. Think about that for a second."[4]

Actual examples not only give your audience a more concrete understanding of some problem but also can help them imagine a solution—perhaps grasping, for the first time, the actual form that an abstract concept may take. In a speech at Georgetown University, President Clinton discussed responsible citizenship and the ways in which all Americans can work together to promote the good of all. He urged everyone to become involved and cited specific examples of organizations that work to improve their communities.

> More of our citizens have got to say, "What should I do in my community?" You know, it's not just enough to bemoan the rising crime rate or how kids are behaving and whatever—that's just not enough. It is not enough. Not when you have example after example from this LEAP Program, the "I Have a Dream" Program, to the world-famous Habitat for Humanity Program, to all these local initiatives, support corporations, that are now going around the country, revolutionizing slum housing and giving poor, working people decent places to live; to the work of the Catholic social missions in Washington, DC, and other places.[5]

Watch the Video
"Untreated Depression" at
MyCommunicationLab

Narratives as Actual Examples   More extended examples may come from your research or your own experiences. The following excerpt from a student speech illustrates the use of a narrative example based on the student's personal experience.

> Did your parents go to college? How about your brothers and sisters, or your cousins? Did you just assume that you would attend college from the time you were a child? I didn't. No one in my family had attended college—not even for a year or two. No one in my family

even talked to me about the possibility of attending college. I think they just thought that I'd work on the farm like everyone else in the family. But when I was in high school, I had a wonderful English teacher who took an interest in my writing. She told me she thought I had some real ability. No one had ever talked to me like that before. She encouraged me to enter a writing contest during my junior year. When I actually won the contest, she started giving me college brochures and urging me to check out some Web sites. Before I knew it, I had applied to three colleges and been accepted by all of them with financial aid packages. Without the kindness, support, and encouragement of this one teacher, I might never have even applied to any college. It is even less likely that I would be about to graduate from one of the best colleges in the state this coming May.

This student went on to talk about the vital role that adults can play in mentoring, encouraging, and serving as role models for youth. She invited her fellow classmates, nearly all graduating seniors, to become role models for other young people in their own communities.

Vivid, engaging examples are usually well received by listeners. During a Remembrance Day ceremony in the Rotunda of the Capitol in April 2009, Fred S. Zeidman, chairman of the United States Holocaust Memorial Council, used a vivid example to make the point that we *can* make a difference, even when the challenges we face seem overwhelming:

We can see the sheer scale of slaughter and surrender to our own feelings of futility. Or we can choose to see the Six Million…as individual faces, and say: I might not be able to save them all. But it is within my power to save one. Or two, perhaps dozens, even hundreds. And what is within our power is also our responsibility. What we do matters.

Therein lies a story—a story of heroism of the truest sort. It began on an infamous ship called the St. Louis, whose Jewish passengers fled Nazi Germany 70 years ago in May 1939, seeking safety in the United States by way of Cuba. Most of you know the shameful result: First Cuba, then our country, turned them away. The story might have ended there. Because people concluded they could not make a difference. That the forces involved were too powerful, the number of individuals too vast, the dangers too distant.

But two individuals, Lawrence Berenson and Morris Troper, who worked for the American Jewish Joint Distribution Committee, felt otherwise. They knew that returning these passengers to Hitler's Germany would doom them. So they…arranged for the passengers to be accepted in…four safe European countries.

The following year, the continent was consumed by war, but the JDC clung to the belief that they could still make a difference for the passengers on the St. Louis. They tracked them one by one as they spread across Europe….Of course, they did not save them all. But they saved some. By the scale of the Holocaust, one might say they saved "few." But the ethic these individuals lived by is the same ethic we celebrate today. What you do matters.

Zeidman's account helped make his point that even ordinary people could make a difference.[6]

Hypothetical Examples   On some occasions, you may choose to use hypothetical rather than real examples to illustrate your point. A hypothetical example is one that plausibly *could* be real, yet it is not an actual, true, or empirically verifiable account. Although it is "made up," a hypothetical example should not be grossly exaggerated or unimaginable; it must be at least realistically believable to be effective.

In a speech to the European Aviation Association, James C. May, CEO of the Air Transport Association of America, used hypothetical examples to illustrate the importance of air cargo. His examples did not refer to actual cases in which critical cargo arrived by air, but they did point to realistic possibilities:

> There's an excellent reason why the cargo carried by air is 89 times more valuable per unit of weight than cargo carried by truck or train. Air cargo fills all kinds of critical needs. If there were no cargo-carrying planes, most of the people waiting in hospitals for organs—hearts, kidneys, livers and lungs—would be out of luck, because live organs are normally delivered by commercial air. If there were no planes, you might think that there would be no interruption in the flow of oil, but even if oil moves by ship, it takes skilled workers to get it out of the ground. Think of how people in the oil field services industry would be affected if they were suddenly unable to get urgently needed tools and replacement parts. And think of the just-in-time inventory systems made possible by worldwide supply chains. Do we want these productivity-enhancing supply chains to collapse?[7]

In a Remembrance Day ceremony in the Rotunda of the U.S. Capitol, speakers used vivid narrative examples to draw out the lessons of the Holocaust.

Narratives as Hypothetical Examples Some speakers may choose to use proverbs, stories, or folktales to illustrate an idea or make a compelling point. When used in this way, narratives rely on the audience's imagination or cultural symbols to convey a moral or life "lesson" instead of describing actual people or events. For instance, in a speech to the 96th Annual Convention of the NAACP, national board member Roslyn Brock shared an African folktale about a band of elephants to make a point about helping others:

> As they were traveling across the terrain, they came upon a river. The big elephants did not have a problem stepping into the rough…waters. However, there were some very small elephants in the group who were afraid to step in the water. Somebody in the middle of the river shouted to the front of the line to those who had crossed over and said, "Brother leaders, we have some folks still standing on the banks of the river who haven't made it into the water to cross over."
>
> Viewing the situation, the larger elephants turned around, got back in the water and stood shoulder to shoulder, allowing their bodies to create a dam that parted the waters to allow those little elephants to cross over on dry ground.
>
> The moral of the story is: once you make it and get to the other side, don't forget…to turn around…and get back in the water and help someone else cross over.[8]

After stating the moral of the story, Brock concluded with a powerful call to action, defining the NAACP as the "conscience of the nation" and urging the group to keep fighting for AIDS education, better urban schools, and prison reform.

Because examples are related to our everyday experiences, they can be a powerful tool for supporting your ideas. Still, some examples are better than others, and you need to choose your examples carefully.

Thinking Critically about Examples   Several criteria should be used in assessing the quality of examples.

Perhaps the best test of an example is its *typicality*. If a speaker supports a claim with examples, we should ask whether those examples are representative of other examples, or whether they represent the normal course of events. If a speaker were to cite just one example of a homeless person arrested for shoplifting, for instance, we should be skeptical of any sweeping claims about homeless people being responsible for the high costs of retail theft. Similarly, we would not conclude that all professors are reckless drivers because we heard about one professor who was arrested in a hit-and-run accident. Both the homeless shoplifter and the hit-and-run professor may be isolated examples; neither seems all that *typical*.

The *importance* of an example must also be considered. An example may rarely occur yet still warrant our attention. Several years ago, for example, a student speaker criticized the Food and Drug Administration for failing to adequately

HIGHLIGHTING SPECIFIC EXAMPLES | On Ratifying the Law of the Sea Convention

Senator Richard Lugar

Richard Lugar, a long-time Senator from Indiana and former Chairman of the Senate Foreign Relations Committee, offers several specific examples of negative consequences if the United States fails to ratify the Convention.

I would like to take a few minutes to thank you for your advocacy on behalf of the United Nations Convention on the Law of the Sea. Ratification of this treaty is vital to U.S. leadership in ocean policy. It has the support of the President, his Cabinet, the Joint Chiefs of Staff, the Navy, the Coast Guard, the U.S. Commission on Oceans Policy, every major ocean industry, and a broad coalition of environmental groups.

Virtually the entire world has ratified the Law of the Sea Convention, which now serves as the accepted international basis for ocean laws and practices. The United States faces intensifying environmental, national security and economic costs if we continue to absent ourselves from the Law of the Sea. If we fail to ratify

this treaty, we are allowing decisions that will affect our Navy, our ship operators, our off-shore industries, and other maritime interests to be made without U.S. representation. Our ability to claim exclusive right to our vast extended continental shelf will be seriously impeded, as will our ability to cooperate with other nations on ocean conservation issues. We will also be forced to rely on other nations to oppose excessive claims to Arctic territory by Russia and perhaps others. We will be dismissing more than a decade of impassioned advocacy from fleet commanders who have told us that U.S. participation in the Treaty will help them operate on the oceans more effectively and with less risk to the men and women they command. And we will not even be able to participate in the amendment process to this treaty, which is far more likely to impose new requirements on our Navy and ocean interests if the U.S. is absent from negotiations.

Source: http://lugar.senate.gov/energy/press/speech/garden.cfm (accessed March 14, 2012). ◢

monitor our food supply. She recalled a specific example of a boy who had died from *Escherichia coli*–related illnesses after consuming some prewashed, bagged spinach—a product sold in grocery stores around the nation. In this case, the example was not typical; thousands of other people had consumed this spinach with no ill effects. Yet given the seriousness of the threat, the one example got people's attention, and the speaker was able to strengthen her argument by noting that more than 100 other people had become sick from the bagged spinach, Again, the typical consumer may not have gotten ill from the product, but there were enough examples of serious, even fatal food-poisoning to warrant concern.

Although examples often provide a "human interest" angle on our topic, they are most compelling when used in tandem with other forms of evidence, such as statistics.

Statistics

Watch the Video "S.A.D.D." at MyCommunicationLab

Speakers commonly use statistics as supporting material. As they attempt to show that a policy or program has had a real impact, for example, speakers may offer statistics to demonstrate how many people signed up for the program or were affected by the policy. They may also use statistics to make predictions about the future. When the executive director of a soup kitchen tells listeners, "We served nearly 80,000 meals last year—an increase of 16 percent over the year before," he means to impress them with the growing need for funds. Statistics provide a numerical method of handling large numbers of cases. When used appropriately, they provide some of the most compelling information available to public speakers.

Understanding Statistical Support   Statistics offer a way of showing how some things are related to others. They may tell us about the typicality of an occurrence and thus validate our examples. In a speech addressing the problem of prison reform, for instance, a speaker noted the example of a young man who had been in and out of jail 63 times over the course of his life! This actual example was coupled with statistical information demonstrating the general problem of repeat offenders, or *recidivism*, which statistically has been on the rise.[9]

Statistics also may be used to show cause-and-effect relationships or at least correlations between certain phenomena. One student, in a speech addressing the problem of ozone depletion, used statistical information to argue that the thinning of the ozone layer corresponds to significant increases in skin cancer and cataracts. And correlations between smoking and serious health risks are so strong as to be viewed generally as cause and effect.

Statistical information can be helpful in pointing out trends over time. For example, we can better appreciate how quickly and significantly unemployment has increased if we can see the rise over the last few years. If you wanted to argue that crime is becoming a more serious problem in suburban and rural areas, you need to produce the figures for the crime rate.

Finally, statistics can highlight or reinforce an important point you wish to make. This may be done by using a presentational aid to depict visually the most important figures. But when delivered effectively by the speaker, excellent statistics can have considerable impact on their own. A speaker urging her fellow students to vote, for example, demonstrated that, although people in their age brackets were getting better at turning out to vote, they still lagged behind older voters:

> There a lot of issues that are of special importance to us. People of our age are concerned about college tuition loan programs, jobs for new graduates, whether military service will lead to career opportunities or likely result in multiple tours of duty in dangerous places. We have good reasons to pay attention to who gets elected to lead our country. It's true we've made some progress in getting involved. According to the latest U.S. Census Bureau statistics, in the presidential election of 2000, 28.4 percent of us between the ages 18 to 20 voted, and 35.4 percent between 21 and 24 went to the polls. By 2008, those numbers had gone up to 41 percent and 46.6 percent. That's the good news. Here's the bad news: voters of every other age bracket voted by larger percentages than we did. When it comes to Congressional elections things are even worse. The election of 2010 was important since it replaced the party in power with its opposition and changed the political situation dramatically. How did we do in that election? 16.4 percent of the youngest voters and 22 percent of 21- to 24-year-olds cast their ballots. Compare this with 51.1 percent of voters between 45 and 64 and 58.9 percent of those 65 and over. Given statistics like this, whose voices do you think politicians will listen to?

Statistics, then, are one important way of making ideas more understandable and believable. They should, however, be used responsibly by the speaker and viewed critically by the listener. You should never assume that a statistic always "proves" something conclusively. It is part of the total structure of evidence and should be considered in light of other supporting material.

Using Averages Reliably Statistics can sometimes be misleading. *Average*, for example, is a notoriously vague measure, even though it seems to give an air of statistical weight when it is used. Many people just assume that the words *mean* and *average* are synonymous, but they are not.

Averages can be computed in different ways, such as by adding up a list of figures and dividing by the number of figures (the mean), by choosing the figure that occurs most often (the mode), or by choosing the figure that is the midpoint between the two extreme figures (the median). These three methods of computing an average may lead to quite different conclusions. The mean is the arithmetic average, but it is not necessarily the best or the preferred average to quote. If there are extreme scores in the distribution of numbers, the mean will reflect a greatly distorted version of the real central tendency.

Consider this example. A city council was holding an open meeting for public comment on the budget. An item in the budget was the salary for a new city manager. A survey of seven nearby communities with city managers showed a range of salaries paid. One member of the council thought that an average salary would be appropriate and suggested the post be budgeted at $60,280. Another member thought this too low because he calculated the average at $65,000. When the discussion was opened for comment, one member of the audience complained that both council members' figures were much too high. The "real" average, he asserted was $50,000. Technically, all of them were right because "average" is such an ambiguous term. Table 7.1 shows how each average was determined.

Considering the difference in the two salaries at either extreme, the median may be the most sensible "average" in this case. But what is important when using

> ### TABLE 7.1
>
> **Differences among Averages**
>
> | | |
> |---|---|
> | Individual salaries | $ 74,000; 70,000; 67,000; 65,000; 50,000; 50,000; 46,000 |
> | Total of all salaries: | $ 422,000 |
> | Mean as "average" (total divided by 7) | $ 60,280 |
> | Median as "average" (the salary in the middle) | $ 65,000 |
> | Mode as "average" (occurs most frequently) | $ 50,000 |

an "average" figure is that the speaker and listener both understand how such an average was determined and what the implications of different "averages" may be.

Descriptive versus Inferential Statistics   Still other issues should be considered when using statistics or listening to speakers using statistics. First, most statistics quoted in speeches are inferential rather than descriptive; that is, they deal with probabilities rather than with observable facts. In inferential statistics, one generalizes from a small group or sample to some larger population. For example, polls taken during an election campaign draw inferences about which candidates are leading particular races based on the opinions of a representative sample of voters. The same is true of exit polls that are often reported as soon as the polls close. When the votes actually come in and are all counted, however, the fact that one candidate got 51 percent of the vote and the other got 49 percent is a descriptive statistic—it describes how the entire population actually voted.

Many times, speakers turn to inferential statistics because it is inconvenient or impossible to obtain descriptive data. Using inferential statistics is acceptable, however, so long as you recognize that whenever you generalize from a sample to a larger population, there is always some margin of error. That margin may be quite small, perhaps three or four percentage points.

But the potential for error is always there, and it may be magnified by a poorly designed sample or badly worded survey questions. Sometimes these statistics prove to be completely meaningless. In the 2011 Iowa Straw Poll, for example, Republican hopeful Michele Bachmann won 28 percent of the vote, followed closely by Ron Paul. This poll, however, was only useful for propaganda purposes because the sample was in no way representative. In the long run, Bachmann came in last in the actual Iowa caucuses and soon dropped out of the race. Ron Paul never came in first in any subsequent primary election. Whether an inferential statistic is sound depends not only on the size and representativeness of the sample but also on the techniques of measurement and other factors.

If you wanted to know how students at your college felt about a particular issue, you would need to gather the opinions of a cross section of the entire college, including first-year and senior students, women and men, different ethnic and racial groups, and students representing different majors. In addition, if there were 10,000 students on your campus, you would need a sample size in the hundreds, not just the opinions of five or ten of your friends. That is why most inferential statistics are collected as part of formal surveys or large-scale research projects. Inferential statistics *can* be a powerful form of evidence, but it is critical that your statistics come from reputable sources using sound sampling and measurement techniques.

If you just wanted to survey your own public speaking class, of course, you could easily get a representative sample or even give a questionnaire to the entire class. In Chapter 4, we explained how you might design such a survey. If *everyone* in your class responded to your audience survey, you would obtain a descriptive statistic.

Thinking Critically about Statistics   Sometimes speakers use statistics in ways that are confusing to listeners. The figures may be accurate, but interpretations of statistics can differ radically.

Statistics by themselves don't always "prove" anything. In the spring of 2012, for example, various indicators pointed to an improvement in the economy. The Democrats pointed to these statistics as "proof" that the president's recovery programs were working, while Republicans charged that they demonstrated that economic growth was too slow, "proving" that the president's programs had failed. In both cases, the statistics themselves didn't necessarily "prove" a point; they were *interpreted* as supporting each party's position.

Like other forms of evidence, statistics should be used only when they provide needed support. No speech should be "padded" with statistics simply because they

HIGHLIGHTING EXAMPLES AND STATISTICS

Combining statistics with a striking example, Ralph W. Basham, commissioner of the U.S. Customs and Border Protection Agency, delivered a powerful speech to a symposium on human trafficking in Washington, DC, on September 9, 2008.

[Human] trafficking generates billions of dollars in profit each year and is one of the world's fastest growing criminal activities. The State Department estimates that between 600,000 and 800,000 people are trafficked across borders each year. As many as 17,000 right here in the United States. The majority are female. Most still children. Most—70 percent— trafficked for sexual purposes. Men, women, and children from Eastern Europe, Latin America, Asia, and Africa, too, are trafficked for forced prostitution, forced labor, and domestic servitude.

Consider Irina's story: Irina is a 16-year-old Russian high school student. She accepted a family friend's offer of $500 to take a quick trip to the Middle East to bring back merchandise to sell. Irina received a passport, a tourist visa, and a plane ticket. When she had her documentation, the story changed. Irina was told she would be a waitress in a local café for $1,000 a month. Her parents were told that if she didn't go, they would owe huge sums of money for the arrangements that had already been made. When she arrived, Irina found that she would not be a waitress, but a prostitute.

Her passport was taken away. She was threatened. Her life became a series of hotel rooms, madams, and clients. She tried to escape, but the madam claimed she had stolen money and the police sent her back. She was resold to another madam…and saddled with a huge debt for her misbehavior. The good news for Irina is that she was able to escape with the help of the Russian Embassy.

But not all are so lucky…

Source: From W. Ralph Basham, "Keynote Remarks from CBP Commissioner W. Ralph Basham." Published 2008 by CBP.gov.

sound impressive. Moreover, too many statistics can overwhelm listeners. When you do use statistics, you may want to present some visual representation or summary of the statistics to help the audience comprehend them.

Every attempt should be made to present the statistics clearly and meaningfully. One student speaker, for example, dramatized the need for improved sanitation at a global level when he said, "In human costs internationally, one child dies every 8 seconds from waterborne disease!...[T]he human and economic costs are staggering."[10]

It is often helpful to translate a statistic into more specific or more personal terms. Instead of saying that a new school will cost $7 million, you may point out that each taxpayer should expect a property tax increase of about $100 per year over a ten-year period. In this way, the audience can understand what the proposal would mean to them personally.

Finally, statistics change rapidly. Although all evidence should be as recent as possible, nothing is more useless than outdated statistics. Always gather statistical information from the most current sources available and cite those sources in your speech.

In short, statistics must be approached cautiously. Both the speaker and the listener should carefully evaluate the place of statistics in the total pattern of evidence.

Testimony

Watch the Video "Get Involved with Big Brothers/Big Sisters" at **MyCommunicationLab**

Another way to support your ideas is to offer testimonial evidence. Whereas statistical evidence seems more "factual" or "objective," testimony consists of the opinions, interpretations, or judgments of other people. There are three kinds of testimonial evidence: personal testimony, lay testimony, and expert testimony.

Personal Testimony　Regardless of the kind of speech you are making, you are likely to offer your personal testimony from time to time. For many topics and in many speaking situations, this is entirely appropriate. We have pointed out in previous chapters that a speaker's ethos or personal appeal can have a significant impact on listeners. However, you should avoid overreliance on your own testimony to the exclusion of other kinds of support. Equally important, you need to ask yourself a fundamental question: To what extent am I perceived by my audience as being a credible source of information on this subject?

If you have high credibility with your listeners, then your personal views may be an extremely convincing source of support. If, for example, you were a campus police officer, you would be a credible source of testimony on the topic of campus safety. Similarly, a nonprofit leader may speak credibly about funding sources for new programs, or a college student may testify personally to the benefits of participating in student organizations. In one classroom speech, a student used her personal experiences to emphasize the need for volunteers to help rebuild towns devastated by an outbreak of tornadoes:

> This past March, I had the opportunity to travel to Southern Indiana, along with a group of other students from around the Midwest, to help rebuild homes and buildings that were destroyed or badly damaged by tornadoes. I'm sure you're familiar with our school's "Learning through Service" program, which takes place during Spring Break. For 8 days, I worked together with about two dozen students to help rebuild homes, schools, and

hospitals. We stayed in trailers or nearby churches and spent a lot of time getting to know the residents of Washington County who had been displaced by the storms. Many worked side by side with us—whether on their own homes, the homes of strangers or neighbors, or on public buildings that would benefit the common good.

Although I've taken a lot of great courses during my three years of college, this was, by far, my most meaningful learning experience. I learned some basic skills—how to rebuild foundations, how to install siding, and even how to put on a roof that is unlikely to easily blow away. But far beyond that, I learned about community and caring and the wonderful resilience of the human spirit.

Personal testimony is not something you will use in all of your speeches. As a college student, you may not have direct experience or expertise on many topics that interest you. You may be interested in alternative energy sources, for example, but that does not make you an expert on the subject. In most cases, then, you will need to go beyond your own experiences and expertise and gather other kinds of testimonial evidence.

Lay Testimony Another kind of opinion evidence is lay testimony. Like personal testimony, lay testimony is based on firsthand experience—except in this instance, the experience is not your own. Nor is it the experience of an expert. Rather, lay testimony comes from ordinary women and men whose personal experiences make their testimony compelling.

Let us say, for example, that you wanted to encourage your classmates to become involved in the kind of "Learning through Service" program described earlier. While conducting your research, you may have discovered excellent statistics on the popularity of these kinds of programs. You may have learned that students who participate in these programs tend to be better students and that, on graduation, they are more likely to become engaged citizens in their communities. But beyond sharing such facts and statistics, you want to convey to your listeners the sorts of personal experiences they may have and how those experiences may impact their thoughts and feelings. In other words, you want to *humanize* the topic. If you have not participated in such a program yourself, you will need to find lay testimony from other students who *have* direct experience with such programs.

How effective is lay testimony? Like other forms of evidence, it depends on how carefully you choose that testimony. Standing alone, lay testimony may be insufficient as evidence. But when used in tandem with other strong supporting material, it can be quite effective. In speaking about the economic recession, for example, you may quote expert testimony from the chairman of the Federal Reserve, but you also may want to quote lay testimony from unemployed workers struggling to pay their bills. Your sources of lay testimony may not have special education or training that qualifies them to speak, but they should have direct, firsthand experience that gives them a unique perspective on your topic.

Expert Testimony One way to make your own speeches more persuasive is to borrow, in effect, the ethos of experts. Expert testimony is among the most frequently used types of evidence, particularly in speeches about complicated or highly technical issues. In such cases, we rely on those whom we regard as experts, or those who have some special education, training, or work-related experience with the subject. In a speech on the Obama administration's economic stimulus program, for example, you may quote expert testimony from the chairman of the Federal Reserve, Ben Bernanke, who asserted in a speech to the Economic Club of New York that "Americans can be confident that every resource is being brought to bear to address the current crisis: historical understanding, technical expertise, economic analysis, financial insight, and political leadership." Or you may choose to quote the part of his speech in which he said, "We now have the tools we need to respond with the necessary force to meet these challenges. Although much work remains and more difficulties surely lie ahead, I remain confident that the American economy, with its great intrinsic vitality and aided by the measures now available, will emerge from this period with renewed vigor."[11]

In using expert testimony, you will need to decide whether you want to quote the exact words the expert used or whether it's enough to simply paraphrase his or her ideas. If you plan to use the expert's *exact* words, you may want to ensure accuracy by writing them out on a note card that you will read while delivering your speech. You will also want to quote the expert's exact words when those words seem especially compelling, eloquent, or memorable. If you wanted to encourage your listeners to get involved in their community, for example, you might want to use a famous quotation from cultural anthropologist Margaret Mead: "Never doubt that a small group of thoughtful, committed people can change the world. Indeed, it is the only thing that ever has."

On other occasions, you may prefer to convey the basic sense of an expert's argument or capture his or her ideas in your own words. In this case, you will name the expert and perhaps say something about his or her credentials, but you will only be paraphrasing the main ideas of the testimony. If you were addressing the issue of generational poverty, for example, you might paraphrase the words of an education expert by saying, "Long-time educator Ruby Payne has written two books that address the issue of generational poverty. In *Bridges Out of Poverty*, she argues that the poor lack access to basic resources such as financial resources, emotional and spiritual resources, and basic support systems. She points out that most of us focus only on the financial aspect, but it is much more complicated than that." You could then go on to offer concrete examples of these resources and explain how lacking such resources can keep people trapped in poverty. In paraphrasing, of course, it is important to fairly and accurately represent the source's views—never exaggerating or distorting.

Good expert testimony is often one of the best ways to demonstrate that you have done your research and know what you're talking about. However, like all forms of evidence, expert testimony must be carefully chosen and critically evaluated.

Thinking Critically about Expert Testimony   Both the ethical speaker and the critical listener need to evaluate expert testimony carefully. By raising questions about the source and the nature of testimony, we can determine whether it is worthy of belief.

First, we need to ask whether our audience considers the source a reputable expert. Are your sources even *known* to your listeners? If not, you may need to identify them—and say something about their credentials—during the speech itself. Thus, you may introduce testimony from an expert on Social Security by saying,

"Professor Martin Wilson, a distinguished Harvard economist, has argued that Social Security is one generation away from complete failure." On other occasions, your audience may recognize the name of your source but not know much about the person's credentials, expertise, or experience with your topic. It never hurts to establish the ethos or credibility of your sources by saying something about why their testimony should be believed.

Sometimes speakers provide only vague references to their sources, saying, "Political analysts have noted that..." or "One member of the New York City police department said that..." In such cases, listeners have a right to be skeptical. "Political analysts" could mean respected political science professors or paid political "spin doctors." The police officer may be the chief of police or some rookie cop. Critical listeners are unlikely to be impressed or persuaded by such ambiguous references.

Another important question that we should ask about testimony is: How timely is it? People's views may change over time; even experts sometimes change their minds as the situation changes. Many members of both political parties, for example, initially supported authorizing President George W. Bush to use military force in Iraq following the 9/11 terrorist attacks. Over time, however, the costs of the war skyrocketed, international support waned, and the number of casualties grew—and many who at first supported the war changed their minds. Obviously, it is important to understand *when* and under what circumstances the testimony was given.

When using testimony, you should never misrepresent the *context* in which it was given. Unfortunately, this happens in political contests too often. In the GOP race for the 2012 presidential nomination, for example, Mitt Romney said, in the course of a speech, "I like to fire people." Using that phrase was a political blunder pounced on by his opponents. But to be fair to the governor, the context made it clear that he was referring to dropping an insurance company that did not serve its customers well. Taken out of context, the phrase was used to paint Romney as cold-hearted and mean. Whenever possible, we should take our testimony from those who have *nothing to gain* from their statements. One would expect the president of a pharmaceutical company to oppose policies that would hurt the industry's profits. Similarly, NASA officials could be expected to support increased government spending on space exploration. Although these people may be authorities in their fields, quoting them may not help your cause because they may be viewed as biased.

Finally, it is important to ask whether a source of testimony has relevant credentials. Unfortunately, we have been conditioned by advertising to accept testimony from celebrities with little or no real knowledge about the products they endorse. We also have become accustomed to movie actors, athletes, and famous singers or musicians endorsing candidates for office or particular political causes. That is their right, of course, but that does not mean we should consider them experts. A famous tennis player may be a good source of testimony on the rules or the history of the game, but that does not mean that he or she knows more than you do about politics or social welfare policies. Although entertainers and sports figures have every right to their opinions, their celebrity does not qualify them as experts on social, political, or economic issues.

Prestige Testimony as Evidence On the other hand, it may sometimes be acceptable, even desirable, to quote a celebrity with high visibility. They may

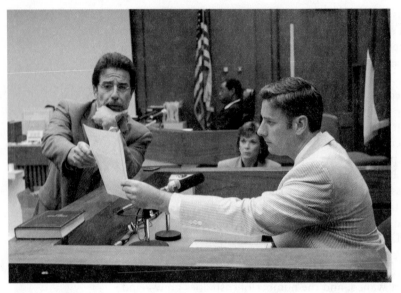

Testimony by those whose experience and credentials qualify them as experts can be especially effective in addressing important and complicated issues.

not be "experts," but prestige testimony *can* provide support for our argument if the source of that testimony is perceived as smart, dedicated, well-educated, or inspirational. Angelina Jolie, for example, has served as a Goodwill Ambassador to the United Nations Commissioner for Refugees, using her high public profile to focus more attention on the plight of refugees throughout the world. The Church World Service, in presenting her with a humanitarian award, cited her as one whose "work on behalf of refugees has made her a role model of individual humanitarian action, an inspiration to people around the world, especially the young. She gives a voice to the often forgotten refugees and displaced persons whose lives have been torn by persecution and war. Her active concern brings the promise of hope."[12] Another example is CBS News former anchor Katie Couric, who used the death of her own husband from colon cancer as inspiration for a personal crusade to promote screening for the disease.

Whenever we use testimony, we have an ethical obligation to assure our listeners that we are quoting or paraphrasing accurately, that we are not taking the testimony out of context, and that the source of the testimony has the expertise or experience to speak authoritatively on the subject. Listeners are not always in a position to judge whether the testimony in a speech is sound, but the critical listener *can* look for signs that it is relevant, timely, and attributed to a credible source.

SUPPORTING IDEAS THROUGH COMPARISON AND CONTRAST

7.2 Understand the ways in which comparisons and contrasts can support ideas.

Preview.   *One of the principal ways we learn is by comparison and contrast. We compare the unknown to the known. We look for similarities and differences between a new experience and an old one. We try to see ways in which new problems are similar to old problems that we have figured out how to solve.*

Comparison and contrast are not evidence in the strictest sense of the word; technically, they are a form of reasoning focusing on similarities and differences. Used with various forms of evidence, however, comparison and contrast can provide strong support for our ideas and enhance the clarity or persuasiveness of our speeches.

Watch the Video "Fear of Public Speaking" at **MyCommunicationLab**

Techniques of Comparison and Contrast

One of the most frequently used ways to make ideas more understandable or believable is by comparing or contrasting the old with the new, the known with the unknown, the familiar with the unfamiliar. New programs are better understood if we consider how they resemble or differ from the programs already in effect. New ideas may seem less "radical" if we show how they compare to ideas we've already had. If our audience is already familiar with a comparable policy, they may be less fearful or more comfortable with a new policy if we can show that it's not all that different. In short, it helps people to understand something new or different if we can compare it to something old and familiar. Comparison and contrast can make people more at ease with the idea of change.

Comparisons are often used by speakers who want to make a difficult or abstract concept more concrete and understandable to listeners. For example, we have all experienced traffic control firsthand. It is relatively easy to understand how a police officer at a sporting event controls the flow of traffic. She allows certain cars to make left-hand turns while oncoming traffic is halted. She might then let traffic proceed both ways or allow those in the right lane to merge right and so forth. In some ways, the management of traffic is like certain functions performed by the brain. By comparing information flow in the brain to traffic management, a speaker might help an audience visualize this much more complicated process.

One of the most striking uses of comparison to simplify a complicated idea occurred in the 1992 presidential campaign. Ross Perot, an independent candidate for president, hoped to refute Bill Clinton's assertion that his success as Governor of Arkansas proved that he would make a great president. Perot countered this with the observation that such a claim was like comparing the successful management of a mom-and-pop grocery store with managing Walmart.[13]

These comparisons take abstract ideas—how the brain functions, how difficult it is to run a country as big and as varied as the United States—and make them more understandable by identifying them with concrete, observable things with which we are familiar.

Whereas comparison focuses on similarities, contrast highlights differences. This can be a compelling form of support when you advocate an alternative to some idea or policy that generally is thought to have failed. Or you may use contrast to distinguish your own credentials or ideas from those of a competitor. During political campaigns, for example, candidates frequently contrast themselves with their rivals for office. Note how the Republican candidates for the presidential nomination in 2012 contrasted their views on an important issue for Michigan voters on the eve of the primary in that state.

Thinking Critically about Comparison and Contrast

Although listeners may find comparison and contrast helpful and persuasive, the basis of comparison should be carefully considered.

Speakers and listeners should ask the same question: Are the people, events, places, or objects being compared actually comparable in essential ways? Some may be similar in obvious or superficial ways, but comparison on such bases could be misleading. Those who urge an American-style democracy for Iraq are accused

◤FOCUS ON CIVIC ENGAGEMENT | Candidates' Contrasting Views

Candidates in the 2012 Republican primary often faced issues on which they basically agreed, but sought to distinguish their views from those of their rivals. In a debate in Michigan, for example, all the candidates were on record as opposing the General Motors and Chrysler rescue by the government but sought to contrast their view with opposing candidates.

Rick Santorum depicted his position as consistent because he had also opposed support for financial institutions, while Mitt Romney supported the Wall Street bailout while opposing propping up the auto companies.

Romney argued that it would have been irresponsible to let banks collapse as Santorum would have done and that his idea of letting the companies go into a structured bankruptcy would still have saved the auto industry but would not have called for government funds to be used.

For his part, Ron Paul distanced himself from other candidates by simply declaring that all bailouts were bad and the government shouldn't ever bail out anyone.

Source: The Detroit Free Press, "GOP Candidates Debate Government Loans to Auto Companies," www.freep.com/article/20120222/NEWS15/120222074/GOP-candidates-debate-government-loans-auto-companies (accessed March 18, 2012). ◢

of setting up a false comparison because the histories, cultures, and values of the two countries are so different. On the other hand, proponents of the war in Iraq reject comparisons to the "quagmire" of the Vietnam war because the geopolitical contexts of the two wars are not at all comparable. So care must be exercised in using comparisons. Speakers and listeners should try to satisfy themselves that the things being compared are really similar in ways that are essential to the argument.

Sometimes speakers use a colorful analogy as a way of dramatizing a comparison or contrast they hope to emphasize. In addressing health care reform, the CEO of AARP, William Novelli, advanced the following bold comparison:

> We might compare fixing our health-care system to wrestling an octopus: Two arms are hugging you, two arms are trying to strangle you, and God knows what the other four arms are doing. Every time you think you're making headway, another arm reaches out and grabs you and pulls you back.

> This octopus that is the American health-care system seems at times to have us by the arms, legs, and throat…and the pocketbook. One reason that it seems to be an octopus rather than a Clydesdale, steadily pulling the wagon along, is that the system is not really a system at all, as many of you know so well.

> As we try to grapple with one part of the octopus—say the affordability of prescription drugs—we find another tentacle threatening us, then another and another….The lack of health insurance, the need for more geriatric training in medical schools, the problems with long-term care. This octopus has more than eight arms.[14]

The critical listener would likely conclude that this comparison works well, so long as the octopus analogy does not unfairly exaggerate the seriousness of the challenge. If judged as fair and reasonable, the listener would also probably see Novelli's comparison as reinforcing the complexity of the challenge Americans face—making it memorable and compelling.

EVALUATING SUPPORTING MATERIAL

Preview. *There are several criteria to use when evaluating the quality of your supporting material: accuracy, completeness, recency, source reliability, and appropriateness for your audience. There are also ethical considerations in testing your evidence. All evidence, regardless of type, should be carefully scrutinized.*

7.3 Apply the criteria of accuracy, completeness, recency, source reliability, appropriateness, and ethical integrity to evaluate the quality of supporting material.

Not all evidence is of equal quality. Simply collecting a great deal of information on a subject is not enough. As you read, talk with individuals, and ponder the information you have unearthed, you have the intellectual and ethical responsibility to carefully judge what should be included in your speech and what should be omitted. In discussing each form of supporting material earlier in the chapter, we explained that each type must be examined critically for its validity, appropriateness, and ethical responsibility. Now we'll consider some tests that may be applied to all forms of support.

Accuracy

Naturally, you want to use evidence that is true and accurate. Accurate information is redundant and verifiable. You should be able to examine several independent sources and discover essentially the same factual or statistical information. For instance, various sources should all pretty much agree on the number of teenage pregnancies in America each year, the amount of money spent on the space program, or the number of crimes committed in major U.S. cities. When serious inconsistencies occur, you should question the accuracy of your sources and continue your research until you feel confident that you have found the most accurate information available. One student, for example, gave a speech on the results of the war in Iraq. At one point, he asserted that an important accomplishment of

---

HIGHLIGHTING SOURCE ACCURACY | Beware of Wikipedia

Wikipedia is a free online encyclopedia that started in 2001. Its content is written collaboratively by users around the globe.

- The site is called *wiki*, meaning that anyone with Web access can add to, correct, or amend it by clicking on an edit function.
- The site has millions of visitors every month, making it one of the most popular sites on the Internet.
- Because of the nature of the site, a sobering possibility for misinformation and vandalism exists.
- Already, political operatives have covertly rewritten—or defaced—candidates' biographical

entries to make their boss look good, or to make the opponent look ridiculous. Altering senators' ages, entering highly personal information, and posting damaging "jokes" are just a few of the problematic practices that have surfaced.

- Experts in communication technology believe that the sheer size of Wikipedia and the huge number of entries make it impossible to monitor or police it in any effective way.

Source: "Wikipedia: An Online Encyclopedia Being Used for Political Tricks," *Bloomington (IN) Herald-Times,* April 30, 2006, D3. ▲

the war was the elimination of Iraq's nuclear weapons. There were allegations that Iraq was developing nuclear weapons, and the student substantiated his contention with quotes and statistics from early on in the conflict. His inadequate research led him to make this completely inaccurate statement.

Completeness

You should also test your information for completeness. Although you cannot know all there is to know on a subject, the more thorough, complete, and well-rounded your knowledge on your topic, the better your speech will be.

Completeness and accuracy are clearly related. As you check for accuracy, you will consult numerous sources, making your evidence more and more complete. The student referred to in *the Highlighting Source Accuracy* feature made inaccurate statements because of incomplete research, failing to consult a wide variety of sources. Having complete information will also help you respond to questions after your speech.

Recency

Generally, you should strive to obtain the most recent information possible. If you are speaking about economic trends, consumer spending, the unemployment rate, or the financial stability of banks and insurance companies, you obviously will want to be armed with the most recent information available. Consider our earlier example of the student speaking on voting patterns of young people. Had she argued that young people were apathetic and cited the 2000 statistic that indicated only 28.4 percent of 18- to 20-year-olds voted, she would have presented a misleading picture of how her peers voted in more recent elections. The recency of your information may not be so important when you are discussing other topics, such as a notorious historical character or an event that took place many years ago. As a general rule, however, it's a good idea to look for the most recent evidence available; the more recent your evidence, the better.

Advances in technology have made it easier than ever to find the most up-to-date information on almost any topic. And because your listeners also have access to computer databases and other sources of up-to-date information, it is more important than ever that you, as a speaker, have the most recent information available.

Watch the Video "Wikipedia as a Primary Source of Information" at **MyCommunicationLab**

Source Reliability

It is also important to assess the reliability of your sources of information. We have already addressed this concern, but we want to stress here that if you find an impressive piece of testimony or a compelling statistic, you must ask yourself about the credibility of the magazine, newspaper, Web site, or other source in which the information appears.

Whenever you test the reliability of a source, you should ask: Is this source known to have some bias on the subject? Are they promoting a particular point-of-view out of prejudice or self-interest? On energy conservation, for example, evidence drawn from the petroleum industry is likely to reflect their interest in promoting more drilling. This may be a defensible position, but don't rely on any one source that has a stake in the outcome of a debate. In general, if you have any reason to doubt a source's objectivity, trustworthiness, or competence, it is best to look elsewhere for information.

Audience Appropriateness

Regardless of the quality of your evidence, it should not be used if it may be considered somehow inappropriate for a particular audience or situation. A human interest story or a personal narrative may be perfectly appropriate in a sermon or an after-dinner speech, but it may seem out of place in a technical report. Similarly, humorous anecdotes may be expected in a speech about a famous entertainer but be considered tasteless when addressing a serious topic such as AIDS or child abuse. The type of speech you are giving, your topic, and your audience's characteristics and values should all be considered as you reflect on the appropriateness of your supporting materials.

Ethical Considerations

In a sense, all the tests of evidence we have discussed raise ethical considerations. If you use evidence that you know to be inaccurate, incomplete, biased, or offensive to your audience, you have violated the ethical trust of your listeners. You have shown them that you do *not* have their best interests at heart. Sometimes speakers simply lose track of their ethical responsibilities. They want, more than anything, to get the audience to respond—to vote a particular way, to contribute to some cause, or to commit to some action. They want these things so badly that they use evidence in ways that they know to be unethical—perhaps quoting expert testimony out of context, distorting statistics, or citing examples that they know are not typical.

Although anyone can make mistakes, you have an ethical obligation to scrutinize your own evidence carefully and to guard against the temptation to "get the job done" even if the audience is misled in the process. Civic responsibility demands a commitment to ethical public speaking.

 Study and Review materials for this chapter are at **MyCommunicationLab**

SUMMARY

 Listen to the Audio Chapter Summary at **MyCommunicationLab**

Supporting Ideas with Evidence

7.1 Identify and understand how to use the principal types of supporting evidence: facts, definitions, examples, statistics, and testimony.

- Even if your ideas have merit, they need to be developed and supported if they are to be understandable and believable to your listeners. Using good evidence is critical.

- Depending on the topic, you will want to use several different types of evidence in your speech:
  - Facts that are accurate and verifiable
  - Definitions that are either informative or persuasive
  - Actual or hypothetical examples that are typical, relevant, and important
  - Statistics that accurately show how things are related and what trends have occurred over time
  - Testimony that is timely and authoritative

Supporting Ideas through Comparison and Contrast

7.2 Understand the ways in which comparisons and contrasts can support ideas.

- Comparisons and contrasts relate the unfamiliar to the familiar or simplify difficult concepts.
- People, events, places, or objects being compared must actually be comparable in essential ways.

Evaluating Supporting Material

7.3 Apply the criteria of accuracy, completeness, recency, source reliability, appropriateness, and ethical integrity to evaluate the quality of supporting material.

- Regardless of the specific kind of supporting material you use, you will want to do the following:
- Carefully consider its accuracy, completeness, and recency.
- Make sure it is appropriate to the audience and the situation and meets high ethical standards.

QUESTIONS FOR REVIEW AND REFLECTION

Supporting Ideas with Evidence

7.1 Identify and understand how to use the principal types of supporting evidence: facts, definitions, examples, statistics, and testimony.

1. Why should public speakers use supporting material?
2. What are the major kinds of evidence that speakers might use? Briefly define each.
3. How will you determine whether factual information is of high quality?
4. Explain the difference between offering an informative definition and a persuasive one. Offer an example of each.
5. Compare and contrast the actual example with the hypothetical example. Which do you think is generally better to use in speech making? Why?
6. Describe how narratives can be especially effective as examples. Think of one narrative you might use with a speech topic of interest to you.
7. Contrast the three different kinds of averages—mean, median, and mode. Under what circumstances might the mode or median be preferable to the mean as a measure of the true average?
8. Whenever you use statistical support in a speech, what criteria will you use to assess its effectiveness?
9. Under what circumstances might you choose to use personal testimony or lay testimony? How will you make sure you do so effectively?
10. If you were going to use expert testimony in a speech, what criteria would you use in choosing this kind of evidence?

11. Under what circumstances would you say prestige testimony is legitimate? When is it misleading or irrelevant?

Supporting Ideas through Comparison and Contrast

7.2 Understand the ways in which comparisons and contrasts can support ideas.

12. How might comparisons or contrasts be compelling as supporting material?
13. Give an example of a comparison you have used when trying to explain something to a friend.
14. Give an example of a contrast you might use in favoring one position over another.

Evaluating Supporting Material

7.3 Apply the criteria of accuracy, completeness, recency, source reliability, appropriateness, and ethical integrity to evaluate the quality of supporting material.

15. What are some basic tests for evidence? Why are they important?
16. How do you determine whether or not you are making ethical decisions when choosing supporting material?

✓ Study and Review the Flashcards at **MyCommunicationLab**

WHY WE NEED UNIVERSAL HEALTH INSURANCE

Robert Stone, M.D., Director, Hoosiers for a Commonsense Health Plan, State Coordinator, Indiana Chapter, Physicians for a National Health Program

Dr. Rob Stone is a strong advocate for universal health care. A dedicated activist, Dr. Stone meets with legislators, addresses rallies, and speaks frequently at local and state groups interested in the issue in order to promote the single-payer or "Medicare-for-all" plan. Dr. Stone routinely conducts extensive question-and-answer sessions following his speeches and encourages listeners to get more information at his organization's Web site. The following is a basic version of the many talks he gives, including a presentation at the First United Methodist Church, Bloomington, Indiana, on April 16, 2009.

Everyone has a story to tell, usually a horror story, about themselves or someone they know. About an outrageous medical bill. About not being able to afford health care. About being afraid of financial ruin due to illness or injury. I see it every day when I work in the ER at Bloomington Hospital, where I have worked the past 23 years.

Recently it was a young fellow who had torn his ACL, a knee ligament that doesn't heal without surgery when it's completely torn. Every time he steps wrong on his leg, the knee swells up and hurts for a week or two. The surgery would cost $15,000. He lost his job that had insurance and his new job doesn't offer any coverage. There's no way he can afford the surgery. He wants to have his life back, to be able to play softball, to be able to work, to be free of fear. He looked at me and asked, "What can I do, Doc? Do I have to keep re-injuring it until I'm completely crippled, go on welfare, and then finally get it fixed?" I had no answer for him. Maybe he can figure a way out of his predicament, and maybe he can't. We have no answer in our current system.

You have seen the miserable statistics by now: 46 million people in this country, 860,000 in Indiana, and 15,000 just in Monroe County have no health insurance. The Institute of Medicine, part of the National Institutes of Health, estimates that 18,000 people a year die simply because they lack health insurance. That's a September 11th catastrophe every two months, but we don't see it.

People without insurance live sicker and die younger. And it's a myth that there is a safety net. In the ER, I work in the safety net. The reason they call it a "net" is because it is full of holes.

Even if you have insurance, it may not be good enough to protect you. If you have Medicaid, it can be hard to find a doctor who will take you. More and more folks find themselves underinsured, with skimpy policies and very high deductibles. To make it worse, insurance companies have a way of canceling policies once you get sick or injured. The cost of insurance is rising much faster than wages or inflation. Small businesses find it harder and harder to cover their employees. The whole system is collapsing.

Here in Monroe County we have seen the community come together around a new entity to serve the uninsured, the Volunteers in Medicine Clinic, which will expand upon our current Community Health Access Program Clinic. We are making a significant effort to address the problems of the uninsured at the local level. We have formed a partnership between the hospital, physicians, and the community, with the support of government,

DR. STONE BEGINS BY ESTABLISHING HIS OWN ETHOS: HE IS AN M.D. WHO HAS PRACTICED FOR 23 YEARS, AND AS AN EMERGENCY ROOM PHYSICIAN, HE HAS SEEN COUNTLESS CASES OF PEOPLE WITHOUT RESOURCES TO PAY MEDICAL BILLS.

THE USE OF A SPECIFIC EXTENDED EXAMPLE HUMANIZES THE PROBLEM. HIS USE OF STATISTICS DEMONSTRATES THE TYPICALITY OF THE EXAMPLE HE HAS JUST USED. THE COMPARISON WITH SEPTEMBER 11 DRAMATIZES THE STATISTIC AND MAKES IT MORE CONCRETE.

HERE HE USES A CLEVER DEFINITION TO CHALLENGE THE WIDESPREAD BELIEF THAT THE "SAFETY NET" REALLY DOES PROVIDE PROTECTION.

THIS ASSERTION IS NOT SUPPORTED BY SPECIFIC EVIDENCE HERE. THE GENERAL PREMISE THAT THE HEALTH CARE SYSTEM IS SERIOUSLY FLAWED IS WIDELY ACCEPTED EVEN IF THE SOLUTIONS ARE CONTESTED. IN ADDITION, DR. STONE TYPICALLY ENLARGES ON THIS POINT WITH SPECIFIC EXAMPLES AND STATISTICS WHEN APPROPRIATE IN THE Q&A.

business, and individuals that has proven potent and exhilarating. This is something that we can and will accomplish.

But we understand at the same time that there are larger, systemic problems we need to consider.

Hoosiers for a Commonsense Health Plan is an Indiana group of health care workers and other interested people working for universal health insurance in the state and at the national level. We urge citizens to get involved, educate themselves, and spread the word. It will take a grassroots effort and a lot of work. In Canada, their national system started in the province of Saskatchewan and then spread to the entire country. We want to push the Indiana legislature to solve this problem, and our congressional representatives in Washington as well.

There are so many problems we face that could be solved if we just had enough money. This isn't one of them. We are already spending enough money on health care. In fact, in the U.S. we spend twice as much per capita as the other wealthy democracies, all of which cover everyone in their populations, and they have better heath statistics than we have, better life expectancy, better infant mortality, and so on. Our problem is that we spend too much money on overhead, inefficiency, and profit. Thirty-one percent of our health care dollars go to overhead, mostly to the private insurance companies. Have you heard how profitable WellPoint/Anthem in Indianapolis is? They have been reporting record earnings this year, and last year their CEO made $25 million. Many studies have shown that if we ran our system as efficiently as Medicare, we would have enough money to cover everyone and have money left over. Compare Medicare with for-profit WellPoint/Anthem. Medicare spends about 3.1 percent of the money it collects on overhead, while WellPoint spends closer to 19 percent. It's not even close.

There are those who reject a single-payer system by labeling it "socialized medicine." But it is not. A single-payer system is one where the government collects and distributes the money, but care is delivered in the private marketplace. Medicare is the classic single-payer system. It was "made in America" and will celebrate its 44th birthday July 30. The sticking point is not that Medicare-for-all is "socialized medicine," but that it would essentially do away with the for-profit insurance as we know it. Congress recently heard from Wendell Potter, former head of corporate communications at Cigna.

He said: "I know from personal experience that members of Congress and the public have good reason to question the honesty and trustworthiness of the insurance industry. Insurers make promises they have no intention of keeping; they flout regulations designed to protect consumers; and they make it nearly impossible to understand—or even to obtain—information we need."

Single-payer Medicare-for-all is the common-sense solution for our broken health care system. Call it Medicare Part E—E is for Everyone. Health care for all is an idea whose time has come. It is not a Democratic issue or a Republican issue. It is an idea to unite us, not divide us. This is the real national security issue. Go to our Web page, HCHP.info. Contact us, get involved, make your voice heard, make a difference!

Source: Reprinted by permission from Robert Stone, "Why We Need Universal Health Insurance" speech. Copyright © 2009 by Robert Stone.

THE EXAMPLE POINTS TO A PROGRAM WITH WHICH THE LISTENERS WOULD BE FAMILIAR. HE RAISES IT IN PART TO RECOGNIZE THAT VARIOUS GROUPS CAN WORK TOGETHER BUT ALSO TO MAKE SURE THE AUDIENCE DOES NOT BELIEVE THAT THIS IS THE SOLUTION.

THE STATISTICS USED HERE ARE DESIGNED TO DISPEL THE NOTION THAT IMPROVING HEALTH CARE WILL COST TOO MUCH MONEY. THE SPECIFIC EXAMPLE OF THE CEO MAKING $25 MILLION REINFORCES HIS POINT ABOUT INSURANCE COMPANY OVERHEAD AND IS ALSO MEANT TO SHOCK LISTENERS.

HERE DR. STONE REFUTES THE ASSERTION THAT HIS PLAN IS "SOCIALIZED MEDICINE" WITH A SHORT DEFINITION OF "SINGLE-PAYER." BECAUSE "SOCIALIZED MEDICINE" IS OFTEN ASSOCIATED WITH AND COMPARED TO EUROPEAN PLANS, DR. STONE DISPELS THAT NOTION WITH HIS DESCRIPTION OF SINGLE-PAYER AS TRULY AMERICAN.

HERE IS TESTIMONY FROM A SOURCE DIRECTLY ASSOCIATED WITH THE INSURANCE INDUSTRY ITSELF OFFERING CRITICISM OF THE INDUSTRY BASED ON HIS PERSONAL EXPERIENCE.

THE SPEECH CONCLUDES WITH AN ASSERTION THAT THIS IS NOT A PARTISAN ISSUE, A REITERATION OF THE IMPORTANCE OF THE ISSUE, AND A CALL TO ACTION.

Organizing Your Speech

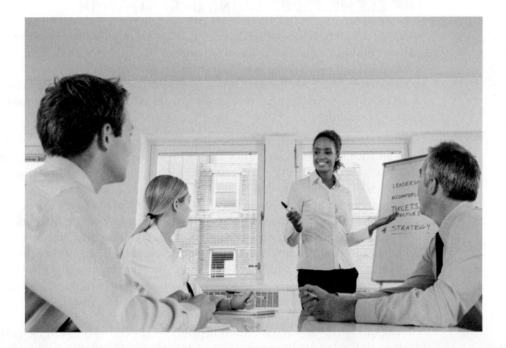

OVERVIEW AND LEARNING OBJECTIVES

The Elements of Sound Organization

8.1 Explain how the quality of your ideas influences the strength of your speech's organization.

How Patterns of Organization Connect Ideas

8.2 Describe basic organizational patterns you might use as you arrange your ideas strategically.

Guidelines for Organizing Your Speech

8.3 List and explain underlying principles of sound organization you will follow, regardless of the specific pattern you choose.

Transitions as Connectives

8.4 Describe different transitional devices you might use in creating a coherent presentation.

Introducing Your Speech

8.5 Identify the key components of a speech's introduction.

Concluding Your Speech

8.6 List different ways of concluding a speech effectively.

Some speakers carefully select and focus their topics, have a clear purpose and thesis, seek out good supporting materials, and still fail to deliver a good speech. Part of their failure may be due to how they have organized their materials. This chapter is devoted to helping you understand how to organize your ideas in a way that will help you achieve your purpose.

THE ELEMENTS OF SOUND ORGANIZATION

8.1 Explain how the quality of your ideas influences the strength of your speech's organization.

Preview. *Nearly everyone recognizes that a speech must have strong content and be delivered effectively. Yet what impact, if any, does the organization of those ideas and supporting materials have on the listeners' response? Research and experience have shown that sound organization can have a significant effect on the audience's willingness and ability to listen and their impressions of the speaker's credibility.*

Effective speakers organize their speeches carefully. They think about what to include and what to leave out. They do not introduce irrelevant or redundant information. The best speakers understand how much background to cover, which issues to address, and how best to allocate their limited time.

Good organization is important for many reasons. Well-organized speakers appear to be competent, focused, and knowledgeable. As a result, listeners perceive them as more credible.[1] A clearly organized presentation also promotes learning and retention.[2] Delivering a well-organized presentation is one of the *best* ways for you to show respect for your listeners. When you take the time and effort to organize your comments clearly and coherently, you show that you care about making yourself understood. No listener should have to struggle to understand a presentation that is disorganized or incoherent.[3]

The quality of your organization depends on the clarity and simplicity of your ideas, as well as their appropriateness to the particular situation and audience. A well-organized speech is clear, straightforward, and easily comprehended by your listeners.

Clarity of Ideas

To be clear, an idea must first be complete. Consider, for example, Amy, who wants to speak on reforming the way appropriations for pet projects (known as *earmarks*) are inserted into legislation by members of Congress. In drafting an outline, she first clarified her specific purpose and thesis statement. These were clearly articulated and reflected the guidelines for such statements in Chapter 5. The draft read like this:

> **Specific purpose:** *I want my audience to agree that the process through which earmarking projects are selected significantly influences the nature and outcomes of those initiatives.*
> **Thesis statement:** *Earmarking can lead to positive outcomes when sound selection procedures are used.*
> **Main Ideas**
>   I. Earmark examples
>   II. Criticism of earmarks

III. How earmarks waste money
IV. Benefits of earmarks
 V. Transparency and accountability

Although Amy's specific purpose and thesis statement were clear, her main points were not. None of her ideas were in the form of a complete sentence; each was undeveloped and unclear. As a result, the main points were not easily distinguished and some even overlapped. The first idea was not a main idea at all, but rather one type of supporting material—examples—that she might use throughout the speech. Amy's second point was too vague; her third point referred to one of several of the criticisms one might make of earmarks. Amy wanted to describe the potential risks and controversies of earmarking. At the same time, she sought to acknowledge that earmarks sometimes produce good results, providing funding for badly needed local projects. Ultimately, her goal was to advocate vigilance in the earmark vetting process to control the abuses sometimes associated with the practice.

Thus, Amy ultimately decided on a problem-solution pattern of organization, identifying pros and cons, and then spelling out the specifics of a sound process for examining and choosing earmarks. Her new outline reflected this pattern:

 I. The process and practice of adding earmarks to legislation in the U.S. Congress have long been controversial.
  A. Some argue that earmarks waste taxpayer dollars, with many going to support trivial projects.
  B. Others believe that legislators promote earmarks because of personal or political gain.[4]
  C. Some have called for a permanent ban on the practice of earmarking.
  D. Earmarks can lead to political corruption.
 II. In spite of these concerns, earmarking can lead to a number of positive outcomes.
  A. Projects financed through earmarking have revitalized communities, saved lives, and improved local economies.[5]
  B. Earmarks are chosen by elected representatives—who presumably are close to their communities and know their legitimate needs and concerns.
  C. The process of choosing projects to earmark can lead to bipartisan collaboration.
III. The key is creating a rigorous vetting process for earmarks.
  A. Keep debates about earmarking open to public scrutiny and accountability.
  B. Maintain current rules that require a written statement by the sponsoring legislator(s) certifying that neither they nor their spouses have a financial interest in the proposed project.
  C. Maintain vigilance and, if necessary, require additional disclosure or documentation as earmarking projects are debated and chosen.

Amy's plan for the speech was now clear, with straightforward main ideas stated in complete sentences. Her subordinate ideas were also clear and coherent, and all that remained was for her to fill in the details with examples, testimony, and other forms of evidence.

Simplicity of Ideas

Audiences must be able to understand your ideas if they are to respond positively. In addition to clarity, the simplicity of your main ideas is important. You want to state your ideas fully and accurately, yet in terms simple enough that your listeners can understand immediately and recall your main ideas pretty much word for word.

To achieve this ideal, ask yourself whether you have stated your ideas in the most basic ways possible. Avoid combining two or three ideas in one main point. Strive for a balance among your main points, so that you allocate approximately the same amount of time to each.

Some speakers try to include too much information or even a whole series of ideas within one main point. Meleia, for example, proposed the following speech:

> **Specific purpose:** *I want my audience to become more actively involved in politics.*
> **Thesis statement:** *Political involvement leads to positive results.*

She stated her first main idea like this:

I. People who take an interest in politics can have a practical impact, help restore idealism to the process, and learn valuable personal skills.

This main point tries to do too much. It is not a single idea. Instead, it is really two and perhaps even three interrelated ideas. Meleia needs to sort out the ideas and focus separately on each. A revised version of this outline might look like this:

I. There are practical benefits to society when more citizens participate in politics.
II. The political system itself also benefits from more citizen participation.
III. Individuals who participate in the political process gain valuable personal skills.

If Meleia can convince her audience that important benefits can be gained from participating in politics, then she will have achieved her purpose. To accomplish this, of course, she will have to take the next step and develop each of her ideas with supporting materials. She will need to enumerate the benefits that come from political participation, show that they are indeed beneficial, and make them real and compelling for her audience.

Simplicity, then, goes hand in hand with clarity as a basic characteristic of a well-stated main point. What seems simple and clear to one audience, however, may not seem that way to a different audience, so it is also important that you consider the situation and audience as you prepare your speech.

Suitability to the Situation

As we emphasized in Chapter 5, a speech is designed for a specific audience. A speech is also influenced by the occasion that prompts it and the setting in which it occurs. Thus, your ideas must not only be clear and simple but also appropriate for the particular audience and context.

The level of complexity of any idea will be significantly influenced by the audience's relationship to the topic. If, for example, you wanted to address the threat posed by the growing federal deficit, you might choose to introduce ideas that are highly technical, sophisticated, and complex if you were addressing a group of economists at a professional conference. If, on the other hand, you were speaking to your classmates, you would probably want to offer more basic information about the deficit, including background information and definitions of key terms. How technical or complex your discussion should be, then, depends on what the audience brings to the speech in terms of their background, experience, and expectations.

HOW PATTERNS OF ORGANIZATION CONNECT IDEAS

Preview. *To make a set of ideas reasonable and coherent for your audience, you need to put the ideas together so that they relate to one another in some logical fashion. To do this, you will use such basic patterns of organization as chronological or sequential, spatial, categorical, climactic, cause-and-effect, problem-solution, and narrative.*

When you have developed a good idea or series of ideas, you then face the job of arranging them in some order. It is important to recognize that most speeches can be organized in a variety of different ways. *Your* task is to choose the most appropriate organizational pattern for the particular topic and situation in which you are speaking.

There are several organizational patterns from which to choose, many of which we will explore further in later chapters. Here, however, we introduce several of the most commonly used organizational patterns.

8.2 Describe basic organizational patterns you might use as you arrange your ideas strategically.

Explore the Concept "Organization" at **MyCommunicationLab**

Chronological or Sequential Order

One commonly used pattern of arrangement is chronological order. You begin with a specific point in time and then move forward or backward, depending on the nature of the subject. Chronological order may be useful with a variety of topics, most notably those that deal with a process or a historical event. Thus, the development of the labor movement in the United States, the events that led up to the dissolution of the Soviet Union, or the evolution of the Tea Party as a national political force might all be appropriate subjects for chronological arrangement.

Here is how one student, providing an historical account of Nazi Germany, arranged his ideas in a chronological pattern:

Specific purpose: *I want my audience to understand how the Nazis came to power in Germany.*
Thesis statement: *Nazism grew out of social and political unrest.*
  I. In 1919, the Treaty of Versailles created several serious problems for Germany.
  II. Financial crises encouraged the National Socialists to attempt an unsuccessful coup in Bavaria in 1923.
  III. By 1930, the National Socialist Party had emerged as a major political party.
  IV. The violent election campaign of 1933 brought the Nazi Party to power.

Similar to the chronological pattern is the sequential pattern, which you would use if you wanted your audience to understand some step-by-step procedure or process. For instance, if you wanted listeners to understand the process involved in applying for government-subsidized housing, you could begin with the first step that the applicant takes and follow the process in order, step by step. You could similarly use a sequential pattern to help listeners understand how the Asian long-horned beetle attacks and destroys trees, how terrorists make dirty bombs, or the steps involved in adopting a child.

Spatial Order

A second common pattern is spatial arrangement. With this pattern, you use space as your ordering principle. A speech explaining the architectural plans for a new library, a presentation describing major tourist attractions of a big city (as one travels from north to south), or a speech describing the most progressive, reform-oriented prisons in the United States may all be appropriate candidates for spatial organization.

The following is an example of how one student arranged ideas in a spatial pattern determined by geography as he addressed the need for emergency preparedness in the United States.

> **Specific purpose:** *I want my audience to recognize the serious natural disasters that increasingly threaten all of our geographical regions.*
> **Thesis statement:** *Natural disasters pose a growing threat throughout the United States.*
>   I. Hurricanes threaten our coasts.
> II. Wildfires threaten our woodlands.
> III. Tornadoes threaten our Midwestern regions.
> IV. Floods threaten low-lying areas along streams and lakes.

The student then went on to offer specific examples of each of these natural disasters, as well as illustrating how each has increased in frequency.

Watch the Video
"Roommates" at
MyCommunicationLab

Categorical Order

Ideas can also be arranged in a pattern that emphasizes distinct topics—a categorical pattern. When you arrange your ideas categorically, you address types, forms, qualities, or aspects of the speech subject. For example, if you were giving a speech on the benefits of higher education, you could develop ideas related to the intellectual, social, or economic advantages of education. Similarly, you might discuss teen pregnancy in terms of those most at risk or prison reform in terms of different models that have been tried.

In the example that follows, the executive director of a small nonprofit agency arranged his ideas categorically as he described the agency's major funding sources to his board of directors:

> **Specific purpose:** *I want my audience to understand the main revenue sources that have supported our agency over the past five years.*
> **Thesis statement:** *Individual donors have provided the vast majority of the financial support that has enabled our agency to exist and thrive.*
>   I. Over the past five years, individual donations have accounted for 65 percent of our total revenue.

II. Faith communities have provided slightly less than 15 percent.
III. Grants from foundations and government agencies have averaged 18 percent.
IV. Businesses have provided only about 2–3 percent.

Under each category, the director developed his remarks by elaborating on the demographics of the individual donors category (e.g., their age, occupation, gender, etc.). He gave specific examples of faith communities most involved with supporting the agency and then commented on the funding cycles, restrictions, and stability of each granting agency with an eye toward future funding. He concluded by exploring possible reasons for underfunding by the business community. This pattern and the other patterns described so far are especially well suited for organizing informative speeches.

Climactic Order

Another way of arranging ideas is to use a climactic pattern, or a sequence that goes from simple to difficult, from least important to most important, or from emotionally neutral to emotionally intense. When the climactic order reflects audience needs and priorities, it can be an especially effective way to arrange ideas if the goal is to gain audience agreement or action. As you assess your ideas or arguments, you would then arrange them to build up to your strongest argument or most compelling idea.

Like a playwright, a speaker may wish to build on the listeners' interests and concerns until a climactic moment is reached. If, for example, you were addressing an audience with a strong concern for ethics, you might talk about a solution to a community problem in terms of its affordability and its benefits to the community, concluding with the moral imperative to act. The following is an example of ideas patterned climactically, from least to most important, with rising emotional intensity:

> **Specific purpose:** *I want my audience to agree that the United States needs a central food inspection agency.*
> **Thesis statement:** *The United States should create a central food inspection agency.*
> I. Oversight by a central agency would yield economic advantages.
> II. Oversight by a central agency would curb food-borne illnesses.
> III. Oversight by a central agency would save lives.

The climactic pattern is most often used in persuasive speeches. By using this pattern, the speaker hopes that audiences will remember and be moved by the last thing they hear.

Causal Order

Ideas can be arranged in an order that leads from cause to effect or from effect to cause. This causal pattern is useful for speakers who want an audience to understand how an idea or event has unfolded or for speakers who want to suggest changes in a chain of relationships that will bring more desirable outcomes. If, for example, you wanted your audience to understand why type 2 diabetes is on the

This speaker used a causal pattern of organization as she argued that subsidized school lunch programs lead to increased achievement scores across academic subjects and improved social skills for children of all ages.

rise, you could arrange your ideas so that they would show the relationship between the disease and the contributing factors (unhealthy diet, lack of exercise). You could also use cause-and-effect order to discuss such topics as the causes of ozone depletion, the effects of gang activities on communities, or the economic factors that typically lead to a recession.

The following is an example of ideas arranged in a causal pattern. Here the president of a neighborhood association argued that the lack of traffic lights and signs produced harmful results and urged the city council to take action.

> **Specific purpose:** *I want council members to agree that a better system of traffic lights and signs is needed in this community.*
> **Thesis statement:** *The present system of traffic control is inconvenient and dangerous.*
> I. *Effect:* Pedestrians, young and old alike, have been struck and killed at unguarded crossings.
> II. *Effect:* At the main mall entrance, several accidents have resulted when oncoming traffic has failed to stop for the red light.
> III. *Effect:* Traffic jams causing long delays occur every weekday during rush hours.
> IV. *Cause:* The real culprit contributing to this safety hazard is poor traffic control procedures.

When using causal arrangement, keep in mind that a chronological relationship does *not* necessarily equal a causal relationship. One event following another may represent chance as easily as cause. In addition, whenever you look at a given effect to seek its causes, you must guard against oversimplification. Identifying a single cause for a complex problem is usually unrealistic. Finally, sometimes cause-and-effect order is incorporated into a problem-solution pattern. Within the structure of a problem-solution speech, you will analyze the problem (effect) in terms of contributing causes, and then go on to propose solutions. The speaker who advances solutions is clearly speaking persuasively, but informative speakers may also occasionally use a causal pattern (see Chapter 13).

Problem-Solution Patterns

The problem-solution pattern is most common in persuasive or political speeches. In such a speech, you might identify an important problem, then propose a solution that you hope the audience will endorse. You might use this approach in proposing

Watch the Video "Emergency Preparedness" at **MyCommunicationLab**

solutions to such problems as credit card fraud, the rise in eating disorders among college students, or the unregulated selling of drugs over the Internet.

Reflective Thinking Sequence The traditional problem-solution pattern is based on educational philosopher John Dewey's Reflective Thinking Sequence[6] and typically addresses these questions:

1. How shall we define and limit the problem?
2. What are the causes and extent of the problem?
3. What are the effects of the problem? Who has been hurt?
4. What are the criteria by which solutions should be judged?
5. What are the possible solutions and the relative strengths and weaknesses of each?
6. What is the best solution?
7. How can we put it into effect?

Depending on the problem and the audience's prior knowledge, you might spend more or less time discussing the nature of the problem and its contributing causes. In situations where the audience is well versed on the problem, you might only briefly describe it and spend most of your speaking time exploring viable solutions.

The following is an example of ideas from a student speech that employs a problem-solution pattern:

Specific purpose: *I want my audience to join in the effort to stop deforestation.*
Thesis statement: *Deforestation must be stopped before its adverse effects make the world unfit for future generations.*

   I. *Problem (causes):* Deforestation has accelerated in recent years for a variety of reasons.
     A. One cause of deforestation is agriculture, which clears forests for farming.
     B. Another cause is cattle ranching, which needs land for grazing.
     C. In developing countries, people still cut down large numbers of trees for shelter and firewood.
     D. In general, overpopulation drives new development that threatens our remaining forests.
  II. *Problem (effects):* The effects of deforestation are often devastating.
     A. With more than 50 percent of the world's plants and animals living in 7 percent of the world's forests, most of them are headed for extinction—thus significantly decreasing biodiversity.
     B. Deforestation also leads to serious erosion and flooding.
     C. Some experts argue that perhaps the most serious effect of deforestation is global warming.
 III. *Criteria for solutions:* The solutions may be weighed against such criteria as feasibility, affordability, and fairness.
 IV. *Possible solutions:* We can take a number of actions to help end deforestation.
     A. We can support *reforestation* legislation, which would prohibit clear-cutting in designated areas and allow trees to grow back naturally.

B. We can tackle population control—by educating developing countries concerning birth control and acting responsibly in building our own families.

C. We can inform others about the problem while setting a good example by not wasting paper and other forest products.

V. *Best course of action:* In this case, all three solutions are interrelated, and all should be pursued. Some actions are personal and immediate; others are more long-range and deal with developing new policies and educational outreach.

The Motivated Sequence as a Special Problem-Solution Pattern   One specific approach to organizing a problem-solution speech is the motivated sequence.[7] This pattern is organized around five steps:

1. *Arouse:* Capture the audience's attention and focus on the problem.
2. *Dissatisfy:* Make listeners understand that this is a serious problem that needs their attention and action.
3. *Gratify:* Reveal the solution to the problem, and assure listeners that it is within *their* power to remedy the situation.
4. *Visualize:* Show listeners *exactly* how much they can improve the situation.
5. *Move:* Appeal to the audience to take a specific action.

The motivated sequence is best suited to topics with emotional as well as logical appeal. It may work best in a speech on the need for safe housing for domestic abuse victims, or on reducing the practice of euthanizing shelter animals, or on creating after-school programs for at-risk teens. The motivated sequence allows you to engage the audience's emotions and urge them to act. It addresses the problem *and* the solution, but it concludes with an appeal designed to motivate the audience to *act.* Above all, it aims to convince the audience that they have the *power* to act, and it helps them visualize *how* they can address the problem in specific ways. Visualizing the outcomes as you conclude the speech can be especially moving. Your own passion and commitment, an awareness of the audience's needs and values, and a thorough understanding of the details of your solution are central to the effective use of this problem-solution pattern.

Narrative Patterns

Because of cultural background or personal preference, some speakers may prefer to use less direct and more organic patterns of organization.[8] For instance, a speech may be organized around telling one or more stories, using a narrative pattern. Rhetorical scholar Walter Fisher points out that the most compelling narratives are coherent, rather than scattered or fragmented.[9] The speaker may begin by introducing a theme, such as the idea that the best government leaders are highly ethical. Then, the speaker would share various stories to illustrate and reinforce the speech's thesis. Or, he or she might pay tribute to a single person by sharing an extended narrative of the person's life. The speech is a continuous narrative with various internal stories drawn out and emphasized. Each would relate to an overarching theme, perhaps by demonstrating how the person being honored lived a courageous life. Narratives should also possess what Fisher calls fidelity—that is, they must "ring

On November 2, 2006, Amanda Cunningham spoke at a Habitat for Humanity fund-raising breakfast. In her moving speech, she shares the story of her parents' courage and determination and reveals how they qualified to become Habitat homeowners. Using a narrative pattern, this speech also functions as a tribute to Amanda's parents and offers testimonial evidence of the impact of Habitat for Humanity on the lives of real people.

My name is Amanda Cunningham. I am a student at Ivy Tech. My parents, Mark and Kim Cunningham, and I are a Habitat for Humanity partner family. Let me tell you a little bit about us. My parents were high school sweethearts and have been married for 24 years now. My dad was laid off from Otis Elevator in 1991 and decided to accept a job offer in Florida to support our family. At the age of 29, two years after moving to Florida, my dad was diagnosed with a rare type of cancer in his sinus cavity. The news from the doctors was not good; they gave my dad a small chance of survival.

After months and months of radiation treatments, the tumor had decreased in size. My brother and I were so young that we do not remember our dad being anything but sick. I remember him coming home from his radiation treatments being so tired that he would just fall asleep on the sofa. I watched him have seizures and feed himself through a tube in his nose.

My dad got very sick, but my mom stood beside him, never once giving up. Mom was not only trying to keep her and Dad's spirits up, but she was also trying to raise two small children and work her job. She ended up working long hours, seven days a week. My dad went through treatments for cancer the entire time we were in Florida. After six years there, we decided to move home to Indiana. We did not know whether the cancer was gone or not.

My dad is now 43 years old. The cancer has been in remission for 14 years, and he has completed college. The years of treatments have left him cancer-free, but his health is not perfect. The effects from the radiation treatments have been significant. Dad is now speech, hearing and visually impaired, and is fed through a tube in his stomach. His immune system is not as strong as all of ours, and we are not ever sure if or when he will end up sick and in the hospital.

My parents are the strongest people I will ever know. Their strength is not only an inspiration to my brother and me, but has also given us a solid foundation for our lives. There *are* heroes left in this world, and I count my parents among them. Giving up has never been an option for our family. Whenever a door closed on my parents, they continued to search for one that was open.

The trailer we live in is cold. It has no insulation and drafty windows and doors. The roof leaks and we have to be careful where we walk because the floor is giving way. It has been our home for the last seven years, and we have been looking for any opportunity to get into a better situation.

That opportunity was provided by Habitat for Humanity. Our family has never been looking for a handout, but rather a hand up. Habitat for Humanity offered us more than the opportunity for a place to live. It offered us an opportunity to help ourselves. *Finally*, my parents will have a home to call their own. You cannot imagine how it feels to know that my parents are going to have a home again. I speak for everyone in my family when I say that Habitat for Humanity of Monroe County is a blessing.

As blessings go, the best of blessings are those that bless others as well. We know as a family that being part of Habitat for Humanity is being part of a bigger family that offers hope for more families that need a window of opportunity like us. We can't wait to start building our home with Habitat this spring!

Now, I would like to introduce you to my parents: Mark and Kim Cunningham.

true" with the stories that listeners know to be true in their own lives.[10] For example, a speaker might explore the meaning of *courage* by sharing a series of stories of courageous acts. While those acts might be admirable and unusual, they must also seem plausible to the audience if they are to "ring true."

If the speaker wants to build in a sense of drama or climax within a narrative pattern, he or she may choose to use a spiraling narrative. For instance, the speaker might give a speech of tribute by sharing stories that build in intensity. A person's simple acts of courage might be shared first, moving to more unusual acts, and perhaps culminating with uncommon acts of valor. Again, each would be united by the general theme. When delivered effectively, narrative patterns can contribute to a powerful, engaging presentation.

This list of organizational patterns is not exhaustive, but it does include the principal ways in which you can arrange your ideas. Some patterns of organization work best with informative speeches, whereas others work better with persuasive speeches. And some topics lend themselves to a chronological or a spatial pattern of organization better than others. In the final analysis, however, it is important to recognize that there is never just one "correct" way to organize a given speech. As you prepare your speech, you may experiment with various ways of arranging your ideas until you come upon the organizational pattern that seems to work best.

GUIDELINES FOR ORGANIZING YOUR SPEECH

8.3 List and explain underlying principles of sound organization you will follow, regardless of the specific pattern you choose.

Preview. *Regardless of the particular pattern of organization you choose, you will want to keep in mind some basic guidelines. It is important to view the choice of an organizational pattern as a strategic decision. At the same time, you will want to consider issues of balance, the number of main ideas to include in your speech, and where to place your strongest, most compelling ideas and information.*

Given the wide variety of organizational patterns from which you can choose, you should keep a few general principles in mind. Select your organizational pattern carefully.

Making the Pattern a Strategic Choice

The way you present your ideas and information should be *strategic*, designed to enhance the chance that you will elicit the audience response you are seeking. If you are talking to an audience about a problem that is quite complicated or one with which they have little knowledge or experience, you will want to devote a good portion of your speech to educating your listeners. A good organizational strategy in this case may be a traditional problem-solution pattern—one in which you devote substantial time to defining and exploring the problem and its causes and effects *before* moving on to propose possible solutions.

Developing Main Ideas with a Concern for Symmetry

Second, give some thought to symmetry or balance. If the idea you are addressing is one of your speech's main points, then you will want to explore it thoroughly and offer a well-developed, substantive treatment. Sometimes you may be discussing an idea that is particularly controversial or complex, so you may need to devote a bit more time to it. In general, however, you should advance the main ideas of your speech in a balanced way, giving each one the emphasis it deserves so that your listeners will understand, recall, and hopefully be moved by what you are saying.

Determining the Number of Main Ideas

Sometimes speakers have questions about how many main ideas they can convey in a single speech. In doing research on an engaging topic, the speaker may be tempted to cover a long list of key points. But including too many main ideas may result in the inadequate development of each. To some extent, the time allowed for the speech will influence how many main ideas can be fully developed. If you are delivering a six- to eight-minute speech (as is common in the classroom), you may be hard-pressed to cover more than two or three main points adequately. A twenty-minute presentation (perhaps in a community setting) may allow you to advance a larger number of main ideas (usually no more than five). But there are two constraints to keep in mind. First, many listeners cannot absorb a large number of main ideas during a single presentation. In addition, a well-formulated specific purpose statement should limit and focus the speech. You can test each idea you are considering by asking whether it advances your speech's specific purpose. If it does not, you will want to eliminate it.

Choosing the Placement of Main Ideas

Finally, be aware of primacy and recency effects. Although researchers do not agree on whether arguments are more memorable and persuasive if they are placed first (primacy) or last (recency), they *do* agree that those two positions are the most powerful—and that information or arguments embedded in the middle of a message are less likely to be as memorable or have as much impact on listeners.[11] In most instances, then, you will want to lead with and conclude with information and ideas that are especially crucial to the case you are making.

TRANSITIONS AS CONNECTIVES

Preview. *Transitions add clarity and smoothness to a speech. Without strong transitions, even a well-organized speech may strike listeners as confusing or disorganized. When crafted well, transitions can contribute significantly to the impact of the speaker's overall message.*

As a responsible speaker, you need to help the audience see the relationships among your ideas. Once you have drafted your speech, you must consider how you will progress from one idea to another so that listeners can see the connections.

A transition is a bridge that connects one idea to another. Listeners cannot be expected to pay complete attention to the speaker, nor can they be expected to understand the sequence of ideas and information as clearly as the speaker does. You must alert your listeners to a new idea about to be introduced and help them see how it relates to your overall message.

As structural elements, transitions are small but mighty. They are, perhaps, the most unappreciated and underused components of effective speech making.

8.4 Describe different transitional devices you might use in creating a coherent presentation.

Explore the Concept "Better Transitions" at **MyCommunicationLab**

A transition links one major idea with another in a speech, showing their relationship to each other. However, a transition does more than show how an idea fits into a speech. It also reinforces an idea that a speaker wishes to share. Transitions often provide a quick glance back at the idea just discussed and then a quick look forward to the next main idea. A transition, then, may function as a miniature review and preview of ideas, reinforcing key ideas in the speech.[12] For example, a speaker identifying factors that have contributed to the rise in rates of type 2 diabetes may make the following two points:

I. Poor dietary choices have contributed to the rise of type 2 diabetes.
II. Sedentary lifestyles have contributed to the rise of type 2 diabetes.

A transition that bridges the two, simultaneously reinforcing the ideas, could be as follows:
Not only does a poor diet make developing type 2 diabetes more likely, so does a lack of exercise.

Sometimes, in longer, more intricately developed speeches, this reviewing and previewing should be done more extensively. When this is the case, the speaker can rely on an internal preview or an internal summary, both of which are extended transitions.

Internal Previews

Explore the Concept "Connecting to Key Ideas" at **MyCommunicationLab**

When moving from one idea to the next, you can give your audience a brief internal preview of the point you are about to make to help focus listeners' attention on what's to come. For example, suppose a speaker has just discussed this point: "Pollution of air and water in this community has direct consequences for your health." The next main idea he plans to take up is the following: "Pollution effects can drastically alter the standard of living in this country." To transition into this second point, he might combine a simple restatement of the first idea with an internal preview in this way:

> Pollution, then, can cost you (and those you love) your health. But its effects are even more far-reaching. If pollution isn't controlled now, drastic steps will have to be taken that will impact the way we live every day. Let us consider now the ways in which our standard of living is at risk because of pollution.

You may benefit from using an internal preview when you want to set the stage for a particular portion of your speech, perhaps by explaining *why* you will focus on the programs you have chosen. Suppose, for example, you have been addressing the problems with public education in the United States, with a particular focus on young children from low-income families. Now, you want to explore programs in your community that represent "best practices" in after-school programming for these children. To transition into this portion of your speech, you might say the following:

> Our community is filled with many interesting after-school programs for children. But three in particular have recently won awards for their excellence and creativity: the Boys and Girls Club After-Hours Program, the Girls, Inc. Leadership Program, and the Mother Hubbard's Cupboard Growing Food for Healthy Bodies Program. In the time that remains, I would like to focus on each of these programs and explore how they have truly enriched the lives of our children.

Internal Summaries

Sometimes, getting from one idea to another has to be more elaborate because the material is complex. In these cases, you may use an internal summary, briefly going over the information covered so far before moving on to the next point. A speaker who is advocating for green burials as an alternative to traditional funerals, for example, used an internal summary in her transition:

> As you can see, green burials are a growing trend in many parts of the United States, with certified green cemeteries in over forty states. We've seen how green burials help protect the environment and ecology by reducing the use of toxic chemicals, nonbiodegradable materials, and fossil fuels. We've seen pictures of peaceful green burial sites that are typically planted with natural grasses and wildflowers that require little or no maintenance. Now let's look at two other advantages of green burials: affordability and family members' feelings of involvement as they participate in laying their loved ones to rest.[13]

This kind of transition—a short summary of what has been said—helps keep the audience mentally on track. It also reinforces key ideas.

Sometimes internal summaries can be brief phrases embedded in new ideas. This is how one speaker used transitions to develop her first main idea in a speech on poverty and dental health:

I. Poor people with impaired dental health confront a variety of problems.
   A. Their general health can be at risk (including heart disease).
   B. *Not only can poor dental health lead to other serious health consequences,* it also adversely influences the individual's ability to get a job.
   C. *In addition to basic health and employment problems,* those with poor dental health often find it challenging to establish meaningful relationships with others in their daily lives.

These sample transitions illustrate how words and phrases can help listeners process information and ideas as they are advanced by the speaker.

Signposts

Watch the Video "The Process of Developing a Speech: Transitions" at **MyCommunicationLab**

In some instances, you may merely want to provide verbal markers to alert your audience to the fact that you are moving from one idea to another by enumerating each point or by signaling the next point to be made. If so, you can rely on what are known as signposts. You may, for example, tell your listeners that you have three good reasons for asking them to sign up for the Big Brothers/ Big Sisters program. You may simply say: "*The second reason* for you to sign up now is that the need is so urgent in our community." As you move into the third reason, you may go on to say: "*A final reason* for volunteering is that you will derive great satisfaction from knowing you have really made a difference in a child's life."

Other signposts include words such as *next, another,* and *finally.* Here are some examples:

"*The next* good reason is…"
"*Another* reason you should sign up is…"
"*Finally,* you should join now because…"

Rhetorical Questions

A speaker can also use rhetorical questions to highlight movement and assist flow, with the added benefit of encouraging listeners' involvement. Rhetorical questions stimulate thought and interest without seeking an oral response. Suppose a speaker has been discussing the need for a Volunteers in Medicine clinic in her community. She has described the medical services currently available in the area. As she moves on to address the issue of those who fall through the cracks of the present system, she asks, *But what happens if you have no health insurance? Who will take care of you when you are sick?*

These rhetorical questions should engage listeners' emotions and make them eager to hear what the speaker has to say. They should also encourage movement in the minds of the audience, allowing the speaker to focus their attention on the community's real need for a VIM clinic.

Taken together, these transitional devices help listeners make the right connections and follow the progression of ideas in your speech. In addition, transitions reinforce ideas and encourage listener involvement.

So far in the chapter, we have discussed organizational principles and approaches that largely apply to the way you will arrange the main ideas in the body of your speech. Now we turn our attention to how you will begin your speech. The effectiveness of your speech's introduction will likely influence the audience's frame of mind as you move into the presentation of your main ideas.

INTRODUCING YOUR SPEECH

8.5 Identify the key components of a speech's introduction.

Watch the Video "Jason Warren Discusses Tips for an Effective Introduction" at **MyCommunicationLab**

Preview.   *Although speech introductions may be structured in different ways, the most effective introductions establish common ground with the audience, capture and hold the listeners' attention, stress the relevance of your topic, establish your credibility as a speaker, clarify your purpose, and provide a preview of your ideas.*

No matter which organizational pattern you follow, you will need to introduce your speech in an effective way. It is not enough to say, "Today I am going to talk with you about why the community needs a free health clinic." Hardly any listener will be riveted by that. Instead, the introduction needs to be structured so that audience members *want* to listen to your speech, view you as a credible source, and have some idea of your speech's purpose and main ideas.

Establish Common Ground

Many speakers seek to establish common ground with listeners as they begin to speak. Audiences tend to listen to speakers with whom they share common experiences, problems, or goals. For example, when giving a speech on student loans in a class with several other working students, Yuko began her speech this way:

> When I get to this class at 8:00 A.M., I have had four hours' sleep. I work full-time as a waitress at Nick's and do not get home until about 2:00 A.M. Like many of you, I need to work to support myself while going to school. Some of you have full-time jobs and some are part-timers. Some of you also have families to care for as well as working and going to school. And I know that at least one of you is also a single parent. For us, getting an education and making ends meet is not easy.

In speaking contexts outside the classroom, the speaker may also want to emphasize similarities between himself or herself and the audience. Perhaps the speaker is perceived as someone whose life experiences have differed significantly from those of the audience. In this case, establishing common ground with listeners creates a sense of "we-ness" that invites the audience to listen. In 1993, President Bill Clinton addressed the convention of the Church of God in Christ in Memphis, Tennessee, speaking from the pulpit where Martin Luther King had given his last sermon. This white president used the occasion to connect with the African-American community by stressing their common goals.

> By the grace of God and your help, last year I was elected President of this great country. I never dreamed that I would ever have a chance to come to this hallowed place where Martin Luther King gave his last sermon. I ask you to think today about the purpose for which I ran and the purpose for which so many of you worked to put me in this great office. I have worked hard to keep faith with our common efforts: to restore the economy, to reverse the politics of helping only those at the top of our totem pole and not the hard-working middle class or the poor; to bring our people together across racial and regional and political lines, to make a strength out of our diversity instead of letting it tear us apart; to reward work and family and community and try to move us forward into the 21st century. I have tried to keep faith.[14]

Establishing common ground (together with other devices described in upcoming sections) may also engage the audience's attention and make them want to hear more.

Capture and Maintain the Listeners' Attention

When you first get up to speak, listeners usually give you their full attention. But that attention may be fleeting. Let us consider several approaches to maintaining the audience's attention and how some speakers have used them.

Watch the Video "Investing in Our Future" at **MyCommunicationLab**

Tell a Story An interesting story—whether it is emotional, humorous, puzzling, or intriguing—commands attention. The story can be real or hypothetical. It can be a personal story that reveals something of your own experience, or it can be something you have read. Speaking to a group of teachers, Carmen Mariano, an assistant superintendent in the Massachusetts public school system, began with this narrative:

> Ernest Hemingway tells the story of a Spanish man who has a bitter argument one morning with his young son, Paco. When he arrived home later that day, the man discovered that Paco's room was empty—he had run away from home.

> Overcome with remorse, the man realized that his son was more important to him than anything else. He went to a well-known grocery store in the center of town and posted a large sign that read, "Paco, come home. I love you. Meet me here tomorrow morning. Signed, your father."

> The next morning, the man went to the store. There, he found his son and seven other young boys who had also run away from home. They were all answering the call for love, hoping it was their dad inviting them home.[15]

Mariano used this opening to lead into the point that teaching children who come from tension-filled homes where they do not feel loved or wanted is a great challenge for teachers in the public school system.

Use Rhetorical Questions   Earlier in the chapter, we discussed how rhetorical questions may assist movement in a speech and encourage involvement. Similarly, in an introduction, rhetorical questions can prompt listeners to think about an issue or idea without seeking an immediate response.

Lin began his speech by raising questions that challenged listeners to consider how they might deal with ethical dilemmas:

> This is an honors public speaking class, and, as honors students, we're all used to getting good grades. Grades are very important to us and we can be very competitive. Well, you might not kill for an A—but, what *would* you do for an A? Would you consider peeking at the answers to someone's exam if you had the chance to do so and were sure you wouldn't get caught? Would you tell a professor that he or she made a mistake in grading an exam if it meant that your grade was lowered? Would you let a friend write a short paper for you and turn it in as your own? Can you think of any time when you've done something that you wouldn't like anyone else to know about to get a good grade? If we're perfectly honest with ourselves, we know that these questions are not so easy to answer in a "socially acceptable" way. Maybe you've never cheated or plagiarized or lied to a friend—but, have you ever been tempted?

Lin's audience will likely find their thinking stimulated by these rhetorical questions that relate directly to their lives as students.

Begin with a Memorable Quotation   No doubt someone has said or written something that captures the thesis of your speech. The idea has been expressed so well, perhaps by a person whom the audience respects and admires, that you know it will get the listeners' interest and attention right away. An esteemed scholar, scientist, or political figure can be quoted. Or you can use the words of a popular entertainer, author, athlete, singer, or other well-known and highly respected figure.

As a concerned citizen, David wanted to persuade his audience to volunteer with a new community initiative called New Leaf, New Life. The program sought to make the local jail a more humane and educational environment and to provide mentors for prisoners who were about to be released. David began his speech by quoting the famous nineteenth-century union organizer and Socialist Party presidential candidate Eugene V. Debs:

> Eugene V. Debs devoted most of his life to seeking justice for the most vulnerable members of society. Debs once said, "While there is a lower class, I am in it; while there is a criminal element, I am of it; and while there is a soul in prison, I am not free."[16]

By quoting Debs, the speaker hoped to move his listeners to seek social justice by participating in what he described as a life-altering program.

Use Humor   Some speakers like to begin a speech with a humorous story, but you need to approach humor with caution. No matter how funny a story may be, it must also be relevant to the point you want to make. Just telling a few jokes is not a good way to begin a speech, and a joke that falls flat is embarrassing. Humor should never be disrespectful or aimed at ridiculing someone or something, so you need to be careful. In the following introduction, Richard Lamm, representing the University of Denver's Center for Public Policy and Contemporary Issues, began his speech to the World Future Society by telling the story of a priest who ended up sitting next to a drunk while riding the subway. The man was disheveled and smelled strongly of liquor. At the same time, he was deeply engrossed in reading a newspaper. Lamm continues:

> After a few minutes, the man turned to the priest and asked. "Excuse me, Father, what causes arthritis?"
>
> [Without hesitation] the priest said roughly, "Loose living, drink, dissipation, contempt for your fellow man and being with cheap and wicked women!"
>
> "That's amazing," said the drunk [as he] returned to his newspaper.
>
> A while later, the priest, feeling a bit guilty, turned to the man and asked nicely, "How long have you had arthritis?"
>
> "Oh," said the man, "I don't have arthritis. I was just reading that the pope did."
>
> The parable, of course, is a lesson on assumptions.[17]

Of course, these techniques are not mutually exclusive; you can use several at once. You may, for example, tell an interesting story that also establishes common ground and arouses curiosity. And you will want to deliver the introduction effectively. For example, pausing after telling a compelling story, posing an engaging rhetorical question, or sharing a memorable quotation may help listeners ponder what you are about to say. The key factor is capturing and holding the audience's attention and interest.

Stress Relevance

Either consciously or unconsciously, your listeners will ask themselves why they should care about your topic. Even when we find something interesting, we soon begin to wonder whether it has any relevance to us or any real impact on the lives of those we care about. In the introduction, you should take the time to establish the significance of your topic, answering for your audience such questions as, "What does this have to do with me?" or "How will this course of action make for a better world?"

Sarah, a student speaker, wanted to get her audience to take an active role in the university's new fund-raiser, the Dance Marathon. In her introduction, she emphasized how her classmates could make a real difference in the lives of children while participating in a wonderful, truly engaging event. She pointed out that dance marathons had been held on campuses around the country, such as Penn State and Indiana University, for quite a few years. This year, however, was to be Southeast Missouri State's first year to host such an event. Here is how she emphasized the importance of her topic:

> Why would anyone force themselves to dance for 48 hours? The student who chaired the Dance Marathon steering committee at Indiana University put it this way: "Dance Marathon is about learning what is a priority in life....A true priority in someone's life should be giving back to others who need your help." As a dancer, you too can discover the incredible experience of knowing you helped save children's lives. One dancer summed up his experience like this: "I love this. My feet hurt, but the feeling in my heart won't go

away." When you participate in the Dance Marathon, you are raising money for the Children's Miracle Network. Money from our marathon will be split between St. Louis Children's Research Hospital and Cardinal Glennon Children's Miracle Center in St. Louis. I have known several children who have been patients at these hospitals, and I know you have too.[18]

No one listening to these introductory remarks could fail to see the importance of this cause and how it could positively impact their lives as well as the lives of countless children.

Well known for his courageous actions during the civil rights movement, Congressman John Lewis possesses strong credibility on issues of social justice and human rights.

Establish Your Credibility

The audience should know of any special relationship you have with the topic that would enhance your ethos. Of course, credibility is an ongoing issue throughout any speech, but the introduction represents an especially critical time for establishing your credentials. For seasoned professionals, this process may be less daunting. We expect doctors to know about medicine, attorneys to know about law, and accountants to be able to answer questions about our taxes. For student speakers, however, establishing ethos can be more challenging.

Yet student speakers can establish their ethos in compelling ways. Let us look at how one student did it. In her speech urging students to volunteer for a summer work project, Kristin began by relating her own experience:

Last year I took a different kind of summer vacation. I did not go to the beach to try to get a fabulous tan. I did not go to a lake and learn to water-ski. I did not go to a big city to visit museums and see shows. I went to a hot, dry desert. There was no air conditioning anywhere. After a night spent sleeping in a sleeping bag on a bare floor, I got up, had breakfast, got into an old truck with about a dozen other kids and took off over a dusty road to a house that badly needed repair. In the hot sun I helped plug cracks in the wall, learned how to mix and apply plaster, and stripped and painted peeling boards.

I did this for nothing. Well, that isn't right. I did not get paid money, but I did get something a lot more valuable. Working as a volunteer in a remote town in an Indian reservation, I learned so many things about a different culture. I made close friends among the people I worked with. I helped to make a real difference in real people's lives. I came back from this experience a different—and richer—person than I was when I went. I am going to tell you today how you can enrich your life, too.

Having established her credibility, this speaker is well positioned to use her personal experience to convince her listeners that they should get involved as well.

If you lack the kind of direct topic-related experience illustrated in the preceding example, you can still establish your credibility as a student speaker by telling your audience that you have had a long-standing interest in your topic and have become motivated to do further research to learn even more about it. You may briefly explain what sparked your interest and then go on to show listeners that you really *are* knowledgeable, widely read, and able to respond to challenging questions.

Clarify Your Purpose/Advance Your Thesis

A key function of the introduction is to advance your speech's thesis—stating, in a single declarative statement, the central idea of your speech. By articulating your thesis as part of the introduction, you help the audience discern your central theme, overarching point, or principal argument. No speaker wants to move into the body of the speech with the audience still wondering, "What's the point? Where is this going?"

One speaker, Joel, decided to give a persuasive speech about the U.S. prison system.[19] In his introduction, he pointed out that the U.S. prison population has increased dramatically over the past 35 years. He noted that one out of every 200 U.S. residents is incarcerated, resulting in steeply rising prison costs.[20] He then advanced his thesis: *The government needs to reform the U.S. prison system.* He went on to argue for lighter sentences, a reduction in mandatory sentencing, and an increased emphasis on rehabilitation.

Often, the thesis statement is soon followed by a preview of the speaker's main ideas.

Preview Your Main Points

Before moving into the body of your speech, you should provide a preview. The preview introduces your main ideas, offering a road map so that listeners can more easily follow your speech. In previewing, you are also signaling what you feel is most important—those things you want the audience to remember and reflect on long after you have finished speaking. By providing a preview, you increase the likelihood they will.[21] If, after giving your preview, you follow through with your plan, you will have further enhanced your credibility by demonstrating your careful organization and preparation.

Consider, for example, the speech given by a student speaker, Erin, whose thesis was as follows: *Students should explore exciting alternatives to traditional college majors before making a final choice.* The speaker began by reminding her audience that more than two-thirds of college students change majors before settling on a final plan of study—some switching three or more times. She pointed out "Many of us think we have to choose a major in a traditional area, such as accounting, English, computer science, or education. But that's not necessarily the case." She then went on to preview the ideas she would develop:

> There are three exciting programs at our university that offer creative alternatives to the traditional college major, and these may be of interest to you if you have not yet found your niche here at I.U. First is LAMP, the Liberal Arts and Management Program, which combines a strong liberal arts education with specialized business skills and knowledge. Second is PACE, the Political and Civic Engagement program which helps you develop skills for participating

in political and civic life. Finally, there is the Individualized Major program, where you literally design your own major from scratch—choosing from courses all over the university.[22]

Having forecast what she planned to do in the speech, the speaker's challenge was to deliver on the promise by developing each point she mentioned in the preview.

Final Tips about Introductions

Remember the power of *first impressions*. Part of your first impression as a speaker will be based on the way you introduce your speech. Following are some tips to keep in mind:

- Craft your introduction with care. Most speakers wait until after they have outlined the body of the speech to develop the introduction. For instance, they may experiment with several different attention-getting devices before they settle on the one they feel is most compelling.
- The length of the introduction will vary with the needs of the speaking situation. Some formal events require the speaker to offer an introduction that refers to the events at hand and acknowledges or thanks several significant persons related to the event. Usually, however, introductions should be *brief*. We have all heard speakers who ramble on for some time, and then say, after ten minutes or so, "What I'd like to talk about today is…" This can prompt the frustrated listener to tune out.
- Each introduction should be tailored to the situation. If the person introducing you fully establishes your credibility, for example, you may have little need of augmenting what has already been said. If the audience is already keenly aware of the significance of the problem you are addressing, you will not need to offer an elaborate justification. Instead, you may simply say, "We are all aware of the urgency of the problem that has brought us here tonight." In short, each introduction should be crafted not according to a formula but based on the demands of the topic, the listeners, and the situation.
- If you develop your introduction carefully and deliver it effectively, you will set the stage for the audience to attend to the main ideas that you will develop throughout the rest of your speech. A strong introduction makes the audience want to hear more.

Bringing your speech to an effective conclusion is also important. Sometimes speakers primarily think about how to arrange and present their main ideas, without paying attention to what they will say at the end of their speech. Yet the conclusion is the last thing the audience hears. If it is memorable and compelling, the conclusion can truly enhance the overall impact of the speech.

Watch the Video "Jason Warren Discusses Tips for an Effective Conclusion" at **MyCommunicationLab**

8.6 List different ways of concluding a speech effectively.

CONCLUDING YOUR SPEECH

Preview. *Carefully planning your speech's conclusion is an essential part of preparing to speak. By summarizing your main ideas, challenging your audience, appealing to your audience, visualizing the future, using good quotations, or referring to the introduction—or by using a combination of these techniques—you can craft an effective ending for your speech.*

Many speakers do not really conclude their speeches—they simply stop talking. Others may stumble through their concluding remarks, reducing the effectiveness of the presentation. Sometimes speakers say something like, "Well, I guess that's about it. Any questions?" The conclusion is very important. If you construct it properly, you will bring your speech to a strategic close and create a final positive impact.

As you approach the speech's conclusion, you will want to signal to the audience that you are, in fact, concluding. One of the major vehicles for signaling the conclusion is a summary of your main points.

Summarize Your Ideas

Summaries are especially important when the speech is complex or long. The summary reinforces your ideas and reminds the audience of your most important points. When combined with the preview in your introduction and the development of each main idea in the body of your speech (including the transitions that connect them), the summary provides a final chance to reiterate key ideas and help the audience remember them.

Watch the Video
"The Process of
Developing a Speech:
Conclusions: Using a Summary"
at **MyCommunicationLab**

Summaries are often used in conjunction with another concluding device. In the summary that follows, Patti, a long-time volunteer with a local nonprofit agency, the Shalom Community Center, offers a summary and extended quotation as she concludes her speech:

> I hope I have been able to help you better understand what critical services the Shalom Community Center provides for people experiencing extreme poverty and homelessness in our community. Shalom offers the basics: food for the hungry—serving breakfast and lunch every weekday, shelter during the day where guests can take a shower, do their laundry, store their belongings, and receive their mail, *and* opportunities for day-by-day problem-solving and empowerment.
>
> As part of their mission statement, Shalom lists their basic values on their Web site. I think they really capture the essence of Shalom:
>
> 1. *Hospitality*—We extend community beyond the margins to include those unserved by society. We invite all people into our safe and welcoming space.
> 2. *Dignity*—We value the worth and dignity of every person, treating all with compassion and respect. We honor the lives, concerns, and stories of people who have been marginalized by society and expect our staff, volunteers and guests to do the same.
> 3. *Empowerment*—We strive to increase the economic and social strength of people in need. We help people develop confidence in their own capacities. We support people in making choices that improve the quality of their lives.
> 4. *Hope*—We believe in the possibility each person possesses to create a sustainable, healthy, and happy life. We work to nurture that hope in all people.[23]
>
> Shalom is a special place. I hope you will join me at the next Shalom open house and Community Conversation on May 10. You will be able to take a tour, meet Shalom's new executive director, chat with volunteers and guests, and learn how you can become involved in serving the most vulnerable citizens of our community.

The speaker then distributed a flyer that offered details about the Community Conversation (including time and place) and provided agency contact information.

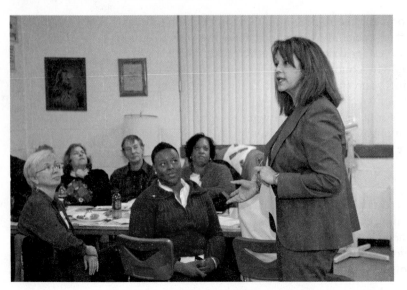

Speakers who feel strongly about their topic will make every effort to challenge their listeners to act.

Challenge Your Audience

Most of the time, summaries do not stand alone. Often they are—or should be—accompanied by some other interesting concluding device. One device that can be effective is a challenge to the audience to act on what you have said. This was the strategy used by then-senator Barack Obama in his keynote speech to the 2004 Democratic Convention:

> Hope—Hope in the face of difficulty. Hope in the face of uncertainty. The audacity of hope!

In the end, that is God's greatest gift to us, the bedrock of this nation. A belief in things not seen. A belief that there are better days ahead.

I believe that we can give our middle class relief and provide working families with a road to opportunity.

I believe we can provide jobs to the jobless, homes to the homeless, and reclaim young people in cities across America from violence and despair.

I believe that we have a righteous wind at our backs and that as we stand on the crossroads of history, we can make the right choices, and meet the challenges that face us.

America! Tonight, if you feel the same energy that I do, if you feel the same urgency that I do, if you feel the same passion that I do, if you feel the same hopefulness that I do—if we do what we must do, then I have no doubt that all across the country, from Florida to Oregon, from Washington to Maine, the people will rise up in November…and this country will reclaim its promise, and out of this long political darkness a brighter day will come.[24]

Appeal to Your Audience

In your conclusion, you can make a final attempt to move your audience to act or believe more strongly about your proposition. Speaking to an audience of representatives of companies honored as *Parents* magazine's "Best Companies for Working Families," Richard Lamm concluded his speech with this appeal:

> I close with a metaphor on the need for cooperation and community.…The metaphor is an Amazon legend which tells of a priest who was speaking with God about heaven and hell.

> "I will show you hell," said God.

> They went into a room that had a delicious beef stew on the table, around which sat people chained to their benches and who looked desperately famished. They held spoons with long handles that reached into the pot, but were too long to put the stew back into their mouths. Their suffering was terrible.

"Now, I will show you heaven," said God.

They then went into an identical room with the savory stew on the table, around which sat people with identical spoons and handles, but they were well nourished and joyous.

The priest was baffled until God said, "Quite simply, you see, these people have learned to feed each other."[25]

Lamm's appeal is for the audience to recognize their responsibility for taking care of *everyone* who is part of the organizational family.

Visualize the Future

In a speech in which you advocate important changes, visualizing the results of those changes is an especially appropriate and powerful way to conclude. This device (which is built into the motivated sequence) allows you to picture or imagine the projected results of your ideas in an appealing way. In a speech delivered to a large group of students at Liberty Baptist University, the late Senator Edward M. Kennedy concluded his speech by offering this compelling vision of America:

I hope for an America where neither "fundamentalist" nor "humanist" will be a dirty word, but a fair description of the different ways in which people of goodwill look at life and into their own souls.

I hope for an America where no president, no public official, no individual will ever be deemed a greater or lesser American because of religious doubts—or religious beliefs.

I hope for an America where the power of faith will always burn brightly, but where no modern Inquisition of any kind will ever light the fires of fear, coercion, or angry division.

I hope for an America where we can all contend freely and vigorously, but where we will treasure and guard those standards of civility which alone make this nation safe for both democracy and diversity.[26]

Kennedy then goes on to invite his listeners, many whose views differed sharply from the speaker's in terms of politics and religion, "to live peaceably with men and women everywhere."

End with a Quotation

Ending your speech with a good quotation can help reinforce your thesis and restate the major points you made. Poetry, plays, songs, speeches, and literary works can all supply effective quotations. Quotations should be pertinent, compelling, and brief. In his speech to the nation on October 1, 1979, President Jimmy Carter concluded with a striking quotation:

The struggle for peace—the long, hard struggle to bring weapons of mass destruction under the control of human reason and human law—is the central drama of our age.

At another time of challenge in our nation's history, President Abraham Lincoln told the American people: "We shall nobly save, or meanly lose, the last best hope of earth."

We acted wisely then, and preserved the nation. Let us act wisely now, and preserve the world.[27]

Refer to the Introduction

You can achieve a sense of symmetry and reinforce your major theme by coming back to the introduction in the conclusion of your speech. This commonly happens when a speaker uses both a preview and a summary, but you can find more interesting ways to do this, often by using one of the techniques we have already discussed in the chapter. For example, you may return to a story, quotation, or rhetorical question that you used in the opening.

Consider the following example from a speech given by Robert C. Purcell, executive director of General Motors Advanced Technology Vehicles, at the 1998 MBA Recognition Ceremony at the Kelly School of Business, Indiana University. He had introduced his speech with a riveting story from May 1961, in which a group of black and white students, riding on a bus together, were attacked by an angry white mob. One young black seminary student, John Lewis, was nearly killed. His life was saved only because a white Alabama public safety officer, Floyd Mann, chased off the crowd by firing shots into the air. Purcell concluded his speech like this:

> There's a postscript to the story I shared with you when I began today. Not long ago, John Lewis, the young seminary student, returned to Alabama, to the site of that historic attack 37 years ago, for the dedication of a civil rights memorial....By that time, Lewis had a long and distinguished career.
>
> As we waited for the ceremony to begin, an older gentleman, who seemed vaguely familiar, came over to him.
>
> "You're John Lewis, aren't you?" the man said. "I remember you from the Freedom Rides."
>
> It was Floyd Mann—the same Floyd Mann who had waded into that mob with his revolver, more than 35 years before.
>
> Lewis was overcome with emotion. "You saved my life," he said. And then he embraced Floyd Mann. Not sure as he did so, if even then, black men and white men hugged each other in contemporary Alabama.
>
> But Mann hugged him back, and John Lewis began to cry.
>
> And as the two men released each other, Floyd Mann looked at Lewis and said, "You know...I'm right proud of your career."
>
> And if there is one hope that I hold for each of you today—it is that 10 or 20 or 30 years from now, when you look back on your careers, you'll be just as proud.[28]

Many speakers use a combination of techniques. Patti combined a summary with an extended quotation. Barack Obama offered a challenge while also visualizing the future. Robert Purcell brought closure to his speech through an extended story that referred to his introduction. These combined approaches are fairly typical and often work more effectively than any one technique used alone.

Final Tips about Conclusions

Just as the introduction of your speech contributes to the audience's first impression of you, the conclusion represents your last chance to reach out to listeners and reinforce your speech's purpose. Guidelines to help you include the following:

- The conclusion should be *brief*; this is no place to introduce new information or to tack on something you forgot to say earlier.
- Speakers sometimes have trouble ending their speeches. A speaker may say, "Let me leave you with this thought," and then ramble on for several more minutes. Or the speaker may pepper his or her remarks with signposts such as *finally* or *in conclusion*—but not stop talking. Soon, listeners will become frustrated or bored. Even a good speech (and a good speaker) can lose ground if the conclusion is poorly crafted and delivered.
- You can signal to the audience that you are concluding by your content and your delivery. Offering a summary clearly communicates that you are approaching the end of your speech, as do signposts such as *finally* or *in closing*. You may also move physically closer to the audience and connect with them directly through eye contact and vocal expressiveness as you offer a concluding quotation, help them visualize the future, or call them to action. Your conclusion is your last opportunity to connect with your audience, and it should never be lost.

 Study and Review materials for this chapter are at **MyCommunicationLab**

SUMMARY

 Listen to the Audio Chapter Summary at **MyCommunicationLab**

The Elements of Sound Organization

8.1 Explain how the quality of your ideas influences the strength of your speech's organization.

- Effective speakers strive to organize their ideas carefully and strategically.
  - Well-organized speakers are usually viewed as competent and knowledgeable.
  - They are also viewed as being invested in their topic and respectful of the audience.
  - The better organized the speaker, the more likely the audience will learn from the speech and be influenced by it.
- The foundation of a well-organized speech is a set of main ideas that are clearly formulated.
  - Design ideas with a specific purpose in mind, making sure that they are clear, simple, and appropriate to the situation.

How Patterns Connect Ideas

8.2 Describe basic organizational patterns you might use as you arrange your ideas strategically.

- Ideas should be organized in a coherent and reasonable fashion. The principal patterns of organization follow:
  - Chronological or sequential (arranged in a time or step-by-step order)
  - Categorical (a pattern that emphasizes distinct topics)
  - Climactic (arranged according to importance, size, or degree of simplicity)
  - Causal (moving from causes to effects or from effects to causes)
  - Problem-solution (a logical progression that moves from perceived difficulties to an examination of alternatives to a best solution)
  - Narrative (based on a story-telling model)

Guidelines for Organizing Your Speech

8.3 List and explain underlying principles of organization you will follow, regardless of the specific pattern you choose.

- Every speech should be organized with underlying principles in mind.
  - Ideas and information should be presented strategically, always guided by the specific purpose of the speech.
  - Each idea should be well developed, with a concern for balance and symmetry.
  - Main ideas should relate directly to your specific purpose and should be limited in number.
  - The most important information and ideas should be presented first or last.

Transitions as Connectives

8.4 Describe different transitional devices you might use in creating a coherent presentation.

- A transition is a connective that provides a bridge as you move from one idea to another. Transitions include the following:
  - Internal previews
  - Internal summaries
  - Signposts
  - Rhetorical questions

Introducing Your Speech

8.5 Identify key components of a speech's introduction.

- Once you have chosen the basic organizational pattern and worked on good transitions, you are ready to think about how to introduce your speech. In most situations, your introduction should do the following:
- Establish common ground with the audience.
  - Capture and hold the audience's attention.
  - Show them why your topic is relevant to them.
  - Establish your credibility.
  - Advance the speech's purpose.
  - Preview your main ideas.

Concluding Your Speech

8.6 Describe different ways of concluding a speech effectively.

- Crafting an effective conclusion is also important. The conclusion is your last opportunity to connect with your audience and realize your specific purpose. Conclusions allow you to do the following:
  - Summarize your main ideas.
  - Challenge your audience.
  - Appeal to listeners.
  - Visualize the future.
  - Offer a memorable quotation.
  - Create balance and closure by referring to the introduction.

QUESTIONS FOR REVIEW AND REFLECTION

The Elements of Sound Organization

8.1 Explain how the quality of your ideas influences the strength of your speech's organization.

1. Why is good organization important?
2. In what ways does the purpose of your speech influence the main ideas?
3. What makes an idea a good one? Examine the main ideas you advanced in your last speech. How do they measure up in light of these criteria?

How Patterns of Organization Connect Ideas

8.2 Describe basic organizational patterns you might use as you arrange your ideas strategically.

4. What are the principal patterns of organization?
5. Why would you choose one pattern over another?

Guidelines for Organizing Your Speech

8.3 List and explain underlying principles of sound organization you will follow, regardless of the specific pattern you choose.

6. How might each of the following concepts be important to you as you go about organizing your next speech?
   a. Strategic organization
   b. Balance/symmetry
   c. The number of main ideas to include
   d. Primacy and recency effects

Transitions as Connectives

8.4 Describe different transitional devices you might use in creating a coherent presentation.

7. What is the function of transitions?
8. What are the different kinds of transitions that you might use as you move through your speech? Briefly define each, and describe whatever advantages each may offer.

Introducing Your Speech

8.5 Identify the key components of a speech's introduction.

9. What are the major components of the speech introduction? Why is each important?
10. Give some examples of how you might capture the listeners' attention in your introduction.
11. As you look toward your next speech, what preliminary ideas do you have for good ways to introduce your topic?

Concluding Your Speech

8.6 List different ways of concluding a speech effectively.

12. What should you accomplish in the conclusion to your speech?
13. What are some devices you might use to conclude your speech in an effective and compelling way?
14. Thinking of your next speech topic, begin to focus on what kind of device might work effectively in your conclusion. Offer an example of one quotation or other device that you might use.

 Study and Review the Flashcards at **MyCommunicationLab**

Outlining Your Speech

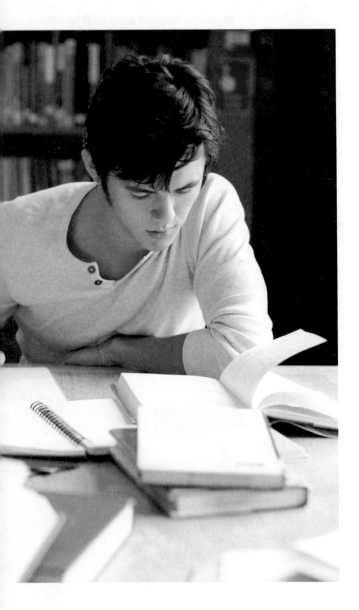

It is easy to view outlining as an academic exercise—something that is required by the instructor but serves no useful purpose. Yet by outlining, you can correct many mistakes in organizational strategy and the use of supporting material *before* you deliver your speech. Outlines can help you sort through ideas to determine which ones work well together. Outlines can also help you determine whether you need to conduct additional research. And outlines can enhance the effectiveness of your delivery.

The outline is something you will develop continuously as you prepare your speech. Most speakers construct a rough outline early, representing their initial thinking and ideas. Later, as they read widely and begin to choose some strategy of organization, the outline grows, changes, and is refined. The outline, then, *evolves* as your ideas emerge and you gather new information. Sometimes it is rearranged; often it is expanded to include more detail or support. The final formal outline will reflect all that has gone into the preparation of your speech.

TYPES OF OUTLINES

Preview. *An outline emerges from careful preparation. Working outlines include your first thoughts and evolving ideas; formal, full-sentence outlines contain fully developed ideas and support; and keyword outlines serve as notes for speakers.*

9.1 Describe the different types of outlines and the purposes served by each.

Although we have spoken of *the* outline, the reality is that you will use several different kinds of outlines as you prepare to speak. Although no two people prepare a speech in exactly the same way, outlining is always an invaluable tool. Through outlining, you can record your early thoughts, experiment with different organizational strategies, consider whether evidence "fits" by observing the relationship between ideas and supporting material, and improve the delivery of your speech.

Working Outlines

First, there is the working outline. This is the outline you develop as you brainstorm ideas, investigate your chosen topic, and reflect on your emerging views. You may change the working outline many times, inserting new information and revising and rearranging main ideas and supporting points. By examining your working outline, you can see if you have given each main idea the appropriate emphasis. You can also note whether you have developed your arguments with sufficient supporting material. You may choose to jot down your working outline(s) in longhand, or, if you prefer, enter your thoughts on your computer.

As you go through the *process* of developing and revising the working outline, you will use your thesis and specific purpose statements to determine which ideas and supporting material belong in your speech. When, for example, you examine some expert testimony or a statistic you think you might use, ask yourself, "How does this supporting material help me realize my specific purpose?" And ask: "To what extent and in what ways does it relate directly to my thesis?" If the answers to these questions are not clear to you, then the wisest route is to keep reading and looking for relevant support.

In short, the working outline is a kind of *diagnostic tool* that helps you see where you've been and where you are going and keeps you focused on your thesis and purpose. You will sketch out several versions of your working outline as you continue to read, learn, and think critically about your topic. Don't rush the process. If you devote time, effort, and critical thinking to your working outlines, they will naturally "flow" into the formal outline—the final product of your efforts.

Formal Outlines

When you have completed your research and are moving toward the delivery of your speech, your instructor may ask you to prepare a formal outline. This full-sentence representation of your speech will also include the bibliography of sources you consulted while preparing your speech. The formal outline displays your ideas and arguments as they are fully developed, complete with supporting material. It serves as a tangible symbol of the time, effort, and thought you have put into your speech.

The formal outline is also a final test for you—a last chance to look carefully and critically at the speech you plan to present. Do your main ideas relate directly to your thesis and specific purpose statement? Is the supporting material sufficient and compelling? Is anything missing or underdeveloped? When *you* are convinced that you have given your best efforts to creating the formal outline—the blueprint for your speech—you are ready to submit it to your instructor.

When your instructor examines your formal outline, he or she can assess whether you have done the following:

- Chosen an effective organizational strategy
- Achieved proper structure with coordinated thesis, main points, and transitions
- Consulted sufficient sources
- Developed your main ideas thoroughly

Sometimes instructors will offer feedback on your formal outline and give you the opportunity to revise it. Or, you and a classmate may be asked to exchange outlines and offer constructive feedback to one another. You can always alter and strengthen your speech right up until the time you must submit the outline in final form and deliver your speech. The more you are able to use the outline to evaluate your own work and incorporate feedback from others, the more you will see your organization improve.

We provide two sample formal outlines later in the chapter. One appears in the *Focus on Civic Engagement* feature on pages 217–219, and the other appears at the end of the chapter.

Keyword Outlines

You will typically use a keyword outline when you deliver your speech. A keyword outline is an abbreviated version of your formal outline, designed to remind you of the ideas you want to convey. You still may want to write out a few things completely, such as important transitions, key statistics, or exact quotations—to make sure you quote your sources accurately. When well constructed, a keyword outline enables you to deliver your speech effectively in an extemporaneous style.

Some speakers make the mistake of carefully preparing a formal outline and then throwing together a keyword outline at the last minute. They fail to allow sufficient time for practicing with their keyword outline. Practicing with your keyword outline is the key to a relaxed, conversational style of delivery. Practicing with your keyword outline also allows you to revise and refine your speaking notes until you feel confident about delivering the speech. Many speakers transfer their keyword outline to note cards for easier handling during delivery. A good example of a keyword outline appears in the *Focus on Civic Engagement* feature on pages 217–219.

BASIC PRINCIPLES OF OUTLINING

Preview. *A basic system of rules governs outlining. These principles identify the key components to be included in each formal outline and the use of consistent labeling through a system of universal symbols. They mandate focusing on one idea at a time in the speech's body and coherently developing ideas with supporting material. The keyword outline has guidelines of its own, such as using words sparingly, writing out key portions, and producing legible notes.*

Although nearly all of us have drafted an outline at some point in our lives, many remain confused about the proper way to develop a formal, full-sentence outline. Following the few simple principles discussed in the following sections will help.

Guidelines for Developing the Formal Outline

The principles that follow are not trivial. Rather, each one is aimed at getting you to think clearly about how your ideas are related, to examine the nature and extent of your supporting material, and to make sure that your ideas are coherently developed.

Include the Key Elements   The sample outlines that appear in the *Focus on Civic Engagement* feature (pages 217–219) and at the end of the chapter (pages 224–227) offer illustrations of outlines broken into distinct parts. Most formal outlines should include the following components, with each clearly labeled:

- **Speech title.** If you are preparing a classroom speech, your instructor may or may not be interested in having you list a title at the top of your outline. Outside the classroom, speakers are often asked to give the program planner a speech title. This title should be placed at the top of your formal outline.
- **Specific purpose and thesis statement.** Both the specific purpose and the thesis statement should be listed at the top of the outline. Articulating your central idea and specific purpose at the beginning allows anyone who reads your outline to discern whether your thesis is supported and your specific purpose advanced by the *way* you have organized and developed your speech. You will also want to include and label your thesis statement as part of your introduction, perhaps highlighting it with italics or bold print.

9.2 Explain and apply basic principles of outlining.

Watch the Video "Outline of: Our Immigrant Story" at **MyCommunicationLab**

Explore the Concept "Using the Microsoft Outlining Tool" at **MyCommunicationLab**

Explore the Concept
"Practicing with the
Microsoft Outlining Tool" at
MyCommunicationLab

- **Introduction, body, and conclusion.** These major elements should be labeled and included in the outline. As we noted in Chapter 8, introductions and conclusions need to be carefully planned in advance. By clearly labeling them on the outline, you will be sure that they are present and well developed. It is also helpful to label the specific components of each, such as the attention-getting device, credibility, justification, thesis, and so forth. (Your instructor may insist that you do so.)

- **Transitions.** Transitions hold the speech together and show the progression of ideas, as well as their relationship to one another. They help listeners follow the speech and see how the ideas advanced form a coherent whole. Entering and labeling transitions on your formal outline will ensure that you *have* included them and given them the attention they deserve. You may also want to italicize them, so that they stand out from the rest of the text.

- **Bibliography.** Normally, a list of sources or works consulted is required at the end of a formal outline. Various forms of bibliographic citations are available for you to use. Your instructor may suggest that you use a specific guide, such as the *Chicago Manual of Style* or the style manuals of the Modern Language Association (MLA) or the American Psychological Association (APA). Bibliographic formats change over time. Once you have selected the format you plan to use, you will want to follow it consistently. For assistance with locating different bibliographic formats, visit the Web, where you will find links to the most current formats available. The formal outline presented on pages 217–219 in the *Focus on Civic Engagement* feature includes a sample bibliography that follows the *Chicago Manual of Style*, whereas the formal outline that appears at the end of the chapter illustrates the MLA bibliographic format.

Use a Consistent System   Use a consistent system of symbols and indentations. Learning a system will help you fix in your mind the relationships between ideas and supporting material that the outline represents and is important in organizing your speech into a coherent structure. These symbols also designate the various components of your speech for your instructor or others you might ask for feedback on your speech. Figure 9.1 illustrates how the system looks when outlining the body of the speech. As with most speeches, some ideas are more fully developed than others, reflecting the speaker's assumptions about the relative importance of each idea and the extent to which each needs to be explained or illustrated.

Focus on a Single Idea in Each Main Point   Each main point in the body of your outline should contain only one idea. Here is an example of a poorly worded main idea:

I. Becoming media literate is important because so much information is communicated through the news; yet we have many excuses for not watching the news.

This example contains several different ideas in a single statement. Here is an improved version, focusing on one idea at a time:

I. Many of us avoid watching the news.
   A. Viewership of TV news has declined dramatically.
   B. Young people, in particular, have "tuned out."

> **FIGURE 9.1**
>
> **Outline Form for the Body of the Speech**
>
> I. MAIN IDEA
> - A. First main subpoint
>   - 1. Support for this subpoint
>   - a. First piece of specific information
>   - b. Second piece of specific information
>   - 2. Additional support for this subpoint
> - B. Second main subpoint
>   - 1. First supporting statement
>   - 2. Second supporting statement
>   - a. Specific information
>   - b. More specific information
>   - (1) Very detailed support
>   - (2) More detailed support
>   - c. More specific information
> - C. Third main subpoint
>   - 1. First supporting statement
>   - 2. Second supporting statement
>
> *Transition*
> II. SECOND MAIN IDEA
> - A. First main subpoint
>   - 1. First supporting statement
>   - 2. Second supporting statement
> - B. Second main subpoint
>   - 1. Support for this subpoint
>   - a. First piece of specific information
>   - b. Second piece of specific information
>   - 2. Second supporting statement
>
> *Transition*
> III. THIRD MAIN IDEA
> And so forth...

II. People give a number of reasons for avoiding the news.
- A. Many people feel that the news is too negative.
- B. Others argue that there's simply too much information to take in—and they feel overwhelmed by it.
- C. Still others are cynical—believing that much of the news has been "managed" or "manipulated" in some way.

Notice the clarity and simplicity that results as we focus on a single idea in each part of the outline. This simplification will assist you as you draft your speech, and it will also assist your listeners, helping them to better process and retain your message.

Coherently Develop Ideas and Supporting Material   Your outline should accurately reflect relationships between ideas and supporting material. The main ideas are listed with roman numerals, the subpoints that support those ideas with capital letters, the material that develops the subpoints with Arabic numbers, the support for these with lowercase letters, and the most specific supporting materials with numbers in parentheses. See Figure 9.1 for a skeletal illustration of proper outlining form.

Explore the Concept "Testing for Relevance of Supporting Ideas" at **MyCommunicationLab**

The outline thus becomes a *visual representation* of the supporting relationships between ideas and evidence. By examining your outline carefully, you should be able to discern whether the supporting material actually develops, supports, or elaborates your main ideas. Consider the following example, which *fails* to coherently represent the relationship among ideas:

I. Negativity and cynicism stand in our way of becoming media literate.
- A. There is a difference between an "informed" citizen and an "informational" citizen.

B. Media gatekeepers make it challenging for anyone to become media literate.
C. Much of the information we must process from the media is cognitive, based on facts.
D. There are several steps we can take to improve our media literacy.

Any one of these ideas might be explored on its own. But they clearly do not fit together, nor do the subpoints all advance the main point (that negativity and skepticism stand in the way of media literacy). Subpoint A offers a definition of an informed citizen, whereas subpoint B explores one of the challenges to media literacy. Subpoint C introduces a model of media literacy, and the final subpoint proposes actions to improve media literacy.

Here is a better approach to this outline:

I. Becoming media literate requires us to develop our ability to think critically.
  A. According to scholar James Potter, we must be able to evaluate facts—separating false information from that which is valid and reliable—using our *cognitive* ability.
  B. Potter argues that we must also understand the *emotional impact* that visual images and moving language can have on our ability to think critically.
  C. Finally, Potter insists that we must strive to separate "art from artificiality"—becoming more capable of dealing with the *aesthetic dimension* of information.[1]
II. Media scholar Carla Brooks Johnston outlines several specific steps we can take to enhance our media literacy.
  A. First, we can develop an *awareness* of how media may be influencing us.
  B. Next, we must exercise our "critical reading/viewing" skills.
  C. We must also reflect on the political, social, economic, and cultural *context* in which information is presented.
  D. Finally, we can engage in media advocacy by demanding that the media meet higher standards.[2]

In this outline, as you can see, the subordinate points illuminate the main ideas. Thus, each of the main ideas is coherently developed. In a complete formal outline, of course, each of these subpoints might be further developed through concise explanations, examples, expert testimony, and other sorts of supporting material.

The formal outlines that appear in the Focus on Civic Engagement feature on pages 217–219 and at the end of the chapter on pages 224–227 illustrate these principles.

The Keyword Outline: Some Special Considerations

Explore the Concept
"Creating a Speaking Outline" at
MyCommunicationLab

Some speakers make the mistake of trying to deliver their speech from their formal outline. But delivering your speech from such a detailed outline may tempt you to read the speech word-for-word. The outline functions almost like a manuscript and may discourage you from interacting more directly with your listeners.

There is nothing magical about transferring your outline onto note cards. Some speakers try to put their entire formal outline onto small note cards, using cramped writing or even using both sides of the cards. This typically does not produce a

FOCUS ON CIVIC ENGAGEMENT | Job Training for the Poor: A Speech of Advocacy

CULINARY ARTS FOR SHALOM: BASED ON A PRESENTATION PREPARED FOR A COMPETITIVE GRANT

Note: The Shalom Community Center is a daytime shelter and resource center for people who are experiencing poverty and homelessness in Bloomington, Indiana. The Shalom Center also operates a hunger relief program—serving breakfast and lunch five days each week. In 2011, Shalom served nearly 80,000 meals.

SPECIFIC PURPOSE: I want my audience to award Shalom Community Center the funding needed to establish a culinary arts job training program.

THESIS: Creating a program that offers certification in the culinary arts will lead to job opportunities for many.

INTRODUCTION

Attention-Getting Device

I recently met a man named Sam who was homeless for five years. He slept in his car until it was towed away. After that, he slept under a bridge. Sam's life turned around when a friend took him in and helped him find a job baking at a small café. Sam had always liked to bake, and he soon became famous for his cakes and pies. After working in the café for a couple of years, Sam went back to school and studied the culinary arts. Now, he has a job as head chef in an upscale restaurant.

You may wonder if Sam's situation is unusual. Will training in the culinary arts actually lead to good jobs?

Credibility

I believe so, and I speak from experience. I am a member of the Shalom board, where I chair the Operations Committee. For seven years, I have also worked as a volunteer in the Shalom kitchen and as a job counselor in the Job Links employment program.

Justification

One of our greatest challenges is helping our guests find decent jobs—jobs that pay a living wage (see Ehrenreich's *Nickel and Dimed*). Our guests often lack education, training, or certification—and this poses a huge barrier to employment. If we could provide training in an industry in which jobs are *growing*—as is true of the restaurant industry—we believe that we could make many of our guests employable.

Thesis

We are convinced that creating a culinary arts job training program at Shalom will lead to job opportunities for many.

Preview

I'd like to begin by telling you why I think a culinary arts job training program is right for Shalom. Then I'll describe the model we will use to develop our program and explain how we will use the grant money.

BODY

I. The restaurant industry is growing—with numerous job opportunities.
   A. Food service jobs are among the most commonly advertised in our community—in restaurants, hospitals, hotels, assisted living facilities, nursing homes, and schools.
      1. This past week alone, nearly 20 food-service ads appeared in the *Bloomington Herald Times*.
      2. More than half of these jobs were in traditional restaurants (i.e., *not* fast-food).
   B. In 2011, the National Restaurant Association reported that over the next ten years the restaurant industry is expected to add 1.3 million positions.
   C. The restaurant industry employs more minority managers than any other industry in the United States.

(*Continued*)

TRANSITION: Clearly restaurants need a trained workforce, and at Shalom we can help meet that need.

II. The Shalom Center is a logical place to offer training in the culinary arts.

A. Our state-of-the-art commercial kitchen is sufficiently large and versatile to provide an effective training arena.

B. We have partners who are interested in helping us develop and offer this kind of program.

1. We already have an ongoing alliance with Ivy Tech Community College.

2. The Bloomington Cooking School has agreed to offer classes.

3. A number of local chefs have also signed on to serve as instructors and mentors.

C. Many Shalom guests have some background working in restaurants—as line and prep cooks, servers, and dishwashers.

TRANSITION: The training we provide will infuse our community with a high-quality workforce.

III. Our program will be available to anyone who qualifies.

A. Applicants must be unemployed or underemployed.

1. They may be working part-time or doing work that is well beneath their skill level (such as the part-time custodian who once worked full-time in a factory).

B. They must pass a basic physical examination.

1. One component of this exam is a drug screening test.

2. They must also be able to stand for extended periods of time, tolerate heat, move quickly, bend easily, demonstrate good eye-hand coordination, and lift at least 30 pounds.

C. Applicants must also pass a basic skills test.

1. Each will be tested for basic literacy (ensuring that they can read recipes and cooking directions).

2. They will also be tested for fundamental math skills (allowing them to make accurate measurements, double recipes as needed, and so forth).

D. They must pass a screening interview.

1. This interview will explore applicants' employment history, drug treatment programs, and educational background.

2. Candidates will also be judged in terms of their communication skills, motivation, work ethic, and appearance.

TRANSITION: The training they receive will be first-rate.

IV. Our program will build on a successful job training model while creating several *new* components of our own.

A. A foundational portion of our program will be modeled after the Second Helpings job training program in Indianapolis.

1. Second Helpings has placed 90 percent of its graduates, and more than 70 percent of those remain employed six months later.

2. Like Second Helpings, we will offer a food handler course that will meet the Indiana law requirements for manager certification in the food service industry.

a. The law requires each establishment to employ at least one individual who is trained and certified in food safety.

B. In addition to the Food Handler's Certification, we anticipate that the Shalom Culinary Arts Certification Program will contain a number of *new* components.

1. A Cooking Fundamentals class will feature special workshops led by local chefs and the Bloomington Cooking School.

2. A Workforce Readiness class will be offered through Work One and our own Job Links program.

3. An Apprenticeship will provide additional hands-on training in local restaurants.

(Continued)

4. A Service Component will require everyone in the program to plan, prepare, and serve at least five meals to families in need who are served by the Shalom Center's hunger relief program.

C. The handouts I distributed show you our proposed budget and tentative timetable for developing the program.

1. As you can see, we have already begun collaborating with our partners.

2. With the funds we receive from your foundation, we hope to establish a new culinary arts administrative position.

a. This person will work with our partners to develop and refine the new program.

b. He or she will also be responsible for overseeing advertising, admissions, and testing.

3. The first students will enter the program in the summer, move through the requirements, be tested, and receive certification by the early fall.

4. After completing brief apprenticeships, graduates will be placed in area restaurants.

5. All graduates will be eligible to receive three credits toward Ivy Tech's Hospitality Administration degree program—thus encouraging them to pursue additional education.

CONCLUSION

Summary

The program we are proposing is easily within our grasp. We have the partners, the facility, and the basic program model in place. With this program, we will be able to offer valuable job training that will lead to employment opportunities and better lives for a number of the guests we serve.

Appeal

Remember the story of Sam that I shared in the beginning? No longer homeless, Sam glows with pride when he talks about his job and home. He is filled with hope and optimism! It is our dream that Sam's story will become a story shared by many others here in our community. With your foundation's support, we can make it so.

BIBLIOGRAPHY

Ehrenreich, Barbara. *Nickel and Dimed: On (Not) Getting By in America.* New York: Holt, 2001.

Ivy Tech Community College, www.ivytech.edu/hospitality-admin/ (accessed March 2, 2012).

Kilty, Keith M., and Elizabeth A. Segal, eds. *Rediscovering the Other America: The Continuing Crisis of Poverty and Inequality in the United States.* Binghamton, NY: Haworth Press, 2003.

Leonhardt, David. "U.S. Poverty Rate Was Up Last Year," *New York Times,* August 8, 2005, A1, A14.

National Restaurant Association, "Restaurant Industry Is Job Creation Engine," www.restaurant.org/pressroom/pressrelease/?ID=2096 (accessed March 1, 2012).

Second Helpings, www.secondhelpings.org (accessed March 3, 2012).

"Poverty: 2010 Highlights," U.S. Census Bureau, September 13, 2011 (last revised), http://www.census.gov/hhes/www/poverty/about/overview/index.html (accessed March 1, 2012).

Shalom Community Center, www.shalomcommunitycenter.org (accessed February 25, 2012).

useful set of speaking notes. Instead, try following these simple guidelines for developing a keyword outline:

Use Words Sparingly   When you create your speaking notes, you should try to write out as *little* as possible so that you will not be tempted to read your notes and risk losing contact with your listeners. Although it makes sense to write out and read direct quotations and specific statistical information, you will stay more focused on the audience if you have practiced enough to deliver the speech without relying on your notes too much.

Write Out Key Portions of the Speech   Even though you want to use notes sparingly, you may want to write out transitions and other key portions of your speech completely to ensure accuracy. When delivering a speech, you are most likely to forget what comes next after completing your discussion of a main idea. Writing out transitions can serve as a memory prompt and will help you emphasize *how* your ideas are connected. You may also wish to write out *parts* of your introduction and conclusion, such as a preview or summary, as well as specific statistics and quotations appearing anywhere in the speech. In fact, when you read statistics or directly quoted material from a note card, you demonstrate to your audience that you are concerned about conveying that information precisely and accurately.

Strive for Legible Notes   You will want to make sure that you can easily read your notes. Keep handwritten entries readable and sufficiently sized. If you type your notes, use a large font and emphasize important words in bold. In either case, leave adequate space between entries. Follow the basic format of your formal outline.

Avoid cramming too much onto any one card. You may want to use 4 × 6 rather than 3 × 5 note cards, so that you can put more notes on each card. Write on only one side of the card to avoid confusion. Number your cards and, of course, practice several times until you are comfortable with your speaking notes. Refer to Chapter 11 for more specific guidelines on how to practice with and use speaking notes.

Give Yourself Delivery Hints   When presenting your speech, it is easy to get caught up in following your notes and end up forgetting to deliver your remarks as effectively as possible. During practice, you will probably realize that you need to guard against certain tendencies, such as speaking too rapidly, forgetting to move or use gestures, or failing to look around the room to include all your listeners. In the margins of your notes, then, you may want to jot down delivery reminders, such as "Pause Here" or "Slow Down!!" You might write or print these in a color that differs from your speaking notes so that the two are not confused.

Consider Your Options   Some speakers prefer to use a sheet of paper instead of note cards for their keyword outline. When using note cards, you can easily carry them with you as you speak, gesturing and moving with ease. However, you *do* have to coordinate moving from card to card. If you use a sheet of paper, you can see the entire outline at a glance, but you will probably need to place the outline on a table or podium because carrying it around while you speak may look awkward and be distracting to your audience. Practice with each method to see which you prefer.

Use Speaking Notes Openly   Unless you have been asked to deliver your speech from memory (which is a rare occurrence), feel free to consult your keyword outline openly as you speak. Hold your cards comfortably or place your full sheet of notes on the podium. Look at your notes as needed, and read from them whenever you are trying to quote precisely. Avoid staring at your notes, however. You should *never* use your speaking notes as a crutch to avoid interacting with your audience. The reason you prepare a keyword outline is so that you can interact *more* with your listeners.

The *Focus on Civic Engagement* feature presents a keyword outline, based on the formal outline on pages 217–219.

Taken together, these outlining tools will assist you throughout the process of preparing and delivering your speech. The working outline will help you brainstorm ideas, conduct research, and think through how best to approach the subject. The formal outline reveals the final product—showing how well each main idea is articulated, developed, and supported—as well as how ideas are arranged and balanced. Finally, the keyword outline provides an aid to delivery that can help boost your confidence and keep you on track. When the audience perceives your speech as well planned and structured, they will be more likely to view you, the speaker, as a credible source of information and a person whose ideas and proposals are worthy of serious consideration.

Good speaking notes allow you to feel confident and stay on track while remaining connected to your listeners.

FOCUS ON CIVIC ENGAGEMENT | A Keyword Outline for a Speech of Advocacy

INTRODUCTION

SHARE STORY OF SAM—leads to question, "Will training in the culinary arts actually lead to a good job?"

SHARE PERSONAL BACKGROUND—at Shalom, working with Job Links.

Eye contact!

JUSTIFY TOPIC—need to find jobs that pay a living wage in a growing industry (refer to Ehrenreich's *Nickel and Dimed*).

Thesis

We are convinced that creating a culinary arts job training program at Shalom will lead to job opportunities for many.

PREVIEW

- I'll explain that this job training program is right for Shalom
- Describe what the model will look like
- Explain how we will use the grant money

Slow down here!

BODY

I. Restaurant industry is growing—with lots of job opportunities
- Nearly 20 food service job ads in *HT* during past week

(Continued)

- More than half in traditional restaurants, schools, hospitals, etc.—not fast-food
- National Restaurant Assoc.—1.3 million new jobs predicted over next decade

TRANSITION: Clearly, restaurants need a trained workforce, and at Shalom, we can help meet that need. `Might move here`

II. Shalom Center—logical place to meet the need
   - State-of-the-art commercial kitchen
   - Partnerships already formed—Ivy Tech, Cooking School, local chefs
   - Shalom guests—cooking backgrounds common

TRANSITION: The training we provide will infuse our community with a high-quality workforce.

III. Program available to anyone who qualifies:
   - Unemployed or underemployed
   - Passes basic skills test
   - Passes screening interview

TRANSITION: Training will be first-rate.

IV. Built on successful Second Helpings model in Indy
   - Program places 90 percent of grads, with high retention rate (over 70 percent)
   - Like SH, we will offer a food handler course `Watch speed!`
   - New Indiana requirement

- Course co-taught by Ivy Tech faculty, plus our own instructor
- New components in our program!
  - Cooking Fundamentals
  - Workforce Readiness
  - Apprenticeship
  - Service
- See handouts for budget and timetable for developing program
- Collaboration with partners ongoing
- With grant money, will hire new administrator
- Early summer through late fall, then apprenticeships and placement
- Grads receive three credits toward Ivy Tech program

CONCLUSION
Summary

- Program within our grasp—have partners, facility, and model in place
- Can offer valuable job training—to enrich lives of guests and benefit the greater community `Eye contact!`

Appeal

- Refer to Sam's story—no longer homeless, filled with hope!
- Others can share this story—with your foundation's support!

 Study and Review materials for this chapter are at **MyCommunicationLab**

SUMMARY

 Listen to the Audio Chapter Summary at **MyCommunicationLab**

Types of Outlines

9.1 Describe the different types of outlines and the purposes served by each.

- As you prepare yourself to speak, an outline will begin to emerge.
- Outlining is important as a diagnostic tool, as well as a visual representation of your speech.

- You will use different types of outlines:
  - Working outlines incorporate preliminary thoughts and emerging ideas.
  - Formal, full-sentence outlines contain fully developed ideas and support.
  - Keyword outlines serve as speaking notes.

Basic Principles of Outlining

9.2 Explain and apply the basic principles of outlining.

- As you craft your formal outline, you should do the following:
  - Include and label key elements (such as the introduction, body, and conclusion, transitions, and bibliography).
  - Use a consistent set of symbols and indentations.
  - Make sure that each point contains only one idea.
  - Develop ideas and supporting material in a coherent manner.

- A keyword outline is used in delivering your speech. You should do the following for this outline:
  - Write it on note cards.
  - Use words sparingly.
  - Include a few extended quotations and statistics.
  - Write it legibly.
  - Include delivery prompts.
  - Use it openly.
- When listeners perceive your speech as well planned and structured, they will be more likely to view you as a credible speaker whose ideas are worthy of their serious consideration.

QUESTIONS FOR REVIEW AND REFLECTION

Types of Outlines

9.1 Describe the different types of outlines and the purposes served by each.

1. List and describe the different kinds of outlines.
2. Why is it important to develop and use each kind of outline as you prepare and deliver your speech?

Basic Principles of Outlining

9.2 Explain and apply the basic principles of outlining.

3. What are the main components that need to be labeled and included in a formal outline? Why is each important?

4. Why is it important to restrict each point in the outline to a single idea?
5. How does the outline reflect relationships between ideas and supporting material?
6. How does the use of a consistent system of outlining symbols and indentation help make these relationships clear?
7. What are the most important guidelines to remember when preparing speaking notes?

 Study and Review the Flashcards at **MyCommunicationLab**

AUTISM: WHY ARE THE RATES RISING?

Kaitlin Rapone

NOTE: This outline is based on a speech that was delivered in a public speaking class at Southeast Missouri State University in 2008.

SPECIFIC PURPOSE: I want my audience to understand some possible explanations for the dramatic increases in the number of children diagnosed with autism.

THESIS: Researchers have offered a variety of different, sometimes competing, explanations for the dramatic increase in the number of children diagnosed with autism.

INTRODUCTION

Attention-Getting Device

Not long ago, my cousin Susan came to visit our family. She brought her 17-year-old son, Michael, with her. Michael does not behave like other teenagers. He rocks back and forth, rarely looks directly at anyone, and will eat only a few different foods, like chicken nuggets and Cheerios. Michael is autistic. Although he has made incredible progress over the years, Susan is worried about his future.

Credibility

I have known Michael for most of my life and have watched his parents agonize over how to help him communicate and learn the skills he needs to live independently. Because of this personal experience, I have been doing research to better understand the causes of this disorder.

IN ORDER TO GET LISTENERS' ATTENTION AND SHOW THE RELEVANCE OF HER TOPIC, KAITLIN SHARES A COMPELLING STORY ABOUT SOMEONE IN HER FAMILY. SHE THEN EMPHASIZES THE LARGE NUMBER OF CHILDREN WHO ARE DIAGNOSED WITH AUTISM.

Justification and Background

Autism is becoming increasingly prevalent in our society. *Every day,* 60 children in our country are diagnosed as autistic. The National Institute of Neurological Disorders and Stroke reports that 6 children out of 1,000 will have what they call an "autism spectrum disorder." Yet most people know very little about this disorder that the Autism Society of America (ASA) describes as a "complex developmental disability."

There is no simple medical test for detecting autism. Instead, children are diagnosed during the first three years of life through careful observation of their communication, their actions, and their interactions. Signs of the disorder include impaired communication, lack of eye contact, repetitive movements such as rocking or twirling, inflexible adherence to specific routines or rituals, and social withdrawal. These behaviors cannot be cured or outgrown, but many autistic children do benefit from education and therapy.

TO HELP THE AUDIENCE UNDERSTAND THE NATURE OF THE DISORDER, KAITLIN ENUMERATES THE GENERAL BEHAVIORS ASSOCIATED WITH AUTISM.

Thesis

Researchers have attributed the increased rates of autism among children to a variety of factors.

Enumerated Preview

Today, I'd like to examine three possible explanations for the rise in autism rates: hereditary factors, environmental factors, and changing definitions of the disorder.

AFTER ADVANCING HER THESIS, THE SPEAKER SETS THE STAGE FOR HER SPEECH BY OFFERING A PREVIEW OF HER MAIN POINTS AND TRANSITIONING INTO HER SPEECH'S FIRST MAIN IDEA—THE THEORY OF HEREDITY.

BODY

I. Some experts believe that heredity plays a major role in the development of autism.
   A. Genetics is one of the most obvious and common explanations for why certain children are autistic.
      1. Twin and family studies strongly suggest that some people have a genetic predisposition or vulnerability to autism.
         a. Identical twin studies show that if one twin is autistic, there is a 90 percent chance the other twin will be affected.
      2. Researchers also believe that children with a family history of autism or similar disabilities have a greater chance of being autistic.
      3. In addition, the ASA notes that children born with certain abnormalities in their brain or nervous system have a higher chance of being autistic.
   B. According to the ASA, many experts believe that when a child is born with a genetic susceptibility to autism, then other external factors may serve as triggers.

KAITLIN SUPPORTS HER FIRST MAIN IDEA WITH RESEARCH ON GENETIC VULNERABILITY, BRAIN ABNORMALITIES, AND SUSCEPTIBILITY TO EXTERNAL FACTORS.

TRANSITION: Along with genetics, our environment could be contributing to increased rates of autism.

II. Some researchers believe that environmental factors could trigger autism.
   A. The ASA explains that complications during pregnancy caused by harmful substances entering the body may cause an unborn child to become more vulnerable to autism.
   B. After birth, exposure to toxins and pollutants, such as lead and pesticides, might also interfere with healthy brain development.
      1. One expert, Dan Orzech, observes: "In the last half-century or so, more than 85,000 industrial chemicals have been registered in the United States, and many of them have found their way into our environment—and our bodies. Children, with their smaller and still-developing bodies, may be the ones most vulnerable to their effects."
      2. The sheer quantity of these harmful substances and the ease with which they find their way into our bodies is of special interest to researchers who believe they might contribute to the rising rates of autism.

TO SUPPORT HER POINT ABOUT ENVIRONMENTAL INFLUENCES, KAITLIN USES EXPERT TESTIMONY AND STATISTICS ON THE NUMBER OF INDUSTRIAL CHEMICALS THAT HAVE BEEN REGISTERED IN THE UNITED STATES.

   C. Finally, some experts have advanced the theory that childhood vaccinations might have played a significant role in the rising rates of autism.
      1. Until 2002, childhood vaccines for measles, mumps, and rubella contained a mercury-based preservative, Thimerosal.
      2. However, because cases of autism have continued to rise *after* Thimerosal was removed from vaccines, other experts, including those at the Centers for Disease Control, no longer believe that vaccines should be a cause of concern.

IN THIS PORTION OF HER SPEECH, KAITLIN EXPLORES THE CONTROVERSIAL THEORY THAT CHILDHOOD VACCINES MIGHT TRIGGER AUTISM IN SOME CHILDREN. SHE SUPPORTS THE ASSERTION THAT A MERCURY-BASED PRESERVATIVE, THIMEROSAL, ONCE IDENTIFIED AS A POSSIBLE CULPRIT, HAS LARGELY BEEN DISCOUNTED BY REFERENCING THE CDC.

TRANSITION: Heredity and environmental factors may well help explain the increase in autism rates, but another explanation has been offered as well, one that focuses on *how* we define and diagnose the disorder.

III. Some experts have argued that the rising number of autism cases may be attributable to nothing more than changes in how we define and diagnose the disorder.

   A. In recent years, as the Centers for Disease Control and Prevention has observed, the definition of autism has broadened significantly.

   B. Because there is no single medical test but rather a growing number of signs or symptoms associated with the disorder, doctors and other health care providers may be stretching the definition further by applying the criteria loosely.

   C. These wide-ranging boundaries for diagnosing autism, as Dr. Janice Hopkins recently pointed out in the *British Journal of Medicine*, could by themselves account for why "the prevalence of autism increased eightfold in the United States" between the early 1980s and the late 1990s.

      1. A good example of how autism may be too readily assumed comes from a study by Susan Bryson, published in *The Canadian Journal of Psychiatry*, which noted that within one group of individuals with various intellectual disabilities, 28 percent were diagnosed with autism.

      2. According to the *Economist*, a similar study by Dorothy Bishop tested 38 individuals who had been diagnosed with language disorders early in their lives and found that 12 of those would have been diagnosed as autistic by today's standards.

      3. The American Psychiatric Association is currently revising its diagnostic manual and may narrow the criteria for autism.

         a. The revised criteria are controversial.

         b. Even if adopted, their impact is uncertain.

TRANSITION: Whatever is responsible, autism rates are likely to continue to rise unless the widely acknowledged definition is narrowed or altered significantly.

CONCLUSION

Refer to Introduction

There are days when my cousin, Susan, nearly loses hope. She has had to educate herself about autism—and sometimes she has even had to educate her son's teachers. She has battled with his doctors. She often asks, "How did this happen to my child?" At the time she became pregnant, she had never known anyone with an autistic child.

Appeal

Today, we are learning more about autism each day. Most of you know at least one autistic person. Maybe you even have someone with autism in your family.

The causes of autism are not fully understood, but the implications are clear for those of us who plan to start a family someday. As future parents, we must be knowledgeable about our family histories. If disorders like autism are prevalent, anyone who becomes pregnant must take extra precautions. Every pregnant woman should talk to her doctor

IN THIS PART OF HER SPEECH, KAITLIN EXPLORES THE EXPANDED DEFINITION OF AUTISM BY QUOTING THE CENTERS FOR DISEASE CONTROL AND PREVENTION.

KAITLIN CITES AN ARTICLE IN A REPUTABLE PROFESSIONAL JOURNAL TO EMPHASIZE THAT DIAGNOSTIC PRACTICES ALONE MIGHT EXPLAIN THE RISE IN AUTISM.

IN CONCLUDING HER LAST MAIN POINT, KAITLIN SUMMARIZES TWO STUDIES THAT DOCUMENT THE EXPANDED DEFINITION OF AUTISM.

THIS QUICK SUMMARY SERVES AS A TRANSITION AS KAITLIN MOVES TOWARD HER CONCLUSION.

AS SHE BEGINS HER CONCLUSION, KAITLIN REMINDS HER LISTENERS OF THE DAILY STRUGGLES OF PARENTS WITH AUTISTIC CHILDREN—REFERENCING THE PERSONAL STORY THAT SHE SHARED IN THE INTRODUCTION.

FINALLY, THE SPEAKER RELATED THE TOPIC TO HER AUDIENCE BY ARTICULATING THE ISSUES THAT LISTENERS WILL WANT TO REMEMBER AS THEY THINK ABOUT HAVING THEIR OWN FAMILIES. SHE ALSO REMINDS THEM OF THE IMPORTANCE OF SUPPORTING RESEARCHERS AS THEY STRIVE TO IMPROVE OUR UNDERSTANDING OF AUTISM.

about what she can do to avoid exposing herself and her baby to dangerous toxins that could adversely affect her child.

We also must support researchers who continue to work to more clearly define autism and strive to create reliable tools for its diagnosis and treatment.

BIBLIOGRAPHY

"Autism Society: Improving the Lives of Those Affected by Autism." February 20, 2010. Autism Society of America. February 22, 2010 <www.autism-society.org/site/PageServer>.

"Autism Spectrum Disorders (ASDs)." 17 Aug. 2009. Centers for Disease Control and Prevention. 20 Feb. 2010 <www.cdc.gov/ncbddd/autism/topics.html>.

Benedict Carey, "New Definition of Autism Will Exclude Many, Study Suggests," *The New York Times*, January 19, 2012, <www.nytimes.com/2012/01/20/health/research/new-autism-definition-would-exclude-many-study-suggests.html?pagewanted=all> (accessed March 3, 2012).

Bryson, Susan. "Prevalence of Autism among Adolescents with Intellectual Disabilities." *Canadian Journal of Psychiatry* 53 (July 2008): 449–59. Academic Search Premier. Ebscohost. SEMO Lib., Cape Girardeau, MO. February 15, 2010 <http://ebscohost.com>.

Hopkins, Janice. "Increase in Autism Due to Change in Definition, Not MMR Vaccine." *British Journal of Medicine* 330 (January 15, 2005): 132 <www.bmj.com/cgi.content>.

"Morbidity and Mortality Weekly Report." February 18, 2010. Centers for Disease Control & Prevention. February 21, 2010 <www.cdc.gov/mmwr>.

National Institute of Neurological Disorders and Stroke, "Autism Fact Sheet" <www.ninds.nih.gov/disorders/autism/detail_autism.htm> (accessed March 4, 2012).

"Not More, Just Different." *Economist* 387 (April 12, 2008): 89. Academic Search Premier. Ebscohost. SEMO Lib., Cape Girardeau, MO. February 10, 2010 <http://web.ebscohost.com>.

Orzech, Dan. "Environmental Toxins and Child Development." *Social Work Today* 7 (March/April 2007): 37 <www.socialworktoday.com>.

Using Language Effectively

*S*tyle is a difficult term to define, partly because we use it in so many different ways. If we say a person has style, we may mean that the person dresses well, sings in a unique voice, or plays basketball with a special flair. In those situations, the context of our remark will clarify what we mean when we say that a person has style. When we talk about a speaker's style, however, we mean something different. We still may mean that, in a general sense, the person has a pleasing style of speaking—that is, he or she projects a good image and relates to audiences effectively. Style, in the ancient tradition of rhetorical theory, has a more specific meaning, however: it refers to how we use language in oral presentations.

This chapter focuses on this more specific meaning of style: how you choose the language for your speech and the effects of those choices on your overall success as a speaker. We will begin by discussing the connections between language and meaning, keeping in mind that the speaker who wants to use clear language must begin with clear thinking. If you first develop a clear grasp of the ideas you hope to communicate, it will be much easier for you to find the right language to get your message across. Then we will discuss how to choose language that is clear, interesting, effective, and appropriate to the particular situation. By the end of the chapter, you should have a better sense of the importance of style and what you can do to improve your style as a public speaker.

LANGUAGE AND MEANING

Preview. *Style is fundamentally concerned with how the speaker uses language. When crafting a speech, it is critical to choose appropriate language. The language you choose has the potential to influence listeners through its symbolic power and its explicit and implicit meanings. Your choices can help you connect with listeners or can create barriers and misunderstandings.*

10.1 Understand the relationship between language and meaning.

Speakers and listeners do not always speak exactly the same language. All of us may speak English, but we do not choose and use language in the same ways. We may come from different backgrounds that provide us with different vocabularies or different meanings for words. Regional uses of English, ethnic uses of language, and generational variations in language can be confusing to those outside a particular linguistic group. Phrases or abbreviations that are commonplace on Facebook or Twitter, for example, may need to be translated for those who do not participate in online social networks. In a sense, we all speak different "languages," and those differences influence how our listeners respond to our speeches.

The words we choose reflect our values, our perceptions, or our attitudes. Depending on our point of view, members of a rebel organization might be labeled *terrorists* or *freedom fighters*. Likewise, an army labeled *invaders* by some might be considered *liberators* by others. During the recent health care debate in America, what some described as needed *reform*, others denounced as *socialized medicine*.[1] As you prepare to speak, it is important to keep in mind that language is symbolic and allows for a variety of meanings.

Watch the Video
"Tree Hugger" at
MyCommunicationLab

The Symbolic Nature of Language

Words are symbols. They are abstractions that allow us to talk about people, places, things, actions, and ideas without providing every detail. The more abstract our words, the more details we omit. Abstract language makes it possible for us to talk about our feelings and values. It permits us to talk about the past and the future and things we can only imagine. We conceptualize ideas—such as love, honor, and beauty—through abstract language. Yet using too many abstract words can also cause problems in communication.

Abstract language is ambiguous language. As we speak more abstractly, ideas can become more and more difficult to grasp, and the chances of misunderstandings increase. If you were to describe a course of action as "the patriotic thing to do," for example, how your audience will respond depends on what *patriotism* means to them. For some, patriotism might demand that they support the War in Afghanistan; others may feel they have a patriotic duty to protest the war. Similarly, some may assume that *supporting our troops* means sending them care packages or letters of encouragement, whereas others may feel that the best way to support our troops would be to bring them home.

Abstractions are a powerful source of personal identity. We live in a diverse country, made up of people of many different cultural and social backgrounds. The word *American*, for example, can apply to all of us, but it is also an abstraction that can be variously interpreted. Consider how listeners might have responded differently when former secretary of state Colin Powell used the word *American* in a speech to the National Volunteer Summit. Urging his listeners to work toward the day when everyone would live the "American Dream," Powell appealed to the widespread belief that America was especially blessed by a "Divine Providence." He also invoked the principle that we must all be "good stewards" of each other:

> Let us make sure that no child in America is left behind, no child in America has their dream deferred or denied. We can do it. We can do it because we are Americans. We are Americans who draw our strength from this place. We are Americans who believe to the depth of our hearts that this is not a land that was placed here by historic accident, it is a land that was put here by Divine Providence who told us to be good stewards of our land, but especially to be good stewards of each other. Divine Providence gave us this land, blessed it and told us always to be proud to call it America. And so we go forward. Let us go save our children.[2]

Powell's use of abstractions was broad enough that many people with different specific convictions could agree with his statement. Yet people with different backgrounds may have had different views of what it meant to be an "American," and people of differing religious beliefs may have reacted differently to his reference to "Divine Providence."

Sometimes speakers exploit ambiguous terms to trick listeners into accepting their ideas without seriously thinking about them. Most of us favor "family values," for example, but Republicans and Democrats often disagree over which policies best promote those values. Similarly, we may all agree that accountability in government is good or that we should all be responsible citizens. But what it means to be accountable or responsible may vary from person to person. When a speaker uses such abstract words, details are lost and differences may be glossed over.

Suppose, for example, that a political candidate claims that we need a "safety net" to protect the poorest and most disadvantaged among us. Does that mean that we need more government spending on social services? Or is the candidate advocating that we rely on private charities to provide a safety net for the disadvantaged? In the sample speech following Chapter 7, one health care expert referred to a "safety net" that was "full of holes." In short, the abstract term *safety net* can be used in a wide variety of ways. The careful listener looks for clues as to how a speaker translates ambiguous terms into specific ideas or policies.

Denotative and Connotative Meaning

Although meaning may vary according to the understanding we bring to abstract words, many words have commonly understood meanings; if this were not so, we could not communicate at all. The meanings of words can be divided into two groups: denotative and connotative meanings. Denotative meaning refers to the literal, objective meaning of words stripped of any emotional baggage they may carry. These meanings tend to be more objective and less susceptible to a wide variety of interpretations. For example, the denotative meaning of *pencil* is "a writing implement consisting of a thin rod of graphite or similar substance encased in wood or held in a plastic or metal mechanical device." Its meaning is relatively objective; not a lot of personal interpretations and feelings are attached to the word *pencil*. When we hear the word, few of us are confused or feel fear, joy, or anger.

Connotative meanings, by contrast, derive from the emotional implications of words and suggest a range of subjective and personal interpretations. Many words in our culture carry strong connotations because of their association with historic events or political controversies. For many U.S. citizens, words such as *terrorist*, *traitor*, or *un-American* carry strong connotations because they automatically provoke feelings of fear, hostility, or even hatred. Words such as *patriot* or *hero*, on the other hand, invoke more positive feelings and emotions.

Connotative meaning is infused into language by the context in which words appear and by the perceptions of the listener. Nonetheless, in our society, some words seem to be more emotionally charged than others: *honor, free enterprise, racist,* and *neo-Nazi* are just a few examples. All of these words are likely to conjure up intense personal feelings, positive or negative.

During a congressional campaign, pollsters for a political action group conducted focus groups to determine connotative responses to certain words. They issued a pamphlet suggesting "good" words for candidates to use in their campaigns when talking about themselves and "bad" words to use when discussing their opponents. Figure 10.1 lists some of the "optimistic" words candidates were urged to use in letters, speeches, and ads. The "bad" words, labeled "contrasting," were to be used when referring to an opponent's "record, proposals and party."[3] If you examine these words closely, you'll see that the "optimistic" words all evoke positive feelings and associations, while the "contrasting" words are meant to raise fears, anxieties, disapproval, or discomfort.

In another example of how seriously political strategists take word connotations, Frank Lutz, a Republican consultant, sent the Senate Republican policy committee suggestions for phrasing their objections to President Obama's proposals

Watch the Video
"President Franklin
D. Roosevelt on the Motion
Picture Industry" at
MyCommunicationLab

FIGURE 10.1

Optimistic		Contrasting	
common sense	passionate	anti-child	greed
courage	pioneer	anti-flag	hypocrisy
dream	pride	betray	incompetent
duty	principle(d)	cheat	lie
empowerment	pro-environment	collapse	radical
fair	prosperity	corruption	self-serving
family	reform	crisis	shallow
freedom	rights	decay	steal
hard work	strength	destroy	taxes
liberty	truth	devour	traitors
moral	"workfare"	failure	welfare

Source: "Language: A Key Mechanism of Control," from *Power Persuasion: Moving an Ancient Art into the Media*, by Cooper and Williams. © 1992 by Educational Video Group. Used by permission.

for health care reform. He recommended one claim that was designed to exploit both fears of losing control over one's own health care and widespread hostility toward the federal government: "A committee of Washington bureaucrats will establish the standard of care for all Americans." He also proposed that the plan be attacked with the claim that it would "deny people treatments they need and make them wait to get the treatments they are allowed to receive." Suggesting that "Washington bureaucrats" would make health care decisions for Americans—instead of their own doctors—and allow or deny some treatments was hardly an accurate description of the administration's health care plan, but it did tap into the negative feelings many Americans have toward the federal government.[4]

Thoughtful speakers and listeners understand the power of words with strong positive or negative connotations, and they look beyond their immediate, surface reactions to the deeper meanings of such words. As speakers, we have an obligation to be sensitive to the emotional power of language. We also need to realize that our language does not automatically mean the same thing to every listener. Your goal as a speaker should be to make yourself as clear as possible, not obscure your real meaning or stir up emotions with highly connotative language.

USING LANGUAGE THAT IS CLEAR AND ACCURATE

10.2 Choose language that is specific, concrete, precise, and clear.

Preview. *The most profound idea, clever remark, or astute observation will have little impact if your listeners cannot grasp it. Clear speakers use language familiar to their audience. They also speak with specificity, concreteness, precision, and clarity. Finally, they avoid the use of clichés, empty words, and distracting language, and they construct their sentences with a concern for good oral style.*

As you consider the ways in which language choices help you connect with your audience, keep in mind that oral style and written style are not the same. In most

Explore the Concept
"Power of words" at
MyCommunicationLab

situations, you will use less formal, more conversational language in speeches than you do in written manuscripts. A good oral style is more informal, simpler, and more repetitious than a written style. Also—and this is important—oral style is more spontaneous. It allows you the flexibility to adapt your language as you speak. In this chapter, we encourage you to make careful and effective language choices. But if you plan to deliver your speech extemporaneously, you probably will not write out every single word of your speech in advance. Rather, you will need to choose appropriate language as you speak.

Also keep in mind that a speech delivered orally is received differently from a written presentation. If you are reading a page and come across difficult or unfamiliar words, you can always reread the passage and try to figure out the meaning of the word from the context, or you can consult a dictionary. Indeed, a good book often challenges readers to learn new words and expand their knowledge of the language. But a speech is a different matter. When you are giving a speech, your listeners cannot stop you and ask you to repeat an unfamiliar word. Nor can they whip out the dictionary and look up a word that they did not understand.

Oral language may be described as "written for the ear." It is language that sounds more informal and is less complex. It usually employs shorter sentences and more contractions than written language. It generally is not as economical either. Although your sentences may be shorter, it may take more sentences—and thus more words—to express an idea. We will address this more fully in Chapter 11 when we discuss delivery, but consider this example of two ideas, one as it might be written, the other as it might be spoken:

- *Written:* Several complex, interrelated factors work together to produce an almost insoluble problem given the political, economic, and social context.
- *Spoken:* This problem doesn't have just one cause. Many factors contribute to the difficult situation we're facing now. And because there are many causes of our problem, there are no simple solutions.

As speakers, we need to be sensitive to the differences between oral and written communication and do all we can to achieve clarity and understanding. If our speaking is to be meaningful, we must make sure that what we say is *instantly* intelligible.

Familiar Language

It is important that you use words familiar to your audience. Most of the great speakers in our history did not use big, pompous, important-sounding words. Rather, they used simple, direct language that listeners could easily grasp. In one of Abraham Lincoln's greatest speeches, given when he was nominated for the U.S. Senate in 1858, for example, he put his suspicions of the power of the slaveholders and their allies into clear, unequivocal words. He began with a simple and familiar biblical phrase:

> "A house divided against itself cannot stand." I believe this government can not endure permanently half slave and half free. I do not expect the Union to be dissolved—I do not expect the house to fall—but I do expect it will cease to be divided. It will become all one thing or all the other. Either the opponents of slavery will arrest the further spread of it,

and place it where the public mind shall rest in the belief that it is in the course of ultimate extinction; or its advocates will push it forward till it shall become alike lawful in all the states, old as well as new—North as well as South.[5]

Nothing in the language of this passage would have been puzzling to listeners. Every single word was familiar to Lincoln's audience. The same is true of the next example. A senior student gave a speech to incoming freshmen at her university with the purpose of encouraging them to become active in significant projects and activities outside the classroom. In her introduction, she used familiar language to get her audience to look at an ordinary phrase in a different way and then led into her suggestions for getting the most out of their college experience:

> "Multitasking" is something that all of us know a lot about. If you were like me when I was in high school, you could listen to music and do your homework at the same time. You could listen to your mom or dad while texting a friend. Well, you can keep on multitasking now that you're in college, but if you're going to get the most out of your four years here, you're going to have to think about what "tasking" means. If it means playing computer games far into the night while blasting your favorite tunes into your headset and then sleeping through your morning class, your stay here might be one year and not four. Today, I want to talk about a different kind of "multitasking" that you can do at this university by exploring how you can better prepare yourself to be a productive, useful contributor to your community and—and this is a very important *and*—a happy, satisfied person.

Because the familiarity of your words is important to the clarity of your speech, it is important that you learn as much as you can about your audience's education and vocabulary. Then you will be able to better choose the language most suitable to them.

Technical Language

You need to remember that listeners may not know the meaning of technical words. It is perfectly appropriate to use technical language in a speech to a specialized audience who will understand it. But in a speech addressed to a general audience, you should avoid using language that excludes people who lack technical expertise. If you *must* employ technical terms, then it is your job to define them for listeners who may not have the knowledge or training to understand their precise meaning. Chemistry majors will know what a *reagent* is, and an accounting major understands what is meant by a *trial balance*. Less specialized audiences, however, will need to have the terms defined.

A student speaking about the challenges of passing a health care reform bill in the U.S. Senate needed to explain two technical terms: *filibuster* and *cloture*. A filibuster occurs when opponents of a bill use extended debate to prevent the legislation from coming to a vote. Cloture is a motion to end the debate, but under Senate rules a motion for cloture requires a three-fifths majority, or 60 votes. When opponents of reform threatened a filibuster, supporters of reform thus needed to line up not just the simple majority needed to pass the bill but also the 60 votes necessary to end a filibuster.

Abbreviations and Acronyms The same is true, of course, of technical or specialized abbreviations or substitutions for longer words or titles. The best example of this is the *acronym*, which is a series of letters that stand for some longer name or title. Few may know that *RFID* stands for *radio frequency identification*, a technology that provides a unique identification system used to carry information. But even more common acronyms may need a quick explanation. Anyone who is interested in broadcasting will know that *FCC* stands for *Federal Communications Commission*, but others in your audience may not be familiar with this acronym. College students all know what a GPA is, but people not associated with the university may not know this shorthand for *grade-point average*. As speakers, we need to be conscious of the fact that our language grows out of our experience and knowledge and sometimes needs to be translated for listeners.

Concreteness and Specificity

Words chosen for their concreteness and specificity increase clarity. Compare the following two brief passages from student speeches given on related topics.

> *Student #1:* The tragedy of civil war falls heavily on women and children. They are displaced from their homes and suffer so many hardships from disease and injuries. They have the most primitive medical care in the large refugee camps and are attacked by lawless militias. It is hard to imagine the hardships they must endure.

> *Student #2:* Women and children are the innocent victims of civil wars raging in Africa. Life in the refugee camps is a constant struggle to get enough food to survive. Lack of clean water and proper sanitation means that diseases like cholera spread rapidly, and diarrhea is rampant. Those who stray just a few feet outside the camp may be attacked by militiamen wielding machetes. It is not uncommon to see children lying, glassy-eyed, on makeshift beds, with missing limbs and flies swarming over the wounds.

The second passage is clearly more moving. "Hardships" are specified; the results of the "attacks" are made real through the choice of concrete language that helps listeners visualize the situation.

Precise Language

Mark Twain once observed that there is no such thing as a synonym; he admonished writers to seek the right word, not its "second cousin." Twain's advice is also good for public speakers. Precise words are important because they allow us to communicate our meaning as accurately as possible.

If you wanted to describe someone walking down the street, how would you do it? Specifically, what verbs would you choose? This would depend entirely on the kind of image you wanted to create. If you wanted to portray the person as being in a hurry, you might use verbs such as *raced, hustled,* or *hurried.* But each of these is different. Which is faster? Which is more informal? To take a different example, suppose you wanted to describe a negative feeling about something. You might say you *disliked* it, but if you felt more strongly, you might choose a verb such as *hated, detested,* or *loathed.* Which conveys the most accurate description of your feeling? In general, you will be more effective with your language if you use words that convey your meaning precisely.

Consider these sentences from student speeches as originally given and as revised to convey more precisely the point the speaker wishes to make:

Original: Many troops have been hurt by these homemade bombs.

Revised: Young American men and women serving in Iraq have been killed or maimed by roadside bombs.

Original: Homeless people increasingly run the risk of random violence.

Revised: People who live in the street have been subjected to beatings with baseball bats; they've been kicked, stabbed, punched, and even killed for no reason other than they're easy targets, and their assailants like to beat up "bums."

Not only do carefully chosen words enhance meaning and promote clarity, they also contribute to the kind of specificity we discussed earlier in the chapter, thus heightening the impact of your message.

Avoid Clichés, Empty Words, and Distracting Language

Effective public speakers avoid using clichés—trite, overused expressions. At one time, these expressions were probably fresh and interesting. *The bottom line* conveys a clear enough meaning, but the phrase has been used so much that it does not show any originality and may have lost its precise meaning: the total cost of something. The same is true of such phrases as "twenty four/seven," "with all due respect," or "it's not rocket science." Because of overuse, clichés are tired and lifeless, and they are less likely to engage listeners' thoughts and hold their interest.

Avoid empty words—those that add nothing but length to your sentences. For instance, why say *a number of*, when you can say *several* or *many*? You might say *because* instead of *due to the fact that*, *after* instead of *subsequent to*, *about* rather than *in connection with*, and *I must* instead of *it will be necessary for me to*.

Even though we may think of a speaking situation as an enlarged conversation, there *are* stylistic differences between the two. A conversation is more interactive. We don't always finish sentences, we may be interrupted from time to time, or others in the conversation may verbalize reactions. Casual conversations are often littered with unnecessary language that may be acceptable in that setting but not in a formal speech. You may say to a friend that "he was, like, very tall and, you know, well built." But "like" and "you know" only clutter your everyday speech and should especially be avoided when giving a public speech.

If you can avoid empty words, clichés, and distracting language in your speaking, you will say more, say it more efficiently, and speak more clearly. And your audience will benefit through greater knowledge and understanding.

Constructing Sentences to Promote Clarity

Individual words must be clear, and so should sentences. Construct sentences with well-chosen words, but arrange those words so that the sentences they form are direct and easy to follow.

For good oral style, craft sentences so that the subject and the verb are close together. This makes the sentence easier to understand, and it sounds more natural. Consider the following sentence, in which the subject and verb have been separated: "This new program, which has been tried at other colleges similar to our own and has been enormously popular, is worthy of your support." Note how the sentence would be more understandable if reworked to say: "This program is worthy of your support. Other colleges like our own have tried it, and it has been enormously popular."

Repetition and Restatement   Speakers may have to repeat certain words, phrases, or ideas to make them stick in listeners' minds. Repetition is especially effective when the speaker wants the audience to remember specific, vivid, or especially meaningful words or phrases. You may wish to use restatement if you want to emphasize or clarify an idea by discussing it in several different ways. Of course, speakers should not overuse these devices. When used carefully, however, they can reinforce your main ideas and make important expressions memorable.

President John F. Kennedy made effective use of repetition in his inaugural address. Speaking directly to "those nations who would make themselves our adversaries," he called upon both sides in the Cold War to "begin anew the quest for peace" and identified some potential areas of cooperation in a series of statements using repetition:

> Let both sides explore what problems unite us instead of belaboring those problems which divide us.
>
> Let both sides, for the first time, formulate serious and precise proposals for the inspection and control of arms...
>
> Let both sides seek to invoke the wonders of science instead of its terror...
>
> Let both sides unite to heed in all the corners of the earth the command of Isaiah—to "undo the heavy burdens...[and] let the oppressed go free."[6]

Through the simple device of repeating a phrase at the end of each example, one student speaker reinforced his contention that all of us are contributing money to large corporations for foolish or wasteful projects:

> Let's take a look at someone like Lockheed Martin, a defense manufacturer. They received only a paltry $25,000 in a tax write-off in 1996. But what did the tax write-off come for? Entertainment expenses that included $20,000 worth of golf balls. That's your tax money at work! Then we have the Walt Disney Corporation, a company whose profits are over $1 billion per year. They received a $300,000 federal subsidy in order to research bigger and better fireworks for their theme parks. That's your tax money at work! But probably the biggest and most insulting federal subsidy of all that I came across happened between 1990 and 1994, when General Motors received $110.6 million in federal technological subsidies under the auspices of a jobs program. During that time period, their profits skyrocketed. And what happened? They laid off 104,000 of their workers—25 percent of their U.S. workforce. That's your tax money at work!

Short, Concise Sentences   In an oral style, you should also keep sentences relatively short. Shorter sentences are easier for listeners to follow. Also avoid needless repetition, unnecessary modifiers, and circumlocutions, such as, "The reason why I think this plan will work is because..." Instead, say "This plan will work because..." One way to eliminate unnecessary words is to use the active voice. Consider the following examples:

> "Great frustration with the lack of progress in enacting a health care reform bill in Congress has been expressed by health care advocates." (*passive voice, too wordy*)

> "Advocates for health care reform have expressed frustration over the lack of progress in passing legislation." (*active voice*)

> "It has been argued by some advocates of the 'cash for clunkers' program that of all the government programs that have been proposed or put in place that this one should be supported because it is very popular with the public and seems to be working as it was intended." (*passive voice, too wordy*)

> "Even many critics of government programs argue that the 'cash for clunkers' program works and should be extended." (*active voice*)

Modifiers It is best to use only necessary modifiers. There are two kinds of modifiers: those that comment and those that define. Commenting modifiers include *very*, *most*, and *definitely*. These modifiers add little; instead they boost the force of the words they modify. Yet, if you select your words precisely, they should be able to stand alone without the assistance of such modifiers. Saying that the president is *very seriously worried* about the future of health care adds little to the statement that the president is *seriously worried*.

By contrast, defining modifiers provide information that the noun standing alone cannot convey. They tell us something we need to know. It is informative to know that a policy is supported by a *narrow majority* of voters or that the government has a *contingency plan* to deal with H1N1 flu. Modifiers are also used to color audience perceptions; depending on whether an idea is described as innovative, brilliant, outdated, or preposterous, listeners will respond to it quite differently.

Watch the Video
"Harry S. Truman's Decision to Drop the Bomb" at
MyCommunicationLab

Simplicity

Simple and precise words and sentences contribute to active speech. Consider, for example, the way President Lyndon Johnson urged members of Congress to support him in passing the Voting Rights Act of 1965. When Johnson delivered this speech at a joint session of Congress, the nation was engulfed in racial turmoil. In Alabama, police and civil rights protesters clashed in bloody confrontations. A sense of great tension and urgency gripped the country. The following passage from LBJ's speech has no exceptional or unusual words and no particularly striking sentence constructions, but the clarity and forcefulness of the language suggest action.

> The bill I am presenting to you will be known as a civil rights bill.

> But in a larger sense, most of the program I am recommending is a civil rights program. Its object is to open the city of hope to all people of all races, because all Americans just must have the right to vote, and we are going to give them that right.

> All Americans must have the privileges of citizenship, regardless of race, and they are going to have those privileges of citizenship regardless of race.

But I would like to caution you and remind you that to exercise these privileges takes much more than just legal right. It requires a trained mind and a healthy body. It requires a decent home and the chance to find a job and the opportunity to escape from the clutches of poverty.

Of course people cannot contribute to the nation if they are never taught to read or write; if their bodies are stunted from hunger; if their sickness goes untended; if their life is spent in hopeless poverty, just drawing a welfare check.

In urging passage of the Voting Rights Act of 1965, President Johnson used simple, direct, and forceful language to demand justice for African Americans.

So we want to open the gates to opportunity. But we're also going to give all our people, black and white, the help that they need to walk through those gates.[7]

Apart from the ideas that are discussed, language can have a force of its own. When used to promote interest, it can help make a speech more persuasive and effective.

USING LANGUAGE THAT IS ACTIVE AND INTERESTING

Preview. *As speakers, we can keep listeners interested by using active language—language that is lively and vivid—and figures of speech. We can also use rhetorical questions and parallelism to promote audience interest and identification with the topic.*

10.3 Choose language that is lively and vivid, using appeals to the senses and figures of speech.

Even if your language is clear—so that listeners understand your main ideas or arguments—you may fail to move them unless it is also compelling. Gaining and maintaining listeners' interest is essential if you hope to achieve your desired response. When you use language that stimulates the listeners' imagination, offers memorable images, and is pleasing to the ear, you will have a better chance of also engaging their minds and hearts.

Use Active, Vivid Language

Action holds interest and commands attention. The way we choose language and the way we put it together can create a sense of action for our listeners. We can create the illusion of action and help listeners understand more precisely what we have in mind by using active, vivid language.

Language promotes a feeling of action when it is lively. Language that gives a realistic and specific description of events, people, and ideas is the liveliest. Further,

Watch the Video "Martin Luther King, Jr." at **MyCommunicationLab**

HIGHLIGHTING ACTIVE AND INTERESTING LANGUAGE

The Rev. Forrest Gilmore, Executive Director of a day shelter for those experiencing homelessness and poverty, began an appeal to gain support for a program called "Permanent Supportive Housing" with a compelling narrative:

I was angry. It's not how I usually feel at a memorial service. But this was not a normal memorial service. This service was for someone who shouldn't have died.

Frank Crawford was homeless. He was also disabled, significantly ill, and addicted to alcohol. He died alone in the middle of the night behind the old Ponderosa back in June.

A few weeks earlier, he had been released from a nursing home. Considered "too healthy" to stay, he was encouraged to find an assisted living facility. But,

of course, there wasn't one for him. So, Frank became homeless…again.

Over many years, Frank had been in and out of nursing homes. He would decline to the edge of death on the streets and then get nursed back to health only to be released to the streets once again.

Every time Frank came back to the Shalom Center, we all sighed with despair, astonished that anyone thought Frank could care for himself. We knew soon enough he would be in a nursing home again, if he was lucky.

Unfortunately, this last time, he wasn't so lucky.

And I was angry.

Because now he's dead.

Source: Forrest Gilmore, "Anger Transformed Into a Passion for Justice." Used by permission. ▴

listeners' emotions are often engaged through the use of vivid descriptions of pleasant or unpleasant situations. In Chapter 7, we noted that telling a story about real people tends to promote identification between the audience and the subject. The simple narrative can make us feel ashamed or angry or experience a host of other emotions.

In using vivid language, speakers often try to appeal to listeners' senses. Through sensory appeals, audience members are encouraged to see, hear, or feel something. Two famous speeches from our history illustrate the power of vivid language to evoke strong feeling.

The first is by the African-American abolitionist, Frederick Douglass, who vividly depicted the inhumanity of slavery: "What, am I to argue that it is wrong to make men brutes, to rob them of their liberty, to work them without wages, to keep them ignorant of their relations to their fellow men, to beat them with sticks, to flay their flesh with the lash, to load their limbs with irons, to hunt them with dogs, to sell them at auction, to sunder their families, to knock out their teeth, to burn their flesh, to starve them into obedience and submission to their masters?"[8]

The second is a speech by Chief Joseph of the Nez Perce tribe, who surrendered after a long and desperate 1,100-mile flight from pursuing U.S. cavalry. Here is his description of his people's plight:

I am tired of fighting. Our chiefs are killed. Looking Glass is dead. Toohulhulsote is dead. The old men are all dead. It is the young men who say yes or no. He who led the young men is dead.

It is cold and we have no blankets. The little children are freezing to death. My people, some of them, have run away to the hills and have no blankets, no food. No one knows where they are—perhaps freezing to death. I want to have time to look for my children and see how many I can find. Maybe I shall find them among the dead.

Hear me, my chiefs. I am tired. My heart is sick and sad. From where the sun now stands, I will fight no more forever.[9]

Listeners exposed to such vivid and detailed narratives have a strong likelihood of identifying with them. With the bulk of the appeal resting on visual images, the result is a more persuasive presentation.

Lively, vivid language is important, but much still depends on your ability to marshal excellent arguments and your listeners' openness to new and alternative viewpoints. Lively, vivid language alone cannot make up for weak ideas.

Using Figures of Speech

Language that is striking or impressive can create interest and contribute to understanding. For centuries, students of rhetoric have studied what are called figures of speech; these are special ways of using language to heighten the beauty of expression, or the clarity of ideas, or the emotional impact of speeches. It is not important for the beginning student of public speaking to understand and identify all the technical names for the different figures of speech. But both listeners and speakers should be aware of some common ways of using language effectively.

Simile   The simile is used when you want to make comparisons. A direct comparison between things that an audience may not see as being similar can help them understand a concept or a particular set of circumstances. You do this by taking something that they will know about or understand and comparing it with the new or unfamiliar idea or situation you want them to understand. This kind of comparison, a simile, is typically introduced by the words *like* or *as*. When President Bush appointed Tony Snow as his new press secretary in May 2006, one reporter used similes to describe the situation Mr. Snow faced: "Any press secretary taking over the podium for the first time comes off *as a substitute teacher trying to take control of a restless high school class*. With the president's standing in the opinion polls this low, *Mr. Snow was more like a stepfather meeting his wife's children for the first time*."[10]

"A day in the life of the college student," one student began her speech, "is like a day at an amusement park. You have ups and downs; you can get spun around; you can do new things you've never done before; you can have a lot of fun; and you can end by throwing up." More eloquently, John F. Kennedy, in a speech on civil rights, used a simile to salute the courage of civil rights workers: "Like our soldiers in all parts of the world they are meeting freedom's challenge on the firing line..."[11]

Metaphor   Like a simile, a metaphor compares objects that the audience may think of as quite dissimilar. In a metaphor, however, the comparison is not so direct and does not use the words *like* or *as*. You will often use metaphor when hoping to express strong feelings or emotions. For example, a freshman college student, was about to join a group heading to southern Indiana after a series of deadly tornados. She had never seen the results of such a natural disaster before, nor had she ever volunteered to help with clean-up. She described her apprehension by using a swimming metaphor: "I think I understand the principles of swimming, but I'm about to find out by jumping into the deep end of the pool; I just hope I can swim to the other end." And, in a moving tribute to the murdered Mahatma Gandhi, Indian prime minister Jawaharlal Nehru expressed the sadness felt by his fellow Indians by comparing Gandhi to the sun: "A glory has departed and the sun that warmed and brightened our lives has set and we shiver in the dark."[12]

These images create a certain feeling or mood in the audience. In this way, they make an important contribution to the audience's total appreciation of a speech.

Antithesis   Antithesis is a way of putting together two things that have sharply different meanings. You would use this device to make contrasts between words or ideas. Through antithesis, ideas can be reinforced and compelling contrasts in thought can be suggested. A definition of *classics*, for example, is that they "are examples of *how* to think, not *what* to think."[13] In a speech criticizing those who polluted the environment in the pursuit of profits, one student speaker used this antithesis: "On this campus we're engaged in an important struggle. We must not support the forces of death and personal profit, but, instead, we must choose the forces of life and personal responsibility." The antithesis pitted life against death, effectively associating those who would put money first with the latter.

Irony   Through irony, you can strongly imply a meaning that is opposite that which is stated. This device can highlight the absurd or bitter disconnect between what is asserted and what is real. Mary Church Terrell was a graduate of Oberlin College, a teacher, the first president of the National Association of Colored Women, and a professional lecturer who spoke out against racism at the beginning of the twentieth century. In a speech given in Washington, DC, in 1906, she used irony to highlight the contradictions between the ideals of our nation's founders and the laws upholding segregation:

> As a colored woman I cannot visit the tomb of the Father of this country, which owes its very existence to the love of freedom in the human heart and which stands for equal opportunity for all, without being forced to sit in the Jim Crow section of an electric car which starts from the very heart of the city—midway between the Capitol and the White House. If I refuse thus to be humiliated, I am cast into jail and forced to pay a fine for violating the Virginia laws.[14]

Irony can be a potent way for you to point out the discrepancies between professed values and real actions.

Alliteration   A repetitive pattern of sounds used to create a more poetic tone and to reinforce key ideas is called alliteration. One returning student, proud of her new U.S. citizenship, said that becoming an American was "more than just a passport to plenty," it was "a doorway to democracy." In a speech to the NAACP in July 2009, President Obama also used alliteration when speaking of the great civil rights leaders of the past: "They knew that the stain of slavery and the sin of segregation had to be lifted in the courtroom, and in the legislature, and in the hearts and the minds of Americans."[15]

Poets commonly use alliteration and other figures of speech. Edgar Allan Poe wrote of the "silken, sad, uncertain rustling of each purple curtain"[16] to capture the sound of wind blowing through an open window. Whether used in a poem or a speech, alliteration can be memorable and pleasing to the ear. Of course, it must not be forced or overdone. A former vice president of the United States, for example, attacked media commentators who had criticized the president by absurdly labeling them "nattering nabobs of negativism."

Personification When you attribute human characteristics to animals or to inanimate objects, you are using personification. One common form of personification is a phrase we hear almost every day: "*The White House says...*" You can use personification to add interest to your speech while enhancing its emotional appeal. A student speaker, for example, observed: "This city can be a very hostile place. It can ignore you, it can frighten you, and it can punish you very severely if you ignore its unwritten rules." This student then went on to talk about such urban problems as loneliness, homelessness, and crime.

Mary Church Terrell actively attacked racism in America in the early twentieth century. She pointed to the irony of an American of color being forced to sit in a segregated section of a trolley car when traveling from the nation's capital to George Washington's tomb at Mount Vernon.

Oxymoron An oxymoron combines seemingly contradictory expressions, such as *thunderous silence* or *cheerful pessimist*. You might use such a device when you want to emphasize the contrast between two things or give an amusing twist of meaning to phrases that are sometimes used in the media, such as *found missing* or *negative increase*. Some oxymorons, such as *virtual reality*, have become so common that we no longer even recognize their contradictory quality. Others are arresting and thought-provoking, and they can reinforce ideas in memorable ways. One student, for example, described the caucus systems used in the presidential primaries as "organized chaos." Similarly, filmmakers sometimes use oxymorons to create memorable titles for their films—for example, *Back to the Future* or *Eyes Wide Shut*.

Rhetorical Questions Speakers sometimes ask listeners questions. When they do so, they are usually not actually looking for an answer from the audience. Instead, they are posing rhetorical questions, which pique the audience's curiosity and stimulate thinking. As we noted in Chapter 8, you might use a rhetorical question to gain your audience's attention at the start of a speech, or you might use rhetorical questions as transitions. But they can also be effective stylistic devices when used anywhere in a speech.

When you pose a rhetorical question, you encourage your audience to think. When you ask a question, you also invite participation in a dialogue. Questions trigger guesses, speculation, and other forms of thought. In short, questions activate your listeners' brains.

As with all stylistic devices, rhetorical questions should be chosen carefully. If the question is unimaginative or simplistic, it will not have the desired effect. "Why should you wear your seat belt?" "Why is smoking bad for you?" The answers to these rhetorical questions are probably too obvious to inspire much thought.

The effectiveness of any rhetorical question depends on its wording, its timing, and the way you develop your own response to the question. Having posed the question, you are, of course, obliged to answer it. For example, one speaker, who wanted audience members to understand the urgency of supporting a local day shelter and hunger relief program, posed this question: "What does the face of hunger look like in our community?" After pausing to let the audience contemplate the question, she then offered these examples:

> A young couple living in their car with their two young children. Unable to afford child care, the mother stays with the children while the father goes to work.
>
> A Vietnam veteran, who lives in a tent in a wooded area west of town. War injuries have made it impossible for him to maintain steady employment.
>
> A young mother, on work release from jail, struggles to rebuild her life while doing volunteer work for a church and working part-time for a local cleaning company.
>
> A 60-year-old woman—a former nurse's aide, working most of her life in nearby hospitals and nursing homes—is diagnosed with leukemia. Too weak to work, she stays at a local emergency shelter.
>
> Is this how *you* pictured poverty and hunger in our community?
>
> These are only a few of the *real* women, men, and children who take their meals at the Shalom Community Center each day.

As a way of getting listeners to think and to engage issues, rhetorical questions can prove very effective.

Parallelism You may use parallelism to bring force, clarity, rhythm, and interest to a speech. Using parallel sentences or phrases of about equal length can also add emphasis to particular ideas. In speaking about the Great Depression, for example, Franklin Roosevelt emphasized the seriousness and widespread nature of the economic problems facing the nation with a series of parallel sentences:

> I see millions of families trying to live on incomes so meager that the pall of family disaster hangs over them day by day.
>
> I see millions whose daily lives in city and on farm continue under conditions labeled indecent by a so-called polite society half a century ago.
>
> I see millions denied education, recreation and the opportunity to better their lot and the lot of their children.
>
> I see millions lacking the means to buy the products of farm and factory and by their poverty denying work and productiveness to many other millions.
>
> I see one-third of a nation ill-housed, ill-clad, ill-nourished.[17]

A student talking about the problem of excessive drinking similarly used parallelism to emphasize the extent of the problem she was addressing in her speech:

Every weekend, a student drinks too much after using a fake ID to get into a bar illegally.

Every weekend, a student drinks too much, gets sick, and even risks death.

Every weekend, a student drinks too much and risks finding herself unable to resist unwanted sexual advances.

Every weekend, a student drinks too much, walks home alone late at night, and risks being attacked or robbed.

Every weekend in this town, students are engaged in one of the most serious problems for college students today: binge drinking.

The language a speaker chooses can make a big difference. Becoming familiar with various stylistic devices and learning to use them effectively will help you become a better speaker. It is important to remember, however, that the stylistic choices you make must be appropriate to the situation in which you are speaking.

HIGHLIGHTING LANGUAGE | John McCain Accepts the 2008 Republican Nomination

Senator John McCain used active, vivid language, along with antithesis and parallelism in his speech accepting the Republican presidential nomination in 2008.

I fight to restore the pride and principles of our party. We were elected to change Washington, and we let Washington change us.

We lost the trust of the American people when some Republicans gave in to the temptations of corruption. We lost their trust when rather than reform government, both parties made it bigger.

We lost their trust when instead of freeing ourselves from a dangerous dependence on foreign oil, both parties—and Sen. Obama—passed another corporate welfare bill for oil companies. We lost their trust when we valued our power over our principles.

We're going to change that. We're going to recover the people's trust by standing up again to the values Americans admire. The party of Lincoln, Roosevelt and Reagan is going to get back to basics.

In this country, we believe everyone has something to contribute and deserves the opportunity to reach their God-given potential, from the boy whose descendents arrived on the Mayflower to the Latina daughter of migrant workers. We're all God's children, and we're all Americans.

We believe in low taxes, spending discipline, and open markets. We believe in rewarding hard work and risk-takers and letting people keep the fruits of their labor.

We believe in a strong defense, work, faith, service, a culture of life, personal responsibility, the rule of law, and judges who dispense justice impartially and don't legislate from the bench.

We believe in the values of families, neighborhoods, and communities. We believe in a government that unleashes the creativity and initiative of Americans, government that doesn't make your choices for you, but works to make sure you have more choices to make for yourself.

Source: From John McCain, "Republican Presidential Nomination Acceptance Address, St. Paul, Minnesota, Sept. 4, 2008." Published 2008 by American Presidency Project. ▲

USING APPROPRIATE AND ETHICAL LANGUAGE

10.4 Understand how language choices relate to audience expectations and have ethical implications.

Explore the Concept "Language" at **MyCommunicationLab**

Preview. *Depending on the situation, you may find yourself employing a formal or a more conversational style of speaking. When choosing your language for any speech, however, you should strive for a style that is appropriate to the situation, gender-inclusive, and consistent with your audience's expectations and ethical standards.*

Your choice of language in a public speech should reflect careful thought about the formality or informality of the speaking situation and the characteristics and expectations of your audience. You should always strive to use language that is appropriate, nonsexist, and consistent with the expectations of your audience. You also should use language consistent with your audience's ethical standards.

Appropriateness

One of the most dramatic examples of contrasting uses of language was demonstrated by the release of the famous Watergate tapes. These recorded conversations illustrated the startling differences between the public and private language of President Richard Nixon and many of his advisers.[18] What shocked people was not so much the use of vulgar words, but the fact that those words were used by the president of the United States in the Oval Office of the White House. Most people had surely heard such words before and perhaps even used some of them themselves, but they seemed especially inappropriate when spoken in the White House.

Your choice of language should be influenced by the context in which you speak. In general, you probably think about language choices and choose your language more carefully in a public speech than in a private conversation. The language you choose to introduce your city's mayor at a public forum, for example, should be more formal than the language you use when talking to a friend.

At the same time, a good speaker never "fakes" language to sound like someone else. For example, it would be inappropriate for a well-educated speaker to use poor grammar or coarse language intentionally to establish common ground with a less-educated audience. Not only would that be unethical, but it might also be interpreted as condescending and insulting. In the 2012 Republican primary, for example, the use of "you all" by a Northern candidate campaigning in Alabama was ridiculed by other candidates as blatant pandering. It would also be unwise for a speaker to use the slang or the technical language of a particular audience if that language did not come naturally to that speaker.

Certain aspects of a situation—the audience, the topic of the speech, and the occasion or setting in which the speech takes place—also have an impact on language choice. Martin Luther King Jr.'s memorable speech at the March on Washington is perhaps the best example of adapting language to the situation. King, standing on the steps of the Lincoln Memorial, began with a reference to Lincoln and the Emancipation Proclamation, a rhetorical move calculated to remind the audience of the long and bloody struggle for racial justice that began with the Civil War over a century earlier.

Gender-Inclusive Language

As we have pointed out, language is a powerful force in shaping our perceptions and beliefs. Research has shown that gendered language—typically language that excludes women—has negative effects on those excluded.[19] Consider the implications of this statement: "If a student expects to get into medical school, he will have to work hard to get excellent grades." This, of course, implies that only men should aspire to become doctors. Speakers often use gendered language thoughtlessly, without thinking about acceptable, gender-neutral alternatives.

The list in Figure 10.2, adapted from a Web site on gender-sensitive language, offers some common examples of gendered language, as well as some possible alternatives. Also, you may consult several guides to nonsexist language, such as the International Association of Business Communication's *Without Bias: A Guidebook for Nondiscriminatory Communication* (Wiley, 1982) or *The Dictionary of Bias-Free Usage: A Guide to Nondiscriminatory Language* (Oryx, 1991).

Typically, your audience will be made up of both men and women, and nowadays most audiences expect the use of gender-inclusive or gender-neutral language.

Ronald Reagan's admonition to the Soviet government to "tear down this wall" was particularly dramatic because of the setting: the Brandenburg Gate that separated East and West Berlin.

Explore the Concept "Sexist Language" at **MyCommunicationLab**

Audience Expectations

Whenever you prepare to speak in public, you should consider what your audience is already likely to know and think about your topic. In choosing language for your speech, you also need to consider your audience—their level of linguistic sophistication and their stylistic expectations. You should consider not only how formal or casual the setting may be but also the nature of the forum, the audience's background and education, and any other factors that could influence their expectations for the kind of language you use.

The wise speaker thinks carefully about audience expectations and makes reasonable and appropriate adjustments. This does not mean that you should change your natural style of speaking in order to pander to your audience. It does mean, however, that you may want to make some different language choices depending on the situation. For one audience, for example, *best guess* may be better than *informed speculation*. You want to remain true to your own voice, but you also want to take your audience's expectations into account and respect their linguistic values.

> **FIGURE 10.2**

Gendered	Gender-neutral
man, men	person, people
mankind	humankind, human beings
waiter, waitress	server
mailman	mail carrier
chairman, chairwoman	chair, chairperson
actress	actor
policeman	police officer
Congressman	representative, Member of Congress

Ethical Language

When you think of speaking appropriately, you may think only about the effectiveness of your speech. But we also have an obligation to speak ethically, choosing language that promotes mutual respect and avoids offending others. Using language that the audience considers offensive or tasteless is not just ineffective; it communicates a lack of respect for their values. Mutual respect, as we've noted throughout this book, is the hallmark of ethical public speaking.[20] You have an *ethical* obligation to choose language that communicates respect for your listeners.

As a speaker, you expect your audience to treat you respectfully. You expect them to make you feel welcome, to not interrupt you while you speak, and to reserve their own questions or comments for the question-and-answer period. If somebody does wish to challenge your views after the speech, you also have a right to expect that they will do so respectfully and without resorting to personal attacks.

These expectations go both ways, of course. If you, as a speaker, do not show respect for your listeners, you should not be surprised if they respond in kind. As partners in the communication process, both speakers and listeners have an obligation to display mutual respect, civility, good taste, and sensitivity to the feelings of others. This obligation extends even to the specific words you choose to use in your speech.

Ethical speakers guard against the use of language that demeans a particular gender, race, religion, or culture. We are not just talking about being "politically correct." We are talking about showing respect for your listeners and others in society. Most of us know that grown women do not want to be referred to as *girls* or *chicks*. Hispanics do not tolerate derogatory labels, and homosexuals rightly take offense at being called degrading or offensive terms. There are, of course, dozens of slurs that one may use to insult or demean people of particular groups. It should go without saying that the use of such slurs is unethical, particularly when they substitute for substantive argument or are intentionally designed to silence or intimidate members of minority groups.

Of course, offensive language is not only unethical; it is ineffective as well. Listeners who are offended by a speaker are not likely to continue listening, much less be persuaded to embrace that speaker's point of view.

RESPONDING CRITICALLY TO A SPEAKER'S STYLE

Preview. *When a speaker has good style, listeners are likely to be moved. Critical listeners are aware that style in language can have an impact. They look for sound arguments, good evidence, and substance of thought—regardless of the speaker's style. They avoid overreacting to style in either a positive or a negative sense.*

10.5 Avoid over-reacting to style by focusing on the substance of a speaker's ideas.

It should be apparent by now that style can have a strong impact on listeners— almost apart from the ideas being expressed. That is, the *way* in which ideas are expressed can be as important as the ideas themselves in influencing the listeners' reactions. A clear and appropriate speaking style can enhance a speaker's ethos, whereas an otherwise good speech can be undermined by poor stylistic choices.

Using Emotional Language Ethically

The ethical public speaker never uses language to whip the audience into an emotional frenzy. As we have made clear, emotional appeals are often appropriate and necessary to move an audience to action. Most people do not respond to reasoned arguments alone if they do not also feel emotionally engaged. Ethical emotional appeals are backed up with strong evidence and sound reasoning. The ethical speaker *wants* the audience to think critically and constructively, and he or she does nothing to discourage that.

Style Substituted for Argument

Speakers have been known to dismiss an idea not by dissecting it, analyzing it, or examining its weaknesses or strengths, but simply by labeling it. For example, a speaker may simply declare that an idea is too "simplistic," too "radical," or perhaps too "reactionary." Such a speaker is substituting style for argument. During the most recent GOP primaries, for example, opponents of Governor Mitt Romney referred to him as the "Massachusetts moderate" in an effort to discredit him within the conservative base of the party. What should you do when you hear such labeling? Good critical listeners ask, What is the basis for calling him that? What does the speaker even mean by "Massachusetts moderate?" Does simply calling Romney a "moderate" prove anything about how his values and policies would affect America? Asking these kinds of questions will help you avoid falling prey to an attempt to substitute style for argument.

In Chapter 7, we discussed the importance of supporting your ideas with evidence. You should keep the same principle in mind when you listen to others use language to persuade you. Be wary of highly emotional language and labeling. Always look for evidence backing up the speaker's claims. Good speakers anticipate an audience of smart, critical listeners, and they know they must provide support for their ideas.

Study and Review materials for this chapter are at **MyCommunicationLab**

SUMMARY

 Listen to the Audio Chapter Summary at **MyCommunicationLab**

Language and Meaning

 Understand the relationship between language and meaning.

- Because all language is symbolic, it has the power to engage our emotions as well as promote understanding. Language is rich in both denotative and connotative meaning.

Using Language That Is Clear and Accurate

 Choose language that is specific, concrete, precise, and clear.

- Good style means promoting the audience's understanding and acceptance through the use of effective language.
  - Using language that is familiar to listeners, as well as concrete, specific, and precise, will help you achieve clarity, which is essential to a good speaking style.
  - It is important to avoid crowding sentences with clichés and empty words. Also avoid constructing sentences that are overly complex and hard for listeners to follow.

Using Language That Is Active and Interesting

 Choose language that is lively and vivid, using appeals to the senses and figures of speech.

- Listeners find active language more engaging than passive language.

- Figures of speech, such as metaphors, antithesis, and alliteration, make language more interesting.

Using Appropriate and Ethical Language

 Understand how language choices relate to audience expectations and have ethical implications.

- Language should be appropriate to the situation—well adapted to the setting, the listeners' expectations and levels of understanding, and the constraints of the occasion.
- Using language ethically entails showing respect for the audience, striving not to offend them, using good judgment and good taste, and encouraging listeners to respond thoughtfully rather than impulsively.

Responding Critically to a Speaker's Style

 Avoid overreacting to style by focusing on the substance of a speaker's ideas.

- The critical listener guards against being swayed by style alone.
  - The critical listener does not respond to emotionally charged words without considering the evidence and reasoning supporting the argument.
  - The critical listener is not persuaded by a speech that substitutes style for substance.

QUESTIONS FOR REVIEW AND REFLECTION

Language and Meaning

 Understand the relationship between language and meaning.

1. What is meant by *style* in public speaking? How does it differ from other notions of style?
2. What is the relationship between language and meaning?
3. Can you identify denotative and connotative language in messages you hear or read? How might emotionally charged language affect your response?

Using Language That Is Clear and Accurate

 Choose language that is specific, concrete, precise, and clear.

4. Explain the differences between oral and written style.
5. In what ways can a speaker strive to make his or her language clearer? Give examples of how you could improve on unclear language choices.
6. What is wrong with using expressions such as *it goes without saying*, *last but not least*, and *due to the fact that* when you speak?

Using Language That Is Active and Interesting

 Choose language that is lively and vivid, using appeals to the senses and figures of speech.

7. Why is active language more interesting to listeners than passive language? Give an example of the same thought expressed in passive and then active language.

8. Provide a good example of each of the following figures of speech and explain how it makes an idea more effective:
   a. Simile
   b. Metaphor
   c. Antithesis
   d. Irony
   e. Alliteration
   f. Personification
   g. Oxymoron
   h. Parallelism
   i. Rhetorical question

Using Appropriate and Ethical Language

 Understand how language choices relate to audience expectations and have ethical implications.

9. To be effective, a speaker must make appropriate language choices. What are three key guidelines for using language appropriately in a public speech?
10. What is the relationship between using language appropriately and using it ethically?
11. What language do you find offensive, and how would you react to a speaker who uses such language?

Responding Critically to a Speaker's Style

 Avoid overreacting to style by focusing on the substance of a speaker's ideas.

12. How might style be used to obscure a flawed argument? Give examples.

 Study and Review the Flashcards at **MyCommunicationLab**

NEW HORIZONS FOR WOMEN

Mrs. Lyndon Baines (Lady Bird) Johnson, Former First Lady, United States of America

The 1960s were a time of turbulence and change. John F. Kennedy was assassinated in November 1963, and Lyndon Johnson became president. The new president announced ambitious domestic reforms—"the Great Society"—and signed two civil rights bills in the summer of 1964. In 1963, Betty Friedan wrote The Feminine Mystique, *in which she urged women to break free of traditional prescribed roles, setting the stage for the establishment of the National Organization of Women, which she founded in 1965. Between those two events, in 1964, Lady Bird Johnson gave this speech. The First Lady, in addressing this audience of home economists— teachers and county agents, all of whom were women—stressed the need for women to become involved at a time when they were beginning to strive for the fulfillment of their rights as citizens.*

ADDRESS TO THE NATIONAL CONVENTION OF AMERICAN HOME ECONOMICS ASSOCIATION IN DETROIT, MICHIGAN, ON JUNE 24, 1964

While we meet here on an evening in June, the horizons of women all over the world are widening from home to humanity—from our private families to the family of man.

A quiet revolution of emancipation has been taking place in the lives of women everywhere— from Detroit to Delhi. Millions of women have achieved the right to vote, to own property, to be educated. Technological marvels now can free women from the total bondage of home chores. You, as home economists, have helped to make it so. You have taught American women to master the intricacies of push-button washer-dryers, automatic ranges, and convenience foods. More and more, you will be exporting this know-how to other parts of the world.

With these newly won rights and with a rising standard of living, women can move beyond the struggle for equal status and for material goods to the challenges and opportunities of citizenship. Increasingly, we are going to be concerned with what my husband calls "the Great Society"—the quality of goals and the achievement of goals which will mean a better life for all.

As American women, we hold a tremendous potential of strength for good. I do not refer to the sense of power that comes from flicking a switch or turning an ignition key. But to the force we exert when we mark a ballot, teach our children, or work for a better community.

The question is: How can we best mobilize this potential? How can the individual woman practice citizenship to the fullest extent, both at home and abroad?

Ernest Hemingway once said, "Talk and write about what you know." One sees change in terms of one's own experiences.

As a girl, my home was in East Texas. It was a place where Spanish moss was draped from age-old cypresses, where alligators slithered down muddy banks into dark, enchanted bayous. While we fished through the long summer days, we enjoyed the illusion that time was standing still. But time never stands still. I grew up, went to college and married a tall Texan. My horizons have been broadening and my involvement getting deeper ever since.

As she begins her speech, Johnson chooses figurative language that announces her theme. In using the phrases "from home to humanity" and "from our private families to the family of man," she suggests that her message to women is to move from personal preoccupations to involvement in larger issues.

Note the many words the speaker chooses throughout the speech that have positive connotations, such as challenges, opportunities, potential, strength, community. All of these suggest bold, positive action.

In the past few years, my own participation has included travel with my husband to all corners of our own land, to Thailand and India, to Senegal and Iceland, and a score of other countries.

This spring, I have been traveling some myself. I have been to areas of serious unemployment and limited opportunities, such as Wilkes-Barre, Pennsylvania, and Breathitt County, Kentucky. For me, it helps me see in human terms the objectives of the war on poverty.

Once in a while I ask myself, "What am I doing here?" Perhaps when I visit, it helps draw the curtain open a little more. Perhaps it gives national attention to a local problem. Perhaps it exposes us to ourselves and says, "This is the other side of America. Look! And act!"

I am only 1 of 65 million American women. Almost all of us are involved, one way or another, in being the best citizens we know how to be. Actually, none of us just sat down and said, "I'm going to get involved." It happens gradually, inspired by husband and family, sometimes triggered by crisis, always influenced by circumstances and opportunity.

For example, let me tell you about one woman who has made a mark on her community and on the lives of many people around her. I went to college with her at the University of Texas. She was—and is—a beautiful girl, gay, filled with character and grace. Then, after she married, she was hit by one of life's hardest blows: her second child was born with cerebral palsy.

After two or three years of fighting this fact, and carrying her child to many, many doctors, she accepted it. She discovered that there were different degrees of this illness, and that in many cases, the victims could be helped. So she went to work.

Largely through her untiring persuasion, she brought together local organizations and city fathers. We now have a clinic in Austin where hundreds of children come from hundreds of miles around for treatment and training. Behind every achievement or success is one dauntless person who keeps gathering together the strength that makes the web of success.

Tonight we met a high school home economics teacher with four children who, I understand, has a daughter born with a physical handicap and a sister-in-law who suffered loss of an arm recently.

Far from restricting her activities because of these family problems, this home economist has gone beyond the call of duty to organize a place of worship for her religious denomination in the community, to initiate and lead a 4-H group, to introduce the National Honor Society in her high school and to serve as the faculty adviser for the student council and the yearbook. And, she is volunteering as bookkeeper for her husband who has just opened his own business! These are just two examples among thousands.

All of us are acquainted with many women working at citizenship. You, yourselves are doing it each day of your lives—bringing home economics know-how to girls and women who have or will have a home of their own.

That has been your role since your association was founded 55 years ago. I like what your founder, Ellen Richards, the first woman graduate from Massachusetts Institute of Technology, said. It is as applicable today as it was in 1909; to apply principles of science to the home so we may have—and these are her words—"Freedom of the home from the dominance of things."

What better formula with which to develop the full potential of the home as a springboard to citizenship!

THROUGHOUT THE SPEECH, JOHNSON USES SIMPLE BUT APPROPRIATE LANGUAGE. IN RELATING SPECIFIC EXAMPLES, SHE DESCRIBES THE EXPERIENCES OF WOMEN USING LANGUAGE CHOSEN TO BE BOTH CLEAR AND INTERESTING.

For, as someone once said, "When you teach a man, you teach an individual; when you teach a woman, you teach a family." And in this age, I would add to that—You also teach a nation and a world."

For me, your work has a very personal meaning. In Texas, our county home demonstration agents have helped homemakers to live better, to make wiser choices, to tackle problems more intelligently within the family and the community. At the ranch, we have always been delighted to see her coming. We know that when she leaves, we shall have learned much in a few hours.

Over the past fifteen years, as Americans moved to town, the home economist has followed them.

I do not need to tell you that the cities reach out for you—to help people in the public housing units and the crowded slum areas who do not know how to cope with the new and unaccustomed conditions of city life.

Indeed, as I consider your profession, there are so many ways in which the nation needs your help in the unfinished business of America.

You have long been alert to the fact that poverty's roots are deepest in the family structure. Now I am delighted you are stepping up your activities for the low-income family.

An education program geared to the family without modern equipment, the family that can read, perhaps not well or not in English, may offer these people the lifeline they need.

Your president, Florence Lowe, tells me of the El Paso Project in which a bilingual set of instructions about Food for Fitness was mailed out to Mexican-American families. It brought tremendous results.

One reason was that the mail got top attention because these families received so little mail.

The all-out war on poverty needs home economists in the front brigade. And I commend all you are doing to be a full participant in this force.

New thinking and teaching is needed if we are to communicate fully to the low-income family. We must reexamine the college curriculum which produces the home economists. As in other professions, this curriculum may be geared too much to the values of the middle-income family.

Our state departments of welfare are realizing, more and more, how important it is to have the home economist to reinforce the case worker. Family problems often stem from a lack of knowledge of wise buying habits. Seventeen states now have full-time home economists on their staffs.

One of the most exciting new horizons for the home economist is helping solve the problems that daily face ten million homemakers in this country who are permanently or temporarily disabled.

The blind woman with the baby needs advice on how to care for it in her own home.

The woman with only one arm needs a little extra attention to learn how to manage her home and bathe the baby.

A mother paralyzed by polio was asked several months ago what she wished she had known when she returned home from the hospital.

"I wish someone had told me to buy a different type of carpet, one that would be right for my wheelchair," she said.

Help from an expert can make life more comfortable and productive.

THE WAR ON POVERTY WAS ONE ASPECT OF PRESIDENT JOHNSON'S GREAT SOCIETY. JOHNSON EMPLOYS THIS METAPHOR TO DIRECTLY INVOLVE HER AUDIENCE, DESCRIBING THEM AS THE "FRONT BRIGADE."

I trust your professional efforts on behalf of women and families in the developing countries will receive a big push in the coming years. The fact that over 300 home economists are in the Peace Corps—some of them women who came out of retirement to volunteer for service in Sierra Leone and Peru—is an indication of your concern for your fellow man around the world.

One of the great joys of your work is that you can see the results. My husband has often told me that the years which gave him the most intense personal satisfaction were those in which he served under President Roosevelt as a state director of the National Youth Administration. Boys were taken from boxcars and given back their self-respect along with part-time jobs which enabled them to stay in school. To watch this happening, to have a part in its happening, was an experience we shall never forget.

For me, it was the beginning of seeing how politics can bring tangible results. I always hope that the very best of our people will go into politics, and I am sure that some of our best are women. It was for this reason that the President began his effort last winter to bring more women into government.

You home economists are examples of women who manage several lives successfully. Most of you have both a home and a professional career. Many of you, like several of the award winners tonight, also have children. You have much to share.

So, I say: "Don't hold back. Don't be shy. Step forward in every way you can to plan boldly, to speak clearly, to offer the leadership which the world needs."

For me, and probably for most women, the attempt to become an involved, practicing citizen has been a matter of evolution rather than choice. Actually, if given a choice between lying in a hammock under an apple tree with a book of poetry and watching the blossoms float down or standing on a platform before thousands of people, I don't have to tell you what I would have chosen 25 years ago. But 25 years and the invention of the nuclear bomb have left us no choice. The hammocks and apple trees are happy memories except for a few short, cherished moments.

Edmund Burke said, almost 200 years ago, "The only thing necessary for the triumph of evil is for good men to do nothing." I hope he would forgive me if I modernize and amend his statement to say, "The only thing necessary for the triumph of evil is for good men *and good women to do nothing.*"

I am sure that will not be.

Source: From Mrs. Lyndon B. Johnson, "New Horizons by Women" Address to the National Convention of American Home Association in Detroit, MI. Published 1964.

HERE, JOHNSON USES SIMPLE, DIRECT LANGUAGE TO CHALLENGE HER AUDIENCE—HER IMMEDIATE AUDIENCE OF HOME ECONOMISTS AS WELL AS THE MILLIONS OF AMERICAN WOMEN SHE HOPES TO ENCOURAGE TO PLAY AN ACTIVE ROLE IN CIVIC AFFAIRS.

SHE ENDS HER SPEECH BY TAKING A FAMOUS QUOTATION AND ADDING TO IT THE WORDS "AND GOOD WOMEN," REINFORCING HER PLEA FOR WOMEN TO GET INVOLVED IN CIVIC AFFAIRS. HER SIMPLE FINAL SENTENCE IS BOTH AN AFFIRMATION OF HER OWN CONVICTION AND A CALL TO ACTION.

Delivering Your Speech Effectively

In 1847, a young woman graduated from Oberlin College and began a career as a reformer, lecturing throughout the country. She first spoke in support of the abolition of slavery and then took up the cause of women's suffrage. In a time when women who dared to speak in public were often subjected to ridicule and abuse, it took conviction, courage, and a commanding presence to appear before such hostile audiences. Her supporters, however, frequently praised her logic and command of the facts. According to one listener, her message was "wholly irresistible to every person who cares for reason or justice." Yet she probably would have failed without a powerful delivery—and that Lucy Stone had. She was, one observer wrote, "small in stature but large of soul...her bearing modest and dignified, her face radiant with feeling, and speaking all over, as it were, in eloquent accord with her earnest voice."[1]

You are not likely to confront the kind of challenges faced by Lucy Stone, and most of us would have a hard time standing up to such challenges. But whenever you speak in public—in the classroom, in a business meeting, or at a town hall meeting—your delivery will play a significant part in your success. Delivery is one of the most obvious aspects of public speaking, and it shapes your listeners' first impressions of your skills as a speaker. Yet you should never count on an engaging delivery to compensate for a speech that is poorly structured or lacking in substance.

SOUNDING GOOD VERSUS BEING SOUND

Preview. *One of your ethical obligations as a speaker is to present a message of substance. Good delivery, though important, is no substitute for sound ideas. Having an ethical and effective delivery means remaining audience-centered, avoiding behaviors that distract from the message, and promoting the listeners' understanding.*

11.1 Explain the ethical issues involved in delivering your speech.

Sometimes you may find yourself thinking that a speaker sounded good but did not have anything important to say. On another occasion, a speaker's delivery may be so dramatic that it actually distracts from the content of the speech. Whether intentional or not, a distracting delivery is not good delivery.

Beyond Delivery: Listening to the Message

As listeners, we sometimes give too much weight to how a speech is delivered. A speaker who is poised and articulate, has a good voice, and appears confident and friendly may impress us. However, such a speaker might be merely facile—he or she can speak easily but may not have much to say. It is important to distinguish between a speaker who *is* sound and a speaker who just *sounds* good.

A sound speaker's ideas pass the tests of evidence and reasoning discussed in Chapters 7 and 15. As much as we might admire the ease and grace of some speakers, we need to be on our guard against the slick, superficial speaker who tries to manipulate or deceive us rather than engage us in a discussion of important ideas.

The Foundation of Ethical Delivery

Ethical delivery grows out of a collaborative, transactional model of communication (as described in Chapter 2). It means communicating with respect for your listeners, never seeking to manipulate them, but aiming instead for a mutually beneficial outcome. The ethical speaker does not put on an "act" but speaks sincerely and authentically—always mindful of the needs, values, and priorities of those assembled to listen.

Ethical delivery does not distract from the content or meaning of the speech. It is appropriate to the situation, including the size and makeup of the audience. By contrast, an unethical speaker may intentionally use overly dramatic gestures, striking movement, or exaggerated vocal patterns to distract the audience from the speech's content. Not only is this kind of delivery ethically questionable, it can also backfire. Effective and ethical delivery should *reinforce* rather than distract attention from the speaker's ideas.

Finally, ethical delivery promotes the listeners' trust and comprehension. When you make a speech, your body, voice, and gestures must be in tune with the mood and nature of your message. Never forget that your audience will form impressions of you and your ideas based, in some measure, on how you deliver your speech. A speaker may have some compelling ideas, but if that speaker seems dull and lifeless—if the speaker does not seem to care—the message may be lost.

PRINCIPLES OF GOOD DELIVERY

11.2 Describe the basic principles of effective delivery.

Explore the Concept "Speech Delivery" at **MyCommunicationLab**

Preview.   *Certain basic principles of effective delivery apply to a wide variety of public speaking situations. You will want to adapt your delivery to the specific situation and to audience expectations. In general, effective delivery is associated with proper attire, good eye contact, appropriate gestures and movement, and facial expressions that reinforce your message. Good delivery also means a dynamic yet conversational speaking voice.*

Most of us recognize the importance of delivery, yet we may become apprehensive at the thought of standing in front of a group of people and delivering a speech.[2] As you prepare to deliver a speech, you will confront many questions: Should I use a podium? Should I move around during my speech? Will everybody be able to hear me? There are no absolute answers to any of these questions. You will need to adjust your style of delivery to the demands of each situation.

In your classroom, these questions are relatively easy to answer; they become more problematic when giving a speech in a different setting. In that case, the person who invited you to speak should be able to offer you guidance concerning the formality of the occasion and the expectations of the audience. It is wise to find out as much as you can about the situation before you begin planning your speech. Above all, you need to think about what sort of delivery style will best help you connect with your audience.

Watch the Video "Martin Cox Discusses Tips for Speech Delivery" at **MyCommunicationLab**

Understand the Situation and Audience Expectations

What is appropriate in one speaking situation may be inappropriate in another. The more you learn about audience members' needs, norms, and preferences, the more likely you will deliver your speech effectively. Do these listeners expect a formal presentation, or do they like to sit in a circle and have the speaker "chat" with them? Is this an after-dinner speech, to be delivered in a hotel conference room equipped with a podium and technological support? If so, will the listeners expect you to speak from behind the podium and make use of that technology?

How you dress when you deliver a speech can also be important. Your appearance can influence how your audience judges your ethos or credibility. Although there are no fixed rules for attire, listeners generally expect an invited speaker to be well groomed and nicely dressed.[3] How the audience itself will be dressed may provide one clue. You do not want to be wearing jeans and a T-shirt if your audience will be dressed in suits and ties.

In your public speaking class, casual attire may be appropriate, but you still want to feel confident and comfortable with the way you look. Avoid shoes that are too tight or clothes that are too snug. Also avoid any attire that detracts from your speech, such as a flamboyant blouse, a T-shirt with written or visual content, or a baseball cap.

Establish Eye Contact

Have you ever talked with someone who did not look you in the eye? Did you feel that the person was uncomfortable? Nervous? Ashamed? Preoccupied? Dishonest? In most cultures, a communicator who does not look us in the eye makes us suspicious.[4] The same is true in formal public speaking. As listeners, we respond more positively to speakers who make eye contact with us.

Of course, there are cultural variations in practices and reactions to eye contact. The *Highlighting Eye Contact* feature provides examples of some of these cultural differences.

Watch the Video "Student Scholarships and Awards Ceremony" at **MyCommunicationLab**

HIGHLIGHTING EYE CONTACT	Acknowledging Cultural Differences in Eye Contact and Gaze

- In Japan, meeting participants often look down or close their eyes while others are talking. By doing so, they show their attentiveness to and even agreement with the speaker.
- African Americans, Native Americans, Chicanos, and Puerto Ricans often avoid eye contact as a nonverbal sign of recognition and respect for an authority-subordinate relationship.
- In some Far Eastern cultures, it is considered rude to look into another person's eyes while talking to him or her.
- For Arabs, the eyes are considered a key to a person's being; looking deeply into

another person's eyes allows one to see another's soul.
- In U.S. culture, establishing eye contact with others conveys a sense of directness, openness, and candor.

Sources: Edward T. Hall and Mildred Reed Hall, *Understanding Cultural Differences* (Yarmouth, ME: Intercultural Press, 1990); Carolyn Calloway-Thomas, Pamela J. Cooper, and Cecil Blake, *Intercultural Communication: Roots and Routes* (Boston: Allyn & Bacon, 1999); and Michelle Le Baron, *Bridging Cultural Conflicts: A New Approach for a Changing World* (San Francisco: Jossey-Bass, 2003).

Whatever our cultural differences, our eyes can be very expressive. As we squint, smile, laugh, frown, or scowl, we communicate many emotions: concern, commitment, joy, or anger. When we fail to establish eye contact, we must rely solely on our words, voice, gestures, or facial expressions to convey emotions. In U.S. culture, we clearly place ourselves at a disadvantage if we do not use our eyes to communicate.[5]

Good eye contact also conveys sincerity. We are more likely to believe a speaker who looks us in the eye while speaking.[6] When we establish eye contact with our listeners, we come across as more truthful, candid, open, and trustworthy.

Finally, looking at the members of the audience gives us a chance to observe their reactions to our speech. How can we clarify what we are saying if we have not even noticed that our listeners look confused? How can we benefit from appreciative smiles and nods of encouragement if we are not looking? With the exception of comments or questions after the speech, the feedback you get from your audience will consist of nonverbal signs, such as nods, smiles, or expressions of excitement or boredom. If you "close your eyes" to such feedback, you will miss out on an important chance to adjust your speech and to engage in more of a dialogue with your audience. When you *do* respond to audience reactions, you show sensitivity and respect.

As you establish eye contact with your listeners, remember to share your attention with everyone. Figure 11.1 highlights several patterns of eye contact to avoid. Of all the principles of effective delivery, maintaining good eye contact with your listeners is among the most important.

▶ **FIGURE 11.1**

Ineffective Eye Patterns

When you deliver your speech, seek to avoid all of the following:

- *Staring at one or two listeners—excluding others and creating discomfort for those who are the focus of your excessive gaze*
- *Directing your gaze to those of particular interest—an attractive classmate, the instructor, the boss, a key competitor, or an elected official*
- *Directing your gaze only to those who are smiling and appear to agree with what you are saying*
- *Looking at one side of the room as if listeners on that side are magnetized*
- *Staring at the floor while speaking and failing to connect with the audience altogether*
- *Looking over listeners' heads and speaking to the back wall*
- *Talking mostly to your speaking notes and only occasionally bobbing up to look briefly at listeners as if making sure they haven't left the room*
- *Directing your eye contact to your presentational aids—speaking directly to a screen, a flip chart, or a handout while losing contact with the audience*
- *Rolling your eyes during audience questions and thus expressing your low regard for the question or the questioner*

Reinforce Ideas through Gestures, Movement, and Facial Expressions

Explore the Concept "Nonverbal Communication" at **MyCommunicationLab**

Most of us use several physical gestures in ordinary conversation. We wave our hands, point, or pound on the table to emphasize a point. How we hold or move our bodies can also communicate information to others, intentionally or unintentionally.[7] If we pace or slouch in our chair, we may imply we are nervous or disinterested. We might move closer to someone to express affection or intimacy, or we might move farther away to create distance or convey aloofness. We communicate a great deal with our faces, too.[8] We might smile broadly, scowl, raise an eyebrow, or clench our teeth to communicate our determination, anger, or stubbornness. Through facial expressions, we can "say" a lot.

Your words and physical actions should be mutually reinforcing.[9] If you were talking to a friend about something that really mattered to you, you might say, "I *really* want you to consider doing this!" At the same time, you might lean forward, look into her or his eyes, and nod your head. In public speaking, you can use similar nonverbal signals to reinforce your message, perhaps gesturing to emphasize a point or moving laterally to reinforce a transition. If, on the other hand, you contradict your words with your nonverbal actions—say, you smile when discussing a serious matter or appear uninterested when claiming to be excited—your audience is likely to give more weight to your nonverbal cues.[10]

Perhaps you are uncertain about whether your movement, gestures, and facial expressions are appropriate. If so, you might ask someone to watch you practice your speech and give you feedback. Here are some questions you may want to consider:

- Does my movement seem to reinforce the flow of the speech?
- Are my gestures distracting in any way?
- Do I rely too much on any one gesture?
- Does my face seem to convey sincerity and reinforce the meaning of my speech?
- Are there different gestures, movements, or facial expressions that might better communicate my intended meaning?
- Does my nonverbal communication consistently convey a respectful attitude toward the audience?[11]

Although you may plan a few basic gestures and movements in advance, *most* should occur spontaneously as you interact with your audience. Your nonverbal delivery will vary as you give your speech at different times, in different rooms, and to different audiences. For instance, the same gestures that you use in ordinary conversation may work well if you are speaking to an audience of 25 or fewer. But if you are speaking to 150 people assembled in an auditorium, you may want to enlarge your gestures so that everyone can see them.

Finally, you should work at avoiding nonverbal behaviors that may come across as nervous or distracting. Figure 11.2 lists some specific gestures and movements to avoid while delivering a speech.

Whenever a gesture calls attention to itself, eliminate it. Gesture and movement can reinforce your ideas, but they can also distract from the message you hope to convey.

> ▶ **FIGURE 11.2**
>
> **Nonverbal Behaviors to Avoid**
>
> Like all other "rules," some nonverbal behaviors will appropriately vary with the speaking situation. In general, however, you should seek to eliminate the following behaviors:
>
> - *Pacing nervously while you speak*
> - *Moving to a different spot in the room for no apparent reason*
> - *Pointing your finger at the audience while making an important point*
> - *Wagging your finger back and forth as if saying, "That's a no-no!"*
> - *Using the same gesture repeatedly*
> - *Using large, expansive gestures in a small room*
> - *Using tiny gestures in a large room*
> - *Stroking your face or hair*
> - *Biting your lip*
> - *Fiddling with your glasses or jewelry*
> - *Leaning on or gripping the podium*
> - *Smiling throughout the speech*
> - *Frowning throughout the speech*
> - *Chewing on your nails while listening to audience questions or comments*

Strive for an Effective Speaking Voice

One of the most obvious aspects of your delivery is your voice. Have you ever listened to a speaker whose voice really bothered you? Perhaps she or he spoke in a monotone, stumbled over words, or inserted *you know* at every pause. Or maybe the speaker's voice sounded too high and squeaky or too low and unvarying. Clearly, our voices can get us into trouble as public speakers. But they can also be used effectively to enhance our messages. When you use your voice effectively, you can add extra emphasis to key ideas, display a variety of emotions, demonstrate your commitment, and enhance your credibility.

How can you improve the vocal aspects of your delivery? You might try speaking into an audio recorder and playing it back to see what your voice sounds like to others. Obtaining feedback from friends can also be helpful. You can modify some features of your voice by recognizing their importance, paying attention to them as you practice your speech out loud, and monitoring them as you speak. The features that you can control and perhaps improve include volume, rate, pitch, and clarity.

Volume   If listeners cannot hear you, they obviously cannot benefit from your message. Nor will they be able to concentrate on your message if you speak so loudly that they feel uncomfortable.

The volume of your delivery should be determined by the setting in which you speak. Naturally, a small room calls for a quieter voice than does a large lecture hall or an outdoor setting. If you are concerned that you cannot be heard, you could simply ask your audience as you begin to speak. Doing so shows your respect for your listeners, and they will be glad to give you feedback.

In some situations, you may need a microphone to amplify your voice. Some microphones clip to your clothing, while others are handheld or attached to a podium. If you use a microphone, make sure it is working properly before you start your speech. If the microphone is attached to a podium, you may need to adjust its height so that you can speak directly into it.

Rate   It is not uncommon for a beginning speaker to sit down after giving a speech, look at the clock, and be amazed to find that the planned ten-minute speech took only seven or eight minutes. Several miscalculations could account for this, but often the problem is that the speaker rushed through the speech. Keep in mind that your audience needs time to absorb and process your speech—especially if you are addressing a complex or thought-provoking issue.

The needs of the listeners should be paramount. Just as they cannot keep up with a speaker who is talking too quickly, they may lose interest in one who speaks too slowly. In most speaking situations, about 125–150 words per minute is considered an appropriate rate of speaking,[12] but you may choose to speak more quickly or slowly, depending on the complexity and novelty of the information you are presenting. Some research suggests that listeners may perceive speakers who speak quickly (though not *too* fast) as more knowledgeable,[13] but you should speak at a rate that fits your own personal style and that allows the audience to process the information you present.

Finally, your speaking rate can be used to emphasize key ideas. The effective use of pauses can give your audience the opportunity to absorb information and ideas. Some speakers even use pauses or silence to reinforce a compelling statistic, quotation, or narrative, in effect saying, "Let's stop to think about this for a moment. This is important." Similarly, you may slow down or use repetition to emphasize an important idea. When you *vary* your rate—by pausing, slowing down, or using restatement or repetition at critical and strategic moments—you enhance your chances of getting your message across.

Pitch   Sometimes a speaker's voice is simply unpleasant to listen to. It may be squeaky or raspy, or it may be pitched so low that you can hardly distinguish one word from the next. *Pitch* refers to the highness or lowness of your voice on a musical scale. It is the voice's upward or downward inflection. A speaker's vocal pitch can be too high, too low, or too unvarying. When the pitch is too high, listeners tend to cringe. When the pitch is too low, listeners may be unable to hear what the speaker is saying. An unvarying pitch is called a monotone—a vocal quality guaranteed to put your audience to sleep.

Rightly or wrongly, listeners often draw conclusions about speakers whose pitch seems inappropriate. A high pitch may be associated with immaturity, inexperience, tension, or excitability. A low pitch or a monotone may cause listeners to view the speaker as bored or disengaged. By contrast, a richer pitch, one with depth and variety, can communicate a sense of authority and competence.[14]

What can you do about the pitch of your voice? Start by audio-recording your voice and listening to how you sound. If you are not satisfied, you may want to use some vocal exercises to improve your pitch. In extreme cases, you may want to seek assistance from someone trained in voice therapy. Here are a few pointers to keep in mind:

- Your pitch will vary throughout your life. It will be higher when you are younger and lower later in life. Working with the pitch of your voice is an ongoing process.
- If you are tense, your pitch tends to rise. Use the relaxation techniques outlined in Chapter 3 to help you manage communication apprehension.
- Strive for variety in your pitch. Avoid repetitive pitch patterns, such as *uptalking* (in which your pitch rises as you seem to question the statement you have just made).[15] You want your voice to be interesting, and you want to use all aspects of your voice to emphasize your most important points.

Clarity   To be effective as a speaker, you must be understood. Although speaking at an appropriate speed can help you communicate more clearly, vocal clarity is also important. A clear vocal style depends on several things: First, strive for distinctness in *articulation*. Dropping the endings off words, slurring sounds, and running words together can interfere with the clarity of your message. For example, if you say "locked out" but you sound like you said "lucked out," you did not articulate clearly. Articulation especially becomes a problem when a speaker rushes through a speech, failing to take the time to articulate each word carefully.

Second, strive for correct pronunciation of the words you use. Whereas articulation refers to the clarity with which we say words, *pronunciation* involves saying words correctly. If you are unsure of the correct pronunciation of an uncommon or unfamiliar word, look it up in a dictionary. Practice aloud so that you are comfortable saying the words you are using, and especially check the pronunciation of words used in quoted material.

Finally, avoid *vocal mannerisms*. It is pointless and distracting to keep saying *you know* every time you pause during speaking. Some speakers also have a habit

---

HIGHLIGHTING THE IMPORTANCE OF A GOOD VOICE | The Practices of Demosthenes

One of the greatest orators of ancient Greece was Demosthenes. According to historians, Demosthenes had difficulties speaking clearly, but he recognized the importance of good articulation, so he did all he could to improve. Plutarch writes the following:

His inarticulate and stammering pronunciation he overcame and rendered more distinct by speaking with pebbles in his mouth; his voice he disciplined by declaiming and reciting speeches or verses when he was out of breath, while running or going up steep places; and in his house he had a large looking-glass, before which he would stand and go through his exercises.

It is told that someone once came to request assistance as a pleader, and related how he had been assaulted and beaten. "Certainly" said Demosthenes, "nothing of the kind can have happened to you." Upon which the other, raising his voice, exclaimed loudly, "What, Demosthenes, nothing has been done to me?" "Ah," replied Demosthenes, "now I hear the voice of one that has been injured and beaten." Of so great consequence towards the gaining of belief did he esteem the tone and action of the speaker.

Source: From Plutarch, "The Practices of Demosthenes," Plutarch's Lives, vol. 12. Published 1909 by P.F. Collier & Son.

of concluding almost every statement with the unnecessary question, "Right?" Also, some regional mannerisms clutter speech and thus reduce clarity, for example, "Ya know?" Other speakers seem to end every sentence with an *at*, as in "He didn't know where I was *at*." These vocal mannerisms often are distracting to listeners.[16]

Remain Flexible

No matter how carefully you plan and practice in advance, some speaking situations will surprise you. Flexibility is the key to responding successfully to these situations. You might find that the podium is missing or the microphone is not working. You might be told at the last minute that you have less time to speak than originally planned and that you will have to cut your speech short. Or, imagine that you expected to deliver a formal speech to a large audience, but when you arrived, only five or six people were present. Rather than standing behind a podium and speaking formally, you might want to adapt to the situation by sitting on the edge of a table and informally "chatting" with the group.

The foundation of flexibility is spontaneity and open-mindedness—a willingness to recognize that there are many different ways to deliver a good speech and an ability to discover a "better" way whenever a situation seems to demand it. Speakers

▶ HIGHLIGHTING FLEXIBILITY | A Dramatic Example

Perhaps the most extraordinary—and certainly unique—example of adapting to the situation came during the presidential campaign of 1912. Former president Theodore Roosevelt, who had failed to secure his own party's nomination, was running for president as a candidate of a third party, the Progressive or "Bull Moose" Party. With scarcely three weeks to go before the election, Roosevelt's campaign pulled into Milwaukee, where he was scheduled to speak before a huge rally of supporters. As Roosevelt left his hotel, a man stepped up to him and fired a gun at point-blank range. The bullet passed through the copy of Roosevelt's speech, which was 50 pages, folded over—long speeches were typical in those days—and his glasses case before lodging in the candidate's chest. Feeling as if he had been "kicked by a mule" but determined to continue, TR refused to go to a hospital, insisting instead that he go on and give his speech. Usually a dynamic speaker with a robust, energetic style, Roosevelt quieted the cheering crowd that greeted him. Raising his arm, he said quietly, "I shall ask you

to be as quiet as possible. I don't know whether you fully understand that I have just been shot; but it takes more than that to kill a bull moose." Opening his coat, revealing the bloodstained shirt, Roosevelt showed the crowd the speech text with the bullet hole. Because "the bullet is in me now," Roosevelt explained, he would not give a very long speech. "But," he said, "I will try my best." Speaking without the bullet-torn manuscript, Roosevelt spoke extemporaneously for a very painful hour and a half before his anxious aides were able to get him off the platform and to a hospital.

This example is, of course, dramatic and makes the loss of a note card or facing a larger audience than you anticipated seem like a small thing. You may never experience such an extreme challenge, but you *will* have times when you will have to deliver your speech under difficult circumstances, and you will need to be flexible.

Sources: See H. W. Brands, *TR: The Last Romantic* (New York: Basic Books, 1997), 720–22; and Nathan Miller, *Theodore Roosevelt: A Life* (New York: Morrow, 1992), 530–31. ▲

need not always stand or use a podium, and they *can* engage the audience in dialogue if doing so seems fitting and consistent with the audience's norms and expectations.

Practice Your Speech

Sometimes speakers think that once they have carefully researched their topic, organized their thoughts, and prepared their outline, all they need to do is read through the outline silently a few times—and they will be ready to go. Nothing could be further from the truth. If you have not practiced your speech aloud several times, chances are you are not prepared to speak.[17]

Here are a few guidelines for practicing your speech:

- *Practice delivering your speech aloud with your keyword outline.* But first read through your notes silently several times until you feel ready to begin.
- *Practice your speech all the way through—noting sections that are rough, rereading and revising your notes, and then practicing again.*
- *Break the speech into parts and practice major sections, such as the introduction, several times in a row.*
- *Always take breaks.* Avoid practicing so much at one time that you begin to lose your energy, voice, or concentration.
- *Practice in front of friends and ask for their constructive feedback.* Over a period of time, practice your speech again several times, all the way through, but do not try to memorize your speech.
- *Incorporate your visual aids into your practice sessions.* If possible, visit the room where you will speak and practice using the equipment there. If you are going to deliver your speech using computer support, such as PowerPoint or Prezi slides, prepare those slides in advance and incorporate them into your practice sessions. Remember that when you deliver the speech, you want to avoid talking to the screen, standing where you might block any projected image, or reading every word appearing on each slide. At the same time, you will want to point to key features of maps or other visuals to direct the audience's attention to key elements of your speech. See Chapter 12 for a more detailed discussion of the preparation and presentation of computer-generated visual aids.
- *Time yourself several times.* If your speech is too long, make appropriate cuts. For instance, you may cut a section that is less important, use fewer examples, or edit long quotations. It is important to remember that practicing your speech is something you do *before* the beginning of class or *before* you are seated in front of your audience. Sometimes speakers read through their notes while others are speaking. Do not fall into this trap. Practice sufficiently beforehand so that you will be able to listen to other speakers. Not only do they deserve your respectful attention, but you might even learn something you can refer to in your own speech.

Seek Out Opportunities to Speak

As you gain experience and confidence as a speaker, you will naturally deliver your speeches more effectively. This is especially true if you ask for listener feedback and strive to improve by addressing whatever weaknesses they identify. In addition, you will speak with more confidence and credibility if you speak about topics that genuinely concern you. When you deliver your remarks with personal conviction, you tend to speak with more force, clarity, directness, and spontaneity—all hallmarks of effective delivery.

Look for opportunities to speak inside *and* outside the classroom. You may join your college's student speakers bureau, run for political office on campus, or volunteer with a local service or nonprofit organization and join *their* speakers bureau. You can also use your vol-

Speakers with deep personal conviction tend to deliver their speeches more effectively.

unteer work as a foundation for bringing your life's passions into the classroom. When you take courses with an emphasis on service learning or civic engagement, you will have more opportunities to make these kinds of connections between your life experiences and the classroom.

SPEAKING EXTEMPORANEOUSLY

Preview. *Extemporaneous speaking requires careful preparation. Using this delivery style and speaking from a keyword outline allows you to be completely involved in your speech. At the same time, you can maintain the flexibility you need to adapt to differing situations.*

Depending on the occasion, listener expectations, and other demands of the situation, speakers may choose to use different styles of delivery. Some of these styles are more informal and spontaneous, whereas others are more formal and scripted. In *most* speaking situations, however, you will probably want to deliver your speech in an *extemporaneous* style.

Extemporaneous speaking should not be confused with *impromptu* speaking, or speaking with no preparation at all. Extemporaneous speaking still requires careful preparation. In preparing an extemporaneous speech, you will thoroughly research your topic, decide how to best organize your ideas, carefully prepare your outline, and practice delivering the speech from notes. An extemporaneous speech is not memorized word for word. Yet neither is it completely spontaneous or delivered "off the cuff."

When delivering a speech extemporaneously, you may commit some key ideas to memory, but your specific words, phrases, and examples may vary both as you practice the speech and during its final delivery. With the extemporaneous style of

11.3 Explain the advantages of delivering your speech extemporaneously.

Watch the Video "Whatever Happened to Sisqo?" at **MyCommunicationLab**

delivery, you have the advantage of being well prepared, yet you can also adapt to changing circumstances if necessary.

Advantages of Speaking from a Keyword Outline

When you deliver a speech extemporaneously, you will typically use speaking notes with a keyword outline, as described in Chapter 9. This outline keeps you on track and reminds you of your main ideas, but it does not lay out the speech word for word. A keyword outline is not something you can use as a crutch. It will keep you on track, reminding you of your main points and perhaps some of your key examples, statistics, or other forms of evidence. But you will still need to think on your feet and interact with your audience. When delivering your speech extemporaneously, you can speak more directly with your audience, watching for their responses, and making any changes in the content or delivery of your speech that may seem necessary.

On occasion, circumstances before your speech may dictate last-minute changes in your own presentation. In your speech class, for example, another student may speak before you and refer to an event or a piece of information that you had planned to discuss. Would you go ahead as planned and just pretend that the other speaker had not already mentioned the matter? Or would you have the flexibility to build on what the other speaker said without just repeating the same information? When you deliver your speech from a keyword outline, you have the flexibility to adapt to changing circumstances. Of course, to take advantage of that flexibility, you need to listen closely to those other speakers and quickly come up with ideas for building on their remarks.

Whenever you do some last-minute fine-tuning on your speech, you demonstrate respect for your fellow speakers and your audience. You show that you have been paying attention to what others have said, and you demonstrate a commitment to dialogue, not just to having your say. In doing so, you help build a sense of community among speakers and listeners. Delivering your speech extemporaneously will not guarantee that it will be a success, but it will give you that flexibility you need to adapt to changing circumstances. In the *Focus on Civic Engagement* feature, we provide a sample of a keyword outline that a speaker might use to deliver a speech about Habitat for Humanity. Also see the sample keyword outline in Chapter 9.

Keep in mind that there are no hard-and-fast rules for constructing your keyword outline. You may choose to record only a few main ideas to jog your memory, or you may elect to write out the speech in more detail, recording both main ideas and more detailed information, such as statistics, quotations, or particular phrasings that you want to use. In either case, practicing with your notes (as well as revising and refining them as you practice) is essential.

Why Use Extemporaneous Delivery?

With an extemporaneous delivery, you can more easily adapt to the audience and the situation. You can make changes, clarify or elaborate with examples or illustrations, omit a minor point if time is running short, and more effectively involve the audience in your speech.

FOCUS ON CIVIC ENGAGEMENT | A Keyword Outline for a Speech about Habitat for Humanity

INTRODUCTION

SHARE STORY—Single-parent domestic abuse survivor
SHARE PERSONAL BACKGROUND WITH HABITAT
IMPORTANCE OF HH—Providing thousands with decent, affordable housing

THESIS

Becoming actively involved with Habitat is an excellent way of making a difference in others' lives.

PREVIEW

- Habitat—mission and background
- International impact
- The Habitat selection system
- How to get involved

TRANSITION: First, I'd like to give you a little background on Habitat.
`Speak fairly quickly`

BODY

I. Habitat—a terrific organization
  - Nonprofit Christian housing ministry (Habitat Web site)
  - Started in the U.S. in 1976
  - Eliminates substandard housing worldwide
  - Adequate housing—a matter of conscience and action

TRANSITION: Habitat has had a huge impact all over the world.
`Point to slide with Habitat map`

II. HH has gained a large following in its 36 years.
  - All 50 states in the U.S.
  - Nearly 100 other countries
  - More than 2,000 total affiliates
  - Local Habitat building 115th house (2012 newsletter)

TRANSITION: How are families chosen to become HH homeowners?
`Point to slide—keep eye contact!`

III. Habitat—developed fair and efficient selection system
  - Selection criteria for homeowners (local Habitat ED, Thomson)
  - Need
  - Ability to repay no-interest mortgage
  - Willingness to put in 300–500 "sweat equity" hours
  - Builds modest homes
  - About 1,100 square feet
  - Low mortgage payments—less than $300 per month
  - Money reverts to a "Fund for Humanity"—supports future projects

TRANSITION: If you agree with me that Habitat is a wonderful organization, you may be wondering, "How can I get involved?"
`Move closer to audience—direct eye contact`

IV. Getting involved is easy!
`Show slides of each program`
  - Find local affiliate
  - Gifts from the heart (financial and food donations)
  - Global village—Habitat volunteer vacation
  - Women Build
  - Campus chapters and programs
  - Jimmy Carter's Work Project (distribute handouts)

CONCLUSION

Revisit personal story—*working with great people, community building.*

(*Continued*)

Summary

We've looked closely at Habitat—what it is, where it operates, how it works, and how you can get involved.

Share quote from HH homeowner: "This is the first time my three children have had a real home. They will be able to attend the same school and live in a safe neighborhood. Without HH, this *never* would have been possible." ▲

Appeal for Action

Sign up today!

Final slide—contact information

Pause for questions

Extemporaneous speaking, however, demands focused concentration. When delivering a speech extemporaneously, you cannot just read from a manuscript or rely on a detailed outline if you lose your train of thought. You cannot just "zone out" or "wing it." Speaking extemporaneously demands careful preparation, good notes, and a clear mind as you speak.

An extemporaneous style works best when you have a genuine passion for your topic. As you speak extemporaneously, you can interject spontaneous comments or include personal observations that reflect your own interests and experiences. If *you* are intellectually and emotionally engaged, you are better able to speak in the moment and communicate the conviction and passion that you feel to your audience. When well done, an extemporaneous style also contributes to your ethos as a committed and effective advocate.[18] For example, former president Bill Clinton, who was well known for connecting personally with his audiences, was at his best when speaking extemporaneously. One journalist writing on Clinton's presidency pointed out that he was at his very best when he spoke, without a manuscript, at political rallies or from the pulpit of host churches.[19]

ALTERNATIVE STYLES OF DELIVERY

11.4 Compare and contrast different styles of delivery, listing strengths and weaknesses of each.

Explore the Concept
"Methods of Delivery" at
MyCommunicationLab

Preview. *Besides the extemporaneous style of delivery, speakers can choose from several other presentation styles that range from very informal to quite formal. The style you choose will depend on your preference, the demands of the speaking situation, and audience expectations.*

Successful speakers develop the ability to use a variety of different styles of delivery because different topics and occasions may call for different approaches to presenting your speech. You would not want to speak to a large, formal meeting with a casual, off-the-cuff style; nor would you want to speak to your classmates about getting involved in student government by writing out and reading a speech word for word. It is important to fit the delivery style to the situation.

In addition to the extemporaneous style, you may want to consider three other styles of delivery: impromptu, manuscript, and memorized speaking. Although the extemporaneous style is appropriate in most situations, one of these alternative approaches may be called for on certain occasions.

The Impromptu Speech

Impromptu speaking is off-the-cuff and casual, delivered with little or no preparation. In general, you should never choose to make an impromptu speech if you have time to prepare in advance. There may be occasions, however, when you find yourself in a situation where impromptu speaking is the only option.

Watch the Video
"Martin Cox Discusses
Types of Delivery" at
MyCommunicationLab

Imagine that you are attending a community forum on heath care, for example, and you feel the need to respond to what some of the speakers have said. Perhaps you want to share a hair-raising experience you once had in the local hospital's emergency room, or maybe you want to argue for a new health care facility for low-income citizens. At your place of work, you may be called on to articulate your point of view, make a brief report, or explain some rule or procedure. Requests for these spontaneous "speeches" are more common than you may think in business and professional settings. As a student, you may be called on to make brief, impromptu speeches during discussions or debates in your classes. It is important to learn how to respond effectively to these demanding situations, even if you have little or no time to prepare.

If your instructor assigns an impromptu speech in your speech class, take advantage of this opportunity to get accustomed to standing up and speaking in front of your classmates without advance preparation. Your impromptu speech does not have to be perfect. Your instructor and classmates will understand that you had no time to prepare, and they won't expect the same polished performance they might expect in a formal speech. So relax! You may even enjoy this opportunity to "think on your feet" and fashion a speech "off the top of your head."

Guidelines for Giving Impromptu Speeches   When giving an impromptu speech, you have limited time to organize your thoughts. Even so, here are a few things you can do to succeed:

- *Anticipate the possibility that you may be called on to speak and be thinking about what you might say.* Every class, conference, business meeting, or community forum will have an agenda. When you attend one of these, become as well versed as possible on issues to be discussed and reflect on what ideas or experiences you might like to share. You may want to jot down a few notes and have them ready if, in fact, you have the opportunity or are called upon to speak.
- *Practice active listening.* During a meeting, be sure to follow the flow of the discussion. You don't want to be daydreaming and then suddenly hear someone say, "Kevin, does this plan make sense to you?" If you are listening to formal presentations by others, you likewise will want to listen actively. We offer more guidelines for engaged and active listening in Chapter 2.
- *Increase your feelings of confidence by reminding yourself that no one expects perfection from impromptu remarks.* Listener expectations are always higher when the speaker is delivering a planned presentation. In impromptu speaking, however, listeners expect less fluent delivery.
- *Use even limited preparation time to your advantage.* At community forums or in professional conferences, you can take notes while listening to a panel or symposium. These notes will help you recall more accurately what others have said and can serve as the foundation for your own impromptu remarks.

- *Use basic principles of speech organization.* Even an impromptu speech should have an introduction, a body, and a conclusion. Within the body, you can still organize your main points in some basic strategic order. You may briefly introduce your remarks, make two or three main points, and perhaps summarize or appeal to listeners. However limited the time you have to prepare, it is always a good idea to sketch out at least a rough outline of the main ideas you want to cover.
- *Speak briefly and concisely.* Regardless of the situation, impromptu speeches should not consume too much time. Nobody appreciates a speaker who tries to dominate the meeting. If you are given the chance to speak, keep your comments brief and on-issue. Always assume that others will want to speak as well, and be respectful of their right to do so.
- *Think of impromptu speaking as an opportunity to practice and improve your delivery skills.* When you speak without notes or with limited notes, you have an opportunity to focus even more on your vocal and physical delivery. Take advantage of that to practice and more closely observe how listeners react to your style of speaking.

The Manuscript Speech

When former president Clinton speaks from a manuscript, he still connects with his audience and preserves his engaging style.

At the other end of the continuum is manuscript speaking. Manuscript speeches are carefully prepared formal speeches. They are speeches designed to be delivered exactly as written, such as a speech on a controversial issue that might be covered by the news media, or a ceremonial address with language carefully crafted to sound eloquent or even poetic. In these situations, the manuscript not only allows you to say precisely what you planned to say but also provides a written transcript of your remarks.

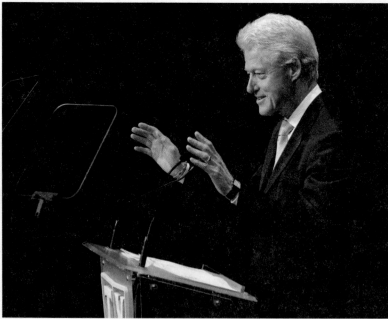

Some settings may call for manuscript speeches because of their formal nature. The president of the United States delivers many important speeches from manuscript, such as the State of the Union address. Commencement addresses are also typically delivered from manuscript. If you were called on to make formal remarks upon the installation of new officers at a civic or fraternal organization, a manuscript speech again may be most appropriate. Using a manuscript allows you to time your speech precisely, choose your words carefully, and decide exactly how to phrase your most important ideas. The underlying principles of good public speaking still apply to the manuscript speech: even though you may be reading from a manuscript, you should pay attention to audience reactions and be responsive to feedback. And it's important that you prepare a copy of the manuscript that you can read easily while speaking.[20]

Guidelines for Giving Manuscript Speeches Delivering a manuscript speech presents special challenges relating to eye contact, movement, the use of your voice, and flexibility. Here are some guidelines to follow:

- *Use a manuscript for the right reasons.* Use a manuscript when it is important to choose your words carefully and say exactly what you mean. Do not use it as a crutch to hide behind or as a way to manage your anxieties.
- *Use good oral style.* Even though you are speaking from a manuscript, you should still use language that is appropriate for oral presentation. This means that you will choose words and construct your sentences in ways that are easily spoken and more readily understood by listeners, as was discussed on Chapter 10.
- *Practice extensively.* You need to know the speech well enough to look at the audience and get back to the manuscript without losing your place. If you're going to deliver the speech from a written manuscript, prepare a clean, double-spaced copy printed in an easily readable font (14, 16, or even 18 points). If you use a more advanced technology to deliver your manuscript speech, such as a laptop or teleprompter, be sure to practice your speech using that technology. And it's always a good idea to prepare a backup manuscript in case the technology fails.
- *Look for opportunities to move and gesture.* When you speak from a manuscript, you will normally be speaking from behind a podium. As a result, you may feel compelled to stand in one place or be tempted to lean on the podium. Resist these temptations. With planning and practice, you can deliver a manuscript speech and still move, use appropriate gestures, and engage your audience through eye contact and facial expressions.
- *Use your voice effectively.* Some speakers sound artificial or flat when delivering a manuscript speech. Their inflection may be less animated than normal, or they may sound monotonous or singsong, as if they were doing a poor job reading a poem. To speak effectively, concentrate on adding variety, color, and emphasis to your voice—just as you do when speaking extemporaneously. You may want to write delivery reminders on the manuscript itself, such as *Slow down*, *Pause for emphasis*, or *Repeat this*. You can also underline or boldface key words or phrases in the manuscript that you want to emphasize with your voice.
- *Maintain flexibility.* Rather than adapting to the moment or reacting to audience feedback, some speakers feel compelled to read from their manuscript word for word, never deviating, no matter what. Yet your manuscript need not be a straitjacket. Although the idea behind speaking from a manuscript may be to deliver the speech exactly as written, that does not mean you should *never* change a single word or improvise in response to audience

reactions. A manuscript speech *can* be changed if circumstances warrant it. You *can* (and often should) elaborate on a point with some spontaneous remarks. When you speak from manuscript, you *can* be flexible, remain connected to your listeners, and respond to their feedback.

The Memorized Speech

You will rarely find yourself in a situation where you will want to give a memorized speech. Some students participate in speaking contests, such as the American Legion Oratorical Contest, where they deliver memorized speeches. Some formal or ceremonial occasions may also call for a short memorized speech, such as a wedding toast or a brief tribute to a colleague at a retirement dinner. In extemporaneous speaking, you may want to memorize key parts of a longer speech, such as the attention-getter, the concluding appeal or challenge, or an especially important quotation or passage from a literary work. Generally, however, memorized speeches are a thing of the past—a form of delivery quite common 100 or 150 years ago but increasingly rare today.

Guidelines for Giving Memorized Speeches   If you *do* find yourself in a situation where you want to speak from memory, keep these pointers in mind:

- *Stay focused on your specific purpose and the key ideas you want to convey.* When you memorize, you may be tempted to focus on the specific language you want to use. You may try to memorize your speech word for word, but don't forget that it's more important to remember your main ideas than your exact phrasing.
- *Speak in the moment.* When speakers deliver a speech from memory, they risk going on "automatic pilot." If this happens, the speech becomes a ritualistic performance rather than a communicative exchange with an audience. Remember: Even if speaking from memory, you should stay focused on your listeners and remember your specific purpose. If you lose yourself in your own thoughts and fail to speak in the moment, you may say all the words you planned, but you will not really be *communicating*.
- *Practice, practice, practice.* To be effective, all speakers must practice, regardless of their method of delivery. The memorized speech, however, may require even more practice. If your speech is long, you may want to read through it several times and practice it in sections before trying to memorize all of it. Practice sessions should be spaced out over time rather than crammed into a few hours to help you resist fatigue and commit the speech to your long-term memory.

Each method of delivery, as we have noted, has its benefits and potential liabilities. Table 11.1 compares the four styles of delivery.

Over time, you will discover your own preferences, and you may even develop a style of delivery that is uniquely your own. Experiment with different speaking styles. Discover the techniques that make you most comfortable and allow you to speak with confidence and conviction. Whatever style you choose, remember that the purpose of public speaking is to communicate with an audience. So however you deliver your speech, it's crucial that you remain connected to your listeners.

> ### TABLE 11.1
>
> #### Comparing Styles of Delivery
>
> Extemporaneous
>
> - Carefully prepared with thorough research, strategic organization of ideas, and practiced delivery
> - Delivered from speaking notes, typically using a keyword outline
> - Offers the opportunity to deliver the speech with flexibility, spontaneity, and directness
> - Encourages audience adaptation
> - Works best when the speaker cares deeply about the topic and can speak with passion and commitment
>
> Impromptu
>
> - Off-the-cuff, casual style that deemphasizes preparation
> - Often called for in business, community, and classroom settings
> - Delivery and organization are helped by informally jotting down notes as impromptu occasions arise
> - Should be seen as an opportunity to practice and improve delivery skills
>
> Manuscript
>
> - Carefully prepared formal speeches, usually delivered precisely as written
> - Sometimes delivered using a teleprompter, often delivered from behind a podium
> - Typically used in important political speeches or on ceremonial occasions
> - Allows for precise, eloquent language and control of speaking time
> - Requires easily readable manuscript and extensive practice for a more natural style of speaking
>
> Memorized
>
> - Delivered from memory without the aid of speaking notes or manuscript
> - Sometimes used by students in speaking contests or by citizens delivering toasts or other short tributes
> - Requires extensive practice and concentration on key ideas

RESPONDING TO AUDIENCE QUESTIONS

Preview. *After you speak, you may be expected to entertain questions. The question-and-answer period is important because it allows you to interact informally with the audience, to provide additional information, to enhance your credibility, and to participate in a mutually beneficial dialogue.*

11.5 Anticipate audience questions and explain appropriate ways of responding to them.

Some speakers give little thought to the question-and-answer period that often follows a formal address. Instead, they focus all their attention on the preparation and delivery of the speech itself. Yet if you don't respond effectively to questions, you can damage your credibility and undermine the success of your speech. You don't want to give a good speech and then appear defensive, ignorant about related issues, or insensitive to your audience's concerns or questions about your speech.

The question-and-answer period is a potentially decisive moment in the audience's ultimate judgment of your speech. It gives your listeners a chance to ask for clarification or elaboration of the points that most interested them. As such, it provides a good barometer of how well your speech came across, as well as one last opportunity

The question-and-answer period following a speech is a time for respectful and mutually influential dialogue.

to address any confusion or skepticism left by the speech itself. You should listen carefully to the questions posed by your audience and strive to engage your listeners in a genuine dialogue.

Preparing for the Question-and-Answer Period

Although you cannot anticipate everything listeners may ask, you certainly can make some educated guesses about their potential questions and concerns. You should expect questions about any controversial issues you may bring up during your speech, and you should give some thought in advance to how you might respond to questions about those matters. Try to anticipate arguments that listeners may use to challenge your ideas, and make sure you have a good command of your sources. A questioner may well ask you to provide additional information or evidence for your claims, and you should be prepared to do so. Consider which parts of your speech may prove most difficult to understand, and be prepared to elaborate on those matters. Try to have additional examples, statistics, and other sorts of evidence "in reserve," ready to use in response to audience questions. When it seems that you *could* have said much more about your topic, you come across as more credible. The more you know about your topic, of course, the better prepared you will be to deal with questions.

Show Respect for Your Listeners   In addition to anticipating questions about the content of your speech, you should think about the sort of attitude you convey as you respond to questions. Will you seem defensive and closed-minded? Or will you strike your listeners as somebody who genuinely respects their opinions and wants to engage in a productive dialogue? Listeners occasionally will challenge you or openly disagree with you. Sometimes they may even do so in ways that you consider disrespectful, abrasive, or even rude. Although being challenged in this way can be unpleasant, you should keep your cool! Always try to respond with class and civility. As the speaker, *you* have a lot of control over the tone of the exchange, and you can refuse to respond in kind to a rude or disrespectful questioner. Should you get a hostile question, it is often best to respond only briefly, and then move on to the next question.

Conducting the Question-and-Answer Period

Decide where you will stand as you receive audience questions. One option is to remain behind the podium. This conveys a sense of formality, maintaining some distance between you and the audience. Another option is to stand at the side or in front of the podium, where you can interact more directly with the audience. Finally, in informal settings, you may sit on a table or a stool and engage in more of a "chat" with your audience. Any of these options may work well, depending on the situation, the audience's expectations, and your own preferences.

The following guidelines will help you conduct the question-and-answer period more effectively.

- *Listen carefully to each question.* If you can't hear a question very well, ask the questioner to stand and repeat it. Or move away from the podium and stand closer to the audience. As you listen, provide a few nonverbal cues, such as nodding your head, to let the questioner know that you understand the question. Generally, you should avoid interrupting audience members while they are asking their questions. Occasionally, however, an audience member will abuse the right to ask a question by making a long, perhaps even belligerent statement. In that case, you may intervene in the interest of allowing others to ask questions. Elizabeth Warren, a candidate for the United States Senate from Massachusetts, faced a hostile questioner who addressed her with a rude epithet. As supporters began to boo, Ms. Warren quieted them and calmly responded to the questioner before moving quickly on to another question. This exchange was recorded on YouTube.[21]
- *If appropriate, repeat each question so that everyone can hear it and keep track of what is happening.* In repeating the question, you may want to rephrase it because audience members sometimes ask poorly phrased or rambling questions.
- *Do not allow one person to dominate.* If many people raise their hands at once, make sure you call on people who have not already spoken. If someone who already asked a question raises his or her hand again, you might ask, "Is there anyone else who has a question?" Occasionally, a persistent questioner may try to engage you for an extended period of time. If that happens, you may invite that person to speak with you later, and then move on to the next question.
- *Do not try to fake your way through a response.* If you do not know the answer to a question or are not familiar with some topic raised by a questioner, it is best to admit it. Perhaps a questioner will ask if you have read a particular book or whether you know about some incident or event. Admitting that you do not know everything will not hurt your credibility. Indeed, we tend to be more suspicious of speakers who pretend to "know it all."

  If a listener poses a difficult question that you can't answer, you can always offer to investigate the matter and get back to the person. It is easy to get a listener's e-mail address following your talk—and then do your research and follow through with a thoughtful response. When you do this, you are showing respect for the listener. At the same time, you are learning more about your topic—and will be better prepared to answer questions the next time you speak.
- *Respect time limits.* Question-and-answer periods should not go on forever. Like speeches, they have time constraints. Sometimes you will be asked to speak briefly and leave plenty of time for audience questions. Other times, you will have only a little time left for interaction with the audience. Ask in advance what the audience expects or desires, and then follow through, limiting the question-and-answer period to the agreed-upon time.[22]

■ *Anticipate the possibility of no audience questions.* On occasion, you may conclude your speech and ask for questions but get no response from the audience. If you have used most of the time available for speaking and responding to questions, you may choose simply to thank them and take your seat. However, if time permits, you may also consider sharing some additional information or experiences that you didn't have the chance to address during your speech. Sometimes listeners need extra time to formulate good questions. By talking just a bit longer (but not too long), you give them the time to think. As a result, they may offer more thoughtful or interesting questions.

 Study and Review materials for this chapter are at **MyCommunicationLab**

SUMMARY

 Listen to the Audio Chapter Summary at **MyCommunicationLab**

Sounding Good versus Being Sound

 11.1 Explain the ethical issues involved in delivering your speech.

■ Ethical delivery grows from a collaborative, transactional approach to public speaking:
  ■ Good speakers try never to distract the audience with their delivery.
  ■ They do all they can to promote audience comprehension and understanding.
  ■ They know that good, ethical delivery not only sounds good, it also grows from a solid foundation—a carefully constructed, thoughtfully reasoned, and well-supported speech.

Principles of Good Delivery

 11.2 Describe the basic principles of effective delivery.

■ Underlying principles of good delivery apply across public speaking situations:
  ■ Understand the speaking context and audience expectations.
  ■ Establish eye contact with listeners.
  ■ Reinforce ideas through gestures, movement, and facial expressions.
  ■ Strive for an effective speaking voice.

Speaking Extemporaneously

11.3 Explain the advantages of delivering your speech extemporaneously.

■ For most public speaking situations, you will likely want to use the extemporaneous

style, which involves meticulous preparation and is typically delivered from a keyword outline:
  ■ When you speak extemporaneously, you are encouraged to speak with flexibility, adapting to audience expectations and to the context.
  ■ As you speak, you are able to establish eye contact with audience members, use appropriate gestures, and make effective use of your voice.
  ■ Extemporaneous delivery also encourages you to speak with passion and conviction.
  ■ Practicing your speech aloud and seeking out opportunities to speak can help you develop an effective extemporaneous style of delivery.

Alternative Styles of Delivery

 11.4 Compare and contrast different styles of delivery, listing the strengths and weaknesses of each.

■ Other styles of delivery may be appropriate on certain occasions, but each presents some special challenges:
  ■ Even impromptu speaking requires some preparation and organization.
  ■ Manuscript speaking demands a special focus on using good oral style, incorporating gestures and movement, and using your voice effectively.
  ■ Speaking from memory requires extensive practice; it challenges you to speak "in the moment" and to stay focused on the ideas you are conveying.

Responding to Audience Questions

 Anticipate audience questions and explain appropriate ways of responding to them.

- The question-and-answer period is an important part of most formal speeches:
  - As you respond to audience questions, you have the chance to show listeners how well informed you are and how quickly you can think on your feet.
  - You can also demonstrate how carefully you listen, how open you are to others' ideas, and how honest you are in responding to difficult questions.
- Anticipate and prepare for possible questions from your audience, and do all you can to establish a climate of respectful and mutually beneficial dialogue.

QUESTIONS FOR REVIEW AND REFLECTION

Sounding Good versus Being Sound

11.1 Explain the ethical issues involved in delivering your speech.

1. Describe the difference between "sounding good" and "being sound."

Principles of Good Delivery

11.2 Describe the basic principles of effective delivery.

2. Your friend has to make an important presentation at a fund-raising event for the local Boys and Girls Club. He comes to you and asks you for advice on how to deliver his speech. What three things would you stress? Why are they important?
3. To what extent may cultural differences influence the way listeners respond to a speaker's delivery?
4. You have heard many people give speeches (classroom speeches, lectures, political speeches, after-dinner speeches, speeches at memorial services). Given your experience as an audience member, what things most annoy you about some speakers' delivery habits or styles? What delivery characteristics do you especially admire?

Speaking Extemporaneously

11.3 Explain the advantages of delivering a speech extemporaneously.

5. How would you describe extemporaneous delivery? Why is this style most appropriate in most public speaking situations?

6. Why is a keyword outline useful in delivering a speech? Can you think of any potential disadvantages to using such an outline? What might you do to minimize any potential disadvantages?

Alternative Styles of Delivery

11.4 Compare and contrast different styles of delivery, listing the strengths and weaknesses of each.

7. Some situations may call for a style of delivery other than extemporaneous. Describe each of these alternative delivery styles:
   a. Impromptu
   b. Manuscript
   c. Memorized
8. Compare and contrast the advantages and disadvantages of each.

Responding to Audience Questions

11.5 Anticipate audience questions and explain appropriate ways of responding to them.

9. You have given a speech, and now it is time for audience questions. How would you deal with each of these situations?
   a. An audience member is hostile.
   b. An audience member asks three questions in a row.
   c. Someone asks you a question and you do not know the answer.
   d. No one asks you a question.

 Study and Review the Flashcards at **MyCommunicationLab**

Supporting Your Ideas Visually

OVERVIEW AND LEARNING OBJECTIVES

Functions of Presentational Aids

12.1 Understand the diverse ways that presentational aids can help you as a speaker.

Options for Presentational Aids

12.2 Describe the types of presentational aids commonly available to speakers.

Guidelines for Preparing Presentational Aids

12.3 Follow basic guidelines for creating presentational aids.

Guidelines for Using Presentational Aids

12.4 Follow basic guidelines for using presentational aids.

Visual material greatly impacts how we react to information. Photographs from inside the Abu Ghraib prison, for example, depicted the mistreatment of detainees by American military personnel and generated outrage in the United States and abroad.[1] Live shots of the tsunami coming ashore in Indonesia and Thailand in 2004—sweeping away all in its path—shocked television viewers around the world, as did media coverage of the earthquake that devastated Haiti in 2010. These images, and the diagrams and charts that experts created to explain them, reminded us of how destructive natural disasters can be and prompted calls for improved early-warning systems and better-coordinated evacuation and relief efforts.[2] From the pictures of a jetliner that survived a crash landing in the Hudson River in January 2009—an event dramatically proclaimed "the miracle on the Hudson"[3]—to the live coverage of the devastation from the earthquake and tsunami that struck Japan in March 2011,[4] visual images play a big role in shaping both our understanding and emotional reactions to events.

It should come as no surprise, then, that visual images can also have an impact when used in a public or classroom speech. The use of such presentational aids increasingly has become the norm in our visually oriented society, so it is important that you learn how to use them effectively.

Using visual or audio aids effectively calls for careful thinking, strategic planning, and practice. There is nothing magical about presentational aids. But it *is* important that you understand some basic principles concerning how they function and that you incorporate them effectively into your verbal presentation.

FUNCTIONS OF PRESENTATIONAL AIDS

Preview. *Presentational aids can help audience members follow, retain, and be moved by the speaker's ideas. They can also enhance the credibility of a speaker. Given these potential benefits, it is important that you learn to create and use presentational aids skillfully.*

Both speakers and listeners can benefit from the effective use of presentational aids. Several noteworthy benefits exist.

Promoting Clarity

Effective presentational aids provide clarity. Researchers have found that "human brains extract valuable information from audiovisuals more quickly and more easily than from purely verbal information" and do so with "a more error-free grasp of information."[5] For this reason, as explained in *Highlighting Visual Perception and Thinking*, a speaker should use visual aids. A simple table depicting a budget provides more clarity than merely describing it in words. Photographs of urban areas in decay provide a clearer understanding of problems confronting American cities than words alone. And listeners who see a statistical trend via a graph are more likely to understand it—and more immediately—than if left to chart it mentally on their own.[6]

It is easy to understand the popularity of graphs and charts; they make quantitative information easy to understand.[7] Speakers who fail to use them appear remiss. When you use statistical support that's the least bit complex, you should provide visual representations to assist comprehension.

12.1 Understand the diverse ways that presentational aids can help you as a speaker.

Explore the Concept "Presentation Aids" at **MyCommunicationLab**

HIGHLIGHTING VISUAL PERCEPTION AND THINKING

Graphic icons populate our dashboard and every lever in our car. Road signs often feature images, not words. Our smartphone's menu is a series of icons. We have increasingly replaced words with images.

We obtain much of our information through graphic images, something experts have long noted. Marty Shelton, a highly acclaimed scholar of visual communication, estimated that visual perceptions provide an astonishing 99 percent of our knowledge about the world around us. This emphasis is quite natural, Shelton noted, because "we are a visual species."

We "don't think much in words *per se*," he contended, but "do most of our thinking in terms of graphic images—visuals such as pictures, icons, and facsimiles."

When we view news broadcasts, read illustrated books, or experience multimedia presentations, visual or graphic images become our "primary medium of thought." Fruitful, practical thought would be nearly unattainable were it not for such "visual stimuli."

Source: From Marty Shelton, "Special Issue: Visual Communication: Introduction." Copyright © 1993 by Technical Communication. ◤

Assisting Retention

Presentational aids make information more understandable *and* more memorable. Research indicates that effective presentational aids can make recall easier, faster, and more accurate than "memories of purely verbal messages."[8] One study even found that people remembered 43 percent more information when visuals were used than when they were not.[9] In short, if you want to bolster understanding and leave a lasting impression, use good presentational aids.[10]

Providing Emphasis

FIGURE 12.1
A list can help your audience follow your speech and remember its main ideas.

A visual aid can help a speaker underscore what is most important. Even a simple list (such as in Figure 12.1)[11] can highlight key ideas as well as help listeners recall them.[12] If you are using a list, consider using graphical icons—such as a dollar sign to designate "money saved." Graphical icons can be even more striking and memorable than a list of keywords.[13]

Clean Energy Economy

- **Restores Economic Competitiveness**
- **Lessens Dependence on Fossil Fuels**
- **Avoids Funding Our Enemies**
- **Lessens International Conflict**
- **Assists Environmental Recovery**

—Source: *Time*, 16 Feb. 2009

Providing Support

Presentational aids can also function as evidence to support your ideas. For example, a speaker might argue that hurricane readiness should be a top priority for key coastal regions of the United States. Displaying a map that documents direct hits by hurricanes (see Figure 12.2) allows listeners to see for themselves the number of hurricanes as well as the widespread extent of the threat.[14]

Hurricane Landfalls in 2008

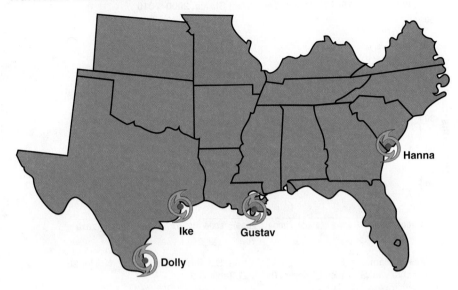

Source: National Oceanic and Atmospheric Administration, 2009.

FIGURE 12.2

A visual aid can communicate efficiently and powerfully.

Basing the map (or any other visual aid) on information from a reputable source also lends support by adding credibility to your ideas. To derive this benefit, as well as meet your ethical obligations, enter the source on your display *and* cite it orally.

To support ideas, speakers often use graphs, and they are wise to do so. Graphs make statistical information more vivid and show relationships. The most familiar and useful kinds of graphs are line graphs, bar graphs, pictographs, and pie graphs. The type of graph used will depend on the type of information to be conveyed.[15]

Line Graphs A line graph is especially well suited to showing comparative relationships through time. For example, a hospital administrator might use a line graph to show how emergency room visits increase over time among populations who lack access to primary health care. The graph allows us to see the tendency.

It is possible to place more than one line on a single graph, but it may be at the expense of clarity. If you plan to use multiple lines or curves, try to use strikingly different colors and restrict yourself to two or three lines. It is also important to guard against distorting a trend by compressing or elongating the space allotted to time periods while keeping the other dimension of the graph constant. Whenever you selectively focus on a particular segment of data, be sure to label the graph so that your audience can fully understand what you have elected to show them.[16]

Figure 12.3 provides an example of a line graph. Using this graph helped underscore the downward trend in teen pregnancies in the United States in recent years.[17]

Bar Graphs A bar graph can be used to show comparisons and contrasts between two or more items or groups. Even if listeners have little background in reading graphs, the bar graph is easy to understand. In addition, these graphs have a

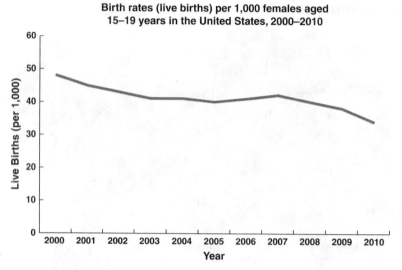

Birth rates (live births) per 1,000 females aged 15–19 years in the United States, 2000–2010

FIGURE 12.3

Line graphs help to reveal trends.

Source: Hamilton, B.E., Martin, I.A., Ventura, S.J. Births: Preliminary data for 2010. National Vital Statistics Reports 2011.6(2). Table S-2

dramatic visual impact. As with line graphs, whenever you focus on a particular segment of data, be sure to label the graph so that your audience can fully understand what you have elected to show them.[18]

Figure 12.4 compares the estimated percentage of overweight boys and girls from several countries. The speaker using this bar graph quoted Dr. Philip James,

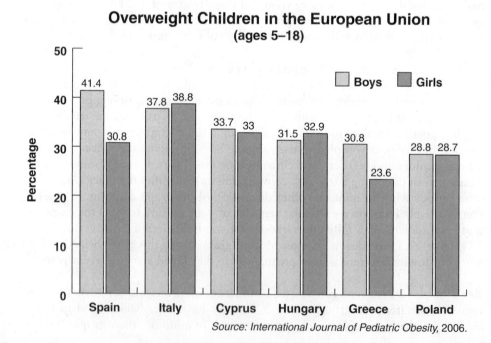

Overweight Children in the European Union
(ages 5–18)

FIGURE 12.4

Bar graphs help to compare and contrast.

Source: International Journal of Pediatric Obesity, 2006.

Drinks per week:

"**A**" student:

"**D**" student:

Source: Columbia University, 2006.

FIGURE 12.5
Pictographs can be powerful and memorable.

chairman of the International Obesity Task Force, in arguing that we have "a truly global epidemic" and detailing its impact on health care systems around the world.[19]

Pictographs   Listeners often find pictographs particularly interesting. In a pictograph, a graphical icon is used to form lines or patterns to convey information in the same way other graphs do. Figure 12.5 shows how a pictograph can communicate information in an interesting and meaningful way. A student speaker used this pictograph to support his argument that students who drink excessively suffer from impaired academic performance in college. Pictographs (such as this one created with Photoshop) are more challenging to construct than traditional graphs. They require more creativity and original labor.

Pie Graphs   The final type of graph is the pie graph, most often used to show numerical distribution patterns. When you need to show how a total figure breaks down into different parts, you will probably want to use a pie graph. Suppose, for example, you're noting the relative amount of our federal dollars spent on defense, Social Security, health care, and various other programs. A pie graph, like the one depicted in Figure 12.6, could efficiently convey that information. Because of their simplicity, pie graphs are easily understood by an audience.

When constructing a pie graph, observe two central guidelines. First, create a two-dimensional, rather than a three-dimensional, pie. As Joel Best, author of *More Damned Lies and Statistics*, explains, "Showing the edge of a tilted pie chart to the viewer (so that it seems to be a three-dimensional disk)...exaggerates the visual importance of those slices that can be viewed edge-on."[20] In addition, use a bold or bright color to set off the sector you hope to highlight or emphasize. For added emphasis, it can be pulled out slightly from the rest of the pie.[21]

You may use several different kinds of graphs in a single presentation. When carefully constructed and used strategically, they can help you depict statistical information in ways that listeners will likely find understandable, interesting, informative, and convincing.

Creating graphs has become increasingly easy because of software like PowerPoint. However, some design options allow a speaker to easily distort data—intentionally or unwittingly. The author of *How to Lie with Charts*, Gerald Everett

**Federal Spending on Defense, Social
Security, & Other Programs**

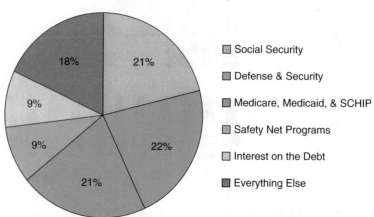

- Social Security
- Defense & Security
- Medicare, Medicaid, & SCHIP
- Safety Net Programs
- Interest on the Debt
- Everything Else

FIGURE 12.6
Pie graphs efficiently convey distribution.

Source: Office of Management Budget, 2007.

Jones, provides some basic pointers for communicating accurately and ethically when presenting data in graphs. See *Highlighting Using Graphs to Communicate Data* on page 287.

To provide support, speakers often use photographs to "document" some phenomenon or otherwise provide "proof." The proliferation of visual imagery requires that speakers and listeners alike develop visual literacy, or the ability to think discerningly about visual images—a matter we take up in *Highlighting Visual Literacy* on pages 288–289.[22]

Encouraging Emotional Involvement

A speaker can use pictures that will elicit greater emotional involvement than if the audience were left to conjure up their own images.[23] During the war in Vietnam,

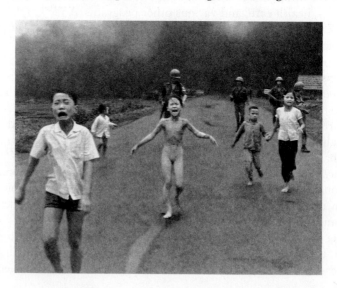

This photo of nine-year-old Kim Phuc, badly burned and fleeing her village during a napalm attack, ignited strong antiwar sentiment during the Vietnam war. The journalist, Nick Ut, helped the children to safety, and his photo won a Pulitzer Prize.

- *Use each type of graph properly.* Pie graphs depict relationships in terms of percentages or ratios. Line graphs emphasize trends, whereas bar graphs emphasize results at each division of a particular point in time. Pictographs compare basic amounts.
- *Adhere to traditional formats.* Line graphs and bar graphs consist of a *y* axis and an *x* axis. As Jones explains, "Quantity goes up and down on the vertical axis—the *y axis.* Time progresses from left to right along the horizontal axis—the *x axis.*"[24] Departing from this conventional arrangement (as many software packages may allow one to do) will impede understanding and/or distort the data. For example, a program may allow you to turn a conventional vertical bar graph on its side, but Jones advises against it. Pictographs, on the other hand, can show increasing magnitude along either axis; each depicted unit of measure can be stacked or can build from left to right, as modeled in Figure 12.5.
- *Be sensitive to the implications of range.* Graphs should always begin with zero on the *y* axis. Notice, too, that expanding or compressing the range of either axis (*y* or *x*) can distort the data and suggest different interpretations of the data. For example, Figure 12.7 takes a long view of homicide rates. If a speaker chose to use only the portion of the graph from 1980–1983, though, such data might suggest a "great decline" in homicides. That interpretation, though, would be misleading; in terms of the long view, the number of homicides would still be high. It may make sense to violate the rule of beginning with zero, so that differences can be better detected when one zooms in to a particular segment. When doing so, just be sure everything is labeled clearly, as well as noted aloud for your audience.
- *Label every element.* Numbers alone will not suffice. Explain their meaning via a simple label. For instance, each sector of a pie graph should be labeled in terms of its category and percentage, as should the meaning of the whole pie.
- *Make labels easily readable.* Employ a simple, easy-to-read style—and a large size—for fonts.

Homicide victimization, 1950–2005
Rate per 100,000 population

Source: FBI, 2006.

FIGURE 12.7

What does this graph suggest about murders in the United States? How might that interpretation change if the source showed data only from 1994 through 2005? Although technically correct, the impression would be different from a graph in which more years are considered.

- *Avoid overwhelming the audience.* Pies should be confined to five or six slices—never more than eight. Line graphs should have no more than two or three lines—each easily distinguished. Bar graphs should feature six or fewer bars (though each bar can be clustered into two or three vertical sectors).
- *Avoid "stacked" bars.* Bars with layered strata of data are harder to read and can obscure relationships.
- *Proofread.* Be careful with spelling, usage, correctness, and so on.
- *Choose colors carefully.* Use colors that yield good contrast so each element depicted is easily distinguished. Make sure, too, that the color scheme can be seen in the lighting conditions under which you will be making your presentation. Be mindful that what appears on your monitor will likely be much more vivid than what is projected on a screen.
- *Reveal your sources.* Cite the source(s) of all information at the bottom of the chart or graph. Also include the date (e.g., Bureau of Labor Statistics, June 2010).

Source: Gerald Everett Jones, *How to Lie with Charts* (San Jose, CA: Authors Choice Press, 2000).

a widely published photograph of Vietnamese children fleeing their village after a napalm attack was credited with igniting strong antiwar sentiment.[25] Pictures of human suffering following the hurricanes that devastated the Gulf Coast in 2005, the earthquake in Haiti in 2010, and the earthquake and tsunami in Japan in 2011 prompted people from all over the world to get involved in the recovery efforts that followed. Images can prompt increased attention to political problems as well. During the so-called Tea Party protests of recent years, pictures of the protestors and their signs resonated with those similarly inclined, as did pictures from the Occupy Wall Street movement, which inspired similar "occupy" protests around the U.S. and the world.

Stimulating Interest

As we have noted, presentational aids can make a speech easier to follow and understand. They also stimulate interest. When you think of the challenges of listening (discussed in Chapter 2), you will quickly recognize the value of presentational

HIGHLIGHTING VISUAL LITERACY | The Visual Dimension of Critical Thinking

Veteran journalist Gregg Hoffmann argues that visual literacy is a "requirement for clear thinking in the twenty-first century." Hoffman makes his case using a major international news story about an uncle's failed attempt to gain custody of and citizenship for his six-year-old Cuban nephew, rescued at sea. The boy's mother died trying to reach Miami by boat to gain refuge for herself and her son, Elian, in the United States. The father, still in Cuba and content to stay there, insisted that his son be returned. He won the legal battle, which ensued for five months. The uncle and other relatives defied the court order to surrender Elian to authorities. The ordeal finally ended with a predawn raid when federal agents removed the boy from a relative's household. Hoffmann writes:

Two photos likely will become symbolic of the Elian Gonzalez story. First is the Associated Press photo of the federal marshal, dressed in riot gear, demanding the boy be turned over. Second is the photo of the boy smiling at his father. People on both sides of the issue point to those photos to support their contentions.

You can see "what happened" in a photo or video, most people would argue. "A picture is worth a thousand words" is a widely accepted statement. Words are another person's abstraction of what happened, but a photo captures reality.

But does it? Is a photo or video simply a mirror of reality, or is it a product of certain premises and processes that then make it susceptible to manipulation? A photo or video grows from a point of view, or a set of premises. The photographer will select his subject, to a large degree, to represent his or her own world view, or to meet what is perceived as the preferences of an audience.

A skilled photographer can capture your senses and then craft the photo or video in such a way that you leap from that sensory level to very high, abstract levels. So, we see the photo of the federal officer and Elian and jump to thoughts of fascism. Or, we see the smiling Elian with his father and jump to thoughts of family values.

In political propaganda, advertising, and other media products, we see these attempts to foster such leaps all the time. The intent is *not* to have the viewer aids. By engaging multiple senses, presentational aids can help keep listeners from feeling bored, distracted, or passive. Research indicates that visual aids bolster interest and involvement.[26]

Color, a common element in visual aids, can stimulate audience interest.[27] Colorful poster boards and vivid graphs attract more attention than black-and-white images.[28] In addition, vivid colors are more striking than lighter shades, with blue, red, and green among those most preferred.[29] Variety also helps maintain audience interest. A presentation accompanied by varied graphs and perhaps a few illustrative pictures will be more interesting than one in which the speaker projects list after list.

Enhancing Your Credibility

Using good presentational aids can enhance your credibility. When you use well-constructed aids, you show the audience that you care enough about your presentation to prepare carefully. A well-constructed graph, for example, shows listeners

These two very different photos illustrating the Elian Gonzalez story evoke contrasting reactions. They show how visual depiction can neutralize logical analysis to capture viewers' emotions and direct their thoughts.

logically analyze or think about the image. The intent is to capture the viewer's senses and then evoke certain emotions and thoughts.

Source: Reprinted with permission of the author and the Institute of General Semantics, publishers of *ETC: A Review of General Semantics*, n.d. ▲

that you took pains with your preparation, and it also shows your concern for their understanding. A speaker who does not use presentational aids may be seen as less organized and less interested in audience understanding.[30]

You also demonstrate your trustworthiness when you use presentational aids. Rather than ask your listeners to rely exclusively on your judgment, you let them "see for themselves" when you share an illustrative photo or chart the numbers.[31] As a result, listeners may see you as more open and honest, more willing to let them share in determining the true meaning of the data. Being seen as trustworthy and fair-minded boosts your ethos—a matter we explored further in Chapter 2.

Facilitating Extemporaneous Delivery

Presentational aids can assist delivery by serving as speaking notes. Speakers often use bulleted lists to help frame their message for the audience. As each item appears on the screen, it functions as a speaking outline, reminding the speaker of what he or she wishes to address next. Some speakers also find that these prompts alleviate communication apprehension.[32]

Of course, you should be aware of the risks of using bulleted lists. For one, a speaker can use too many lists. Constantly displaying and quickly removing list after list can confuse the audience, just as leaving one up long after it is useful can bore or distract them. A speaker also should avoid visuals that feature too many words, or that simply duplicate his or her oral presentation. If you put your whole outline on a transparency, listeners will concentrate on the display instead of on you.[33] At the other extreme, simply posting keywords and failing to supply a needed graph, chart, or other aid may diminish your effectiveness and tarnish your image.

OPTIONS FOR PRESENTATIONAL AIDS

12.2 Describe the types of presentational aids commonly available to speakers.

Preview. *Presentational support can range from the low-tech chalkboard to sophisticated computer-generated graphics. A variety of options can reinforce your speech visually or through sound.*

What kind of presentational aids should you use? The answer to this question depends on many factors—such as listeners' expectations, available equipment, and whether the room lends itself to the kind of aid you have in mind. If a room cannot be adequately darkened, for instance, you would be hard-pressed to use slides effectively. In short, consider what options will work best in the setting, for the particular audience and occasion, and for the content of the speech.

Watch the Video "The Process of Developing a Speech: Using Presentation Aids" at **MyCommunicationLab**

Watch the Video "Writing Position Papers" at **MyCommunicationLab**

Computer-Generated Slide Shows

The classic movie *Star Wars* (1977) was ahead of its time, illustrating for moviegoers the power of computer-generated slide shows. Near the film's end, Luke Skywalker and his fellow pilots receive instructions on how to destroy the Death Star. The military strategist projects computer-generated graphics to provide an overview of the enemy's massive battleship, close-ups of its surface, and diagrams

HIGHLIGHTING PREZI | An Attractive Alternative to PowerPoint

Move over, PowerPoint. You've got serious competition. Prezi has arrived with much acclaim—even landing a coveted spot in *PC World*'s "100 best products of 2010." Given its ease of use, features, and ongoing, real-time updates, we can see why.

■ Its introductory tutorial (at prezi.com) gets you started in a matter of minutes, and other, equally brief tutorials allow you to hone your skills. You'll be amazed at what you can do and how quickly you can do it. Prezi's design is nicely intuitive, simplifying its use.

■ Prezi's features make it highly attractive. Rather than a linear slide show, you place images, text, and embedded video (e.g., a YouTube clip) on a canvas—and Prezi allows you to move to and fro and to zoom in and out. As its creators caution, you'll just want to be a bit conservative with the movement to avoid making your audience dizzy or seasick. With purposeful, well-choreographed moves, you can emphasize connections and produce good flow. And if you'd rather use Prezi than PowerPoint but already have a PowerPoint devised—no worries! Prezi allows you to insert PowerPoint slides!

■ Prezi lives in "the cloud," not only making it available anywhere there's an Internet connection but also allowing it to continuously evolve with real-time updates, further simplifying an already easy-to-use program and adding to its array of desirable features. ▲

of its infrastructure. The visual display—complete with movement—allows the speaker to provide this information to Luke and his squadron with clarity, impact, and efficiency.

What was once confined to science fiction has become commonplace. We regularly view full-motion weather maps, graphical depictions of what has happened on Wall Street, and computer-generated models of what likely occurred during a tragic accident or natural disaster.

Software such as PowerPoint or Prezi puts this same power in our hands. We can easily create slides and integrate images, sound, and video clips. We can enter data and select the type of graph, chart, or other device that is best suited for conveying the information. Digital images we have taken, scanned, or found online (if eligible for fair use, as discussed at www.copyright.gov/) allow us to easily insert them into a slide show. We can even design our own graphics, such as the pictograph in Figure 12.5. In addition, a presentational aid created via computer can easily be modified or updated, even during a presentation.

Meeting rooms and classrooms often allow computer assistance. If not, you might use the computer indirectly. Simply print any graph, table, or other visual display that you have created using PowerPoint or even a basic word-processing program. Use it as a handout, print it on transparency stock for use with an overhead projector, or have a copy shop—such as Staples or FedEx Office—print a poster-sized version.

In any case, you'll want to recognize the strengths of this technology and learn to use it competently and comfortably, following the guidelines we provide

HIGHLIGHTING HOW *NOT* TO USE POWERPOINT

We have synthesized various authors' advice—some empirically based—to offer these surefire ways to irritate, insult, and otherwise alienate an audience when using PowerPoint (or any other slideware). We hope you enjoy this tongue-in-cheek look at some of the more common infractions. (And we bet you've seen many of them!)

1. Use a lot of slides. The more the better! Always have something posted on-screen.
2. Read your slides to your audience (and preferably with your back to your listeners, facing the screen).
3. Give your audience a handout, before your speech, that duplicates the slides you will read to them.
4. Write out what you intend to say, completely, with full sentences, filling up each slide as much as possible.
5. If you use bullets, post them all at once, rather than bring them up individually.
6. For textual content, use a font that is itsy-bitsy or otherwise difficult to read.
7. Avoid charts, graphs, and graphical icons. Stick to text-based content.
8. If you must use charts, graphs, or graphical icons, do not fret over their substance, such as whether they actually convey or clarify information central to the meaning of your speech.
9. Do not fret over explaining any chart, graph, or depiction. Let the audience figure it out on their own, while you are plodding ahead.
10. When using any graph, chart, or other visual content, simply flash it onto the screen, giving the audience only a millisecond or two to process it.
11. Use auto-timing features to advance your slides—never mind that you may have to speed up or slow down or even stop from time to time to keep pace with your slide show.
12. Present multiple ideas on a single slide, and do not bother explaining their connection or lack thereof.
13. Do not obsess over spelling, grammatical correctness, and the like.
14. Use lots of special effects. Always have something spinning or pulsating on-screen. Accompany visual effects with sound effects—squealing and rat-a-tat-tats and the like!
15. Do not worry about a backup plan in case the slide show cannot be used. Simply insist on rescheduling your speech.
16. Remember: The screen is king! Serve the screen!

Selected Sources

Keith Barker et al., "To Read or Not to Read PowerPoint Slides," *Teaching Professor* 18 (November 2004): 4.

Jean-Luc Doumont, "The Cognitive Style of PowerPoint: Slides Are Not All Evil," *Technical Communication* 52 (February 2005): 64–70.

T. Trent Gegax, "Not Another PowerPoint Presentation!" *Newsweek*, (May 9, 2005) E29.

Peter Norvig, "PowerPoint: Shot with Its Own Bullets," *Lancet* 362 (August 2, 2003): 343–44.

Geoffrey Nunberg, "The Trouble with PowerPoint," *Fortune*, December 20, 1999, 330–31.

Thomas A. Stewart, "Ban It Now! Friends Don't Let Friends Use PowerPoint," *Fortune*, (February 5, 2001) 4. ▲

in this chapter. Also review the lighthearted cautionary notes in *Highlighting How Not to Use PowerPoint*. Because so many people use presentational software poorly (prompting many detractors), you will want to study the guidelines carefully.[34] We also offer pointers for Prezi in *Highlighting Prezi: An Attractive Alternative to PowerPoint*, as well as in our general guidelines for using presentational aids.

Chalkboard or Whiteboard

The chalkboard (now commonly replaced by a whiteboard) remains a useful device for speakers who have no other option or who wish to compile a list while working cooperatively with an audience. The chalkboard allows the speaker to highlight information visually and put terms, diagrams, or sketches on the board as an explanation unfolds or a list develops. In addition, moving to and from the board allows the speaker to be active in communicating his or her ideas and can also help the speaker channel nervous energy.

Of course, the chalkboard has its limitations. Because it is so familiar to most audiences, it may seem less interesting or original than other types of visual aids. Poor handwriting and a tendency to look at the board rather than at the audience can also diminish a speaker's effectiveness. In most cases, it is wise to choose a different vehicle for visually enhancing your presentation.

Flip Charts

A flip chart is essentially an oversized writing tablet, offering the same advantages and disadvantages as chalkboards. Flip charts are commonly used in business, conference, and workshop settings. In these settings, speakers often use flip charts to record ideas generated during discussions or brainstorming sessions. if you use a flip chart, remember that you will need a tripod for displaying it.

Poster Board Drawings and Displays

Watch the Video
"Sweat (Hyperhidrosis)" at
MyCommunicationLab

Poster board drawings and displays can be constructed well in advance and can be either simple or sophisticated. They can also be colorful and engaging. The advantages end there, however. Aside from the time, effort, and artistic ability necessary to construct content for posters, they are clumsy to transport and handle. You must also make sure that you will be able to display them. For example, will a tripod be available? Will thumbtacks be necessary? If you decide to use poster boards, make sure to investigate the speech setting and prepare adequately.

Handouts

Handouts are helpful when listeners need to be able to recall information accurately for use at a later time, but they can distract when made available during a speech. Consider selecting another means of visual assistance *during* your presentation. For example, you might present a budget on-screen and tell listeners you will distribute a handout containing the budget at the end of your speech. If you distribute multiple handouts, you may want to use a different color for each handout to better distinguish them.

Handouts can also help promote action. If you urge listeners to voice their opinion about a particular issue, you can provide a handout with specific contact information. By simplifying the task for listeners, you'll increase the chances that they will follow through.[35]

Watch the Video
"The Cocker Spaniel" at
MyCommunicationLab

Objects

Sometimes an object is suitable as a presentational aid. For example, when raising awareness about methamphetamine, law-enforcement officers often display some of the common items used to manufacture the drug. Presenting the actual items makes the information more concrete, vivid, and memorable.

Avoid small items that need to be passed around. Circulating something while you are talking can present problems. First, only one person will have the object while you are describing it; other listeners will be in the dark. Moreover, the act of passing something around will distract your listeners, taking their attention away from your speech.

Models

Some speeches call for a model as a visual aid. When informing classmates about "green" architectural design, one student brought in a simple model she had constructed to illustrate how a wide overhang, positioned to work with the angle of the sun in winter versus summer months, can reduce energy consumption. Holding a flashlight at different angles, representative of the different seasons, she showed how the overhang allowed direct light in the windows during the winter months but shaded the windows in the summer, allowing only indirect light to enter.

Obviously, constructing a three-dimensional model requires skill and effort. Many times, our students have been able to borrow models, thus simplifying the task.

Transparencies and Overhead Projectors

Overhead projectors, particularly those used to display transparencies, remain common in many meeting rooms. When computer projection is not available, they are the next-best thing. They allow a speaker to project lists, figures, charts, graphs, and other information onto a large screen in supersize form. Transparencies are also easy to transport, allowing a speaker to use several in a single presentation. If your printer will not accept transparency stock, check with a local copy shop to see if they can assist. (*Note*: If you're lucky, the overhead projector may work with a regular paper printout. Many classrooms feature these next-generation projectors.)

Audio and Video Materials

Some topics cannot be explained by using only words and still images. The quickness with which a particular crime can be perpetrated, the force and fury of a hurricane, and the precision and lightning speed of a Hellfire missile are but a few examples. In addition, in an increasingly media-oriented society, many listeners have grown accustomed to audio and video support. These sensory experiences, as we have noted earlier in the chapter, help generate interest and involvement. Using them successfully, though, requires careful planning and preparation. In general, the more heavily your presentation depends on any form of technology, the more time and effort you must devote to creating your materials and making sure the appropriate equipment will be available and in working order. Also, the room in which you will be speaking must lend itself to using these aids effectively.

Fortunately, most presentational software allows insertion of an audio or video clip, making for a more seamless and trouble-free multimedia presentation. Be mindful that clips should be short because they are used to illustrate a single idea. Showing a clip that takes up most of your speaking time is not using a presentational aid; it is substituting an audiovisual presentation for a major portion of your speech. Be sure to consult your instructor if you contemplate using video materials. He or she will likely have particular guidelines regarding their use.

In short, whenever you choose presentational aids, do so with the audience, setting, and occasion in mind. Find out which options are available and expected in a particular setting—including your classroom. Once you know your options, you can select which one(s) will best serve your needs. Whatever the option, prepare your presentational aids for maximum impact.

The force, speed, and destruction of a tsunami as it rushes onshore cannot be captured adequately with a single picture. A short video clip may be necessary.

GUIDELINES FOR PREPARING PRESENTATIONAL AIDS

12.3 Follow basic guidelines for creating presentational aids.

Preview. *Presentational aids must be carefully planned and prepared for maximum impact. In this section, we offer some basic guidelines for constructing presentational materials, including practical tips and ethical considerations.*

Over the years, we have seen speakers, in the classroom and in the community, use a variety of presentational aids. We have seen aids that were thoughtfully devised, those that made no real contribution to the speech, and some that actually detracted from the speech. In these latter instances, what was *supposed* to be an aid became a hindrance. A few guidelines can help ensure that you prepare presentational aids that genuinely contribute to your presentation.

Employ an Actual Aid Make sure the presentational aid you are planning to use is truly an aid. As you contemplate your speech, note places where a presentational aid would help. Keep in mind that an aid achieves one or more of the following:

- Adds clarity or promotes understanding
- Encourages interest or emotional involvement
- Helps your listeners remember what you have said

If a presentational aid does not fulfill one of these functions, it will not contribute to your speech; it may only distract the audience.

There are exceptions, of course. A prop can sometimes add a healthy element to a speech. A prop is any visual or audio material that enlivens a presentation but is not integral to its success. For example, a student who advocated gardening as a means of rehabilitation for troubled teens had a flat of plants, a watering can, and a hand trowel arranged on a table, simply to set the mood. A prop may be appropriate if it does not distract listeners' attention from the content of the speech.

Design Your Aid for Quick Processing Your listeners should be able to grasp the meaning of the aid with minimal effort. When preparing *visual aids*, follow these guidelines:

- Make them large enough to be seen. Your audience should never have to strain to see.
- Be smart with fonts. Choose a font that is easy to read. Sans serif fonts, such as Arial and Helvetica, are excellent choices. Be sure the font style you select is supported by the computer you will use during your presentation. Otherwise, the text will be garbled. Size the characters so that they can be read; this will depend on the size of the room. Experiment with bold versus plain characters to see which provides the most clarity.
- Employ good contrast. Contrast promotes clarity.[36] Start with a light or dark background and choose an opposite (dark or light) color for the text (see Figure 12.8).[37] For computer-generated color slides, a dark blue background with white content works best.[38] Use the opposite scheme for black-and-white transparencies: dark content on a white or clear background. The contrast between dark and light helps prevent washout of a projector's beam

so you can leave the lights up a bit. When using colors, be mindful that they are less vivid when projected than they appear on a computer monitor or printout.

Ground Cover: Advantages

✓ **Less maintenance**
✓ **Less pollution**
✓ **Less runoff**

- Consider using fill patterns. Dots or stripes for sectors of a pie graph or bar graph can assist anyone who has trouble distinguishing colors.

- Keep everything simple. Use as few words as possible for labels and listings. Your audience should be able to process what is on the screen with a glance. Feature only those terms or expressions that categorize or highlight what you want to discuss. Ignore rules such as "limit each bullet point to six words, with no more than five bullets per slide."[39] Concentrate, instead, on using as few words as possible, rarely if ever exceeding one line per bulleted entry.[40] For other visuals, avoid complicated details; show only the essentials and illustrate only one idea in each chart, graph, or diagram.[41] The idea suggested by the content should be stated at the top.

- Be careful with handwriting. Handwriting (as in the case of using a flip chart) should be large, legible, neat, and—if appropriate—color coded for clarity.

FIGURE 12.8
When creating a slide, keep things simple and use good contrast.

When you prepare *audiovisual aids*, keep these guidelines in mind:

- Sound and video recordings should offer sufficient quality for easy viewing or listening.
- Limit sound and video recordings to a brief clip that illustrates a single idea.
- Inquire about the feasibility of using audiovisual material. Find out whether using this kind of aid is possible in the classroom or community setting in which you will speak.
- Avoid razzle-dazzle. Presentational aids are there to support, emphasize, and clarify key points and information. They are not a show unto themselves. They should not compete with (or merely duplicate) what you are saying. They should *support* your presentation, not *become* your presentation. Avoid too much distracting detail or too many effects, such as having a new element come flying and spinning in, accompanied by a dramatic sound. Effects can be distracting as well as annoying. When using Prezi, pan with minimal movement from item to item so to avoid making the viewer dizzy, woozy, or nauseated. Your listeners should not have to take motion sickness medication to sit through your presentation! Likewise, use moderation with any background or border for a slide. Your visual displays should not upstage you as the speaker.[42]

Strive for Professional Quality   The best results can be achieved by computer. If you must rely on a poster or some similar option, take great pains to make it of superior quality.

Employ "Silence" Avoid using too many visual displays or sounds. Display blank slides or (with Prezi) a "hidden," empty frame when you want listeners focused on your spoken words rather than something on-screen. These can be your most important slides or frames in a presentation, even helping to accentuate subsequent slides or frames containing visual content. When a slide or frame with content appears *after* a blank screen, the audience will be even more attracted to it.

Anticipate Problems Much can go wrong, especially when technology and electricity are involved. It pays to have a backup plan, such as a handout of an all-important graph. In this way you can safeguard against potential disaster if the computer malfunctions, a server goes down or is too slow, or you encounter software incompatibility.

GUIDELINES FOR USING PRESENTATIONAL AIDS

12.4 Follow basic guidelines for using presentational aids.

Preview. *Presentational aids must be used properly for maximum impact. In this section, we offer some basic guidelines for using presentational materials, including practical tips and ethical considerations.*

Even when presentational aids are well designed, speakers sometimes fail to *use* them effectively. We have endless examples we could provide, such as presenters unintentionally blocking a projector's beam and others who placed transparencies upside down on a projector. You likely have witnessed similar mishaps. The following guidelines will help you avoid embarrassment.

Practice! Many speakers practice their speeches aloud several times, yet fail to practice using their presentational aids. Perhaps it never occurs to them or they think it is not necessary. Practicing with those aids, though, allows one to present more smoothly and confidently and to avoid unwelcome surprises (such as undesirable animation in a slideshow).

Preview in the Venue Check out the actual setting ahead of time, if possible, to become familiar with any equipment you will use. Test for sight and sound—from different areas of the room. Audience members who must squint to see the print on a slide or strain to hear the words on a recording can easily become frustrated and tune out the speaker. Too loud a volume, of course, can be annoying. If you are using a projector on a rolling stand, you may need to move it closer or farther away from the screen for an appropriately sized image. Also note where you should stand to avoid blocking the audience's view or interfering with the beam. It is easy to unwittingly cast a large shadow on the screen. Determine, too, how well you will be able to see your speaking notes under the specific lighting conditions.

Have Everything Set To Go For example, have presentational software positioned on the first slide or frame (a blank image, so not to interfere with your introduction). Have audiovisuals cued to the proper spot with the proper volume. If using a marker, make sure it has ink. Put any handouts in the proper order. With everything ready to go, you can relax and get off to a good start.

Use Only When Needed Display a visual aid long enough for the audience to process the information and make sense of it, and then remove when it is no longer relevant to the point being made. Visual images attract attention and can easily upstage a speaker. Keep them out of sight unless you need to refer to them. Doing so will help you maintain control of the audience's attention. (*Note*: If you are using presentational software, accomplish this by inserting blank slides or frames between content slides or frames and at the beginning and end of the slide show.)

Help Listeners Focus The effective public speaker uses presentational aids so that the audience knows what to focus on, and the speaker helps them process the aids. If, for example, your visual aid has more than one part, direct the audience's attention to the part being discussed by pointing to it with your finger, a pencil, or a laser pointer. Rather than project an entire bar graph, you might display and discuss it one bar at a time to help the audience process the information. Presentational software (such as PowerPoint) may allow you to bring up one element at a time. Otherwise, you can duplicate a slide or frame several times and

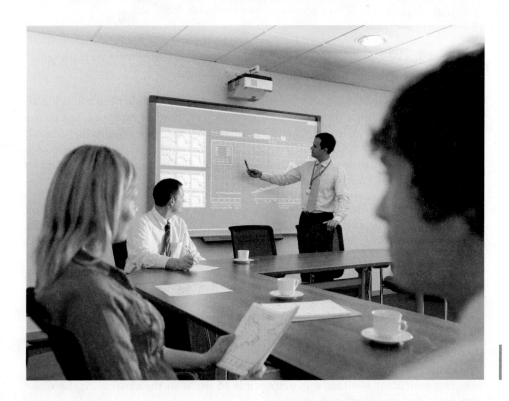

Many speakers do not use visual aids effectively.

HIGHLIGHTING PRESENTATIONAL AIDS AND ETHICS

■ *Recognize and respect the power of visual symbols.* Media scholars such as James Potter have pointed out that visual symbols function as powerful means of influencing our ideas and behavior. Visuals can attract and sustain attention, enhance emotional appeals, and even function as proof. Using them judiciously, fairly, and along with other substantiating evidence, then, becomes paramount.

■ *Use presentational aids to promote understanding—never seeking to distract or mislead the audience.* Listeners can be overwhelmed by too many handouts, too many images or those that move too fast, or by "aids" that cannot be easily viewed or heard with clarity.

■ *Select visuals that fairly represent the data you are presenting.* Avoid using graphs that exaggerate trends, for example.

■ *Recognize that presentational aids function as a form of evidence, and follow the criteria for using evidence presented in Chapter 7.* Give credit to your sources, and always strive to present accurate, recent, and complete information.

■ *Openly acknowledge visual manipulation.* If, for example, you "enhance" a picture to dramatize an effect or encourage an emotional reaction, you should alert listeners to the changes you have made. Changing colors, for example, can impact the tone and feeling of an image, as in the classic case of *Time* magazine darkening a cover photograph of O. J. Simpson to "achieve a brooding, menacing quality."[43]

■ *Make sure your speech can stand on its own; never substitute visual representations for sound argument.* Although presentational aids can greatly enhance your speech, the substance of your speech should remain strong, even if technology were to fail you.

Source: W. James Potter, *Media Literacy*, 3rd ed. (Thousand Oaks, CA: Sage Publications, 2005). ◣

then work backward, deleting one element at a time so that during your presentation a click or pan forward results in an added element.

Stay Connected With Your Listeners   As you direct the audience's attention to your visual aid, monitor your bodily movement. Talk to your audience, not to the aid. Avoid turning away from them and facing the screen, for example. Be mindful, too, that even though a room may be darkened, the audience will be able to see you, especially after their eyes have adjusted to the dim lighting. It is important to maintain eye contact with the audience.

Use Presentational Aids Ethically   Speakers often create their own visuals. You might create, for instance, a simple graph to illustrate a statistical trend. Remember that you will need to reveal the source of the data—orally and with a written acknowledgment on the visual aid for the audience to see. Reveal the source on the bottom of the display, simply by noting, for instance, "Source: *Newsweek*, May 7, 2012." (Notice how the sample presentational aids presented throughout this chapter consistently cite their sources.)

Sometimes a speaker discovers an existing visual, such as a graph in *USA Today* or another publication. In most settings, it is permissible to use this material (blown up and transferred onto a transparency, for example), but you must acknowledge the source orally *and* on the visual. Before using existing visual material, be sure to ask your instructor whether it is permissible to use it in the classroom; she or he may want you to design your own.

In any case, remember that citing the sources you have drawn upon for creating presentational materials is part of being an ethical public speaker.

 Study and Review materials for this chapter are at **MyCommunicationLab**

SUMMARY

 Listen to the Audio Chapter Summary at **MyCommunicationLab**

Functions of Presentational Aids

 Understand the diverse ways that presentational aids can help you as a speaker.

- Most public speakers use presentational aids. In an increasingly visual society, using aids helps engage listeners' senses.
- From the speaker's perspective, using carefully prepared presentational aids is an excellent way to enhance a speech. By using presentational aids, the speaker can do the following:
  - Clarify and support main ideas.
  - Facilitate understanding.
  - Engage listener emotions.
  - Deliver the speech effectively.
  - Enhance his or her credibility.
- From the listeners' perspective, presentational aids can do the following:
  - Focus their attention on what is especially important in the presentation.
  - Make the presentation more interesting and engaging.
  - Aid in comprehension and retention.

Options for Presentational Aids

 Describe the types of presentational aids commonly available to speakers.

- Almost any speech can benefit from the use of presentational aids.
- Diverse options abound, such as the chalkboard and computer-generated slide shows.

Guidelines for Preparing Presentational Aids

 Follow basic guidelines for creating presentational aids.

- Each aid should be carefully chosen and constructed, with the audience, the speech, and the setting in mind. In many speaking contexts, including the community and the classroom, listeners *expect* speakers to use presentational aids.
- In developing effective presentational aids, keep these guidelines in mind:
  - Make sure that each aid truly assists the presentation.
  - Design all aids for quick processing by listeners.
  - Strive for professional quality.
  - Learn to employ "silence" (i.e., avoid using too many visuals or sounds).
  - Anticipate potential problems by always having backups.

Guidelines for Using Presentational Aids

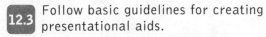 Follow basic guidelines for using presentational aids.

- As you use presentational aids, follow these guidelines:
  - Practice your speech *with* the aids.
  - Preview the speaking venue, if possible.
  - Have everything set up, tested, and ready to go before listeners arrive.
  - Reveal presentational aids for as long as needed, but only for as long as needed.
  - Direct the audience's attention to the part of the aid you are discussing and explain and clarify as you move through the presentation.
  - Remain connected with the audience—avoid talking to the aid.
  - Use all presentational aids (graphs and images alike) with a concern for accuracy and integrity.

QUESTIONS FOR REVIEW AND REFLECTION

Functions of Presentational Aids

 Understand the diverse ways that presentational aids can help you as a speaker.

1. What are some ways that using presentational aids can help speakers?
2. How do presentational aids assist audience members as they try to listen attentively to a speech?
3. Can you think of any topic for which no presentational support would be needed? Explain.
4. What are some ways that graphs can be used to clarify and illuminate ideas and information?

Options for Presentational Aids

 Describe the types of presentational aids commonly available to speakers.

5. What are the major presentational aids available to most public speakers? What are the potential advantages and disadvantages of each?
6. How might audience expectations influence your choice of presentational aids?

Guidelines for Preparing Presentational Aids

12.3 Follow basic guidelines for creating presentational aids.

7. How will you go about developing your presentational aids to maximize the chances that they will enhance the effectiveness of your presentation?

Guidelines for Using Presentational Aids

12.4 Follow basic guidelines for using presentational aids.

8. What are the key principles you will want to remember as you are setting up and using your presentational aids?
9. In what ways might the motto "less is more" be advisable for the speaker planning to frame her or his presentation with bulleted lists?

 Study and Review the Flashcards at **MyCommunicationLab**

Speaking to Inform

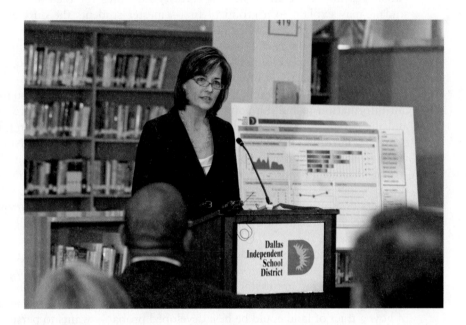

OVERVIEW AND LEARNING OBJECTIVES

Functions of Informative Speeches

13.1 Describe the different functions of informative speeches.

Types of Informative Speeches

13.2 Compare and contrast the different types of informative speeches.

Organizing the Informative Speech

13.3 Use appropriate strategies to organize your informative presentations.

How Audiences Learn from Informative Speeches

13.4 Describe the different ways that speakers can make information interesting and memorable to an audience.

As a professional and as a citizen, you frequently will be called on to deliver informative speeches. In informative speeches, you aim to educate or enlighten rather than persuade. You act as a teacher, not an advocate, providing facts and other information but not taking a stand on controversial issues. Thus, for example, an attorney may enlighten a group of concerned citizens about new laws governing the release of convicted child molesters. The leader of a task force may explain how his organization will generate and administer aid to newly arrived citizens displaced by a natural disaster. A security expert may brief the Parent-Teacher Association on new security measures for their school. A senior student may explain to a group of first-semester students the different ways of becoming involved with student government. You, too, will inevitably be called on to give informative presentations—in the classroom, on your job, or in your community. You may speak in workshops, orientation and training sessions, business meetings, board meetings, or community forums.

Some informative speeches may be preliminary to persuasion. You may transmit information to build a common ground of understanding before urging the audience to support a given point of view or to act in a certain way. In these cases, providing information might become the foundation for persuasion. Nevertheless, when we speak of informative speaking in this chapter, we are thinking of a speech whose ultimate purpose is to help the audience gain some understanding of a theory, concept, process, program, procedure, or other phenomenon. Informative speakers do not advocate for any particular position in a public controversy, but rather seek to educate or enlighten audiences about matters they will find interesting or useful.

Listeners should be skeptical about speakers who attempt to disguise persuasive speeches as "merely" informative. A political candidate who just wants to "explain" her plan for improving Social Security really wants to *convince* you that her plan should be accepted. A builder who says he only wants to "inform" you of how a tract of land could be best developed probably wants to persuade you to accept his scheme for using the land. Speakers who disguise a persuasive message as informative by claiming to be "objective" are acting in an unethical manner. Furthermore, if an audience sees through the speaker's deception, that speaker's ethos is undermined.

FUNCTIONS OF INFORMATIVE SPEECHES

13.1 Describe the different functions of informative speeches.

Watch the Video
"Informative Presentations" at
MyCommunicationLab

Preview. *All informative speeches seek to foster audience understanding. Yet they may function in different ways. Different types of informative speeches may describe, demonstrate, explain, or report on some process or phenomenon of interest.*

When you give an informative speech, you often will be imparting new information—helping listeners understand something for the first time. On other occasions, you may present a new or different way of thinking about a familiar topic. Although informative speeches function in a variety of ways, they all impart ideas and information. Your goal as an informative speaker is to help your audiences gain understanding.

Sharing Ideas and Information

Perhaps the most common function of an informative speech is to provide information or to share ideas. The speaker may decide that the audience needs to be briefed, taught, or informed about some data, program, issue, or problem. He or she aims to stimulate learning and gain understanding.

For instance, one student decided to give an informative speech about biometric scanners. He was not trying to get everyone in the class to purchase one of these scanners. Rather, he wanted to make them aware of what a biometric scanner is, how the technology works, and the purposes it serves.[1] He described its history as an outgrowth of fingerprinting—a tool used in law enforcement since the early 1900s. In the final section of his speech, he discussed the ways this new technology has been adapted for use by civilians and businesses (such as allowing employees to clock in and out of work or for monitoring access to high-security areas).

Raising Awareness

We are surrounded by a dazzling array of information—from the Internet, television, newspapers, and lectures. It is impossible to take it all in. We have our own interests and information sources, and we tend to limit ourselves as we strive to become well versed on a manageable number of subjects. Inevitably, we overlook many important issues.

Sometimes you may wish to call an audience's attention to something worthy of their consideration. When you do that, you are saying, "Here is something worth knowing. This could prove helpful, enriching, or worthy of further exploration." One speaker may talk about new careers in health care made possible by advances in technology. Another might teach us about the history of New Harmony, Indiana, the site of two of America's most famous utopian communities in the nineteenth century.[2] Still another might describe the principles of feng shui, the Chinese science and art of creating harmony between inhabitants and their environment.[3] In these situations, the speaker's purpose is to raise your awareness, to arouse your interest and curiosity, and to educate or enlighten you. The goal, again, is to promote understanding, not change listeners' opinions about controversial issues.

Articulating Alternatives

Most complex issues can be addressed in a variety of ways. Often we are not aware of our options, or we may know of only a few possibilities when in fact many others exist. Sometimes a speaker will give a presentation aimed at helping listeners grasp the number, variety, and quality of alternatives available to them. A pharmacist may speak to a group of soon-to-be senior citizens about the alternatives among the new Medicare prescription drug benefit plans. An academic adviser may speak to a group of college students about the latest alternatives for completing a semester abroad while simultaneously completing the university's requirements for a service learning certificate.

In articulating alternatives in an informative speech, the speaker must be certain that he or she presents the information in a fair and unbiased manner. The speaker who secretly favors one program or plan but feigns objectivity with listeners commits a serious ethical breach. Trustworthy speakers should be able to set aside their own biases in the interest of helping listeners make good choices from among the available alternatives.

TYPES OF INFORMATIVE SPEECHES

13.2 Compare and contrast the different types of informative speeches.

Explore the Concept "Informative Speeches" at **MyCommunicationLab**

Preview. *Speakers may be called on to present several different types of informative speeches. They may prepare and deliver informative speeches that describe, demonstrate, explain, or report on some process or phenomenon of interest.*

As noted earlier in the chapter, the major purpose of any informative speech is to share knowledge and ideas with the hope of promoting the audience's understanding or competence. Even so, several different types of informative speeches exist. Understanding their differences can help you prepare and deliver each type more effectively.

The Speech of Description

Sometimes speakers want to describe a place, an event, or a person. By giving a speech of description, they hope to help the audience get a clear picture of their subject. Topics that have worked well for students in the past include green spaces in urban planning, life on a Native American reservation, public transportation options in major metropolitan areas, the wetlands of North America, and experiences while serving in the army in Afghanistan.

If you decide to give a descriptive speech, you will want to take great pains with your language. Precision, color, and clarity are essential. You might also use presentational aids. A computer-generated slide show, for example, may be useful in showing the beauty of nearly extinct birds in North America, the grandeur of old homes in your community, or the ravages of war. However, avoid being overly reliant on visuals. Do the best you can to describe the subject of your speech without them, and then add the visuals to clarify certain points or to help explain ideas too complex or difficult to communicate in words alone.

The Speech of Demonstration

Watch the Video "Internet Blogs" at **MyCommunicationLab**

If you aim to teach an audience how something works or how to do something, you might give a speech of demonstration. A lawn-care expert, for example, might demonstrate how listeners can care for their lawns and gardens in environmentally friendly ways. An exercise science major might demonstrate fitness routines that can reduce stress and lower our health care costs. The leader of a Habitat for Humanity crew might demonstrate to a group of volunteers how to build a backyard storage shed. In each case, the speaker is demonstrating some sort of process.

The speech of demonstration may focus on application along with understanding. In some cases, the speaker wants the audience to apply certain principles or steps—to learn how to do something during the course of the speech. The exercise science major would want her audience to apply each step in the fitness program she advocates. The Habitat for Humanity crew leader expects that the volunteers who listened to her presentation will be able to build that shed by following the procedures and specifications she described.

On other occasions, the speaker may be describing a more complicated process, simply hoping that the audience will grasp that process, not necessarily perform it. For instance, a nurse in a hospital's cardiovascular unit might use a dummy to teach a group of heart patients about the preparations for their surgery, the surgery itself, and their subsequent recuperation. She wants her listeners to understand what to expect, not necessarily to do anything themselves.

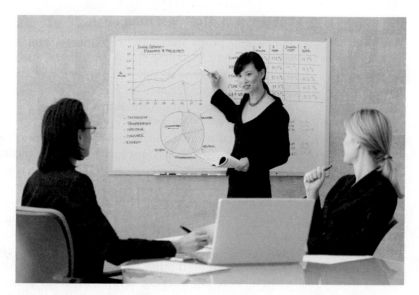

Most speeches of demonstration involve the use of visual aids to show, clarify, and make the information more memorable. Many use a sequential pattern of organization. To make sure the audience clearly understands the demonstration, you should allow ample time after your speech for questions from your audience.

The Speech of Explanation

A speaker who wants to help the audience understand concepts that are complicated, abstract, or unfamiliar will give a speech of explanation. The explanatory speech demands that the speaker be knowledgeable about the topic and be able to explain it clearly to the audience.

A professor's lecture may be considered a speech designed to explain abstract or difficult concepts to students. Skilled teachers carefully define concepts being introduced, explain their importance or relevance, offer good clarifying examples, and give students the chance to show what they have learned through some kind of application exercise.

If you are giving a speech of explanation, you typically will define the key terms or concepts in the speech, explain their significance, and offer examples that illustrate them. One student speaker gave a speech whose purpose was to help his classmates understand the meaning of *Learning Disabled (LD).*[4] He began with the legal definition of LD, gave examples of some of the most common learning disabilities, explained how LD students were typically placed in special education classes in the past, but now are usually mainstreamed into regular classes, and concluded by examining how various types of disability influenced the student's ability to learn in different classroom environments.

When you illuminate a concept that your listeners previously did not understand, you can make a real contribution to their learning. Because explanations of unfamiliar or difficult concepts can be challenging, you again will want to allow plenty of time for audience questions after your speech.

When presenting an informative speech, speakers often use presentational aids to enhance listeners' understanding. This speaker points to a line graph as she explains how students with different learning styles progress as they go from kindergarten through college.

Watch the Video "Marriage Equality" at **MyCommunicationLab**

The Informative Oral Report

In business, professional, and community settings, people are often called on to present an informative oral report. In some cases, these reports are given informally (perhaps even to one or two listeners) and may be quite brief. On other occasions, the speaker may be asked to prepare a more formal presentation, often technical in nature, to inform others in the organization of recent events, discoveries, or other vital information.

The need to give an informative oral report can arise in business and professional contexts, but is not limited to these settings.[5] For instance, one of this book's authors volunteers with a homeless shelter and recently attended a conference on "supported employment."[6] Upon her return, she was asked to present an oral report to the shelter's employment task force concerning the various forms of supported employment that were being used successfully by similar agencies around the state. Or, in a different context, a student was elected to the student senate and was later asked to represent the senate at an important meeting of the university's board of trustees. At this particular meeting, the trustees were considering several different plans for substantially increasing student tuition—a possibility that had attracted the concern of students and parents alike. The next time the senate met, the student was asked to present an oral report detailing the main features of each of the options the trustees were considering. To clarify the options, she prepared some handouts to accompany her presentation.

Informative reports often provide background that a group will use in making decisions or solving problems. For example, the report on "supported employment" resulted in the homeless shelter hiring a new caseworker to specialize in employment issues. Following a report (or even a series of reports), a group may go ahead with other business.

Although the primary purpose of a speech may be to report, explain, demonstrate, or describe, any speech can include a combination of these goals. For example, a speaker reporting on an innovative product would almost certainly devote part of that speech to describing the product or perhaps even demonstrating how it works. The various types of informative speeches are not always distinct, but they all share a common goal: increasing audience understanding.

ORGANIZING THE INFORMATIVE SPEECH

13.3 Use appropriate strategies to organize your informative presentations.

Preview. *Several different organizational patterns are particularly well suited for organizing informative speeches. You will want to select one of these patterns, and some examples provided in this section will help illustrate how those patterns may work with different informative topics.*

The basic principles of organization that we discussed in Chapter 8 should guide your efforts as you begin to organize your informative presentation. In that chapter, we presented several different organizational patterns, some of which work particularly well with informative speeches. These include chronological/sequential, spatial, categorical, and causal patterns. Table 13.1 presents guidelines

TABLE 13.1

Guidelines for Choosing an Organizational Pattern

Pattern	Use When...	Possible Topics
Chronological/ Sequential	You want to discuss an event, phenomenon, or concept over time, *or* you want to show a step-by-step progression	■ Trends in public schooling from the twentieth century to the present ■ The changing demographics of the United States ■ How our voting procedures have evolved from paper and pencil to machine voting ■ How to organize a successful town hall meeting
Spatial	You want to help the audience visualize something you are describing, *and/or* you want to describe something by moving from point to point through space	■ The spread of AIDS in Africa ■ Introducing the new Volunteers in Medicine clinic ■ Homeland security expenditures: regional differences ■ Options for bike trails in our community
Categorical	You want to emphasize the significance of the categories or divisions in some way, *or* you are interested in a flexible approach to organization	■ Bringing education to prison: innovative programs ■ How presidential primaries work in our state ■ Environmentally-friendly vehicles ■ New drugs for treating HIV ■ Award-winning service-learning programs
Causal	You want your audience to understand the factors (causes) that have contributed to some outcome (effects), *or* you want your audience to understand the impact (effects) of some problem or phenomenon	■ Factors that influence civic engagement ■ Media influences on women's body image ■ The decline of math scores in the United States ■ Academic misconduct on our campus

for choosing an organizational pattern for an informative speech, along with some sample speech topics.

Here are some examples of how each pattern may work with a particular informative topic.

A Chronological Illustration

Suppose you are particularly interested in the role of women in U.S. history. For your informative speech, you decide to help your classmates gain an understanding of the women's suffrage movement that culminated in ratification of the Nineteenth Amendment. You choose to organize your remarks chronologically as you trace the women's suffrage movement over 72 years.

Thesis: The passage of the Nineteenth Amendment was the conclusion of a long and difficult struggle.

I. The fight for women's right to vote experienced high and low points during its first phase, in the mid-nineteenth century.

    A. The suffrage movement began at a women's rights convention held in Seneca Falls, New York, on July 19–20, 1848.

        1. This was the first large gathering of women to discuss women's suffrage.

        2. Elizabeth Cady Stanton's famous *Declaration of Sentiments* was introduced at the convention.

        3. Although the convention was widely ridiculed in the press, women across America began talking openly about suffrage.

    B. When the Civil War started in 1861, movement leaders Stanton and Susan B. Anthony had to make a tough decision—whether to continue to fight for suffrage or support the Union effort to abolish slavery.

        1. After much debate, the women decided to assist in the war effort.

        2. Women played diverse roles—serving as nurses, scouts, and spies for the army and as seamstresses making uniforms and sewing bandages.

        3. They anticipated that their service would earn them suffrage at the end of the war.

    C. After the War, Anthony and other movement leaders felt "betrayed" by the government.

        1. In 1870, the Fifteenth Amendment was passed, giving black men the right to vote.

        2. Anthony saw this amendment as simply expanding male suffrage—leaving women behind.

        3. Movement leaders did not agree among themselves about the next step, leading to a split in leadership.

            a. Lucy Stone, who wanted to work for suffrage through the individual states, separated from Anthony and Stanton, who wanted to fight for a constitutional amendment.

            b. The two groups of suffrage advocates led separate, unsuccessful campaigns over the next 20 years.

    D. It was not until 1890 that the three women reunited to form the National American Woman Suffrage Association (NAWSA).

Transition: After many turbulent years, the debate over women's rights finally reached Congress during the so-called Progressive Era.

II. The fight for women's suffrage concluded with prolonged struggles in Congress and in state legislatures.

    A. America's entrance into World War I in 1917 initially delayed the debate over suffrage.

    B. In 1917, the House of Representatives began to debate the bill and finally passed the suffrage amendment in January 1918.

C. As the amendment moved to the Senate, suffrage leader Carrie Catt pleaded with senators to approve it, but they were too distracted by the war.
   1. A brutal flu outbreak in 1918 killed some senators opposed to the amendment, and they were replaced by senators more sympathetic to the cause.
   2. In September 1918, however, the Senate finally voted on the amendment and it was narrowly defeated.
D. At President Woodrow Wilson's urging, a new Congress finally passed the amendment in 1919, some 71 years after the beginning of the suffrage movement.
E. Yet it was not yet the law of the land.
   1. For the Nineteenth Amendment to become law, at least 36 states had to ratify it.
   2. After a tough battle, Tennessee became the last state needed to win ratification.
   3. On August 26, 1920, the Nineteenth Amendment was finally signed into law.
   4. The women who had fought so long and so hard for the right to vote could finally celebrate a new amendment to the U.S. Constitution: "The right of the citizens of the United States to vote shall not be denied or abridged by the United States or by any State on account of sex" (see Linda Monk's *The Words We Live By*).

By using this sort of chronological pattern, you would be able to dramatize the long and difficult struggle of the women who finally made it legal for females to vote.

A Spatial Illustration

A long-time volunteer with an overnight winter shelter that serves men and women experiencing homelessness decides to speak to a citizens' group in her community. The shelter is open every night from November 1 through the end of March and rotates among four churches. The speaker hopes to enhance her audience's understanding of the actual experience of people who are homeless. She organizes her speech spatially as she invites listeners to walk in the shoes of a homeless person staying in the shelter.

Thesis: Imagining the experience of someone staying in a homeless shelter may help us empathize with the plight of men and women who have no place else to sleep.

I. You arrive at the church early in the evening and find that the doors are locked.
   A. You have been told that because of other programs going on in the church, the shelter space is not available until 8:30 at night.
   B. You peer through the door and see volunteers moving furniture, organizing the registration desk, and otherwise preparing the church rooms that will be used for the shelter.

    C. As you wait outside, you huddle together with others as you try to stay as warm as possible.

        1. Everyone hopes that the doors will be opened earlier than usual.

        2. Most are weary from trudging across town with heavy backpacks or duffle bags that contain all of their earthly possessions.

        3. You notice that two disabled guests are accompanied by service dogs.

Transition: *After waiting as patiently as possible in the cold, you are relieved when the church is unlocked so that you and the other guests can enter the shelter.*

II. The doors open and you enter the church atrium—a large room with several "stations" through which you and your fellow shelter guests will pass.

    A. You move into a rapidly forming line as you wait for the registration process to begin.

        1. As you wait in line, you worry that you or someone else will be turned away tonight (because of the church's limited sleeping space).

        2. You notice that some guests are tense and irritable, while others use humor or tell stories.

    B. The registration process begins at last as a church volunteer asks you for your name, age, veteran's status, and so forth.

        1. A volunteer shows you a chart of the sleeping areas and asks you to choose the numbered mat that you will sleep on tonight.

            a. Once you pick your mat, the volunteer gives you a piece of masking tape with your number on it to help you remember which mat you selected.

            b. That same number will be used to identify any possessions you store in the shelter storage area for the night.

        2. You overhear some guests making special requests.

            a. One needs a wake-up call at 5:15 A.M. so she can get to her job as a laundry attendant.

            b. Another needs to be awakened at 2:00 A.M. to take her antiseizure medication.

    C. Once registered, you move to the north end of the atrium where a security coordinator scans your body and backpack with a screening wand.

        1. You know that he is searching for knives, tools, or any potential weapons made of metal.

            a. He will ask you to relinquish any metal object he finds—to be returned to you in the morning.

            b. Anyone who refuses to cooperate will not be allowed to stay in the shelter that night.

    D. The final stop in the atrium is a long table where you place your coat and backpack.

        1. A volunteer packages your possessions, marking them with your name and mat number.

        2. Another volunteer takes them to a storage room where they will be kept until you depart in the morning.

Transition: *Now that you have completed registration, you are allowed to move into the shelter's sleeping areas.*

III. The shelter has two sleeping areas divided by gender.
   A. Because far more men than women stay at the shelter, the men's room is much larger than the women's.
      1. You have noticed, though, that more women seem to be coming to the shelter as the winter wears on.
         a. Someone told you that the number of women has tripled since the shelter opened three years ago.
      2. You try to remember the sleeping chart as you search for a mat with your number in the men's sleeping area.
         a. You see that everyone's mat also has a pillow and blanket placed on top of it.
         b. You locate your mat in one corner of the room—not too far from the hallway that leads to the restroom.
            (1) You put your sweatshirt on your mat so others will notice that your spot has been claimed.
         c. You notice that the blanket on your mat looks thin, and you wonder if you will be able to get another one if you get cold during the night.
            (1) You are grateful for the shelter and don't want to be too demanding.
         d. You notice that the mats are closer together than ever before as the church tries to shelter as many people as possible.
            (1) You worry about what will happen if they run out of room.
   B. Because the church was not originally designed to serve as an overnight shelter, restrooms are not very close to the sleeping areas.
      1. From the men's dorm, you have to walk down a long hallway to get to a small restroom.
      2. Women must walk through the dining area to get to an even smaller restroom.
      3. You are grateful for the facilities, but you sometimes wish that the restrooms were more accessible and plentiful.

Transition: *The winter shelter's mission is to provide a warm, safe place for homeless people to sleep. Even so, shelter volunteers also prepare and serve a late soup supper.*

IV. The kitchen and dining hall are located between the men's and women's dorm areas.
   A. Church volunteers provide an evening meal consisting of hot soup, crackers, cheese cubes, fruit, and cookies.
      1. As a last stop before going to bed, you go into the dining hall and stand in line as you wait to be served some soup.
         a. You are grateful for the kindness of the volunteers.
         b. The hot soup helps most people relax a little before going to bed.
   B. Even though most food disappears within the first hour, the dining hall is open all night.
      1. Late arrivals sometimes find a pot of soup waiting for them, but there are no guarantees.

    2. Decaf coffee and cookies are always available throughout the night.

    3. Unlike the rest of the shelter, the dining hall remains lit by the soft glow of lamps so that sleepless guests and late arrivals will have a place to sit.

V. Quiet time begins at 10:30 P.M.

  A. With the exception of nightlights, all other lights are turned out.

  B. Most guests have found their mats long before this time and are already asleep.

    1. Sleep comes quickly for most because being homeless is exhausting.

    2. For others, however, falling asleep is really difficult.

      a. You hear one man who suffers from mental illness muttering softly to himself.

      b. Another man weeps because this is his first night in a homeless shelter.

    3. Guests hope to get as much rest as possible before volunteers awaken them at 6:00 A.M.

As she continues to use the spatial pattern, the speaker goes on to trace guests' steps through the shelter space as the night wears on and morning arrives. She points out that guests travel from the sleeping area to the kitchen for coffee in the morning before retrieving their bags and leaving through the atrium entrance by 7:00 A.M. From there, they will walk half a mile to a day shelter/resource center where they will eat breakfast, meet with caseworkers, and try to tackle the challenges of finding affordable housing, dealing with addictions and mental illness, and finding a job that pays a living wage.

A Categorical Illustration

A student speaker who was volunteering at a local food pantry, Mother Hubbard's Cupboard, decided to speak about the pantry in her public speaking class. After briefly tracing the history of the organization, she went on to use a categorical pattern of organization to discuss the agency's three major programs: the food pantry, nutrition education, and community gardening.

Thesis: Mother Hubbard's Cupboard provides healthful, wholesome food to people in need, while educating them about nutrition and developing useful new skills.

I. Mother Hubbard's Cupboard is perhaps best known for its food pantry, which emphasizes healthful, wholesome food.

  A. The pantry offers a welcoming and positive environment.

Community gardens allow low-income people to grow their own healthy foods.

B. On a typical day, MHC patrons take home bags full of fresh produce, organic dairy products, tofu, and locally baked breads.

1. More traditional foods, such as canned goods, snack foods, and meats are also available.

2. In 2011, MHC provided 86,758 bags of groceries to patrons (up 10 percent from 2010, according to an MHC newsletter published earlier this year).

   a. Nearly *one-third* of those served were children.

   b. Compared to 2010, MHC saw a *23 percent* increase in services to ill or disabled patrons.

3. Practically every day volunteers see new faces in the pantry.

   a. In 2011, 3,852 *new* patrons used the pantry services.

C. Patrons at MHC enjoy free choice of food items.

1. Each family gets one visit per week without a cutoff period.

2. Each family can fill one grocery bag per visit.

3. Every patron signs in but is *not* asked to justify their need.

4. More than 85 percent of the volunteers at MHC are also patrons who wish to "give back" to the program by helping others.

Transition: One major food source for the food pantry is another MHC program, the Community Gardens.

II. The Community Gardening Program promotes self-reliance and self-care by teaching people how to grow their own healthy foods.

A. In this innovative program, MHC teaches low-income patrons the life skill of organic gardening.

1. Patrons plant, tend, and harvest produce that goes directly to the MHC food pantry and to their own kitchens.

2. Over the eleven years of this program, the MHC staff and volunteers have raised close to 18,000 pounds of organic fruits and vegetables for the MHC food pantry.

3. In 2012, MHC will tend gardens at three different locations around the community and hold garden education workshops at these sites.

Transition: Not all MHC educational programs focus on gardening. Their third major program emphasizes nutritional education.

III. MHC's nutritional education program aims to provide patrons with the knowledge needed to make positive, healthy food and lifestyle choices for themselves.

A. The program teaches how to cook healthy meals at home, how to select the most nutritious meals on a tight budget, and how to preserve food grown in gardens.

B. Workshops are offered on such subjects as bread baking, soup making, and making homemade baby food.

1. Twenty-one workshops were offered in 2011.

2. Six of those were designed for parents with young children.

C. The program also features an in-store library on nutrition and health and offers recipes and handouts on nutritional issues for patrons to take home.

Watch the Video
"Banned Books" at
MyCommunicationLab

D. The store also offers displays and labels to educate patrons about the foods on the pantry shelves as well as a sample table to expose them to new foods.

After providing her classmates with an excellent overview of the MHC programs, this student speaker distributed copies of the most recent agency newsletter and responded to questions about her volunteer experiences and upcoming events.[7]

A Causal Illustration

Suppose you are a student at a university where there is no service-learning requirement. You have considered taking a service-learning course (in which performing community service is part of the class requirements),[8] but you are uncertain whether you have the time, or even if you would find taking it all that valuable. You decide to do some research on the topic and share your findings with your public speaking class.

Thesis: Most students who take service-learning courses benefit greatly from the experience.

I. Students benefit in a variety of ways from taking service-learning (SL) courses.
   A. An extensive study of more than 22,000 students by the Higher Education Research Institute at UCLA reported an impressive array of positive student outcomes.
      1. Students' academic performance was enhanced (measured in terms of GPA, writing skills, and critical-thinking skills).
      2. Positive values were also promoted, including stronger commitments to civic engagement and social justice.
   B. Other studies have reported that SL students learn more of the course content than those who take standard versions of the same class.
      1. These studies examined all kinds of courses, including political science, criminal justice, communication, environmental studies, business, anthropology, and sociology.
      2. This learning is further enhanced if students are asked to share their experiences with fellow students and reflect on their service experience through papers or personal journals.
   C. SL students also report that they intend to participate in service or volunteer activities after college.
      1. A recent study of hundreds of alumni suggests that these students' intentions are lived out after graduation because most SL alums reported a high degree of involvement with service in their communities.[9]
      2. This post-graduation involvement seemed to depend on whether the SL course emphasized the theme of civic engagement.
   D. Finally, SL students are more likely than others to choose a career in service—in some cases switching majors in order to do so.

Transition: Although nearly all SL outcomes are positive, a couple of caveats are in order.

II. Students benefit *most* from SL courses that are thoughtful and well designed.
   A. First, those courses must be grounded in realistic expectations.
      1. The typical SL class requires students to volunteer for two or three hours each week (at a minimum).
      2. SL classes typically have a few extra requirements, including reflection papers and journals.
   B. It is also important to anticipate logistical challenges.
      1. SL students may have to coordinate their schedules with other students if the class is organized around group work.
      2. Some students may have transportation problems because some nonprofit agencies are off bus routes or far from campus.
   C. Finally, approaching SL classes with genuine discipline and commitment is a must.
      1. Distribute service-learning hours throughout the semester.
         a. If you don't get started with your service early in the semester, you may have difficulty completing all of your class assignments.
         b. It is tough to catch up once you fall behind in SL classes.
      2. Recognize, too, that the hours your instructor requires you to volunteer are actually a *minimum*.
         a. The more time you spend working with your agency, the more you will learn and the better you will perform in the class.
         b. Genuinely giving something back to the agency may require you to go the extra mile.

This student describes his group's project and its impact on the community at a recent Service Learning Conference in Albuquerque, New Mexico.

You might then conclude your speech by pointing out that when students approach service-learning courses with a real sense of commitment, both they *and* their agencies reap many benefits. At the same time, you might warn students who cannot make this kind of commitment that an SL course may not be right for them.

In choosing your organizational pattern, you should let your specific purpose be your guide. What pattern is most likely to produce the response you hope to get from your audience? What strategy is most likely to assist in raising their awareness and understanding?

HOW AUDIENCES LEARN FROM INFORMATIVE SPEECHES

13.4 Describe the different ways that speakers can make information interesting and memorable to an audience.

Preview. *Listeners who are motivated to learn make the speaker's job much easier. Often, however, listeners are not as motivated as the speaker may hope, challenging the speaker to find ways to capture and maintain their interest and attention.*

Speakers need to understand the strategies available for heightening listener interest and helping them learn and retain information.[10] A good place to start is by thinking about how listeners are motivated to listen.

The Role of Listener Motivation

Perhaps you have heard the old saying: "You can lead a horse to water, but you can't make it drink." Any teacher will tell you that the learning process works like that: you can give people information, but you cannot make them learn. In informative speaking, much depends on the listeners and the understanding, beliefs, and attitudes they bring to the speaking situation. The ideal listener, as we discussed in Chapter 2, is the motivated listener, who is intrinsically interested in the topic, willing to work at listening, and eager to gain some new understanding. When listeners are motivated to listen and learn, the speaker's job is much easier.

Unfortunately, listening sometimes takes place under less-than-ideal circumstances. Sometimes audience members do not have the background they need to be truly prepared to listen. Sometimes they resent having to listen to a presentation. At other times, they are simply bored. Under these circumstances, trying to impart information can be challenging.

Usually when we are called on to make informative presentations, audience members are a mixed bag. Some are eager, some knowledgeable, and others less than motivated. Fortunately, there are things you can do to heighten listeners' interest and overcome, or at least reduce, initial inertia and apathy.

Capturing and Maintaining the Audience's Attention

A good place to begin is with thinking about how to interest listeners in what you are saying. Interest motivates learning.[11] In general, audience members respond with interest to ideas and information that are relevant, novel, and varied.[12]

Relevance   In Chapter 5, we discussed the importance of choosing a topic that the audience will perceive as relevant and important. Some topics will easily be viewed as relevant. How presidential primaries function in selecting a party's nominee was of obvious interest to many in 2008 (when the nomination was so hotly contested between Democrats Clinton and Obama) and again in 2012 (as Romney, Gingrich, and Santorum vigorously competed for the Republican nomination). However, relevance is not always obvious. In some cases, you will want to establish the relevance of your topic right away, during the introduction of your speech. Why should your listeners want to hear about hybrid cars or the proposed community public transit system? One student speaker established her topic's relevance by pointing this out:

> Did you ever imagine yourself being the victim of some kind of natural disaster—such as an earthquake, flood, tornado, wildfire, or tsunami? Probably not—but neither did the people of Japan expect an earthquake, nor the citizens of New Orleans, a devastating flood. Recently, I read that the leaders of FEMA and the American Red Cross have asked every household to purchase an emergency supplies kit. They argue that it is especially important to have one if you live in a region that is vulnerable to natural disasters. As you know, our college is located in an area where wildfires are quite common. There were three within 20–30 miles of our community over the past 18 months. So, knowing what items to collect for this kind of emergency kit should be a real priority for us.

Of course, the relevance of your topic should be clear throughout the speech, not just during the introduction. Your listeners will probably not learn much if, midway through your speech, they begin to think: "Wait a minute! What does this have to do with me?"

Novelty   Listeners are often interested in things they find startling, unusual, or new. Novelty gains attention. By contrast, overly familiar or commonplace topics are often perceived as boring or unimaginative. Of course, topics that lack novelty for some audiences may be fine for others. For example, a speaker who explains how to organize a town hall meeting to an audience of seasoned community leaders would likely find her listeners bored by what for them is a familiar subject. However, the same topic may be seen as novel and engaging by an audience of listeners who want to organize such a meeting but have had no experience doing so.

Whether information is seen as novel, then, will depend on the audience and what they already know. If listeners know little about urban sprawl, how to protect themselves from identity theft, or recognizing Internet scams, such topics may generate interest. With any topic, some initial audience interest must exist—a readiness to learn or at least openness to becoming interested. If a topic is seen as bizarre or irrelevant, the fact that it is also seen as new or unusual may not help much.

Sometimes a speaker can approach a topic in a novel or unusual manner and immediately gain the audience's interest. In general, when a speaker has personal, direct experience with a topic, he or she brings a fresh perspective that audience members may find interesting. During National Homelessness and Hunger Awareness Week in 2008, several citizens in a small Indiana community agreed to live on the budget of a federal food stamp recipient—$21.00 for the entire week. At the end of the week, they participated in a community forum, where they addressed the challenges they had faced and the feelings they had experienced. The speakers included the publisher of the local newspaper, the city's mayor, a county judge, a prominent real estate agent, and a woman living in poverty. By far, the most interesting and engaging presentation was given by the woman who had had actual, long-term experience with homelessness and poverty. As she spoke about her and her family's months of homelessness, her quest for a job that paid a living wage, and her ongoing struggles to provide nutritious food for her two children, the audience sat riveted. Because of her direct and extensive experience, she provided a unique perspective on the topic—one the audience found illuminating and memorable.

Variety Most of us have had the experience of being bored during others' presentations. Speakers can be predictable, overly repetitive, or dull. Longer presentations entail special challenges in this regard, because listener attention spans are often far too short.[13]

Speakers can help sustain the audience's interest by introducing some variety into their presentations. Variety is not so much about the topic chosen for a speech as it is about the *way* the speaker presents it. Variety can come in many forms. Speakers may mix humor with more serious speech segments. They may use presentational aids in imaginative ways to create visual variety. Speakers may deliver a speech with varied movement, voice, and facial expressions. In almost all cases, they will want to use a variety of supporting material, such as testimony, statistics, comparison, and narrative. These are just a few of the options available to help sustain listener attention. With variety comes unpredictability—a certain level of suspense and increased interest.

In a speech to a group of donors, the executive director of a hunger relief program varied his presentation by using colorful slides that showed the faces of some of the men, women, and children who had benefited from the program. He also presented graphs that revealed a statistical increase in poverty in the community, and he concluded with a brief video in which the program's patrons thanked the donors in their own words. At the same time, the speaker varied his movement and gestures, walking to the screen to point out specific points on the graphs and stepping out into the audience as he responded to their questions.

An effective speaker will use these sorts of attention-capturing techniques in combination and in varying ways throughout his or her speech. For instance, a novel topic may be of little interest to the audience unless the speaker can show its importance. And even the most relevant topic may seem uninteresting if the speaker presents it in a less-than-engaging way. Establishing and maintaining the audience's attention should be an ongoing concern for every speaker.

Watch the Video
"Learn CPR" at
MyCommunicationLab

Helping Listeners Learn

In Chapter 2, we discussed the audience's listening challenges, including ways to help them better attend to messages. If you are to give a successful informative speech, you have to present information that is, among other things, new to your listeners. However, new information can also be overwhelming if it is not presented effectively. You will want to pace yourself carefully, provide visual reinforcement as needed, and use language that is well adapted to the audience's existing knowledge and background.

We have discussed other ways to promote listener attentiveness and learning throughout this book. You can help listeners learn when you limit the number of main points you address (as discussed in Chapter 8). You can also avoid presenting excessive details, and you should translate statistics into terms that listeners can understand (see Chapter 7). Ask yourself, "What is essential for my audience to understand, recall, and perhaps use?" When you decide that something is really important, you will want to emphasize it—perhaps by using restatement or repetition (Chapter 10) or by altering your delivery to signal its significance (Chapter 11). You will also want to take the time to respond to audience questions. For an extended discussion of the question-and-answer period, refer to Chapter 11.

Cognitive experts agree that people learn far more when they are actively involved in the learning process than when they remain passive.[14] Do all you can to engage your audience. Choose a topic that allows you to share relevant, important, or novel information that you hope the audience will find intrinsically interesting. Beyond that, you may pose provocative rhetorical questions, quiz listeners with a few select questions that simultaneously review and reinforce what you covered, or ask them to write down their own questions.

With a longer presentation, such as a workshop, you may build in all sorts of activities, such as small discussion groups or exercises. You may present a concept, illustrate it with a brief video example, and then follow up with an audience discussion. You may provide breaks, which allow time for informal chitchat. Be creative in thinking of ways to get the audience involved. A student speaker recently gave an informative presentation on the barriers faced by disabled students at the university. As part of her presentation, she asked listeners to try to exit the room in a wheelchair, to climb a stairway with a leg brace, and to brush their teeth using only one arm.

Ethical Considerations

When you give an informative speech, be certain of the accuracy of the information you present. Invite the audience to investigate on their own, encourage them to listen to you critically and constructively, and give them sufficient time to raise questions and clear up misunderstandings. When they do ask questions, respond honestly, indicating when you are uncertain or when you need to do further research.

Of primary importance is the point we made earlier in the chapter: it is inherently unethical to camouflage a persuasive purpose by portraying it as informative. To reinforce the value of ethical communication, you may want to think of yourself as a teacher. Ask yourself, "What have I learned from good teachers?" You know that good teachers have your best interests at heart. They go to great pains to make sure that you understand. They strive to be clear as they make abstract concepts concrete through excellent examples. They watch for your confusion and respond to it. They ask you questions to make sure you are following. They encourage you. Striving for this degree of integrity lies at the heart of effective and ethical informative speaking.

 Study and Review materials for this chapter are at **MyCommunicationLab**

SUMMARY

 Listen to the Audio Chapter Summary at **MyCommunicationLab**

Functions of Informative Presentations

 13.1 Describe the different functions of informative speeches.

- Informative speeches are commonly delivered in diverse business, professional, classroom, and community settings.

- Such speeches should not be given when the speaker's aim is really persuasive, as is the case with most issues of public controversy.
- In presenting an informative speech, the speaker may hope to do the following:
  - Share ideas and information
  - Shape listeners' perceptions
  - Articulate alternatives

Types of Informative Speeches

13.2 Compare and contrast the different types of informative speeches.

- Even though all informative speeches aim to help listeners gain understanding, several different types of informative presentations can be distinguished:
  - The speech of description
  - The speech of demonstration
  - The speech of explanation
  - The informative oral report

Organizing the Informative Speech

13.3 Use appropriate strategies to organize your informative presentations.

- Various organizational strategies are available for arranging informative speeches. Among the organizational patterns commonly used for informative speaking are the following:
  - Chronological/sequential
  - Spatial
  - Categorical
  - Causal
- Like other speeches, informative speeches can be approached in a variety of ways, depending on the speaker's specific purpose.

How Audiences Learn from Informative Speeches

13.4 Describe the different ways speakers can make information interesting and memorable to an audience.

- Every informative speaker must be concerned with how listeners learn.
  - Unfortunately, not all listeners are intrinsically motivated to learn.
  - If listeners are resentful, bored, or simply not convinced that they need to know what is being discussed, they can present real challenges for the speaker.
- Listeners pay more attention if the speaker can show how his or her ideas are relevant, useful, and novel.
- The informative speaker should think about the learning process and strive to help listeners acquire information with a concern for ethical communication.
  - Learning is more likely to take place if the speaker limits main points and details, provides emphasis, responds to audience questions, and actively engages the audience.
  - The ethical informative speaker avoids giving a persuasive speech under the guise of an informative one and has the listeners' best interests at heart.

QUESTIONS FOR REVIEW AND REFLECTION

Functions of Informative Speeches

13.1 Describe the different functions of informative speeches.

1. What is the overarching purpose of an informative speech?
2. What are the three functions of informative speeches discussed in this chapter? Describe special issues and challenges associated with each.

Types of Informative Speeches

13.2 Compare and contrast the different types of informative speeches.

3. What are some topics that may be appropriate for a speech of description? How important are visual aids to this kind of speech?

4. Under what circumstances might a speaker be asked to present a speech of demonstration?
5. What are some of the key points you will want to address in giving a speech of explanation?
6. Think of one context in which a speaker (student, community leader, or professional) might be called on to give an informative oral report. What are the keys to effectiveness in this situation?

Organizing the Informative Speech

13.3 Use appropriate strategies to organization your informative presentations.

7. Which patterns of organization are especially well suited to organizing informative presentations? Under what circumstances might you use each?

8. Table 13.1 lists possible speech topics that would work well with each of the informative organizational patterns. What other topics might you add to the list?

How Audiences Learn from Informative Speeches

 Describe the different ways that speakers can make information interesting and memorable to an audience.

9. Describe the role of listener motivation in informative speaking.

10. What are some ways speakers can make their ideas and information interesting to listeners? Which are the most important and why? Can you think of other ways of capturing the audience's attention?

11. The informative speaker's challenge is to help listeners learn. Think of your most effective teachers. What do they do to facilitate your learning in the classroom? How can you apply what they do to your own informative presentations?

12. When you listen to someone make an informative presentation, how do you determine whether he or she is communicating ethically? How will you ensure that *you* communicate ethically?

✓ Study and Review the Flashcards at **MyCommunicationLab**

PREPARING STUDENTS FOR COMMUNITY INVOLVEMENT

Cecilia Orphan

Cecilia Orphan is a Ph.D. student in the Higher Education Division of the Graduate School of Education at the University of Pennsylvania. Prior to coming to Penn, Ms. Orphan directed the American Democracy Project (ADP), an initiative of the American Association of State Colleges and Universities (AASCU), which focuses on higher education's role in preparing informed, engaged citizens. In 2011, she was awarded the John Saltmarsh Award for Emerging Leaders in Civic Engagement. In the speech that follows, Ms. Orphan helps listeners understand the vital role the ADP has played in colleges and universities by encouraging students' engagement in civic affairs. She has delivered versions of this speech to audiences of students, faculty, and administrators.

One of the most celebrated features of American society is its democratic government. Indeed, many countries around the world have sought to replicate the unique form of democracy that is enjoyed by citizens of the United States. Yet democracy in the U.S. is not guaranteed as a permanent feature of American culture. In the words of the political philosopher John Dewey, "democracy must be reborn in every generation." For a democracy to work, an informed, engaged citizenry must guide the country through times of prosperity and difficulty. Historically, Americans have been deeply engaged in their communities and local and federal government. However in the last 50 years, there has been a drop-off in certain forms of engagement, most notably voting, political activities, and participation in voluntary associations. Because of this decrease in civic engagement, American democracy is suffering. While young people are volunteering at high rates, their service activity is not often extended into deeper acts of civic engagement such as voting, protesting, and community organizing. We can look to one form of political engagement to demonstrate this trend. Young people do not vote as much as their older counterparts. Tufts University's Center for Learning and Research on Civic Learning and Engagement report that only 24 percent of college-aged youth voted in the 2010 midterm election, and 62 percent voted in the 2008 presidential election. Additionally, public knowledge about democratic institutions is very low. For example, in 2011, the Pew Research Center reported that just over half (56 percent) of Americans correctly identify John Boehner as Speaker of the House, while only 47 percent know that Justice Roberts is conservative, and only 43 percent know that Republicans have a majority in the House.

So what is being done to reverse this tide of ignorance and disengagement in the United States? Leaders in higher education have taken notice of these alarming trends and are working to reclaim the democratic dimensions of their work. Starting with Campus Compact, an organization focused on creating opportunities for community service as part of the college curriculum, a movement has gained momentum to leverage the vast intellectual and human resources of the academy to prepare the next generation of informed, engaged citizens. In 2003, the American Association of State Colleges and Universities (AASCU) launched the American Democracy Project (ADP) in order to shift the trends of disengagement toward deeper involvement. What began as a set of marginal, celebratory, and

CECILIA GAINS HER LISTENERS' ATTENTION BY WARNING THEM THAT THE KIND OF DEMOCRACY U.S. CITIZENS TAKE FOR GRANTED IS NOT GUARANTEED. SHE SUPPORTS HER ASSERTION WITH A COMPELLING QUOTATION FROM PHILOSOPHER JOHN DEWEY.

SHE BRINGS THE PROBLEM OF DECREASED CIVIC ENGAGEMENT INTO SHARP FOCUS BY SHARING SOBERING STATISTICS ON LOW VOTER TURNOUT BY YOUNG PEOPLE IN RECENT ELECTIONS. SHE ALSO OFFERS SPECIFIC EXAMPLES OF DRAMATICALLY POOR PUBLIC KNOWLEDGE ABOUT DEMOCRATIC INSTITUTIONS.

AS CECILIA TRANSITIONS INTO THE BODY OF HER SPEECH, SHE USES A RHETORICAL QUESTION TO ENGAGE THE AUDIENCE'S INTEREST IN LEARNING MORE ABOUT STEPS THAT U.S. COLLEGES AND UNIVERSITIES HAVE TAKEN TO ADDRESS THE PROBLEM.

episodic activities on just over 100 college campuses has now grown into a national effort on 240 campuses to prepare informed, engaged citizens for our democracy. Since its beginnings, ADP has focused on building the civic agency of undergraduate students. Civic agency can be defined as an individual's ability and desire to engage in their community and political institutions. Civic agency involves the development and use of civic skills that are used in community-based problem solving and political engagement efforts. By focusing on building the civic agency of undergraduate students, ADP has become a national leader in higher education's effort to strengthen American democracy.

In the last ten years of the project, ADP has made many important discoveries. The first and perhaps most promising discovery is the deep desire on the part of young people to solve local problems. This desire is evidenced by the high volunteer rates of college-aged citizens. Indeed, young people around the country are eager for meaningful opportunities for civic engagement. In addition to this important finding, the leaders of ADP have learned four important lessons through their work to prepare students as citizens. The first is that for students to become engaged and politically knowledgeable, they must have multiple opportunities to develop their democratic skills throughout their undergraduate careers. This means that universities must take a holistic approach to civic education and institutionalize civic efforts throughout all aspects of the undergraduate experience. ADP found that those campuses that were able to produce the largest gains in student civic agency were ones that provided a variety of opportunities for civic engagement in major requirements, general education, extracurricular activities, and campus/community partnerships.

Another important lesson the ADP leaders learned was to let 1,000 flowers bloom. AASCU is a membership association composed of 400 universities and colleges. AASCU institutions are highly diverse in terms of size, location, local circumstances and academic focus. Some examples include: San Francisco State University, Rhode Island College, Texas Women's University, the University of North Carolina at Greensboro, Massachusetts College of Liberal Arts, and Wayne State University in Detroit. Given this great institutional diversity, the leaders of ADP quickly discovered that they could not be prescriptive about what the project should entail. It became apparent very quickly that for the project to work, campuses would have to adapt the national initiative to their own specific environments. Maintaining a focus on institutional intentionality, as I mentioned earlier, ADP campuses have created a dynamic set of best practices that can be shared throughout all of higher education because they represent the varied landscape of American academia. Thus, letting 1,000 flowers bloom has been an integral part of ADP's success.

Because of the large number of campuses involved, ADP found that the project was most useful to its members when it served as an umbrella organization that housed many different coordinated efforts. This discovery gave birth to the Civic Engagement in Action (CEIA) Series. CEIA is a set of initiatives that allow smaller groups of campuses to experiment with programs and develop a set of best practices. The leaders of ADP often refer to the CEIA

Series as laboratories for democracy because campus leaders are able to experiment with best practices for educating students for civic engagement and then share these findings with the rest of the campuses in ADP. For example, ADP partnered with the Yellowstone Foundation to lead faculty through a week-long institute where they learned about controversies facing Yellowstone National Park and how the public can get involved in finding solutions to these controversies. The faculty then brought their knowledge of this process back to their own campuses where they taught their students how to become involved in *local* controversies and work constructively with other solution-seekers from around the community. The CEIA Series is now an important source for innovative strategies for campuses to use to educate students as citizens.

SHE ILLUSTRATES THE WAYS THAT ADP ADAPTS TO SPECIFIC INSTITUTIONS BY ENCOURAGING EACH TO DEVELOP THEIR OWN "BEST PRACTICES." TO CLARIFY AND DEVELOP THIS POINT, SHE THEN OFFERS A SPECIFIC ILLUSTRATION OF HOW A PARTICULAR "LAB-ORATORY FOR DEMOCRACY" WORKED.

The final lesson that was learned is the need for meaningful student leadership. This realization grew out of the eCitizenship: New Tools, New Strategies, New Spaces initiative, which is part of the CEIA Series. As the name implies, ADP faculty members and leaders had the goal of using online spaces to enhance student civic development. Because social networking sites and tools are often foreign territory for professors, ADP leaders quickly decided that they would need student leadership in the design and implementation of the project. The leaders of ADP were so impressed with the student involvement in eCitizenship that they decided to incorporate student leadership into all ADP initiatives. After all, who else is better equipped to design civic engagement opportunities that will appeal to undergraduate students than students themselves?

ONCE AGAIN, THE SPEAKER USES A RHETORICAL QUES-TION AS SHE SEEKS TO HELP LISTENERS REALIZE THE CRITICAL IMPORTANCE OF STUDENT LEADERSHIP IN DESIGNING ENGAGING NEW INITIATIVES.

ADP stands as one of many civic engagement efforts in higher education. These efforts are extremely important because the future of American democracy depends on our ability to educate informed, engaged citizens. I mentioned John Dewey in the introduction to this speech. The second half of this quote helps us understand the importance of education in protecting American democracy. Dewey believed that democracy must constantly be evolving and that education was its midwife. Thanks to the efforts of the American Democracy Project and other similar organizations, higher education is stepping up to serve in this important role.

Source: Reprinted by permission from Cecilia Orphan, "Preparing Students for Community Involvement."

Persuasive Speaking in a Democratic Society

OVERVIEW AND LEARNING OBJECTIVES

The Anatomy of Public Controversy

 Define *public controversy* and discuss what it means to *deliberate in good faith*.

Questions of Fact, Value, and Policy

 Distinguish among the three different types of persuasive issues: fact, value, and policy.

Ethical Proof in Persuasive Speaking

 Define *ethos* and discuss what contributes to strong credibility.

Appealing to Audience Emotions

 Discuss the techniques and ethics of appealing to an audience's emotions.

Astudent urges his fellow students to boycott a speech by a controversial public figure. A public health nurse urges the distribution of condoms in the local high schools. A lawyer argues against imposing limits on the money juries can award in medical malpractice cases. The president of the United States goes on national television to urge public support for his economic policies.

Every day, all sorts of people—from ordinary citizens to world leaders—try to persuade other people. That is, they seek to influence the beliefs, values, or actions of others or "make the case" for a new policy or program. Sometimes you try to persuade others about trivial or purely personal matters. You may persuade a friend to go to a movie, for example, or to take up yoga. In a democracy, however, persuasion takes on greater significance. Persuasion is the chief mechanism through which we select our leaders, determine our civic priorities, resolve controversies and disputes, and choose among various policies. Indeed, the reliance on persuasion rather than force is what most clearly distinguishes a democracy from a dictatorship.

Perhaps you have studied persuasion in another public speaking class. Or you may have studied persuasion in psychology, sociology, or public relations and advertising. In all of these fields, persuasion is important, because to understand persuasion is to understand human behavior. In this chapter, however, we are concerned with the role of persuasion in our democratic society. We will consider, first, how public controversies invite persuasion and the sorts of issues we debate as citizens in a democracy. Then we will reflect on some of the means of persuasion and the ethical constraints on persuasion in a democracy.

THE ANATOMY OF PUBLIC CONTROVERSY

14.1 Define *public controversy* and discuss what it means to *deliberate in good faith*.

Watch the Video "Bill Gates Criticizes America's High Schools" at **MyCommunicationLab**

Preview. *Persuasion is rooted in controversy. We deal with personal controversies every day, but not all controversies involve matters of public importance. When you speak about a public controversy, you have a responsibility to do more than simply express your opinion. As a citizen, you have an obligation to back up your opinions with arguments and evidence and to "test" those opinions in the give-and-take of public debate.*

Prayer in the schools. The future of Social Security. Illegal immigration. Affirmative action. Health care reform. Same-sex marriage. All of these issues spark controversy because people have strong yet conflicting opinions. They are *public* controversies because they affect large numbers of people—and because they require that we make decisions about new laws, how to spend our tax dollars, or what programs and policies to adopt. Not every difference of opinion leads to a public controversy, of course. You may have disagreed with your parents over which college you should attend, or perhaps you have debated with your friends over where to go on spring break. These issues may be important to you personally, but they are not *public* controversies. Public controversies involve the choices we must make as *citizens*; they affect the whole community, perhaps even the nation or the world.

Some public controversies literally involve matters of life or death. When we debate whether the government should restrict stem cell research, for example, our decision could affect tens of thousands who potentially may benefit from such research. So, too, do people's lives hang in the balance when we debate how much aid to send to the scene of a natural disaster or whether to send troops to some trouble spot on the other side of the globe. Obviously, not all public controversies have such grave implications. Sometimes we may address little-known controversies or try to call attention to some problem that we believe has been ignored. In just the past decade or so, for example, we have begun to hear warnings about the environmental hazards posed by "e-waste,"[1] and now we also hear warnings of a new "health care crisis": a projected shortage of trained nurses.[2] Every day, new controversies arise over our nation's economic, social, and political problems and policies. As citizens, we need to participate in public discussions of these important issues. Indeed, that's what it *means* to be a citizen in a democracy: participating in the process of governing ourselves.

Let us begin by reflecting on one recent controversy and what that controversy can teach us about the anatomy—that is, the shape, structure, and parts—of a public controversy. Since at least 2004, there has been an ongoing debate over the use of so-called enhanced interrogation techniques by U.S. military and intelligence personnel in the war against terrorism. Inspired by allegations of torture and prisoner abuse, this debate has pitted former members of the George W. Bush administration against a variety of critics, including Bush's successor as president, Barack Obama. In one of his first major foreign policy addresses as president, Obama denounced "so-called enhanced interrogation techniques" as both ineffective and immoral. "I know some have argued that brutal methods like waterboarding were necessary to keep us safe," he stated. "I could not disagree more." In Obama's view, such methods not only were ineffective, they also undermined the "rule of law," alienated our allies, and served as a "recruitment tool for terrorists." They also risked the lives of American troops by making it less likely that enemy combatants would surrender and more likely that captured Americans would be tortured. Those who defended such techniques were simply "on the wrong side of the debate, and the wrong side of history," Obama argued. "We must leave these methods where they belong—in the past. They are not who we are. They are not America."[3]

On the other side of the debate, former vice president Dick Cheney defended enhanced interrogation techniques as both lawful and effective. According to Cheney, the legal authority for such methods was drawn from the Constitution and from a congressional resolution authorizing the Bush administration to use "all necessary and appropriate force" to protect the American people after the 9/11 attacks. Calling the interrogations "legal, essential, justified, successful, and the right thing to do," Cheney insisted that such methods were used only on "hardened terrorists" after "other efforts failed," and he claimed that the information gathered had prevented the "violent death of thousands, if not hundreds of thousands, of innocent people." From the start, Cheney explained, "there was only one focused and all-important purpose" for the interrogations, and that was to obtain "specific information on terrorist plans." That purpose was fulfilled and terrorist plots were "averted." To rule out such techniques in the future, Cheney concluded, would be "recklessness" and "make the American people less safe."[4]

Like most complex public controversies, the debate over enhanced interrogation techniques raised a number of factual questions: What sorts of interrogation techniques were actually employed by U.S. agents, and what exactly did waterboarding and other such methods entail? How many alleged terrorists were subjected to such techniques, and what information was obtained from them? How, if at all, did that information help the U.S. avert terrorist attacks? Was President Obama right that such methods hurt America's reputation around the world and helped to recruit new terrorists? Or was Dick Cheney right that such methods are necessary to save innocent lives? Beyond these questions, the whole controversy raised larger, more difficult questions about the legal and ethical justifications for such actions. Did the Bush administration have the legal authority to authorize such techniques? What rights, if any, do alleged terrorists have? In time of war, are such methods really necessary to protect our national security? Are they morally justifiable? These are just a few of the larger and more difficult questions raised by the debate.

In today's political climate, some people inevitably try to exploit such controversies for personal or political gain. On talk radio and TV debate shows, politicians and representatives of various special interests put their own spin on the controversy, eager to score points. For most Americans, however, the debate over enhanced interrogation methods was not about who might gain the political advantage. Rather, it was about finding the truth and striking the right balance between equally worthy goals—upholding our ideals and protecting our national security. Unfortunately, answers to the factual, legal, and political questions raised by the controversy were neither simple nor obvious. Historians will someday judge whether the Bush administration acted properly in authorizing such methods. But the larger issue will always be with us: how far are we willing to go to protect our national security?

As citizens in a democracy, we have a right to our opinions on such controversial issues. If we express those opinions in public, however, we assume a greater responsibility—the responsibility to back up our opinions with *arguments*. By speaking out in public, we also invite those who disagree to speak out as well. As citizens, we have an ethical obligation to respond sincerely and respectfully to those who accept that invitation. The success of our democracy depends on our willingness to subject our ideas to the scrutiny of public debate—and to be open-minded and respectful toward those who disagree.

Deliberating in Good Faith

In Chapter 1, we introduced the phrase deliberating "in good faith." Among other things, we noted that deliberating in good faith means making *arguments* in support of your opinions. But what is a good argument? What does deliberating in good faith mean in terms of your responsibilities as a speaker?

First, it means telling the truth, at least as you see it. Your beliefs and opinions may not always turn out to be right. Yet speakers who *deliberately* misrepresent the facts, or speakers who publicly advocate ideas that they do not *sincerely* believe, are not merely mistaken; they are unethical. They deserve to be condemned by all who value free and open debate.

Second, deliberating in good faith means backing up your personal opinions with evidence and reasoning. In public debate, you have an obligation not only to be honest but also to *prove* your claims. Proving one's claim does *not* mean presenting conclusive or irrefutable evidence; it does *not* mean settling an issue once and for all. It *does* mean presenting a *reasonable* argument—one at least worthy of serious consideration and further debate.

Third, deliberating in good faith means accepting your burden of proof, or your responsibility to meet a certain standard of proof in a particular context. Perhaps you have heard the phrase *burden of proof* in a legal context. In a courtroom, the burden of proof refers to the level of proof necessary for the prosecution to win the case. Depending on the type of case, that burden of proof may range from a *preponderance of the evidence*—the standard typical in a civil case—to the much higher

The "rules" of democratic deliberation often break down on TV talk shows, where participants sometimes seem more interested in "scoring points" than in finding common ground.

standard required in criminal cases: *beyond a reasonable doubt.* In public debate, the burden of proof is not so clearly defined, yet we expect some advocates to meet a higher standard of proof than others. As in the courtroom, those who accuse others of wrongdoing carry a heavier burden of proof than those who speak in self-defense. Likewise, those who advocate new policies carry a heavier burden of proof than those who defend well-established or existing policies. After all, the existing policy at least has a track record, and there is always some risk to trying something new. In public debate, of course, there will be no judge to instruct you on your burden of proof or to enforce the rules of debate. Nevertheless, it is important that you understand the expectations and standards of proof in public debate.

We will return to the practical implications of meeting your burden of proof in Chapter 15. For now, it is enough to understand that public deliberations, like courtroom debates, are governed by *rules* and that you have an obligation to live up to those rules—however irresponsible or unconstrained other speakers may seem. No doubt you have seen speakers attack their political opponents, cite dubious evidence, or stir up ugly emotions. That does not mean you have a right to resort to the same tactics. The fact that other speakers may be irresponsible is all the more reason for you to uphold higher standards. By following the rules yourself, you can set a good example and contribute to more constructive public discussion.

QUESTIONS OF FACT, VALUE, AND POLICY

Preview. *Persuasive issues revolve around questions of fact (what is true), value (what is good or bad), and policy (what we should do in the future). As you prepare to speak about a particular topic, you need to identify the types of issues surrounding that topic and focus your efforts on unresolved controversies.*

14.2 Distinguish among the three different types of persuasive issues: fact, value, and policy.

Watch the Video
"Dirty Hands
across America" at
MyCommunicationLab

Is That the Truth?

Normally, we use the word *fact* to describe something that is already established as true. We think of a fact as something that we can just look up in a reference book or that we can establish by using the appropriate measurement device. Thus, we may say that it is a fact that Peru is in Latin America or that it is currently 80 degrees—based on a thermometer reading. These are not the sorts of facts that are disputed or debated. In ordinary usage, a fact is something that we all agree is true.

On many occasions, however, we disagree over the facts relating to a particular subject, and we discuss and debate what may or may not be "true." Does the Loch Ness Monster really exist? How many people are currently unemployed in this country? Do artificial sweeteners cause cancer? What might account for the rash of hurricanes in recent years? These are the sorts of issues where the "facts" themselves are in dispute. Many public controversies, such as the debate over Social Security and disagreements over the causes of global warming, rest on unresolved or debatable questions of fact.

A question of fact typically involves issues of existence, scope, or causality. We would address a controversy over *existence* if, for example, we tried to persuade our audience that the ivory-billed woodpecker, a bird once thought extinct, still survives in remote forests of the American Southeast. Issues of *scope* may emerge in debates over how many Americans are unemployed or the extent of a flu epidemic, whereas we debate *causality* when we disagree over the causes of juvenile delinquency or the epidemic of obesity in the United States. In addition to involving different sorts of questions, some factual controversies may revolve around questions about the past (How many people have died from breast cancer in the past decade?), whereas others may involve predictions about the future (Will the Obama administration's plan to discourage "outsourcing" through tax incentives bring manufacturing jobs back to the United States, as the president promised in his 2012 State of the Union address?).[5]

Whatever the specific focus, issues of fact invite empirical proof: real examples, statistics, and testimony from experts. In addition, we typically try to resolve questions of fact *before* we debate questions of value or policy. If, for example, we cannot agree about the existence or causes of global warming, it makes little sense to discuss possible solutions. Similarly, before we debate how best to control illegal immigration, we should first answer some factual questions: How many immigrants enter America illegally each year? Where and how do they enter the country? And what motivates them to risk arrest or even death to get into the United States? Again, an analogy to courtroom debates may help clarify how controversies evolve. In a criminal trial, lawyers must first establish the *facts of the case*. Only then do they debate which laws may have been violated. And only after the court has decided which laws have been broken do the lawyers debate the appropriate sentence. In public controversies, the rules are less clearly defined, but the process is essentially the same: only after we have resolved major factual controversies does it make sense to debate how to *evaluate* those facts or how to *act* in response.

Is This Good or Bad?

A question of value focuses on what we consider good or bad, right or wrong, just or unjust, and moral or immoral. Questions of value focus not just on what we believe to be true but what we consider appropriate, legal, ethical, or moral. Advocates of animal rights try to persuade us that medical experiments on animals are morally wrong, for example, whereas their opponents deem them necessary to save human lives. Opponents of affirmative action contend that racial preferences violate our commitment to equal treatment under the law, whereas those who favor such preferences deem them necessary to "level the playing field." In both of these debates, it is not so much the facts that are in dispute as the differing *values* applied to those facts by the advocates involved. That is what debates over questions of value are all about: determining how we should *evaluate* specific facts, ideas, or actions.

In a courtroom, the law itself provides the general principles we use to evaluate facts. Yet it is not always clear which laws ought to apply in a particular case, and the meaning of the law itself is sometimes in dispute. Once they have determined the facts of the case, for example, lawyers in a murder trial still might debate whether the facts warrant a verdict of first- or second-degree murder. Outside the courtroom, the general principles or criteria that we use to evaluate ideas and actions are even more diverse and unsettled—and hence more "debatable." During the civil rights debates of the 1960s, for example, some people condemned civil rights protestors for deliberately breaking local laws that segregated the races in the South, whereas the activists themselves invoked "higher laws"—the Constitution's guarantee of equal rights under the law, for example, or even "God's law" that all people are created equal.

How do we choose and define the general principles that we employ in value arguments? In some cases, we may find such principles written in a law book or in a professional code of ethics. In other cases, we might rely on reputable authorities to suggest the appropriate principles or criteria of judgment. If we wish to judge the constitutionality of a particular action, for example, we may consult with experts in constitutional law. If we wish to render a moral judgment, we should consult whomever our audience considers a credible moral authority—a religious leader, perhaps, or maybe a well-known philosopher or ethicist. In many cases, the best source of the standards or criteria we employ in our arguments will be the audience itself because such arguments work best when they are grounded in our listeners' own value systems. Only after we have convinced our audience that a problem exists or that some wrong has been done does it make sense to move on to the highest level of controversy: issues of policy.

What Are We Going to Do?

A question of policy has to do with our actions in the future: there is something wrong in our world, and we need to correct it; we have a problem that needs to be solved. Yet even when we agree that we have a problem, we still may not agree about how best to solve it. In our complex society, we inevitably have a variety of options for addressing various problems. And in considering each option, we must weigh not only its effectiveness in solving the problem but also its costs, its feasibility, and any advantages or disadvantages that it might have.

Watch the Video "Citizens for Community Justice" at **MyCommunicationLab**

We may all agree that health care for the poor and the elderly in the United States is a serious problem. Yet we continue to debate how best to respond to that challenge, with some arguing for universal health care coverage and others emphasizing "market solutions." Likewise, everybody seems to agree that our current income tax system should be reformed. Still, we debate a wide variety of policy alternatives, ranging from minor changes in the existing tax code to a "flat tax" or even a national sales tax that would eliminate income taxes altogether.

Even when we all agree on a particular approach to some problem, we may find ourselves debating the details of implementation, financing, or administration. We may agree that wealthy nations should do more to fight the spread of AIDS in developing nations. But exactly how much should the United States contribute to that effort? And where should our aid go? People worried about the effects of television on children likewise seem to agree that there are problems with children's programming. But does that mean we need more government regulations? What should those regulations say, and how would they be enforced? And how, if at all, do we balance the protection of children with the rights of those who produce and advertise on children's television?

Whatever issues you address in your speeches, it is important that those choices be grounded in thorough research and analysis of both your topic and your audience. Controversies evolve, and what were once hotly contested issues may no longer be seriously debated. At one time, for example, there was a vigorous debate over whether cigarette smoking caused cancer—a question of fact. That debate has largely been settled now, of course, and the debate over smoking now revolves around questions of policy: Should smoking be banned in more public places? Should tobacco companies be held liable for the health costs of smoking? In some persuasive speeches, your sole purpose may be to establish a disputed fact, whereas in other speeches, your audience may already agree that there is a serious problem. In that case, you can focus on policy issues. Whatever your purpose, it should reflect the current status of the public controversy surrounding your topic and the existing beliefs and opinions of your audience.

It is important that you make your persuasive purpose clear when you speak. Given the nature of the issue and the existing attitudes of your audience, do you

HIGHLIGHTING THE CHALLENGE OF PERSUADING OTHERS | Will You Give Blood?

In a study of people's willingness to donate blood, a group of people reluctant to donate were asked to listen to a powerfully emotional speech, delivered by a young hemophiliac. Immediately following the speech, a questionnaire revealed an impressive change in attitudes. More than 70 percent of those who previously had refused to give blood now indicated that they *would* donate blood if given the opportunity! Yet when presented with official Red Cross blood donation sign-up cards, nearly 80 percent of those with "changed" attitudes *still* declined to commit themselves to the *action* of donating blood. The authors concluded from this study that it is one thing to change minds, but motivating people to *act* is an even greater challenge.

Source: Patricia Hayes Andrews and John E. Baird Jr., *Communication for Business and the Professions*, 6th ed. (Madison, WI: Brown & Benchmark, 1995), 359–60.

hope merely to stimulate their thinking—that is, to get a previously apathetic or indifferent audience thinking about some issue? Or do you aspire to change minds, persuading listeners to reconsider their opinions? Do you hope to inspire your audience to *act* in some way, perhaps by sending money to some organization or volunteering their time? As you might imagine, getting people to *do* something is harder than getting them merely to *think* about it.

ETHICAL PROOF IN PERSUASIVE SPEAKING

Preview. *Since ancient times, theorists of persuasion have recognized three broad categories or "modes" of proof: ethos, pathos, and logos. We begin our examination of the modes of proof with ethos, or ethical proof, which refers to the audience's perception of the credibility of the speaker and his or her sources. The constituents of strong ethos are trustworthiness, competence, open-mindedness, and dynamism. Your ethos as a speaker is shaped by the content, structure, and clarity of your speech as well as by how you deliver it*

14.3 Define *ethos* and discuss what contributes to strong credibility.

Watch the Video
"Grant Proposal Presentations" at **MyCommunicationLab**

Have you ever responded negatively to a speech, only to realize later that it was not the content of the speech that bothered you so much as the person delivering it? Perhaps the speaker's voice irritated you. Or maybe the speaker belonged to a group or political organization that you have always distrusted. On the other hand, you may also have followed someone's advice not so much because he or she gave you good reasons, but because that person seemed knowledgeable and trustworthy. For good or ill, we all react to messages on the basis not only of what is said but of who says it. The perception we have of a speaker—whether that perception is positive or negative—constitutes that person's ethos.

Students of public speaking have long recognized the importance of ethos. More than 2,000 years ago, the Greek rhetorician and philosopher Aristotle identified the speaker's character, intelligence, and goodwill as the most important dimensions of ethos.[6] Later theorists have refined and modified Aristotle's original concept. Modern researchers have stressed that ethos depends on what an audience *thinks* about the speaker, and they have noted that people sometimes have very different *perceptions* of the same speaker. In other words, ethos refers to *how the audience sees a speaker*, not to the *actual intelligence or character* of that person.

Ethos is not the same thing as *ethics*, but the two concepts are closely related. A person who is perceived as ethical has a good reputation—a positive ethos—even before he or she speaks. If, on the other hand, a speaker is perceived as unethical, we may find his or her arguments less convincing. Whatever the speaker's true ethical commitments, what is important, again, is our *perception* of the speaker.

Scholars have identified several specific qualities that influence our perceptions of a speaker.[7] From their research, we can identify four major qualities that contribute to a positive ethos:

- Trustworthiness
- Competence
- Open-mindedness
- Dynamism

Trustworthiness

Not surprisingly, we are more likely to listen to and act on the advice of people who we think are honest and concerned about our best interests. Integrity and sincerity are qualities that inspire trust. Suppose, for example, you were trying to decide what to do after you graduate from college. An older friend whom you trust—a teacher, a counselor, or a family friend—suggests that you join Teach for America, a program in which college graduates spend two years teaching in public schools in economically depressed areas. You are more likely to take this advice if you believe this person not only is knowledgeable about the program but also has your best interests at heart.

Public figures rely heavily on perceptions of their trustworthiness to persuade listeners. In 1986, for example, President Ronald Reagan survived the biggest scandal of his career by assuring Americans that he had *tried* to do the right thing in trading arms for American hostages being held in Iran. In his 1987 State of the Union address, Reagan admitted his mistakes but asked Americans to *trust* that his intentions were good:

> I have one major regret. I took a risk with regard to our action in Iran. It did not work, and for that I assume full responsibility. The goals were worthy. I do not believe it was wrong to try to establish contacts with a country of strategic importance or try to save lives. And certainly it was not wrong to try to secure freedom for our citizens held in barbaric captivity. But we did not achieve what we wished and serious mistakes were made trying to do so.[8]

Reagan survived the so-called Iran-Contra affair because of his strong personal ethos.

In contrast to Reagan, former Illinois governor Rod Blagojevich inspired only skepticism and ridicule when he denied any wrongdoing following his arrest on federal corruption charges on December 9, 2008. Accused of trying to "sell" the U.S. Senate seat vacated by Barack Obama, Blagojevich was impeached and removed from office by the Illinois Senate, despite more than a dozen TV appearances and a 47-minute "closing argument" before the senators themselves. In proclaiming his innocence, Blagojevich insisted that he "never, ever intended to violate the law" and that there was "no evidence, zero" that he had done so. Yet not a single senator rose to his defense, and he was impeached by a unanimous vote, with senators calling him a "devious, cynical, crass, and corrupt politician" and an "unusually good liar."[9] In *Time* magazine, commentator James Poniewozik compared Blagojevich to one of those "bad auditioners" on *American Idol*: "Does he really have no idea how he sounds to other people? It's gotta be an act, right?"[10] Obviously, Blagojevich had lost the *trust* of his fellow politicians; his personal ethos had been destroyed.

"Oh, he's jolly enough, but he lacks credibility."

Source: Reprinted by permission from www.cartoonstock.com.

Competence

Listeners tend to be persuaded more easily by speakers they view as intelligent, well informed, or personally competent. Whether it comes from native intelligence, education and training, or firsthand experience, the perceived competence of a speaker is a crucial part of his or her ethos. Indeed, competence is often *the* issue in a political campaign, especially when candidates have similar views on policy questions. In announcing his bid for the 2012 Republican nomination for president, for example, Mitt Romney reminded voters of his vast experience, both as a businessman and as a public servant. After leaving a "steady job" to start his own business, Romney explained, he grew that business from "ten employees to hundreds" and then became "deeply involved" helping other businesses to succeed, "from innovative startups to large companies going through tough times." Subsequently, he left his own business to head the organizing committee for the 2002 Winter Olympics in Salt Lake City, helping to get that effort "back on track." Finally, he went home to Massachusetts to serve as Governor, digging that state out of a "$3 billion budget hole" and balancing the budget each of his first four years in office. "All of these experiences," Romney concluded—"starting and running businesses for 25 years, turning around the Olympics, governing a state"—helped "shape who I am and how I lead."[11]

By emphasizing his extensive experience, of course, Romney hoped to contrast himself with President Barack Obama, who came into office in 2009 without much experience in either business or politics. Concerns about Obama's youth and lack of experience—his *competence* to assume perhaps the most challenging job in the world—were common during the 2008 presidential campaign. They were the main reason many voters supported his rival in that year's presidential election, Senator John McCain of Arizona.

Open-Mindedness

A speaker's ethos is also influenced by the impressions listeners have of his or her open-mindedness. Nobody is perfectly objective. But audiences value speakers who seem willing to enter into a dialogue, consider various points of view, and search for common ground. Of course, open-mindedness is not the same thing as empty-headedness; a speaker has the right to take sides in a controversy. Yet that does not mean you should distort, exaggerate, or otherwise misrepresent the facts to "win" a debate. Nor does it give you the right to dismiss the arguments, values, or feelings of those who disagree with you. To say that you are open minded is not to say that you are wishy-washy. Rather, it means that you are willing to listen to others, treat their ideas fairly, and remain open to at least the possibility of changing your own mind.

In many situations, a speaker's objectivity may be in doubt because of his or her position or reputation or because of the setting in which the speech takes place. In one of the most celebrated political speeches in history, for example, an African-American congresswoman from Texas, Barbara Jordan, rose above partisanship and displayed a broader vision of America's promise at the 1976 Democratic National Convention. Jordan had become famous for denouncing President Richard Nixon during the Watergate scandal, and some of her fellow Democrats might have expected a hard-hitting attack on the Republicans. Instead, Jordan talked about our common dreams and the need for all Americans to come together:

> I could easily spend this time praising the accomplishments of this party and attacking the Republicans but I don't choose to do that.
>
> I could list the many problems Americans have. I could list the problems which cause people to feel cynical, angry, frustrated;…I could recite these problems and then I could sit down and offer no solutions. But I don't choose to do that either.
>
> The citizens of America expect more. They deserve and they want more than a recital of problems.
>
> We are a people in a quandary about the present. We are a people in search of our future. We are a people in search of a national community.
>
> We are a people trying to solve the problems of the present…but we are attempting on a larger scale to fulfill the promise of America. We are attempting to fulfill our national purpose; to create and sustain a society in which all of us are equal.[12]

Jordan was hardly an objective observer. But by rising above partisanship, she earned a positive ethos and delivered a speech that we still remember as one of the great keynote addresses in U.S. history.

Dynamism

Finally, audiences look positively on speakers who are energetic and enthusiastic—in other words, speakers who are dynamic. Dynamism does *not* mean ranting and raving; it means achieving the right balance of enthusiasm and self-control. It means setting the right tone for the occasion. On the one hand, we want to avoid appearing as if we're just "going through the motions," talking in a colorless monotone or focusing more on our notes than our listeners. On the other hand, we do not want to scream at our audience, engage in distracting physical gyrations, or appear so intense that our audience thinks we're crazy! A dynamic speaker takes the middle ground, enthusiastically engaging the audience but not getting "in their face." Dynamic speakers talk *with* us rather than *at* us, communicating their personal enthusiasm but remaining "tuned in" to our reactions.

Perhaps the best way to summarize ethos is to think about it as a kind of filter: everything you say is filtered through the *perception* your audience has of your trustworthiness, competence, open-mindedness, and dynamism. What an audience thinks of a speaker—a speaker's ethos—may sometimes be determined by his or her past reputation. Still, every speech should be viewed as an opportunity to improve your ethos by demonstrating that *you* have the qualities we admire in a speaker.

How Context Affects Ethos

Although ethos is always important, the characteristics that we admire in speakers may vary from situation to situation. If we attend a public briefing on a new sewage-treatment plant, we may not care whether the engineers explaining the system are dynamic or open minded. We are more concerned with whether they can explain technical aspects of the plant clearly—whether they have the *competence* to answer our questions about how the plant would work. Conversely, we do not expect everybody at a town hall meeting to be an "expert" on every issue. Not everybody understands the tax laws or the best way to build a bridge. In that situation, we may be more concerned with the speaker's sincerity and open-mindedness, or we may be impressed by how passionately a speaker feels about some issue.

The context in which we speak thus determines what characteristics—or combination of characteristics—will affect our ethos. As speakers, we should reflect on which of the constituents of ethos may be most important to our audience in particular situations. As citizens, we should ask whether other speakers have *earned* the right to be trusted. Do they have the experience or knowledge necessary to speak convincingly about that issue?

In today's society, we are often tempted to judge the credibility of speakers by standards that have little to do with their background or training. Many advertisers, for example, pay celebrities to endorse their products. Perhaps it makes sense for a basketball player to endorse Nike shoes or a nutritional supplement. But even before he famously crashed his Cadillac Escalade following a domestic dispute, did we really believe golfer Tiger Woods when he claimed to drive a Buick? Is stock car driver Mark Martin really a good source of information about the prescription drug Viagra? Should we believe Jessica Simpson when she tells us that Proactiv cured her acne? Does anybody really believe that Paris Hilton eats at Hardee's? Perhaps these celebrities have at least *tried* some of the products they endorse. But it would be naïve to think that their endorsements have nothing to do with the millions of dollars they get from advertisers.

Sometimes factors beyond our control influence our ethos. When Barbara Bush was invited to deliver a commencement address at Wellesley College in 1990, some students objected that she had done nothing to earn that honor— besides marrying the president of the United States! To her credit, Bush won over her audience by establishing her *own* ethos during the course of the speech. Reflecting on the challenges of balancing life as a mother with her role as First Lady, Bush concluded on a humorous note: "And who knows? Somewhere out in this audience may even be someone who will one day follow in my footsteps, and preside over the White House as the president's spouse. And I wish *him* well!"[13] Disarming her critics with humor, Mrs. Bush also communicated that she shared the ideals of her listeners at this progressive women's college.

Depending on the context, the same individual may have both a highly negative and a highly positive personal ethos. Indeed, many public figures who might be described as *controversial* or *polarizing* provoke widely differing audience responses, depending on the situation. On February 28, 2009, for example, talk show host Rush Limbaugh received an "immense ovation" when he delivered the keynote address at the Conservative Political Action Conference (CPAC) in Washington, DC. Given his frequent criticisms of "feminazis" and "environmental wackos," however, he likely would have been greeted differently at a conference of the National Organization of Women (NOW) or the Sierra Club. Similarly, the Reverend Jesse Jackson Sr., a longtime civil rights activist, received a warm reception when he addressed an NAACP fund-raising dinner in Detroit on May 3, 2009. Had he been speaking instead to the American Jewish Committee, the reception might have been cooler. Among many in that group, resentment still lingers over Jackson's 1984 reference to Jews as "Hymies" and New York City as "Hymietown."[14]

At this point in your life, you probably do not have to worry about how past indiscretions or media coverage of your life might affect your ethos. Each time you speak, however, people will form impressions of you, so it is important to keep the components of ethos in mind. Even in your speech class, your listeners will draw conclusions about your trustworthiness, competence, open-mindedness, and dynamism. It is never too early to begin building a positive ethos—a reputation that will help you succeed as a public speaker.

So what can you do to enhance your ethos? There is no simple answer, because everything you do affects how listeners perceive you: the content of your speech, how you organize and deliver it, and how you come across in general. But here are some specific things you can do to strengthen your ethos.

Show Your Audience That You Share Their Experiences and Concerns   Showing your audience that you have something in common with them can strengthen your ethos. We feel a natural attraction to people we perceive to be like ourselves; we assume they face the same challenges and understand our values and priorities. In a speech advocating tougher penalties for academic cheating, for example, one student recalled the pressures he felt from his parents and others to get into a top college. At one point, he even admitted that he had been tempted to cheat to get better grades. The students listening to the speech not only appreciated the fact that he had chosen a topic relevant to their lives but also that he shared their aspirations and understood the pressures they faced. He was honest enough to admit that he had been tempted to cheat, yet in the end he realized he would only be cheating himself.

Bolster Your Own Ethos with the Ethos of Reputable Experts   When you give speeches on highly complex or technical issues, you need information from experts. Your own lack of expertise on such topics need not undermine your ethos. When your remarks are supported by acknowledged experts, your audience can still have confidence in what you say. In Chapter 7, we explored the use of expert testimony in detail, but it is worth repeating here that you can bolster your own ethos by using testimony from highly reputable sources.

Suppose, for example, that you wish to speak about the effects of global warming on weather patterns or our forest ecosystems. You may have read many newspaper articles on the subject, and perhaps you have seen several reports on TV about global warming. But does that make you an expert? Of course not. You are a concerned citizen, and perhaps you know more about the topic than the average citizen. Yet if you hope to be persuasive, you still need testimony from reputable experts who have studied the problem, such as meteorologists and climatologists.

If you are genuinely open-minded, you might modify your own opinion as you read what leading experts have to say. But once you have settled on a firm opinion, the challenge is to communicate your conclusions, along with support for those conclusions from credible experts. Remember, a speech is not like a term paper, where you can just footnote your sources. Rather, you need to identify and establish the credibility of your expert sources *in the speech itself*. That means both naming your sources and saying something about their credentials. If you were to cite Paul Krugman in a speech on the economy, for example, you might identify

Watch the Video "We Don't Have to Live in Slums" at **MyCommunicationLab**

▶ HIGHLIGHTING CREDIBILITY

Credibility is an essential quality for any politician. Following are excerpts from former presidential candidate Mike Huckabee's speech to the Republican National Convention in September 2008. Notice how, even in defeat, Huckabee worked to build a positive ethos. By recalling the civil rights movement and expressing "great respect" for Barack Obama, he demonstrated his goodwill, open-mindedness, and devotion to the good of the country. In recalling his childhood, he reminded his audience of his humble background and displayed his sense of humor. At the same time, he countered negative images of Republicans as a party of the rich.

> I grew up at a time and in a place where the civil rights movement was fought. I witnessed firsthand the shameful evil of racism. I saw how ignorance and prejudice caused people to do the unthinkable to people of color not so many years ago.

> So I say with sincerity that I have great respect for Senator Obama's historic achievement to become his party's nominee—not because of his color, but with indifference to it. Party or politics aside, we celebrate this milestone because it elevates our country...

> I really tire of hearing how the Democrats care about the working guy as if all Republicans grew up with silk stockings and silver spoons. In my little hometown of Hope, Arkansas, the three sacred heroes were Jesus, Elvis, and FDR, not necessarily in that order.

> My own father held down two jobs, barely affording the little rented house I grew up in. My dad worked hard, lifted heavy things, and got his hands dirty. The only soap we had at my house was Lava.

> Heck, I was in college before I found out it wasn't supposed to hurt to take a shower.

> I'm not a Republican because I grew up rich, but because I didn't want to spend the rest of my life poor, waiting for the government to rescue me.

Source: Reprinted by permission from Associated Press, Mike Huckabee's Speech. Copyright © 2008 by Associated Press. ▶

him as an economist from Princeton University who won the 2008 Nobel Prize in Economics. By offering support from such renowned experts, you can improve your own ethos and make a more convincing argument.

Strengthen Your Ethos with Personal Experiences   You are more likely to be seen as trustworthy and competent when you have had some personal experiences related to your topic. A student aiming to help her audience understand the plight of Native Americans, for example, established her special qualifications to speak on this topic by recalling how she had spent three weeks on an Indian reservation, helping to repair homes and paint schools. Of course, you will not always have firsthand experience with the issues you speak about. But when you do, you can strengthen your ethos by talking about those experiences.

Strive to Be Clear and Interesting   Listeners appreciate speakers who make their ideas understandable and who make an effort to keep the audience interested. Unfortunately, some speakers try to impress their audiences with "big words." Other speakers make little effort to organize their speeches so they're easy to follow. Still others may come across as not genuinely interested in their topic. We have all sat through dull and uninteresting speeches—speeches that hardly provide any "news" at all. Typically, it is not the topic itself that is the problem, but the failure of the speaker to consider ways to make the speech relevant and interesting to the audience.

You should try to gain the audience's attention and interest from the outset of the speech—in your introduction. Doing so creates a positive first impression and improves your ethos throughout the speech. You can also maintain interest by citing examples that are familiar and relevant to the audience and by speaking directly *to* your listeners rather than staring down at your notes or reading from a manuscript. Sometimes little things make all the difference in whether your audience develops a positive view of your ethos. For example, some speakers hurt their ethos simply by talking too long. By showing respect for your audience's comfort and expectations, you can enhance your ethos as a speaker.

A dynamic delivery can contribute to your ethos as a sincere, passionate, and committed speaker.

Show Your Audience That You Have Considered Different Points of View If you can show that you have considered other people's opinions, you will demonstrate that you are both well informed and open minded. For example, when the Indiana Department of Natural Resources proposed a two-day hunt to thin

the deer population in Brown County State Park, both experts and ordinary citizens disagreed passionately over the idea. A student who favored the hunt began by showing that she initially shared some of the emotions felt by its opponents. She then explained how she changed her mind after carefully researching the topic and discovering all the problems caused by overpopulation, including disease and starvation in the deer herd. Recalling her interviews with both activists opposed to the hunt and DNR officials who favored it, she showed that she was open minded and had considered both sides of the controversy.

Develop a Dynamic, Audience-Centered Delivery How you deliver your speech can dramatically affect your ethos. One student with a well-prepared speech about crime and personal safety on campus failed to persuade her audience simply because listeners had trouble hearing her. Sitting in the back of the room and straining to hear what she said, some listeners became irritated and concluded that the speaker did not care about her topic or her audience. Likewise, speakers who use lots of vocalized pauses—*um, you know,* and *like,* for example—often irritate listeners and come across as inarticulate or even unintelligent. Finally, speakers who read rapidly through written manuscripts, without looking up or otherwise engaging listeners, may damage their own ethos.

Dynamic speakers remain in touch with their audiences. Speakers who seem bored or detached cannot expect their audiences to respond any differently, and they may even be perceived as less knowledgeable, competent, or sincere. As we suggested in Chapter 11, you can do many things to improve your presentational skills. Vocal variation, gestures, facial expressions, and eye contract can all have a significant effect on your ethos. Delivery may not be the only thing affecting your ethos, but it *can* make a difference.

Your audience's perceptions of your intelligence, character, and sincerity can affect the success of your speech. You can bolster your ethos by establishing common ground with your audience, by showing that you share common concerns, by citing reputable experts, and by mentioning personal experiences that qualify you to speak on your topic. Making an effort to be clear and interesting can also help

FOCUS ON CIVIC ENGAGEMENT | Former Presidents Bury the Political Hatchet

Former presidents George H. W. Bush and Bill Clinton were bitter political rivals. During the 1992 presidential campaign, Bush attacked the challenger Clinton as a "tax-and-spend liberal" and, in a moment of uncharacteristic enthusiasm, even called him a "bozo." For his part, Clinton portrayed Bush as an agent of "privileged private interests" who had betrayed his promise of a "kindler, gentler" America. In his speech accepting the Democratic nomination in 1992, Clinton accused Bush of talking a "good game" but having "no game plan to rebuild America."[15]

Imagine people's surprise, then, when the two former presidents joined hands to lead the U.S. relief effort following the devastating tsunami in the Indian Ocean in 2004. Traveling to the region and raising millions of dollars to help rebuild homes and lives ravaged by the disaster, they used their ethos as former presidents and political rivals to make an important point: that even in an era of deep partisan divisions, people can work together for the common good. Following Hurricane Katrina, the two again joined forces to raise more than $120 million for rebuilding colleges and churches devastated by the storm. The "Odd Couple," as Barbara Bush has characterized them, not only did a lot of good but

also became close personal friends. Perhaps most important, they took advantage of their return to the public spotlight—and their unique ethos as former presidential rivals—to call for more civility and cooperation in American politics. Following the shooting of Congresswoman Gabrielle Giffords and nineteen other people in January 2011, Bush and Clinton again teamed up to serve as honorary chairmen of a new National Institute for Civil Discourse at the University of Arizona. "Politics doesn't have to be uncivil and nasty," Clinton said when asked about his relationship with Bush. "Where we can find common ground and do something for the future of the country and for the future of our children and grandchildren, I think we ought to do it."

Sources: Michael Duffy, "Bill Clinton and George H. W. Bush," *Time,* May 8, 2006, www.time.com/time/specials/packages/article/0,28804,1975813_1975847_1976609,00.html (accessed February 27, 2012); ABC News, "People of the Year: Bill Clinton and George H. W. Bush," *World News Tonight,* December 27, 2005, http://abcnews.go.com/WNT/PersonOfWeek/story?id=1446477#.T0uhgHm-y50 (accessed February 27, 2012); and JoAnne Allen, "Former Presidents Bush, Clinton Team Up for Civility," *Reuters,* February 21, 2011, http://blogs.reuters.com/talesfromthetrail/2011/02/21/former-presidents-bush-clinton-team-up-for-civility/ (accessed February 27, 2012). ▲

your ethos, as can showing your audience that you have considered other points of view. Finally, you can enhance your ethos by delivering your speech effectively. By engaging your audience and delivering your speech with enthusiasm, you can show your listeners that you care about them and your topic.

APPEALING TO AUDIENCE EMOTIONS

14.4 Discuss the techniques and ethics of appealing to an audience's emotions.

Preview. *If you hope to persuade your audience, you need to engage their emotions. You can engage your audience's emotions by using strong, affective language; appealing to shared social values; providing specific, vivid details; helping listeners visualize what you are talking about; and comparing the unfamiliar to the familiar. Emotional appeals, however, can be deceptive and manipulative and should never substitute for reasoned arguments.*

Listeners who have little or no emotional involvement in a speech are unlikely to be persuaded. Appealing to an audience's emotions is fundamental to motivating them to act. You may even need to engage their emotions to get them to listen in the first place. If people are not emotionally involved in a topic, they are not likely to be persuaded.

Fear, pride, anger, reverence, hatred, compassion, and love—all are strong emotions and can be powerful motivators. Successful speakers know that listeners can be motivated by appeals to such emotions. Notice how former president Ronald Reagan, a president remembered as the "Great Communicator," used emotional appeals to build support for dramatic increases in military spending.

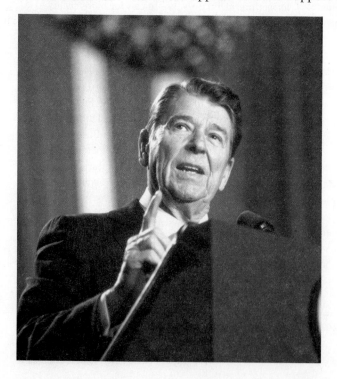

Former president Ronald Reagan, the Great Communicator, used emotional appeals to build support for dramatic increases in military spending.

Instead of reviewing the "long list of numbers" in his defense budget, Reagan tapped into some of his audience's most basic emotions: their fear of nuclear war, their sense of "duty" as citizens, and their concern for protecting their children and their "free way of life":

> The subject I want to discuss with you, peace and national security, is both timely and important....This subject involves the most basic duty that any president and any people share, the duty to protect and strengthen the peace.

> At the beginning of this year, I submitted to the Congress a defense budget which reflects my best judgment of the best understanding of the experts and specialists who advise me about what we and our allies must do to protect our people in the years ahead. That budget is much more than a long list of numbers, for behind all the numbers lies America's ability to prevent the greatest of human tragedies and preserve our free way of life in a sometimes dangerous world.[16]

Appeals to your audience's emotions should never substitute for reasoned arguments backed by the best available evidence. Yet neither can we ignore the role of emotions in human behavior, especially if we hope to motivate our audience to act. A speech that fails to engage the audience's emotions is dull, boring, and lifeless—and, in the end, probably ineffective. The characteristics of speech that engage your audience emotionally include affective language, shared values, vivid detail, visualization, and familiar references.

Affective Language

Affective language is strong language that plays on emotions or feelings. Consider the emotional impact of this series of statements:

"I see things differently from Bob."

"I think Bob's statement is not quite accurate."

"What Bob is saying seems misleading."

"Bob is a liar."

To call Bob "a liar" is to use strong, affective language. As a persuader, you must choose your language carefully, taking into account both the ideas you hope to convey and the emotional connotations of the words you choose.

Eugene Debs, a four-time Socialist candidate for president of the United States, passionately opposed American involvement in World War I. Yet in the pro-war climate of the time, Congress passed laws that limited the right to criticize the government's war policies. Along with other antiwar speakers, Debs was arrested, tried, and convicted under one of these laws, the Sedition Act of 1917. At his sentencing, however, Debs refused to tone down his rhetoric. Instead, he spoke out against social injustice in emotionally powerful language:

> Your Honor, years ago I recognized my kinship with all living beings, and I made up my mind that I was not one bit better than the meanest on earth. I said then, and I say now, that while there is a lower class, I am in it, while there is a criminal element, I am of it, and while there is a soul in prison, I am not free…
>
> I am thinking this morning of the men in the mills and the factories; of the men in the mines and on the railroads. I am thinking of the women who for a paltry wage are compelled to work out their barren lives; of the little children who in this system are robbed of their childhood…and forced into the industrial dungeons, there to feed the monster machines while they themselves are being starved and stunted, body and soul. I see them dwarfed and diseased and their little lives broken and blasted because…money is still so much more important than the flesh and blood of childhood…
>
> Your Honor, I ask no mercy and I plead for no immunity.…I never so clearly comprehended as now the great struggle between the powers of greed and exploitation on one hand and upon the other the rising hosts of industrial freedom and social justice.
>
> I can see the dawn of a better day for humanity. The people are awakening. In due time they will and must come to their own.[17]

By today's standards, Debs's language may seem excessive, even "over the top." Nowadays we do not often hear talk about children "robbed" of their childhood, "dwarfed and diseased," their "little lives broken and blasted." But nearly 70 years later, César Chavez used equally emotional language to describe the plight of migrant farmworkers in America. In a speech before the Commonwealth Club of California in 1984, Chavez began by describing what motivated him to fight for the rights of migrant workers:

> Today, thousands of farmworkers live under savage conditions, beneath trees and amid garbage and human excrement near tomato fields in San Diego County....Vicious rats gnaw at them as they sleep. They walk miles to buy food at inflated prices and they carry in water from irrigation ditches.

> Child labor is still common in many farm areas. As much as 30 percent of Northern California's garlic harvesters are underaged children....Some 800,000 underaged children work with their families harvesting crops across America. Babies born to migrant workers suffer 25 percent higher infant mortality rates than the rest of the population. Malnutrition among migrant workers' children is 10 times higher than the national rate. Farmworkers' average life expectancy is still 49 years, compared to 73 years for the average American. All my life, I have been driven by one dream, one goal, one vision: to overthrow a farm labor system in this nation that treats farmworkers as if they were not important human beings. Farmworkers are not agricultural implements; they are not beasts of burden to be used and discarded.[18]

Chavez, of course, had statistics to back up his argument, but it was his affective language—his references to "savage conditions," living amid "garbage and human excrement," sleeping among "vicious rats," and so on—that gave his speech its emotional power.

Shared Values

Listeners are more likely to be emotionally engaged when their own values are involved. One way to involve your listeners emotionally is to identify values that you share with them and show how your ideas or proposals relate to those values.

After Barack Obama's election in November 2008, the new president used a series of weekly "transition" addresses to rally the country behind his agenda, reminding Americans of their shared values and urging them to work together. In his first address just a week after the election, he observed that "in America we can compete vigorously in elections and challenge each other's ideas, yet come together in service of a common purpose once the voting is done." America faced "the most serious challenges of our lifetime," he reminded his listeners, but America was "a strong and resilient country," and he expressed confidence that those challenges could be overcome if we could just "put aside partisanship and work together as one nation." A week later, he again suggested that we would "rise or fall as one nation, as one people" and argued that the difficult challenges of our time would "require not just new policies but a new spirit of service and sacrifice, where each of us resolves to pitch in and work harder and look after not only ourselves, but each other." Finally, in his third address, he put the burden of success or failure squarely on the people, calling on every citizen to recapture that spirit of service and devotion to the common good that historically had made America great:

> The survival of the American Dream for over two centuries is not only a testament to its enduring power, but to the great effort, sacrifice, and courage of the American people. It has thrived because in our darkest hours we have risen above the smallness of our divisions

to forge a path toward a new and brighter day. We've acted boldly, bravely, and above all, together. That is the chance our new beginning now offers us, and that is the challenge we must rise to in the days to come. It is time to act.[19]

Not everybody embraced Obama's vision of a "new beginning," of course. But many did respond to his call to service, especially young people. On an official government Web site entitled *United We Serve*, people of all ages and backgrounds from all around the country share their stories about how they have responded to President Obama's call to serve their communities through volunteer work. The site's "National Service Blog" includes stories about volunteers responding to the devastating tornadoes that struck Joplin, Missouri, and other cities and towns in 2011, a program to feed the hungry in eastern Pennsylvania, and a program in Montana to provide tax-filing assistance to returning military veterans.[20] These and many other stories appeal to our emotions because they invoke shared values: sympathy for the less fortunate, honoring those who have served, devotion to the common good, and even personal sacrifice and courage.

Vivid Detail

Using vivid detail can help your audience relate to your topic emotionally. Listeners respond more positively to concrete examples and stories than they do to abstractions. Charities that raise money to help sick children, for example, often choose a "poster child" who represents thousands of other children afflicted with disease. The "poster child" gives potential donors somebody they can relate to emotionally—a real person whose suffering they can help relieve.

Persuasive speakers engage audiences' feelings by reinforcing their ideas with vivid details. Before the Civil War, for example, the great abolitionist Frederick Douglass painted a vivid portrait of slavery that enhanced the emotional power of his most famous speech, "What to the Slave is the Fourth of July?" Highlighting the irony of slavery in a nation founded on liberty and freedom, Douglass argued logically that slavery violated America's most sacred ideals. At the same time, however, he made a powerful emotional appeal by vividly describing the scene with a slavemaster, "armed with pistol, whip and bowie-knife," who drove a group of a hundred men, women, and children "from the Potomac to the slave market at New Orleans." "Mark the sad procession," Douglass continued, "as it moves wearily along," with an "inhuman wretch" barking out orders. "Hear his savage yells and his blood-chilling oaths, as he hurries on his affrighted captives!" Describing the sights and sounds of the scene in vivid detail, Douglass encouraged his listeners to "see the old man, with locks thinned and gray," and the young mother, "shoulders…bare to the scorching sun, her briny tears falling on the brow of the babe in her arms." He also urged his listeners to "see" a girl of thirteen, "weeping, yes, weeping, as she thinks of the mother from whom she has been torn!" As the march continues, "heat and sorrow" finally overcome the slaves, and "suddenly you hear a quick snap, like the discharge of a rifle; the fetters clank, and the chain rattles simultaneously; your ears are saluted with a scream, that seems to have torn its way to the center of your soul!" That "crack," Douglass explained, "was the sound of the slave-whip; the scream you heard, was from the woman you saw with the babe." Douglass concluded with still more vivid images of the auction itself, where the men were "examined like horses" and the women "rudely and brutally exposed to the shocking gaze of…slave-buyers." As the slaves were "sold and scattered forever," Douglass helped his listeners to "hear" the "deep, sad sobs" of the "scattered multitude."[21]

Visualization

In an effort to make messages more concrete, speakers often employ visualization, or techniques that allow their audience to "see" what they are talking about. By helping your listeners visualize some problem or crisis, you can stir their emotions, get them thinking more deeply about your topic, and clarify information that otherwise may be vague or unclear.

The most obvious way to help your audience visualize a problem is, of course, to show them a picture. Perhaps you have heard the old saying "Pictures don't lie." In an age of digitally altered photos, of course, pictures *can* lie. But used responsibly, they can communicate information that may be difficult to communicate in words. Pictures can also have a strong emotional impact on your audience. "A picture is worth a thousand words," goes another old saying, and that is especially true for pictures that surprise, shock, scare, or otherwise engage our emotions.

Sometimes pictures can provide powerful, irrefutable evidence for a speaker's claims. During the Cuban Missile Crisis in 1962, for example, the American ambassador to the United Nations, Adlai Stevenson, confronted the Russian ambassador with high-altitude reconnaissance photos that dramatically disproved Russia's denial that nuclear missiles had been stationed in Cuba. On other occasions, photos may be used simply to increase the emotional impact of an argument. Mothers Against Drunk Driving, for example, personalize their statistics with photos of young victims of alcohol-related crashes. Similarly, supporters of a strong defense invoke images of those two hijacked planes crashing into the Twin Towers of the World Trade Center on September 11, 2001. By rekindling the feelings of horror and anger many Americans felt on that day, they hope to build support for a more aggressive war against terrorism.

Visualization is not just something you do by showing pictures to your audience. By painting "word pictures,"

Blow-ups of high-altitude reconnaissance photos provided dramatic support for U.S. Ambassador Adlai Stevenson's speech to the U.N., in which he accused the Soviet Union of stationing offensive nuclear missiles in Cuba.

you can use language to help your audience visualize a problem, "see" an abstract idea, or grasp an otherwise incomprehensible statistic. During the building of the Panama Canal 100 years ago, for example, journalists helped their audiences back home visualize the magnitude of the project with mind-boggling comparisons. One wrote of how the dirt removed from the canal route would build 63 pyramids the size of the Great Pyramid of Egypt. Others compared the canal to digging a tunnel 14 feet in diameter "through the very heart of the earth," or building a longer version of the Great Wall of China—"from San Francisco to New York." One account even reported that the soil excavated for the canal would fill a train long enough to encircle the earth four times—a train that could be pulled only by a string of locomotives stretching from "New York to Honolulu."[22]

Visualization also can be used to contrast a troubling present with a brighter future. In a famous speech at the 1992 Democratic National Convention, for example, former New York governor Mario Cuomo asked his audience to visualize a parade like those we stage to honor military heroes. This time, however, the parade would celebrate safe communities, affordable housing, adequate health care, and economic security. Like parades celebrating the safe return of our soldiers, this parade would be spirited and jubilant. The people would sing "proud songs, happy songs," and the parade would include blue-collar workers "who have a real stake in their company's success," parents glad to be living in safe neighborhoods "where children can be children," and young people who have the opportunity to attend college and someday own their own homes. At the end of the parade, there would be fireworks and still more celebration, with the citizens giving thanks for the nation's strong economy and for our success at "outproducing and outselling our overseas competitors."[23] Regrettably, Cuomo concluded, we rarely saw this sort of parade. We often witnessed parades honoring soldiers returning from war, but we seldom celebrated our victories in education, housing, health care, or the economy. By allowing his audience to "see" such a parade, at least in their mind's eye, Cuomo helped them imagine how things might be different under new leadership.

Familiar References

Speakers often relate new ideas, plans, or proposals to familiar things, not so much to prove their value but to help listeners *feel* more comfortable with something new. By this means, complicated and even controversial ideas can be made to seem more familiar and "everyday"—and hence more acceptable. Before America entered World War II, for example, Franklin Delano Roosevelt defended his controversial plan to supply ships and other war materials to the British—his "lend-lease" plan—by comparing it to how you might help a neighbor whose house was on fire. Logically, perhaps, the two situations were not really comparable. Yet FDR's illustration helped many Americans *feel* that his lend-lease plan was a good idea—the "neighborly" thing to do:

> Well, let me give you an illustration: Suppose my neighbor's home catches fire, and I have got a length of garden hose four or five hundred feet away; but, by Heaven, if he can take my garden hose and connect it up with his hydrant, I may help him to put out his fire. Now what do I do? I don't say to him before the operation, "Neighbor, my

garden hose cost me $15; you have got to pay me $15 for it."...I don't want $15—I want my garden hose back after the fire is over. All right. If it goes through the fire all right, intact, without any damage to it, he gives it back to me and thanks me very much for the use of it. But suppose it gets smashed up—holes in it—during the fire....I say to him, "I was glad to lend you that hose; I see I can't use it anymore, it's all smashed up." He says, "How many feet of it were there?" I tell him, "There were 150 feet of it." He says, "All right, I will replace it." Now, if I get a nice garden hose back, I am in pretty good shape. In other words, if you lend certain munitions and get the munitions back at the end of the war, if they are intact—haven't been hurt—you are all right; if they have been damaged or deteriorated or lost completely,...you have them replaced by the fellow that you have lent them to.[24]

By comparing a complicated governmental policy to the familiar act of helping the folks next door, FDR made his lend-lease policy *feel* like the neighborly thing to do.

The Ethics of Emotional Appeals

In advertising, we are constantly bombarded with emotional appeals. Yogurt commercials feature an elderly man and his even older mother, implying that if we eat yogurt, we, too, can live to a ripe old age. Ads for athletic shoes exploit the dreams and ambitions of young people, suggesting that if they wear the same shoes as their heroes, they, too, can be superstars. Political ads show candidates sympathizing with the sick or the elderly, or they try to frighten us into thinking that the other candidate may take away our Social Security or blow up the world. Advertisers know that successful marketing often depends on an audience's emotional reactions. Thus, they persuade us by associating their products with personal success, physical or economic security, or love and "family values."

Emotional appeals, however, can be deceptive and manipulative. More than 2,000 years ago, the rhetorician Aristotle warned that emotional appeals could warp an audience's judgment, producing hasty or ill-considered decisions.[25] When feelings such as fear, anger, love, rage, and guilt are stirred, the results can be powerful and unpredictable. Ethical public speakers respect the power of emotions. They never use emotional appeals to distract, disorient, or manipulate their listeners.

In speaking persuasively, you should never short-circuit the reasoning process or provoke an emotional overreaction on the part of your listeners. Vivid stories about brutal crimes, the suffering of victims of natural disaster, or the horrors of war may sometimes be appropriate, depending on the situation and the audience. However, we all have heard speakers who go too far. In striving to stir audience emotions, some speakers use crude or tasteless language and images, justifying such tactics as necessary to get people "fired up." Apart from the possibility that such tactics may backfire, the ethical speaker avoids overwhelming listeners with emotions so strong that they can hardly think. Appeals to emotion should supplement and complement well-reasoned arguments, not undermine reasoned deliberation or provoke hasty, violent actions.

When in doubt, ask yourself this question: Underneath the emotional appeal, do I have a sound argument—a substructure of evidence and reasoning—that can withstand critical scrutiny? You do not want your audience members to respond unthinkingly. Rather, you want to appeal to their minds while recognizing that emotions play an important role in human behavior.

SUMMARY

The Anatomy of Public Controversy

 14.1 Define *public controversy* and discuss what it means to *deliberate in good faith*.

- Persuasion is rooted in public controversy, or disagreements over matters of political or social significance.
- As citizens in a democracy, we have an obligation to deliberate "in good faith," respecting our fellow citizens and backing up our opinions with good reasons and evidence.

Questions of Fact, Value, and Policy

14.2 Distinguish among the three different types of persuasive issues: fact, value, and policy.

- Public controversies typically revolve around questions of fact, value, or policy.
  - Questions of fact involve controversies over existence, scope, or causality.
  - Questions of value revolve around how ideas and actions should be evaluated or judged.
  - Questions of policy involve choices among future courses of action.

Ethical Proof in Persuasive Speaking

 14.3 Define *ethos* and discuss what contributes to strong credibility.

- Ethical proof, or *ethos*, refers to the audience's perceptions of the credibility of the speaker and his or her sources.
  - The constituents of ethos are trustworthiness, competence, open-mindedness, and dynamism.
  - Your ethos will be influenced by the context or situation in which you speak.
  - You can enhance your ethos by showing your audience that you share their concerns, citing reputable sources, relating personal experiences, striving to be clear, considering different points of view, and delivering your speech effectively.

Appealing to Audience Emotions

 14.4 Discuss the techniques and ethics of appealing to an audience's emotions.

- Emotional appeals can be powerful motivators.
  - You can engage the emotions of your audience by using affective language, identifying shared values, using vivid detail, using visualization, or comparing the unfamiliar to the familiar.
  - Emotional appeals should never be used to deceive or manipulate or to *replace* well-reasoned arguments.

QUESTIONS FOR REVIEW AND REFLECTION

The Anatomy of Public Controversy

 14.1 Define *public controversy* and discuss what it means to *deliberate in good faith*.

1. Define *public controversy* and identify two or three public controversies that you think are important today. Do you believe that public debate over those controversies has helped clarify the issues involved or the options for resolving those controversies?

2. What does it mean to deliberate "in good faith"? Do you think most politicians today deliberate in good faith? What about the political commentators and representatives of interest groups and "think tanks" that you hear on radio or TV talk shows? Do they deliberate in good faith?

Questions of Fact, Value, and Policy

14.2 Distinguish among the three different types of persuasive issues: fact, value, and policy.

3. What are the differences between questions of fact, value, and policy? Can you think of a major public controversy today that revolves mostly around questions of fact? Can you identify other controversies that focus more on questions of value or policy?

Ethical Proof in Persuasive Speaking

14.3 Define *ethos* and discuss what contributes to strong credibility.

4. The following is a list of well-known public figures. How would you describe the ethos of each, and what do you think have been the most important influences shaping their ethos?
- Barack Obama
- Mitt Romney
- Hillary Clinton
- Oprah Winfrey
- Rush Limbaugh
- Angelina Jolie
- Tiger Woods

Appealing to Audience Emotions

14.4 Discuss the techniques and ethics of appealing to an audience's emotions.

5. What, in your opinion, determines whether appeals to emotion are ethical? Are there certain types of emotional appeals—or appeals to certain emotions, such as fear or hatred—that you think are always unethical? Does a speaker's purpose influence your assessment of whether his or her emotional appeals are ethical?

 Study and Review the Flashcards at **MyCommunicationLab**

Arguing Persuasively

Democracies are fragile things. They require committed, honest leaders, and they depend on ordinary citizens to assume the responsibility of governing themselves. That means that citizens must participate in public deliberations and learn to distinguish between good and bad arguments. They must be committed to deliberating in good faith, and they must be willing to put the common good ahead of their own selfish interests. In a diverse democratic society, it is sometimes difficult to reconcile all the competing interests in a major public controversy. That is all the more reason that we must learn *how* to deliberate. If our democracy is to thrive, we must learn to discuss and debate public issues with intelligence, civility, and respect for our fellow citizens.

Historically, America has not always lived up to this ideal. In the 1950s, for example, a reckless demagogue named Joseph McCarthy rose to power by exploiting the fears and uncertainty of the Cold War era. Claiming that "card-carrying" communists had infiltrated the government, McCarthy inspired anticommunist "witch hunts" across the nation, throwing our political system into chaos and destroying innocent lives. At another time, McCarthy's outrageous accusations might have been ignored. In an era of fear, uncertainty, and political complacency, however, he caused a national sensation and became the most feared man in America.[1]

Today we live in another era of widespread apathy and uncertainty. Pointing to low voter turnout and declining involvement in civic affairs, some worry that another great demagogue might throw the nation into turmoil. Could a modern-day Joseph McCarthy exploit today's economic problems or our fears of terrorism to advance a dangerously reactionary political agenda? Are we so ill-informed and complacent that we would fall for such tactics again? Or have we learned the lesson of the McCarthy era: that as citizens in a democracy, we must guard against those who seek to manipulate and deceive us? In this chapter, we pick up where we left off in the previous chapter, exploring in greater depth the role of persuasion in our democratic society. Specifically, we will distinguish between persuasion and demagoguery, defining persuasion as "reason-giving argument" and contrasting it with the deceptive and manipulative techniques of the demagogue. Then we will reflect more practically on what it means to construct a *reasonable* argument, examining the components of a complete argument and identifying some of the most common fallacies or errors in reasoning and evidence. Contrary to what one might conclude from watching TV talk shows, arguing about civic affairs does *not* have to mean attacking your political enemies or stirring up public passions. To the contrary, it can and *should* mean engaging your fellow citizens in a constructive dialogue about issues of mutual concern.

PERSUASION AND DEMAGOGUERY IN A FREE SOCIETY

15.1 Distinguish between persuasion and demagoguery.

Preview. *Persuasion is an essential tool of democratic governance. Indeed, reliance on persuasion to resolve conflicts and induce social cooperation is the main difference between a democracy and a totalitarian or authoritarian state. Yet precisely because they depend so much on persuasion, democracies are especially vulnerable to demagoguery, or deceptive and manipulative speech. With advances in technology, demagoguery has become an even greater threat. If we hope to* *sustain our democratic way of life, we must understand the differences between persuasion and demagoguery and demand high ethical standards from all who speak in public.*

Watch the Video
"Same Sex Marriage" at
MyCommunicationLab

Persuasion, as we have emphasized throughout this book, is an essential tool of democratic citizenship. The earliest treatises on persuasion, such as Aristotle's *Rhetoric*,[2] prepared citizens to participate in the judicial and legislative assemblies of the Greek city-state. Passed down over centuries, this classical tradition evolved in response to changing social and political conditions, but its essential purpose remained the same: to educate people for citizenship. As part of that education, citizens were taught to distinguish between good and bad arguments, between the legitimate techniques of democratic persuasion and the tricks of the propagandist or the demagogue.

America's founders were well schooled in this classical rhetorical tradition. Taught to view demagoguery as "the peculiar vice to which democracies were susceptible," they designed our constitutional system to guard against what Alexander Hamilton described as the "temporary delusions" of a public misled by those who might "flatter their prejudices to betray their interests." As James Madison observed, there would be times in any democracy when the public might be "misled by the artful misrepresentations of interested men." In those "critical moments," Madison looked to the Senate—the legislative branch more insulated from public opinion—to moderate public passions until the people regained their "cool and deliberate" judgment.[3]

More than a hundred years later, a young scholar named Woodrow Wilson echoed the founders' concerns. As a student of oratory and politics, Wilson wrote at length about protecting our democracy against demagoguery by properly educating both our leaders and our citizens. Like the ancient rhetoricians, Wilson drew a clear, *ethical* distinction between the responsible, civic-minded orator— a leader he dubbed the orator-statesman—and those "artful dialecticians" who manipulated public opinion through "subtle word-play," "dialectic dexterity," or "passionate declamation." As an educator, Wilson taught that "high and noble thoughts" were the hallmarks of the orator-statesman, and he professed faith in the ability of ordinary citizens to "exercise intelligent discretion."[4] As Wilson wrote early in his career, "A charlatan cannot long play the statesman successfully while the whole country is looking critically on."[5]

Today, some doubt the public's ability to "exercise intelligent discretion." Many Americans lack even the most basic understanding of our nation's institutions and traditions,[6] and advances in communication technologies have created new possibilities for the manipulation of public opinion. So how, in today's world, can we protect ourselves against demagoguery? In an age of global propaganda and the politics of spin, does the ancient distinction between persuasion and demagoguery still have meaning?

We believe that it does, for regardless of the political context or the technologies of communication, we can still distinguish between sound and unsound arguments. The ancient Greeks lived in very different times, but their basic lesson remains relevant: if democracy is to thrive, every citizen must learn to evaluate arguments. Today, as in ancient times, *reasoned* arguments are the substance of democratic deliberation, while demagoguery relies on personal and emotional appeals. Claiming special powers to discern the truth, demagogues cultivate a charismatic ethos, setting themselves apart from ordinary citizens by insisting that they have "supernatural, superhuman, or at least specifically exceptional powers or qualities."[7] Appealing to our fears and prejudices, demagogues use *pathos* as a distraction, substituting passion for argument and concocting various scapegoats and "enemies." Demagogues do *not* appeal to what Abraham Lincoln called the "better angels of our nature."[8] To the contrary, they exploit the envy, resentment, hatred, and fears of their audiences.[9]

FOCUS ON CIVIC ENGAGEMENT | The Politics of Outrageousness

In her 2006 book *Godless: The Church of Liberalism*, political commentator Ann Coulter took her reputation for making outrageous statements a step further by accusing four women who had lost their husbands in the September 11 terrorist attacks—the so-called Jersey Girls—of exploiting their personal loss for political purposes. "These broads are millionaires, lionized on TV and in articles about them, reveling in their status as celebrities and stalked by grief-arrazies," Coulter wrote. "I've never seen people enjoying their husbands' deaths so much." And just for good measure, Coulter added: "And by the way, how do we know their husbands weren't planning to divorce these harpies?"

Broads? Harpies? Had Coulter "gone off the deep end," as some observers suggested? Or were her remarks simply a marketing ploy, an effort to "rise above the din" of the 24-hour news cycle and to stand out in the "blogosphere," where such rhetorical excess has become common?

At one level, perhaps, Coulter made a reasonable argument: that simply because they lost loved ones in the 9/11 attacks, the Jersey Girls should not be given a free pass to criticize the Bush administration or to make partisan speeches without backing up their claims. At another level, however, Coulter was obviously trying to provoke people because she deliberately used offensive language. Whatever her point, Coulter crossed the line of propriety and civility. Not only did Senator Hillary Clinton protest the remarks as "vicious" and "mean-spirited," but New York's Republican Governor George Pataki and even Fox News commentator Bill O'Reilly criticized her as well.

Of course, Coulter is not the only practitioner of the politics of outrageousness. Radio talk show hosts have perfected the form, and public figures on both the left and the right have become known for offensive or outrageous remarks. In our media-saturated culture, the politics of outrageousness may be one way to rise above the din and attract attention to one's self. But as concerned citizens, we ought to be asking other questions: Does such rhetoric contribute anything constructive to the public dialogue? Does it help us understand or resolve important public controversies? Does such talk encourage citizens to participate in politics and civic affairs? In short, does the politics of outrageousness serve the public good?

Ann Coulter and the other practitioners of the politics of outrageousness have a right to their opinions—and even to their confrontational and polarizing ways of expressing those opinions. But as citizens, we do *not* have to listen, much less take them seriously. Calling Coulter a "hater," at least one newspaper editor, Bob Unger of the *Centre Daily Times* in State College, Pennsylvania, quit carrying her syndicated column, provoking cries of censorship from her admirers. But does refusing to publish hateful rhetoric constitute censorship? Do media "gatekeepers" have a right to decide who gets to be heard? Should newspapers banish columnists on both the right and the left whom they consider hateful? In principle, Unger has a point: Coulter and others like her poison the public dialogue. Yet who gets to decide who will be censored or silenced? Ultimately, it is up to us—as citizens—to decide who has crossed the line of acceptable public debate. Coulter and others like her may have a right to talk, but we also have the right *not* to listen.

Source: Jocelyn Noveck, "Outrageousness an Art Form for Top Practitioners," *Centre Daily Times*, June 14, 2006, A2.

As rhetorical scholar James Darsey has reminded us, the agitator, even the political *provocateur*, has a role to play in our democratic system. Occasionally, we *need* speakers to shake things up, shattering our complacency and motivating us to act. Radical speakers *can* be a source of democratic inspiration and renewal, reminding us of our revolutionary heritage and demanding that we live up to our ideals.[10] But in the day-to-day business of democratic governance, we still must guard against rhetorical excess and extremism. The hard work of self-governance cannot be done by a divided and polarized citizenry.

As we discuss what it means to *argue persuasively*, our emphasis will be on the constituents of a *reasonable* argument. We will first examine the various components of an argument and the major types of reasoning. Then we will discuss some of the most common errors or *fallacies* of reasoning and evidence. As we shall see, arguing persuasively is not about getting your own way or manipulating an audience. Rather, it is about coming together with your fellow citizens to discuss and debate the issues of the day.

CONSTRUCTING REASONABLE ARGUMENTS

Preview. *A good argument is not one that echoes our own views, nor is a good argument simply one that "works." To the contrary, a good argument is one that adheres to certain rules of evidence and reasoning. A good argument may not always win the day. Indeed, the best argument may be one that forces us to reconsider our own opinions. Good arguments engage our listeners' emotions and draw strength from our ethos. But in the final analysis, a good argument is one that meets certain tests of reasoning and evidence and fulfills its burden of proof.*

15.2 Define *argument* and discuss what it means to make a complete and "reasonable" argument.

Watch the Video
"The Process of Developing a Speech: Building a Persuasive Argument" at **MyCommunicationLab**

We all know that there are good and bad arguments. But what do we mean when we make that judgment? Unfortunately, many of us seem to think that a good argument is one that confirms what we already believe—an argument that has us shaking our head in agreement. Others take a more pragmatic view: a "good" argument is one that "works"—one that persuades other people. That, too, seems a bit shortsighted. As we have noted, a demagogue's arguments may "work," but they have *ethical* shortcomings—they twist the truth, or they appeal to ugly emotions. Obviously, we do not want to praise a speaker for being an effective liar.

Like any artistic creation, an argument can be judged not only in terms of how it is received but also by certain theoretical and ethical principles. We already have suggested some of those principles: truth, for example, and a commitment to the common good. Those are ethical standards we already have discussed. But what does it mean to say that an argument is *theoretically* sound? What, in theory, defines a "good" argument, and how do we go about evaluating an argument?

Unfortunately, there is no simple list of rules defining a "good" argument. The whole tradition of rhetorical studies, dating back more than 2,000 years, might be seen as a search for such rules. Today, some even reject the need for rules altogether, arguing that any such rules reflect cultural biases or "silence" some voices.[11] Yet most who study speech would still agree on a couple of points. First, a good argument must be complete—that is, it must have all the basic components of the so-called Toulmin Model of Argument (see Figure 15.1): a claim, evidence

FIGURE 15.1

The Toulmin
Model of
Argument

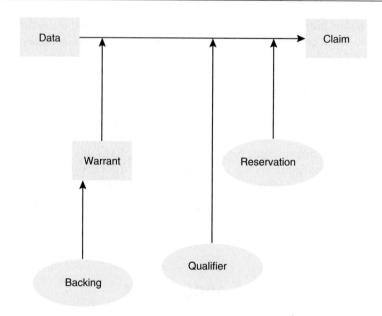

to back it up, and a *warrant* (or general principle) that links the evidence to the claim.[12] Second, a good argument must be *reasonable*—that is, it must be worthy of serious consideration by a hypothetical listener who is reasonably intelligent, well informed, and fair minded. Perhaps you have heard of the *reasonable person* test in a court of law.[13] Something like that test can help us distinguish between reasonable and unreasonable arguments in public debate.

Watch the Video
"Untreated Depression" at
MyCommunicationLab

Claims

Claims are the debatable assertions put forward by a speaker. They are the contested positions you want your audience to accept, such as the claim that illegal immigration poses a threat to our national security or the claim that capital punishment deters crime. When you make a claim, you do not expect your listeners to automatically nod their heads in agreement. By definition, a claim takes sides on a controversial matter and invites debate. If you hope to prevail in that debate, you still need to *prove* your claims, or provide convincing evidence and reasoning in support of those claims.

Claims take many different forms, mostly arising out of the types of persuasive issues or controversies discussed in Chapter 14. If we are debating whether something exists, what *caused* something to happen, or the *scope* or *magnitude* of some phenomenon, we are debating *claims of fact*. If we are debating whether something is good or bad, we are considering *claims of value*. Value claims assume a variety of forms, including claims about what's effective or ineffective, just or unjust, moral or immoral, legal or illegal, and beneficial or harmful. In debates over what we should do—debates over future courses of action—we make *claims of policy*. These are, by their very nature, the hardest to prove because they involve, in effect, predicting the future.

Precisely because they are the hardest to prove, policy claims tend to come more heavily qualified than other sorts of claims. Qualifiers are words that indicate our level of confidence in our claims—words such as *possibly*, *probably*, or *beyond any doubt*. So, for example, we may qualify a factual claim if our evidence is not conclusive: "The major cause of increased levels of mercury in fish is *probably* emissions from coal-fired power plants." If we overqualify our claims, of course, we sound unsure or wishy-washy, but if we do not qualify our claim at all, we may overstate our case. A reasonable argument is qualified at a level appropriate to the strength of the reasoning and evidence supporting it.

Reservations are exceptions to our claim, or stipulated conditions under which we no longer hold to our claim. Thus, for example, the chairman of the Federal Reserve might argue that a proposed increase in interest rates will be sufficient to control inflation—*unless* energy prices continue to escalate. As with qualifiers, reservations can be overdone, leaving virtually no conditions under which you still hold to your claim ("I predict that inflation will remain low *unless* prices for food, shelter, clothing, and energy go up!"). By identifying one or two major reservations, however, you can assert your claim more confidently ("Inflation will *almost certainly* remain low, *unless* energy prices go up.") and still make a reasonable argument.

Whatever sorts of claims you make, you will be expected to back them up with evidence or other supporting materials. Evidence, as we discussed in Chapter 7, may include statistics, testimony, examples, or comparison/contrast. But whatever types of evidence you choose, you need to use it properly and make sure that it meets certain tests of quantitative and qualitative sufficiency.

Evidence

When attempting to persuade an audience to accept a factual claim, you might use statistics, specific examples, testimony by experts, and other sorts of evidence. When long-distance telephone companies sought approval from the public utilities commission for a reduction in the fees they paid to local phone companies, for example, one student used a variety of evidence to persuade his audience that consumers would save little, if any, under the plan. His factual claim and supporting material looked like this:

The proposed reduction in fees will not result in lower costs for consumers.
  A. According to the *New York Times*, documents filed by AT&T indicate that basic rates on One Rate plans would increase by 66 percent. *(statistic)*
  B. According to a spokesperson for the Consumers Union, new per-minute fees would go up every day except Sunday, resulting in higher bills for low-volume callers. *(testimony)*
  C. A customer who made 45 minutes of long-distance calls on Saturday would pay $4.95 under the old plan and $13.05 under the new plan. *(statistics/contrast)*
  D. Even if the companies changed to a flat 5-cents-per-minute rate, the cost to consumers would still go up an average of $8.55. *(example/statistics)*

In proving claims of value—claims about good and bad, right and wrong—you need more than just factual evidence. Not only must you cite examples, statistics, and other empirical evidence, but you must also consider the *criteria* or *standards* that support your *evaluations* of those facts. In a murder case, for example, it is one thing to prove that that the accused pulled the trigger, resulting in the death of the victim. It is quite another to convince a jury that the defendant committed first-degree murder—that he pulled the trigger as part of a premeditated plan to commit murder. Depending on the circumstances, the same action—shooting another person dead—might be considered first-degree murder, or it may be reckless homicide or even self-defense. In this sort of case, the facts alone do not determine the verdict. The facts must be considered *in light of the law*.

· In public policy debates, the standards of judgment are rarely as clear as they are in a court of law. Still, it is important that we reflect on the rules, principles, or standards we employ in making our judgments. In a speech on medical malpractice, for example, one student cited the example of her uncle, who had undergone what was supposed to be a routine operation but ended up seriously disabled. She also cited other examples of people hurt by medical errors. Yet in order to convince her listeners that medical malpractice was a "very serious problem" in America, she needed some broader basis for her judgment. She was able to establish that basis with statistics on the leading causes of death and through comparisons to other, more familiar health threats such as car accidents and various diseases. With this evidence, she was able to show that medical malpractice posed as "serious" a threat as these other, more familiar dangers.

Policy arguments pose the greatest challenge because they involve choices about what we *should* do in the future. Because we cannot present *direct* evidence of a proposed policy's feasibility, costs, or effects, we typically must rely on comparisons to similar policies, or we may use testimony from experts in the field. If we wish to propose a new program for recycling high-tech waste, for example, we might look for evidence of how similar programs have worked in other communities. Or we might turn to experts in waste management for testimony on the value, cost, feasibility, and benefits of such programs. In the final analysis, however, we really cannot say for sure how a policy that may have worked well elsewhere in the past will work under different circumstances in the future.

Whatever sort of evidence you use, it needs to be sufficient, both quantitatively and qualitatively, to convince a "reasonable person" that your claims are worthy of serious consideration. There are three basic tests of the adequacy of your evidence.

First, the quality of the evidence should justify the audience's acceptance. As we discussed in Chapter 7, certain questions should always be asked about particular types of evidence, such as the following:

- Are the examples representative?
- Are the statistics reliable?
- Is the testimony authoritative?
- Are the comparisons sound—that is, are the objects or ideas being compared really comparable?

Beyond these questions, there are some general "tests" of evidence that we should always apply: Is the evidence accurate, recent, and complete? Is the source of the evidence credible?

Second, the evidence must be relevant to the claim. Evidence can be accurate and truthful and still not prove the claim. Consider, for example, Meagan's argument in favor of voting for Josh as student government president:

> What we need most in a president is strong leadership. Josh has been my friend since we arrived here at the university. He has always been there for me, often putting aside his own problems or needs to help me when I needed help.
>
> Everyone likes Josh. He has a great sense of humor. When things got tense in our study group, Josh always found something funny to say to break the tension.

Everything that Meagan said about her friend may be true; Josh is no doubt a nice guy. But is that relevant to Meagan's claim? Does the fact that Josh has been a good friend to Meagan, or the fact that he makes people laugh, prove that he would be a strong leader?

Third, the amount of evidence used must be sufficient to support the claim. Your evidence must not only be true and relevant but must also be quantitatively sufficient. Of course, what constitutes a sufficient *amount* of evidence depends on your topic and your audience. If you are addressing a highly controversial issue or an especially skeptical audience, you will need to present more evidence. If your topic is relatively uncontroversial and your audience is open minded, less evidence may be required.

Consider, for example, what would be "sufficient" evidence to refute claims made by former player Jose Canseco that steroid use is widespread in Major League Baseball (MLB). To fans of sluggers Barry Bonds and Sammy Sosa, the players' denials that they used performance-enhancing drugs might be sufficient. When the scandal reached Congress in March 2005, however, members of the House Government Reform Committee demanded more proof. Sosa, Rafael Palmeiro, and Mark McGwire all denied—or at least refused to admit—that they had used illegal substances. Yet when MLB executives appeared before the committee, the legislators "all but scorned" their denials that baseball had a drug problem. Despite more than eleven hours of testimony, the committee remained unconvinced. "I have not been reassured one bit," Representative Steven Lynch of Massachusetts concluded.[14] Obviously, the baseball executives failed to provide *sufficient* evidence to overcome the committee's doubts.

There are, of course, no set rules to determine what constitutes sufficient evidence. In the final analysis, that depends on your audience—their existing knowledge and beliefs, their attitude toward the topic and the speaker, and their willingness to take the evidence you present at face value. That is one more reason to always analyze your audience carefully.

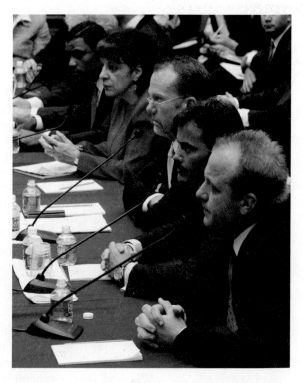

Major League Baseball players Sammy Sosa (sitting next to his translator, Patricia Rosell), Mark McGwire, Rafael Palmeiro, and Curt Schilling appear before a congressional committee investigating steroid use in baseball. The committee appeared unconvinced by the testimony at the hearings.

Warrants

Warrants are the general assumptions, principles, or rules that connect our evidence to our claims. Suppose, for example, that a politician claims that his opponent in the election is "unfit for office." And suppose further that he bases that claim on the fact that his opponent never served in the military. In this debate, the evidence may not be in dispute; the candidate's service record is a matter of public record. But does fitness for office *require* military service? Is the claim that the candidate is unfit for office *warranted* by the fact that she did not serve in the military? In this case, the argument turns not on the evidence but on a general principle: that politicians who have not served in the military are unfit for office. For most Americans, of course, that would be a dubious assumption. Military service may *contribute* to one's fitness for office, but few would agree that military service is a *necessary* qualification.

Some warrants may already be accepted by your audience and may go unstated in your argument. In the United States, for instance, most listeners would agree that under our Constitution, everyone is entitled to fair and equal treatment under the law. Thus, we may use that warrant to link evidence about a particular policy—say, racial profiling by police—to the claim that the policy is unconstitutional. In that argument, there would be little need to back up or even state the warrant; most Americans agree that our Constitution entitles us to fair and equal treatment. Our main burden, then, would be to prove that racial profiling does exist, and that it violates the principle of "fair and equal treatment" under the law.

When we invoke general rules or principles that are themselves controversial, we may need to provide backing for those warrants. Returning to our earlier example, suppose that our hypothetical candidate claimed that his opponent was unfit for office because she was divorced or because she was gay. Does either of these characteristics warrant the argument that she is unfit for office? Fifty or sixty years ago, many people *did* view divorce as a moral failing that disqualified people from high political office. Today, some people still think one's sexual preference is a relevant political credential. Yet in an age of greater social tolerance, divorced candidates are now routinely elected to political office, and in many communities, homosexuality is no longer a political liability. The point, of course, is that warrants themselves are sometimes controversial and that you may need to back them up with additional support.

The Burden of Proof

There is no such thing as an argument that is "reasonable" under any and all circumstances. What qualifies as a reasonable argument in one situation may not seem so reasonable in another, depending on the audience and the situation. One way to anticipate what might be considered a reasonable argument is to reflect on your burden of proof. Although meeting your burden of proof does not guarantee that you will "win" a debate, it does mean that you have made an argument that is at least reasonable enough to warrant serious consideration and further debate.

As we noted in the previous chapter, the theory of presumption and burden of proof is most familiar in the legal context. We have all heard how, in a court of law, we are *presumed* innocent until *proven* guilty. That means that a defendant has the *presumption* of innocence; the prosecution has the burden of proof. In civil cases, that burden of proof means that the prosecution must prove the defendant guilty by a *preponderance of evidence*, whereas in criminal cases, the burden of proof is greater: *beyond a reasonable doubt*. Because more is at stake in a criminal trial, it makes sense that our system demands a higher burden of proof.

In public debates, the burden of proof is not so clearly defined, but there are certain expectations about what constitutes a *reasonable* case. In debates over public policy, for example, advocates of change have the burden of proof because change involves risk—because it means abandoning the known for the unknown. Advocates of new policies are therefore expected to establish, first, that there is some *need* for change. Then we expect them to present a specific *plan*, not only describing their proposed policy or program, but also explaining how it is to be implemented, funded, and enforced or administered. Finally, we expect policy advocates to prove that their plan is *workable*—that is, it is feasible, will solve some problem, and perhaps even produce some benefits or advantages over other possible solutions. In sum, a reasonable argument for a policy change provides at least preliminary answers to these questions: Why do we need a new policy? What would that new policy entail? How would the plan be implemented? Would it be workable and solve the problem? And why should we prefer that plan over other alternatives?

A reasonable argument does not end but begins the discussion. If you make an argument that is, on its first face, reasonable (in Latin, a *prima facie* case), you have a right to expect that your listeners will take it seriously. At the same time, you should be willing to defend your position, perhaps responding to questions or even offering additional arguments and evidence. Part of making a reasonable argument is remaining open to further discussion. Democratic deliberation is an ongoing conversation, and you should never expect to have the "final word."

THE FORMS OF REASONING

Preview. *The process of reaching a sound conclusion involves reasoning, or the process of drawing inferences from known facts. Reasoning always involves some mental leap from the known to the unknown. There are four common types of reasoning: inductive, deductive, causal, and analogical. Understanding these types of reasoning and how they work can help you build solid, well-reasoned persuasive speeches.*

 15.3 Identify the different *types* of reasoning and discuss what makes each different type "reasonable."

 Watch the Video "Interstate Commerce Clause" at **MyCommunicationLab**

Rarely do the facts speak for themselves. More commonly, we must *reason* from facts to conclusions, asking our audience to accept certain *inferences* we make. Thus, for example, we may know that 1,200 respondents to a poll said they planned to vote for the incumbent in an upcoming election—by a margin, say, of 55 to 45 percent. But to predict the outcome of the election based on that evidence involves several assumptions and inferential leaps. First, of course, we assume that the respondents did not lie to the pollster. More important, we trust that those 1,200 respondents are *representative* of the larger population. Finally, we assume that no major events will change voters' minds between the time the survey was taken and election day. In short, we assume *a lot* when we reason from a poll to a prediction of how an election will turn out. All that we *really* know is how 1,200 people said they *planned* to vote. To predict the outcome of the election from that evidence requires an inferential leap.

The process of making inferential leaps is called reasoning, and it commonly assumes one of four forms: (1) *inductive reasoning*, where we reason from specific instances to a more general conclusion, (2) *deductive reasoning*, or reasoning from an accepted generalization to a conclusion about a particular case, (3) *causal reasoning*, which means reasoning from cause to effect or effect to cause, and (4) *analogical reasoning*, in which we reason that what is true of one case will be true of a similar case. Each of these types of reasoning involves inferences; none leads to conclusions that are absolute or certain. All lead to *probable* conclusions, with the strength of those conclusions dependent on the strength of our evidence and the *quality* of our reasoning.

Inductive Reasoning

Inductive reasoning involves reasoning from a set of specific examples or a series of observations to a general conclusion. So, for example, we may investigate ten medical malpractice cases in order to draw a more general conclusion about the typical case—and whether such cases tend to be justified or frivolous. Polls and surveys also rely on inductive reasoning, of course, because they generalize from a small but representative sample to some larger population. So, too, do many other kinds of scientific research rely on inductive reasoning: the forester reasons inductively about the threat posed by pine beetles after examining only a sample of trees; the sociologist interviews a sample of juvenile delinquents before drawing conclusions about what, in general, motivates such bad behavior; and the communication researcher tests reactions to violent images on a small group of experimental subjects before drawing larger conclusions about the effects of media violence.

The strength of inductive reasoning rests on the number of cases examined and the representativeness of those cases. The first questions one should ask about inductive reasoning are thus obvious: How many examples support the generalization? And is that a sufficient number to warrant the generalization? Representativeness is a trickier matter because it requires us to think about the characteristics that might be most relevant to the generalization. When designing election surveys, for example, pollsters go to great lengths to design samples that reflect all the characteristics that they think might affect how one votes: age, gender, race, education, income, occupation, party affiliation, and so on. Similarly, it would be crucial to ask, when generalizing about the problem of medical malpractice, whether the cases examined were *typical* of malpractice suits. Did the cases involve errors *commonly* made by doctors? Or were they the sort of "freak accidents" that make headlines but do not commonly occur?

When reasoning inductively, you should qualify your claims carefully, avoiding sweeping generalizations based on just one or two examples. You might also attach reservations to your claim, identifying conditions under which your generalization may not hold true. Thus, a pollster might conclude that the incumbent president will win reelection—*unless* there is a major crisis or an economic downturn before election day.

Finally, inductive reasoning can be strengthened by testimony and statistics that establish the reliability or representativeness of your examples. Are experts willing to testify that your examples are typical of those they have encountered in their research? Do statistics show that the examples you cite are common or widespread? In inductive reasoning, it is important not only that you have *enough* examples but also that your examples are both true and typical.

Deductive Reasoning

Deductive reasoning is the process of drawing conclusions about specific cases based on inferences from a generally accepted premise or principle. A classic example of deductive reasoning, called a *syllogism*, looks like this:

A. All Democrats are liberal. *(major premise)*
B. My neighbor Tim is a Democrat. *(minor premise)*
C. Therefore, we may conclude that Tim is a liberal. *(conclusion)*

Most of us do not think or talk this formally, of course, and in the real world very few universal premises—like "all Democrats are liberal"—hold true. As a practical matter, then, we more commonly reason from *qualified* premises ("Most Democrats are liberal") to *probable* conclusions ("My neighbor Tim is probably liberal").

Suppose, for example, that you were trying to persuade an audience that we cannot win the war in Afghanistan because we are fighting an indigenous, or "homegrown," religious insurgency. Your claim is that we cannot win; perhaps you have evidence that the insurgency is indigenous and motivated by religious beliefs. What's missing, of course, is what we earlier called the *warrant*: the assumption that, in general, indigenous religious insurgencies are difficult to defeat. Of course, history may show that it is not *always* true that indigenous religious insurgencies prevail in wars on their home turf, and you may also discover evidence that some of the Afghan insurgents are neither homegrown nor religiously motivated. Thus, you would want to *qualify* your argument: "It will be *difficult* to win the war in Afghanistan because *many* of the insurgents are indigenous and motivated by strong religious beliefs."

Often speakers do not even state their premises because they are already accepted by their audience. That is, they assume that the audience will supply the missing premise from their own store of beliefs and values. Thus, for example, we might assume that our audience already believes that "politicians who have lied in the past will lie in the future." If we can prove that a particular politician has lied in the past, our audience will probably accept the conclusion that he or she is likely to lie again. This sort of reasoning is called a *rhetorical syllogism*, or enthymeme. It reflects how we typically construct deductive arguments in everyday talk. If our audience does, in fact, already accept our general premises, these arguments can be persuasive.

If your audience is likely to be skeptical of your premises, you should not only state them but also provide evidence to back them up. Suppose, for example, that you want to argue for a ban on selling carbonated soft drinks in school vending machines. Your deductive reasoning may look something like this:

Major premise: Sugary carbonated sodas are the major cause of an epidemic of obesity and related health problems in America.

Minor premise: School vending machines are the chief source of carbonated sodas for millions of young people.

Conclusion: Therefore, banning the sale of carbonated sodas in school vending machines is the best way to combat the epidemic of obesity and related health problems.

As with all deductive reasoning, the persuasiveness of this argument depends, in part, on whether you can prove that school vending machines are the "chief source" of carbonated sodas consumed by young people. But it also depends on whether your audience is willing to accept the major premise: "Sugary carbonated sodas are a major cause of an epidemic of obesity and related health problems in America." Thus, just to be sure, you might provide backing for that warrant, quoting something like the following statement from the Center for Science in the Public Interest:

> More than two-thirds of Americans are overweight or obese, and soft drinks are the only food or beverage that has been shown to increase the risk of…obesity. Obesity costs $95 billion a year in medical expenditures.…Obesity also causes numerous other problems, including reduced self-esteem and lower productivity…

> Several scientific studies have shown that soft drinks are directly related to weight gain. Weight gain is a prime risk factor for type 2 diabetes, heart attacks, strokes, and cancer. Frequent consumption of soft drinks is also linked to osteoporosis, tooth decay, and dental erosion.[15]

Causal Reasoning

Another everyday form of inference is causal reasoning—reasoning from effect to cause, or from cause to effect. Suppose, for example, that we notice a significant increase in crime or a decrease in the number of traffic deaths across the nation. We naturally want to know about the causes of these trends. By the same token, we often want to know what effects might result from some change in policy. What impact will a proposed welfare reform policy have on the number of people on welfare? Would allowing Social Security recipients to invest in private accounts help solve the system's financial crisis or provide more secure retirements for the elderly? These sorts of questions invite causal reasoning.

Causal reasoning is at the heart of all scientific investigation. In trying to solve the mysteries of the world, researchers routinely reason from cause to effect and effect to cause. What causes some volcanoes to violently explode, while others lay dormant for centuries? What caused the great chestnut forests of the eastern United States to disappear? What are the causes of the increase in high school dropouts in recent years?[16] Why do some people become sexual predators, preying on innocent children? These are just a few of the questions scientists and social scientists are trying to answer through causal reasoning.

Scientists know just how difficult it can be to establish causation. In the natural world, causation is often complex, involving multiple causes or chains of causation. What is *the* cause of declining songbird populations? The answer is that there *is* no single cause. Some ornithologists point to climatic change, acid rain, or disappearing habitat as the primary culprits. Others emphasize the destruction of nesting habitats resulting from the planting of nonnative shrubs, competition or parasitism among different species of birds, or the proliferation of such predators as domestic cats, gray squirrels, and raptors. No doubt still more causes will be discovered as the research continues. The decline in songbird populations is a complex problem with multiple and dynamic causes. It is impossible to point the finger at any single cause.

Imagine how much more difficult it can be to prove what causes humans to do some of the things they do! What causes the anorexic literally to starve herself to death, or the bulimic to binge and purge? What leads people to a life of crime or to a life of violence against others? Why do some people become obsessive about their work, neglecting their families and all of the pleasures of life just to "get ahead"? Again, these are complex questions with no simple answers. Even more than the natural world, human behavior involves systems of multiple and interrelated causes that even the best experts have difficulty sorting out.

In short, establishing causation is rarely simple. The responsible speaker recognizes the difficulty of proving causation and seeks out the best information and evidence available from reputable sources. The responsible advocate also *qualifies* his or her causal claims, acknowledging that we can rarely assert causal claims with absolute certainty or talk about any single factor as *the* cause of a complex problem.

Analogical Reasoning

Consider the following two arguments, both of which you have probably heard before in one form or another:

1. Our economy is headed toward another Great Depression. We must act boldly to shore up the banking industry, stimulate the economy, and create new jobs before our entire financial system collapses, as it did in the 1930s.
2. Politics is like a horse race. It doesn't matter who's first out of the gate, and even the best horses occasionally stumble. True champions have stamina, perseverance, and the courage to let others take the early lead. But as the race heats up, true champions emerge out of the pack, charging to the front with the race on the line. They have a nose for the finish line.

Both of these arguments are based on comparisons. Both illustrate analogical reasoning, where we conclude that what is true of one case will also be true of the other. Yet are the two arguments equally logical? Of course not. In the first example, we are comparing one economic crisis to another. This is what we call a literal analogy, comparing two similar examples. In the second, we are comparing electoral politics to a horse race. That is a *figurative* analogy, like the metaphors discussed in Chapter 10. Figurative analogies may be useful for illustrating a point or giving a speech stylistic color. But they rarely *prove* anything. If we hope to make serious, logically compelling analogical arguments, we should rely upon *literal* analogies.

The explanation for this is simple: the logical strength of analogical reasoning rests on the degree of similarity between the cases being compared. So, for example, if we really hoped to convince people that we are headed for "another

THE GREAT POLITICAL RACE!

STAKES, $25,000 A YEAR!

The LINCOLN Horse is ahead, free and unencumbered, while the others are in the back-ground loaded down with their favorite riders.

FIGURE 15.2

Political cartoonists historically have compared the presidential election to a horse race. In this cartoon from 1860, Abraham Lincoln is depicted as the lead horse in the race for the White House, while his chief competitors are slowed by riders representing slavery, the Dred Scott decision, and a newspaper that obstructs the rider's vision.

Great Depression," it would be important to establish as many similarities as possible between today's economic conditions and those of the 1930s. Similarly, if we advocated a new recycling program for our city, it would be important to establish that such a program has worked well in a similar city—a city with the same population, perhaps, or one that has similar waste management problems. In short, the more similar the cases, the stronger the analogical argument. That is why figurative analogies carry little persuasive weight.

Analogical reasoning is most frequently used in policy arguments. When proposing a new policy, you should investigate whether similar policies have been tried elsewhere. Then you can draw your evidence from places where the policy already has worked. During the late 1990s, for example, welfare reform swept the nation, with state after state setting tougher eligibility requirements and adopting a variety of new policies to encourage aid recipients to find work. Overall, these reforms reduced the welfare rolls nationwide by more than half. Yet what worked in one state did not necessarily work in another, even though all the policies reflected the Clinton administration's goal of "ending welfare as we know it."[17]

Like all forms of reasoning, analogical reasoning involves a leap from the known to the unknown. In policy arguments, we may know that a particular program has worked in the past. But we never know for certain what the future will bring, nor can we identify all the circumstances that might affect how well a particular policy works. Thus, analogical arguments, like all arguments, should be *qualified* at the appropriate level of certainty. Based on the fact that a policy has worked in the past, we can conclude that it *may* or even *probably will* work in the future. But we can never say that with certainty; the future is always, to some extent, unknown.

FALLACIES OF REASONING AND EVIDENCE

Preview. *Arguments are unsound when they have flaws of reasoning or evidence, called fallacies. Common fallacies occur when speakers draw irrelevant conclusions, employ faulty reasoning, provide insufficient evidence, or indulge in personal attacks.*

As we have pointed out, any claim is only as good as the reasoning and evidence that support it. Many things can go wrong during the reasoning process, leading one to draw a faulty conclusion. Following are some common fallacies of reasoning and evidence that ought to be avoided by speakers—and rejected by listeners. Also sometimes known by the Latin names given to them centuries ago, the fallacies may be categorized as follows:

15.4 Define and describe some common fallacies of reasoning and evidence.

Explore the Concept "Perception" at **MyCommunicationLab**

- Fallacies of relevance
- Fallacies of faulty reasoning
- Fallacies of inadequate evidence
- Fallacies of personal attack

Fallacies of Relevance

Fallacies of relevance occur when a speaker, in effect, changes the subject, talking about matters that are simply not relevant to the issue at hand. Fallacies of relevance are sometimes deliberately employed to distract audiences and divert attention away from the real issues.

Appeal to Ignorance (*Ad Ignorantiam*) Speakers sometimes try to convince us that because something has never been proven wrong, it must be right! If a friend told you that it has never been proven that aliens from other planets have *not* visited earth, would that persuade you that aliens *have* visited us? Of course not! Yet we hear similar arguments every day from people who do not really have any evidence to prove their claims. A legislator, for example, might offer the following argument:

> I am convinced that my bill to require teachers to lead schoolchildren in reciting the Pledge of Allegiance each day will increase patriotism among young people. So far, no one has proven that I'm wrong about this. Why would anyone oppose teaching our kids to be more patriotic?

True, nobody can prove that reciting the Pledge will *not* make children more patriotic. Yet neither does this legislator cite any evidence that it *would* increase patriotism.

The *ad ignorantiam* fallacy may assume the opposite form as well: just because something has *not* been proven true does not mean that it is false. In the following example, a student committed the *ad ignorantiam* fallacy in an argument about television's effects on children:

> So we've seen that while there are instances of some children acting violently after watching television—and while some studies indicate that television violence can desensitize children to violent acts—no one has been able to establish a direct link between TV and violence. We can only conclude that television is not to blame for violent behavior among children.

This student may be right that nobody has established a "direct link" between TV and violence. But his own evidence suggests the *possibility* of such a link, and the fact that nobody has proven that connection conclusively does not prove that there is *no* link between TV and violence.

Appeal to Popular Beliefs (*Ad Populum*)   Sometimes known as a bandwagon appeal, this fallacy occurs when a speaker urges listeners to accept something simply because so many others accept it. Many of us are tempted to "follow the crowd," and public speakers sometimes take advantage of this by urging us to do something because "everybody is doing it." Knowing that other people support an idea or a policy is certainly one piece of information that you may want to take into account. But that fact alone should not be persuasive.

In a democracy, the majority rules, of course, so the fact that 63 percent of Americans support some plan may be *one* reason for adopting it. But majority support does not prove that it is a *good* policy—that it will solve some problem or serve the national interest. In American history, the majority has been proven wrong on more than one occasion, and over time minority views sometimes *become* the majority view. In the following excerpt, for example, we hear a line of argument commonly used to silence debate over controversial wars. It was an argument heard during the Vietnam War, which most Americans initially supported but *later* came to oppose:

> The polls are clear, the people have spoken: the vast majority of Americans supports this war. The time for dissent has passed, and now is the time to support our men and women in uniform, no matter how we feel about the war.

There may well be good reasons for supporting our troops regardless of how we feel about a war. And in a democracy, majority opinion must be respected. Yet in a free society, we should never allow an appeal to popular beliefs to silence debate over the merits of an idea or policy.

The *Non Sequitur*   *Non sequitur* is Latin for "it does not follow." In other words, this fallacy occurs when a conclusion does not follow logically from the arguments and evidence that precede it. In a sense, all logical fallacies are more specific types of *non sequiturs*. But when the problem with an argument is that, in general, the evidence is simply not relevant to the claim, we say that the speaker has committed a *non sequitur*.

To continue with our previous example, suppose now that our pro-war speaker began the same way: "The polls are clear…the vast majority of Americans supports this war." Instead of concluding that we should stop criticizing the war because a majority supports it, however, suppose that our speaker now says the following: "So, as we can see, the president's decision to go to war was constitutional under his powers as commander in chief." Here the problem is not that the speaker is asking us to jump on the bandwagon, but that public support for the war simply has nothing to do with whether the president's actions were legal under the Constitution. That is a question for experts in constitutional law, not a matter to be resolved by public opinion.

Appeal to Tradition (*Ad Verecundiam*)   You have probably heard this fallacy expressed this way: "We've never done it that way before." Or perhaps you have heard it expressed another way: "This is the way we've always done it." People get set in their ways, and speakers sometimes exploit this fact to argue against change. An advocate of change *does* have the burden of proof in a policy debate, but that does not mean that those who oppose change can simply respond, "We've always done it this way." Tradition is not, in itself, a good reason for sticking with the status quo.

Appeals to tradition are often heard in contexts where the ideas or policies being challenged have a long history. So, for example, the Virginia Military Institute (VMI) appealed to tradition for many years to justify excluding women from its programs. In 1996, however, the Supreme Court, in *United States v. Virginia et al.*, ruled that women had a right to attend VMI under the equal protection clause of the Constitution.[18] Similarly, students at Texas A&M University resisted for many years efforts to end a 90-year tradition of building "the world's largest bonfire" on the eve of their annual football rivalry with the University of Texas. Yet after the 59-foot-high structure collapsed in 1999, killing 12 students and injuring 27 others, arguments about safety and liability finally prevailed over appeals to tradition.[19]

Tradition can be a good thing, of course, but it is unreasonable to use it as a shield against compelling arguments for change. Change involves risk, and advocates of change must meet their burden of proof. But if they meet that

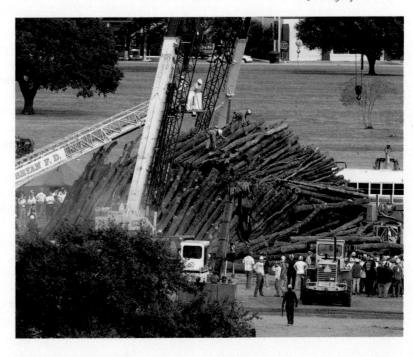

At Texas A&M University, it took a terrible tragedy to overcome appeals to tradition, as a log structure built for the "world's largest bonfire" collapsed, killing twelve students. Rescue workers are shown here responding to the tragedy.

burden, they have a right to a real debate, not a deflection of their arguments by appeals to tradition.

The Red Herring Fallacy The term red herring comes from an old practice of using the strong odor of smoked herring to throw hunting dogs off the track of a fox, either as a training exercise or to keep them out of farmers' fields. In argumentation theory, a red herring is an attempt to throw an audience off track by raising an irrelevant, often highly emotional issue that prevents critical examination of an issue. In a debate over whether prayer ought to be allowed in the public schools, for example, an advocate may divert attention from the real issues by declaring, "The issue here is whether we are going to allow atheists to determine what happens in our schools." Many who oppose prayer in schools, of course, are not atheists at all, but are simply concerned about the separation of church and state. The real issue is not the threat posed by atheists, but whether school prayer violates the Constitution.

Consider another example of how a red herring might distract attention from the real issue at stake. Imagine a defense lawyer saying the following:

> My client is a fine, upstanding citizen who has spent his life in community service. He was a Boy Scout leader, sang in his church choir, and coached Little League. This man has lived in this town all his life and never has been charged with a crime. Would such a man embezzle money from his employer?

Perhaps it is hard to imagine such a man embezzling money, but his attorney has avoided the real issue here. The man's guilt or innocence must be established by the evidence, not by a recitation of his personal virtues. The introduction of his exemplary life is a red herring, designed to distract attention from the real issue at hand.

The Straw Man Fallacy In the straw man fallacy, a speaker attributes a flimsy, easy-to-refute argument to his opponent, and then proceeds to demolish it. In the process, of course, the speaker misrepresents the opponent's real position. In some cases, the speaker may even try to make the opponent look silly for making such a ridiculous argument. So, for example, an environmentalist might portray a so-called wise use advocate—one who supports *some* logging or mining on public lands—as favoring "the sale of our national forests to the highest bidder." That exaggerates the position of the wise use advocate, creating a straw man that is easy to attack.

Straw men have been prominent in debates over welfare reform in the United States. The following example is hypothetical, but it sounds like some of the arguments actually heard during the welfare debates of the late 1990s:

> We need to find ways to reform the welfare system so that our tax dollars are not wasted on those who just want a free handout. Opponents of reform believe that anyone who doesn't want to work shouldn't have to. They argue that if a woman wants to have children out of wedlock, well, that's her right, and the state should take care of those children. I, for one, disagree with those who think that taxpayers' money ought to be used to encourage people not to work, not to get married, or to have more children out of wedlock. My opponents want to continue this culture of welfare dependency that has cost taxpayers billions of dollars. I say the time has come for a new approach.

Opponents of welfare reform never made such arguments, of course. At the time, almost everybody agreed about the need for reform. The real debate was over what *sorts* of policies might get people off welfare and end the "culture of dependency." The welfare advocate who *favored* "free handouts" and *wanted* to see more children born out of wedlock was a straw man.

These fallacies—appeal to ignorance, appeal to popular beliefs, the *non sequitur*, appeal to tradition, the red herring, and the straw man—all produce conclusions that do not follow logically from the evidence. They are all ways to distract attention from the real issues at stake. When employed intentionally, they violate the spirit of deliberating in good faith.

Fallacies of Faulty Reasoning

Fallacies of reasoning are errors in analogical or causal arguments, or they might involve "arguing in circles" or creating false choices. Like fallacies of relevance, fallacies of faulty reasoning may be unintentional, reflecting only fuzzy thinking on the part of a speaker. Or they may be used deliberately as propaganda techniques.

The False Dilemma   The false dilemma is a fallacy that occurs when a speaker suggests that we have only two alternatives, when, in fact, more than two alternatives exist. Typically this takes the form of an either/or proposition: "Either we fight to win in Afghanistan, or we 'cut and run' as we did in Vietnam." This reasoning is faulty, of course, because there are a number of policy options between the extremes of all-out escalation and total retreat.

The false dilemma is routinely evident in budget debates. Consider, for example, the following passage:

> The budget deficit has once again become a serious threat to our economy and to the future welfare of our children. The only way to make sure that the budget deficit doesn't continue to grow out of hand is to cut social programs. Some people may be hurt by this, but we have no choice—either we cut these programs, or we run the risk of huge budget deficits that will stop our economic growth and create a huge burden for the next generation of American taxpayers.

The problem here, of course, is that other choices are possible. One choice is to do nothing and see whether an improving economy takes care of the budget deficit. Another is to raise taxes to bring down the deficit. Still another is to combine cuts in social programs with tax increases. Perhaps radical cuts in social programs really are needed, but that remains to be proven. To say that we must *either* make drastic cuts *or* suffer huge budget deficits is a false dilemma.

The false dilemma may assume more complex forms, of course, proposing three or more false alternatives. Thus, for example, an advocate may say that we *must* do one of three or four things—or face horrible consequences. Again, what determines whether such reasoning is fallacious is not the number of alternatives per se, but whether the advocate has listed *all* the realistic alternatives. In dealing with complex issues, we typically have many options, so we should always be suspicious of those who say that we have only one or two choices.

Begging the Question   Begging the question occurs when a speaker makes a claim that *assumes* the very thing he or she hopes to prove. This typically takes the form of circular reasoning, in which the speaker offers no support for a claim, but instead simply restates the claim itself in different words. Thus, for example, a speaker may claim that "illegal immigrants are a drain on our nation's economy." When asked for evidence, the response may be: "Well, we all know that illegal immigrants use expensive social services yet pay no taxes." Here the speaker has not offered any evidence for the original assertion, but has simply restated the original claim in different, more specific terms. In effect, the speaker is offering one unsupported assertion as support for the other.

Speakers often attempt to disguise efforts to beg the question with words such as *obviously*, *of course*, or *as we all know*. So, for example, a speaker may say the following:

> As we all know, capital punishment deters crime. Obviously, potential criminals will think twice before committing a crime if they know they will be executed if they are caught. With capital punishment reinstated in every state, we would, of course, see a dramatic reduction in the murder rate.

This speaker claims that capital punishment deters crime. But what is her evidence? When forced to support her contention, she simply restated the same claim in another way, speculating that criminals "obviously" would "think twice" if they faced execution.

The Faulty Analogy   As we noted earlier, the strength of analogical reasoning depends on the similarity of the two things being compared. When speakers compare things that are not, in fact, similar, they commit the fallacy of faulty analogy. There are no specific rules for when an analogy becomes "faulty," but *figurative* analogies—almost by definition—are logically faulty. Literal analogies *may* provide support for an argument, but the legitimacy of such comparisons is always open to debate. Suppose, for example, that an opponent of stricter gun control made the following argument:

> Gun control is not a new idea. In Nazi Germany, guns were confiscated to prevent any groups from taking actions that might have undermined Hitler. In Cuba, Castro made sure that no one but his own Communist followers had guns. Whenever dictators want to stifle opposition, they take away people's guns. Now we have men and women in Washington who want to pass new gun control legislation and take away your guns.

Is the speaker's comparison of gun control advocates in America to Hitler and Castro legitimate? Are the similarities between the United States and Nazi Germany—or between the United States and Cuba—sufficient to warrant such comparisons? The analogies used by this speaker certainly add *pathos* to the argument, but scaring listeners is not the same as arguing logically. From a logical point of view, this may well be a faulty analogy, ignoring important political and cultural differences between the nations being compared. In addition, the analogy wrongly equates all gun control measures with the *confiscation* of guns. Not only is this argument based on a faulty analogy, but it also creates a straw man.

The Slippery Slope   The fallacy of the slippery slope occurs when a speaker claims that some cause will *inevitably* lead to undesirable effects, ultimately resulting in some worst-case scenario. If you take the first step down the slippery slope—or so the reasoning goes—you will quickly slide all the way to the bottom. Again, opponents of gun control are probably guilty of this fallacy when they insist that any gun control legislation inevitably will lead to the confiscation of all guns. The slippery slope can also be heard in debates over rising tuition costs, as in this passage from a student speech:

> The Board of Trustees is once again considering raising tuition next year. This is a dangerous action and threatens to undermine the very foundation of public education. A state university is supposed to serve the interests of the citizens of the state; if this tuition increase is implemented, it will be the first step in an ever-increasing spiral of rising costs for students. Eventually, only the rich will be able to attend our state universities and have the opportunity to get a college education.

Of course, it is not necessarily fallacious to argue that some action will lead to bad consequences down the road. We reason like that every day—for example, in arguing that bad eating habits lead to health problems. The slippery slope, however, treats *probable* or *possible* causal links as certain and inevitable, and it preys on fears of the worst-case scenario.

These fallacies—false alternatives, begging the question, the faulty analogy, and the slippery slope—are all perversions of otherwise legitimate forms of reasoning. It is not the form of reasoning *per se* that leads to fallacious arguments, but rather faulty assumptions and unwarranted inferential leaps in otherwise legitimate forms of reasoning.

Fallacies of Inadequate Evidence

Fallacies of inadequate evidence occur when a speaker simply does not have sufficient evidence to back up his or her claim. Generally, speakers who commit these errors have some but not enough evidence to prove their claims.

False Cause (*Post Hoc, Ergo Propter Hoc*)   The false cause fallacy occurs when a speaker confuses a chronological relationship with a causal one. It is often known by its Latin name, *post hoc, ergo propter hoc*—"after this, therefore because of this." Simply because one event precedes another, of course, does not mean that it *caused* it. Crime may decline after a new gun control law is passed, but that does not prove that the legislation *caused* the decline. The economy may improve in the wake of tax cuts, but that does not mean that tax cuts *caused* the improvement. As we noted earlier, most political, economic, and social trends have complex, often multiple causes that may be difficult to sort out. In their effort to simplify explanations, advocates sometimes *oversimplify* causation, and that often takes the form of the *post hoc* fallacy.

The Hasty Generalization   The hasty generalization fallacy occurs when a speaker generalizes from too few examples. Perhaps the speaker observed but a handful of students at one university before concluding that all college students are binge drinkers. Or maybe she talked to just three senior citizens before generalizing that all seniors suffer from depression. In either case, the speaker committed a hasty generalization. He or she drew a sweeping generalization based on too few examples.

HIGHLIGHTING THE *POST HOC* FALLACY | The Gun Control Debate

As is often the case in long-running, highly emotional public debates, both sides in the gun control debate have been guilty of logical fallacies. Indeed, one can often find the same logical fallacies committed by advocates both for and against gun control. Consider, first, the following argument against gun control:

"The only policy that effectively reduces public shootings is right-to-carry laws. Allowing citizens to carry concealed handguns reduces violent crime. In the 31 states that have passed right-to-carry laws since the mid-1980s, the number of multiple victim public shootings and other violent crimes has dropped dramatically. Murders fell by 7.65 percent, rapes by 5.2 percent, aggravated assaults by 7 percent, and robberies by 3 percent."

Handgun control advocates respond that the evidence actually shows that gun control laws work, particularly at the state and local level. Some cite the 1974 Bartley-Fox law in Massachusetts, which required licensing for carrying a handgun outside of one's home or office. Enforced with a mandatory prison sentence, the law reportedly reduced homicides in Massachusetts by 50 percent and armed robberies by 35 percent. Supporters of the law cited research by Glenn Pierce and William Bowers of Northeastern University in support of their argument.

Unfortunately, both sides in the debate committed the post hoc fallacy, reasoning that because a drop in crime occurred after some new legislation was passed, the legislation must have caused the drop. In the quoted example, from the Phyllis Schlafly Report,

an advocate opposed to gun control claims that "right-to-carry" laws "effectively reduce[d]" public shootings and violent crime. This claim is supported by statistics on falling crime rates since the mid-1980s in states that have passed such laws. In response, the pro-handgun control advocates argue that stricter state and local gun control laws "work" to lower handgun crime—another causal claim. Again, the claim is supported by statistics on falling crime rates.

Violent crime fell generally in the United States in the late 1980s and 1990s, and a number of factors may have contributed to that trend. Moreover, neither Schlafly nor the gun control advocates provide us with the comparative data necessary to prove that declining crime rates can be attributed to the passage of new legislation. Schlafly provides no data from states that did not pass "right to carry" laws, so we have no way of knowing whether crime declined any faster in states that passed such laws than in those that did not. Likewise, the pro-gun-control argument provides no basis for comparison to other states. In addition, it doesn't even make clear when Massachusetts's drop in crime occurred, except that it occurred "after"—post hoc—passage of the new handgun control law. Gary N. Curtis, author of The Fallacy Files, concludes, "The very fact that comparative information is not supplied in each argument is suspicious, since it suggests that it would have weakened the case."

Source: "Post Hoc," *The Fallacy Files*, www.fallacyfiles.org/posthocf.html (accessed April 6, 2012). ◤

Consider the following argument from a student speech about funding for public schools in poor neighborhoods. Drawing on his personal experience, the student made the following argument:

Last spring I spent three weeks as an observer in one of these poor schools. What I saw was lazy teachers and lazy students. Everyone seemed to be going through the motions. Students weren't motivated to learn and teachers were just too tired and frustrated to try to get anything out of these kids. I don't believe that pouring money into these poor schools will help them much. People just won't do things they don't want to do.

In this case, of course, the student probably did not actually observe "everyone" in the school. Moreover, all of the teachers and students he observed were from just this one school. To generalize about *all* "poor schools" based on this limited experience would be to commit a hasty generalization. Most reasonable people would agree that generalizing from just one school is unwarranted and fallacious.

These two fallacies—the false cause (*post hoc*) and the hasty generalization—occur when conclusions are drawn without sufficient evidence to support them. Evidence that one thing occurred after another does not prove causation, and sound inductive reasoning requires more than just one or two examples.

Fallacies of Personal Attack

Personal attacks are perhaps the most troubling fallacies because they contribute to the negative tone of our politics and "turn off" many citizens. Fallacies of personal attack are sometimes used deliberately to shift attention away from the real issues at hand. They substitute name-calling or character assassination for engagement of other people's arguments.

The *Ad Hominem* Fallacy   Unfortunately, the *ad hominem* fallacy has become increasingly familiar in our political life. Although the character, integrity, or even intelligence of a political candidate may be a legitimate "issue" during an election campaign, too often attacks on the person are substituted for arguments about a candidate's ideas or proposals.

Here is an example of an *ad hominem* fallacy that may sound vaguely familiar:

> The congressman's criticism of the president is hypocrisy of the worst sort. The congressman has, for many years, had an extramarital affair. Who is he to attack the president for moral indiscretions? The congressman himself has behaved immorally, displaying his own lack of commitment to "family values."

Now it may be true that the congressman is a hypocrite. If he attacked the president for his personal misconduct, perhaps it is only fair that he be subjected to the same sort of criticism. Still, this argument commits the *ad hominem* fallacy because it sidesteps the accusations against the president. The response does not deny the charges against the president, nor does it defend the president's actions. Instead, it attacks the person who raised the issue, in effect changing the subject.

Guilt by Association   The guilt-by-association fallacy arises when we judge an idea, person, or program solely on the basis of their association with other ideas, persons, or programs. If you view yourself as a political liberal, for example, you may be tempted to dismiss any idea or proposal that comes from the likes of Newt Gingrich or Rush Limbaugh. If you consider yourself conservative, you may be equally likely to dismiss—without serious thought or analysis—the ideas of liberals such as Howard Dean or Nancy Pelosi. Research shows that many people rate an idea, an essay, a speech, or even a painting higher if they are told that it came from a person they respect.[20] This, of course, illustrates the power of *ethos*. Put in more negative terms, however, it also suggests how we may discredit an otherwise good idea simply by associating it with an unpopular source.

Guilt by association refers to attacking the worth of people or their ideas solely on the basis of their associations. Rather than assessing the quality of an idea or argument, guilt by association dismisses it by connecting it to something already discredited in the minds of the audience. Consider, for example, the following hypothetical argument:

> How can we believe that this proposal is made with our best interests in mind? Mr. Morgan says it will save us a lot of money. But Mr. Morgan once belonged to an investment club in which many of the investors lost everything. One member of that club was actually indicted for fraud, while others pulled out just in time to make a lot of money at the expense of their fellow members.

Mr. Morgan was not the one indicted for fraud, nor was he likely one of the members who pulled out "just in time." If he had been guilty of either of those things, his critic probably would have mentioned it. Indeed, Mr. Morgan may have been one of the victims himself. But bent on discrediting Morgan's proposal, the speaker suggests that his plan is suspect simply because of his former associations. This is fallacious because it diverts attention from the real issue at hand—whether the proposal is a good idea—by discrediting the source.

Arguments that are based on personal attacks—the *ad hominem* attack and guilt by association—are flawed because they sidestep the real issues. More than that, they debase the quality of our public discourse, undermining the politics of ideas with what former president Bill Clinton once called "the politics of personal destruction."

The fallacies we have discussed are not the only forms of faulty reasoning. Scholars of argumentation have identified hundreds of fallacies and propaganda devices, all of which can detract from the quality of our public deliberations. As responsible citizens, we should avoid committing fallacies in our own speeches, and we should learn to recognize and speak out against the fallacious arguments of others. Fallacies are among the techniques that demagogues and propagandists use to deceive and mislead the public. As citizens in a democracy, we need to recognize and resist such techniques and speak out against those who use them.

 Study and Review materials for this chapter are at **MyCommunicationLab**

SUMMARY

 Listen to the Audio Chapter Summary at **MyCommunicationLab**

Persuasion and Demagoguery in a Free Society

 Distinguish between persuasion and demagoguery.

- Persuasion is a legitimate, essential tool of democratic deliberation, whereas demagoguery subverts reasoned deliberation with charismatic and emotional appeals.

Constructing a Reasonable Argument

 Define *argument* and discuss what it means to make a complete and "reasonable" argument.

- A good argument is not one that confirms our existing beliefs or "works" to persuade an audience, but one that is complete, reasonable, and meets certain tests of reasoning and evidence.

- *Claims* are debatable assertions about fact, value, or policy that we put forward in a persuasive speech.
- *Evidence* provides support for our claims and should meet certain tests of quantitative and qualitative sufficiency.
- *Warrants* are general assumptions, principles, or rules that connect our evidence to our claims.
- The burden of proof is the level of proof necessary to warrant serious consideration of an argument.

The Forms of Reasoning

15.3 Identify the different *types* of reasoning and discuss what makes each different type "reasonable."

- The process of drawing inferences from known facts is called *reasoning*.
- The four common types of reasoning are inductive, deductive, causal, and analogical:
  - Inductive reasoning draws a general conclusion from a set of specific examples.
  - Deductive reasoning draws conclusions about specific cases from a generally accepted premise or principle.
  - Causal reasoning makes inferences from cause to effect or effect to cause.
- Analogical reasoning infers that what is true of some known case is or will be true of a similar case.

Fallacies of Reasoning and Evidence

15.4 Define and describe some common fallacies of reasoning and evidence.

- Fallacies are errors or flaws of reasoning and evidence.
- The four major categories of fallacies are fallacies of relevance, fallacies of reasoning, fallacies of inadequate evidence, and fallacies of personal attack:
  - Fallacies of relevance include the appeal to ignorance, the appeal to popular beliefs, the disconnected conclusion (or *non sequitur*), the appeal to tradition, the red herring, and the straw man.
  - Fallacies of faulty reasoning include the false dilemma, begging the question, the faulty analogy, and the slippery slope.
  - Fallacies of inadequate evidence include the false cause (*post hoc*) and the hasty generalization.
  - Fallacies of personal attack include the attack against the person (*ad hominem*) and guilt by association.

QUESTIONS FOR REVIEW AND REFLECTION

Persuasion and Demagoguery in a Free Society

15.1 Distinguish between persuasion and demagoguery.

1. How would you distinguish between persuasion and demagoguery? Can you identify one or two public figures today whom you would consider demagogues? Why do you think they deserve that label?

Constructing a Reasonable Argument

15.2 Define *argument* and discuss what it means to make a complete and "reasonable" argument.

2. What makes for a good argument? Is a good argument always *persuasive*? Is there such a thing as a *reasonable* argument that people do not find *persuasive*? What, exactly, does it mean to say that an argument is *reasonable*, and what sorts of standards or tests might we use in judging arguments?

3. Distinguish among the different types of *claims* discussed in this chapter, and think of one example of each type of claim. Can you think of a major public controversy that still revolves around claims of fact? What about claims of value and policy?

4. What is meant by *burden of proof*, and who would have the burden of proof in debates over (a) an allegation of wrongdoing by a public official and (b) a proposal for a new tax policy? If you meet your burden of proof, what does that mean? Does that mean you "win" the debate?

The Forms of Reasoning

 15.3 Identify the different *types* of reasoning and discuss what makes each different type "reasonable."

5. Distinguish among the four types of reasoning discussed in this chapter and discuss what makes for strong inductive, deductive, causal, and analogical reasoning. Besides the examples given in the book, can you think of one or more examples of each type of reasoning that you have heard in a speech or public debate?

Fallacies of Reasoning and Evidence

 15.4 Define and describe some common fallacies of reasoning and evidence.

6. Which of the *fallacies of relevance* discussed in this chapter do you think are most common in today's political environment? In other words, do we hear more red herrings than straw man fallacies? More appeals to popular belief than appeals to tradition?

7. Are the fallacies discussed in this book *always* errors in reasoning? Are they *always* "illogical"? Is there ever a time, for example, when an appeal to popular beliefs is reasonable? Is an appeal to tradition ever legitimate? Is it ever reasonable to attack the person or to discredit the source of an argument because of the people or groups they associate with ("guilt by association")?

✓ Study and Review the Flashcards at **MyCommunicationLab**

GLOBAL CLIMATE CHANGE

Kathryn Gromowski

In this speech delivered at a public speaking contest in 2008, Penn State student Kathryn Gromowski urged her listeners to support legislation to combat global warming. Although the bill she advocated did not become law, similar legislation is still being debated in Congress, and many of her arguments remain relevant to the ongoing debate over climate change. Kathryn uses causal reasoning, statistical evidence and expert testimony, and a simple problem-solution organization to meet her burden of proof and make a reasonable argument for the legislation. She reinforces the logical reasoning of the speech with credible sources (ethos) and mild but effective emotional appeals (pathos) grounded in fears of a climatic disaster.

We have all seen these pictures. Ice caps shrinking. Cities going underwater. People displaced with nowhere to go due to storms and expanding oceans. They are terrifying, but to many of us, they are just images. Soon, however, they may become realities if we continue to stand by and do nothing about global climate change. According to David Elliot Cohen, author of a best-selling book about climate change, those scary pictures may "someday be the iconic images of our decade…because they presage the images we will spend this century viewing—on our screens, and out our windows." If we are to prevent this from becoming a reality, we need to start by finally doing something to curb global warming, and that means tackling carbon emissions more aggressively. A bill currently before Congress, the Sanders-Boxer Global Warming Pollution Reduction Act, is America's best hope for preventing further damage from global warming. Today, I will discuss the problem we face, describe the provisions of the Sanders-Boxer Act, and explain why it is the best horse to bet on in the race for our planet's survival.

Although climate change might refer to any number of natural or human-caused environmental changes, the greatest danger we face is global warming. Global warming is caused by atmospheric gases through a phenomenon known as the greenhouse effect. According to the Environmental Protection Agency, or EPA, "The greenhouse effect is a natural phenomenon that helps regulate the Earth's temperature. Greenhouse gases…act like an insulating blanket, trapping solar energy that would otherwise escape into space." Over the last century or so, human activities have dramatically increased the natural greenhouse effect, causing the earth's average temperature to rise.

The primary greenhouse gases are carbon dioxide, methane, and nitrous oxide, but the real killer is carbon dioxide. According to the Carbon Dioxide Information Analysis Center, the concentration of CO_2 as of September 2008 is 383.9 parts per million, which may not seem like much, but over the entire surface of the earth that amount of CO_2 causes a warming effect equivalent to roughly 141 billion 60-watt lightbulbs. In fact, a *New York Times* article from February 6, 2007, stated that, "if greenhouse gas emissions continue unabated, they will most likely warm the earth by about 3 to 7 degrees Fahrenheit by the end of this century," with an even greater effect of up to 12 degrees possible. Also, the EPA indicates that this atmospheric buildup of CO_2 and other greenhouse gases is, and I quote, "largely the result of human activities such as the burning of fossil fuels."

KATHRYN BEGINS WITH A CONCISE INTRODUCTION, GRABBING HER AUDIENCE'S ATTENTION BY REFERRING TO FAMILIAR IMAGES BUT THEN GETTING RIGHT TO THE POINT: SHE WANTS HER AUDIENCE TO SUPPORT A BILL IN CONGRESS THAT WOULD "AGGRESSIVELY" COMBAT GLOBAL WARMING.

KATHRYN DESCRIBES SOME FAIRLY TECHNICAL MATTERS IN TERMS HER AUDIENCE CAN EASILY UNDERSTAND, COMPARING THE "GREENHOUSE EFFECT" TO AN "INSULATING BLANKET" AND THE INCREASE IN TEMPERATURE TO THE HEAT PRODUCED BY 141 BILLION LIGHTBULBS!

This buildup of greenhouse gases could have serious repercussions. As you can see from this graph from the Pew Center on Global Climate Change [Figure 15.3], the earth's temperature over the last 400,000 years, shown in orange, has closely tracked the amount of CO_2 in the atmosphere, shown in blue. Those CO_2 levels have now reached unprecedented heights, due to the human-contributed CO_2 shown in green toward the right of the graph. If we don't act quickly to reduce these levels of greenhouse gases, we could soon see temperatures rise to correspondingly high levels. These temperature increases could have catastrophic effects. The Pew Center has noted that global warming already appears to be causing more frequent and more severe hurricanes, changes in precipitation that cause flooding in some areas and droughts in others, and widespread melting of the polar ice caps, which in turn is causing sea levels to rise. The Pew Center has predicted that sea levels could rise by as much as one meter by 2100, which would cause many low-lying areas around the world to be flooded.

A *New York Times* article from November 2008 indicates just how real this threat is for some people in the world. In the Maldives, for example, the president-elect has promised to

FIGURE 15.3

Reprinted by permission from "Climate Change 101: Science and Impacts." Copyright © 2009 by PEW Center on Global Climate Change.

Sources: Surface temperature: Brohan, P., J. J. Kennedy, S. F. B. Tett, and P. D. Jones. "Uncertainty estimates in regional and global observed temparature changes: A new dataset from 1850," *Journal of Geophysical Research* 111, no. D12106 (2006): doi: 20.2092/2005JD006548. Ocean heat: Domingues, C. M., J. A. Church, N. J. White, P. J. Gleckler, S. E. Wijffels, P. M. Barker, and J. R. Dunn. 2008. "Improved estimates of upper ocean warming and multi-decadal sea-level rise," *Nature* 453: 1090–1093.

establish an investment fund for buying up new lands for the people who now live in the 1,200 islands that make up this nation. Many in the Maldives now live less than three feet above sea level and will be displaced if global warming raises the sea level of the Indian Ocean.

Stephan Schneider, a climate scientist at Stanford University, summed things up nicely in a September 2008 article in *USA Today*, stating that if the trend of increased greenhouse emissions continues over the next century, we'd be "luckier than hell for it to just be bad, as opposed to catastrophic." Obviously, we face a serious problem. What can be done about this threat? What are the best ways to reduce global warming? A good start would be passage of the so-called Sanders-Boxer Act, which is the most comprehensive of several climate change bills now being considered in Congress.

The Sanders-Boxer Act has the potential to significantly reduce CO_2 levels across the planet. How can it do that by restricting carbon dioxide emissions only in the U.S.? The answer is simple. According to a *New York Times* article from February 3, 2007, "The United States, with about 5 percent of the world's population, contributes about a quarter of greenhouse gas emissions, more than any other country." While a good portion of the industrialized world falls under the blanket of the Kyoto Protocol, which was ratified in February 2005 and caps emissions in 39 other industrialized countries, the U.S. refused to ratify the agreement. Now, the Kyoto Protocol is due to expire in 2012, and by that time we might be able to renegotiate the treaty to include not only the U.S. but also rapidly industrializing countries, such as China and India. In the meantime, however, we need the Sanders-Boxer Act. We cannot afford to wait another four years before cutting back on the amount of greenhouse emissions in the United States.

The Sanders-Boxer Act is the right combination of aggressive and flexible measures. As you can see from this second chart from the Pew Center on Global Climate Change [Figure 15.4], there are a number of proposals before Congress for addressing the problem. The orange line on the graph represents how carbon emissions will continue to increase if we choose to do nothing. The blue line, which represents the projected effects of the Sanders-Boxer Act, shows the most dramatic *decrease* in emissions over the next half century. The Sanders-Boxer Act aims for an overall reduction in emissions of 80 percent by 2050. The projected effects of another popular bill in Congress, the Boxer-Lieberman-Warner Climate Security Act, is represented by this green line on the graph. This bill is popular with industry because it demands little action by polluters until the year 2036 and it sets a less-dramatic goal of reducing emissions by 71 percent by the year 2050. Some argue that bill would allow the economy time to adapt, but according to the Sierra Club and other environmental groups, it simply doesn't go far enough.

The Sanders-Boxer Act will achieve its more dramatic results through a variety of methods. First, it would regulate all greenhouse gases rather than just those covered by cap-and-trade provisions, which pertain only to certain industries, according to the Pew Center. It does this at the national level, relying heavily on the EPA to measure and enforce limitations on how much carbon dioxide can be produced. Secondly, it imposes limits on vehicle emissions that must be met by 2016, according to the Library of Congress. It also directs that all gasoline sold in the U.S. contain a certain percentage of renewable fuel. Lastly, it includes

383

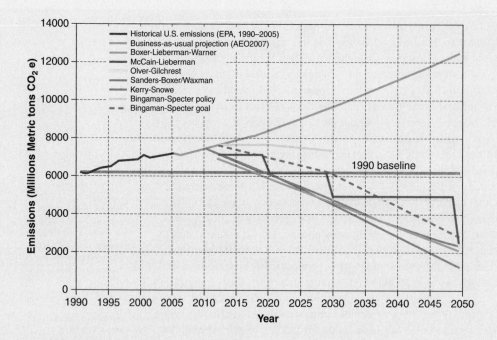

FIGURE 15.4

Reprinted by permission from "Climate Change 101: Science and Impacts." Copyright © 2009 by PEW Center on Global Climate Change.

a cap-and-trade program for dealing with problem industries, much like the one utilized effectively in the 1990 Clean Air Act.

According to the Center for American Progress, a cap-and-trade program essentially allows companies to buy from the government the right to emit a certain number of carbon "units." This would provide a steady source of revenue of up to $300 billion a year. This money in turn would be allocated as shown in this graph [Figure 15.5], with most of the money going to research and development of new clean air technologies and aid to American consumers coping with higher energy costs. Companies that buy more carbon units than they need would be free to resell them to companies that underestimated their emissions. An article in the *New York Times* in January 2007 indicates that "such a market, already in effect in Europe," would "stimulate innovation in technologies that would reduce emissions or produce goods or power without the same high emissions common today." So why is the Sanders-Boxer Act the best option among the several bills now being debated in Congress?

The Sanders-Boxer Act is the best choice because it addresses all the sources of carbon emissions, not just some of them. As I mentioned earlier, its chief competition in Congress is the Climate Security Act, sponsored by Senators Boxer, Lieberman, and Warner. According to the

KATHRYN PROVIDES A CONCISE SUMMARY OF THE COMPARATIVE ADVANTAGES OF THE BILL AND PROCLAIMS IT POLITICALLY FEASIBLE.

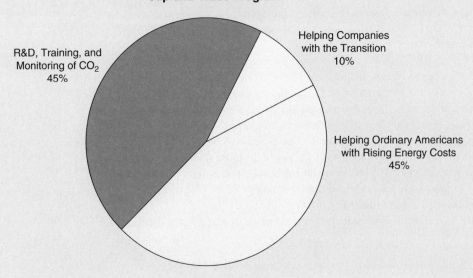

Allocation of Funds Collected from Cap-and-Trade Program

R&D, Training, and Monitoring of CO_2
45%

Helping Companies with the Transition
10%

Helping Ordinary Americans with Rising Energy Costs
45%

FIGURE 15.5
Reprinted by permission from "Economy-wide Cap-and-Trade Proposals in the 110th Congress, Includes Legislation Introduced as of January 30, 2008." Copyright © 2008 by PEW Center on Global Climate Change.

National Resources Defense Council, the Climate Security Act would regulate only 86 percent of the total carbon emissions because it only applies only to capped industry emissions. Also, the Climate Security Act simply isn't aggressive enough. Although the 9 percent difference between the two bills in the projected emission reductions might not seem like much, it could make a huge difference in the long run. In a report on CNN in 2007, world-renowned climatologist James Hansen stated that we have only "eight more years to reverse the flow of carbon into the atmosphere" before we suffer serious and perhaps irreversible harms. The Climate Security Act has a great deal of political support, but it simply does not do as much as the Sanders-Boxer Act to reverse the dangerous trend toward ever-increasing emissions.

The Sanders-Boxer Act has the potential to pull the world out of its predicament. It addresses all of the carbon being emitted by our economy, in both the industrial and the transportation sectors. It is also the most aggressive bill proposed. According to Senator Bernie Sanders, one of the two authors of the bill, "simply raising our fuel-efficiency standards to forty miles per gallon would save roughly the same amount of oil as we import from Saudi Arabia." The Sanders-Boxer Act also would use an organization already in place, the EPA, to regulate emissions, and it would allow for a market-based system so that companies that need extra time

KATHRYN CLOSES BY QUOTING FROM THE BOOK ON CLIMATE CHANGE THAT SHE MENTIONED AT THE START OF THE SPEECH. HER SPEECH CONCLUDES WITH AN OMINOUS WARNING ABOUT WHAT MAY HAPPEN "IF WE DO NOTHING."

to comply with the new emission standards will literally be able to buy it. Lastly, the Sanders-Boxer Act is politically realistic. President-Elect Obama, Vice-President-Elect Joe Biden, and Senator Hillary Clinton have all pledged to support it, and the bill already has 16 co-sponsors in the Senate. At the moment, the Climate Security Act has broader political support, but it simply is not as good a bill as the Sanders-Boxer Act.

In conclusion, I have discussed the problem of global warming, how the Sanders-Boxer Act will address the problem of carbon emissions, and why the Sanders-Boxer Act is the best of several bills now before Congress. The root problem we face today is global warming, which is caused by greenhouse gases, and specifically, carbon dioxide. The Sanders-Boxer Act proposes to use a variety of methods to reduce carbon emissions in the U.S. It seeks to do this in a more comprehensive and aggressive manner than the rival Climate Security Act. With our atmospheric carbon levels rising every second, now is not the time to be timid. As David Elliot Cohen says, "the next few years are a kind of final exam for the human species. Does that big brain really work or not? It gave us the power to build coal-fired power plants and SUVs...but does it give us the power...to build a world that isn't bent on destruction?" Unfortunately, only time will tell. But one thing is certain: if we do nothing, the world as we know it will one day cease to exist.

Speaking on Special Occasions

OVERVIEW AND LEARNING OBJECTIVES

Ceremonial Speaking in a Free Society

16.1 Discuss the role of ceremonial speaking in a free society.

Social Values in Ceremonial Speaking

16.2 Explain how ceremonial speeches define and reinforce social values.

The Forms of Ceremonial Speech

16.3 Identify and describe different types of ceremonial speeches.

Style and Delivery in Ceremonial Speaking

16.4 Define *eloquence* and discuss the importance of style and delivery in ceremonial speaking.

At some point in your life, you will be asked to deliver a ceremonial speech—the type of speech that the ancient Greeks called epideictic. This is the sort of speech you deliver when you pay tribute to someone, present or accept an award, or mark some special occasion or event. Ceremonial speeches are often associated with culturally significant occasions: weddings, funerals, graduations, awards banquets, conferences and conventions, or major political events. We also deliver ceremonial speeches to mark important dates in our history, such as Memorial Day or the Fourth of July.

Traditionally, ceremonial speeches were considered less "serious" than informative or persuasive speeches. In Aristotle's *Rhetoric*, for example, epideictic speeches were treated as mere "display," a sort of "poetic" speech in which speakers showed off their speaking skills but did not say anything of great political or social significance. According to Aristotle, epideictic speakers engaged in "praise and blame," and they focused on the present rather than the past or the future. Some have interpreted this to mean that the audiences for such speeches act as mere "observers," appreciating the "skill of the orator" but not making important judgments or collective decisions. In this view of epideictic speech, the speaker aims not to elicit action but only to influence "the general attitude of the audience toward a particular person or behavior."[1]

Today, we recognize that ceremonial speaking plays an important role in defining and sustaining our civic culture. More than a mere display of the speaker's skill, ceremonial speeches shape our collective identity, remind us of our history and traditions, and imagine the world "as it ought to be rather than as it is."[2] Epideictic speeches bring us together as members of a community, and they remind us of our responsibilities as citizens. Honoring our heroes and commemorating important events, ceremonial speeches articulate and reinforce important social values and strengthen the bonds that unite us. In short, ceremonial speeches help sustain our civic culture.

We begin this chapter by reflecting on the role of ceremonial speaking in a free society. Identifying four important functions of ceremonial speaking, we examine how epideictic speeches remind us of our heritage, celebrate our heroes, identify important social values, and give us inspiration and encouragement. Then we will consider in more detail the role of ceremonial speeches in articulating and reinforcing social values. In the third section of the chapter, we will review the wide variety of epideictic speeches we encounter in everyday life, ranging from brief speeches of introduction to historic inaugural and keynote addresses. Finally, we will discuss the importance of language and delivery in ceremonial speaking, reflecting on what it means to be *eloquent* and offering some tips for writing and delivering ceremonial speeches.

CEREMONIAL SPEAKING IN A FREE SOCIETY

16.1 Discuss the role of ceremonial speaking in a free society.

Preview. *Ceremonial speeches are often presented on formal occasions and may be associated with important cultural rituals. Through ceremonial speeches, we remember the past, honor our heroes, celebrate shared beliefs and values, and offer inspiration and encouragement.*

Speeches given on ceremonial occasions are rich in symbolic content. They help define who we are as a people and bind us together as members of a group, community, or nation. As we honor our heroes, pay tribute to those we love or have lost, or celebrate our accomplishments, we remind ourselves of our shared history and traditions. We articulate and reinforce our shared beliefs and values and find inspiration and encouragement to take on new challenges. Ceremonial speeches comfort us, inspire us, and reinforce our faith in ourselves and in one another. Ceremonial speeches may be ritualistic and symbolic, but in some ways that makes them even more important than other types of speeches.

Remembering the Past

In 1863, Abraham Lincoln pledged in his Gettysburg Address that the world would "never forget" the soldiers who "gave the last full measure of devotion" to assure that "government of the people, by the people, for the people" would not "perish from the earth." A century and a half later, New York mayor Rudy Giuliani, in an address to the 2004 Republican National Convention in New York, recalled that sunny September morning when he looked up and saw smoke pouring out of the World Trade Center—and realized that the world had changed forever. Giuliani mourned those who had died in the "worst attack in our history," and he pledged to never forget the scene he had witnessed on that fateful day: the twin towers engulfed in "the flames of hell" as people jumped to their deaths. In just those few seconds, Giuliani recognized that we were "facing something that we had never, ever faced before": a new "creed of terrorism" aimed not only at killing Americans but also at destroying our culture and way of life.[3] Like Lincoln in his Gettysburg address, Giuliani helped his listeners understand the historical significance of the moment, as well as its implications for the future. Never before had something like this happened, he suggested, and we had a duty to make sure that it never happened again.

Remembering historic events is more than mere ritual. When we remember the past, we come to a clearer understanding of ourselves and the challenges we face. We also look to the past for "lessons of history." In a variety of settings, ceremonial speakers recall past events to help define who we are, what we stand for, and where we are headed in the future.

Consider how just one historical event, the American Revolution, has supplied inspiration and guidance for generations of Americans. For the first generation of Americans, of course, the Revolution was a live memory, and for more than a decade large crowds gathered in Boston to commemorate an incident that took place on March 5, 1770: the so-called Boston Massacre. According to scholars, the Boston "massacre" was little more than a "barroom brawl" between "wharf-side rabble" and a few "surly" British soldiers. Yet between 1771 and 1783, some of the most famous orators in America came to Boston every year to reflect on the "massacre" and its "lessons."[4] Speaking on the fourth anniversary of the incident, for example, John Hancock, one of the signers of the Declaration of Independence, spoke about the threat posed by standing armies

In this famous engraving by Paul Revere, a British commander orders his troops to fire into a crowd of civilians in Boston. Historians doubt the accuracy of the depiction, but Revere's engraving, along with annual speeches commemorating the "massacre," helped inspire the American Revolution.

in a free society and declared: "[L]et our misfortunes teach posterity to guard against such evils for the future."[5]

During the Civil War, Abraham Lincoln also drew inspiration from the Revolution. Lincoln began his famous Gettysburg Address by referring to the founding and reminding his audience of the principles that more than 360,000 union soldiers died for during that bloody conflict: "Fourscore and seven years ago our fathers brought forth on this continent a new nation, conceived in liberty, and dedicated to the proposition that all men are created equal." After the war, a progressive Southerner, Henry Grady, also recalled the Revolution but for a different purpose: to urge Northerners to forget the "Old South" and embrace the "New South" of "union and freedom." As Grady reminded his audience, both Northerners and Southerners "were lost in the storm of the first Revolution," and out of that storm was born the "American citizen," who taught the whole world about the blessings of democracy.[6]

Today, we still invoke the Revolution as the source of our ideals and inspiration. Yet so, too, do we remember a long list of other historical events that have shaped our character and purposes as a nation: the Civil War, the abolition of slavery, the Great Depression, two world wars, the Cuban Missile Crisis, and the assassinations of John F. Kennedy and Martin Luther King Jr., to name just a few. Many of those memories are painful, but they serve as important reminders. When speakers urge us to "Remember the Alamo" or the sacrifices of D-Day, they hope to inspire respect for our men and women in uniform. When they recall building the Panama Canal or landing a man on the moon, they hope to rekindle our "can-do" spirit and inspire us to take on new challenges.

For today's generation, of course, the terrorist attacks of September 11, 2001, represent an important public memory. Already that day has been commemorated in countless ceremonial speeches, ranging from eulogies and dedications to keynote and commencement addresses. Whatever the occasion, the events of 9/11 have become a fertile source of "lessons"—both positive and negative—about the principles and ideals that define us as a nation. In the years to come, 9/11 will continue to both sadden and inspire, as speakers invoke memories of that fateful day in a variety of ceremonial settings.

Honoring Heroes

Part of remembering the past is celebrating our heroes. In honoring our heroes, we emphasize themes of *character* and *personal virtue*, hoping to inspire others by holding up role models worth emulating. In praising our heroes, we remind ourselves of the ideals that define the life well lived.

Some of our heroes are "larger than life," while others are ordinary people—our parents, teachers, neighbors, or friends. But whomever we count as a hero, we honor their achievements, invite them to share their wisdom with us, and mourn them when they die. Honoring our heroes allows us to speak about the personal characteristics we admire and to reflect on the social values we share as a community. Like remembering the past, honoring our heroes is an educational act, illuminating the lessons to be learned from their lives.

Some of the most famous speeches in our history have been eulogies to our national heroes. Campaigning for the Democratic presidential nomination in 1968, for example, Robert F. Kennedy delivered an impromptu eulogy to Dr. Martin Luther King Jr. just moments after learning that King had been assassinated in Memphis, Tennessee. After sharing the news with his predominantly African-American audience, Kennedy summarized, in but a single sentence, the essence of King's "dream": "Martin Luther King dedicated his life to love and to justice between fellow human beings." Next, he elaborated on the lesson to be learned from King's life: "What we need in the United States is not division; what we need in the United States is not hatred; what we need in the United States is not violence and lawlessness, but…love and wisdom, and compassion toward one another, and a feeling of justice toward those who still suffer within our country, whether they be white or whether they be black." Finally, Kennedy urged his audience to rededicate themselves to the ancient ideals King championed: "Let us dedicate ourselves to what the Greeks wrote so many years ago: to tame the savageness of man and make gentle the life of this world. Let us dedicate ourselves to that, and say a prayer for our country and for our people."[7]

Over the course of American history, ceremonial speakers have celebrated a remarkable array of heroes: presidents, explorers, military heroes, movie stars, great writers, and popular musicians. We still honor the founders of our nation, of course—George Washington, Thomas Jefferson, and Benjamin Franklin, among others. We also honor many of the presidents who came later: Lincoln, Roosevelt, and Kennedy, to name just a few. Yet ceremonial speakers have also paid tribute to philanthropists such as Andrew Carnegie, great thinkers and writers such as Einstein and Harriet Beecher Stowe, and successful entrepreneurs from Henry Ford to Bill Gates and Steve Jobs. Mother Teresa has been honored for her charitable work, and aviation pioneer Amelia Earhart for her courage and determination. Even controversial figures have sometimes found redemption in ceremonial speeches. Although she was widely criticized in her own day, for example, we now honor Susan B. Anthony for her tireless efforts to win the right to vote for women.

Occasionally, we even elevate ordinary citizens to the status of national heroes. In his 1982 State of the Union address, for example, President Ronald Reagan introduced the nation to a government worker named Lenny Skutnik, who had helped rescue people from a jetliner that had crashed into the Potomac River. "We don't have to turn to our history books for heroes," Reagan began. "They're all around us." Reagan then introduced Skutnik, who was sitting in the audience:

> Just two weeks ago, in the midst of a terrible tragedy on the Potomac, we saw again the spirit of American heroism at its finest—the heroism of dedicated rescue workers saving crash victims from icy waters. We saw the heroism of one of our young government employees, Lenny Skutnik, who, when he saw a woman lose her grip on the helicopter line, dived into the water and dragged her to safety.[8]

On January 15, 2009, another ordinary American became an overnight hero. After his Airbus A320 struck a flock of birds and lost both engines, US Airways pilot Chesley B. "Sully" Sullenberger skillfully landed the disabled jetliner on the Hudson River and then made sure that all 155 people onboard made it to rescue boats. New York governor David Paterson proclaimed it the "Miracle on the Hudson," and New York City mayor Michael Bloomberg praised Sullenberger for a "masterful job." Before workers could even lift the 81-ton plane out of the river, Sullenberger "vaulted to fame nationwide and across cyberspace," with more than 10,000 people joining his Facebook fan club in a single day.[9] Later, he was honored with invitations to President Barack Obama's swearing-in ceremony and to the new president's speech before a joint session of Congress on February 24, 2009.[10]

Honoring our heroes is not just a meaningless ritual. In doing so, we define the personal virtues and social values that we admire as a culture, and we create role models for others, especially young people. Occasionally, of course, we also recall notorious or infamous figures in history, such as Adolf Hitler or Osama bin Laden. In doing so, however, our mission remains essentially the same: to teach important lessons about personal character, morality, or civic virtue.

Celebrating Shared Beliefs and Values

Chesley B. "Sully" Sullenberger and the Airbus A320 jetliner that he crash-landed on the Hudson River in New York City on January 15, 2009.

Ceremonial speeches articulate and reinforce common beliefs and values. As you think about delivering an epideictic speech, you should ask: What is the occasion for this speech? What defines the audience as a group? Which of the group's victories or accomplishments inspire the most pride? What do they believe most deeply, and what principles do they cherish? These questions may lead you to an inventory of beliefs and values shared by your audience and, then, to the major themes of your speech. The shared beliefs and values you identify may be philosophical or practical, religious or political, social or economic. But whatever their nature, they reflect the audience's collective understanding of themselves.

In their inaugural addresses, U.S. presidents typically emphasize those beliefs and values that unite *all* Americans, regardless of party. In his celebrated inaugural address, for example, John F. Kennedy identified "freedom" as just such a value and embraced the responsibility of "defending freedom in its hour of maximum danger."[11] Similarly, Dwight D. Eisenhower concluded his second inaugural address by reemphasizing the themes of freedom and peace. Like Kennedy, Eisenhower articulated the ideals that he believed were shared by all Americans: "May the light of freedom, coming to all darkened lands, flame brightly—until at last the darkness is no more. May the turbulence of our age yield to a true time of peace, when men and nations shall share a life that honors the dignity of each, the brotherhood of all."[12]

Other ceremonial speeches revolve around the beliefs and values of smaller groups or subcultures, or they emphasize values associated with a specific occasion. In delivering the keynote address to a conference of newspaper editors, for example, a speaker might celebrate our constitutional guarantee of a free press, while commencement addresses invariably stress the value of education. Similarly, it may be appropriate for a minister to praise Jesus in a sermon before an audience of believers. In addressing a religiously diverse audience of civic leaders, however, the same preacher might celebrate the constitutional separation of church and state.

It is important to recognize that the shared beliefs and values of one group may be controversial or rejected altogether within another community. In a keynote address to the National Organization for Women, for example, one might expect to hear a celebration of feminist values, whereas speakers before a more conservative group may praise traditional family values. By the same token, the beliefs and values celebrated in some types of ceremonial speeches may be wholly inappropriate in others. In a humorous after-dinner speech, for example, one might "roast" the honoree by recalling some embarrassing flub or failure. At that same person's funeral, however, it might be considered bad taste to recall such an incident.

Offering Inspiration and Encouragement

Watch the Video
"Elegy for a Special Person" at
MyCommunicationLab

When speakers present awards, pay tribute to individuals, speak at commencements, or deliver keynote addresses, they offer encouragement and inspiration to their listeners. In effect, they deliver motivational speeches. A life well lived provides an example for all of us. Thus, the speaker accepting an award might suggest to the audience: "You can do this, too! I have confidence in you." Similarly, the commencement speaker does not simply congratulate the graduates, but encourages them to continue striving—to "reach for the stars." Even a eulogy can be inspirational, reminding us that life is short and inspiring us to live life to the fullest. Whatever the specific type of speech, the goal remains the same: to inspire and encourage people to be good citizens, do good work, and "give back" to their communities.

Occasionally, speakers are called on to sustain people's morale through difficult times. That is precisely what British prime minister Winston Churchill did in one of his best-known speeches during World War II, an address to the House of Commons on June 4, 1940. In this famous speech, Churchill reported on a "colossal military disaster"—the evacuation of Dunkirk, in which French and British forces were driven off the European continent by the advancing German army. Churchill also mourned the loss of 30,000 men and warned of an impending invasion of the British homeland. Yet pledging to "defend to the death" his "native soil," Churchill reassured his fellow citizens that their cause would prevail and promised a vigorous response to the Nazi threat wherever it might appear— whether in France or in Britain, whether on land, in the air, and on the open seas. Projecting total confidence, Churchill famously declared, "we shall fight on the beaches, we shall fight on the landing grounds, we shall fight in the fields and in the streets, we shall fight in the hills; we shall never surrender...."[13] And in Churchill's pledge to "never surrender," the British people not only found the strength to survive but also the courage to regroup, rally, and fight on to ultimate victory. Churchill's ringing declaration of his nation's determination and resolve demonstrated the power of words to sustain public morale through even the most trying of times—and to change the course of history.

SOCIAL VALUES IN CEREMONIAL SPEAKING

Preview. *Ceremonial speeches do more than merely entertain us. They perform important educational and cultural functions. Most important, they reinforce the shared social values that define us as a community. Sometimes ceremonial speeches affirm traditional values and work to preserve things as they are. Yet ceremonial speeches can also be powerful agents of change, challenging prevailing values or pointing to contradictions between our ideals and our actions.*

16.2 Explain how ceremonial speeches define and reinforce social values.

In an informative speech, you hope to teach your audience something new. In a persuasive speech, you aim to change your audience's beliefs or opinions. In a ceremonial speech, however, your purpose typically is to articulate and reinforce *existing* social values. As the speaker on a ceremonial occasion, you aim to give eloquent expression to the beliefs and values *already* held by the audience.

Consider, for example, how a eulogy differs from an informative or persuasive speech. In delivering a eulogy, we may safely assume that the audience knows the deceased; people generally do not attend the funerals of strangers. So there's no need for an informative speech. Nor does the eulogist typically persuade, trying to convince us that the dearly departed was not such a bad fellow after all. Instead, the eulogist's job is to give voice to the shared feelings of love and loss among family and friends. Put another way, the eulogist tries to "put into words" the feelings already held by the audience.

Ceremonial speeches supply the "glue" that holds our communities together. Even in ancient times, when ceremonial speeches were viewed as a kind of artistic performance, it was recognized that they also served important educational and cultural functions. In Greek funeral orations, for example, listeners were called on to imitate the virtues of the deceased.[14] The Roman rhetorician Quintilian viewed teaching itself as a form of epideictic rhetoric.[15] Today, we recognize even more clearly the political, social, and cultural importance of ceremonial speaking. In a wide variety of contexts, ceremonial speakers not only help us celebrate special occasions but also remind us of the values, traditions, and aspirations we share as a people. They also work to define our collective identities, defining what it means to be an American or a member of some other group with distinct social values. Sometimes they even make implicit political arguments by honoring people associated with particular ideas and policies. In those cases, epideictic speeches become something of a hybrid form, containing characteristics of a deliberative or policy speech as well.

Some argue that ceremonial speeches are inherently conservative because they articulate and reinforce *existing* social values.[16] Historically, however, ceremonial speeches have been powerful agents of change, invoking "shared values as a basis for promoting a vision of what could be."[17] That certainly was true of the most famous ceremonial speech in U.S. history: Martin Luther King Jr.'s "I Have a Dream" speech. It is also true of many other ceremonial speeches, ranging from abolitionist and suffrage speeches in the nineteenth century to contemporary speeches marking Earth Day or Gay Pride Week.

One of the most famous ceremonial speeches in our history was a Fourth of July speech delivered in 1852 by a former slave named Frederick Douglass. Calling slavery "the great sin and shame of America," Douglass chose to mark Independence Day with an ironic speech highlighting the contradictions between our revolutionary ideals and the institution of slavery. Posing a famous question, Douglass called attention to the hypocrisy of a nation founded on the principle of liberty, yet built on the labor of slaves:

> What to the American slave is your Fourth of July? I answer, a day that reveals to him…the gross injustice and cruelty to which he is the constant victim. To him, your celebration is a sham; your boasted liberty, an unholy license; your national greatness, swelling vanity; your sounds of rejoicing are empty and heartless; your denunciations of tyrants, brass-fronted impudence; your shouts of liberty and equality, hollow mockery; your prayers and hymns,…are to him mere bombast, fraud, deception, impiety, and hypocrisy—a thin veil to cover up crimes which would disgrace a nation of savages. There is not a nation on the earth guilty of practices more shocking and bloody than are the people of these United States, at this very hour.[18]

Calling on the nation to live up to its professed ideals, Douglass's speech illustrates how ceremonial speeches can be powerful agents of social change.

On occasion, ceremonial speeches even provide an opportunity for groups or communities to reassess their *own* traditions, beliefs, or social values. In a speech to the National Association for the Advancement of Colored People (NAACP) in 2004, for example, actor Bill Cosby asked his audience to honor the pioneers of the civil rights movement by facing up to problems still plaguing the African American community, including the breakdown of traditional families, teen pregnancies, and high drop-out rates among black students. The speech drew criticism from black leaders who complained that Cosby was blaming the victims of racism and failed governmental policies. But Cosby refused to apologize, accusing his critics of trying to hide the black community's 'dirty laundry.'"[21]

THE FORMS OF CEREMONIAL SPEECH

16.3 Identify and describe different types of ceremonial speeches.

Preview. *There are many different kinds of ceremonial speeches: introductions, presentation and acceptance speeches, welcome and farewell speeches, commemoration and commencement speeches, tributes and eulogies, inaugural and keynote addresses, after-dinner speeches, and even some sermons. Each type of ceremonial speech is unique, but all share the same basic mission: to reflect on the significance of a special occasion and to give voice to the shared beliefs and values of the audience.*

What does a commencement address have in common with a eulogy? A keynote address with an after-dinner speech? The answer, as we have already suggested, is that they are all ceremonial speeches, or what the ancient Greeks called *epideictic*. They are all speeches delivered on special occasions, when people gather to honor other people or to celebrate some special anniversary or event. Those special occasions vary widely, of course, so there are important differences between, say, an inaugural address and a eulogy. Yet all ceremonial speeches have the same basic mission: to reflect on the larger meaning of the occasion and to "put into words" the shared beliefs and values of the audience.

The Speech of Introduction

The speech of introduction sometimes sounds like an informative speech, introducing us to an unknown speaker. More commonly, it celebrates the achievements of a well-known speaker who has been invited to speak on a special occasion.

Many people who introduce other speakers underestimate the importance of their role. They prepare very little, hastily scratching down a few notes or quickly underlining a few points on the speaker's résumé. Some cop out completely, saying, "I'm delighted to welcome our speaker tonight, a person who needs no introduction." Others go to the opposite extreme, giving a lengthy introduction to a person already quite familiar to the audience. When introducing other speakers, keep in mind that your purpose is to *introduce* another speaker, not to steal the spotlight yourself. You should never take away from the principal speaker's time or try to upstage his or her message.

The effective speech of introduction should do three things. First, it should extend a genuinely warm welcome to the speaker. Second, it should reinforce the speaker's ethos by emphasizing key educational or professional accomplishments. Finally, it should provide listeners with any information they may need to understand or process the speech. At the very least, the person introducing the main speaker should mention the topic or title of the speech, and the introductory speaker also might indicate whether the speaker will take questions following the address.

Here are just a few tips for preparing a good speech of introduction:

- *Do your homework.* The speech of introduction should be well researched. Study any materials the speaker has provided, such as a biographical sketch or résumé. Call and chat with the speaker if you lack information, and make sure to ask about the topic or title of the speech.
- *Look for connections between the speaker and the audience.* The speaker you introduce may have accomplished many things. You cannot cover them all. You will want to highlight information that would be important for your group to know. What does the speaker have in common with this particular audience? What values do they share? If you make these connections, you will help the speaker establish common ground with the audience.
- *Stay focused on the speaker.* Your purpose should be to introduce the speaker, not focus attention on yourself. Some people end up sharing stories about how they met the speaker or talk about their common experiences. It may be fine to share a brief anecdote, but do not get carried away.

Watch the Video
"Richard Nixon's
Resignation" at
MyCommunicationLab

Welcome and Farewell Addresses

Comings and goings do not, under ordinary circumstances, inspire speech making. When you come back from your vacation, you do not expect your neighbor to deliver a speech. When the president of the United States visits another country, however, we *do* expect speeches, both on his arrival and as he prepares to depart. In addition, politicians and other prominent people often give "farewell addresses" at the end of their careers, reflecting on their years of service or giving advice to their successors.

Welcome addresses are not just for world leaders. They are also common at conventions, festivals, trade shows, and other large public gatherings. When a college or university hosts an academic conference, for example, it is common for a dean or even the president of the university to offer a few words of welcome. Similarly, when a city attracts a major business conference or trade show, the mayor or some other local official typically welcomes the group. Generally, the task of the speaker in such situations is simple: on behalf of the hosts, convey a sincere welcome. When welcoming a group, you also might offer tips for making the most out of their visit. The mayor's welcome may mention some local attractions, for example, while a conference organizer might preview some highlights of the upcoming meeting.

Farewell addresses are sometimes short, simple expressions of gratitude. Yet even short farewells can be powerfully moving. On July 4, 1939, for example, one of the greatest players in the history of baseball, Lou Gehrig, delivered a farewell address that was barely 250 words long, but it said everything that needed to be said to the 62,000 fans at Yankee Stadium. Struck down in the prime of his career by amyotrophic lateral sclerosis (ALS), a rare degenerative disease later named *Lou Gehrig's disease*, the all-star player began by mentioning his "bad break"—a reference to the terrible disease that would take his life just two years later. The all-star player famously described himself as a lucky man, thanked all who had made it possible for him to play professional baseball, and fought back tears as he concluded by recalling his positive experiences during seventeen years in the big leagues. When he was finished, there was 'not a dry eye in Yankee Stadium,' and the speech remains "one of the most poignant and emotional moments in the history of American sports."[22]

Not nearly so sentimental was Dwight D. Eisenhower's famous "farewell address" on January 17, 1961. Stepping down after two terms as president, Eisenhower took to the airwaves "with a message of leave-taking and farewell," including just a "few final thoughts" about matters of politics and national security. Those "few thoughts" turned into a somber and famous warning about "the acquisition of unwarranted influence" by what he labeled the "military-industrial complex." Warning his fellow citizens against becoming "captive" to the "scientific-technological elite," Eisenhower worried out loud about how the technology of war was outpacing human understanding. He then closed with a hope and a prayer: that "in the goodness of time, all peoples will come to live together in a peace guaranteed by the binding force of mutual respect and love."[23]

Not all welcome and farewell addresses are so historic or philosophical, of course. Many consist of little more than a few brief remarks, thanking a visitor for coming or bidding a fond farewell. Like all ceremonial speeches, however, welcome and farewell addresses should be carefully prepared and adapted to the particular audience and situation in which they are given.

Presentation and Acceptance Speeches

Award ceremonies may or may not be occasions for formal speeches. Nowadays, most presentation and acceptance speeches consist of a few brief remarks, with presenters announcing the winner of the award and the winner simply thanking the presenter and perhaps a few other people. On a few occasions, however, an award ceremony calls for a longer, more substantive speech. If you someday win the Nobel Peace Prize, for example, you will be expected to deliver a formal speech before a distinguished audience of royalty and Nobel laureates in Oslo, Norway. With the king and queen of Norway and several hundred guests in attendance, you will express your gratitude and reflect on the larger significance of the Nobel Prize.

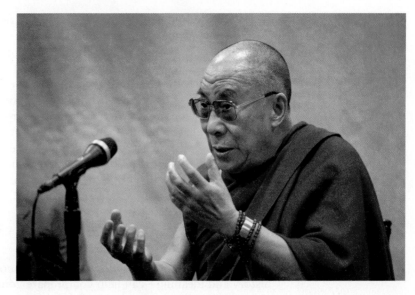

His Holiness the Dalai Lama, winner of the 1989 Nobel Prize for Peace.

Watch the Video "2007 Clarion Award, Kevin Spacey" at **MyCommunicationLab**

That is precisely what His Holiness the Dalai Lama did in his Nobel Prize acceptance speech in 1989. Like most acceptance speeches, the Dalai Lama's address began with an expression of gratitude and humility: "I am very happy to be here with you today to receive the Nobel Prize for Peace. I feel honored, humbled and deeply moved that you should give this important prize to a simple monk from Tibet." Then, he interpreted the award itself as "recognition of the true value of altruism, love, compassion and non-violence." Accepting the award "on behalf of the oppressed everywhere," the Dalai Lama spoke of the injustices against his own Tibetan people and his determination, despite their suffering, to see that their "long struggle" remain "non-violent and free of hatred." Transcending that immediate conflict, he then articulated the broader, more universal principles that motivated his efforts to build a more peaceful world:

> I believe all suffering is caused by ignorance. People inflict pain on others in the selfish pursuit of their happiness or satisfaction. Yet true happiness comes from a sense of brotherhood and sisterhood. We need to cultivate a universal responsibility for one another and the planet we share. Although I have found my own Buddhist religion helpful in generating love and compassion,... I am convinced that everyone can develop a good heart and a sense of universal responsibility with or without religion.[24]

Generally, the formula for *presenting* an award is simple: introduce yourself and your purpose in speaking, say a few words about the significance or history of the award itself, and then extol the virtues of the recipient. Sometimes the winner will be known in advance; on other occasions, you may reveal the recipient in your speech. In either case, your goal is to honor the recipient and give expression to the social values associated with the award.

When *accepting* an award, you want to convey a sincere sense of gratitude but also humility, perhaps by acknowledging the support of others who contributed to your success. This does not mean that you should read a long list of names, including everyone who has ever done you a favor. But you do want to thank those most responsible for your moment in the limelight—a teacher or a coach who prepared you for a competition, perhaps, or a partner or spouse who supported you. Finally, you might acknowledge the deeper meaning of the award, using language that fits the dignity of the occasion. Of course, you also want to show that you genuinely appreciate the honor.

Whether presenting or accepting an award, it is important that you do the following:

- *Learn as much as you can about the award.* Knowing about the award—its history and meaning—can help you prepare your speech. If you are the first person to present or receive the award, you may want to note that fact. If other people have received the award previously, you may want to acknowledge one or two of those previous winners.
- *Plan and practice your speech in advance.* A person asked to *present* an award typically prepares a speech in advance, but some people think it is wrong or even "bad luck" to prepare to *accept* an award. That may explain why we hear so many bad speeches at the Academy Awards! Generally, however, you will be told in advance if you have won some award and whether you are expected to speak at the awards ceremony. In that case, you definitely should prepare the speech ahead of time. Even if you will not know whether you have won an award until the ceremony itself, you can still sketch out some brief remarks—just in case you *do* win. Then, if you win, you can deliver those remarks extemporaneously, without pulling notes or a manuscript out of your pocket. After all, you do not want to look *too* prepared, as if you fully *expected* to win!
- *Make your tone and language fit the occasion.* Presentation and acceptance speeches are usually delivered in formal settings, and your language should reflect that. Your tone should be dignified and sincere. This is a time to speak formally, yet "from the heart."
- *Make your speech brief.* Most presentation and acceptance speeches should be very brief, probably no longer than a minute or two. In many settings where awards are presented, there is other business to conduct, perhaps even a keynote speaker. So a brief yet carefully crafted speech is usually expected and appreciated.

Commemoration and Commencement Speeches

A commemorative speech marks an important date or event, whereas a commencement address celebrates one specific type of event: a graduation ceremony. Commemorative speeches are heard on a wide variety of occasions, ranging from national holidays, to dates with special significance for particular groups, to personally significant occasions, such as birthdays or wedding anniversaries. We may hear a commemorative speech on the Fourth of July, or we may hear one marking Black History Month. We still hear speeches commemorating the bombing of Pearl Harbor on December 7, 1941—a "date which will live in infamy," as FDR predicted. We also hear speeches commemorating more positive events, such as the Wright Brothers' first flight at Kitty Hawk or astronaut Neil Armstrong's first step on the moon. Some people reserve formal commemorative speeches for public holidays, while others may view their own birthday or retirement party as an occasion for speech making. People still toast the bride and groom at wedding receptions, although toasts typically consist of a few impromptu remarks rather than prepared speeches.

The commencement address, of course, is a special kind of commemorative speech. Delivered at graduation ceremonies, commencement speeches have acquired an unfortunate reputation for being dull, predictable, and lacking in substance. Indeed, graduation speakers often joke about the insignificance of commencement speeches and promise to keep their remarks brief. Speaking to the graduates of Howard University in 1994, for example, former secretary of state Colin Powell cited a make-believe poll on student attitudes toward commencement addresses and then joked about how most people forget their commencement speaker:

> The real challenge…of being a commencement speaker…is trying to figure out how long you're gonna talk. If you ask the students, the answer is very, very simple. Talk for about four minutes and then sit down. Polls have been taken that show that 10 years after the event, 80 percent of all graduating students don't have a clue who their commencement speaker was. Well, you ain't gonna do that to me. The name is Powell, P-o-w-e-l-l.[25]

Despite their bad reputation, commencement addresses have played an important role in American history. Indeed, some of the most famous speeches in our history have been delivered at graduation ceremonies. With Hitler's armies overrunning Europe in 1940, for example, Franklin Delano Roosevelt used a commencement address at the University of Virginia to condemn the invasion of France by Mussolini's Italian fascists. "On this tenth day of June 1940," the president solemnly intoned, "the hand that held the dagger has stuck it into the back of its neighbor."[26] President John F. Kennedy delivered another historic commencement address at American University on June 10, 1963. Speaking at the height of the Cold War, Kennedy used the occasion to reflect on the horrors of modern war. Kennedy's address had a remarkable effect on world opinion and is still considered one of the greatest speeches in U.S. history. Far from a series of platitudes about the "challenges of life," Kennedy's speech was a thoughtful reflection on the insanity of war in the atomic age:

> I speak of peace because of the new face of war. Total war makes no sense in an age where great powers can maintain large and relatively invulnerable nuclear forces and refuse to surrender without resort to those forces. It makes no sense in an age where a single nuclear weapon contains almost ten times the explosive force delivered by all the allied air forces in the Second World War. It makes no sense in an age when the deadly poisons

produced by a nuclear exchange would be carried by wind and water and soil and seed to the far corners of the globe and to generations yet unborn.

Today the expenditure of billions of dollars every year on weapons acquired for the purpose of making sure we never need them is essential to the keeping of peace. But surely the acquisition of such idle stockpiles—which can only destroy and never create—is not the only, much less the most efficient, means of assuring peace....I realize the pursuit of peace is not as dramatic as the pursuit of war, and frequently the words of the pursuers fall on deaf ears. But we have no more urgent task.[27]

Not all commencement speeches address such weighty and serious topics, of course. Most focus on the immediate event—the graduation ceremony—and offer advice on how to find success and happiness in life. Like all commemorative speeches, commencement addresses should reflect on the larger significance of the day and offer inspiration and guidance. But they are also part of a celebration and should, as a rule, be positive and upbeat in tone.

Tributes and Eulogies

Watch the Video "Tribute to a Mentor, Mildred Ball" at **MyCommunicationLab**

We commemorate events, but we pay tribute to *people*. And, of course, there are no more important speeches than those with which we celebrate our heroes and honor our dead. In paying tribute to people—living or dead—we both reinforce our shared social values and define the meaning of *virtue* and *character*. By recognizing the special talents, unique accomplishments, and extraordinary contributions of people we admire, we define the life well lived and create role models for the next generation.

Television star Oprah Winfrey speaking at a memorial service for Rosa Parks in Washington, DC, on October 31, 2005.

Tributes to living people are delivered on many occasions, such as award ceremonies, birthdays, anniversaries, and retirement celebrations. Whatever the occasion, the purpose remains the same: to highlight the person's unique contributions or talents and to praise him or her as an individual. In a speech honoring composer John Williams at the Kennedy Center for the Performing Arts, for example, filmmaker Steven Spielberg called Williams a "national treasure" and "as American as apple pie."[28] At a White House ceremony, Secretary of Defense Donald Rumsfeld praised a very different man in similar terms, calling economist Milton S. Friedman "a rare talent—indeed, a talent to be treasured." Praising this champion of free markets for "unleashing the power of human freedom," Rumsfeld marked Friedman's 90th birthday by celebrating how he changed "the course of history."[29]

Funerals are typically private affairs, with eulogists mourning the loss and giving voice to the pain and grief of loved ones. When famous people die, however, eulogists typically say more, proclaiming the deceased an inspiration, perhaps even a national "hero." Speaking at the funeral of civil rights pioneer Rosa Parks, for example, Oprah Winfrey recalled how her father had told her about "this colored woman who had refused to give up her seat," and she imagined that Parks must have been "really big"— "at least a hundred feet tall." When she actually met Parks, of course, she was in for a surprise. "Here was this petite, almost delicate lady who was the personification of grace and goodness." At that meeting, Winfrey thanked Parks for all she had done for African Americans, and she thanked her again at her funeral, crediting Parks with all that she had achieved in life: "That day that you refused to give up your seat on the bus, you, Sister Rosa, changed the trajectory of my life and the lives of so many other people in the world."[30]

The death of a president or other political leader likewise tends to inspire eulogies that go beyond simple mourning. Typically, eulogies for political leaders urge us to honor their legacy by continuing their work. In a speech to Congress two weeks after the assassination of President Kennedy, for example, Lyndon Johnson mourned Kennedy's death, lamenting that the "greatest leader of our time" had been "struck down by the foulest deed of our time." Giving voice to millions of Americans, he added: "No words are sad enough to express our sense of loss." Yet then Johnson declared "let us continue," repeating the phrase several times and declaring it our "duty" to carry on Kennedy's crusade for civil rights and world peace. He concluded by assuring his listeners that "John F. Kennedy did not live or die in vain."[31]

Inaugural and Keynote Addresses

Inaugural addresses are speeches we give upon assuming a new office or position. Inaugural addresses may be delivered by newly appointed corporate CEOs, incoming officers of private clubs or fraternal associations, or newly elected politicians. The best-known inaugural addresses, of course, are delivered every four years by the president of the United States. Indeed, a handful of presidential inaugural addresses—those of Thomas Jefferson, Abraham Lincoln, Franklin Delano Roosevelt, and John F. Kennedy—are counted among the greatest speeches in U.S. history.[32] Like all inaugural addresses, presidential inaugurals

Watch the **Video**
"Inauguration Speech:
Dwight D. Eisenhower" at
MyCommunicationLab

perform certain rituals of office taking, such as articulating one's "vision" of the future. Yet presidential inaugurals also perform other political functions, such as reunifying the nation after a divisive campaign and laying the groundwork for the new president's legislative agenda.

The power of an inaugural address to build unity after a divisive election is perhaps best illustrated by Thomas Jefferson's celebrated inaugural address in 1801. During the election of 1800, sharp partisan divisions emerged for the first time in U.S. history. The Federalists, led by John Adams and Alexander Hamilton, favored a strong central government. The Republicans, led by Jefferson, wanted government to play a more limited role. Both parties claimed to be the true heirs to the American Revolution, and both suspected the other of conspiratorial designs, even disloyalty. The campaign was one of the most bitter in all of American history; some doubted that the Federalists would relinquish power peacefully. When he delivered his inaugural address, few expected Jefferson to reach out to the Federalists in a spirit of reconciliation. Yet he did just that, calling the election a mere "contest of opinion" and declaring that, *of course*, all would now "unite in common efforts for the common good." Noting that "every difference of opinion is not a difference of principle," Jefferson then delivered the most famous lines of the address: "We are all Republicans; we are all Federalists. If there be any among us who would wish to dissolve this Union or change its republican form, let them stand undisturbed as monuments of the safety with which error of opinion may be tolerated where reason is left free to combat it."[33]

Other inaugural addresses have been more like deliberative or policy speeches, sketching at least the broad outlines of the new president's agenda. In his first inaugural address, for example, Franklin D. Roosevelt proposed no detailed plan for combating the Great Depression, but he did promise "action, and action now." He then articulated the major aims of his New Deal policies: "put people to work," make better use of natural resources, support agriculture, stop foreclosures on homes and small farms, "drastically reduce" the costs of government, unify relief activities, and establish "national planning" and "supervision of all forms of transportation and of communications…that have a definitely public character."[34] Similarly, John F. Kennedy's inaugural address foreshadowed his administration's aggressive Cold War policies by sounding a metaphorical trumpet and calling his fellow Americans to "a long twilight struggle." Speaking as the voice of a "new generation" of Americans— "born in this century, tempered by war, disciplined by a hard and bitter peace, [and] proud of our ancient heritage"—Kennedy made clear his determination to defend freedom around the world: "Let every nation know, whether it wishes us well or ill, that we shall pay any price, bear any burden, meet any hardship, support any friend, oppose any foe to assure the survival and the success of liberty."[35]

Keynote addresses are featured speeches at meetings, conferences, or other formal gatherings. Keynote addresses typically give expression to the purposes and significance of the group and its gathering. The best-known keynote addresses, of course, are those delivered every four years at the presidential nominating conventions of the two major political parties. Although these keynotes have become increasingly partisan in recent years, they still include some of the most timeless and celebrated speeches in U.S. history.

One of the most memorable keynote addresses in our history is Texas congresswoman Barbara Jordan's speech to the 1976 Democratic National Convention in New York City. As an African-American woman, Jordan began by noting that, in the past, it would have been "most unusual for any national political party to ask a Barbara Jordan to deliver a keynote address." Thus, her very presence on the podium became, for Jordan, "evidence that the American Dream need not forever be deferred." The rest of the speech was a classic keynote address, articulating the ideals of the Democratic Party and celebrating the values shared by all Americans. In the wake of the Watergate scandal, Jordan also acknowledged people's skepticism toward government and called on her fellow politicians to accept responsibility for the problem. "We as public servants must set an example for the rest of the nation," she declared at a time of widespread political cynicism. "More is required...of public officials than slogans and hand-shakes and press releases....We must hold ourselves strictly accountable. We must provide the people with a vision of the future."[36]

You may never be elected president of the United States or address a national political convention, but you can emulate the spirit of the great inaugural and keynote addresses. Whether speaking as the new president of a local civic club or as the keynote speaker at a professional conference, your goal should be the same: to give eloquent expression to the shared beliefs and values of your group or community.

The After-Dinner Speech

Watch the Video
"Ignite Your Life" at
MyCommunicationLab

Sometimes epideictic speeches are delivered after lunch or dinner, perhaps at a business meeting or conference. Although after-dinner speeches are often entertaining, they also may address more serious topics. If Federal Reserve chair Ben Bernanke is asked to deliver an after-dinner speech, for example, people expect him to say something significant about the economy. In other situations, an after-dinner speaker may be asked to pay tribute to a person or to deliver something akin to a keynote address. In these situations, the speaker is also expected to say something substantive yet still be entertaining or perhaps even amusing.

Not surprisingly, after-dinner speeches can pose quite a challenge. Not only have audience members just eaten a meal, but they may also have been in meetings all day, with the dinner as their "reward." As a result, the after-dinner speaker must look for ways to enliven the speech, perhaps by telling anecdotes or stories or by delivering the speech in a more spontaneous and energetic style.

Humor, of course, is one way that speakers make after-dinner speeches more entertaining, but humor can be tricky. Some people seem to have a knack for telling amusing stories; others do not. Some seem to have good comic timing; others stumble over punch lines. The point is not that you should avoid humor in an after-dinner speech. But if you do aspire to be funny, you need to think carefully about what your audience may or may not find amusing.

Generally, an after-dinner speech should not be too long, perhaps no more than five or ten minutes. Stay in touch with how the audience is responding during the speech. Build your speech flexibly, so that you can cut some material during the speech if the audience appears to be losing interest. The most common complaint about an after-dinner speech is that it was too long. One rarely hears people complain that an after-dinner speech was too short!

Finally, keep in mind that audiences expect to walk away from an after-dinner speech with something to think about, remember, or talk about with others attending the event. Some after-dinner speeches might even provide the basis for further discussion and action. However much your audience may enjoy themselves, it is important that they also get something meaningful out of the speech. Even a humorous after-dinner speech can be used to communicate a serious message, as when we pay sincere tribute to somebody by "roasting" him or her at a banquet.

Sermons

Sermons and other religious speeches may or may not be epideictic addresses, depending on their purpose and audience. When we seek to convert somebody to our religion, we obviously are trying to persuade. But when we celebrate and reaffirm our audience's existing faith—when we "preach to the choir"—the sermon functions like other ceremonial speeches, reinforcing or strengthening existing beliefs and values.

The line between epideictic and persuasive speaking is sometimes blurred in sermons that urge believers to cleanse themselves of sin. In the early nineteenth century, for example, a revivalist preacher named Lyman Beecher delivered a series of famous sermons on the "evils of intemperance," elaborating on the "deleterious influence" of alcohol on both individuals and the nation. Most of Beecher's followers already agreed with him about the evils of alcohol. Yet tempted by sin, many still drank. So Beecher took it upon himself to warn the nation (in the metaphorical style of epideictic) that "our sun is fast setting" and that "the darkness of an endless night is closing in upon us." At one level, of course, Beecher was trying to persuade his flock not to drink. At another level, however, his sermons were simply reinforcing their existing beliefs, urging them to have the strength of their convictions and resist the temptation to drink.[37]

STYLE AND DELIVERY IN CEREMONIAL SPEAKING

16.4 Define *eloquence* and discuss the importance of style and delivery in ceremonial speaking.

Preview. *Speakers tend to sound more "poetic" on ceremonial occasions because they strive to give eloquent expression to the significance of the occasion and the shared social values of the audience. This emphasis on "eloquence" focuses more attention on the speaker's language. When preparing a ceremonial speech, you should choose your language carefully, using vivid language and figures of speech to create memorable images and a poetic rhythm and cadence. And because of the emphasis on style, most ceremonial speeches are delivered word-for-word from a manuscript.*

Throughout this chapter, we have emphasized how ceremonial speakers perform important educational and cultural functions, shaping listeners' identity as members of a community and reinforcing shared social values. Yet ceremonial speakers do more than honor our heroes or teach us about our traditions. They also *inspire* us with their eloquence, touching our hearts or motivating us to reaffirm our civic and cultural commitments. In Chapter 11, we discussed the resources of language, including some of the ways that you might make your language more lively and interesting. In the remainder of this chapter, we revisit that discussion of style, focusing on how you might exploit the resources of language to make your ceremonial speeches more memorable.

Vivid Language and Imagery

The difference between a dull and lifeless ceremonial speech and one that is inspirational and eloquent often boils down to the speaker's choice of words. As we noted in Chapter 10, one way to make your speech more lively and interesting is to strive for *vivid* language, or language that is specific and concrete and appeals to your listeners' physical senses. Specific, concrete words allow your audience to see, hear, smell, taste, or feel what you are talking about, and that sort of language can enhance the emotional impact of your speech. In the following passage, notice how former president Ronald Reagan used vivid, concrete language to re-create the scene on D-Day in 1944 as he commemorated the 40th anniversary of that fateful day in Pointe du Hoc, France:

> We stand on a lonely, windswept point on the northern shore of France. The air is soft, but 40 years ago at this moment, the air was dense with smoke and the cries of men, and the air was filled with the crack of rifle fire and the roar of cannon. At dawn, on the morning of the sixth of June, 1944, 225 Rangers jumped off the British landing craft and ran to the bottom of these cliffs. Their mission was one of the most difficult and daring of the invasion: to climb these sheer and desolate cliffs and take out the enemy guns...
>
> The Rangers looked up and saw the enemy soldiers...shooting down at them with machine guns and throwing grenades. And the American Rangers began to climb. They shot rope ladders over the face of these cliffs and began to pull themselves up. When one Ranger fell, another would take his place. When one rope was cut, a Ranger would grab another and begin his climb again. They climbed, shot back, and held their footing. Soon, one by one, the Rangers pulled themselves over the top, and in seizing the firm land at the top of these cliffs, they began to seize back the continent of Europe. Two hundred and twenty-five came here. After two days of fighting, only 90 could still bear arms.[38]

So powerful were Reagan's images—so vivid was his re-creation of the scene on D-Day 40 years earlier—that some of the grizzled old veterans in his audience actually broke down in tears during the speech.

Imagery refers to the "word pictures" that our language creates, and Reagan painted a vivid one. So, too, did Theodore Roosevelt in a famous speech delivered at the dedication of a new federal office building in 1906. In "The Man with the Muck Rake," Roosevelt compared the irresponsible journalists of his day to a

President Ronald Reagan used a visually dramatic setting and vivid language and imagery to commemorate the 40th anniversary of D-Day at Point du Hoc, Normandy, in 1984. In his audience were many of the surviving U.S. Army Rangers who stormed the cliffs on that fateful day.

famous literary figure from Bunyan's *Pilgrim's Progress*—the man with the muck rake, who "could look no way but down." Refusing to see anything positive or "lofty," he instead fixed his eyes "with solemn intentness only on that which is vile and debasing." To Roosevelt's mind, that perfectly described those journalists who reported nothing but bad news and engaged in "hysterical exaggeration" of America's problems. "Hysterical sensationalism is the poorest weapon wherewith to fight for lasting righteousness," Roosevelt declared in summarizing his point. And the imagery stuck: to this day, we use the term "muckraker" to describe journalists who specialize in sensational exposés.

Ceremonial speakers often use *figurative language* or specific *figures of speech* to create imagery. In his presidential inaugural address, as we already noted, John F. Kennedy sounded a metaphorical trumpet as he called his fellow Americans to a "long twilight struggle." He also deployed a variety of other metaphors throughout the address to create memorable imagery and a more poetic tone. Early in the address, for example, he invoked images of a torchlight parade or an Olympic marathon as he declared that the "torch has been passed to a new generation of Americans." A bit later, he summarized a lesson he hoped to teach to the nonaligned nations, warning that in the past those who have "foolishly sought power by riding the back of the tiger" have often "ended up inside." Then came another, quite different metaphor, directed at our "sister republics" to the south: a pledge to help them cast off "the chains of poverty" and effect a peaceful "revolution of hope." Finally, Kennedy put the rest of the world on notice that the western hemisphere intended to remain "master of its own house," while at the same time he urged all nations to renew the "quest for peace" before the "dark forces of destruction" prevailed.[39]

You may not have Kennedy's gift of eloquence. Yet by using more specific, concrete words or a striking metaphor or two, you can enhance the imagery and eloquence of your ceremonial speech. Writing a ceremonial speech is not like writing poetry, yet neither is it the same as writing a persuasive or informative speech. In a ceremonial speech, you should pay closer attention to language and choose your words carefully to achieve a more eloquent tone. Not all epideictic speeches are flowery or poetic, but all should reflect careful attention to language and style.

Rhythm and Cadence

As you prepare your ceremonial speech, pay special attention to its rhythm and cadence. That is, write the speech with a view toward how well it will "flow" when delivered. In general, strive for a smooth, balanced rhythm, paying special attention to the length and structure of the speech's phrases and sentences. You also may employ stylistic devices that contribute to a more "poetic" rhythm, such as antithesis, parallelism, or simple repetition.

When writing an epideictic speech, keep in mind that you are writing for oral delivery. It is crucial that your speech *sound* good when delivered out loud. Generally, this means that you should strive for shorter sentences, perhaps even using phrases or sentence fragments that might be inappropriate in a written essay. You want a speech that you can deliver smoothly, without stumbling over words that are difficult to pronounce or sentences that are awkwardly constructed. It is always a good idea to practice your speech out loud before you deliver it.

We remember some of the most famous ceremonial speeches in history not only for their imagery but also for their rhythm and cadence. In his inaugural address, for example, John F. Kennedy not only employed metaphors but also made effective use of antithesis, most notably in the best-known line of the address: "Ask not what your country can do for you—ask what you can do for your country." Yet that was not the only example of antithesis in the speech. Kennedy also used a complex, extended antithesis to open the speech: "We observe today not a victory of party but a celebration of freedom—symbolizing an end as well as a beginning—signifying renewal as well as change." Midway through the speech, he employed antithesis again: "Let us never negotiate out of fear. But let us never fear to negotiate." Finally, he concluded by echoing the most famous line of the address, directing a similar antithesis to "citizens of the world": "Ask not what America will do for you, but what together we can do for the freedom of man."[40]

President Barack Obama's inaugural address was likewise noteworthy for its rhythm and cadence, primarily because of his use of repetition and parallelism. Early in the speech, he repeated the phrase "on this day" to create a rhythmic parallelism emphasizing what his inauguration represented to those who supported him: "On this day, we gather because we have chosen hope over fear, unity of purpose over conflict and discord. On this day, we come to proclaim an end to the petty grievances and false promises, the recriminations and worn-out dogmas that for far too long have strangled our politics." A bit later in the speech, he again created a rhythmic parallelism by repeating just two words at the start of four consecutive sentences:

> We will build the roads and bridges, the electric grids and digital lines that feed our commerce and bind us together.
>
> We will restore science to its rightful place and wield technology's wonders to raise health care's quality and lower its costs.
>
> We will harness the sun and the winds and the soil to fuel our cars and run our factories. And we will transform our schools and colleges and universities to meet the demands of a new age.

Then, bringing that parallelism to a climax, Obama concluded with two short, punchy sentences, again exploiting the power of repetition to create a poetic cadence: "All this we can do. All this we will do."[41]

Again, you may not possess the natural eloquence of a Kennedy or an Obama, and not every ceremonial occasion calls for a speech poetic in tone. In preparing your own ceremonial speeches, however, you *should* strive for a more eloquent style, and that means paying close attention to the language, rhythm, and cadence of your speech.

Speaking from a Manuscript

On most occasions, you will deliver your ceremonial speech from a manuscript rather than from an outline or brief notes. That is, you will take care to present the speech exactly as written. This is not to say that you should stand before your audience, eyes glued to your manuscript, and simply read the speech. To the contrary, you should have the same concern with delivering your ceremonial speech effectively as you would any other speech.

The reason most ceremonial speeches are delivered from manuscript should be obvious: because of the emphasis on language and style, it is important that we deliver the speech precisely as written. That is not to say that you should never diverge from your manuscript or "ad lib" a few lines. Yet when you invent that memorable turn of phrase or come up with the perfect metaphor—that is, when you carefully craft the language of your speech—you want to deliver those lines exactly as written. In his first inaugural address, Franklin Roosevelt knew exactly what he wanted to say: the "only thing we have to fear is fear itself." Imagine if FDR had delivered that line extemporaneously, concerned only with the idea behind it. Instead of that famous line, he instead might have said: "Let's not be paralyzed by our fears." Or even just this: "Don't be scared!"

Unfortunately, delivering a speech from manuscript poses special challenges. Most speakers find it more difficult to maintain eye contact, use physical movement and gestures, sustain the appropriate rate and volume, and react to audience feedback while reading from a manuscript. Delivering a speech from manuscript requires that you write the speech in a good oral style, using words and sentence constructions that you will not stumble over as you speak. It also requires that you make a special effort to maintain a slow, deliberate pace that allows you to stay connected to your audience. In Chapter 11, we offered some other tips for delivering a manuscript speech, including ways to move and gesture and use your voice effectively while speaking from a manuscript. But perhaps the best advice for delivering a manuscript speech is simple: never forget that you are delivering a *speech*, not simply reading out loud.

 Study and Review materials for this chapter are at **MyCommunicationLab**

SUMMARY

 Listen to the Audio Chapter Summary at **MyCommunicationLab**

Ceremonial Speaking in a Free Society

 16.1 Discuss the role of ceremonial speaking in a free society.

- Ceremonial speeches perform important cultural functions in a free society.
  - They help us remember the past.
  - They honor our heroes.
  - They celebrate shared beliefs and values.
  - They provide inspiration and encouragement.

Social Values in Ceremonial Speaking

16.2 Explain how ceremonial speeches define and reinforce social values.

- Ceremonial speeches articulate and reinforce shared social values.
  - Most ceremonial speeches reaffirm existing values and traditions.
  - Some ceremonial speeches promote social reform or encourage groups to reassess their values and priorities.

The Forms of Ceremonial Speech

16.3 Identify and describe different types of ceremonial speeches.

- There are many different forms of ceremonial speeches, each unique but all with the same basic mission: to celebrate a special person or occasion.
  - Speeches of introduction should be brief and focused on the featured speaker.

- Speeches of welcome or farewell often offer instruction or guidance.
- Presentation and acceptance speeches may focus on the virtues of an award recipient or the significance of the award itself.
- Commemoration and commencement addresses mark special dates or events.
- Tributes and eulogies honor people and teach us about character and personal virtue.
- Inaugural and keynote addresses articulate the "vision" of a new leader or the key principles of some group.
- After-dinner speeches combine entertainment and a serious message.
- Sermons may be considered *epideictic* speeches when they celebrate and reinforce the faith of believers.

Style and Delivery in Ceremonial Speaking

 16.4 Define *eloquence* and discuss the importance of style and delivery in ceremonial speaking.

- Ceremonial speeches should be written with careful attention to language and typically are delivered from manuscript.

QUESTIONS FOR REVIEW AND REFLECTION

Ceremonial Speaking in a Free Society

 Discuss the role of ceremonial speaking in a free society.

1. What are some of the main purposes of ceremonial speeches in a free society?
2. If you were asked to deliver a ceremonial speech on the Fourth of July, what events in the past might you mention? What heroes would you recall, and what shared beliefs and values would you celebrate?

Social Values in Ceremonial Speaking

 Explain how ceremonial speeches define and reinforce social values.

3. Do ceremonial addresses always reinforce *traditional* social values? Can you think of a speaker or speakers who have delivered ceremonial addresses that challenged traditional values?

The Forms of Ceremonial Speech

16.3 Identify and describe different types of ceremonial speeches.

4. Suppose you learn that you are going to receive an award and have to give a brief acceptance speech. Would you talk more about yourself, other people, or the award itself?

5. Do you remember any of the commemorative or commencement speeches you have heard in the past? What made those speeches memorable?
6. Think of an important public figure, celebrity, or other notable person, living or dead, whom you admire. If you were to deliver a tribute or eulogy to that person, what character attributes or personal virtues would you emphasize?
7. What are the major differences between an inaugural address and a keynote address?

Style and Delivery in Ceremonial Speaking

 Define *eloquence* and discuss the importance of style and delivery in ceremonial speaking.

8. What does the word *eloquence* mean to you? What do you think makes some speeches more eloquent than others?
9. What are some of the stylistic devices that contribute to vivid imagery or create a poetic rhythm and cadence in a ceremonial speech?

✓ Study and Review the Flashcards at **MyCommunicationLab**

LIBERTY UNIVERSITY COMMENCEMENT ADDRESS

John McCain

After labeling the Reverend Jerry Falwell an "agent of intolerance" during the 2000 presidential campaign, Senator John McCain (R-Arizona) accepted an invitation to deliver the 2006 commencement address at Falwell's Liberty University. McCain used the occasion to talk about humility, patriotism, tolerance, respect, and forgiveness. He also celebrated free speech in America and urged his listeners to devote themselves to a cause greater than themselves.

May 13, 2006

Thank you. Thank you. Thank you. Thank you, Dr. Falwell. Thank you, faculty, families and friends, and thank you Liberty University Class of 2006 for your welcome and your kind invitation to give this year's commencement address. I want to join in the chorus of congratulations to the Class of 2006. This is a day to bask in praise. You've earned it. You have succeeded in a demanding course of instruction. Life seems full of promise, as is always the case when a passage in life is marked by significant accomplishment. Today, it might seem as if the world attends you.

But spare a moment for those who have truly attended you so well for so long, and whose pride in your accomplishments is even greater than your own—your parents. When the world was looking elsewhere your parents' attention was one of life's certainties. So, as I commend you, I offer equal praise to your parents for the sacrifices they made for you, for their confidence in you and their love. More than any other influence in your lives they have helped you—make you the success you are today and might become tomorrow.

Thousands of commencement addresses are given every year, many by people with greater eloquence and more original minds than I possess. And it's difficult on such occasions to avoid resorting to clichés. So let me just say that I wish you all well. This is a wonderful time to be young. Life will offer you ways to use your education, industry, and intelligence to achieve personal success in your chosen professions. And it will also offer you chances to know a far more sublime happiness by serving something greater than your self-interest. I hope you make the most of all your opportunities.

When I was in your situation, many, many years ago, an undistinguished graduate—barely— of the Naval Academy, I listened to President Eisenhower deliver the commencement address. I admired President Eisenhower greatly. But I must admit I remember little of his remarks that day, impatient as I was to enjoy the less formal celebration of graduation, and mindful that given my class standing I would not have the privilege of shaking the president's hand. I do recall, vaguely, that he encouraged his audience of new Navy ensigns and Marine lieutenants to become "crusaders for peace."

I became an aviator and, eventually, an instrument of war in Vietnam. I believed, as did many of my friends, we were defending the cause of a just peace. Some Americans believed we were agents of American imperialism who were not overly troubled by the many tragedies of war and the difficult moral dilemmas that constantly confront our soldiers. Ours is a noisy, contentious society, and always has been, for we love our liberties much. And among those liberties we love most, particularly so when we are young, is our right to self-expression. That passion for self-expression sometimes overwhelms our civility, and our presumption that those with whom we may have strong disagreements, wrong as they might be, believe that they, too, are answering the demands of their conscience.

When I was a young man, I was quite infatuated with self-expression, and rightly so because, if memory conveniently serves, I was so much more eloquent, well informed, and wiser than anyone else I knew. It seemed I understood the world and the purpose of life so much more profoundly than most people. I believed that to be especially true with many of my elders, people whose only accomplishment, as far as I could tell, was that they'd been born before me, and, consequently, had suffered some number of years deprived of my insights. I had opinions on everything, and I was always right. I loved to argue, and I could become understandably belligerent with people who lacked the grace and intelligence to agree with me. With my superior qualities so obvious, it was an intolerable hardship to have to suffer fools gladly. So I rarely did. All their resistance to my brilliantly conceived and cogently argued views proved was that they possessed an inferior intellect and a weaker character than God had blessed me with, and I felt it was my clear duty to so inform them. It's a pity that there wasn't a blogosphere then. I would have felt very much at home in that medium.

It's funny, now, how less self-assured I feel late in life than I did when I lived in perpetual springtime. Some of my critics allege that age hasn't entirely cost me the conceits of my youth. All I can say to them is, they should have known me then, when I was brave and true and better looking than I am at present. But as the great poet Yeats wrote, "All that's beautiful drifts away, like the waters." I've lost some of the attributes that were the object of a young man's vanity. But there have been compensations, which I have come to hold dear.

We have our disagreements, we Americans. We contend regularly and enthusiastically over many questions: over the size and purposes of our government; over the social responsibilities we accept in accord with the dictates of our consciousness [conscience] and our faithfulness to the God we pray to; over our role in the world and how to defend our security interests and values in places where they are threatened. These are important questions worth arguing about. We should contend over them with one another. It is more than appropriate: it is necessary that even in times of crisis, especially in times of crisis, we fight among ourselves for the things we believe in. It is not just our right, but our civic and moral obligation.

Our country doesn't depend on the heroism of every citizen. But all of us should be worthy of the sacrifices made on our behalf. We have to love our freedom, not just for the private opportunities it provides, but for the goodness it makes possible. We have to love it as much, even if not as heroically, as the brave Americans who defend us at the risk and often the cost of their lives. We must love it enough to argue about it, and to serve it, in whatever way our abilities permit and our conscience requires, whether it calls us to arms or to altruism or to politics.

I supported the decision to go to war in Iraq. Many Americans did not. My patriotism and my conscience required me to support it and to engage in the debate over whether and how to fight it. I stand that ground not to chase vainglorious dreams of empire; not for a noxious sense of racial superiority over a subject people; not for cheap oil (we could have purchased oil from the former dictator at a price far less expensive than the blood and treasure we've paid to secure those resources for the people of that nation); not for the allure of chauvinism, to wreck [wreak] destruction in the world in order to feel superior to it; not for a foolishly romantic conception of war. I stand that ground because I believed, rightly or wrongly, that my country's interests and values required it.

War is an awful business. The lives of the nation's finest patriots are sacrificed. Innocent people suffer. Commerce is disrupted, economies damaged. Strategic interests shielded by years of statecraft are endangered as the demands of war and diplomacy conflict. Whether the cause was necessary or not, whether it was just or not, we should all shed a tear for all that is lost when war claims its wages from us. However just or false the cause, however proud and noble the service, it is loss—the loss of friendships, the loss of innocent life, the innocence—the loss of innocence; and the veteran feels most keenly forevermore. Only a fool or a fraud sentimentalizes war.

Americans should argue about this war. They should argue about it. It has cost the lives of nearly 2,500 of the best of us. It has taken innocent life. It has imposed an enormous financial burden on our economy. At a minimum, it has complicated our ability to respond to other looming threats. Should we lose this war, our defeat will further destabilize an already volatile and dangerous region, strengthen the threat of terrorism, and unleash furies that will assail us for a very long time. I believe the benefits of success will justify the costs and the risks we have incurred. But if an American feels the decision was unwise, then they should state their opposition, and argue for another course. It is your right and your obligation. I respect you for it. I would not respect you if you chose to ignore such an important responsibility. But I ask that you consider the possibility that I, too, am trying to meet my responsibilities, to follow my conscience, to do my duty as best as I can, as God has given me light to see that duty.

Americans deserve more than tolerance from one another; we deserve each other's respect, whether we think each other right or wrong in our views, as long as our character and our sincerity merit respect, and as long as we share, for all our differences, for all the noisy debates that enliven our politics, a mutual devotion to the sublime idea that this nation was conceived in—that freedom is the inalienable right of mankind, and in accord with the laws of nature and nature's Creator.

We have so much more that unites us than divides us. We need only to look to the enemy who now confronts us, and the benighted ideals to which Islamic extremists pledge allegiance—their disdain for the rights of man, their contempt for human life— to appreciate how much unites us.

Take, for example, the awful human catastrophe under way in the Darfur region of the Sudan. If the United States and the West can be criticized for our role in this catastrophe it's because we have waited too long to intervene to protect the multitudes who are suffering, dying because of it.

Twelve years ago, we turned a blind eye to another genocide, in Rwanda. And when that reign of terror finally, mercifully exhausted itself, with over 800,000 Rwandans slaughtered, Americans, our government, and decent people everywhere in the world were shocked and ashamed of our silence and inaction, for ignoring our values, and the demands of our conscience. In shame and renewed allegiance to our ideals, we swore, not for the first time, "never again." But "never" lasted only until the tragedy of Darfur.

Now, belatedly, we have recovered our moral sense of duty, and we are prepared, I hope, to put an end to this genocide. Osama bin Laden and his followers, ready, as always, to sacrifice anything and anyone to their hatred of the West and our ideals, have called on Muslims to rise up against any Westerner who dares intervene to stop the genocide, even though Muslims, hundreds of thousands of Muslims, are its victims. Now that, my friends, is a difference, a cause, worth taking up arms against.

It is not a clash of civilizations. I believe, as I hope all Americans would believe, that no matter where people live, no matter their history or religious beliefs or the size of their GDP, all people share the desire to be free; to make by their own choices and industry better lives for themselves and their children. Human rights exist above the state and beyond history—they are God-given. They cannot be rescinded by one government any more than they can be granted by another. They inhabit the human heart, and from there, though they can be abridged, they can never be wrenched.

This is a clash of ideals, a profound and terrible clash of ideals. It is a fight between right and wrong. Relativism has no place in this confrontation. We're not defending—we're not defending an idea that every human being should eat corn flakes, play baseball, or watch MTV. We're not insisting that all societies be governed by a bicameral legislature and a term-limited chief executive. We're insisting that all people have a right to be free, and that right is not subject to the whims and interests and authority of another person, government, or culture. Relativism, in this context, is most certainly not a sign of our humility or ecumenism; it is a mask for arrogance and selfishness. It is, and I mean this sincerely and with all humility, not worthy of us. We are a better people than that.

We're not a perfect nation. Our history has had its moments of shame and profound regret. But what we have achieved in our brief history is irrefutable proof that a nation conceived in liberty will prove stronger, more decent, and more enduring than any nation ordered to exalt the few at the expense of the many or made from a common race or culture or to preserve traditions that have no greater attribute than longevity.

As blessed as we are, no nation complacent in its greatness can long sustain it. We, too, must prove, as those who came before us proved, that a people free to act in their own interests will perceive those interests in an enlightened way, will live as one nation, in a kinship of ideals, and make of our power and wealth a civilization for the ages, a civilization in which all people share in the promise and responsibilities of freedom.

Should we claim our rights and leave to others the duty to the ideals that protect them, whatever we gain for ourselves will be of little lasting value. It will build no monuments to virtue, claim no honored place in the memory of posterity, offer no worthy summons to the

WHILE CONCEDING THAT WE ARE NOT A "PERFECT" NATION, McCAIN CELEBRATES AMERICA'S ACHIEVEMENTS AS "IRREFUTABLE PROOF" OF THE STRENGTH AND DECENCY OF A FREE NATION. WARNING AGAINST COMPLACENCY, HE ALSO REMINDS HIS LISTENERS OF THEIR DUTY TO "SACRIFICE FOR A CAUSE GREATER THAN YOURSELF."

world. Success, wealth, and celebrity gained and kept for private interest is a small thing. It makes us comfortable, eases the material hardships our children will bear, purchase[s] a fleeting regard for our lives, yet not the self-respect that, in the end, matters most. But sacrifice for a cause greater than yourself, and you invest your life with the eminence of that cause, your self-respect assured.

All lives are a struggle against selfishness. All my life I've stood a little apart from institutions that I willingly joined. It just felt natural to me. But if my life had shared no common purpose, it would not have amounted to much more than eccentricity. There is no honor or happiness in just being strong enough to be left alone. I've spent nearly 50 years in the service of this country and its ideals. I have made many mistakes, and I have many regrets. But I've never lived a day, in good times or bad, that I wasn't grateful for the privilege. That's the benefit of service to a country that is an idea and a cause, a righteous idea and cause. America and her ideals helped spare me from the weaknesses in my own character. And I cannot forget it.

When I was a young man, I thought glory was the highest attainment, and all glory was self-glory. My parents had tried to teach me otherwise, as did my church, as did the Naval Academy. But I didn't understand the lesson until later in life, when I confronted challenges I never expected to face.

In that confrontation, I discovered that I was dependent on others to a greater extent than I had ever realized, but neither they nor the cause we served made any claims on my identity. On the contrary, they gave me a larger sense of myself than I had had before. And I am a better man for it. I discovered that nothing in life is more liberating than to fight for a cause that encompasses you but is not defined by your existence alone. And that has made all the difference, my friends, all the difference in the world.

Let—let us argue with each other then. By all means, let us argue. Our differences are not petty. They often involve cherished beliefs, and represent our best judgment about what is right for our country and humanity. Let us defend those beliefs. Let's do so sincerely and strenuously. It is our right and duty to do so. And let's not be too dismayed with the tenor and passion of our arguments, even when they wound us. We have fought among ourselves before in our history, over big things and small, with worse vitriol and bitterness than we experience today.

Let us exercise our responsibilities as free people. But let us remember, we are not enemies. We are compatriots defending ourselves from a real enemy. We have nothing to fear from each other. We are arguing over the means to better secure our freedom, promote the general welfare, and defend our ideals. It should remain an argument among friends; each of us struggling to hear our conscience, and heed its demands; each of us, despite our differences, united in our great cause, and respectful of the goodness in each other. I have not always heeded that injunction myself, and I regret it very much.

I had a friend once, who, a long time ago, in the passions and resentments of a tumultuous era in our history, I might have considered my enemy. He had come once to the capitol of the country that held me prisoner, that deprived me and my dearest friends of our most basic rights, and that murdered some of us. He came to that place to denounce our country's involvement in the war that had led us there. His speech was broadcast into our cells. I thought it a grievous wrong then, and I still do.

A few years later, he had moved temporarily to a kibbutz in Israel. He was there during the Yom Kippur War, when he witnessed the support America provided our beleaguered ally. He saw the huge cargo planes bearing the insignia of the United States Air Force rushing emergency supplies into that country. And he had an epiphany. He had believed America had made a tragic mistake by going to Vietnam, and he still did. He had seen what he believed were his country's faults, and he still saw them. But he realized he has—he had let his criticism temporarily blind him to his country's generosity and the goodness that most Americans possess, and he regretted his failing deeply. When he returned to his country he became prominent in Democratic Party politics, and helped [elect] Bill Clinton president of the United States. He criticized his government when he thought it wrong, but he never again lost sight of all that unites us.

We met some years later. He approached me and asked to apologize for the mistake he believed he had made as a young man. Many years had passed since then, and I bore little animosity for anyone because of what they had done or not done during the Vietnam War. It was an easy thing to accept such a decent act, and we moved beyond our old grievance.

We worked together in an organization dedicated to promoting human rights in the country where he and I had once come for different reasons. I came to admire him for his generosity, his passion for his ideals, and for the largeness of his heart, and I realized he had not been my enemy, but my countryman, my countryman, and later my friend. His friendship honored me. We disagreed over much. Our politics were often opposed, and we argued those disagreements. But we worked together for our shared ideals. We were not always in the right, but we weren't always in the wrong either, and we defended our beliefs as we had each been given the wisdom to defend them.

David [Ifshin] remained my countryman and my friend, until the day of his death, at the age of 47, when he left a loving wife and three beautiful children, and legions of friends behind him. His country was a better place for his service to Her, and I had become a better man for my friendship with him. God bless him.

And may God bless you, Class of 2006. The world does indeed await you, and humanity is impatient for your service. Take good care of that responsibility. Everything depends upon it.

And thank you, very much, for the privilege of sharing this great occasion with you.

Source: From John McCain, "Liberty University Commencement Address, May 13, 2006." Published 2006 by John McCain.

MCCAIN USES A LONG PERSONAL ANECDOTE TO ILLUSTRATE HIS THEME THAT EVEN BITTER POLITICAL ENEMIES CAN FIND COMMON GROUND. THE STORY IS ABOUT ANTIWAR PROTESTOR DAVID IFSHIN, WHO DENOUNCED THE WAR IN VIETNAM OVER RADIO HANOI WHILE MCCAIN WAS STILL BEING HELD THERE AS A POW. LATER, IFSHIN BECAME A CAMPAIGN AIDE TO PRESIDENT BILL CLINTON, AND MCCAIN NOT ONLY BECAME FRIENDS WITH IFSHIN BUT ALSO WORKED WITH HIM TO PROMOTE HUMAN RIGHTS.

IN CONCLUSION, MCCAIN REINFORCES THE IMPORTANCE OF THIS BASIC THEME—THAT HIS LISTENERS HAVE A RESPONSIBILITY TO SERVE HUMANITY.

Speaking and Deliberating in Groups

OVERVIEW AND LEARNING OBJECTIVES

Understanding Public Deliberation

17.1 Explain the role, importance, and potential benefits of public deliberation.

Group Structures That Encourage Dialogue and Deliberation

17.2 Describe group structures that promote effective deliberation and dialogue.

Factors That Influence Effective Group Deliberation

17.3 List some of the factors that influence how deliberative groups function.

Group Presentations

17.4 Discuss how to prepare and present your ideas in a public discussion.

Guidelines for Deliberating in Groups

17.5 Describe the attitudes and communication behaviors associated with effective group deliberation.

By speaking out in public, we fulfill one of our most important responsibilities as citizens: to work together with our fellow citizens to build stronger communities and a better world. Most of this book focuses on formal speeches, in which you deliver carefully prepared remarks to an audience of listeners. In many instances, however, your listeners will not be passive receivers but active participants in a discussion. In these group settings, you may still engage in advocacy, but your "speeches" will be less formal and more spontaneous. This process of communicating within a group—with speakers and listeners frequently exchanging roles—is called *deliberation*. In group deliberations, you may still be an advocate for a particular point of view, but your ultimate goal may be consensus building, information sharing, or conflict resolution.

We all participate in a variety of formal and informal group deliberations. Professionally, we may spend many hours attending staff meetings or meeting with clients or customers. In our local community, we may participate in a community forum, attend a school board meeting, or work on a task force appointed to tackle some problem. As you interact in such groups, you will learn from others, form friendships, and contribute knowledge and skills vital to the success of the group's efforts. Deliberating in a group is not the same as talking individually with another person or working alone to solve some problem. A group is both dynamic and complex. Done right, group deliberations may lead to long-term, productive relationships and inspire creative decision making. When they go badly, however, they can cause tension and prevent action. This chapter focuses on ways to promote healthy, productive group deliberations.

The frequency with which you deliberate in groups is itself reason enough to read this chapter carefully. Your effectiveness in any organization or community will be influenced by how well you communicate in groups. As businesses and nonprofit organizations have become increasingly team oriented, group communication skills have also become more important in the workplace. Knowing how to be a team player, how to interact effectively with others to complete projects, and how to provide group leadership are all highly valued skills in the twenty-first century.[1]

Group communication skills learned in one setting are usually applicable to others. Whether you are deliberating as a board member of a nonprofit agency, as a citizen in a community group, or as a member of your work team, you will be more effective if you prepare carefully, thoughtfully analyze the problem, maintain an open and flexible attitude, and listen respectfully. When you communicate effectively in a group, you are likely to exert more influence and rise to a position of leadership. You will also find it easier to maintain a civil and respectful atmosphere as you collaborate with others to solve problems. The more involved you become as a citizen in your community, the more frequently you will work in groups dealing with such issues as education, crime and public safety, or housing and environmental policy. Your ability to contribute constructively to groups will affect your community's ability to solve its problems. For all these reasons, developing the ability to work effectively in groups is vital. We begin by examining the form that group communication typically takes in a civic or community setting: the process known as public deliberation.

UNDERSTANDING PUBLIC DELIBERATION

Preview. *Deliberative forums vary in size and purpose, but the same basic principles of effective and responsible deliberation govern them all. Public deliberation differs from debate; it is not a contest with winners and losers, but a process of engaging in dialogue to promote understanding or solve problems. At its best, deliberation can lead to a variety of positive outcomes. When not characterized by a spirit of dialogue, however, deliberation will not have such positive results.*

The concept of public deliberation grows out of democratic theory. According to political scientist Simone Chambers, the theory of deliberative democracy focuses on the communicative processes of opinion formation that precede voting.[2] Although the act of voting itself is a personal decision, the process of deliberation is concerned with public "account giving"—how people articulate, explain, and justify their political opinions and policy preferences to their fellow citizens. In other words, the theory of democratic deliberation is talk-focused. In a sense, then, public deliberation is the process through which democracy is enacted.[3]

Communication scholar John Gastil defines public deliberation as "judicious argument, critical listening, and earnest decision making."[4] Gastil echoes educational philosopher John Dewey, who described *full* deliberation as a careful examination of a problem or issue, including identifying possible solutions, establishing evaluative criteria, and using those criteria in identifying the best solution.[5] Of course, deliberation in the real world does not always work so neatly. But by striving to deliberate as fully and completely as possible, citizens can improve its process and outcomes.

Public deliberation, then, is discourse among citizens—as they engage in dialogue, explore ideas, and strive to reach common understandings and agreements about community problems or courses of action. Public deliberation is a real measure of civic engagement—as much so as voting, attending meetings, working for a political party, or participating in voluntary organizations. Deliberating with others provides the opportunity for citizens to develop and express their views, learn from the ideas of others, identify shared concerns and preferences, and come to common understandings and judgments about matters of public concern. These exchanges can be a "central way of clarifying and negotiating deep divisions over material interests and moral values."[6] At the same time, they can provide a mechanism for airing disagreements that have *not* been articulated and point the way toward resolving differences within a community.

There are many different forms of public deliberation. Some deliberations take place in large, formal settings, such as a town hall meeting between elected officials and their constituents. Other deliberations take place in homes, schools, churches, libraries, or community centers. Public deliberation can also involve face-to-face exchanges, phone conversations, e-mail exchanges, and Internet forums. It may focus on local issues and problems or matters of national or even international significance.

17.1 Explain the role, importance, and potential benefits of public deliberation.

Watch the Video "Tobacco Ordinance Public Hearing (Shirley Lindsay Sears)" at **MyCommunicationLab**

Watch the Video "Tobacco Ordinance Public Hearing (Paul Hager)" at **MyCommunicationLab**

FOCUS ON CIVIC ENGAGEMENT | **Civic Learning and Democratic Engagement in the Twenty-First Century**

The U.S. Department of Education recently released a report calling on colleges and universities to renew their commitment to making "civic learning" a central part of students' undergraduate experience. The report emphasizes skills, values, and actions that are central to civic engagement and discourse. The following illustrates some of these:

Skills

- Seeking, engaging, and being informed by multiple perspectives
- Deliberation and bridge building across differences
- Collaborative decision making

Values

- Open-mindedness
- Tolerance
- Empathy
- Responsibility to a larger good

Collective Action

- Integrating knowledge, skills, and examined values to inform actions taken in concert with others
- Compromise, civility, and mutual respect

Source: The National Task Force on Civic Learning and Democratic Engagement, *A Crucible Moment* (Washington, DC: Association of American Colleges and Universities, 2012).

Engaging in Dialogue

Whether the goal of public deliberation is education, consensus building, conflict resolution, or advocacy,[7] the deliberative process is more likely to be successful if the participants engage one another in a respectful dialogue. As award-winning author Daniel Yankelovich points out, dialogue is most easily understood by contrasting it with the kind of debate in which the goal is to *win* an argument. Debate emphasizes finding flaws in others' positions and winning arguments, while dialogue focuses on working with others to achieve common ground and finding strengths in others' views.[8]

Journalist Scott London points out that deliberative dialogue differs from other forms of public discourse because its objective is to *think together*, "not so much to reach a conclusion as to discover where a conclusion might lie."[9] Thinking together involves listening deeply and with empathy to other points of view. In many discussions, participants bat ideas back and forth, but they seem more interested in articulating their *own* views than in truly understanding what others are saying.

When you participate in deliberations, it's important to approach the dialogue in a spirit of equality. As Yankelovich maintains, "In genuine dialogue, there is no arm-twisting, no pulling of rank, no hint of sanctions for holding politically incorrect attitudes, no coercive influences of any sort, whether overt or indirect."[10] In many contexts, of course, differences of status may exist among the participants, making it more difficult to achieve a genuine dialogue. In that case, those of higher rank or status must take the initiative to build trust and make everybody feel comfortable about airing their views.[11] Differences of power or status can make deliberating more challenging, but those differences *can* be overcome.

The deliberative process usually revolves around problem solving, but it can also be used simply to increase knowledge, understanding, or empathy for different perspectives. London notes that the Greeks believed that individuals could uncover the truth for themselves by reasoning with others. He inventories what they envisioned, writing:

> By questioning and probing each other, carefully dissecting and analyzing ideas, finding inconsistencies, never attacking or insulting, but always searching for what they could accept between them, they could gradually attain deeper understanding and insight.[12]

In this spirit, deliberative dialogue aims at establishing a framework for mutual understanding and a common purpose that transcends individual ideas and opinions. Although it may not produce consensus, it *can* produce collective insight and judgment that reflects the thinking of the group as a whole. When the deliberative process works well, it links people's private ideas and interests with public knowledge and *public values*—knowledge and values that are clarified and corroborated through the process of group inquiry.

Understanding How Deliberative Dialogue Works   While there is no fixed procedure for organizing a deliberative dialogue, certain steps or stages are fairly typical. To begin, a facilitator welcomes participants, invites self-introductions, and quickly reviews and responds to questions about the guidelines for dialogue.

Participants then enter into *exploratory dialogue*—a potentially awkward time when some sit back and watch or express their views tentatively as they size up others in the group or scrutinize the procedures. As individuals begin to relate personal stories of their relationship to the issue at hand, a more comfortable group dynamic begins to unfold. Through the exploratory phase, group members may begin to establish trust and cohesiveness. They also grapple with "naming" the issue—a process that may take them in new and perhaps unanticipated directions. They may discover, for example, that the issue they thought they had come to

---

FOCUS ON CIVIC ENGAGEMENT | **The Exchange: A Marketplace of Student Ideas**

Nobody is born with the habits and skills of civic engagement. We *learn* how to be good citizens, and the National Constitution Center in Philadelphia has developed an innovative program to help high school students do just that: The Exchange: A Marketplace of Student Ideas. Using Internet-2 videoconferencing technologies, The Exchange brings together students from across the nation for live discussions of some of the most pressing issues of the day, including religion in the public schools, health care reform, immigration, and same-sex marriage. Funded by the Annenberg Foundation and the National Endowment for the

Humanities, The Exchange is hosted by former MTV news correspondent SuChin Pak and other guest moderators. The program teaches students the difference between competitive debate and collaborative deliberation, and it cultivates a variety of skills necessary for engaged democratic citizenship, including research, critical listening, public speaking, and group deliberation skills.

For a brief video introduction to The Exchange, visit http://vimeo.com/26973374. For more information and other video clips from The Exchange, visit http://constitutioncenter.org/the-exchange/.

discuss is only a part, or a symptom, of a deeper and more complex issue. So a community group might initially come together because they are concerned about neighborhood crime, but as they deliberate, they may end up focusing on a broader set of concerns, such as poverty or at-risk youth.

Later, the dialogue shifts from inquiry and exploration to *purposeful deliberation* as the group begins to wrestle with what may look like competing choices. Conflict and disagreement are almost certain as the group seeks to identify core group values that transcend individual differences. Participants help generate productive dialogue when they indicate that their ideas are tentative, not cast in stone, and signal their willingness to listen, to grow, and to change. Participants also advance a spirit of dialogue when they give everybody a chance to speak, so that no one dominates the conversation. Finally, participants show their commitment to dialogue by establishing a supportive environment where mutual respect is the norm.[13]

Deliberative groups come together for different reasons and with different outcomes in mind. Some are content to set an agenda for further study or to arrive at a shared sense of how best to address an issue. Others aim for a collective judgment about the best course of action to pursue. Whatever the goal, the deliberative process ends when the facilitator sums up what has been said (or asks group members to do so), points out areas of agreement and lingering disagreement, articulates the overarching concerns that have been shared, allows for final comments, and identifies the "next steps" for the group.

Based on his studies of a number of deliberative groups, London argues that what distinguishes an ordinary from an extraordinary dialogue is the "presence of some transforming moment, or critical turning point." At this crucial point, participants move away from their own perspective and entertain the possibility of developing a collective understanding of the issue at hand.[14]

Compelling personal narratives may trigger this kind of turning point, making abstract and ideological views more concrete and understandable. When individuals in the group recount their personal struggle with drug addiction, their experience of living on the streets, their battle with mental illness, or their anger and despair at being the target of racist or homophobic remarks, others in the group may be moved, perhaps for the first time. Personal narratives give each problem a human face.[15]

Benefits of Public Deliberation

The potential benefits of public deliberation are many. The following are among the most consistently cited:

- Citizens become more engaged and active in civic affairs.
- Tolerance for opposing points of view increases.
- Citizens improve their understanding of their own preferences and can better justify those preferences with arguments.
- People in conflict set aside their "win-lose" approach as they begin to sense their interdependence.
- Faith in the democratic process is enhanced as citizens feel empowered.
- Political decisions become more considered and informed by relevant reasons and evidence.
- Collective decision making grows in frequency and quality.[16]

Under the right circumstances, public deliberation can produce impressive results. Gastil, for example, has documented numerous real-world deliberative initiatives, such as a community "visioning process" held in Chattanooga, Tennessee. This deliberative process involved 50 community activists and volunteers who met over a 20-week period. Their deliberations produced a list of priorities and solutions, including a shelter for abused women and a riverfront park. The organizers next developed a series of neighborhood associations and new nonprofit organizations. Eight years later, most of the solutions that emerged from the forums had been implemented.[17]

Participants often emerge "changed" by the process of deliberating. Research on the National Issues Forums has shown that deliberation can produce an array of positive results, including increasing the participants' sense of community, enhancing their interest in politics, and making them more open minded in their political conversations.[18] An extensive survey of another group of participants in small group deliberations revealed that, as a result of their deliberations, those participants donated money to charitable organizations (57 percent), became more interested in politics or social issues (45 percent), volunteered in the community (43 percent), changed their mind about a political or social issue (40 percent), or participated in a political rally or political campaign (12 percent).[19]

Potential Problems

Public deliberation does not always yield such positive outcomes. Much depends on participants' expectations, the deliberative format used, the facilitator's skill, and whether group members feel that their deliberations have any real impact. For example, one study reported on the feelings of frustration experienced by members of a deliberative group that had made specific recommendations for health care reform and environmental regulation. When the federal government failed to enact any sort of reform, they felt that their deliberations had been in vain.[20] In general, when participants feel that they are "just talking" and that their talk will not have any real impact on policy making, they will experience post-deliberation frustration.[21]

Participating in deliberative forums may also increase participants' sense of *self*-efficacy while reducing their sense of *group* efficacy. One study found that participants left a challenging forum more confident in their own ability to take effective individual action but more skeptical of the efficacy of group-based political action. However, the reactions of participants seemed to depend on the nature of their experiences in the forums. Those who engaged in relatively successful forums—with well-prepared participants, clear guidelines, effective facilitators, and adequate time devoted to deliberation—reported greater attitude changes and more positive feelings about the group experience.[22] In cases where deliberative forums do not go well, however, participants may end up feeling even more powerless and ineffectual.

Facilitators must be well trained and skilled, capable of providing adequate structure while allowing plenty of room for exploring diverse ideas. They must also be able to help group members achieve a sense of closure. Either too much intervention (so that group members are not freely deliberating) or too little (so that the group rambles out of control) can lead to poor outcomes and dissatisfaction.[23] In addition, facilitators must create a climate in which all participants feel they can express their views without fear of reprisal.

GROUP STRUCTURES THAT ENCOURAGE DIALOGUE AND DELIBERATION

17.2 Describe group structures that promote effective deliberation and dialogue.

Preview. *Several foundations and educational groups have developed programs to promote more open, constructive, and engaged public deliberations. These programs provide models for deliberative groups of differing sizes and purposes.*

Although many different types of deliberative groups exist, including citizen juries, roundtables, and public hearings, we focus here on three of the most common models: study circles, town hall meetings, and National Issues Forums.

Study Circles

The Study Circles Resource Center (SCRC) was created by the Topsfield Foundation in 1989 to advance deliberative democracy and improve the quality of public life in the United States. The center was renamed "Everyday Democracy" in 2002. Its goal is to help create communities that work better for everyone because all voices are included in problem solving, and to link that work to creating a stronger democracy.[24] Everyday Democracy offers assistance to communities in which people of different backgrounds are committed to working together to solve public problems. They offer tools, resources, and sometimes technical assistance with community organizing and creating and sustaining dialogue that leads to action and change.

At the heart of their approach is the study circle—a dialogue-to-change group that typically consists of eight to twelve participants guided by an impartial facilitator. Study circle members are encouraged to consider many perspectives, rather than advocating for a particular point of view. Ground rules set the tone for a respectful, productive discussion. Participants are encouraged to listen attentively to one another and to work at building trusting relationships. A typical study circle meets over multiple sessions, with members initially sharing personal experiences and then examining diverse points of view and seeking common ground (while respecting individual differences). Ultimately, the goal is to devise creative strategies for action. Facilitators remind group members that they *can* make a difference.

Individual study circles are often part of a community-wide effort in which several study circles meet simultaneously to address an issue of common concern. These groups contain men and women of all ethnic backgrounds and income levels. They also involve individuals and organizations from different sectors of the community, such as the Chamber of Commerce, the faith community, the media, local government, the United Way, the police department, the YMCA, the Urban League, and various neighborhood associations. Each brings unique tools, knowledge, and grassroots connections to the partnership.

Community-wide study circles are designed to involve the whole community in public dialogue and problem solving. At the end of the process, members of different study circles assemble in a community-wide meeting in which they learn

FOCUS ON CIVIC ENGAGEMENT | Study Circle Success Stories

Syracuse, New York. The Community-Wide Dialogue to End Racism began in 1997. Since then, over 6,000 people of all ages have taken part in the nation's longest-running efforts to address racism and racial inequities. Over the years, this initiative has led to several outcomes:

- Implementing fair-lending practices at a local bank
- Increasing the number of people of color on local boards
- Pairing city and suburban schools for a high school exchange program in which students discuss such topics as the effects of white privilege and racism
- Launching dialogues between the refugee community and American-born residents—including a police-community forum that addressed racial tensions between police and refugees and a peace march in which over 500 people took part
- Addressing the gap in student achievement between whites and students of color by expanding reading lists to include authors of color, reworking the American and World History curriculum to more accurately reflect contributions of people of color, and decorating classrooms to reflect images and cultures of people of color.

New Haven, Connecticut. Community Mediation, Inc. took the lead on a city-wide effort aimed at creating a "culture of dialogue," neighborhood by neighborhood. Guided by a diverse group of community leaders, *New Haven 2020: It Starts Now* brought neighbors together to address issues affecting the well-being of youth. So far, about 120 citizens have taken part in these community-based dialogues. In 2009, action teams formed in four neighborhoods. Some of their accomplishments include the following:

- Better relations between teens and police
- Improved student literacy in both English and Spanish
- Increased involvement of children in neighborhood reading programs
- The creation of a community garden that connects youth with mentors

Working with local nonprofits, the police department, city officials, and concerned citizens, New Haven 2020 aims to involve more people every year.

Source: "Long-time Project in Syracuse, NY, Tackles Student Achievement Gap," www.everyday-democracy.org/en/Article.1196.aspx (accessed March 21, 2012); "New Haven, CT, Residents Take Action to Address Youth Issues," www.everyday-democracy.org/en/Article.1197.aspx (accessed March 25, 2012). ▲

how others are working to make a difference. They may begin to discern how their contribution might fit into the larger picture. Some groups may decide to join forces and work together, whereas others will choose to remain independent. In either case, everyone has the chance to exchange ideas with public officials and other community members about public policy and discover ways to collaborate and bring about real change in policies and institutions.[25]

Town Hall Meetings

Traditionally, a town hall meeting is a gathering where the citizens of an entire geographic area are invited to deliberate over administrative, political, or legislative issues. Typically, everyone in the community is invited to attend, voice their concerns and opinions, and hear responses from public figures and elected officials.

The town hall meeting is a kind of democratic forum that has been used in the United States since the 1600s. Early town meetings brought citizens together

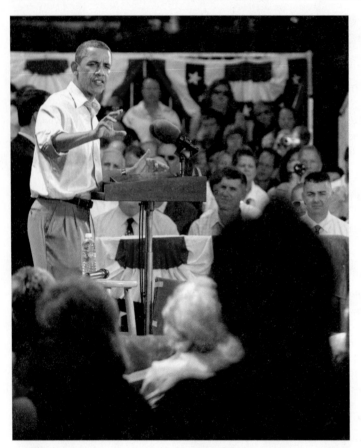

President Obama responds to a listener's question at a recent town hall meeting.

to discuss and vote on policies and budgets for their community. Today, however, town hall meetings are often forums for people to state their views but are not truly deliberative forums, where ordinary citizens decide on policies. U.S. politicians now commonly hold what they call "town hall meetings" as campaign events. In 2008, Senators John McCain and Barack Obama both staged town hall meetings as part of their presidential campaigns. Following the election, President Obama continued to conduct these meetings in the United States and around the globe. In some cases, he has used the Internet to engage citizens from around the country—responding to questions from a live audience and also addressing questions submitted by thousands of citizens who "tune in" and cast their votes on the most critical issues facing the nation.[26]

During the summer of 2009, bitter partisan divisions over a variety of economic issues, including an overhaul of the health care system, resulted in angry confrontations at town hall meetings across the country. Members of Congress were "shouted down, hanged in effigy, and taunted by crowds"[27] as they attempted to engage citizens in dialogue about the proposed reforms. In several cities, noisy demonstrations led to fistfights, arrests, and even injuries. Although a few representatives claimed to enjoy the lively debate, many appeared to agree with the media's portrayals of the protests as "town brawls."

The issue of health care reform has been hotly contested for years. Yet the magnitude and intensity of the 2009 town hall protests took many by surprise. Democrats accused conservative lobbying groups, like Freedom Works, of organizing protesters and training them in confrontational, disruptive tactics.[28] Republicans argued that the protests grew naturally from deep opposition to the administration's proposals. Whatever the causes, responsible deliberation could not take place, and the voices of average citizens—those with questions about the proposed reforms but no strong opinion either way—were lost in the shuffle.

More recently, town hall meetings have focused on a wider array of issues, including climate change, raising the debt ceiling, jobs and the economy, taxes, and health care reform. Although the communication climate at these meetings has been less hostile than it was during the summer of 2009, many meetings continue to be characterized by too much speaking and too little listening, an undercurrent of anger and frustration, and a general sense of frustration with Congressional gridlock.[29] Some analysts point to the impact of YouTube, radio talk shows, and more aggressive strategies from activist groups on both sides. David Fahrenthold, a writer for the *Washington Post*, argues, "Somehow, an event that was once all about listening has become all about shouting."[30]

Some have suggested that the traditional town hall format may *not* be the best way for lawmakers to connect with their constituents. James Fishkin, director of the Center for Deliberative Democracy at Stanford University, argues that town hall meetings work better in smaller communities but are less effective for large populations. He points to the "illusion that a district of 650,000 potential voters can be represented by the unscientifically self-selected who decide to show up." He goes on to note that these meetings become unpredictable, "open invitations for interest groups and grass roots campaigns to capture the public dialogue."[31] Fishkin thus recommends the use of *deliberative polls*, in which a survey is used to identify the range of attitudes in a particular district *before* inviting a randomly selected, representative sample of constituents to attend one of the meetings. Trained moderators then guide the discussion so that all voices are heard, and participants are asked to deliberate thoughtfully and respectfully. The Center for Deliberative Democracy has conducted more than 50 deliberative polls around the world, with excellent results.[32]

Other organizations that help communities organize and conduct town hall meetings suggest these guidelines for organizing a productive meeting[33]:

- *Assemble an organizing committee.* Make sure that the organizers will be seen as neutral or represent all major shades of opinion. The more points of view the committee encompasses, the more successful the project is likely to be.
- *Define the issue or goals.* The committee will have to agree on exactly what issues to tackle and what the meeting is expected to accomplish.
- *Attract broad participation.* Seek endorsements for the meeting from groups and individuals who have large followings in the community and span a wide range of opinions.
- *Maximize public and media interest.* The meeting will have the greatest impact on the community if it draws a big turnout and is covered by local media. Prepare and distribute a press kit that explains how the meeting could lead to resolving an issue that greatly concerns the community.

When town hall meetings are conducted with a concern for inclusiveness and respectful participation—when citizens become actively involved in working *together* to find solutions to their common problems—they *can* be a source of creative and effective solutions that win widespread public support.

National Issues Forums

National Issues Forums (NIF) is a nonpartisan, nationwide network of locally sponsored public forums on important public policy issues. NIF is rooted in the simple notion that people in a democracy need to come together to reason and to talk—to deliberate about common problems.[34] The NIF network has grown to include thousands of civic clubs, religious organizations, libraries, schools, and many other groups who meet to discuss critical public issues. Scholars have described the NIF process as the most pervasive model of small group deliberation in the United States, used yearly by as many as 15,000 groups.[35] Forum participants range from teenagers to retirees, from prison inmates to community leaders, and from community residents to university students.

NIF formats are varied and may include small groups, such as study circles, or large group gatherings similar to town hall meetings. NIF does not advocate specific solutions or points of view. Rather, it provides citizens of diverse views and experiences with the opportunity to carefully study an issue, consider a range of choices (weighing the pros and cons of each), and discuss those options with others. The goal is to identify common concerns and, if possible, to discover areas of agreement about the best course of action.

Although all NIF forums are locally organized, moderated, and financed, the materials they use are produced by the Kettering Foundation and distributed by the National Issues Forums Institute. Prior to an NIF forum, organizers encourage participants to read an "issue book" from the NIF Institute. Each book provides factual information and outlines three or four broad policy choices for addressing an issue. During the forums, trained moderators encourage participants to consider the nature of the problem being discussed, the pros and cons of each approach to solving the problem, and the values underlying each choice. Forum moderators are trained to maintain neutrality and to steer participants away from digressions, logical pitfalls, indecisiveness, or disruptive comments.[36] Recent NIF issue books include the following:

- *What Should Go on the Internet? Privacy, Freedom, and Security Online*
- *Crime and Punishment: Is Justice Being Served?*
- *America's Role in the World: What Does National Security Mean in the 21st Century?*
- *The Environment at Risk: Responding to the Growing Dangers*
- *Youth and Violence: Reducing the Threat*
- *Social Security: How Can We Afford It?*
- *Preparing Today's Kids for Tomorrow's Jobs: What Should Our Community Do?*[37]

These issue books all address large national and even international problems, but they also have implications for the local communities where the NIF forums are held.

Whatever form deliberations take, nearly 60 years of group communication research have taught us that specific factors influence whether they have good results.

FACTORS THAT INFLUENCE EFFECTIVE GROUP DELIBERATION

17.3 List some of the factors that influence how deliberative groups function.

Preview. *As groups work to complete tasks or grapple with difficult problems, they may interact in ways that enhance the quality of their decisions and form strong bonds within the group, or they may deliberate less effectively because they fail to recognize some of the complex dynamics of group communication.*

A variety of factors influence the effectiveness of group deliberations, whatever the context. How groups handle these factors determines whether the deliberations prove empowering and productive for participants or only increase their frustrations or feelings of powerlessness.

Conflict

Whenever people deliberate about important and controversial issues, conflict is likely to occur. It can emerge over differences in opinions, values, or goals, or it can result from personal incompatibilities, status differences, or cultural misunderstandings. Ultimately, conflict results from deficiencies in information, understanding, and communication.[38]

In public life, conflict is inevitable. It is difficult to imagine any community—especially in a diverse society—where there are no differences of interests or opinion. The freedom to express those differences is fundamental to the process of democratic deliberation. Deliberation is all about finding ways to live with, work through, and resolve our conflicting ideas and interests. The challenge is to find ways to make conflict *productive* rather than polarizing and destructive. Although study circles, town hall meetings, and National Issues Forums are a good start, we need to create still more democratic arenas in which everyday people can productively explore their differences.

Public controversies are often treated as zero-sum games, in which one side must win and the other must lose. Antagonisms among some may overshadow the eagerness of most people to search for common ground and to find solutions to their problems.[39] We may underestimate the ability of the community and society as a whole to come together to solve public problems. The media, of course, often play a role in this, emphasizing stories of seemingly intractable conflict over news of cooperation, compromise, and productive collaboration. The nuances of complex issues and the moderation or ambivalence of most people may be lost in the media's search for a good story.

In situations of conflict, it is up to ordinary citizens to come together and voice their interest in overcoming their differences and finding solutions. By involving large numbers of people in addressing issues of shared concern, communities can balance the voices of those who have exceptionally strong opinions with voices of moderation and compromise. It is important that those who feel ambivalent or uncertain *not* be left out of conversations about such critical public issues as education, poverty, jobs, youth issues, and immigration.[40] In the absence of such voices, we may get a distorted view of public opinion, concluding that people appear angrier or more polarized than they really are.

Whether conflict functions in a positive or negative way depends on how it is viewed and managed. Although many of us try to avoid conflict, we must recognize that conflict *can* lead to enhanced creativity, a deeper understanding of complex problems, and better solutions. Conflict is not so much to be avoided or feared as *managed* constructively.[41]

Role Structure

The **norms** that develop in deliberative groups typically suggest (or require) appropriate modes of conduct for all group members. Some groups expect that all participants will have read up on the issue to be discussed and will arrive well informed and aware of the various perspectives. Other groups establish norms of respectful dialogue or actively encourage participants to remain open minded. In addition, individual participants in group deliberations often assume particular roles, either formally or informally. Your group or committee may elect a chair, for example, to keep the discussion on track and enforce the rules of engagement. Other members of groups assume their roles more informally, taking it upon themselves to do things necessary for the group to function effectively.

The importance of various roles and deliberative functions varies from group to group. In one group, for example, a member may use humor to relieve tension or to build group cohesiveness. Another may ask questions to elicit necessary information or to introduce the next issue that needs to be discussed. Of course, both humor and questions *can* be used negatively; sarcastic humor is sometimes used to diminish or silence other members of a group, and questions *can* be phrased as a challenge or a put-down ("What would *you* know about working in a minimum-wage job?"). Thus, it is important that you choose to play a *constructive* role in your group, helping it accomplish the task at hand and contributing to its morale and cohesiveness.[42]

Task roles contribute to the group's ability to solve problems, make decisions, exchange information, and resolve conflicts. One man who serves on the board of a nonprofit organization, for example, excels at offering financial data, explaining the budget, and providing clarification for anyone who is confused. Another listens thoughtfully to everyone, probes for additional information and opinions, and then integrates what others have said into a coherent summary. Sometimes, he offers suggestions for new ways of approaching a problem. Both of these men play important roles on the board, keeping it on task and enhancing its ability to make effective decisions.

Other major roles help build and maintain the group—or help develop and sustain the interpersonal relationships within it. Group members who play these roles help others feel positive about their participation and interact harmoniously

HIGHLIGHTING THE WRITTEN RECORD | Keeping Meeting Minutes

Many groups designate a person to record the minutes of each meeting. In formal groups, such as a board of directors, a secretary is elected to perform that task, whereas in smaller, more informal groups, an elected chair both runs the meeting and records the minutes. Regardless, the minutes should include the following:

- The name of the assembled group and the date, time, and meeting location
- A list of those present, those absent, and the name of the person presiding
- A brief summary of key committee reports

- A list of actions taken by the group (with or without a summary of the discussion surrounding each issue, depending on the customs of the group)
- The vote taken on each action item; for example, a set of minutes might read like the following: "The board voted (9–3) to participate in a collaborative fund-raiser with other local nonprofit agencies."
- A list of announcements
- The time at which the meeting adjourned
- The date, time, and place of the group's next meeting ◣

and respectfully with others. On the same board mentioned previously, one woman excels at mediating conflict and reconciling differences of opinion. She also encourages reticent group members to speak. Another man does an exceptional job of praising others for offering creative or interesting ideas. By performing these group maintenance roles, these board members encourage cooperation among others and help build a spirit of solidarity within the group.

In contrast to the positive roles, of course, some group members occasionally assume negative or destructive roles—roles that promote their own self-interests, or roles that undermine the cohesiveness or productivity of the group. One group member, for example, may dominate the conversation, with little regard for giving others their turn to speak. Another may be overly critical of others' ideas or even engage in personal attacks on others in the group. These self-serving or disruptive roles can get the group seriously off track and lead to tensions.

In general, when positive roles are enacted and shared in deliberative groups and negative roles minimized, groups have more constructive outcomes, including enhanced morale and better decision making.[43] Those who assume such positive roles are often recognized as the leaders of the group and credited with its success in accomplishing its goals.

Tolerance of Dissent

Sometimes we lose patience with the slow processes of democratic deliberation. We may want to make a decision quickly. We may feel that we have been grappling with a problem for a long time, with no agreement on a course of action. Or we become annoyed by a person who raises objections or suggests a different way of viewing things. When an individual or a small minority expresses a dissenting opinion, the majority may react with intolerance. If the majority of the group decides that it's time to move on, they may pressure those who stand in the way to fall in line.

Group pressure for uniformity can be quite powerful. One early study found that if those in the majority within a group simply state their opinions, those in the minority often pretend to agree, even if there is no pressure on them to do so.[44] Giving in to group pressure can be especially tempting for those who really value their group membership or strongly identify with the group.[45]

Situational factors may play a significant role, too.[46] In general, we are more likely to conform to group pressures in situations that are ambiguous or confusing, when other group members are unanimous in their views, or when the group contains people of higher status. We may also feel a lot of pressure when the group appears highly cohesive, or if a crisis or state of emergency exists. Under such circumstances, the group may be under external pressure to come to a quick decision.[47]

Those in the majority may use a variety of tactics to pressure minority members into yielding, ranging from teasing to hostile questioning or ridicule. Often great pressure is put on those who stand in the way of consensus.[48] How a group responds to a dissenter may depend on his or her status in the group. Groups sometimes tolerate more "deviation" from those of higher status.[49]

How should you respond to group pressures? Some people tend to "go with the flow," preferring to fit in with the group rather than risk being perceived as "making waves." Others may come to agree with the group's perceptions—either because they are, in fact, genuinely persuaded, or have begun to question the validity of their own views. Finally, some individuals simply refuse to give in. Challenging the group's authority in this way can result in a variety of outcomes, including rejection or punishment. Organizational communication scholar Phil Tompkins recounts the story of the engineer who unsuccessfully argued against launching the ill-fated space shuttle *Challenger*, which exploded shortly after takeoff in 1986. Even though several other engineers had expressed reservations about the launch, they eventually went along with the management team's decision to proceed with the launch. The lone dissenting engineer lost his job and was socially ostracized.[50]

When we tolerate or even encourage dissent, we bring a broader range of views into the discussion. Those who disagree with the prevailing view may even end up carrying the day. The *way* those in the minority articulate their views can make a huge difference. If they hope for tolerance of their dissenting views, they, too, have an obligation to be well informed and to debate in a spirit of respectful dialogue.[51]

Group Cohesiveness As citizens deliberate in groups over time, they may develop a strong sense of group loyalty. Although cohesiveness *may* function positively, it can also lead to intolerance of dissent and impaired decision making. One of the most extensive investigations of the potentially negative impact of cohesiveness on group decision making was conducted by psychologist Irving Janis.[52] Janis examined the decision-making processes leading to several historic military and political fiascoes, including the decision to escalate the Korean War, the Kennedy administration's invasion of Cuba at the Bay of Pigs, the escalation of the war in Vietnam, and the decisions surrounding the Watergate cover-up. More recently, others have used his framework to examine the U.S. decision to go to war with Iraq.[53]

Janis introduced the term groupthink to describe how cohesive groups sometimes make bad decisions. Groupthink is "a model of thinking that people engage in when they are deeply involved in a cohesive in-group, when the members' striving for unanimity overrides their motivation to realistically appraise alternative courses of action."[54] He also pointed out that those caught up in groupthink tend to seek consensus "prematurely," cutting off full and free discussion of alternative courses of action.[55] Janis identified a number of factors that commonly lead to groupthink, including an illusion of invulnerability, an unquestioned belief in the group's inherent morality, a shared illusion of unanimity, self-censorship, and, of course, direct pressure exerted on dissenters.[56]

Fortunately, not all cohesive groups fall prey to groupthink. In fact, participating in a highly cohesive group can be a productive and satisfying experience. Much depends on the group norms that develop—whether everyone is committed to hard work and the constructive and critical examination of everyone's ideas. Later in the chapter, we discuss how the group's leader can play a key role in setting a positive climate for group deliberations.

Status and Power

Although much research on group roles has taken place in laboratory settings, enacting roles in real-life civic or professional settings is more complex. When individuals deliberate in task forces, community groups, study circles, or workplace teams, they bring to such meetings their professional identity as well as their status within the community. For example, one of the authors of this book recently joined a community group, the "social entrepreneurship" committee. The committee's task is to pool community resources and seek ways to help nonprofit organizations become more self-sustaining by starting their own businesses and generating their own revenue. The committee consists of the executive directors of several prominent nonprofits (including two that are already running successful businesses), the director of the United Way, a well-known judge, a member of the city council, a representative of the mayor's office, the president of the Chamber of Commerce, the director of the local university's Center on Social Entrepreneurship, and a few concerned citizens.

In real-life groups like this, members vary in their *status* (the value, importance, or prestige associated with their given position) and *power* (their potential for controlling resources and/or influencing others). In general, members of the social entrepreneurship committee possess high status. Still, there are significant differences. Some bring success stories to the group. Others have labored with social justice issues in the community for more than three decades. Still others bring impressive academic credentials or strong ties to potential sources of financial support. A few are new to their positions or are simply eager to get involved. Who will have the most influence as this group deliberates over time? Who will help the group advance its goals? Will those with less experience or knowledge participate actively? Much will depend on how those with the *greatest* power and status conduct themselves.

The bases of power are many.[57] Some people are powerful because they have the capacity to reward or punish. The United Way director, for example, can influence which nonprofits receive financial support from the United Way. Others—those with compelling success stories—are held up as experts or as role models. Still others have the connections to make things happen because of their positions or their political networks (the judge and the social justice leader, for example). Some have several sources of power. The center director from the university, for example, is charismatic, has resources, is knowledgeable about successful entrepreneurship models throughout the United States, and is politically well connected.

Whenever deliberative groups are composed of people with varying degrees of power and status, group members do not communicate as equals, and this inequality may serve as an obstacle to effective interaction and decision making. When communicating with someone of higher status, those of lower status often communicate cautiously, attempting to win approval by downplaying "bad" news or acting deferentially.[58] In this kind of communication climate, it can be a challenge to find out what people *really* think.

Leadership

Leaders of deliberative groups are in a position to encourage and empower others. They can insist on hearing from everyone. They can ask other group members to help with specific leadership functions (such as attending an important meeting in their place and reporting back to the group). They can listen intently, ask probing questions, insist on hearing dissenting points of view, encourage constructive

Explore the Concept "Teams" at **MyCommunicationLab**

conflict, and make sure they do not dominate the conversation. They can create a climate of shared leadership, shared problem solving, and shared responsibility for the outcome of the group's deliberations. Although there are many factors to consider when choosing a leadership style, most groups work more effectively when important roles are shared and the climate encourages all to participate without fear of embarrassment or retribution.

When Irving Janis studied group decision making, he looked at groups of individuals who had worked with and advised U.S. presidents. Based on his

---

HIGHLIGHTING LEADERSHIP | Avoiding the Pitfalls of Meetings: Practical Tips for Leaders

Group leaders devote a lot of time to planning and conducting meetings. Following are some common pitfalls in organizing and conducting meetings and brief suggestions on how to avoid them.

- *Lack of Clarity about the Meeting's Purpose:* Why is the group meeting? Sometimes we hold meetings, whether or not they are needed. The effective leader should be able to answer this question: What results should this meeting produce?

- *Inadequate Leader Preparation:* For a meeting to work well, the leader needs to address some basic issues in advance: Why are we meeting? Who will be present? How long will the meeting last? Where is the best place to meet? What is the agenda (and priorities within the agenda)? What problem-solving approach will work best? What must I do to be on top of the issues and prepared to direct the flow of the deliberation? What information will others need so that they can also be well prepared and ready to intelligently and thoughtfully discuss and deliberate?

- *A Haphazard Decision-Making Process:* Group meetings provide the context in which many boards, community groups, and business organizations make important decisions. Yet many know little about how to approach group deliberation and communication. As a result, many meetings are frustrating and nonproductive. The leader needs to be knowledgeable about the factors that impact group deliberation and savvy

about selecting an agenda that is well suited to the task at hand.

- *Jumping to Conclusions:* As they work through a complex problem, group members may be unaware of the criteria or standards that are guiding their decisions. They may tend to jump to conclusions or make hasty decisions. An effective group leader will choose an agenda that asks the group to define and explore the problem, to reflect on causes and effects, and to establish criteria for a good decision (cost, fairness, innovativeness, etc.) before moving on to examine possible solutions.

- *Overdeveloped Egos:* Some meetings end up not being about problem solving at all. Ideas may not be accepted by their merits, but on the competing interests of those around the table. The leader must anticipate ego issues, recognize that some group members bring their own agendas to the meeting, and establish and reinforce norms that keep the deliberation focused on issues, not on personalities.

- *Insufficient Follow-up:* Meetings typically end with people being assigned to carry out various tasks. These assignments need to be accompanied by a timeline and procedures for reporting back to the group. Meeting minutes should accurately reflect actions taken by the group and who was assigned various responsibilities.

Source: Edward Prewitt, "Pitfalls in Meetings and How to Avoid Them," *Harvard Management Update* 3 (June 1998): 9–10. ◢

research, he concluded that leaders need to take some direct actions to make their groups healthy and effective. Specifically, he encouraged leaders to do the following:

- Assign to everyone the role of critical evaluator.
- Avoid stating personal views, particularly at the outset.
- Bring in outsiders representing diverse interests to talk with and listen to the group.
- Play the devil's advocate and ask others to take turns in that role.
- Let the group deliberate without the leader from time to time.
- Hold a "second-chance" meeting after a decision is made, asking each member to express as strongly as possible any residual doubts.[59]

The judicious use of authority to encourage the free expression of ideas and to reward initiative and innovative thinking can go far in eliminating the doubts and skepticism of less powerful group members.

As we have noted throughout this chapter, groups may deliberate in private settings as part of a committee or task force, or they may deliberate in public spaces as part of a community forum. On other occasions, individuals speak in public on behalf of a group, presenting the findings or recommendations of the group.

GROUP PRESENTATIONS

Preview. *When we deliberate as part of a group, we may also be expected to communicate with others outside the group. In doing so, we hope to deepen others' understanding of the issues we view as important. We may not view ourselves as experts. Nevertheless, we may be called upon to speak on behalf of some group that the larger community looks to for advice, guidance, or recommendations.*

17.4 Discuss how to prepare and present your ideas in a public discussion.

Public discussions often bring together representatives from several different groups or organizations, all of whom may have some expertise or differing perspectives on the issue. For example, a recent community forum on hunger and poverty in Bloomington, Indiana, brought together the executive directors of five local agencies: Martha's House (a transitional housing unit for the homeless), Mother Hubbard's Cupboard (a food pantry), the Community Kitchen (an agency that provides free meals to those in need), the Shalom Community Center (a day shelter and resource center for the homeless), and the Hoosier Hills Food Bank (another food pantry). Each director made a brief presentation, followed by an extensive question-and-answer period with the audience.

As you gain knowledge and assume a leadership role within a group, you may be asked to speak on behalf of the group at a panel discussion or symposium. To help prepare you for this role, you should take advantage of opportunities at school to learn about the various forms and functions of group presentations. Although group presentations share some similarities with delivering a speech, there also are some special considerations when speaking as part of a group.

Panel Discussions

Group presentations assume a variety of forms. Panel discussions and symposia are two of the most common. In a panel discussion, participants interact directly and often spontaneously under the guidance of a moderator. No single participant delivers a long, formal speech. Instead, each speaks briefly, frequently, and in conversation with others on the panel. Here are some guidelines for preparing for and participating in panel discussions:

- *Know the group.* Find out who the other panel members are and what organizations or positions they represent. Having this information, as well as information about the group's size, will help you tentatively plan what you want to say and how much you will want to talk.
- *Obtain an agenda for the discussion.* The moderator should have some plan for how he or she wishes to organize the panel discussion. Use the agenda as your guide to prepare for the discussion. Make a few notes, although most of your remarks should be spontaneous.
- *Participate actively, but share the floor with others.* The moderator may start the panel discussion with a brief statement or by posing a question. He or she may also ask each participant for any opening remarks they may have. Otherwise, you should feel free to jump in and comment whenever you have something significant to say. Make your comments succinct and to the point. Take turns with other panel members. The best panel discussions are freewheeling, lively, and dynamic, yet also civil and inclusive. All participants should have the opportunity to speak and to get a respectful hearing.
- *Use good interpersonal communication skills.* Listen to others attentively. If you do need to interrupt, do so politely and tactfully. Build on others' comments, if possible. Establish good eye contact with listeners while also communicating directly with other panelists. Cooperate with the moderator.

Symposium Presentations

A more formal type of group presentation is the symposium, in which discussants prepare brief speeches representing their viewpoints. Each group member speaks in turn without interruption or interaction. The symposium leader usually introduces the group members and provides a summary at the end of the discussion. During the actual discussion, however, it should not be necessary for the moderator to interrupt or intervene in the presentations, except to provide a transition between speakers. Here are some guidelines for participating in a symposium:

- *Know your assigned role.* Understand what you are expected to talk about as well as what other members of the symposium will be expected to do. Make sure you do not talk about subjects that others have been assigned. Once you know your topic, prepare your symposium presentation just as you would any other speech.
- *Respect group norms.* Stay within the time limits you have been given so that everyone will have a fair chance to speak. When you are not speaking,

listen attentively to others. You are part of the group but also part of the audience. If possible, adapt your style of delivery to that of others in the group. If others remain seated while speaking (and you are comfortable doing so), remain seated as well. If others step up to a podium in a more formal style, you should follow suit.

■ *Maintain a cooperative attitude.* Being asked to speak as part of a group

In a symposium, each member of the group speaks in turn without interruption; typically, a question-and-answer session follows.

Watch the Video
"US Involvement in Iraq" at
MyCommunicationLab

can raise competitive feelings. You want to come across well to the audience, of course, but you should never try to "show up" others on the panel. Stay focused on communicating as effectively as you can, and commit to doing all you can to make the symposium as a whole a success.

Both the panel discussion and the symposium are almost always followed by a question-and-answer period. During this time, members of the audience will not only ask questions but also express their opinions. The forum is generally guided by the moderator, and questions may be directed to individual members or to the group as a whole. In either case, it is important that you anticipate responding to audience questions and that you not become defensive or quarrelsome in response to comments or questions from the audience.

Regardless of the format, certain guidelines will serve you well as you speak or deliberate in groups. In the final section of the chapter, we offer some tips for participating successfully in group deliberations.

GUIDELINES FOR DELIBERATING IN GROUPS

Preview. *Regardless of the context in which you are deliberating—whether you are part of a study circle, participating in a National Issues Forum, or serving as a member of a task force at work or in your community—you can do a variety of things to contribute to the success of the group's deliberations.*

17.5 Describe the attitudes and communication behaviors associated with effective group deliberation.

A group deliberation is only as good as its participants. Informed, active members contribute to a deeper understanding of the issue or task before the group, and they also enhance the chances that good decisions will be made. Uninformed, uninvolved, or unskilled participants, on the other hand, almost guarantee the group's failure. In this section, we describe some of the ways you can contribute to more positive group outcomes.

Prepare Carefully for Each Meeting

Every group member needs to be as knowledgeable as possible regarding the subject of the discussion or deliberation.[60] It is probably inevitable that some members of your group will be better informed than others. It is also inevitable that some will understand certain aspects of the topic better than others. But everybody has *some* knowledge or experience worth contributing, and you can always contribute even more by preparing carefully in advance of a meeting. Do your homework. Reflect on the important issues that are likely to arise. And jot down a few notes to yourself in advance of the deliberation.

Often the group's chair distributes an agenda in advance of the deliberations. The agenda sets forth the plan for the meeting—providing a list of issues to be addressed, as well as the order in which they will be discussed. Group leaders should distribute the agenda well before the meeting, allowing ample time for everyone to read and think about the issues the group will discuss. Sometimes a *proposed* agenda is sent to participants, asking if they have any additions or corrections. Examine that agenda carefully—it can have a powerful effect on the direction and substance of the group's deliberations. If an issue is *not* on the agenda, it probably will not be addressed at all. If an issue appears near the end of a long agenda, there may not be time to discuss it fully; or the issue might even be postponed to a later meeting. Pay attention to the proposed agenda, offer input if you have the chance, and come to the meeting prepared to talk about the issues on the agenda.

Adopt a Collaborative Attitude and Participate Actively

We previously noted the importance of approaching group interactions in a spirit of collaboration. Avoid making judgments in advance of the group's deliberations. Allow for judgments and decisions to emerge out of the group as it deliberates over time. Each person shares some responsibility for the success or failure of the entire group. Whenever you allow personal ambitions to overwhelm your commitment to the group, you are undermining the group's success.

Every group member should take an active part in the discussion and activities of the group. If you sit back silently during group meetings, you contribute nothing to the group or to your own credibility. On the other hand, if you participate actively and make positive contributions, you help the group achieve its goals, improve your own standing within the group, and build a reputation as a valued asset to the community. That reputation may in turn lead to other opportunities to become involved in group deliberations and problem solving.

Keep an Open Mind

When working in groups, it is important that you not only have a collaborative attitude but also keep an open mind. Over the course of a group's deliberations, you may hear a diversity of opinions, some of which you may find misguided or even offensive at first. Rather than try to "shoot down" such opinions, you should encourage the group to explore a broad diversity of opinions and viewpoints. As the group's deliberations proceed, you might even find yourself rethinking your own point of view. It is a good idea *not* to assert your own opinions too strongly early in the process. An effective group participant is one who remains open to changing his or her own mind as the discussion proceeds.

Pay Attention to Nonverbal Communication and Listen Carefully

When we work in groups, we tend to focus on what other participants are saying. But it is also important to watch how they are acting.[61] Lack of eye contact may signal disengagement, poor preparation, or interpersonal tensions. Folded arms could suggest dissatisfaction with what others are saying or the course of action being pursued. Of course, differences in cultural norms and practices should be taken into consideration.[62] In general, however, the nonverbal signs that some group members may be uncomfortable or disengaged are easy to read; as a participant devoted to the success of the group, you should take action to ensure that all participants feel valued and engaged in the group's work.

When others are talking, listen carefully and try to understand their points of view. Even if you do not agree, give their opinions fair consideration. Try to offer constructive suggestions that move the discussion forward. At the same time, do not hesitate to question someone who seems vague or who fails to articulate ideas clearly. Research has shown that effective groups are careful and rigorous in the way they explore ideas and evaluate alternatives.[63] Good group members take each other seriously and have a healthy respect for one another, but they are not afraid to challenge each other's ideas.

HIGHLIGHTING DIVERSITY | Recognizing Cultural Differences in Nonverbal Communication

As the groups we work with increasingly include people with diverse cultural backgrounds, it is important that we improve our skills in interpreting nonverbal behaviors. Rather than interpreting others' behavior in terms of our own cultural norms, we should be respectful of cultural differences. Here are a few examples:

- North Americans prefer to maintain a greater personal distance with other parties than do those from the Middle East or Latin America. Many Arabs and Latin Americans see North Americans as distant and cold, whereas North Americans see the others as invading their personal space.
- Americans expect others to look them in the eye as a way of exhibiting trust, openness, and sincerity, while other cultures consider this sort of

eye contact impolite or even insulting. Africans, for example, are taught to avoid eye contact when listening to others.

- Arabs tend to use elaborate and ritualized forms of communication, especially during greetings. Wide gestures and animated faces may come across as boisterous, loud, and unprofessional to Americans.
- Although the Japanese are comfortable with silence and may even close their eyes when they are deeply concentrating, others (including Arabs and Americans) may perceive silence as a sign that something is wrong.

Sources: Michelle Le Baron, Bridging Cultural Conflicts: A New Approach for a Changing World (San Francisco, CA: Jossey-Bass, 2003); Richard D. Lewis, When Cultures Collide, rev. ed. (London: Brealey, 2000). ◣

Play Different Roles

Group communication scholars have identified nearly 20 different roles that group members may play, ranging from information giver to harmonizer (see Figure 17.1). It is easy to get into a rut and perform only one or two roles. For instance, a well-informed or dominant participant might provide ideas and information and control the flow of the conversation. That person could develop a more balanced approach, perhaps, by *also* eliciting others' ideas or offering praise for a good plan

> **FIGURE 17.1**
>
> **Constructive Roles in Groups**
>
> Task Roles
>
> - **Initiator**—Proposes new ideas, procedures, goals, and solutions; gets the group started
> - **Information giver**—Supplies evidence and other information relevant to the issue being discussed
> - **Information seeker**—Asks for information or clarification from other group members and endeavors to make sure that relevant information is not overlooked or ignored
> - **Opinion giver**—Offers his or her own views; is willing to take a position, although not without sensitivity to others' views
> - **Opinion seeker**—Actively seeks opinions and reactions of others
> - **Elaborator**—Clarifies and illuminates ideas by offering examples, comparisons, or explanations, with a consistent concern for relevance and brevity
> - **Integrator**—Clarifies the relationships among facts, opinions, and suggested courses of action; integrates ideas that have been advanced
> - **Orientor**—Helps keep the group directed toward its goal, sometimes summarizing the discussion and moving the group forward
> - **Evaluator**—Offers assessment of ideas and information; applies agreed upon criteria to solutions/courses of action the group is considering
> - **Procedural specialist**—Helps organize the group's work; suggests an agenda or way of approaching deliberation and problem solving
> - **Consensus tester**—Asks if the group has reached a decision acceptable to all, or if there is agreement on a course of action that everyone can support
>
> Building and Maintenance Roles
>
> - **Supporter**—Praises ideas or contributions of others and contributes to an inclusive, supportive communication climate
> - **Harmonizer**—Attempts to mediate conflict, suggests compromises, and tries to reconcile differences
> - **Tension reliever**—Encourages a relaxed atmosphere by reducing formality and interjecting appropriate humor
> - **Gatekeeper**—Encourages reticent group members, discourages those who are monopolizing the discussion, and seeks diversity of opinion
> - **Norm creator**—Suggests preferred ways of deliberating; may challenge unproductive ways of communicating
> - **Solidarity builder**—Expresses positive regard or respect for other group members; reinforces a sense of group cohesiveness
> - **Encourager**—Invites group members to remain hopeful and not give up as they seek solutions to tough problems; asks them to dream and think creatively

HIGHLIGHTING ETHICS | Communicating Ethically in Groups

Embedded in all the other suggestions in this chapter is a concern for the ethics of deliberation. Here are some guidelines:

- Show concern for others' ideas, respect for their feelings, and a willingness to give them time to reflect on new information.
- Develop a collaborative attitude that is less concerned with who "wins" the argument than with finding common ground and building consensus.
- Refuse to allow the group to become a platform for special interests or for your own self-interest.
- Remain as eager to listen to and learn from others as you are to offer them your opinions and advice.
- Approach group deliberations in a spirit of dialogue.

- Be willing to take extra time, even if additional meetings are necessary, for the sake of a better, more fully informed decision.
- Develop a sense of responsibility for the good of the group as a whole.
- Demonstrate the maturity to realize that other legitimate groups may have different priorities and perspectives.
- Recognize that no matter how hard your group deliberates or how well it performs, others work hard as well and have legitimate needs to be fulfilled.

In sum, the ethical group member is a good thinker, a good listener, a hard worker, and a responsible member of the community.

of action. When roles are shared and participants play several different roles in deliberative groups, everyone benefits.

Focus on Substance, Not Personalities

Every group member should concentrate on substantive concerns, not personality differences. Every deliberative group has a task to accomplish. The individuals composing the group, however, are human beings who possess personalities that occasionally conflict. Severe personality clashes can damage the group's ability to find common ground and make good decisions.

As a group member, you will inevitably find some of your fellow members insensitive, uninformed, or even lacking in intelligence. Some may seem domineering or rude. Even so, the success of the group depends on *all* members, so you seek ways to overcome conflicts or irritations rooted in personality differences. In a sense, overcoming personality differences is part of your *ethical* responsibility as a member of a group.

 Study and Review materials for this chapter are at **MyCommunicationLab**

SUMMARY

 Listen to the Audio Chapter Summary at **MyCommunicationLab**

Understanding Public Deliberation

17.1 Explain the role, importance, and potential benefits of public deliberation.

- Deliberating in groups is common in our professional and civic lives. In deliberating, we share

information, gain new perspectives, seek common ground, and make decisions.
- Organizations are increasingly team-based, and citizens encounter many opportunities to help solve problems in their communities by deliberating with others in all kinds of groups.

- In community settings, citizens often gather to deliberate about important public issues.
  - Ideally, these deliberations lead to positive outcomes such as increased civic engagement, deeper understanding of the issues, increased tolerance for opposing points of view, and enhanced faith in the democratic process.
  - Whether these positive outcomes are realized depends on such contextual factors as the facilitator's skill, participant expectations and preparation, and whether the group's deliberations have any practical impact.
  - The more citizens interact in a respectful spirit of dialogue, the better their chances of having a successful experience.

Group Structures That Encourage Dialogue and Deliberation

 Describe group structures that promote effective deliberation and dialogue.

- Certain group structures and formats, such as study circles, town hall meetings, and National Issues Forums, encourage informed, cooperative deliberations with a view toward more effective problem solving.

Factors That Influence Effective Group Deliberation

 List some of the factors that influence how deliberative groups function.

- Many factors influence the effectiveness of a group's deliberations.
  - Learning to manage conflict constructively plays a huge role in any group's comfort levels, creativity, and productivity.
  - In healthy groups, members tend to play a variety of task and maintenance roles, with self-serving behaviors minimized.
  - Welcoming diverse views and tolerating dissent is another key factor. If majority group members pressure those with differing views to "go along with the group," their ability to make judicious decisions may be impaired.
  - Highly cohesive groups whose members are strongly bonded may be vulnerable to

groupthink—leading them to seek agreement before fully exploring alternative courses of action and listening to dissenters. Cohesive groups with positive norms, however, can function quite effectively.
  - Power and status differences must be carefully managed. The burden is on those of higher status to establish an environment of trust.
  - Leaders set the tone for the deliberations and have the opportunity to foster an open and empowering communication climate.

Group Presentations

 Discuss how to prepare and present your ideas in a public discussion.

- On occasion, you may be called on to make public presentations as part of a group.
  - Sometimes these group presentations take the form of a panel (complete with spontaneous interaction under the guidance of a moderator); others are organized more formally in the form of a symposium (with each group member making a short speech).
  - Following group presentations, listeners usually ask questions. The question-and-answer period often leads to extensive sharing of ideas and information and a great deal of interaction between speakers and members of the audience.

Guidelines for Deliberating in Groups

 Describe the attitudes and communication behaviors associated with effective group deliberation.

- In all group settings, public or private, small or large, participants should strive to do the following:
  - Be well prepared.
  - Embrace a group orientation.
  - Participate actively.
  - Maintain an open mind.
  - Listen thoughtfully.
  - Play different constructive roles.
  - Pay attention to nonverbal communication (including cultural variations).
  - Focus on matters of substance.
  - Communicate with the highest concern for ethics.

QUESTIONS FOR REVIEW AND REFLECTION

Understanding Public Deliberation

 Explain the role, importance, and potential benefits of public deliberation.

1. Why is it important for you to be knowledgeable about deliberating effectively in groups?
2. Explain your understanding of "public deliberation." Have you ever witnessed or participated in any kind of event or meeting that you would characterize as public deliberation? If so, describe how it worked.
3. What does it mean to communicate in a spirit of dialogue?
4. What are the potential benefits of public deliberation?
5. Describe some of the challenges of public deliberation as well as some of the ways that the group's facilitator might help manage these challenges.

Group Structures That Encourage Dialogue and Deliberation

17.2 Describe group structures that promote effective deliberation and dialogue.

6. Compare and contrast the following group structures that can encourage deliberative dialogue:
   - Study circles
   - Town hall meetings
   - National Issues Forums
7. What are some topics in your community that might be fruitfully explored through one of these formats?

Factors That Influence Effective Group Deliberation

17.3 List some of the factors that influence how deliberative groups function.

8. How might the following factors influence the effectiveness of any deliberative group? Think of concrete examples from your own group experiences.
   - Conflict
   - Role structure
   - Intolerance of dissent
   - Group cohesiveness
   - Norms
   - Status and power differences among group members
   - Leadership

Group Presentations

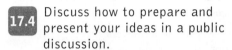 Discuss how to prepare and present your ideas in a public discussion.

9. Compare and contrast a panel discussion with a symposium as particular forms of group presentations.
10. How would you prepare for participating effectively in each of these? If you have ever presented as part of a panel or symposium, describe your experience.

Guidelines for Deliberating in Groups

17.5 Describe the attitudes and communication behaviors associated with effective group deliberation.

11. This chapter describes several guidelines for effective participation in deliberative groups. Which do you think are especially important? Why? Can you think of any others that may also matter in particular contexts? If so, explain.
12. What roles do you typically play in groups? What are some other roles you might be able to play to diversify and enrich the contributions you make to the group's deliberations?
13. Have you ever worked in deliberative groups whose members were culturally diverse? If so, how did cultural differences impact the way you communicated with others and the overall effectiveness of the group?
14. What does ethical group deliberation mean to you? You can use the discussion here as a foundation, and then add your own perspective and experience.

✓ Study and Review the Flashcards at **MyCommunicationLab**

GLOSSARY

acceptance speeches   Ceremonial or epideictic speeches in which the speaker expresses gratitude for an award or some other recognition and gives credit to those who contributed to his or her success.

acronyms   Abbreviated titles for places, organizations, plans, or objects, usually consisting of the first letters of the words in the full or complete title.

active listening   Channeling our energies and efforts so that we actively concentrate on the speaker's complete message.

actual examples   Real-life cases or specific instances.

ad hominem   The fallacy that occurs when a speaker substitutes an attack on a person for a refutation of that person's arguments.

aerobic exercise   Physical activity that increases one's heart rate and respiration and, as a result, lessens tension.

affective language   Strong, provocative language that stirs up an audience's emotions.

after-dinner speeches   Ceremonial speeches designed to entertain while still saying something significant.

alliteration   A repetitive pattern of initial sounds in a sequence of words, used to gain attention and reinforce an idea.

analogical reasoning   Inferring that what is true of one case will be true of another, similar case.

antithesis   A stylistic device in which two contrasting ideas are placed in opposition through the use of parallel phrases or clauses.

appeal to tradition   A fallacy in which a speaker offers past ways of doing things as the only reason for or against doing something now or in the future.

argument   A series of ideas, each one supported by evidence, used to advance a particular position on an issue.

attitudes   Mental constructs that represent people's positive or negative views or feelings toward other people, places, things, or events.

backing   In the Toulmin model, additional support for a disputed or controversial warrant, or general principle, in an argument.

bandwagon appeal   The fallacy that occurs when a speaker urges listeners to accept something simply because so many others accept it.

bar graph   A graph in which a series of bars depict comparative amounts of certain features or elements.

begging the question   The fallacy that occurs when a speaker makes a claim that assumes the very thing he or she hopes to prove, thus arguing in a circle.

beliefs   The ideas or assumptions we have about what is true or factual in the world.

brainstorming   The process of thinking creatively and imaginatively to come up with new ideas, temporarily suspending critical judgments or analysis of those ideas.

bulleted list   A list of key words or phrases, presented one-by-one during a presentation and marked by a typographical symbol such as an arrow, a circle, a square, or a diamond.

burden of proof   The standards or expectations that define a "reasonable argument" in a particular situation, or the proof necessary to warrant serious consideration and further debate over an advocate's claims.

captive audience   An audience that is required to attend a presentation.

categorical pattern An organizational pattern in which several independent, yet interrelated, categories are used to advance a larger idea.

causal pattern An organizational pattern in which ideas focus on causes or effects, or are arranged to reveal cause-to-effect or effect-to-cause relationships.

causal reasoning Reasoning that aims to prove relationships between effects and causes.

chronological pattern An organizational pattern in which ideas are arranged in a logical, time-based or sequential order.

citizen-critic A citizen educated to critically evaluate the claims, reasoning, and evidence he or she encounters in public deliberations.

civic engagement Actively participating in community or public affairs, not only by voting, but also by keeping up with the news, discussing issues with fellow citizens, and participating in civic and volunteer activities.

civic literacy The historical, political, and cultural knowledge necessary to participate actively as a citizen in a democracy.

civic virtue The attitudes and behaviors of good, ethical citizenship in a democracy.

claims The debatable assertions put forward by a speaker.

clichés Trite, overused expressions.

climactic pattern An organizational pattern in which the ideas being advanced in a speech are arranged so that they build in intensity.

closed question A question—often a "yes" or "no" question—in an interview or survey that restricts responses to a limited number of options.

cohesiveness A group dynamic that produces unity, agreement, and sometimes pressure on dissident group members to go along with the majority.

commemorative speech A ceremonial speech marking an important date or event.

commencement address A type of ceremonial speech—more specifically, a type of commemorative speech—celebrating the social values associated with graduation from an educational institution.

commenting modifiers Modifiers that attempt to boost the meaning of a word but reveal nothing new.

communication apprehension Feelings of anxiety a speaker may experience before or during a public presentation.

connotative meanings The subjective or emotional meanings associated with particular words or phrases.

critical listening Listening analytically, carefully evaluating all that is said and assessing the relevance, accuracy, timeliness, and validity of the speaker's message.

databases Immense, searchable collections of materials (indexes, abstracts, and full text) available in electronic form.

decode To interpret the verbal and nonverbal content of a message so as to give it meaning.

deductive reasoning Reasoning from an accepted generalization to a conclusion about a particular case.

deep breathing Expanding the diaphragm to increase one's intake of air, to assist with relaxation and enhance vocal delivery.

defining modifiers Modifiers that provide new, needed information.

definitions Meanings provided for words that are unfamiliar to listeners or technical in nature.

deliberating "in good faith" Debating and discussing controversial issues in a spirit of mutual respect, with a commitment to telling the truth, backing up arguments with sound reasoning and evidence, and remaining open to changing one's mind.

deliberative dialogue A respectful exchange aimed at establishing a framework for mutual understanding and a common purpose that transcends individual ideas and opinions.

demagoguery Deceptive or manipulative speech, often relying upon the charismatic ethos of the demagogue and appealing to "dark" emotions like hatred or fear.

demographics Audience characteristics, such as age, gender, and race, that shape listeners' beliefs, values, and attitudes.

denotative meaning Meaning that is considered literal, objective, or universally accepted.

descriptive statistic A statistic that quantifies or characterizes a dataset without drawing inferences about some larger population.

Dewey's Reflective Thinking Sequence A problem-solution pattern that takes listeners through a thorough problem exploration before considering possible solutions and arguing for the preferred course of action.

empathic listening Listening supportively to another with the goal of understanding his or her feelings or point of view.

encode To put ideas or information into a particular format for transmission over a particular channel, as when a speaker chooses the specific language to communicate his or her ideas in a speech.

enthymeme A "rhetorical syllogism," or a form of deductive reasoning in which the speaker draws inferences from a general principle or rule, often unstated, that is already accepted by the audience.

epideictic The ancient Greek term for ceremonial speeches, or speeches presented on special occasions.

ethical delivery Speaking authentically, with respect for one's listeners and concern for their well-being.

ethnocentrism The belief that one's own racial or ethnic heritage is superior to all others.

ethos The ancient Greek term for ethical proof, or the audience's perception of the speaker's credibility, intelligence, and motives.

eulogies Ceremonial speeches paying tribute to a recently deceased person.

evidence The body of fact and opinion that you present in support of your arguments, including statistics, examples, testimony, or comparisons.

expert testimony Testimony based on those whose expertise and experience make them especially trustworthy.

extemporaneous speaking The presentation of a thoroughly prepared speech using an abbreviated set of speaking notes, often in the form of a keyword outline.

facts Data that can be verified through empirical observation.

fair use The doctrine in copyright law that allows for educators, scholars, and students to use limited amounts of copyrighted material for noncommercial purposes without obtaining formal permission.

fallacies Flaws in reasoning or evidence that render arguments logically unsound.

false cause (*post hoc ergo propter hoc*) The fallacy that occurs when a speaker assumes that because one event precedes another, it must have caused it.

false dilemma The fallacy that occurs when a speaker suggests that we have only two alternatives, when in fact more than two alternatives exist.

farewell addresses Ceremonial or epideictic speeches in which the speaker bids a formal farewell to his or her hosts during an extended visit, or to employees, supporters, or constituents after serving for a time in a particular office or position.

faulty analogy The fallacy of analogical reasoning that occurs when speakers compare things that are not, in fact, similar.

feedback Constructive criticism, comments, and other helpful information about your speech given to you by your instructor, your peers, or other members of your audience.

fidelity Narratives that seem authentic to listeners because they ring true with their own life experiences.

figures of speech Stylistic devices, such as metaphors or personification, that heighten the beauty of one's language or make that language clearer, more meaningful, or more memorable.

flip chart An oversized writing tablet that speakers can place on a tripod for use during a presentation, interactive workshop, or brainstorming session.

formal outline An outline in which ideas and their development are articulated completely and precisely, usually using full sentences.

gendered language Language that reinforces or perpetuates gender stereotypes.

gender identity One's sense of sexual identity, of male and female tendencies and characteristics, as shaped by social norms and expectations that vary across cultures and change over time.

general purpose A speaker's ultimate goal in speaking, whether that goal is to gain audience understanding, change minds and win agreement, motivate to action, or simply reinforce existing beliefs and values.

ghostwriting Writing a speech for another person to deliver as his or her own.

glass ceiling An invisible barrier of prejudices and discrimination that hampers one's ability to rise to the top of some organization or profession.

graphical icons A symbol, such as a dollar sign, which is widely understood and used in place of verbal representations.

group pressure for uniformity The pressure exerted by majority group members on those in the minority in an attempt at getting the minority to conform.

groupthink A group mindset that hinders the group's ability to critically appraise ideas and express lingering concerns; seeking agreement on a course of action before the group has thoroughly and thoughtfully analyzed the problem and allowed everyone to express their points of view.

guilt by association The fallacy that occurs when an advocate judges an idea, person, or program solely on the basis of its association with other ideas, people, or programs.

hasty generalization The fallacy that occurs when a speaker generalizes from too few examples.

hate speech Language that demeans or degrades whole classes of people based on their race, ethnicity, religion, or other characteristics.

hypothetical examples Examples that describe actions or events that did not actually happen but that might or could plausibly occur.

impromptu speaking Casual, off-the-cuff delivery used when a speaker has little or no time for preparation.

inaugural addresses Ceremonial addresses given upon assuming a new office or position.

incorporation Determining if and where specific information and ideas belong in a speech.

inductive reasoning Reasoning from particular instances or examples to a general conclusion.

inferential statistics Statistics that generalize from a small group to a larger population, based on probability.

informational listening Listening in order to learn and expand knowledge.

information literacy Understanding when information is needed and knowing how to locate, gather, and evaluate information and use it responsibly.

informative oral report An informative presentation, often technical in nature, intended to assist a group's performance or decision making.

Informative Speech A speech whose goal is to help the audience gain understanding.

internal preview A quick look ahead at what will be covered under one of the main points or within a particular section of a speech.

internal summary A brief review of what one has presented under a main point or within a particular section of a speech.

irony The use of language to imply a meaning that is the total opposite of the literal meaning of a word or expression.

isometric exercise Tensing a muscle and holding it for a short time, followed by complete relaxation of the muscle.

keynote addresses Ceremonial speeches designed to set the tone and sound the key themes of a meeting, conference, or other formal gathering.

keyword outline An abbreviated outline that serves as a speaker's notes during the delivery of a speech.

lay testimony Testimony based on the experiences of ordinary men and women whose direct experiences make their testimony compelling.

line graph A graph in which one or more lines depict a trend or trends over time.

listening Actively attending to and processing the verbal and nonverbal elements of a message.

loaded questions Biased questions, or questions phrased in such a way that they lead respondents to a particular answer.

manuscript speaking Presenting a speech from a prepared text, often in formal ceremonial settings.

margin of error The range of possible error associated with the sampling procedures used in inferential statistics.

Maslow's Hierarchy A scale of human needs ranging from very basic physiological needs to higher-order psychological needs, such as the need for self-actualization.

mean The mathematical average.

median The number representing the midpoint between the largest and the smallest numbers within a particular set of numbers.

memorized speech A prepared speech presented from memory, without the assistance of speaking notes.

metaphor An implicit comparison in which two dissimilar objects are compared.

mode The most frequently occurring number within a particular set of numbers.

monotone Use of the same vocal pitch without variation.

motivated sequence An organizational pattern for a persuasive speech that is based on psychological studies of what engages people's emotions and motivates them to act.

narrative example An extended example that tells a story, based either on true experiences or on symbolism, perhaps in the form of proverbs.

narrative pattern An indirect, organic organizational pattern that often uses a coherent series of stories to convey the main ideas of the speech.

National Issues Forums (NIF) A nonpartisan, nationwide network of locally sponsored public forums for the consideration of public policy issues.

noise Any interference that distorts or interrupts message flow within the communication process.

non sequitur A fallacy that occurs when a conclusion simply does not follow logically from the arguments and evidence that precede it.

nonverbal communication Facial expressions, vocal qualities, and physical movements that reinforce or contradict one's verbal messages.

norms A set of assumptions or expectations held by a particular group concerning what is good, appropriate, or acceptable language or behavior.

objectivity The audience's perception of a speaker's honesty or fair-mindedness in considering diverse points of view.

open question A question in an interview or survey that allows for open-ended responses and more detailed elaboration.

oral style Language that is chosen with a listener in mind, characterized by short, simple, straightforward sentences and familiar word choices and repetition; generally more informal/conversational than a written style.

orator-statesman Woodrow Wilson's term for the ethical, civic-minded public speaker.

oxymoron An expression that presents, in combination, seemingly contradictory terms.

panel discussion A public discussion format in which the participants interact directly and spontaneously under the guidance of a moderator.

parallelism The use of a series of sentences with similar length and structure to signify the equality of ideas.

paraphrasing Summarizing or restating another person's ideas in your own words.

passivity syndrome Denying one's accountability as a listener and assuming that the burden of effective communication resides wholly with the speaker.

personal testimony Testimony based on your own personal experiences and beliefs.

personification A description of an inanimate form or thing as if it were human.

persuasion The chief mechanism through which citizens in a democracy select their leaders, determine their civic priorities, resolve controversies and disputes, and choose among various policies.

persuasive definition A definition that reflects the speaker's way of looking at a controversial subject.

persuasive speech A speech that seeks to influence the beliefs, values, or actions of others or "make the case" for a new policy or program.

pictograph A graph that relies on a set of self-explanatory icons to depict growth or decline over time or between situations.

pie graph A graph, in the shape of a circle, in which segments of the circle (cut into slices, like those of a pie) depict the relative size of particular features or elements within the whole.

plagiarism Taking all or part of your speech from a source without proper attribution.

poster board A type of display board, made of thin cardboard, suitable for drawings or for affixing flat, printed material or small objects.

presentational aids Visual or audiovisual materials that help clarify, support, and/or strengthen the verbal content of a speech.

presentation speeches Ceremonial or epideictic speeches in which the speaker formally announces the winner of some award or other recognition and reminds the audience of why the recipient is worthy of the recognition.

prestige testimony The views of a popular or famous person who, though not an expert, expresses a genuine commitment to the cause.

presumption In a courtroom debate, the idea that the accused is presumed innocent until proven guilty by the prosecution.

preview A glimpse of the major points one will be treating in a speech or in a section of a speech.

primacy effects The presumed impact of placing the most compelling information or arguments first in a speech.

problem-solution pattern An organizational pattern in which a problem is identified and one or more specific solutions are proposed.

prop Visual or audio material that enlivens a presentation but is not a necessary element.

public controversies Controversies that affect the whole community or nation and that we debate and decide in our role as citizens in a democracy.

public deliberation The discursive process through which people in a democracy articulate, explain, and justify their political opinions and policy preferences to their fellow citizens.

public values Values that are clarified and corroborated through the process of group inquiry.

qualifiers In the Toulmin model, the words or phrases that indicate the level of confidence we have in our claims.

question of fact A question about existence, scope, or causality.

question of policy A question about what policy or program we should adopt, or what course of action we should take.

question of value A question about whether an idea or action is good or bad, right or wrong, just or unjust, moral or immoral.

racism The prejudicial denial of the essential humanity of people of a particular race, often manifested in claims about the superiority and/or inferiority of particular races.

reasoning Reaching a conclusion on the basis of supporting evidence.

recency effects The presumed impact of saving the strongest argument or the most important information for near the end of a speech.

red herring A fallacy in which the speaker attempts to throw an audience off track by raising an irrelevant, often highly emotional issue that prevents critical examination of an argument.

repetition Repeating, word for word, key elements presented in a message.

reservations In the Toulmin model, the stated exceptions to our claims, or the conditions under which we no longer hold to our claims.

restatement Rephrasing, in slightly different language or sentence construction, the key elements in a message.

rhetorical questions Questions posed by a speaker to stimulate audience interest and thought, not to solicit information or answers.

saliency The level of interest or concern that our listeners have in a particular issue or topic.

sample The portion of some larger population that we actually test, interview, or otherwise gather information about in order to draw generalizations about the larger group.

sans serif A style of typeface lettering devoid of any embellishments (such as "feet") that might blur the separation between letters in a word or a line of text. A common type of font in electronic or online texts.

self-actualization needs The desire to achieve to the fullest extent of our capabilities; the highest need level in Maslow's hierarchy.

self-inventory Thinking about what you really know and care about in order to generate possible topics that are both meaningful to you and significant for your audience.

sensory appeals Vivid language that attempts to evoke one of our five senses: seeing, hearing, smelling, tasting, or feeling.

sequential pattern An organizational pattern in which the various steps of a process or phenomenon are identified and discussed, one by one.

sermons Religious speeches that may be either persuasive or ceremonial (epideictic), depending on the occasion, purpose, and audience.

signposts Words that alert listeners to where you are in your speech, particularly in relation to the speech's overall organization.

simile A figurative comparison made explicit by using the word *like* or *as*.

slippery slope The fallacy that occurs when a speaker claims that some cause will inevitably lead to undesirable effects, ultimately resulting in some worst-case scenario.

socially constructed The process by which roles and behaviors are judged as appropriate within different cultures with different cultural norms.

spatial pattern An organizational pattern in which ideas are arranged according to their natural spatial and/or geographical relationships.

specific purpose A precise statement of how the speaker wants the audience to respond to his or her message, which serves to direct the research and construction of the speech.

speech of demonstration An informative speech intended to teach an audience how something works or how to do something.

speech of description An informative speech intended to provide a clear picture of a place, event, person, or thing.

speech of explanation   An informative speech intended to help an audience understand complicated, abstract, or unfamiliar concepts or subjects.

speech of introduction   A type of ceremonial or epideictic speech in which the speaker's purpose is to welcome and introduce another speaker, reinforce that speaker's credibility, and provide any background information necessary for the audience to understand the featured speech.

spiraling narrative   A narrative pattern that builds in intensity from the beginning to the end of the speech.

state anxiety   Anxiety caused by worrisome factors in a specific speaking situation.

statistics   A numerical method of interpreting large numbers of instances to display or suggest such factors as typicality, cause and effect, and trends.

stereotyping   Making assumptions about someone based on such factors as race or gender without considering the person's individuality.

straw man fallacy   The fallacy that occurs when a speaker attributes a flimsy, easy-to-refute argument to his opponent, then proceeds to demolish it, in the process misrepresenting the opponent's real position.

study circle   A diverse small group of people that is guided by an impartial facilitator and that meets over several sessions to tackle community problems and devise creative strategies for action through respectful deliberation.

style   A speaker's choice and use of language.

subscription database   An immense, searchable collection of indexes, abstracts, or full-text materials compiled by a private vendor (such as EBSCOhost or ProQuest) and made available on the Internet by subscription or through library databases.

supporting material   Information that you present in your speech to substantiate and strengthen your main ideas.

symmetry   Using a balanced approach to developing and presenting ideas in a speech, so that each idea is developed with a similar level of elaboration.

symposium   A public discussion in which each group member speaks in turn without interruption or interaction, with the moderator providing introductions, transitions, and closure.

target audience   Those whom the speaker would most like to influence with the message.

technical language   Any language that has precise meaning within a particular field or endeavor.

temporal context   Previous, current, and anticipated events that affect what can or should be said and how it might be received.

testimony   Opinions, interpretations, or judgments quoted from other people, including personal testimony, lay testimony, and expert testimony.

thesis statement   A single, simple, declarative sentence that expresses the principal idea of a speech that the speaker would have the audience understand or accept.

town hall meeting   A community-wide meeting that brings together a diverse array of citizens representing different and often conflicting interests in an effort to find common ground or solutions to community problems.

trait anxiety   Internal anxiety that an individual brings to the speaking situation; not dependent on the specific situation.

transactional communication   The process of constructing shared messages or understandings between two or more individuals.

transition   A word, phrase, or sentence that helps the audience perceive the relationship of ideas and the movement from one main idea to another.

tributes   Ceremonial speeches honoring a person, group, event, organization, town, or community.

values   Things that we consider good and desirable.

visualization   Using language that creates "word pictures" and helps your audience "see" what you are talking about.

visual literacy   The ability to think critically and discerningly about visual images and depictions.

warrants   In the Toulmin model, the general assumptions, rules, or principles that connect evidence to claims.

washout   The reduction in brilliance of an image being projected onto a screen due to interference by light.

welcome addresses   Ceremonial or epideictic speeches in which the speaker formally welcomes some honored guest or dignitary or some group of participants to a convention, fair, or similar public event.

Wikipedia   A free, online encyclopedia to which anyone can contribute information, and whose accuracy cannot be effectively monitored.

working outline   Early drafts of your speech outline, representing your work in progress.

working thesis   A tentative thesis, meant to articulate the overall idea being examined in a speech, that is formulated to guide one's investigation and writing.

WorldCat   An electronic catalog of the holdings for more than 53,000 libraries from around the world.

x axis   The horizontal axis of a graph, often depicting the progression of time.

y axis   The vertical axis of a graph, typically depicting an amount or quantity.

NOTES

CHAPTER 1

1. Judith Forman, "Grass-Roots Activism Is Thriving; Causes Differ, but Aim Is Better Communities," *Boston Globe*, November 1, 2001, 1.

2. Paul Rogat Loeb, *Soul of a Citizen: Living with Conviction in a Cynical Time* (New York: St. Martin's Press, 1999), 4–6, 199–200.

3. Peter D. Hart and Mario A. Brossard, "A Generation to Be Proud Of," *Brookings Review* 20 (Fall 2002): 36–37.

4. Michael Olander, "How Young People Express Their Political Views," Center for Information and Research on Civic Learning and Engagement, Fact Sheet, July 2003, www.civicyouth.org/PopUps/FactSheets/FS_How_Young_Express_Views.pdf (accessed February 1, 2012).

5. Mark Hugo Lopez, Peter Levine, Deborah Both, Abby Keisa, Emily Kirby, and Karlo Marcelo, *The 2006 Civic and Political Health of the Nation: A Detailed Look at How Youth Participate in Politics and Communities* (College Park, MD: Center for Information and Research on Civic Learning and Engagement, 2006), 3, 9.

6. See Infoplease, "National Voter Turnout in Federal Elections: 1960–2010," www.infoplease.com/ipa/A0781453.html (accessed February 1, 2012).

7. Center for Voting and Democracy, "International Voter Turnout, 1991–2000," http://archive.fairvote.org/turnout/intturnout.htm (accessed February 1, 2012).

8. Mark Hugo Lopez, et al., *The Youth Vote 2004, With a Historical Look at Youth Voting Patterns, Circle Working Paper 35, July 2005*, www.civicyouth.org/PopUps/WorkingPapers/WP35CIRCLE.pdf (accessed February 2, 2012).

9. Putnam, *Bowling Alone*, 31–47. Declining attention to the news is particularly evident among young people. See David T. Z. Mindich, *Tuned Out: Why Americans under 40 Don't Follow the News* (New York: Oxford University Press, 2005), esp. 18–33.

10. Putnam, *Bowling Alone*, 43–45.

11. Robert Putnam, "Bowling Together," *American Prospect*, February 11, 2002, 20–22.

12. According to the Center for Information and Research on Civic Learning and Engagement (CIRCLE), turnout among voters between ages 18 and 24 increased by about 5.8 percent in 2004, rising to 42.3 percent from just 36.5 percent in the 2000 election." See Center for Information and Research on Civic Learning and Engagement, "Youth Voting in the 2004 Election," Fact Sheet, November 8, 2004 (updated January 25, 2005), www.civicyouth.org/PopUps/FactSheets/FS-PresElection04.pdf (accessed February 1, 2012).

13. "Turnout in Presidential Elections Hit 40-Year High," *Politico*, December 15, 2008, www.politico.com/news/stories/1208/16576.html (accessed January 16, 2012).

14. Eric Hoover, "Freshman's Views: Politics, Admissions, and Marijuana," *Chronicle of Higher Education*, January 30, 2009, A18.

15. Center for Information and Research on Civic Learning and Engagement and Rock the Vote, *Young Voter Registration and Turnout Trends*, February 2008, www.civicyouth.org/PopUps/CIRCLE_RtV_Young_Voter_Trends.pdf (accessed February 2, 2012).

16. Russell J. Dalton, *The Good Citizen: How a Younger Generation Is Reshaping American Politics* (Washington, DC: CQ Press, 2008).

17. See Elham Khatami, "Spring Breakers Skip Cancun for Volunteer Work," *CNN.com*, March 4, 2009, www.cnn.com/2009/TRAVEL/getaways/03/04/alternative.spring.break.travel/index.html (accessed February 1, 2012); Eleni Berger, "Students Look beyond the Beach for Spring Break," *CNN.com*, March 12, 2003, www.cnn.com/2003/TRAVEL/02/27/spring.service/ (accessed February 2, 2012); and Jane Engle, "For This Party over Spring Break, Bring Your Own Hammer," *LATimes.com*, February 20, 2005, www.latimes.com/travel/la-tr-insider20feb20,1,2302870.column (accessed February 1, 2012).

18. "The Saguaro Seminar: Civic Engagement in America," www.hks.harvard.edu/saguaro/ (accessed February 1, 2012).

19. "Our Purpose," *The Strauss Report: A Publication of the Annette Strauss Institute for Civic Participation*, 2005–2006 edition, n.p.

20. Jeffrey R. Young, "Persuading Students to Care: Eugene Lang's Program Aims to Prod Colleges into Encouraging Civic Involvement," *Chronicle of Higher Education*, April 11, 2003, A47.

21. See Campus Compact, "About Us," www.compact.org/about/ (accessed February 1, 2012).

22. Abby Kiesa, Alexander P. Orlowski, Peter Levine, Deborah Both, Emily Hoban Kirby, Mark Hugo Lopez, and Karlos Barrios Marcelo, *Millennials Talk Politics: A Study of College Student Political Engagement* (College Park, MD: Center for Information and Research on Civic Learning and Engagement, 2007).

23. A study done at UCLA found that more than 55 percent of Internet users aged 18–34 obtain news online in a typical week, and a Nielsen/NetRatings study showed that traffic to the 26 most popular sites in 2003 grew by 70 percent from May 2002 to October 2003. Pew Charitable Trusts, "State of the News Media 2004 Fact Sheets," www.pewtrusts.org/news_room_detail.aspx?id=22562 (accessed February 1, 2012).

24. Morris P. Fiorina, *Culture War? The Myth of a Divided America* (New York: Pearson, 2005), 102.

25. Eric Hoffer, *The True Believer* (New York: Harper & Brothers, 1951).

26. Fiorina, *Culture War?*, 111.

27. "THON: Penn State IFC/Panhellenic Dance Marathon," www.thon.org (accessed November 11, 2011).

28. See Takis Poulakos, *Speaking for the Polis: Isocrates' Rhetorical Education* (Columbia: University of South Carolina Press, 1997).

29. Quintilian, *Institutes of Oratory*, trans. J. S. Watson (London: G. Bell & Sons, 1913), 2: 391.

30. See Rosa A. Eberly, *Citizen Critics: Literary Public Spheres* (Urbana IL: University of Illinois Press, 2000).

31. Stephen R. Goldzwig, "A Social Movement Perspective on Demagoguery: Achieving Symbolic Realignment," *Communication Studies* 40 (1989): 202–28. For Aristotle's classical definition, see William A. Dunning, "The Politics of Aristotle," *Political Science Quarterly* 15 (1900): 273–307.

32. Bruce Cole, "Our American Amnesia," *Wall Street Journal*, June 11, 2002, www.neh.gov/wtp/newsroom/wsjarticle.html (accessed February 1, 2012).

33. Benjamin Franklin, "On the Constitution," in *A Choice of Worlds: The Practice and Criticism of Public Discourse*, ed. James R. Andrews (New York: Harper & Row, 1973), 100.

34. Abraham Lincoln, "Second Inaugural Address," in *American Voices: Significant Speeches in American History, 1640–1945*, ed. James R. Andrews and David Zarefsky (New York: Longman, 1989), 294–96.

35. Kathy Slobogin, "Survey: Many Students Say Cheating Is OK," *CNN.com*, April 5, 2002, http://articles.cnn.com/2002-04-05/us/highschool.cheating_1_plagiarism-cheating-students?_s=PM:fyi (accessed February 2012).

36. Office of the Provost, Northwestern University, "How to Avoid Plagiarism," www.northwestern.edu/provost/students/integrity/plagiarism.html (accessed February 1, 2012).

37. See the home page for Turnitin.com, http://turnitin.com/en_us/home (accessed February 1, 2012).

38. See Jim Geraghty, "Biden His Time," *National Review*, January 22, 2003, www.nationalreview.com/articles/205595/biden-his-time/jim-geraghty (accessed February 1, 2012).

39. Erin Neff, "Gibbons' Speech Plagiarism: 15 Paragraphs Came from Copyrighted Talk by Alabama Woman," *Las Vegas Review-Journal*, March 4, 2005, www.reviewjournal.com/lvrj_home/2005/Mar-04-Fri-2005/news/25992087.html (accessed February 1, 2012).

40. "Reporter Says He 'Never Meant to Hurt Anyone,'" *CNN.com*, March 1, 2004, www.cnn.com/2003/US/Northeast/06/06/nytimes.blair/index.html?iref=newssearch (accessed February 1, 2012).

41. Lois Einhorn, "Ghostwriting: Two Famous Ghosts Speak on Its Nature and Its Ethical Implications," in *Ethical Dimensions of Political Communication*, ed. Robert E. Denton Jr. (New York: Praeger, 1991), 115.

42. Kennedy's speechwriter, Theodore C. Sorensen, not only wrote speeches but also served as one of Kennedy's closest and most trusted advisers. Sorensen later wrote a best-selling biography of the 35th president. See Theodore C. Sorensen, *Kennedy* (New York: Harper & Row, 1965).

43. See Peggy Noonan, *What I Saw at the Revolution: A Political Life in the Reagan Era* (New York: Ivy Books, 1990).

44. Einhorn, "Ghostwriting," 127–30.

45. Among the former presidential speechwriters who have become well-known celebrities are William Safire, Patrick Buchanan, television personality Ben Stein, and former presidential press secretary Tony Snow. Some may question the ethics of speechwriters profiting from inside accounts or going directly from the White House into journalism, but we generally respect speechwriters who are honest about what they do.

46. See Wynton C. Hall, "The Invention of 'Quantifiably Safe Rhetoric': Richard Wirthlin and Ronald Reagan's Instrumental Use of Public Opinion Research in Presidential Discourse," *Western Journal of Communication* 66 (2002): 319–46.

47. Dick Morris, *Behind the Oval Office: Getting Reelected against All Odds* (Los Angeles: Renaissance Books, 1999).

48. For more on this debate, see J. Michael Hogan et al., "Report of the National Task Force on the Presidency and Public Opinion," in *The Prospect of Presidential Rhetoric*, ed. James Arnt Aune and Martin J. Medhurst

(College Station: Texas A&M University Press, 2007), 293–316.

49. Qtd. in Fiorina, *Culture War?*, ix.

50. William Norwood Brigance, *Speech Communication*, 2nd ed. (New York: Appleton Century-Crofts, 1955), 2.

51. Charles W. Lomas, *The Agitator in American Society* (Englewood Cliffs, NJ: Prentice Hall, 1968), 18.

52. Qtd. in T. Harry Williams, *Huey Long* (New York: Knopf, 1969), 411.

53. Reinhard H. Luthin, "Some Demagogues in American History," *American Historical Review* 57 (1951): 22, 45.

54. J. Justin Gustainis, "Demagoguery and Political Rhetoric: A Review of the Literature," *Rhetoric Society Quarterly* 20 (1990): 155–61.

55. Sally J. Walton, *Cultural Diversity in the Workplace* (New York: Irwin Professional, 1994).

56. Pew Hispanic Center/Kaiser Family Foundation, *The 2004 National Survey of Latinos: Politics and Civic Participation*, July 2004, 73.

CHAPTER 2

1. David K. Berlo, *The Process of Communication* (New York: Holt, Rinehart & Winston, 1960).

2. Raymond G. Smith, *Speech Communication: Theory and Models* (New York: Harper & Row, 1970), 14.

3. Steve Duck and David McMahon, *The Basics of Communication: A Relational Perspective* (Thousand Oaks, CA: Sage, 2009), 9.

4. William Norwood Brigance, *Speech: Its Techniques and Disciplines in a Free Society*, 2nd ed. (New York: Appleton-Century-Crofts, 1961), 20.

5. The International Listening Association defines *listening* as "the process of receiving, constructing meaning from, and responding to spoken and/or nonverbal messages."

6. See, for example, Kay Lindahl, *The Sacred Art of Listening* (Woodstock, VT: Skylight Paths, 2002).

7. Periodically, the NIF publishes reports to communicate the outcomes of forums held across the nation about a particular issue. These publications can be accessed online at http://www.nifi.org/reports/index.aspx.

8. Carl Rogers and Richard E. Farson, "Active Listening," in *Organizational Communication*, 2nd ed., ed. Stewart D. Ferguson and Sherry Ferguson (New Brunswick, NJ: Transaction, 1988), 319–34.

9. Joseph A. DeVito, *The Interpersonal Communication Book*, 10th ed. (Boston: Allyn & Bacon, 2003), 64.

10. Megan Thee-Brenan, "From Poll: A Snapshot of Fox News Viewers," *The Caucus: The Politics and Government Blog of the New York Times*, http://thecaucus.blogs.nytimes.com/2010/09/29/from-poll-a-snapshot-of-fox-news-viewers/ (accessed May 7, 2012).

11. For an extended discussion of these ideas, see Susan Bickford, *Listening, Conflict, and Citizenship: Dissonance Democracy* (Ithaca, NY: Cornell University Press, 1996).

12. David Zarefsky, *Lincoln, Douglas, and Slavery: In the Crucible of Public Debate* (Chicago: University of Chicago Press, 1990), x.

13. See Robert Remini, *Daniel Webster: The Man and His Time* (New York: Norton, 1997), esp. chap. 9, "The Plymouth Oration," 178–87, and chap. 18, "The Webster-Hayne Debate," 312–31.

14. Debby Applegate, *The Most Famous Man in America: The Biography of Henry Ward Beecher* (New York: Doubleday, 2006), esp. 215–19.

15. Joan Middendorf and Alan Kalish, "The Change-Up in Lectures," *National Teaching and Learning Forum* 5 (1996): 1–4.

16. Peter J. Frederick, "The Lively Lecture: 8 Variations," *College Teaching* 34 (1986): 43–50; A. H. Johnstone and F. Percival, "Attention Breaks in Lectures," *Education in Chemistry* 13 (1976): 49–50.

17. See, for example, Patricia Hill Collins, *Black Feminist Thought: Knowledge, Consciousness, and the Politics of Empowerment*, 2nd ed. (New York: Routledge, 2000); and bell hooks, *Black Looks: Race and Representation* (Boston: South End Press, 1992).

18. Walter Lippmann, *Public Opinion* (New York: Harcourt, Brace, 1922), 75–89.

19. *The American Heritage College Dictionary*, 3rd ed., s.v. "Stereotype."

20. See, for example, Jon Hurwitz and Mark Peffley, "Public Perceptions of Race and Crime: The Role of Racial Stereotypes," *American Journal of Political Science* 41 (1997): 375–401; Debra L. Oswald and Richard D. Harvey, "Hostile Environments, Stereotype Threat, and Math Performance among Undergraduate Women," *Current Psychology* 19 (2000): 338–56; and Shani H. Peterson et al., "Images of Sexual Stereotypes in Rap Videos and the Health of African American Female Adolescents," *Journal of Women's Health* 16 (2007): 1157–64.

21. We know, for example, that interviewers form early impressions of job applicants, rarely changing their judgments after the first five minutes. See Robert W. Eder and Michael M. Harris, ed., *The Employment Interview Handbook* (Thousand Oaks, CA: Sage, 1999); and Charles B. Stewart and William B. Cash, *Interviewing: Principles and Practices*, 10th ed. (New York: McGraw-Hill, 2003).

22. Paul Martin Lester, *Visual Communication: Images with Messages* (Belmont, CA: Wadsworth Thomson Learning, 2000).

23. Kathleen H. Jamieson, *Eloquence in an Electronic Age* (New York: Oxford University Press, 1988), 114–17.

24. Burley-Allen, "Listen Up," 119–20; "Train Yourself in the Art of Listening," *Positive Leadership* (July 1998): 10.

25. See K. Bosworth and J. Hamilton, ed., *Critical Thinking and Collaborative Learning: Underlying Processes and Effective Techniques* (San Francisco: Jossey-Bass, 1994); Rosabeth Moss Kanter, "Thinking across Boundaries," *Harvard Business Review* 68 (1990), editor's foreword; and S. Holly Stocking et al., *More Quick Hits: Successful Strategies by Award-Winning Teachers* (Bloomington: Indiana University Press, 1998), esp. "Fostering Critical and Creative Thinking," 40–57.

26. For recent insights on note taking, see Rick Reis, "Tomorrow's Professor Message #163: More Effective Note-Taking Strategies," Stanford Center for Teaching and Learning; and Rick Reis, "Tomorrow's Professor Message #172: Teaching Students to Take Better Notes," Stanford Center for Teaching and Learning, http://cgi.stanford.edu/~dept-ctl/tomprof/postings.php (accessed May 18, 2012).

27. Carol A. Carrier, "Note-Taking Research: Implications for the Classroom," *Journal of Instructional Development* 6 (1983): 19–25; J. L. Fisher and M. B. Harris, "Effect of Note Taking and Review on Recall," *Journal of Educational Psychology* 65 (1973): 321–25.

28. Cited by James Brewer Stewart, *Wendell Phillips: Liberty's Hero* (Baton Rouge: Louisiana State University Press, 1986), 46.

29. Margaret Chase Smith, "A Declaration of Conscience," Washington, DC, June 1, 1950, http://gos.sbc.edu/s/chasesmith.html (accessed May 20, 2012).

30. Robert Alexander Kraig, *Woodrow Wilson and the Lost World of the Oratorical Statesman* (College Station: Texas A&M University Press, 2004), 131–33.

31. See Karlyn Kohrs Campbell, *Man Cannot Speak for Her: A Critical Study of Early Feminist Rhetoric*, 2 vols. (New York: Praeger, 1989), 51–58.

32. T. K. Kim, "Hate Website Stormfront Sees Rapid Growth of Neo-Nazi Community," *Southern Poverty Law Center*, www.splcenter.org/intel/intelreport/article.jsp?aid=551 (accessed May 20, 2012).

CHAPTER 3

1. James Thomas Flexner, *George Washington and the New Nation: 1783–1793* (Boston: Little, Brown, 1969), 188.

2. Letter to Abigail Adams, March 17, 1797, in *John Adams: A Biography in His Own Words*, ed. James Bishop Peabody (New York: Harper & Row, 1973), 359.

3. "What Are Americans Afraid Of?" *Bruskin Report* 53 (July 1973): 8.

4. Jerry Seinfeld, *SeinLanguage* (New York: Bantam Books, 1993), 120.

5. "Mental Stress Test Indicator of Future Cardiac Problems," *Bloomington (IN) Herald-Times*, June 5, 1996, A6.

6. James C. McCroskey, "Oral Communication Apprehension: A Summary of Recent Theory and Research," *Human Communication Research* 4 (1977): 78–79.

7. James C. McCroskey and Virginia P. Richmond, "Communication Apprehension and Shyness: Conceptual and Operational Distinctions," *Central States Speech Journal* 33 (1982): 458–68.

8. James C. McCroskey and Janis F. Andersen, "The Relationship between Communication Apprehension and Academic Achievement among College Students," *Human Communication Research* 3 (1976): 73–81.

9. James C. McCroskey and Rod W. McVetta, "Classroom Seating Arrangements: Instructional Communication Theory versus Student Preferences," *Communication Education* 27 (1978): 99–111.

10. James C. McCroskey, "Communication Apprehension: What Have We Learned in the Last Four Decades," *Human Communication* 12 (2009): 157–71.

11. McCroskey, "Communication Apprehension," 161.

12. McCroskey, "Communication Apprehension," 167–68.

13. H. Thomas Hurt and Katherine Joseph, "The Impact of Communication Apprehension in the Process of Social Change," paper presented at the Eastern Communication Association, New York City, 1975.

14. Over the past two decades, communication apprehension has continued to be the subject of much scholarly research. See, for example, Ralph R. Behnke and Chris R. Sawyer, "Milestones of Anticipatory Public Speaking Anxiety," *Communication Education* 48 (1999): 165–72; Ralph R. Behnke and Chris R. Sawyer, "Public Speaking Anxiety as a Function of Sensitization and Habituation Processes," *Communication Education* 53 (2004): 164–73; Amy M. Bippus and John A. Daly, "What Do People Think Causes Stage Fright? Naive Attributions about the Reasons for Public Speaking Anxiety," *Communication Education* 48 (1999): 63–72; and Rebecca B. Rubin, Alan M. Rubin, and Felecia F. Jordan, "Effects of Instruction on Communication Apprehension and Communication Competence," *Communication Education* 46 (1997): 104–14.

15. See Virginia P. Richmond and James C. McCroskey, *Communication: Apprehension, Avoidance, and Effectiveness*, 5th ed. (Boston: Allyn & Bacon, 2000), for an extended discussion of the nature, types, and causes of communication apprehension.

16. Joe Ayres, "Situational Factors and Audience Anxiety," *Communication Education* 29 (1990): 283–91.

17. Marion Woodman, *Addiction to Perfection* (Toronto: Inner City Books, 1982).

18. James C. McCroskey, "The Communication Apprehension Perspective," in *Avoiding Communication Shyness, Reticence, and Communication Apprehension*, ed. John D. Daily and James McCroskey (Beverly Hills, CA: Sage, 1984), 13–84.

19. Theodore Clevenger, "A Synthesis of Experimental Research in Stage Fright," *Quarterly Journal of Speech* 45 (1959): 135–59.

20. Michael J. Beatty, "Situational and Predispositional Correlates of Public Speaking Anxiety," *Communication Education* 37 (1988): 28–39.

21. Cicero, *De Oratore*, vol. 1, trans. E. W. Sutton (Cambridge: Harvard University Press, 1942), 29.

22. James C. McCroskey and Virginia P. Richmond, "The Impact of Communication Apprehension on Individuals in Organizations," *Communication Quarterly* 27 (1979): 55–61.

23. Waldo W. Braden, *Abraham Lincoln: Public Speaker* (Baton Rouge: Louisiana State University Press, 1988), 3.

24. Harold Holtzer, *Lincoln at Cooper Union: The Speech That Made Abraham Lincoln President* (New York: Simon & Schuster, 2004), 28.

25. See Joe Ayres, "Speech Preparation Processes and Speech Apprehension," *Communication Education* 45 (October 1996): 228–35, for an interesting study on how the nature of speaking preparation is vital to the quality of the speech as delivered.

26. Joe Ayres and Tim Hopf, *Coping with Speech Anxiety* (Norwood, NJ: Ablex, 1993), 5–21.

27. In the interpersonal communication and interviewing literature, *active listening* refers to a listening approach in which the listener participates in the conversation by summarizing, paraphrasing, and occasionally interrupting the speaker with clarifying, supportive questions. We are using the term in a different way here.

28. James McCroskey, *An Introduction to Rhetorical Communication*, 7th ed. (Boston: Allyn & Bacon, 1997), 39–61.

CHAPTER 4

1. See The Pew Charitable Trust, "Public Divided on Alaska Drilling, as Well as Social Security," www.pewtrusts.org/news_room_detail.aspx?id=23134 (accessed May 17, 2012).

2. "Value Differences Across Three Generations," www.jstor.org/stable/2786279 (accessed May 17, 2012).

3. See A. Cann and W. D. Siegfried, "Sex Stereotypes and the Leadership Role," *Sex Roles* 17 (1987): 401–08.

4. T. A. Stewart, "Gay in Corporate America," *Fortune*, December 6, 1991, 43–56.

5. Richard D. Alba, *Ethnic Identity: The Transformation of White America* (New Haven, CT: Yale University Press, 1990).

6. According to the findings of the Human Genome Project on Race, "DNA studies do not indicate that separate classifiable subspecies (races) exist within modern humans. While different genes for physical traits such as skin and hair color can be identified between individuals, no consistent patterns of genes across the human genome exist to distinguish one race from another. There is also no genetic basis for divisions of human ethnicity. People who have lived in the same geographic region for many generations may have some alleles in common, but no allele will be found in all members of one population and in no members of any other."

7. See L. Barna, "Stumbling Blocks in Intercultural Communication," in *Intercultural Communication: A Reader*, ed. L. Samovar and R. Porter (Belmont, CA: Wadsworth, 1988), 322–30. Barna has found that individuals are often so steeped in their own culture that they do not recognize how it influences their thinking, views, beliefs, norms, and values, and they assume that others think, perceive, and value things similarly.

8. To help all communicators better understand and communicate with one another, researchers have studied how people in racially mixed groups interact. See, for example, Melanie Booth-Butterfield and Felecia Jordan, "Communication Adaptation among Racially Homogeneous and Heterogeneous Groups," *Southern Communication Journal* 54 (1989): 253–72.

9. Sheel Pandya, "Racial and Ethnic Differences Among Older Adults in Long-Term Care Service Use," AARP Public Policy Institute, June 2005, www.aarp.org/home-garden/livable-communities/info-2005/fs119_ltc.html (accessed May 17, 2012).

10. Erica Goode, "How Culture Molds Habits of Thought," *New York Times*, August 8, 2000, D1, D4.

11. Ohio State University Extension Fact Sheet: Family and Consumer Sciences, "Working with Diverse Cultures," n.d., www.ohioline.osu.edu/bc-fact/0014.html (accessed May 17, 2012).

12. Myron W. Lustig and Jolene Koester, in *Intercultural Competence*, New York: Harper Collins, 1993: 104, note several value differences among people of different cultures. For instance, they point out that "the fast, hectic pace of European Americans, governed by clocks, appointments, and schedules, has become so commonly accepted that it is almost a cliché. The pace of life in cultures such as India, Kenya, and Argentina and among African Americans is less hectic, more relaxed, and more comfortably paced."

13. Arnold D. Hunt, Marie T. Crotty, and Robert B. Crotty, eds., *Ethics of World Religions*, rev. ed. (San Diego: Greenhaven Press, 1991).

14. Jim Kuhnhenn, "Obama Unveils Deficit Reduction Plan, 'Buffett Rule' Tax On Millionaires," 09/19/11, www.huffingtonpost.com/2011/09/19/obama-deficit-plan-buffet-rule-taxes-medicare_n_969403.html (accessed May 17, 2012).

15. Abraham H. Maslow, *Motivation and Personality* (New York: Harper & Row, 1954).

16. Daniel Goleman, *Emotional Intelligence* (New York: Bantam Books, 1995).

17. James R. Andrews, "Reflections of the National Character in American Rhetoric," *Quarterly Journal of Speech* 57 (October 1971): 316–24.

18. George Cheney, "On the Various and Changing Meanings of Organizational Membership: A Field Study of Organizational Identification," *Communication Monographs* 50 (1983): 342–62; George Cheney and Phillip K. Tompkins, "Coming to Terms with Organizational Identification and Commitment," *Central States Speech Journal* 38 (1987): 1–15.

19. "Poverty Rate in U.S.," www.physicsforums.com/archive/index.php/t-86870.html (accessed May 17, 2012).

20. "Why Are People Homeless?" National Coalition for the Homeless, September 2002, www.nationalhomeless.org/publications/facts/Why.pdf (accessed May 17, 2012).

21. Barbara Liston, "Caught in a Gunfight," *Time*, February 20, 2006, 17.

22. "Contacts," Indiana Memorial Union, www.imu.indiana.edu/board/contacts.shtml (accessed May 17, 2012).

23. "Student Programming Association," Penn State University, www.spa.psu.edu/about/about.html (accessed May 17, 2012).

24. There are many excellent books on interviewing. See, for example, Jeanne Tessier Barone and Jo Young Switzer, *Interviewing Art and Skill* (Boston: Allyn & Bacon, 1995); Arnold B. Kanter, *The Complete Book of Interviewing: Everything You Need to Know from Both Sides of the Table* (New York: Times Books, 1995); and Charles J. Stewart and William B. Cash Jr., *Interviewing: Principles and Practices*, 11th ed. (Boston: McGraw-Hill, 2006).

25. Priscilla Salant, *How to Conduct Your Own Survey* (New York: Wiley, 1994).

26. Jeane M. Converse and Stanley Presser, *Survey Questions: Handcrafting the Standardized Questionnaire* (Newbury Park, CA: Sage, 1986); see also Floyd J. Fowler Jr., *Survey Research Methods* (Newbury Park, CA: Sage, 1993), for an excellent discussion of how to construct survey questions.

27. Stanley L. Payne, *The Art of Asking Questions* (Princeton, NJ: Princeton University Press, 1980). Also see Robert W. Eder and Michael M. Harris, eds., *The Employment Interview Handbook* (Thousand Oaks, CA: Sage, 1999). Although this book is focused on the employment interview, it contains an excellent section on questioning as related to structured and unstructured interviews (pp. 143–216).

28. For additional information about survey construction, see Paul Rosenfeld, Jack E. Edwards, and Marie D. Thomas, "Improving Organizational Surveys," *American Behavioral Scientist* 36 (1993): 414–26; and Sam G. McFarland, "Effects of Question Order on Survey Responses," *Public Opinion Quarterly* 45 (1981): 208–15.

CHAPTER 5

1. Researchers in cognitive psychology find that an important element of creativity is to find a task interesting, exciting, or personally challenging. People are more creative when they have this sort of intrinsic motivation. See Mary Ann Collins and Teresa M. Amabile, "Motivation and Creativity," in *Handbook of Creativity*, ed. Robert J. Sternberg (New York: Cambridge University Press, 1999), 297–312.

2. See Richard L. Johannesen, *Ethics in Human Communication*, 5th ed. (Prospect Heights, IL: Waveland Press, 2002).

3. For a special issue devoted to communication ethics, see *Communication Quarterly* 38 (Summer 1990): 208–90.

4. For an account of the functions of ceremonial rhetoric, see Celeste Michelle Condit, "The Function of Epideictic: The Boston Massacre Orations as Exemplar," *Communication Quarterly* 33 (1985): 284–98.

5. Raymond Cohen, *Negotiating across Culture: Communication Obstacles in International Diplomacy* (Washington, DC: Institute of Peace, 1991).

6. Ronald Reagan, "Tribute to the Challenger Astronauts," January 28, 1986, www.americanrhetoric.com/speeches/ronaldreaganchallenger.htm (accessed March 5, 2012).

7. Barack Obama, "Remarks by the President on Memorial Day," May 25, 2009, www.whitehouse.gov/the_press_office/Remarks-by-the-President-on-Memorial-Day (accessed March 8, 2012).

8. See Kenneth R. Andrews, "Ethics in Practice," *Harvard Business Review* 67 (September–October 1989): 99–109.

CHAPTER 6

1. John Walsh and Susan Schindehette, *Tears of Rage: From Grieving Father to Crusader for Justice: The Untold Story of the Adam Walsh Case* (New York: Pocket Star Books, 1997), 53–143.

2. Ibid., 158.

3. Ibid., 158–60.

4. Ibid., 169.

5. Ibid., 191.

6. *America's Most Wanted*, "Captures," www.amw.com/captures/ (accessed May 19, 2012).

7. Bryan Walsh, "How to Prepare for a Pandemic," *Time*, May 18, 2009, 30–33.

8. For information about CREDO, go to http://corp.credoreference.com/.

9. For example, major newspapers often endorse a particular candidate. For a listing of papers and whom they endorse, go to http://wheretodoresearch.com/Political.htm.

10. Stephen K. Reed, *Cognition, Theory and Application*, 3rd ed. (Pacific Grove, CA: Brooks/Cole, 1992), 223.

11. Ilan Yaniv and David E. Meyer, "Activation and Metacognition of Inaccessible Stored Information: Potential Bases for Incubation Effects in Problem Solving," *Journal of Experimental Psychology: Learning, Memory, and Cognition* 13 (1987): 187–205. Also see Peggy Milam, "The Power of Reflection in the Research Process," *School Library Media Activities Monthly* 21 (February 2005): 26–29.

12. Renate Nummela Caine et al., *12 Brain/Mind Learning Principles in Action: The Fieldbook for Making Connections, Teaching, and the Human Brain* (Thousand Oaks, CA: Corwin Press, 2005).

13. Ronald A. Finke et al., *Creative Cognition: Theory, Research, and Applications* (Cambridge, MA: MIT Press, 1992), 149–50. Also see Steven M. Smith, "Getting Into and Out of Mental Ruts: A Theory of Fixation, Incubation, and Insight," in *The Nature of Insight*, ed. R. J. Sternberg and J. E. Davidson (Cambridge, MA: MIT Press, 1995), 229–51.

14. John B. Best, *Cognitive Psychology*, 5th ed. (Belmont, CA: Brooks/Cole Wadsworth, 1999), 420–23.

15. Finke et al., *Creative Cognition*, 166. Also see David N. Perkins, *The Eureka Effect: The Art and Logic of Breakthrough Thinking* (New York: Norton, 2001); and Mihaly Csikszentmihalyi, *Creativity: Flow and the Psychology of Discovery and Invention* (New York: HarperCollins, 1996).

16. Steven Pressfield, *The War of Art: Break through the Blocks and Win Your Inner Creative Battles* (New York: Warner Books, 2002).

17. Peter Elbow, *Writing with Power: Techniques for Mastering the Writing Process* (New York: Oxford University Press, 1981).

18. See Tony Buzan and Barry Buzan, *The Mind Map Book: How to Use Radiant Thinking to Maximize Your Brain's Untapped Potential* (New York: Penguin Books, 1993). For concept mapping, see Joseph D. Novak and D. Bob Gowin, *Learning How to Learn* (New York: Cambridge University Press, 2002). We also recommend doing an advanced search on Google, specifying .edu extensions only as the search parameters for either of these types.

19. R. Keith Sawyer, *Explaining Creativity: The Science of Human Innovation* (New York: Oxford University Press, 2006). Sawyer also emphasizes the importance of an early start and the other strategies we have discussed.

20. For concise advice about taking notes while researching, see Dorothy U. Seyler, *Read, Reason, Write: An Argument Text and Reader*, 8th ed. (Boston: McGraw-Hill, 2008).

21. Linda Flower and John R. Hayes, "A Cognitive Process Theory of Writing," *College Composition and Communication* 32 (1981): 380–81.

22. Jean Wyrick, *Steps to Writing Well: A Concise Guide to Composition*, 6th ed. (New York: Harcourt, Brace, 1996), 103.

23. Peggy Noonan, *What I Saw at the Revolution: A Political Life in the Reagan Era* (New York: Ivy Books, 1990), 77. To learn more about how a president's speeches are written, go to http://millercenter.org/academic/americanpresident.

24. Ibid.

25. Public Broadcasting Service, "Forum Featuring Presidential Speechwriters," www.pbs.org/newshour/inauguration/speech3.html (accessed May 19, 2012).

26. David Greene, "Bush Prepares to Deliver State of Union Address," National Public Radio, 2006, www.npr.org/templates/story/story.php?storyId=5179164&ft=1&f=1001 (accessed May 19, 2012).

27. Jay Newton-Small, "How Obama Writes His Speeches," *Time*, August 28, 2008, www.time.com/time/politics/article/0,8599,1837368,00.html (accessed May 19, 2012).

28. Ibid.

29. Carrie Budoff Brown, "A Peek at Obama's Inaugural Plan," *Politico.com*, January 16, 2009, www.politico.com/news/stories/0109/17515.html (accessed May 19, 2012).

30. Sondra Perl, "Understanding Composing," *College Composition and Communication* 31 (1980): 363–69.

31. Flower and Hayes, "A Cognitive Process Theory of Writing," 365–87.

32. Quintilian, *The Institutio Oratoria of Quintilian*, trans. H. E. Butler (New York: Putnam, 1992), 109–11.

33. American Library Association, *Information Literacy Competency Standards for Higher Education* (Chicago: Association of College and Research Libraries, 2000), 2–3.

34. Ibid.

35. Ibid.

36. Jon Udell, "Wikipedia's Future," *InfoWorld* 28 (January 9, 2006): 30.

37. Cornell University Library, "Introduction to Research: Distinguishing Scholarly from Non-Scholarly Periodicals: (articles and papers)," www.library.cornell.edu/resrch/intro#2Findingbooks,articles,andothermater (accessed May 19, 2012).

38. Ibid.

39. Ibid.

40. Ibid.

41. Penn State University Libraries, "How to Evaluate the Information," http://www.libraries.psu.edu/psul/lls/students/research_resources/evaluate_info.html (accessed May 19, 2012).

42. Lee Rainie, "Internet Librarians Own the Future," *Information Today* 22 (January 2005): 42.

43. Steven Levy, "All Eyes on Google," *Newsweek*, March 29, 2004, 54.

44. Michael Gorman, "The Corruption of Cataloging," *Library Journal* 120 (September 15, 1995): 34.

45. John M. Broder, "Clinton's Drug Plan Attacked by Industry," *New York Times*, June 28, 2000, A22.

46. Purdue University Online Writing Lab, "Evaluating Print vs. Internet Sources," http://owl.english.purdue.edu/owl/resource/553/04 (accessed May 19, 2012).

47. Sandy Whitely, ed., *The American Library Association Guide to Information Access: A Complete Research Handbook and Directory* (New York: Random House, 1994), xvii.

48. Levy, "All Eyes on Google."

49. A study by the OCLC found that less than 35 percent of college students reported that they had used online databases, whereas 82 percent responded that they had used search engines (13). See Online Library Computer Center, "Libraries and Information Sources—Use, Familiarity, Favorability," in *Perceptions of Libraries and Information Resources* (Part I), www.oclc.org/reports/pdfs/Percept_pt1.pdf (accessed May 19, 2012).

50. Whitely, The American Library Association Guide to Information Access, 34.

51. For a discussion of alternatives to popular search engines and their advantages, see Brad Stone, "Little Engines That Can," *Newsweek*, March 29, 2004, 59.

52. Go to www.library.cornell.edu/resrch/intro#2Findingbooks,articles,andothermater.

53. David J. Jefferson, "America's Most Dangerous Drug," *Newsweek*, August 8, 2005, 42.

54. Ibid., 47.

55. John C. Reinard, "The Empirical Study of the Persuasive Effects of Evidence: The Status after Fifty Years of Research," *Human Communication Research* 15 (1988): 3–59.

56. William Norwood Brigance, *Speech: Its Techniques and Disciplines in a Free Society*, 2nd ed. (New York: Appleton-Century-Crofts, 1952), 211.

57. See, for example, Char Miller, "In the Sweat of Our Brow: Citizenship in American Domestic Practice during WWII—Victory Gardens," *Journal of American Culture* 26 (2003): 395–409.

58. See Michael Pollan, "Farmer in Chief," *New York Times Magazine*, October 9, 2008, www.nytimes.com/2008/10/12/magazine/12policy-t.html?pagewanted=1&_r=1 (accessed May 19, 2012).

CHAPTER 7

1. "General Information on Domestic Violence and Sexual Assault," http://middlewayhouse.org/violence.html (accessed March 20, 2012).

2. Taken from *Healthwise*, Richard A. DeVaul's weekly radio program, broadcast on Texas A&M's National Public Radio affiliate, KAMU, 90.9 FM, September 12, 1996.

3. David K. Shipler, *The Working Poor: Invisible in America* (New York: Knopf, 2004), x–xi.

4. J. Edward Hill, "Priorities in Prevention," *Vital Speeches of the Day* 72 (1995): 88.

5. From Bill Clinton, "Remarks by the President on Responsible Citizenship and the American Community," Georgetown University, July 6, 1995, http://clinton1.nara.gov/White_House/EOP/OP/html/book1.html (accessed May 17, 2012).

6. Reprinted by permission from Fred S. Zeidman, "Remembrance Day Ceremony in the Rotunda of the Capital, April 2009," www.ushmm.org/remembrance/dor/years/view_video.php?content=2009&f=info&video=zeidman (accessed May 17, 2012). Copyright © 2009 by United States Holocaust Memorial Museum.

7. James C. May, "Connecting and Protecting Our Planet" October 30, 2008, *Airlines for America*,

www.airlines.org/Pages/Speech-by-James-C-May-Connecting-and-Protecting-our-Planet.aspx. (accessed May 18, 2012), Copyright © 2009 by Air Transport Association.

8. Reprinted by permission from Roslyn Brock, "A Refueling Stop on the Road to Freedom," *Vital Speeches of the Day* 71 (2005): 654.

9. For a detailed description of this and related problems, visit www.therapeuticjustice.com, where you will find a description of the "Community Model," based on the writings of Morgan Moss.

10. Steve Loranger, "How Do We Begin to Solve the Problems?" *Vital Speeches of the Day* 71 (2005): 364.

11. Ben Shalom Bernanke, "Speech to the Economic Club of New York," October 15, 2008, www.americanrhetoric.com/speeches/benbernankenewyorkeconomicclub.htm (accessed March 20, 2012).

12. "UNHCR Goodwill Ambassador Angelina Jolie Receives First Church World Service Humanitarian Award," August 23, 2002, http://www.ncccusa.org/news/02news81.html (accessed March 15, 2012).

13. See, Peter Goldman, et. al, *Quest for the Presidency: 1992* (College Station, TX: Texas A&M University Press, 1994), 577.

14. Reprinted by permission from William D. Novelli. "Transforming the Healthcare System" speech, from the AFCEA Solution Series. Copyright © 2005 by AARP.

CHAPTER 8

1. James C. McCroskey and R. Samuel Mehrley, "The Effects of Disorganization and Nonfluency on Attitude Change and Source Credibility," *Communication Monographs* 36 (1969): 13–21.

2. Studies generally show that organized speeches are better understood than those that are less well-organized. See, for example, Ernest C. Thompson, "An Experimental Investigation of the Relative Effectiveness of Organizational Structure in Oral Communication," *Southern Speech Communication Journal* 26 (1960): 59–69.

3. When listeners are forced to listen to a disorganized presentation, they are unlikely to respond in a way that is consistent with the speaker's specific purpose. See Raymond G. Smith, "An Experimental Study of the Effects of Speech Organization upon Attitudes of College Students," *Communication Monographs* 18 (1951): 292–301.

4. For example, a Michigan legislator sponsored a $486,000 earmark to add a bike lane to a bridge within walking distance of her home. See David S. Fallis, Scott Higham, and Kimberly Kindy, "Congressional Earmarks Sometimes Used to Fund Projects near Lawmakers' Properties," www.washingtonpost.com/investigations/congressional-earmarks-sometimes-used-to-fund-projects-near-lawmakers-properties/2012/01/12/gIQA97HGvQ_story.html (accessed February 10, 2012).

5. See Peg McGlinch, "Don't Ban Earmarks—Fix Them," www.usnews.com/opinion/blogs/peg-mcglinch/2012/02/09/dont-ban-earmarks-fix-them (accessed February 12, 2012).

6. John Dewey, *How We Think* (Boston: Heath, 1910).

7. This pattern was originally introduced by Alan H. Monroe in *Principles and Types of Speech* (New York: Scott, Foresman, 1935) and has been refined in later editions. See, for example, Kathleen M. German, Bruce E. Gronbeck, Douglas Ehninger, and Alan H. Monroe, *Principles of Speech Communication*, 17th edition (Upper Saddle River, NJ: Pearson, 2010).

8. See Karen Zediker, "Rediscovering the Tradition: Women's History with a Relational Approach to the Basic Public Speaking Course," paper, Western States Communication Association, Albuquerque, New Mexico, 1993.

9. Walter R. Fisher, "Narration as a Human Communication Paradigm: The Case of Public Moral Argument," *Communication Monographs* 51 (1984): 1–22.

10. Ibid.

11. See James C. McCroskey, *An Introduction to Rhetorical Communication*, 7th ed. (Boston: Allyn & Bacon, 1997), 205–22; and Howard Gilkinson, Stanley F. Paulson, and Donald E. Sikkink, "Effects of Order and Authority in an Argumentative Speech," *Quarterly Journal of Speech* 40 (1954): 183–92.

12. Assuming that recipients find the message relevant, moderate repetition (such as that provided by transitions, a preview, and a review within a speech) prompts listeners to better understand and better recall what is said as well as process it more deeply. See, for example, Heather M. Claypool, Diane M. Mackie, Teresa Garcia-Marques, Ashley McIntosh, and Ashton Udall, "The Effects of Personal Relevance and Repetition on Persuasive Processing," *Social Cognition* 22 (2004): 310–35. Also see Robert F. Lorch Jr., Elizabeth Pugzles Lorch, and W. Elliot Inman, "Effects of Signaling Topic Structure on Text Recall," *Journal of Educational Psychology* 85 (1993): 281–90.

13. Bob Scott, "Green Burials Gaining Popularity," *The Herald-Times,* Sunday, January 29, 2012, A2.

14. From Bill Clinton, "Memphis Church of God in Christ Convention Address," November 13, 1993. Published 1993 by Bill Clinton.

15. Carmen Mariano, "You as Teachers Are Saving the World," *Vital Speeches of the Day* 71 (October 1, 2005): 642.

16. From Eugene Debs, "Statement to the Court," Federal Court of Cleveland, September 18, 1918.

17. Richard Lamm, "Unexamined Assumptions: Destiny, Political Institutions, Democracy and Population," *Vital Speeches of the Day* 64 (September 15, 1998): 712.

18. Reprinted by permission from Sarah Snyder. Published 2007 by SC 105 Speakers Showcase.

19. Joel Grass, "When Prisons Suffer We All Suffer," Persuasive Speech Two on the Website for SC 105: Fundamentals of Oral Communication, http://cstl-cla.semo.edu/williams/sc105/samples.htm (accessed February 24, 2012).

20. See, for example, Michael Jacobson, *Downsizing Prisons* (New York: New York University Press, 2005).

21. See Claypool et al., "The Effects of Personal Relevance and Repetition on Persuasive Processing"; and Lorch et al., "Effects of Signaling Topic Structure on Text Recall."

22. Office of Admissions, Indiana University, "Academic Opportunities," http://admit.indiana.edu/academics/opportunities.shtml (accessed February 1, 2012).

23. To read more about Shalom Community Center, go to http://shalomcommunitycenter.org/about/our-mission (accessed February 7, 2012).

24. From Barack Obama, "Keynote Address to the 2004 Democratic National Convention," July 26, 2004. Published 2004 by BarackObama.com.

25. Richard Lamm, "Family Friendly Institutions," *Vital Speeches of the Day* 72 (October 15, 2005): 30.

26. Edward M. Kennedy, "Faith, Truth and Tolerance in America," http://www.americanrhetoric.com/speeches/tedkennedytruth&tolerance.htm (accessed: February 7, 2012).

27. Jimmy Carter, "U.S. Response to Soviet Military Force in Cuba," *Vital Speeches of the Day* 42 (1970): 4.

28. Robert C. Purcell, "Values for Value: Integrity and Stewardship," *Vital Speeches of the Day* 64 (October 1, 1998): 766.

CHAPTER 9

1. See W. James Potter, *Media Literacy*, 5th ed. (Thousand Oaks, CA: Sage, 2010).

2. See Carla Brooks Johnston, *Screened Out: How the Media Control Us and What We Can Do about It* (Armonk, NY: Sharpe, 2000).

CHAPTER 10

1. For more on how language choices affect the way we think and view the world, see James R. Andrews, *A Choice of Worlds: The Practice and Criticism of Public Discourse* (New York: Harper & Row, 1973); George Lakoff and Mark Johnson, *Metaphors We Live By* (Chicago: University of Chicago Press, 1980); and Gilles Fauconnier and Mark Turner, *The Way We Think* (New York: Basic Books, 2002).

2. Colin Powell, "Sharing the American Dream," *Vital Speeches of the Day* 62 (June 1, 1997): 485–86. Copyright © 1997 by Colin Powell. Reprinted by permission.

3. Martha Cooper and Mary Rose Williams, *Power Persuasion: Moving an Ancient Art into the Media* (Indianapolis, IN: Educational Video Group, 1992). Reprinted by permission.

4. "Senate GOP Plans Attack on Health Care Bill," *Bloomington (IN) Herald-Times*, May 8, 2009, E2.

5. From Abraham Lincoln, "A House Divided." Published 1858.

6. John F. Kennedy, "Inaugural Address," in *American Rhetorical Discourse*, 3rd ed., ed. Ronald F. Reid and James F. Klumpp (Long Grove, IL: Waveland, 2005), 788–789.

7. From Lyndon B. Johnson, "The Voting Rights Act of 1965." *Great Speeches for Criticism and Analysis*, ed. Lloyd Rohler and Roger Cook, 231–32 (Greenwood, IN: Alistair Press, 1988).

8. Frederick Douglass, "What to the Slave is the Fourth of July, July 5, 1852." http://americanrhetoric.com/speeches/frederickdouglassslaveto4thofjuly.htm (accessed May 22, 2012).

9. Chief Joseph of the Nez Perce, "Chief Joseph Speaks," Archives of the West, www.pbs.org/weta/thewest/resources/archives/six/jospeak (accessed May 22, 2012).

10. Alessandra Stanley, "At White House Briefing, Polish Replaces Testiness," *New York Times*, May 17, 2006, A19.

11. John F. Kennedy, "Civil Rights Message," June 11, 1963, http://americanrhetoric.com/speeches/jfkcivilrights.htm (accessed May 22, 2012).

12. Qtd. in Jane Blankenship, *A Sense of Style: An Introduction to Style for the Public Speaker* (Belmont, CA: Dickenson, 1968), 70.

13. Eugene E. Brussell, ed., *Webster's New World Dictionary of Quotable Definitions* (New York: Prentice Hall, 1988): 91.

14. Mary Church Terrell, "What it Means to be Colored in the Capital of the United States," *Man Cannot Speak for Her: A Critical Study of Early Feminist Rhetoric*, 2 vols., ed. Karlyn Kohrs Campbell (New York: Praeger, 1989), 2:422.

15. Remarks of Barack Obama at the NAACP 100th Anniversary Convention, New York, New York, July 16, 2009, www.presidentialrhetoric.com/speeches/07.16.09.html (accessed May 22, 2012).

16. Edgar Allan Poe, "The Raven," in *The Viking Book of Poetry of the English Speaking World*, ed., Richard Aldington vol. 2 (New York: Viking Press, 1959), 866.

17. Franklin Roosevelt, "Second Inaugural Address, January 20, 1937," www.presidentialrhetoric.com/historicspeeches/roosevelt_franklin/second_inaugural.html (accessed May 22, 2012).

18. See Dennis S. Gouran, "Communicative Influences on Decisions Related to the Watergate Coverup: The Failure of Collective Judgment," *Central States Speech Journal* 34 (1984): 260–68.

19. See, for example, Julia Wood, *Gendered Lives: Communication, Gender, and Culture*, 4th ed. (Belmont, CA: Wadsworth, 2001).

20. See Richard L. Johannesen, "The Emerging Concept of Communication as Dialogue," *Quarterly Journal of Speech* 57 (1971): 373–82; and Maurice S. Friedman, *Dialogue and the Human Image: Beyond Humanistic Psychology* (Newbury Park, CA: Sage, 1992).

CHAPTER 11

1. Doris G. Yoakam, "Women's Introduction to the American Platform," *History and Criticism of American Public Address*, vol. 1, ed. William Norwood Brigance (New York: McGraw-Hill, 1943), 74–76.

2. See, as examples, Joe Ayres, "Speech Preparation Processes and Speech Apprehension," *Communication Education* 45 (1996): 228–35; Joe Ayres and Tim Hopf, *Coping with Speech Anxiety* (Norwood, NJ: Ablex, 1993); Ralph R. Behnke and Chris R. Sawyer, "Anticipatory Anxiety Patterns for Male and Female Speakers," *Communication Education* 49 (2000): 187–95; and Thomas Robinson II, "Communication Apprehension and the Basic Public Speaking Course: A National Survey of In-Class Treatment Techniques," *Communication Education* 46 (1997): 188–97.

3. See John T. Molloy, *Dress for Success* (New York: Warner Books, 1975), one of the first books to address the importance of appearance in the professional world. For a more recent work, see Molloy's *New Women's Dress for Success* (New York: Warner Books, 1996).

4. For a classic work on nonverbal communication, see Edward T. Hall, *The Silent Language* (Garden City, NY: Doubleday, 1959). More recent works include Edward T. Hall, *The Dance of Life* (New York: Doubleday, 1983); and Mark Knapp and Judith Hall, *Nonverbal Communication in Human Interaction* (Philadelphia: Harcourt Brace Jovanovich, 1997).

5. You can learn more about these differences by enrolling in a course in intercultural communication.

6. Virginia P. Richmond and James C. McCroskey, *Nonverbal Behavior in Interpersonal Relations*, 3rd ed. (Boston: Allyn & Bacon, 1995).

7. Nathan Bierma, "Hand Gestures May Expand, Express Unspoken Thoughts," *Chicago Tribune*, August 5, 2004, sec. 5, 2.

8. Paul Ekman, *Emotions Revealed: Recognizing Faces and Feelings to Improve Communications and Emotional Life* (New York: Holt, 2004), 84–112.

9. Knapp and Hall, *Nonverbal Communication in Human Interaction*, 58–74.

10. Albert Mehrabian, *Silent Messages: Implicit Communication of Emotions and Attitudes,* 2nd ed. (Belmont, CA: Wadsworth, 1982); Paul Ekman and Erika Rosenberg, *What the Face Reveals* (New York: Oxford University Press, 1998).

11. For an excellent collection of readings on all aspects of nonverbal communication, see Laura K. Guerrero, Joseph A. DeVito, and Michael L. Hecht, eds., *The Nonverbal Communication Reader: Classic and Contemporary Readings*, 2nd ed. (Prospect Heights, IL: Waveland Press, 1999).

12. PBS Home Programs, www.pbs.org/standarddeviantstv/transcript_public.html#rate (accessed March 13, 2012).

13. Richmond and McCroskey, *Nonverbal Behavior in Interpersonal Relations*, 68–70.

14. "A Powerful Tool: Your Voice," *Costa Connection*, June 2004, 9.

15. See, for example, Deborah Tannen, *You Just Don't Understand: Men and Women in Conversation* (New York: Quill, 2001). Tannen and other linguists have noted that men and women often exhibit different speech patterns, with women more inclined to use inflectional patterns that appear to seek validation from listeners. When using a rising inflection at the end of a statement (as in, "We really have to find a permanent home for the new shelter, don't you think?"), the speaker suggests an attitude of uncertainty. Especially if used often, this kind of vocal pattern can undermine a speaker's credibility.

16. For an extensive guide on vocal communication, see Jeffrey C. Hahner, Martin A. Sokoloff, and Sandra L. Salisch, *Speaking Clearly: Improving Voice and Diction*, 5th ed. (New York: McGraw-Hill, 1996).

17. John O. Greene, Marianne S. Sassi, Terri L. Malek-Madani, and Christopher N. Edwards, "Adult Acquisition of Message-Production Skills," *Communication Monographs* 64 (1997): 181–200. This article emphasizes the importance of practicing speech delivery.

18. See Herbert W. Hildebrandt and Walter W. Stevens, "Manuscript and Extemporaneous Modes of Delivery in Communicating Information," *Communication Monographs* 30 (1963): 369–72.

19. John F. Harris, *The Survivor: Bill Clinton in the White House* (New York: Random House, 2005), 10.

20. For one of the best guides on the techniques of manu-script speaking, see James C. Humes, *Talk Your Way to the Top* (New York: McGraw-Hill, 1980), 125–35.

21. Elizabeth Warren, www.youtube.com/watch?v= vQ3zt3YlNSU (accessed March 13, 2012).

22. For additional advice on managing question-and-answer sessions, see Thomas K. Mira, *Speak Smart* (New York: Random House, 1997), 115–23.

CHAPTER 12

1. See, for example, Stephen Kinzer and Jim Rutenberg, "Grim Images Seem to Deepen Nation's Polarization on Iraq," *New York Times*, May 13, 2004, A11; "Abu Ghraib—An Indelible Stain on U.S.," *Christian Science Monitor*, May 7, 2004, 9; Charles Krauthammer, "Abu Ghraib as Symbol," *Washington Post*, May 7, 2004, A33; and Michael M. Phillips, "The Abu Ghraib Fallout: Marines in Iraq See Prison Photos Creating Enemies," *Wall Street Journal*, May 10, 2004, A10.

2. See *Newsweek*'s special report: "After the Tsunami," *Newsweek*, January 10, 2005, 22–45; and *Time* maga-zine's special report on Hurricane Katrina: "An American Tragedy," *Time*, September 12, 2005, 28–85. See *Time*'s special report: "Haiti's Tragedy," *Time*, January 25, 2010, 30–37.

3. See Robert D. McFadden, "Pilot Is Hailed after Jetliner's Icy Plunge," *New York Times*, January 15, 2009, www.nytimes.com/2009/01/16/nyregion/16crash.html?ref=robertdjrmcfadden (accessed May 19, 2012).

4. See Martin Fackler, "Powerful Quake and Tsunami Devastate Northern Japan," *New York Times*, March 11, 2011, www.nytimes.com/2011/03/12/world/asia/12japan.html?ref=martinfackler (accessed May 19, 2012). Also see Jenna Fisher, "Another Earthquake Shakes Japan; Fukushima Evacuated: A Nuclear Timeline," *The Christian Science Monitor*, March 15, 2011, 8.

5. Doris A. Graber, "Say It with Pictures," *Annals of the American Academy of Political and Social Science 546* (1996): 85–96. These findings continue to hold up. See William E. Hockley, "The Picture Superiority Effect in Associative Recognition," *Memory & Cognition 36* (2008): 1351–1359. Also see Georg Stenberg, "Conceptual and Perceptual Factors in the Picture Superiority Effect," *European Journal of Cognitive Psychology 18* (2006): 813–47.

6. Shu-Ling Lai, "Influence of Audio-Visual Presentations on Learning Abstract Concepts," *International Journal of Instructional Media 27* (2000): 199–207.

7. Priti Shah and James Hoeffner, "Review of Graph Comprehension Research: Implications for Instruction," *Educational Psychology Review 14* (2002): 47–51. Also see Julie A. Edell and Richard Staelin, "The Information Processing of Pictures in Print Advertisements," *Journal of Consumer Research 10* (1983): 45–61.

8. Graber, "Say It with Pictures," 86. Also see Carol L. Hodes, "Processing Visual Information: Implications of the Dual Code Theory," *Journal of Instructional Psychology 21* (1994): 36–43.

9. Claire Morrison and William Jimmerson, "Business Presentations for the 1990s," *Video Manager* (July 1989), 18.

10. Lih-Juan Chanlin, "The Effects of Verbal Elaboration and Visual Elaboration on Student Learning," *International Journal of Instructional Media 24* (1997): 333–39. Also see Carol L. Hodes, "Processing Visual Information: Implications of the Dual Code Theory," *Journal of Instructional Psychology 21* (1994): 36–43; Glenda C. Rakes, "Teaching Visual Literacy in a Multimedia Age," *Tech Trends 43* (1999):14–18.

11. See, for example, Michael Grunwald, "How to Spend the Stimulus," *Time*, February 16, 2009, 20–22.

12. Michael P. Verdi and Janet T. Johnson, "Organized Spatial Displays and Texts: Effects of Presentational Order and Display Type on Learning Outcomes," *Journal of Experimental Education 65* (Summer 1997): 303–17.

13. Ibid., 303–05.

14. Maria L. Berg and James G. May, "Parallel Processing in Visual Perception and Memory: What Goes Where and When?" *Current Psychology 16* (1998): 247–83. Also see Lih-Juan Chanlin, "Visual Treatment for Different Prior Knowledge," *International Journal of Instructional Media 26* (1999): 213–19.

15. Ibid., 253–54.

16. Joel Best, *More Damned Lies and Statistics: How Numbers Confuse Public Issues* (Berkeley: University of California Press, 2004), 45–46.

17. Berg and May, "Parallel Processing in Visual Perception and Memory," 254–62.

18. Best, More Damned Lies and Statistics, 45–46.

19. "Study Predicts Number of Fat Children Will Rise," *Bloomington (IN) Herald-Times*, March 6, 2006, C7.

20. Best, More Damned Lies and Statistics, 49. Also see Gerald Everett Jones, *How to Lie with Charts* (San Jose, CA: Authors Choice Press, 2000), 30.

21. Jones, How to Lie with Charts, 28–29.

22. B. A. Chauvin, "Visual or Media Literacy?" *Journal of Media Literacy 23* (2003): 119–28.

23. Graber, "Say It with Pictures," 90–93.

24. Jones, *How to Lie with Charts*.

25. Read about Kim Phuc and the iconic photograph at http://news.bbc.co.uk/2/hi/4517597.stm (accessed May 19, 2012).

26. Hodes, "Processing Visual Information," 36–40.

27. Elizabeth Keyes, "Typography, Color, and Information Structure," *Technical Communication* 40 (November 1993): 638–54.

28. It is important to remember that some listeners may be unable to distinguish among colors. In addition to the correctives we offer, there are other ways of dealing with this issue. See William Horton, *Illustrating Computer Documentation* (New York: Wiley, 1991), 219–44.

29. There is considerable research on effective color combinations that consider hue, value, and saturation. See Edward Tufte, *Envisioning Information* (Cheshire, CT: Graphics Press, 1990).

30. A study conducted at Indiana University found that an instructor received much better course evaluations when she projected keywords to outline her lecture's main points than when she gave the identical lecture without using visuals.

31. It is important to recognize that speakers *do* exercise judgment in choosing photographs, deciding how to display data, and so forth. The ethical speaker chooses never to knowingly distort information. Likewise, the ethical speaker is mindful of the *potential* for bias when using visual images to present information and offers support for arguments.

32. Joe Ayres, "Using Visual Aids to Reduce Speech Anxiety," *Communication Research Reports* 8 (1991): 73–79.

33. Chanlin, "The Effects of Verbal Elaboration and Visual Elaboration on Student Learning," 333–39.

34. Cornelius B. Pratt, "The Misuse of PowerPoint," *Public Relations Quarterly* 48 (2003): 20–26.

35. James Price Dillard, ed., *Seeking Compliance: The Production of Interpersonal Influence Messages* (Scottsdale, AZ: Gorsuch Scarisbrick, 1990).

36. Tufte, Envisioning Information, 26–64.

37. Amy C. Bradshaw, "Effects of Presentation Interference in Learning with Visuals," *Journal of Visual Literacy* 23 (2003): 41–68.

38. We have found this color scheme to be the best—even in rooms with minimal dimming—and it's also recommended by Jones, *How to Lie with Charts*, 215.

39. Jeremy Caplan, "Tips on Talks," *Time*, November 15, 2005, 93.

40. Jean-Luc Doumont, "The Cognitive Style of PowerPoint: Slides Are Not All Evil," *Technical Communication* 52 (2005): 64–70.

41. Chanlin, "Visual Treatment for Different Prior Knowledge," 213–19.

42. See, for example, L. Rieber, "Animation as a Distractor to Learning," *International Journal* of Instructional Media 23 (1996): 53–57.

43. Arthur Goldsmith, "Digitally Altered Photography: The New Image Makers," *Britannica Book of the Year: 1995* (Chicago: Encyclopedia Britannica, 1995), 135.

CHAPTER 13

1. Paul Korzeniowski, "Fingerprinting Plays a Key Role in Biometrics Boom," *TechNewsWorld*, January 18, 2005, www.technewsworld.com/story/39467.html (accessed February 5, 2012).

2. See, for example, William E. Wilson, *The Angel and the Serpent: The Story of New Harmony* (Bloomington: Indiana University Press, 1984).

3. See, for example, Simon Brown, *Practical Feng Shui* (London: Ward Lock, 1997).

4. Lois Burke et al., *A Cornucopia of Strategies for Working with LD and ADD Students* (Columbus: Ohio State University Office for Disability Services, 1999).

5. Laura J. Gurak, *Oral Presentations for Technical Communication* (Boston: Allyn & Bacon, 2000).

6. "Supported employment" refers to providing employment and advancement opportunities for people with disabilities. See the Web site of the Association for Persons in Supported Employment (APSE), www.apse. org/ (accessed February 19, 2012).

7. For additional information about Mother Hubbard's Cupboard, visit their Web site at www.mhcfoodpantry. org (accessed January 20, 2012).

8. See, for example, Wisconsin Department of Public Instruction, "Service-Learning: Definition and Philosophy," dpi.wi.gov/sl/sldppage.html (accessed February 10, 2012). Service learning is often defined as a form of experiential learning where students apply academic knowledge and critical-thinking skills to address genuine community needs.

9. See, for example, Yan Wang and Robert Rodgers, "Impact of Service-Learning and Social Justice Education on College Students' Cognitive Development," *NASPA Journal* 43, no. 2 (2006): article 7; and various articles in the *Michigan Journal of Community Service-Learning*, www.ginsberg.umich. edu/mjcsl/ (accessed February 19, 2012).

10. For a discussion of retention, see Robert L. Greene, *Human Memory: Paradigms and Paradoxes* (Hillsdale, NJ: Erlbaum, 1992).

11. Abraham Maslow, *Motivation and Personality* (New York: Harper & Row, 1954).

12. See Jane Blankenship, *A Sense of Style: An Introduction to Style for the Public Speaker* (Belmont, CA: Dickenson, 1968); Pamela J. Cooper, *Communication for the Classroom Teacher*, 5th ed. (Scottsdale, AZ: Gorsuch Scarisbrick, 1995); and James C. McCroskey, *An Introduction to Rhetorical Communication*, 7th ed. (Boston: Allyn & Bacon, 1997).

13. See, for example, Joan Middendorf and Alan Kalish, "The 'Change-up' Lectures," *National Teaching and Learning Forum* 5 (1996): 1–4.

14. See William J. McKeachie, *Teaching Tips: Strategies, Research, and Theory for College and University Teachers* (Boston: Houghton Mifflin, 1999), 209–15; and Martha Petrone, "Teaching and Learning as a Transactional Process," in *Teaching and Learning in College: A Resource for Educators*, 4th ed., ed. Gary S. Wheeler (Elyria, OH: Info-Tec, 2002), 143–76.

CHAPTER 14

1. Brad Stone, "Tech Trash, E-Waste: By Any Name, It's an Issue," *Newsweek*, December 12, 2005, 11.

2. American Association of Colleges of Nursing, "Nursing Shortage," July 15, 2011, www.aacn.nche.edu/media-relations/fact-sheets/nursing-shortage (accessed February 21, 2012).

3. Barack Obama, "Remarks by the President on National Security," National Archives, Washington, DC., The White House, Office of the Press Secretary, news release, May 21, 2009, www.whitehouse.gov/the_press_office/Remarks-by-the-President-On-National-Security-5-21-09/ (accessed March 3, 2012).

4. Richard B. Cheney, "Remarks by Richard B. Cheney," May 21, 2009, *American Enterprise Institute*, http://www.aei.org/article/foreign-and-defense-policy/regional/india-pakistan-afghanistan/remarks-by-richard-b-cheney/ (accessed March 2, 2012).

5. Dave Jamieson, "Obama Economic Plan to Discourage Outsourcing, Reward 'Insourcing,'" *The Huffington Post*, January 25, 2012, www.huffingtonpost.com/2012/01/25/obama-economic-plan-insourcing_n_1231666.html (accessed February 21, 2012).

6. *The Rhetoric of Aristotle*, trans. George Kennedy (New York: Oxford University Press, 1991).

7. Gary Cronkhite and Jo Liska, "A Critique of Factor Analytic Approaches to the Study of Credibility," *Communication Monographs* 43 (1976): 91–107; James C. McCroskey and Thomas J. Young, "Ethos and Credibility: The Construct and Its Measurement after Three Decades," *Central States Speech Journal* 32 (1981): 24–34; and Jack L. Whitehead, "Factors of Source Credibility," *Quarterly Journal of Speech* 54 (1968): 59–63.

8. Ronald Reagan, "State of the Union Address," in *Three Centuries of American Rhetorical Discourse*, ed. Ronald F. Reid (Prospect Heights, IL: Waveland Press, 1988), 743.

9. Ray Long and Rick Pearson, "Impeached Gov. Blagojevich Has Been Removed from Office," *Chicago Tribune*, January 30, 2009, www.chicagotribune.com/news/local/chi-blagojevich-impeachment-removal,0,5791846.story (accessed March 3, 1012).

10. James Poniewozik, "Blago Talks! (And Talks…)," *Time*, January 29, 2009.

11. "Mitt Romney Announced his 2012 Run for the Presidency," *Mitt Romney Central*, June 2, 2011, http://mittromneycentral.com/speeches/2011-speeches/060211-mitt-romney-announces-his-2012-run-for-president/ (accessed February 26, 2012).

12. Barbara Jordan, "1976 Democratic National Convention Keynote Address," *American Rhetoric*, www.americanrhetoric.com/speeches/barbarajordan1976dnc.html (accessed March 3, 2012).

13. Barbara Pierce Bush, "Commencement Address at Wellesley College," *American Rhetoric,* www.americanrhetoric.com/speeches/barbarabush wellesleycommencement.htm (accessed July 23, 2012).

14. Larry J. Sabato, *Feeding Frenzy: How Attack Journalism Has Transformed American Politics* (New York: Free Press, 1993), 12.

15. William Jefferson Clinton, "1992 Democratic National Convention Acceptance Address," *American Rhetoric*, www.americanrhetoric.com/speeches/wjclinton1992dnc.htm (accessed March 3, 2012).

16. Ronald Reagan, "Address to the Nation on Defense and National Security," March 23, 1983, www.reagan.utexas.edu/archives/speeches/1983/32383d.htm (accessed March 3, 2012).

17. Eugene Debs, "Address to the Court," Cleveland, Ohio, September 18, 1918, *Emerson Kent.com*, www.emersonkent.com/speeches/address_to_the_court.htm (accessed March 3, 2012).

18. Cesar Chavez, "Address by Cesar Chavez, The Commonwealth Club of San Francisco, November 9, 1984, http://chavez.cde.ca.gov/ModelCurriculum/teachers/Lessons/resources/documents/Commonwealth_Club_SanFrancisco_11-9-84.pdf (accessed March 3, 2012).

19. Barack Obama, "President-Elect Obama's Weekly Address," November 22, 2008 www.youtube.com/watch?v=m17pz0R_qZo (accessed March 3, 2012).

20. National Service Blog, *United We Serve*, www.serve.gov/stories_all.asp (accessed March 3, 2012).

21. Frederick Douglass, "What to the Slave is the Fourth of July," July 5, 1852, *Teaching American History*, http://teachingamericanhistory.org/library/index.asp?document=162 (accessed March 3, 2012).

22. J. Michael Hogan, *The Panama Canal in American Politics* (Carbondale: Southern Illinois University Press, 1986), 49.

23. From Mario Matthew Cuomo, "1984 Democratic National Convention Keynote Address," *American*

Rhetoric, www.americanrhetoric.com/speeches/mariocuomo1984dnc.htm (accessed March 3, 2012).

24. Franklin D. Roosevelt, "Franklin Roosevelt's Press Conference, December 17, 1940," *Our Documents: Lend-Lease*, http://docs.fdrlibrary.marist.edu/odllpc2.html (accessed March 3, 2012).

25. *Rhetoric of Aristotle*, 235.

CHAPTER 15

1. See Albert Fried, *McCarthyism: The Great American Red Scare: A Documentary History* (New York: Oxford University Press, 1997).

2. Aristotle, *Rhetoric*, trans. W. Rhys Roberts (Chicago: University of Chicago Press, 1952).

3. See Jeffrey K. Tulis, *The Rhetorical Presidency* (Princeton, NJ: Princeton University Press, 1987), 27–39.

4. See J. Michael Hogan, *Woodrow Wilson's Western Tour: Rhetoric, Public Opinion, and the League of Nations* (College Station: Texas A&M University Press, 2006), 27–41.

5. Woodrow Wilson, "Congressional Government," in *The Papers of Woodrow Wilson*, ed. Arthur S. Link et al., 69 vols. (Princeton, NJ: Princeton University Press, 1966–1994), 1: 565–66.

6. In a survey sponsored by the McCormick Tribune Freedom Museum, for example, it was found that only about one out of four Americans could name more than one of our First Amendment guarantees, but more than half could name at least two members of the cartoon family, the Simpsons. Only one in a thousand Americans could name all five of their First Amendment rights. Interestingly, Americans also misidentified First Amendment rights in the survey, with about one in five people claiming that the right to own a pet was protected by the First Amendment and 38 percent identifying the right against self-incrimination contained in the Fifth Amendment as a First Amendment right. See "D'oh! More Know Simpsons than Constitution," *MSNBC*.com, March 1, 2006, www.msnbc.msn.com/id/11611015/ns/us_news-life/t/doh-more-know-simpsons-constitution/#.T37lUNmP-mA (accessed April 6, 2012).

7. Max Weber, *The Theory of Social and Economic Organization*, trans. A. M. Henderson and Talcott Parsons (New York: Oxford University Press, 1947), 358.

8. Abraham Lincoln, "First Inaugural Address (1861)," in *American Voices: Significant Speeches in American History, 1640–1945*, ed. James R. Andrews and David Zarefsky (New York: Longman, 1989), 290.

9. For more on the rhetorical techniques of demagogues, see J. Justin Gustainis, "Demagoguery and Political Rhetoric: A Review of the Literature," *Rhetoric Society Quarterly* 20 (1990): 155–61.

10. James Darsey, *The Prophetic Tradition and Radical Rhetoric in America* (New York: New York University Press, 1997).

11. See J. Michael Hogan and Dave Tell, "Demagoguery and Democratic Deliberation: The Search for Rules of Discursive Engagement," *Rhetoric and Public Affairs* 9 (Fall 2006), 479–87.

12. See Stephen E. Toulmin, *The Uses of Argument* (Cambridge, UK: Cambridge University Press, 1958). Also see Wayne Brockriede and Douglas Ehninger, "Toulmin on Argument: An Interpretation and Application," *Quarterly Journal of Speech* 46 (1960): 44–53.

13. In law, the "reasonable person" is a "legal fiction" used primarily in negligence and contract law cases. Under this test, the court imagines how a "reasonable person"—a hypothetical person who is intelligent, informed, aware of the law, and fair minded—might react to arguments before the court. So, for example, a negligence case might raise the question of whether a defendant took the necessary precautions to avoid an accident—with those "necessary precautions" defined, of course, by the "reasonable person" test. Would the reasonable person have anticipated the circumstances that led to the accident? What kinds of precautions would the "reasonable person" have taken? What would the "reasonable person" have recognized as his or her legal rights and obligations in the aftermath of the accident?

14. David Thigpen, "Hall of Shame," *Time*, March 20, 2005, www.time.com/time/magazine/article/0,9171,1039703,00.html (accessed April 6, 2012).

15. Reprinted by permission from "Why Tax Soft Drinks?" *Liquid Candy: How Soft Drinks Are Harming Americans' Health*, www.cspinet.org/liquidcandy/whytax.html (accessed April 6, 2012). Copyright © n.d. by Center for Science in the Public Interest.

16. See Nathan Thornburgh, "Dropout Nation," *Time*, April 17, 2006, 31–40.

17. See R. Kent Weaver and Thomas Gais, "State Policy Choices under Welfare Reform," CCF Policy Briefs Number 21, Brookings Institution, April 2002, www.brookings.edu/papers/2002/04welfare_gais.aspx (accessed April 6, 2012).

18. See Legal Information Institute, Cornell School of Law, "*United States v. Virginia et al.* (94–1941), 518 U.S. 515 (1996)," *Supreme Court Collection*, www.law.cornell.edu/supct/html/94-1941.ZO.html (accessed April 6, 2012).

19. See "History of Bonfire and Bonfire Memorial," *Remembering Bonfire*, http://bonfire.tamu.edu/history (accessed April 6, 2012).

20. Jack L. Whitehead, "Factors of Source Credibility," *Quarterly Journal of Speech* 54 (1968): 59–63.

CHAPTER 16

1. Dale L. Sullivan, "A Closer Look at Education as Epideictic Rhetoric," *Rhetoric Society Quarterly* 23 (1993): 71–72.

2. George Kennedy, *The Art of Persuasion in Greece* (Princeton, NJ: Princeton University Press, 1963), 160.

3. From Rudy Giuliani, "2004 Republican National Convention Address," *American Rhetoric*, www.americanrhetoric.com/speeches/convention2004/rudygiuliani2004rnc.htm (accessed April 9, 2012). Copyright © 2004 by Rudy Giuliani.

4. See Celeste Michelle Condit, "The Functions of Epideictic: The Boston Massacre Orations as Exemplar," *Communication Quarterly* 33 (1985): 284–99.

5. John Hancock, "Boston Massacre Oration," in *American Rhetorical Discourse*, 3rd ed., ed. Ronald F. Reid and James F. Klumpp (Long Grove, IL: Waveland Press, 2005), 103.

6. Henry W. Grady, "The New South," in *American Rhetorical Discourse*, 494–95.

7. Robert F. Kennedy, "On the Death of Martin Luther King," *The History Place*, www.historyplace.com/speeches/rfk-mlk.htm (accessed April 9, 2012).

8. Ronald Reagan, "1982 State of the Union Address," *American Experience,* www.pbs.org/wgbh/americanexperience/features/primary-resources/reagan-1982-address/ (accessed April 9, 2012).

9. Alex Altman, "Chesley B. Sullenberger III," *Time*, January 16, 2009, www.time.com/time/nation/article/0,8599,1872247,00.html (accessed April 6, 2012).

10. Jonathan Martin, "Hero Pilot to Attend Obama Speech," *Politico.com*, February 24, 2009, www.politico.com/news/stories/0209/19229.html (accessed April 6, 2012).

11. John F. Kennedy, "Inaugural Address," in *American Rhetorical Discourse*, 789.

12. Dwight D. Eisenhower, "Second Inaugural Address: The Price of Peace," in *The Presidents Speak*, ed. Davis Newton Lott (New York: Holt, 1994), 310.

13. Winston Churchill, "We Shall Fight on the Beaches," *The Guardian*, www.guardian.co.uk/theguardian/2007/apr/20/greatspeeches1 (accessed April 9, 2012). Copyright © 1940 by British Crown and Churchill Family.

14. See Nicole Loraux, *The Invention of Athens: The Funeral Oration in the Classical City*, trans. Alan Sheridan (Cambridge, MA: Harvard University Press, 1986).

15. Sullivan, "A Closer Look at Education as Epideictic Rhetoric," 76–79.

16. Writing in the late 1950s, for example, scholars Chaim Perelman and Lucie Olbrechts-Tyteca observed that epideictic speeches were typically delivered by "those who, in a society, defend the traditional and accepted values, those which are the object of education, not the new and revolutionary values which stir up controversy and polemics." Chaim Perelman and Lucie Olbrechts-Tyteca, *The New Rhetoric: A Treatise on Argumentation*, trans. John Wilkinson and Purcell Weaver (Notre Dame, IN: University of Notre Dame Press, 1969), 51.

17. Cynthia Miecznikowski Sheard, "The Public Value of Epideictic Rhetoric," *College English* 58 (1996): 755–56.

18. From Frederick Douglass, "What to the Slave is the Fourth of July, July 5, 1982," in *American Rhetorical Discourse*, 343.

19. Jabari Asim, "Did Cosby Cross the Line," *Washington Post*, March 24, 2004, www.washingtonpost.com/wp-dyn/articles/A51273-2004May24.html (accessed April 6, 2012).

20. For Dyson's point-by-point rebuttal of Cosby's speech, see "Talking Points: Bill Cosby vs. Michael Eric Dyson," www.michaelericdyson.com/cosby/points.html (accessed April 6, 2012).

21. Bill Cosby, "Pound Cake Speech," *American Rhetoric*, http://www.americanrhetoric.com/speeches/billcosbypoundcakespeech.htm (accessed September 21, 2012). Also see "Cosby Stands His Ground," *CBS News*, February 11, 2009, www.cbsnews.com/stories/2004/07/02/national/main627156.shtml (accessed April 6, 2012).

22. See *Lou Gehrig: The Official Web Site*, www.lougehrig.com/about/speech.htm (accessed April 6, 2012).

23. Dwight D. Eisenhower, "Farewell Address," in *Great Speeches for Criticism and Analysis*, ed. Lloyd Rohler and Roger Cook (Greenwood, IN: Alistair Press, 1988), 316–19.

24. Reprinted by permission from Dalai Lama, "His Holiness the Dalai Lama's Nobel Prize Acceptance Speech, University Aula, Oslo, December 10, 1989." Copyright © 1989 by Dalailama.com.

25. Colin Powell, "Commencement Address," in *Great Speeches for Criticism and Analysis,* 343. Copyright © 1994 by Colin Powell.

26. Franklin D. Roosevelt, "Address at University of Virginia, June 10, 1940," *The American Presidency Project*, www.presidency.ucsb.edu/ws/index.php?pid=15965&st=&st1= (accessed April 9, 2012).

27. John F. Kennedy, "1963 Commencement," *American University*, www1.media.american.edu/speeches/Kennedy.htm (accessed April 9, 2012).

28. See Tatiana Morales, "A Tribute to 'Rebels': Warren Beatty and Elton John among Kennedy Center Honorees," *The Early Show*, December 6, 2004, www.cbsnews.com/stories/2004/12/06/earlyshow/main659314.shtml (accessed April 9, 2012).

29. Donald H. Rumsfeld, "Lucky Us: A Tribute to Milton Friedman," *National Review Online*, www.nationalreview.com/nrof_document/document073102.asp (accessed April 9, 2012).

30. Oprah Winfrey, "Eulogy for Rosa Parks," *American Rhetoric*, www.americanrhetoric.com/speeches/oprahwinfreyonrosaparks.htm (accessed April 9, 2012).

31. Lyndon Baines Johnson, "Let Us Continue," *American Rhetoric*, www.americanrhetoric.com/speeches/lbjletuscontinue.html (accessed April 9, 2012).

32. In a survey of rhetorical scholars to determine the top 100 speeches of the twentieth century, FDR's first inaugural and Kennedy's inaugural address were ranked third and second, respectively, behind another epideictic speech, Martin Luther King Jr.'s "I Have a Dream." Jefferson and Lincoln's inaugural addresses were not part of the ranking, of course, because they were not delivered in the twentieth century. But they are included in almost all anthologies of great American speeches. See Stephen E. Lucas and Martin J. Medhurst, ed., *Words of a Century: The Top 100 American Speeches, 1900–1999* (New York: Oxford University Press, 2008).

33. Thomas Jefferson, "First Inaugural Address (1801)," in *American Voices: Significant Speeches in American History, 1640–1945*, ed. James R. Andrews and David Zarefsky (New York: Longman, 1989), 115–16.

34. Franklin D. Roosevelt, "First Inaugural Address," in *American Rhetorical Discourse*, 749.

35. John F. Kennedy, "Inaugural Address," in *American Rhetorical Discourse*, 788–90.

36. Barbara Jordan, "Keynote Address," in *Great Speeches for Criticism and Analysis*, 53–55.

37. Lyman Beecher, "The Evils of Intemperance," in *American Rhetorical Discourse*, 278–85.

38. Ronald Reagan, "On the 40th Anniversary of D-Day," *The History Place*, www.historyplace.com/speeches/reagan-d-day.htm (accessed April 9, 2012).

39. Kennedy, "Inaugural Address," in *American Rhetorical Discourse*, 788.

40. Kennedy, "Inaugural Address," in *American Rhetorical Discourse*, 787, 789–90.

41. Barack Obama, "Inaugural Address," *The American Presidency Project*," www.presidency.ucsb.edu/ws/index.php?pid=44#axzz1s71PXwlI (accessed April 13, 2012).

CHAPTER 17

1. David A. Whetten and Kim Cameron, *Developing Management Skills*, 8th ed. (Englewood Cliffs, NJ: Prentice Hall, 2010), 390–450.

2. Simone Chambers, "Deliberative Democratic Theory," *Annual Review of Political Science* 6 (2003): 307–26.

3. Michael X. Delli Carpini, Fay Lomax Cook, and Lawrence R. Jacobs, "Public Deliberation, Discursive Participation, and Citizen Engagement: A Review of the Empirical Literature," *Annual Review of Political Science* 7 (2004): 315–44.

4. John Gastil, *By Popular Demand: Revitalizing Representative Democracy through Deliberative Elections* (Berkeley and Los Angeles: University of California Press, 2000).

5. Randy Y. Hirokawa and Kathryn M. Rost, "Effective Group Decision-Making in Organizations," *Management Communication Quarterly* 5 (1992): 267–88.

6. Carpini, Cook, and Jacobs, "Public Deliberation," 319.

7. Mark Button and Kevin Mattson, "Deliberative Democracy in Practice: Challenges and Prospects for Civic Deliberation," *Polity* 31 (1999): 612–13.

8. Daniel Yankelovich, *The Magic of Dialogue* (New York: Simon & Schuster, 1999).

9. Scott London, "Thinking Together: The Power of Deliberative Dialogue," http://media.wiley.com/assets/80/84/jrnls_ncr_jb_mccoy9102.pdf (accessed March 28, 2012). This essay was adapted from an essay by the same name, published in *Public Thought and Foreign Policy*, ed. Robert J. Kingston (Dayton, OH: Kettering Foundation, 2005).

10. Yankelovich, *The Magic of Dialogue*, 41–6.

11. Some scholars have argued that setting aside status differences is a naïve expectation. See Mary Tonn, "Taking Conversation, Dialogue, and Public Therapy," *Rhetoric and Public Affairs* 8 (2005): 405.

12. London, "Thinking Together."

13. Jack Gibb, "Defensive Communication," *Journal of Communication* 11 (1961): 141–8; Sharon Ellison, *Don't Be So Defensive* (Kansas City, KS: Andrews McMeel, 1998).

14. London, "Thinking Together"; Connie Gersick, "Time and Transition in Work Teams: Toward a New Model of Group Development," in *Small Group Communication: Theory and Practice*, 8th ed., ed. Randy Y. Hirokawa et al. (Los Angeles: Roxbury, 2003), 59–75. Gersick points to the transformative potential and power of "transitional moments" in determining successful or unsuccessful group outcomes.

15. London, "Thinking Together"; David M. Ryfe, "Narrative and Deliberation in Small Group Forums,"

Journal of Applied Communication Research 34 (2006): 72–93.

16. Both Gastil, *By Popular Demand*, and Carpini, Cook, and Jacobs, "Public Deliberation," do an excellent job of summarizing the arguments in favor of public deliberation.

17. See Gastil, *By Popular Demand*, 149–60.

18. Michael K. Briand, *Practical Politics: Five Principles for a Community That Works* (Urbana IL: University of Illinois Press, 1999); Michael Delli Carpini, "The Impact of the 'Money + Politics' Citizen Assemblies on Assembly Participants," report to the Pew Charitable Trusts, Philadelphia, Pennsylvania, 1997.

19. Robert Wuthnow, Sharing the Journey: America's New Quest for Community (New York: Free Press, 1994).

20. Mark Lindeman, "Opinion Quality and Policy Preferences in Deliberative Research," in *Research in Micropolitics: Political Decisionmaking, Deliberation, and Participation*, ed. Michael X. Delli Carpini, Leonie Huddy, and Robert Y. Shapiro (Greenwich, CT: JAI Press, 2002), 195–221.

21. Button and Mattson, "Deliberative Democracy in Practice," 609–37.

22. John Gastil, "The Effects of Deliberation on Political Beliefs and Conversation Behavior," paper, International Communication Association, San Francisco, California, 1999.

23. Ryfe, "Narrative and Deliberation in Small Group Forums," 72–93.

24. "What We Do" www.everyday-democracy.org//en/Page.WhatWeDo.aspx (accessed March 24, 2012).

25. Martha L. McCoy and Patrick L. Scully, "Deliberative Dialogue to Expand Civic Engagement: What Kind of Talk Does Democracy Need?" *National Civic Review* 91 (2002), www.ncl.org/publications/ncr/91-2/ncr91-2_article.pdf (accessed March 24, 2012); "The Basics of Dialogue to Change," www.everyday-democracy.org//en/Page.Organizing.aspx (accessed April 6, 2012).

26. Sheryl Gay Stolberg, "Obama's Interactive Town Hall Meeting," http://thecaucus.blogs.nytimes.com/2009/03/26/obamas-interactive-town-hall-meeting/ (accessed April 4, 2012).

27. Ian Urbina, "Beyond Beltway, Health Debate Turns Hostile," *New York Times*, August 8, 2009, sec. A, 1.

28. Urbina, "Beyond Beltway," 1.

29. Craig Schneider and Jeremy Redmon, "Anger at Congress Surfaces at Town Hall Meetings, *The Atlanta Journal-Constitution*, August 11, 2011, www.acj.com/news/anger-at-congress-surfaces-1099345.html (accessed March 30, 2012).

30. David Fahrenthold, "American Town Hall Meetings More Contentious than Ever, in Part by Design," *The Washington Post*, August 27, 2011, http://www.washingtonpost.com/politics/american-town-halls-more-contentious-than-ever-in-part-by-design/2011/08/25/gIQAhKWHjJ_story.html (accessed March 30, 2012).

31. James Fishkin, "Town Halls by Invitation," *New York Times*, August 16, 2009, Week in Review Section, 9.

32. Ibid.

33. See, for example, America Speaks: Engaging Citizens in Governance, http://americaspeaks.org/?gclid=CLS2oaTIoK8CFYZoKgodn2rFdQ (accessed April 1, 2010).

34. John Gastil, "Adult Civic Education through the National Issues Forums: Developing Democratic Habits and Dispositions through Public Deliberation," *Adult Education Quarterly* 54 (2004): 311; National Issues Forums, www.nifi.org (accessed March 27, 2012).

35. Keith Melville, Taylor Willingham, and John Dedrick, "National Issues Forums: A Network of Communities Promoting Deliberation," in *The Deliberative Democracy Handbook: Strategies for Effective Civic Engagement in the Twenty-First Century*, ed. John Gastil and Peter Levine (San Francisco, CA: Jossey-Bass, 2005), 35–58.

36. Gastil, *By Popular Demand*, 116–17.

37. National Issues Forums, "Issue Books," www.nifi.org/issue_books/index.aspx (accessed March 27, 2012).

38. Whetten and Cameron, *Developing Management Skills*, 390–450.

39. Joseph P. Folger, Marshall Scott Poole, and Randall K. Stutman, *Working through Conflict*, 3rd ed. (New York: Longman, 1997).

40. Several books have addressed the need for communities to handle conflicts constructively. See, as examples, Daniel Yankelovich, *Coming to Public Judgment: Making Democracy Work in a Complex World* (Syracuse, NY: Syracuse University Press, 1991); *Civic Index: Measuring Your Community's Civic Health* (Washington, DC: National Civic League, 2003); and Linda Ellinor and Glenna Gerard, *Dialogue: Rediscover the Transforming Power of Conversation* (New York: Wiley, 1998).

41. Robert R. Blake and Anne A. McCanse, *Leadership Dilemmas—Grid Solutions* (Houston, TX: Gulf, 1991).

42. Kenneth D. Benne and Paul Sheats, "Functional Roles of Group Members," *Journal of Social Issues* 4 (1948): 41–9.

43. Michael E. Mayer, "Behaviors Leading to More Effective Decisions in Small Groups Embedded in Organizations," *Communication Reports* 11 (1998): 123–32.

44. Solomon E. Asch, "Studies of Independence and Conformity: A Minority of One against a Unanimous

Majority," *Psychological Monographs* 70 (1956): No. 416.

45. George Cheney, "On the Various and Changing Meanings of Organizational Membership: A Field Study of Organizational Identification," *Communication Monographs* 50 (1983): 342–62.

46. Patricia Hayes Andrews, "Ego-Involvement, Self-Monitoring, and Conformity in Small Groups: A Communicative Analysis," *Central States Speech Journal* 36 (1985): 51–61.

47. For a more extended discussion of social pressure and conformity, see Patricia Hayes Andrews, "Group Conformity," in *Small Group Communication: Theory and Practice*, 7th ed., ed. Robert S. Cathcart, Larry. A. Samovar, and Linda D. Henman (Madison, WI: Brown & Benchmark, 1996), 225–35.

48. Carl L. Thameling and Patricia Hayes Andrews, "Majority Responses to Opinion Deviates: A Communicative Analysis," *Small Group Research* 23 (1992): 475–502.

49. Dennis S. Gouran and Patricia Hayes Andrews, "Determinants of Punitive Responses to Socially Proscribed Behavior: Seriousness, Attribution of Responsibility, and Status of Offender," *Small Group Behavior* 15 (1984): 524–44; Edwin P. Hollander, "Conformity, Status, and Idiosyncrasy Credit," *Psychological Review* 65 (1958): 117–27.

50. Phillip K. Tompkins, *Organizational Communication Imperatives: Lessons of the Space Program* (Los Angeles: Roxbury, 1993). Also see Dennis S. Gouran, Randy Y. Hirokawa, and Amy E. Martz, "A Critical Analysis of Factors Related to Decisional Processes Involved in the *Challenger* Disaster," *Central States Speech Journal* 37 (1986): 119–35.

51. See, for example, Andrews, "Group Conformity," 225–35; and Renee Meyers et al., "Majority-Minority Influence: Identifying Argumentative Patterns and Predicting Argument-Outcome Links," *Journal of Communication* 50 (2000): 3–30.

52. Irving Janis, *Groupthink*, 2nd ed. (Boston, MA: Houghton Mifflin, 1982), 3.

53. Senate Intelligence Committee Report on Pre-War Intelligence on Iraq, July 9, 2004, http://intelligence.senate.gov/080605/phase2a.pdf (accessed March 30, 2012).

54. Janis, *Groupthink*, 9.

55. Rebecca Cline, "Detecting Groupthink: Methods for Observing the Illusion of Unanimity," *Communication Quarterly* 38 (1990): 112–26.

56. Janis, *Groupthink*, 197–8.

57. John R. P. French and Bernard Raven, "The Social Bases of Power," in *Studies in Social Power*, ed. Dorwin Cartwright (Ann Arbor, MI: Institute for Social Research, 1959), 65–84.

58. Dennis S. Gouran and Randy Y. Hirokawa, "Counteractive Functions of Communication in Effective Group Decision-Making," in *Communication and Group Decision-Making*, ed. Randy Y. Hirokawa and Marshall Scott Poole (Beverly Hills, CA: Sage, 1986), 81–90.

59. Cline, "Detecting Groupthink," 120–6; and Irving Janis, "Vigilant Problem Solving," in Crucial Decisions: Leadership in Policymaking and Crisis Management, ed. Irving Janis (New York: Free Press, 1989), 89–117.

60. Hirokawa and Rost, "Effective Group Decision-Making in Organizations"; Randy Y. Hirokawa and Robert Pace, "A Descriptive Investigation of the Possible Communication-Based Reasons for Effective and Ineffective Group Decision Making," *Communication Monographs* 50 (1983): 363–79.

61. See, for example, Mark L. Knapp and Judith A. Hall, *Nonverbal Communication in Human Interaction* (Belmont, CA: Wadsworth, 2005).

62. William Gudykunst, *Cross-Cultural and Intercultural Communication* (Thousand Oaks, CA: Sage, 2003).

63. Randy Y. Hirokawa, Larry Erbert, and Anthony Hurst, "Communication and Group Decision-Making Effectiveness," in *Communication and Group Decision-Making*, ed. Randy Y. Hirokawa and Marshall Scott Poole (Beverly Hills, CA: Sage, 1986), 269–300.

INDEX

PHOTO CREDITS

TEXT CREDITS

Additional Materials by Mary E. Triece, University of Akron, School of Communication

Welcome to the University of Akron's
General Education Speech Course

Get ready for a rigorous and rewarding semester. The University of Akron's general education speech courses—Effective Oral Communication (EOC) and Introduction to Public Speaking (IPS)—introduce students to principles and theories of effective public speaking. The courses emphasize the importance of being a participant in the broader public sphere/community in which decision-making and problem solving, speech-making, debate, and critical listening shape and determine social welfare.

Undoubtedly, you will find your speech class to be one of the most important courses you experience while attending the University of Akron. The concepts and skills that you acquire will enable you to succeed in a wide variety of contexts, from the workplace to your community, even in other classes you take at UA.

Both EOC and IPS further advance the goals of the General Education Program, which include ensuring that students possess:

- the capacity for critical, independent thought
- a personal sense of values and a regard for the rights of others
- the ability to use language effectively as a medium of both thought and expression
- the analytical skills necessary to make sound qualitative and quantitative judgments

To ensure a successful semester, consider the following helpful tips:

TIP #1: Do all required readings on time. The chapters of this textbook contain the important information you need to help you research, organize, and deliver effective speeches.

TIP #2: Review your class syllabus regularly. Your syllabus contains important information regarding due dates for readings and assignments.

TIP #3: Attend class regularly. Your speech class has a mandatory attendance policy. (Review your syllabus for policy specifics). Excessive absences will have a negative impact on your final grade. Additionally, when you miss class, you miss important information concerning your assignments.

TIP # 4: In general, it's always a good idea to notify your instructor if you know ahead of time that you will have to miss class. Your instructor can then inform you of any readings, assignments, etc. you need to complete.

If you must miss class unexpectedly (e.g., your car breaks down), notify your teacher at your very earliest convenience. When you return to class, be sure to ask your instructor about assignments or handouts you might have missed on the day of your absence. Get class notes from a fellow student.

TIP #5: Visit your instructor in her/his office hours. Seeing your instructor outside of class provides a number of benefits. First, talking one-on-one with your instructor gives him/her a chance to get to know you better—your strengths, weaknesses, concerns, etc. Second, when you visit your instructor during office hours, you can obtain additional assistance on assignments. For instance, your instructor can provide additional help to deal with communication apprehension (see Chapter 3) and can give you that extra boost of confidence you may need to help you succeed with the assignment.

Useful Resources

Libraries	**Main Library**, **Bierce Library**, 330-972-7234, www.uakron.edu/libraries/ **Law Library**, School of Law, 330-972-7330, www.uakron.edulaw/library **Science and Technology Library**, ASEC 104, 330-972-7195 http://www3.uakron.edu/scilib/index.html **Wayne College Library**, Wayne College F-Wing, 330-684-8789, http://www.wayne.uakron.edu/library/
Computers	**Computer Based Assessment** (interactive computer programs and computer-based testing) Schrank Hall North 152, 330-972-6511, http://cbt.uakon.edu/labhours.htm **Computer Solutions** (sales, hardware, software, and computer accessories) Student Union Room 307, 330-972-5308, www.uakron.edu/its/hoss/compstore.index.php **Zip Support Center**—Walk-in Computer Support (Troubleshooting for login, e-mail, and basic computing problems) Bierce Library 52C; Exchange Residence Hall 146; Polsky 267, 330-972-6888, www.uakron.eduits/hoss/helpdesk/index.php **Laptop Checkout** (valid Zipcard and 2nd photo ID for verification required for checkout) Bierce Library 361; Exchange Residence Hall 146; Polsky 267; Student Union Information Center on 2nd floor

Student Computer Support Services-SCSS
(student/faculty/staff computer repair)
Lincoln Building 103, 330-972-7626
Atomic Learning Library From Zipline, log-on using
your UANet ID and password. Click on the student tab
at the top of the screen and under "Computer Software
Help!" you will see Atomic Learning. Click on Atomic
Learning and explore more than 100 software learning
tutorials available at your fingertips.

Student Services

The Office of Multicultural Development,
Simmons Hall 124, 330-972-6769,
http://www.uakron.edu/omd/
UA Adult Focus, Schrank Hall North 260,
330-972-5793, http://www.uakron.edu/uaaf

Disability Services

Office of Accessibility, Simmons Hall 105,
330-972-7928, TTY/TDD: 330-972-5764,
www.uakron.edu/access

Financial

Office of Student Financial Aid (grants, loans,
scholarships, and work-study), Simmons Hall 202,
330-972-7032, www.uakron.edu/finaid
Office of Student Accounts (accounts receivable,
cashier's office, and collections), Simmons Hall 106,
330-972-5100,
www.uakron.edu/busfin/studentfin/index.php
Installment Payment Plan (allows fees to be paid
on payment basis), Simmons Hall 110, 330-972-5100
www.uakron.edu/busfin/studentfin/paymentoptions.php

**Financial Aid,
Registration, and
Cashier's Services**

Student Services Center (In-person assistance
with financial aid, registration, and cashiers),
Simmons Hall Lobby, 330-972-7272 (information desk)

Health & Wellness

Counseling Center (personal and confidential
counseling and support services conducted by licensed
professionals) Simmons Hall 306, 330-972-7082.
http://www3.uakron.edu/counseling/counsel.htm
Department of Psychology Counseling Clinic
(personal and career counseling conducted by
Graduate students) College of Arts & Sciences Building
342, http://www3.uakron.edu/psychology/clinic.html

Health Services (medical care for uncomplicated illnesses and injuries provided by registered nurses, nurse practitioners, and doctors; wellness programming) Student Recreation and Wellness Center 260, 330-972-7808, www.uakron.edu/studentaff/health

Reading and Study Skills

College Reading and Study Skills (course: practice in reading comprehension skills and study techniques) Course #2010:062
Study Skills Center (professional diagnosis and assistance) Polsky 332, 330-972-6551, www.uakron.edu/colleges/univcoll/studyskills.php
College Survival Kit (academic performance workshops presented by Counseling and Testing Center) Simmons Hall 306, 330-972-7082
http://www.uakron.edu/counseling

Testing Services

Counseling Center, Testing services include ADHD and learning disorder assessments and many national exams such as CLEP, PRAXIS, and ACT. Simmons Hall 304, 330-972-7084.

Tutorial Services

Academic support and peer tutoring for math and writing courses, Bierce Library and Polsky Building, http://www.uakron.edu/tutoring

Writing Skills

Basic Writing (course: Intensive practice in basic composition skills) Course #2010:042

Learning Studio

To videotape and watch yourself speaking. Bierce Library 274, 330-972-7234

Accessing the Information Literacy Tutorial on Springboard

THE INFORMATION LITERACY TUTORIAL IS ONLY ACCESSIBLE VIA SPRINGBOARD AT THE FOLLOWING LOG-IN SCREEN: HTTPS://SPRINGBOARD.UAKRON.EDU/

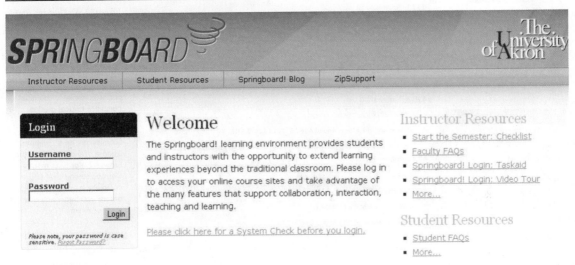

SIMPLY TYPE YOUR UANETID AND PASSWORD IN THE APPROPRIATE BOXES. THEN YOU WILL SEE YOUR PERSONAL SPRINGBOARD HOMEPAGE:

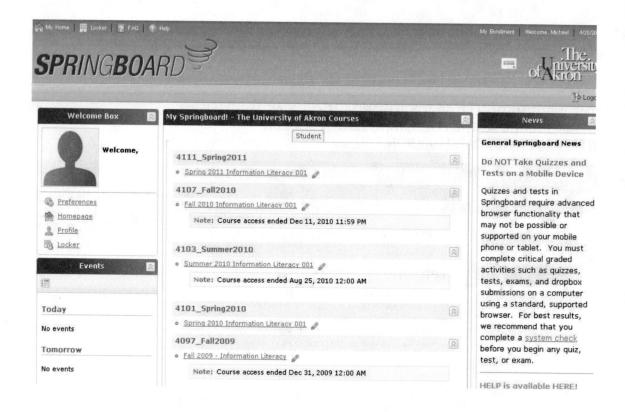

THE INFORMATION LITERACY TUTORIAL WILL BE LABELED AS "INFORMATION LITERACY" PRECEDED BY THE SEMESTER.

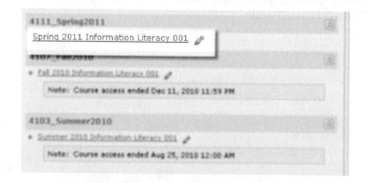

NOTE THAT THE TUTORIAL IS LISTED AS A COMPLETELY SEPARATE, STAND-ALONE COURSE. IT IS NOT A PART OF A COMMUNICATION COURSEPAGE OR STUDENT SUCCESS SEMINAR COURSEPAGE.

TO BEGIN THE TUTORIAL, CLICK ON ITS LINK, AND ON THE SUBSEQUENT WELCOME SCREEN, CLICK ON THE CONTENT LINK IN THE MENU BAR ALONG THE TOP OF THE SCREEN:

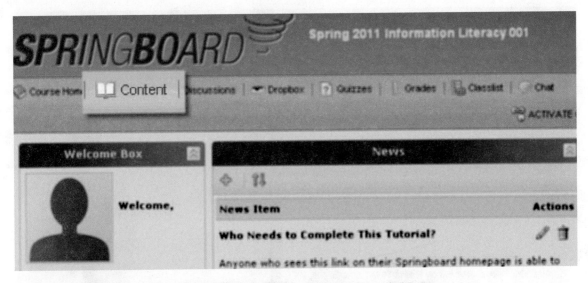

THE CONTENT LINK WILL SHOW THE SCREENS YOU WILL NEED TO READ THROUGH IN ORDER TO COMPLETE LESSON 1 OF THE TUTORIAL.

Content Items

Spring 2011 Information Literacy 001

⊟ ☐ ⚬ Module 1 - Recognizing the Information Need

    ☐ 📄 1.01. What is research?

    ☐ 📄 1.02. Why do I need research skills?

    ☐ 📄 1.03. Assessing, observing, and reading

    ☐ 📄 1.04. How do I define and focus my information need?

    ☐ 📄 1.05. Step 1: Form a question based on your information need

    ☐ 📄 1.06. Knowledge check #1

    ☐ 📄 1.07. Knowledge check #2

    ☐ 📄 1.08. Step 2: Identify key concepts and terms that describe the information need

    ☐ 📄 1.09. Step 3: Eliminate the overly general or non-specific terms from your question

    ☐ 📄 1.10. Step 4: Determine what kind of information you need

    ☐ 📄 1.11. Step 5: Determine how much information you need

    ☐ 📄 1.12. Step 6: Determine if you need popular or scholarly sources

    ☐ 📄 1.13. Module Summary

AFTER YOU HAVE READ THROUGH ALL OF THE SCREENS FOR THAT LESSON, YOU CAN THEN CLICK ON THE QUIZZES LINK IN THE MENU AT THE TOP OF THE SCREEN:

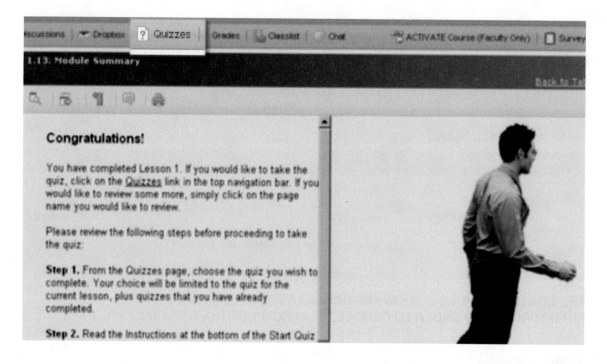

YOU SHOULD THEN SEE A LINK TO THE QUIZ FOR LESSON 1:

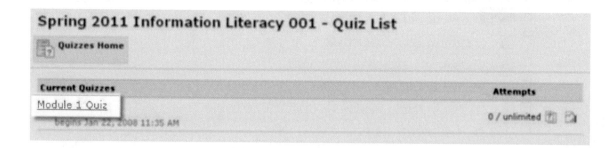

ON THE NEXT SCREEN, CLICK ON THE "START QUIZ!" LINK:

THE ACTUAL QUIZ QUESTIONS WILL APPEAR NEXT:

Please Note: It is recommended that you save your response as you complete each question.

Question 1 (1 point)

For an art history assignment, you must find three scholarly articles on your topic. Which of the following articles meets this requirement?

○ Madoff, Steven Henry. "Publicist, Prankster, Parvenu: Andy Warhol Was the Pan of Modern Art." Time 151, no. 22 (1998): 77.

○ Smith, Charles Saumarez. "I Try to Make Everybody Look Great: Andy Warhol and the Idea of the Twentieth-Century Portrait." Modern Painters 14, no. 2 (2001): 54-7.

○ O'Sullivan, Michael. "Warhol: Another 15 Minutes." New York Times, 8 December 2000.

Save

Question 2 (1 point)

For an effective oral communication class, your assignment is to report on a significant aspect of another culture. Which set of terms below represents the key concepts in the following research question?

"How does the religion of the Amish help them to maintain a distinct culture within modern American society?"

○ culture / Amish / maintain

○ religion / Amish / culture

○ religion / Amish / distinct

○ religion / help / Amish

IMPORTANT: YOU MUST GET AT LEAST 4 OF THE 5 MULTIPLE CHOICE QUESTIONS HERE CORRECT IN ORDER TO MOVE ON AND SEE THE CONTENT FOR THE NEXT LESSON, AND SO ON TO THE END OF THE TUTORIAL. ALSO, QUIZZES CAN BE RE-TAKEN! IF YOU DO NOT GET A 4 OR 5 AT FIRST, TRY AGAIN.

WHEN YOU PASS QUIZ 6, THE LAST ONE OF THE TUTORIAL, YOU WILL SEE A LINK TO A CERTIFICATE WHICH YOU CAN PRINT OUT TO PROVE YOUR COMPLETION. THE CERTIFICATE IS LOCATED UNDER THE CONTENT MENU:

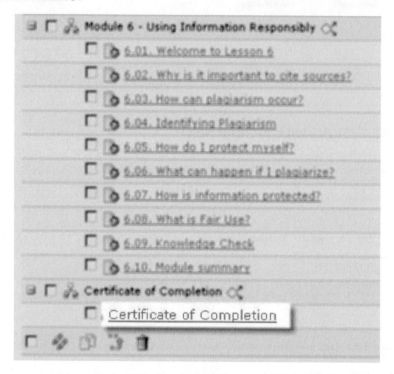

FINAL NOTES: IF YOU DO NOT FINISH THE ENTIRE TUTORIAL ALL AT ONCE, YOU DO NOT NEED TO DO ANYTHING TO SAVE YOUR WORK UP TO THE POINT THAT YOU STOP. THE TUTORIAL WILL AUTOMATICALLY SAVE ANY QUIZZES YOU HAVE COMPLETED. FOR EXAMPLE, IF YOU STOP AND LOG OUT AFTER COMPLETING QUIZ 3 AND DO NOT LOG INTO THE TUTORIAL AGAIN UNTIL THE NEXT DAY, YOU CAN JUMP RIGHT INTO LESSON 4 AND PROCEED FROM THERE. ALSO, ONCE YOU'VE COMPLETED THE TUTORIAL, YOU CAN LOG IN ANY TIME TO ACCESS AND PRINT A COPY OF YOUR CERTIFICATE OF COMPLETION.

***IF YOU DO NOT SEE THE LINK TO THE TUTORIAL ONCE YOU ARE LOGGED INTO SPRINGBOARD, PLEASE CONTACT MIKE TOSKO AT 330-972-2648 OR TOSKO@UAKRON.EDU

The Importance of Practicing Your Speech

Perhaps the number one way that speakers improve their speaking skills is by practicing. The importance of practice cannot be overstated. By going over your speech numerous times BEFORE the day you perform it, you 1.) familiarize yourself with the material; 2.) improve your delivery skills, i.e., eye contact improves, enthusiasm is cultivated; 3.) increase your confidence.

One week prior to your assigned speaking date: Practice your speech from your formal outline. Keep practicing until you become familiar with the main ideas and supporting materials. When you feel comfortable with the material, transfer key words and phrases from your formal outline to index cards to make a keyword outline (Chapter 9).

Then begin practicing the speech from the keyword outline on your index cards. Be willing to tweak and/or redo your keyword outline if you find that the material on your index cards is not clearly written or useful in enabling you to deliver your speech extemporaneously.

Practice from your keyword outline numerous times. As you practice from your keyword outline, your delivery will improve and you will become more confident.

You will also need to time yourself as you practice to ensure the speech falls within the required time limit. (Ask your instructor what the time limit is for each assignment). If the speech falls short of the time limit, you will need to further develop your main ideas. If the speech goes over the time limit, you will need to edit out material.

Deliver your speech in front of friends or family. This will give you an opportunity to practice making direct eye contact.

On the day of your speech: Go over in your mind what you want to say and how you want to sound. **Visualize** yourself giving a successful speech with a dynamic delivery. Practice **cognitive restructuring**, replace negative thoughts ("I'm going to sound stupid") with positive ones ("I have an important message to share"). **Breath deeply. Enjoy sharing the fruits of your labor!**

Citing Sources

Why do I need to cite sources?

For each speech assignment, you are required to do library research. Refer to Chapter 6, pages 142–145, Where To Start Your Research, for information on how to conduct library research.

From the sources you gather, you will find the evidence (Chapter 7) you need to develop your main points. Any time you provide your audience/reader information from an outside source, e.g., a book, web site, news article, etc, you must cite the source from which it came. Giving credit to the source through a citation is important for at least two reasons: 1). Citing your sources ensures that you do not plagiarize; 2). Citing your sources bolsters your own credibility by demonstrating that you have done library research.

Where do I cite sources?

There are two places that you must cite your sources. You will explicitly cite sources throughout the delivery of your speech. You will also cite your sources in full bibliographic format in a Works Cited or References page that you will turn in to your instructor with your formal outline.

How do I cite sources?

1. During the speech: As you deliver your speech, you will be sharing with your audience facts, statistics, examples, definitions, etc. about your chosen topic. These pieces of evidence (Chapter 7) come from your library resources. Any time you provide information from an outside source, *you must cite the source from which it came,* at that place in the speech where you give the information. You will cite the source both when you paraphrase the information and when you quote directly.

    a. paraphrasing: "Paraphrasing refers to putting the ideas or insights of others into your own words" (Chapter 1, p. 12). Most of your presentation will consist of information that you have phraprased from your outside sources.

    The citation should include:
- author(s) name
- author(s) credentials, if available
- title of book or periodical
- date
- if a web site, do not give the URL. Provide the name of the organization/group/person sponsoring the site.

Work the citation smoothly into the presentation. This will require practice on your part. Consider the following suggestions:

> According to the 2010 book, *Obama's Race*, by Tesler and Sears, Barack Obama provided the American public with messages of racial unity and hope.

> In the 2010 book, *Obama's Race*, Tesler and Sears note that Barack Obama provided the American public with messages of racial unity and hope.

Note how the citation information is given *before* providing information from the source. Also note that page numbers and volume numbers are not provided in these citations.

b. quoting directly: You may also decide to provide direct quotes from your sources. When you quote, you are using the exact wording provided in the source. Use direct quotes sparingly, only when the source says something better than you could have said it in your own words. When quoting directly, the citation should include the components mentioned above for paraphrasing.

As with paraphrasing, work the citation smoothly into the presentation. This will require practice on your part. Say "quote" at the beginning and "unquote" at the end of the passage to indicate to your audience where you are taking exact words from the source. Consider the following suggestions:

> According to the 2010 book, *Obama's Race*, by Tesler and Sears, Barack Obama's *quote* self-imposed role as a racial bridge builder was clearly on display in the racially charged aftermath of Hurricane Katrina *unquote*.

> In the 2010 book, *Obama's Race*, Tesler and Sears note that Barack Obama's *quote* self-imposed role as a racial bridge builder was clearly on display in the racially charged aftermath of Hurricane Katrina *unquote*.

2. Works Cited or References page: You will also provide complete bibliographic information in a Works Cited or References page. The bibliography must follow an accepted format, either MLA or APA. Be sure to keep track of the bibliographic information of your sources as you do

504

your research so that you can put together a complete References/Works Cited page. Remember:

- include only those sources used in giving the speech
- list the sources in alphabetical order
- do not number the sources
- according to APA, personal communication (e.g., interviews, emails) are not included in the References. That information is included in parentheses in text. E.g., (J. Smith, personal communication, March 20, 2012).
- according to the MLA, personal interviews are included in the Works Cited. E.g., Smith, J. Personal interview. 20 March, 2012.
- follow the specified format (MLA or APA) *precisely*

Works Cited (MLA format)

Campbell, Karlyn Kohrs and Kathleen Hall Jamieson. *Presidents Creating the Presidency: Deeds Done in Words*. Chicago: The University of Chicago Press, 2008.

Cheney, Michael and Crystal Olsen. "Media Politics 2.0: An Obama Effect." *The Obama Effect: Multidisciplinary Renderings of the 2008 Campaign*. Eds. Heather E. Harris, Kimberly R. Moffitt, and Catherine R. Squires. Albany: State University of New York Press, 2010. 49-64.

Joseph, Peniel E. *Dark Days, Bright Nights: From Black Power to Barack Obama*. New York: Basic Books, 2010.

Terrill, Robert E. "Unity and Duality in Barack Obama's 'A More Perfect Union.'" *Quarterly Journal of Speech* 95 (2009): 363-386.

References (APA format)

Campbell, K. K., Jamieson, K. H. (2008). *Presidents creating the presidency: Deeds done in words*. Chicago: The University of Chicago Press.

Cheney, M. and Olsen, C. (2010). Media politics 2.0: An Obama effect. In H. E. Harris, K. R. Moffitt, and C. R. Squires (Eds.), *The Obama effect: Multidisciplinary renderings of the 2008 campaign*, pp. 49-64. Albany: State University of New York Press.

Joseph, P. E. (2010). *Dark days, bright nights: From Black Power to Barack Obama*. New York: Basic Books.

Terrill, R. E. (2009). Unity and duality in Barack Obama's "A More Perfect Union." *Quarterly Journal of Speech, 95*, 363-386.

The University of Akron University Libraries

Where to Start Your Research

The best place to start your research is the University of Akron Library's Web Site: http://www.uakron.edu/libraries

The Web Site gives you access to three essential research tools:

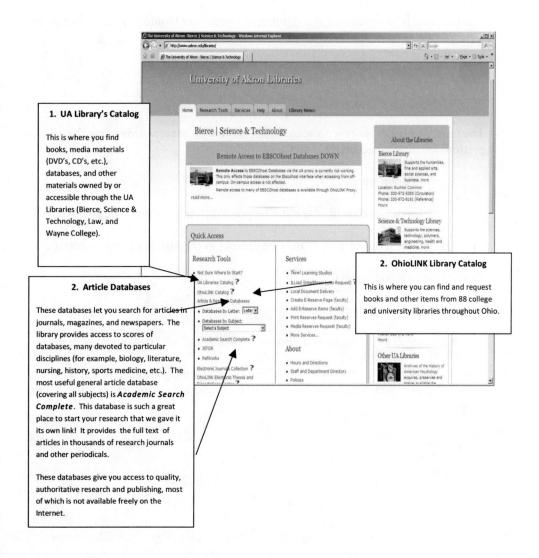

1. UA Library's Catalog

This is where you find books, media materials (DVD's, CD's, etc.), databases, and other materials owned by or accessible through the UA Libraries (Bierce, Science & Technology, Law, and Wayne College).

2. Article Databases

These databases let you search for articles in journals, magazines, and newspapers. The library provides access to scores of databases, many devoted to particular disciplines (for example, biology, literature, nursing, history, sports medicine, etc.). The most useful general article database (covering all subjects) is *Academic Search Complete*. This database is such a great place to start your research that we gave it its own link! It provides the full text of articles in thousands of research journals and other periodicals.

These databases give you access to quality, authoritative research and publishing, most of which is not available freely on the Internet.

2. OhioLINK Library Catalog

This is where you can find and request books and other items from 88 college and university libraries throughout Ohio.

How to Do A Boolean Search

Boolean searching, named after 19ᵗʰ century mathematician George Boole, is the most effective way to search an article database like **Academic Search Complete**.

Let's say this is your topic for research:

The dangers of texting while driving.

The first step is to determine the significant words you would expect to find in an article's title or abstract (summary):

Texting

Driving

The next step is to construct a search statement with these words using the appropriate Boolean connectors:

Boolean connectors:

AND (each word or phrase must be present in the article's title or abstract)

OR (either word or phrase may be present in the article's title or abstract)

Example search statements:

Example 1: Texting and driving

Example 2: (Texting or cell phones or distracted) and driving

—note the use of parentheses to "nest" one search within another in Example 2. Example 2 may retrieve more articles than Example 1, because it is not limited to texting.

Here is one way to enter your search in Academic Search Complete. Notice that this search brought up 159 results (journal articles).

Here is another way to enter the same search, by using two search boxes and the "AND" Boolean connector supplied by the database. The same 159 results were retrieved.

Here is how to enter our example search #2. Notice that far more results were retrieved (820), because we have expanded the search to include any article descriptions that mention the words "cell phones" or "distracted" as well as "texting."

Searching the UA Library's Catalog

This is the main search screen for the UA Library's Catalog.

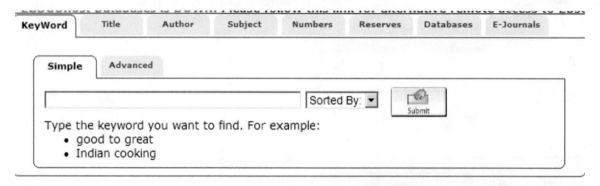

The tabs at the top let you search in various ways. The most common types of searches are:

KeyWord – Here you can search for words appearing book titles, subject headings, and chapter titles. The Boolean search techniques described earlier work here in a KeyWord search.

Title – Type in the title, or the first few words of the title, for a book or other item.

Author – Type in an author's last name, followed by first name.

Subject – Type in a subject category.

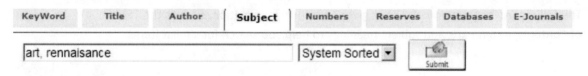

Information about Books and Other Items in the Catalog

Here is the **brief screen** for an item in the Catalog:

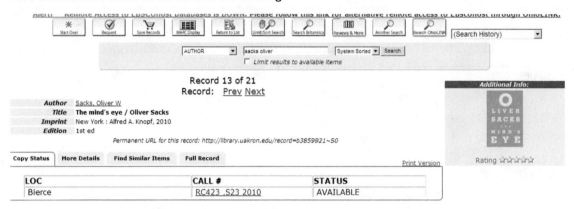

The information given in the sections labeled *Author, Title, Imprint, Edition,* is the bibliographic information about this particular item. This is the information you would use to cite this book in the bibliography.

Other information is given about this particular copy:

LOC – this is the location of the book, in this case Bierce Library. Other locations are Science (for the Science & Technology Library), Law (the Law School Library), and Wayne (Wayne College Library).

CALL # - the book's call number. This is the location of the book in the stacks.

STATUS – this tells us that this particular book is available to be checked out.

The **full record** for this particular book gives additional information, such as the Table of Contents, a summary, and subject headings to help you search for similar items.

Author	Sacks, Oliver W
Title	**The mind's eye / Oliver Sacks**
Imprint	New York : Alfred A. Knopf, 2010
Edition	1st ed

Permanent URL for this record: http://library.uakron.edu/record=b3859921~S0

Copy Status	More Details	Find Similar Items	**Full Record**		Print Versio

Call #	RC423 .S23 2010
Phys Descr	xii, 263 p. : ill. ; 22 cm
Edition	1st ed
Note	"A Borzoi book" -- T.p. verso
Bibliog	Includes bibliographical references (p. [241]-252) and index
Contents	Sight reading -- Recalled to life -- A man of letters -- Face-blind -- Stereo Sue -- Persistence of vision: a journal -- The mind's eye
Summary	Includes stories of people who are able to navigate the world and communicate with others despite losing what many of us consider indispensable senses and faculties: the power of speech, the capacity to recognize faces, the sense of three-dimensional space, the ability to read, and the sense of sight. This book is a testament to the complexity of vision and the brain and to the power of creativity and adaptation, and it provides a whole new perspective on the power of language and communication, as we try to imagine what it is to perceive through another person's eyes, or another person's mind
ISBN	9780307272089
	0307272087
Author	Sacks, Oliver W
Subject	Communicative disorders -- Popular works
	Cognition disorders -- Popular works
	Face perception -- Popular works
	Perception -- Popular works
	Neurology -- Anecdotes
	Show similar items
OCLC #	505417145

LOC	CALL #	STATUS
Bierce	RC423 .S23 2010	AVAILABLE

Requesting a Book Through OhioLINK

If a book is checked out of or not owned by the UA Libraries, you can often request it
through OhioLINK, the combined catalog of 88 college and university libraries
throughout Ohio.

Here is a book that is checked out of UA Libraries:

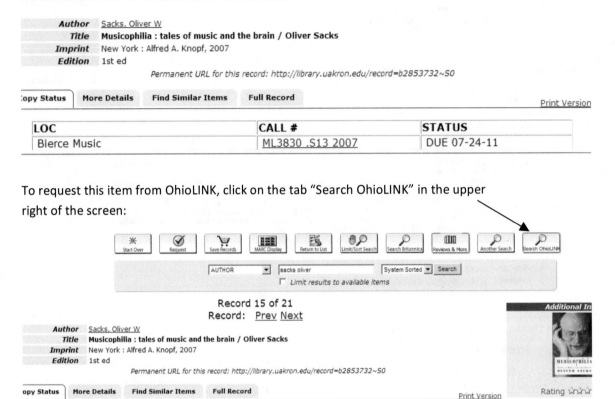

Author	Sacks, Oliver W
Title	Musicophilia : tales of music and the brain / Oliver Sacks
Imprint	New York : Alfred A. Knopf, 2007
Edition	1st ed

Permanent URL for this record: http://library.uakron.edu/record=b2853732~S0

Copy Status | More Details | Find Similar Items | Full Record   Print Version

LOC	CALL #	STATUS
Bierce Music	ML3830 .S13 2007	DUE 07-24-11

To request this item from OhioLINK, click on the tab "Search OhioLINK" in the upper right of the screen:

Start Over | Request | Save Records | MARC Display | Return to List | Limit/Sort Search | Search Britannica | Reviews & More | Another Search | Search OhioLINK

AUTHOR ▾ sacks oliver   System Sorted ▾ Search
☐ Limit results to available items

Record 15 of 21
Record: Prev Next

Author	Sacks, Oliver W
Title	Musicophilia : tales of music and the brain / Oliver Sacks
Imprint	New York : Alfred A. Knopf, 2007
Edition	1st ed

Permanent URL for this record: http://library.uakron.edu/record=b2853732~S0

Additional In

MUSICOPHILIA
OLIVER SACKS

Rating ☆☆☆

Copy Status | More Details | Find Similar Items | Full Record   Print Version

LOC	CALL #	STATUS
Bierce Music	ML3830 .S13 2007	DUE 07-24-11

The same book will be displayed in the OhioLINK Central Catalog. Click on the request tab and follow directions to request this book. You will be asked for your institutional affiliation (University of Akron) as well as your UA ID and password.

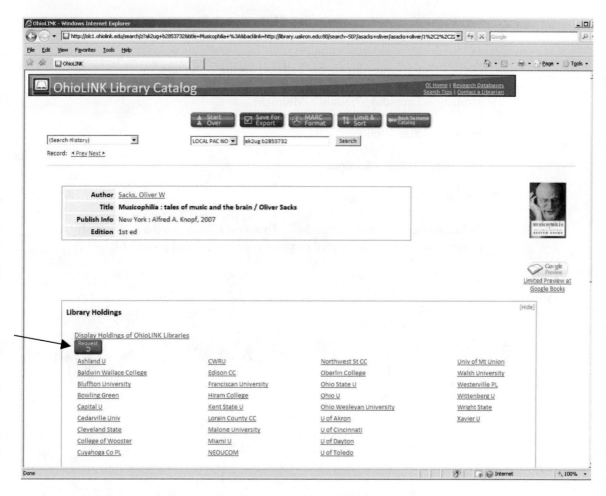

OhioLINK books can be checked out for an initial period of 3 weeks, with 3 renewals.

Library Hours and Access

Bierce Library hours during the Fall and Spring Semesters:

Monday – Thursday: 7:30am – Midnight

Friday: 7:30am – 9:00pm

Saturday: 9:00am – 8:00pm

Sunday: Noon - Midnight

Online resources are available 24/7. To access library databases from off campus, you will be prompted to enter your UA ID and password.

Name:

Audience Analysis
Exercise by Bonnie Keiper

Read Chapter 4, Diverse Audiences in a Democratic Society, before completing this exercise.

Part 1, Questionnaire

Assignment: Create a questionnaire to distribute to your audience so you can understand the following: audience knowledge level, audience psychographic information, and how best to proceed with your persuasive speech.

Demographic (age, race, gender, income, etc.)
-generally not necessary for an audience analysis

Psychographic (attitude, belief, behavior)
-very necessary for an audience analysis

Question Categories:
-Attitude (positive or negative feeling)
-Belief (conviction that something is true or real)
-Behavior (overt action)

Write two questions from each category.

Part 2, Audience Analysis Report

Include your name and your working thesis at the top of the page.

1. What is the audience's attitude about your topic?
2. What is the audience's belief about your topic?
3. What is the audience's behavior in relation to your topic?
4. What forms of reasoning will best work to persuade your audience? Explain why. (inductive, deductive, causal, analogical)
5. What emotion will you elicit from your audience? How will you do this?

Please do not summarize the information from the questionnaire. Draw conclusions. Answers should be about two sentences each.

Please type this report. Please proof read.

Obtaining Evidence From Your Sources

Read Chapter 7, Supporting Ideas, before you complete this exercise.

In an earlier exercise, you located books, articles, and web sites relevant to your informative topic.

1. Locate testimony (expert or lay) in one of your sources. Paraphrase the testimony and write it here. Write the name of the source.

2. Locate another testimony (expert or lay) in one of your sources. Write the direct quote here. Be sure to put quotation marks around the direct quote. Write the name of the source.

3. Locate a statistic in one of your sources. Paraphrase the information and write it here. Write the name of the source.

4. Locate an example (actual or hypothetical) in one of your sources. Paraphrase the information and write it here. Write the name of the source.

Name:

Identifying Main Ideas and Supporting Materials

Read Chapter 8, Organizing Your Speech, before completing this assignment.

Below you will find a list of statements for a speech on how to mat and frame a picture. Identify which statements are main points and write them into the outline format in the appropriate place. Then identify which statements constitute supporting materials and write them into the outline format under the corresponding main points.

* You must have drawing equipment.
* Begin by drawing the lines for cutting.
* Before you buy or do anything you should plan your project.
* Make the actual cut.
* The final step in the process is actually matting and framing the picture.
* Determine the size of the mat.
* You will need cutting equipment.
* Place the matted picture in the frame and anchor it by pushing down the staples.
* Your second step will be to obtain the equipment you will need.
* Attach the picture to the mat so that it is properly centered.
* The third step is actually cutting the mat.
* Decide what color you want the mat to be.
* Prepare the frame by cleaning the glass with alcohol and water.

I.

      A.

      B.

II.

    A.

    B.

III.

    A.

    B.

IV.

    A.

    B.

    C.

Name:

Abolitionist Frederick Douglass and the Power of Language

Read Chapter 10, Using Language Effectively, and read the speech, "The Hypocrisy of American Slavery," on the following pages. Answer the following questions.

1. Identify two places where Douglass employed vivid language. In what ways did his vivid language appeal to your emotions or senses?

2. Identify at least 2 figures of speech used by Douglass. Write the sentence(s) from the speech and the figure of speech it illustrates.

3. What impact might this speech have had on Douglass's listeners who were gathered to celebrate the Fourth of July in 1852?

Frederick Douglass, "The Hypocrisy of American Slavery"

Delivered July 4, 1852

Fellow citizens, pardon me, and allow me to ask, why am I called upon to speak here today? What have I or those I represent to do with your national independence? Are the great principles of political freedom and of natural justice, embodied in that Declaration of Independence, extended to us? And am I, therefore, called upon to bring our humble offering to the national altar, and to confess the benefits, and express devout gratitude for the blessings resulting from your independence to us?

Would to God, both for your sakes and ours, that an affirmative answer could be truthfully returned to these questions. Then would my task be light, and my burden easy and delightful. For who is there so cold that a nation's sympathy could not warm him? Who so obdurate and dead to the claims of gratitude, that would not thankfully acknowledge such priceless benefits? Who so stolid and selfish that would not give his voice to swell the hallelujahs of a nation's jubilee, when the chains of servitude had been torn from his limbs? I am not that man. In a case like that, the dumb might eloquently speak, and the "lame man leap as an hart."

But such is not the state of the case. I say it with a sad sense of disparity between us. I am not included within the pale of this glorious anniversary! Your high independence only reveals the immeasurable distance between us. The blessings in which you this day rejoice are not enjoyed in common. The rich inheritance of justice, liberty, prosperity, and independence bequeathed by your fathers is shared by you, not by me. The sunlight that brought life and healing to you has brought stripes and death to me. This Fourth of July is yours, not mine. You may rejoice, I must mourn. To drag a man in fetters into the grand illuminated temple of liberty, and call upon him to join you in joyous anthems, were inhuman mockery and sacrilegious irony. Do you mean, citizens, to mock me, by asking me to speak today? If so, there is a parallel to your conduct. And let me warn you, that it is dangerous to copy the example of a nation (Babylon) whose crimes, towering up to heaven, were thrown down by the breath of the Almighty, burying that nation in irrecoverable ruin.

Fellow citizens, above your national, tumultuous joy, I hear the mournful wail of millions, whose chains, heavy and grievous yesterday, are today rendered more intolerable by the jubilant shouts that reach them. If I do forget, if I do not remember those bleeding children of sorrow this day, "may my right hand forget her cunning, and may my tongue cleave to the roof of my mouth!"

To forget them, to pass lightly over their wrongs and to chime in with the popular theme would be treason most scandalous and shocking, and would make me a reproach before God and the world.

My subject, then, fellow citizens, is "American Slavery." I shall see this day and its popular characteristics from the slave's point of view. Standing here, identified with the American bondman, making his wrongs mine, I do not hesitate to declare, with all my soul, that the character and conduct of this nation never looked blacker to me than on this Fourth of July.

Whether we turn to the declarations of the past, or to the professions of the present, the conduct of the nation seems equally hideous and revolting. America is false to the past, false to the present, and solemnly binds herself to be false to the future. Standing with God and the crushed and bleeding slave on this occasion, I will, in the name of humanity, which is outraged, in the name of liberty, which is fettered, in the name of the Constitution and the Bible, which are disregarded and trampled upon, dare to call in question and to denounce, with all the emphasis I can command, everything that serves to perpetuate slavery—the great sin and shame of America! "I will not equivocate - I will not excuse." I will use the severest language I can command, and yet not one word shall escape me that any man, whose judgment is not blinded by prejudice, or who is not at heart a slave-holder, shall not confess to be right and just.

But I fancy I hear some of my audience say it is just in this circumstance that you and your brother Abolitionists fail to make a favorable impression on the public mind. Would you argue more and denounce less, would you persuade more and rebuke less, your cause would be much more likely to succeed. But, I submit, where all is plain there is nothing to be argued. What point in the anti-slavery creed would you have me argue? On what branch of the subject do the people of this country need light? Must I undertake to prove that the slave is a man? That point is conceded already. Nobody doubts it. The slave-holders themselves acknowledge it in the enactment of laws for their government. They acknowledge it when they punish disobedience on the part of the slave. There are seventy-two crimes in the State of Virginia, which, if committed by a black man (no matter how ignorant he be), subject him to the punishment of death; while only two of these same crimes will subject a white man to like punishment.

What is this but the acknowledgment that the slave is a moral, intellectual, and responsible being? The manhood of the slave is conceded. It is admitted in the fact that Southern statute books are covered with enactments, forbidding, under severe fines and penalties, the teaching of the slave to read and write. When you can point to any such laws in reference to the beasts of the field, then I may consent to argue the manhood of the slave. When the dogs in your streets, when the fowls of the air, when the cattle on your hills, when the fish of the sea, and the reptiles that crawl, shall be unable to distinguish the slave from a brute, then I will argue with you that the slave is a man!

For the present it is enough to affirm the equal manhood of the Negro race. Is it not astonishing that, while we are plowing, planting, and reaping, using all kinds of mechanical tools, erecting houses, constructing bridges, building ships, working in metals of brass, iron, copper, silver, and gold; that while we are reading, writing, and ciphering, acting as clerks, merchants, and secretaries, having among us lawyers, doctors, ministers, poets, authors, editors, orators, and teachers; that we are engaged in all the enterprises common to other men—digging gold in California, capturing the whale in the Pacific, feeding sheep and cattle on the hillside, living, moving, acting, thinking, planning, living in families as husbands, wives, and children, and above all, confessing and worshipping the Christian God, and looking hopefully for life and immortality beyond the grave— we are called upon to prove that we are men?

Would you have me argue that man is entitled to liberty? That he is the rightful owner of his own body? You have already declared it. Must I argue the wrongfulness of slavery? Is that a question for republicans? Is it to be settled by the rules of logic and argumentation, as a matter beset with great difficulty, involving a doubtful application of the principle of justice, hard to understand? How should I look today in the presence of Americans, dividing and subdividing a discourse, to show that men have a natural right to freedom, speaking of it relatively and positively, negatively and affirmatively? To do so would be to make myself ridiculous, and to offer an insult to your understanding. There is not a man beneath the canopy of heaven who does not know that slavery is wrong for him.

What! Am I to argue that it is wrong to make men brutes, to rob them of their liberty, to work them without wages, to keep them ignorant of their relations to their fellow men, to beat them with sticks, to flay their flesh with the lash, to load their limbs with irons, to hunt them with dogs, to sell them at auction, to sunder their families, to knock out their teeth, to burn their flesh, to starve them into obedience and submission to their masters? Must I argue that a system thus marked with blood and stained with pollution is wrong? No - I will not. I have better employment for my time and strength than such arguments would imply.

What, then, remains to be argued? Is it that slavery is not divine; that God did not establish it; that our doctors of divinity are mistaken? There is blasphemy in the thought. That which is inhuman cannot be divine. Who can reason on such a proposition? They that can, may - I cannot. The time for such argument is past.

At a time like this, scorching irony, not convincing argument, is needed. Oh! had I the ability, and could I reach the nation's ear, I would today pour out a fiery stream of biting ridicule, blasting reproach, withering sarcasm, and stern rebuke. For it is not light that is needed, but fire; it is not the gentle shower, but thunder. We need the storm, the whirlwind, and the earthquake. The feeling of the nation must be quickened; the conscience of the nation must be roused; the propriety of the nation must be startled; the hypocrisy of the nation must be exposed; and its crimes against God and man must be denounced.

What to the American slave is your Fourth of July? I answer, a day that reveals to him more than all other days of the year, the gross injustice and cruelty to which he is the constant victim. To him your celebration is a sham; your boasted liberty an unholy license; your national greatness, swelling vanity; your sounds of rejoicing are empty and heartless; your shouts of liberty and equality, hollow mock; your prayers and hymns, your sermons and thanksgivings, with all your religious parade and solemnity, are to him mere bombast, fraud, deception, impiety, and hypocrisy - a thin veil to cover up crimes which would disgrace a nation of savages. There is not a nation of the earth guilty of practices more shocking and bloody than are the people of these United States at this very hour.

Go search where you will, roam through all the monarchies and despotisms of the Old World, travel through South America, search out every abuse and when you have found the last, lay your facts by the side of the everyday practices of this nation, and you will say with me that, for revolting barbarity and shameless hypocrisy, America reigns without a rival.

Delivering Your Speech Effectively

Read Chapter 11, Delivering Your Speech Effectively, before completing this assignment. Your instructor will choose a speech for you to view. Answer the following questions.

1. Elaborate on the speaker's use of eye contact. Was it effective or not? Explain.

2. Identify 2 other points with regards to delivery that you believe the speaker executed well. Explain.

3. Give the speaker at least 1 suggestion for improving his/her delivery.

Effective Use of Visual Aids

Read Chapter 12, Supporting Your Ideas Visually, before completing this assignment. Your instructor will select a speech for you to view. Answer the following questions.

1. Identify at least 3 reasons to use a visual aid when presenting a speech.

2. Discuss at least 3 ways the visual aid used in the speech you viewed facilitated the speaker's purpose to inform or persuade. See pp. 281–290 on the Functions of Presentational Aids.

3. Identify 3 guidelines for presenting visual aids. Did the speaker follow each of these guidelines? Explain.

Barack Obama Speaking to Inform on Race

Read Chapter 13, Speaking to Inform, and the Barack Obama speech, "A More Perfect Union," on the following pages before completing this assignment.

1. What is the central idea that Obama is trying to get across to his audience?

2. Identify at least 2 types of evidence Obama used to convey his ideas on race in America and provide an example of each (refer to Chapter 7).

3. Chapter 13 explains that by creating informative speeches that contain relevance, novelty, and variety, speakers can capture and maintain audience attention and interest. Identify at least 2 ways that Obama employed relevance, novelty, or variety in order to capture audience attention on the issue of race in America. Provide an example of each.

Barack Obama, "A More Perfect Union"

Delivered March 18, 2008, Philadelphia, PA

Thank you so much. Thank you. Thank you. Thank you so much. Thank you. Thank you. Let me begin by thanking Harris Wofford for his contributions to this country. In so many different ways, he exemplifies what we mean by the word "citizen." And so we are very grateful to him for all the work he has done; and I'm thankful for the gracious and thoughtful introduction.

"We the people, in order to form a more perfect union." Two hundred and twenty one years ago, in a hall that still stands across the street, a group of men gathered and, with these simple words, launched America's improbable experiment in democracy. Farmers and scholars, statesmen and patriots who had traveled across the ocean to escape tyranny and persecution finally made real their Declaration of Independence at a Philadelphia convention that lasted through the spring of 1787.

The document they produced was eventually signed, but ultimately unfinished. It was stained by this nation's original sin of slavery, a question that divided the colonies and brought the convention to a stalemate until the founders chose to allow the slave trade to continue for at least 20 more years, and to leave any final resolution to future generations. Of course, the answer to the slavery question was already embedded within our Constitution—a Constitution that had at its very core the ideal of equal citizenship under the law; a Constitution that promised its people liberty and justice, and a union that could be and should be perfected over time.

And yet words on a parchment would not be enough to deliver slaves from bondage, or provide men and women of every color and creed their full rights and obligations as citizens of the United States. What would be needed were Americans in successive generations who were willing to do their part—through protests and struggles, on the streets and in the courts, through a civil war and civil disobedience, and always at great risk—to narrow that gap between the promise of our ideals and the reality of their time.

This was one of the tasks we set forth at the beginning of this presidential campaign: to continue the long march of those who came before us, a march for a more just, more equal, more free, more caring, and more prosperous America. I chose to run for President at this moment in history because I believe deeply that we cannot solve the challenges of our time unless we solve them together, unless we perfect our union by understanding that we may have different stories, but we hold common hopes; that we may not look the same and may not have come from the same place, but we all want to move in the same direction: towards a better future for our children and our grandchildren. And this belief comes from my unyielding faith in the decency and generosity of the American people. But it also comes from my own story.

I'm the son of a black man from Kenya and a white woman from Kansas. I was raised with the help of a white grandfather who survived a Depression to serve in Patton's army during World War II, and a white grandmother who worked on a bomber assembly line at Fort Leavenworth while he was overseas. I've gone to some of the best schools in America and I've lived in one of the world's poorest nations. I am married to a black American who carries within her the blood of slaves and slave owners, an inheritance we pass on to our two precious daughters. I have brothers, sisters, nieces, nephews, uncles, and cousins of every race and every hue scattered across three continents. And for as long as I live, I will never forget that in no other country on earth is my story even possible. It's a story that hasn't made me the most conventional of candidates. But it is a story that has seared into my genetic makeup the idea that this nation is more than the sum of its parts—that out of many, we are truly one.

Now throughout the first year of this campaign, against all predictions to the contrary, we saw how hungry the American people were for this message of unity. Despite the temptation to view my candidacy through a purely racial lens, we won commanding victories in states with some of the whitest populations in the country. In South Carolina, where the Confederate flag still flies, we built a powerful coalition of African Americans and white Americans. This is not to say that race has not been an issue in this campaign. At various stages in the campaign, some commentators have deemed me either "too black" or "not black enough." We saw racial tensions bubble to the surface during the week before the South Carolina primary. The press has scoured every single exit poll for the latest evidence of racial polarization, not just in terms of white and black, but black and brown as well.

And yet, it's only been in the last couple of weeks that the discussion of race in this campaign has taken a particularly divisive turn. On one end of the spectrum, we've heard the implication that my candidacy is somehow an exercise in affirmative action; that it's based solely on the desire of wild and wide-eyed liberals to purchase racial reconciliation on the cheap. On the other end, we've heard my former pastor, Jeremiah Wright, use incendiary language to express views that have the potential not only to widen the racial divide, but views that denigrate both the greatness and the goodness of our nation and that rightly offend white and black alike.

Now I've already condemned, in unequivocal terms, the statements of Reverend Wright that have caused such controversy, and in some cases, pain. For some, nagging questions remain: Did I know him to be an occasionally fierce critic of American domestic and foreign policy? Of course. Did I ever hear him make remarks that could be considered controversial while I sat in the church? Yes. Did I strongly disagree with many of his political views? Absolutely, just as I'm sure many of you have heard remarks from your pastors, priests, or rabbis with which you strongly disagree.

But the remarks that have caused this recent firestorm weren't simply controversial. They weren't simply a religious leader's efforts to speak out against perceived injustice. Instead, they expressed a profoundly distorted view of this country, a view that sees white racism as endemic and that elevates what is wrong with America above all that we know is right with America; a view that sees the conflicts in the Middle East as rooted primarily in the actions of stalwart allies like Israel instead of emanating from the perverse and hateful ideologies of radical Islam.

As such, Reverend Wright's comments were not only wrong but divisive, divisive at a time when we need unity; racially charged at a time when we need to come together to solve a set of monumental problems: two wars, a terrorist threat, a falling economy, a chronic health care crisis, and potentially devastating climate change—problems that are neither black or white or Latino or Asian, but rather problems that confront us all.

Given my background, my politics, and my professed values and ideals, there will no doubt be those for whom my statements of condemnation are not enough. Why associate myself with Reverend Wright in the first place, they may ask? Why not join another church? And I confess that if all that I knew of Reverend Wright were the snippets of those sermons that have run in an endless loop on the television sets and YouTube, if Trinity United Church of Christ conformed to the caricatures being peddled by some commentators, there is no doubt that I would react in much the same way.

But the truth is, that isn't all that I know of the man. The man I met more than twenty years ago is a man who helped introduce me to my Christian faith, a man who spoke to me about our obligations to love one another, to care for the sick and lift up the poor. He is a man who served his country as a United States Marine, and who has studied and lectured at some of the finest universities and seminaries in the country, and who over 30 years has led a church that serves the community by doing God's work here on Earth—by housing the homeless, ministering to the needy, providing day care services and scholarships and prison ministries, and reaching out to those suffering from HIV/AIDS.

In my first book, *Dreams From My Father*, I described the experience of my first service at Trinity, and it goes as follows:

People began to shout, to rise from their seats and clap and cry out, a forceful wind carrying the reverend's voice up to the rafters.

And in that single note—hope—I heard something else; at the foot of that cross, inside the thousands of churches across the city, I imagined the stories of ordinary black people merging with the stories of David and Goliath, Moses and Pharaoh, the Christians in the lion's den, Ezekiel's field of dry bones.

Those stories of survival and freedom and hope became our stories, my story. The blood that spilled was our blood; the tears our tears; until this black church, on this bright day, seemed once more a vessel carrying the story of a people into future generations and into a larger world. Our trials and triumphs became at once unique and universal, black and more than black. In chronicling our journey, the stories and songs gave us a meaning to reclaim memories that we didn't need to feel shame about—memories that all people might study and cherish and with which we could start to rebuild.

That has been my experience at Trinity. Like other predominantly black churches across the country, Trinity embodies the black community in its entirety—the doctor and the welfare mom, the model student and the former gang-banger. Like other black churches, Trinity's services are full of raucous laughter and sometimes bawdy humor. They are full of dancing and clapping and screaming and shouting that may seem jarring to the untrained ear. The church contains in full the kindness and cruelty, the fierce intelligence and the shocking ignorance, the struggles and successes, the love and, yes, the bitterness and biases that make up the black experience in America.

And this helps explain, perhaps, my relationship with Reverend Wright. As imperfect as he may be, he has been like family to me. He strengthens my faith, officiated my wedding, and baptized my children. Not once in my conversations with him have I heard him talk about any ethnic group in derogatory terms or treat whites with whom he interacted with anything but courtesy and respect. He contains within him the contradictions—the good and the bad—of the community that he has served diligently for so many years.

I can no more disown him than I can disown the black community. I can no more disown him than I can disown my white grandmother, a woman who helped raise me, a woman who sacrificed again and again for me, a woman who loves me as much as she loves anything in this world, but a woman who once confessed her fear of black men who passed her by on the street, and who on more than one occasion has uttered racial or ethnic stereotypes that made me cringe.

These people are part of me. And they are part of America, this country that I love.

Now, some will see this as an attempt to justify or excuse comments that are simply inexcusable. I can assure you it is not. And I suppose the politically safe thing to do would be to move on from this episode and just hope that it fades into the woodwork. We can dismiss Reverend Wright as a crank or a demagogue, just as some have dismissed Geraldine Ferraro in the aftermath of her recent statements as harboring some deep—deep-seated bias.

But race is an issue that I believe this nation cannot afford to ignore right now. We would be making the same mistake that Reverend Wright made in his offending sermons about America: to simplify and stereotype and amplify the negative to the point that it distorts reality. The fact is that the comments that have been made and the issues that have surfaced over the last few weeks reflect the complexities of race in this country that we've never really worked through, a part of our union that we have not yet made perfect. And if we walk away now, if we simply retreat into our respective corners, we will never be able to come together and solve challenges like health care or education or the need to find good jobs for every American.

Understanding—Understanding this reality requires a reminder of how we arrived at this point. As William Faulkner once wrote, "The past isn't dead and buried. In fact, it isn't even past." We do not need to recite here the history of racial injustice in this country. But we do need to remind ourselves that so many of the disparities that exist between the African-American community and the larger American community today can be traced directly to inequalities passed on from an earlier generation that suffered under the brutal legacy of slavery and Jim Crow. Segregated schools were, and are, inferior schools. We still haven't fixed them, 50 years after *Brown versus Board of Education*. And the inferior education they provided, then and now, helps explain the pervasive achievement gap between today's black and white students.

Legalized discrimination, where blacks were prevented, often through violence, from owning property, or loans were not granted to African-American business owners, or black homeowners could not access FHA mortgages, or blacks were excluded from unions, or the police force, or the fire department meant that black families could not amass any meaningful wealth to bequeath to future generations. That history helps explain the wealth and income gap between blacks and whites and the concentrated pockets of poverty that persist in so many of today's urban and rural communities. A lack of economic opportunity among black men and the shame and frustration that came from not being able to provide for one's family contributed to the erosion of black families, a problem that welfare policies for many years may have worsened. And the lack of basic services in so many urban black neighborhoods—parks for kids to play in, police walking the beat, regular garbage pick-up, building code enforcement—all helped create a cycle of violence, blight, and neglect that continues to haunt us.

This is the reality in which Reverend Wright and other African-Americans of his generation grew up. They came of age in the late '50s and early '60s, a time when segregation was still the law of the land and opportunity was systematically constricted. What's remarkable is not how many failed in the face of discrimination, but how many men and women overcame the odds, how many were able to make a way out of no way for those like me who would come after them.

But for all those who scratched and clawed their way to get a piece of the American Dream, there were many who didn't make it—those who were ultimately defeated, in one way or another, by discrimination. That legacy of defeat was passed on to future generations—those young men and increasingly young women who we see standing on street corners or languishing in our prisons, without hope or prospects for the future. Even for those blacks who did make it, questions of race, and racism, continue to define their world view in fundamental ways. For the men and women of Reverend Wright's generation, the memories of humiliation and doubt and fear have not gone away, nor has the anger and the bitterness of those years.

That anger may not get expressed in public, in front of white co-workers or white friends, but it does find voice in the barbershop or the beauty shop or around the kitchen table. At times, that anger is exploited by politicians to gin up votes along racial lines or to make up for a politician's own failings. And occasionally it finds voice in the church on Sunday morning, in the pulpit and in the pews. The fact that so many people are surprised to hear that anger in some of Reverend Wright's sermons simply reminds us of that old truism that the most segregated hour of American life occurs on Sunday morning.

That—That anger is not always productive. Indeed, all too often it distracts attention from solving real problems. It keeps us from squarely facing our own complicity within the African-American community in our own condition. It prevents the African-American community from forging the alliances it needs to bring about real change. But the anger is real; it is powerful, and to simply wish it away, to condemn it without understanding its roots only serves to widen the chasm of misunderstanding that exists between the races.

In fact, a similar anger exists within segments of the white community. Most working and middle-class white Americans don't feel that they've been particularly privileged by their race. Their experience is the immigrant experience. As far as they're concerned, no one handed them anything; they built it from scratch. They've worked hard all their lives, many times only to see their jobs shipped overseas or their pensions dumped after a lifetime of labor. They are anxious about their futures, and they feel their dreams slipping away. And in an era of stagnant wages and global competition, opportunity comes to be seen as a zero sum game, in which your dreams come at my expense. So when they are told to bus their children to a school across town, when they hear that an African American is getting an advantage in landing a good job or a spot in a good college because of an injustice that they themselves never committed, when they're told that their fears about crime in urban neighborhoods are somehow prejudice, resentment builds over time.

Like the anger within the black community, these resentments aren't always expressed in polite company. But they have helped shape the political landscape for at least a generation. Anger over welfare and affirmative action helped forge the Reagan Coalition. Politicians routinely exploited fears of crime for their own electoral ends. Talk show hosts and conservative commentators built entire careers unmasking bogus claims of racism while dismissing legitimate discussions of racial injustice and inequality as mere political correctness or reverse racism. And just as black anger often proved counterproductive, so have these white resentments distracted attention from the real culprits of the middle class squeeze: a corporate culture rife with inside dealing, questionable accounting practices, and short-term greed; a Washington dominated by lobbyists and special interests; economic policies that favor the few over the many. And yet, to wish away the resentments of white Americans, to label them as misguided or even racist without recognizing they are grounded in legitimate concerns, this, too, widens the racial divide and blocks the path to understanding.

This is where we are right now.

It's a racial stalemate we've been stuck in for years. And contrary to the claims of some of my critics, black and white, I have never been so naive as to believe that we can get beyond our racial divisions in a single election cycle or with a single candidate, particularly—particularly a candidacy as imperfect as my own. But I have asserted a firm conviction, a conviction rooted in my faith in God and my faith in the American people, that, working together, we can move beyond some of our old racial wounds and that, in fact, we have no choice—we have no choice if we are to continue on the path of a more perfect union.

For the African-American community, that path means embracing the burdens of our past without becoming victims of our past. It means continuing to insist on a full measure of justice in every aspect of American life. But it also means binding our particular grievances, for better health care and better schools and better jobs, to the larger aspirations of all Americans—the white woman struggling to break the glass ceiling, the white man who's been laid off, the immigrant trying to feed his family. And it means also taking full responsibility for our own lives—by demanding more from our fathers, and spending more time with our children, and reading to them, and teaching them that while they may face challenges and discrimination in their own lives, they must never succumb to despair or cynicism. They must always believe—They must always believe that they can write their own destiny.

Ironically, this quintessentially American—and, yes, conservative—notion of self-help found frequent expression in Reverend Wright's sermons. But what my former pastor too often failed to understand is that embarking on a program of self-help also requires a belief that society can change. The profound mistake of Reverend Wright's sermons is not that he spoke about racism in our society. It's that he spoke as if our society was static, as if no progress had been made, as if this country—a country that has made it possible for one of his own members to run for the highest office in the land and build a coalition of white and black, Latino, Asian, rich, poor, young and old—is still irrevocably bound to a tragic past. What we know, what we have seen, is that America can change. That is true genius of this nation. What we have already achieved gives us hope—the audacity to hope—for what we can and must achieve tomorrow.

Now, in the white community, the path to a more perfect union means acknowledging that what ails the African-American community does not just exist in the minds of black people; that the legacy of discrimination—and current incidents of discrimination, while less overt than in the past—that these things are real and must be addressed. Not just with words, but with deeds—by investing in our schools and our communities; by enforcing our civil rights laws and ensuring fairness in our criminal justice system; by providing this generation with ladders of opportunity that were unavailable for previous generations. It requires all Americans to realize that your dreams do not have to come at the expense of my dreams, that investing in the health, welfare, and education of black and brown and white children will ultimately help all of America prosper.

In the end, then, what is called for is nothing more and nothing less than what all the world's great religions demand: that we do unto others as we would have them do unto us. Let us be our brother's keeper, Scripture tells us. Let us be our sister's keeper. Let us find that common stake we all have in one another, and let our politics reflect that spirit as well.

For we have a choice in this country. We can accept a politics that breeds division and conflict and cynicism. We can tackle race only as spectacle, as we did in the O.J. trial; or in the wake of tragedy, as we did in the aftermath of Katrina; or as fodder for the nightly news. We can play Reverend Wright's sermons on every channel every day and talk about them from now until the election, and make the only question in this campaign whether or not the American people think that I somehow believe or sympathize with his most offensive words. We can pounce on some gaffe by a Hillary supporter as evidence that she's playing the race card; or we can speculate on whether white men will all flock to John McCain in the general election regardless of his policies. We can do that. But if we do, I can tell you that in the next election, we'll be talking about some other distraction, and then another one, and then another one. And nothing will change.

That is one option.

Or, at this moment, in this election, we can come together and say, "Not this time." This time we want to talk about the crumbling schools that are stealing the future of black children and white children and Asian children and Hispanic children and Native-American children. This time we want to reject the cynicism that tells us that these kids can't learn; that those kids who don't look like us are somebody else's problem. The children of America are not "those kids,"—they are our kids, and we will not let them fall behind in a 21st-century economy. Not this time. This time we want to talk about how the lines in the emergency room are filled with whites and blacks and Hispanics who do not have health care, who don't have the power on their own to overcome the special interests in Washington, but who can take them on if we do it together.

This time we want to talk about the shuttered mills that once provided a decent life for men and women of every race, and the homes for sale that once belonged to Americans from every religion, every region, every walk of life. This time we want to talk about the fact that the real problem is not that someone who doesn't look like you might take your job; it's that the corporation you work for will ship it overseas for nothing more than a profit. This time—This time we want to talk about the men and women of every color and creed who serve together, and fight together, and bleed together under the same proud flag. We want to talk about how to bring them home from a war that should've never been authorized and should've never been waged. And we want to talk about how we'll show our patriotism by caring for them, and their families, and giving them the benefits that they have earned.

I would not be running for President if I didn't believe with all my heart that this is what the vast majority of Americans want for this country. This union may never be perfect, but generation after generation has shown that it can always be perfected. And today, whenever I find myself feeling doubtful or cynical about this possibility, what gives me the most hope is the next generation—the young people whose attitudes and beliefs and openness to change have already made history in this election.

There's one story in particular that I'd like to leave you with today, a story I told when I had the great honor of speaking on Dr. King's birthday at his home church, Ebenezer Baptist, in Atlanta. There's a young, 23-year-old woman, a white woman named Ashley Baia, who organized for our campaign in Florence, South Carolina. She'd been working to organize a mostly African-American community since the beginning of this campaign, and one day she was at a roundtable discussion where everyone went around telling their story and why they were there. And Ashley said that when she was 9 years old, her mother got cancer. And because she had to miss days of work, she was let go and lost her health care. They had to file for bankruptcy, and that's when Ashley decided that she had to do something to help her mom.

She knew that food was one of their most expensive costs, and so Ashley convinced her mother that what she really liked and really wanted to eat more than anything else was mustard and relish sandwiches—because that was the cheapest way to eat. That's the mind of a 9 year old. She did this for a year until her mom got better. And so Ashley told everyone at the roundtable that the reason she had joined our campaign was so that she could help the millions of other children in the country who want and need to help their parents too.

Now, Ashley might have made a different choice. Perhaps somebody told her along the way that the source of her mother's problems were blacks who were on welfare and too lazy to work, or Hispanics who were coming into the country illegally. But she didn't. She sought out allies in her fight against injustice.

Anyway, Ashley finishes her story and then goes around the room and asks everyone else why they're supporting the campaign. They all have different stories and different reasons. Many bring up a specific issue. And finally they come to this elderly black man who's been sitting there quietly the entire time. And Ashley asks him why he's there. And he doesn't bring up a specific issue. He does not say health care or the economy. He does not say education or the war. He does not say that he was there because of Barack Obama. He simply says to everyone in the room, "I am here because of Ashley." "I'm here because of Ashley."

Now, by itself, that single moment of recognition between that young white girl and that old black man is not enough. It is not enough to give health care to the sick, or jobs to the jobless, or education to our children. But it is where we start. It is where our union grows stronger. And as so many generations have come to realize over the course of the 221 years since a band of patriots signed that document right here in Philadelphia, that is where perfection begins.

Thank you very much, everyone. Thank you.

Persuasive Speaking and Hillary Rodham Clinton's speech, "Women's Rights Are Human Rights"

Read Chapter 14, Persuasive Speaking in a Democratic Society, and Hillary Rodham Clinton's speech, "Women's Rights are Human Rights," on the following pages before completing this assignment.

1. Is Clinton's speech based on a question of fact, value, or policy?

2. Identify 2 types of evidence Clinton uses in order to appeal to audience emotion. Provide an example of each.

3. Identify at least 2 ways that Clinton cultivates her ethos in the speech. Provide an example of each.

Name:

Reasoning and Hillary Rodham Clinton's speech, "Women's Rights are Human Rights"

Read Chapter 15, Arguing Persuasively, and Hillary Rodham Clinton's speech, "Women's Rights are Human Rights," on the following pages before completing this assignment.

1. What is Clinton's claim?

2. Chapter 15 explains 4 forms of reasoning. Identify at least 1 form of reasoning used in Clinton's speech. Give examples from the speech to illustrate your answer.

Hillary Rodham Clinton, "Women's Rights are Human Rights"

Remarks to the U.N. 4th World Conference on Women
Plenary Session

September 5, 1995, Beijing, China

Thank you very much, Gertrude Mongella, for your dedicated work that has brought us to this point, distinguished delegates, and guests:

I would like to thank the Secretary General for inviting me to be part of this important United Nations Fourth World Conference on Women. This is truly a celebration, a celebration of the contributions women make in every aspect of life: in the home, on the job, in the community, as mothers, wives, sisters, daughters, learners, workers, citizens, and leaders.

It is also a coming together, much the way women come together every day in every country. We come together in fields and factories, in village markets and supermarkets, in living rooms and board rooms. Whether it is while playing with our children in the park, or washing clothes in a river, or taking a break at the office water cooler, we come together and talk about our aspirations and concern. And time and again, our talk turns to our children and our families. However different we may appear, there is far more that unites us than divides us. We share a common future, and we are here to find common ground so that we may help bring new dignity and respect to women and girls all over the world, and in so doing bring new strength and stability to families as well.

By gathering in Beijing, we are focusing world attention on issues that matter most in our lives—the lives of women and their families: access to education, health care, jobs and credit, the chance to enjoy basic legal and human rights and to participate fully in the political life of our countries.

There are some who question the reason for this conference. Let them listen to the voices of women in their homes, neighborhoods, and workplaces. There are some who wonder whether the lives of women and girls matter to economic and political progress around the globe. Let them look at the women gathered here and at Huairou—the homemakers and nurses, the teachers and lawyers, the policymakers and women who run their own businesses. It is conferences like this that compel governments and peoples everywhere to listen, look, and face the world's most pressing problems. Wasn't it after all—after the women's conference in Nairobi ten years ago that the world focused for the first time on the crisis of domestic violence?

Earlier today, I participated in a World Health Organization forum. In that forum, we talked about ways that government officials, NGOs, and individual citizens are working to address the health problems of women and girls. Tomorrow, I will attend a gathering of the United Nations Development Fund for Women. There, the discussion will focus on local—and highly successful—programs that give hard-working women access to credit so they can improve their own lives and the lives of their families.

What we are learning around the world is that if women are healthy and educated, their families will flourish. If women are free from violence, their families will flourish. If women have a chance to work and earn as full and equal partners in society, their families will flourish. And when families flourish, communities and nations do as well. That is why every woman, every man, every child, every family, and every nation on this planet does have a stake in the discussion that takes place here.

Over the past 25 years, I have worked persistently on issues relating to women, children, and families. Over the past two-and-a half years, I've had the opportunity to learn more about the challenges facing women in my own country and around the world.

I have met new mothers in Indonesia, who come together regularly in their village to discuss nutrition, family planning, and baby care. I have met working parents in Denmark who talk about the comfort they feel in knowing that their children can be cared for in safe, and nurturing after-school centers. I have met women in South Africa who helped lead the struggle to end apartheid and are now helping to build a new democracy. I have met with the leading women of my own hemisphere who are working every day to promote literacy and better health care for children in their countries. I have met women in India and Bangladesh who are taking out small loans to buy milk cows, or rickshaws, or thread in order to create a livelihood for themselves and their families. I have met the doctors and nurses in Belarus and Ukraine who are trying to keep children alive in the aftermath of Chernobyl.

The great challenge of this conference is to give voice to women everywhere whose experiences go unnoticed, whose words go unheard. Women comprise more than half the world's population, 70% of the world's poor, and two-thirds of those who are not taught to read and write. We are the primary caretakers for most of the world's children and elderly. Yet much of the work we do is not valued—not by economists, not by historians, not by popular culture, not by government leaders.

At this very moment, as we sit here, women around the world are giving birth, raising children, cooking meals, washing clothes, cleaning houses, planting crops, working on assembly lines, running companies, and running countries. Women also are dying from diseases that should have been prevented or treated. They are watching their children succumb to malnutrition caused by poverty and economic deprivation. They are being denied the right to go to school by their own fathers and brothers. They are being forced into prostitution, and they are being barred from the bank lending offices and banned from the ballot box.

Those of us who have the opportunity to be here have the responsibility to speak for those who could not. As an American, I want to speak for those women in my own country, women who are raising children on the minimum wage, women who can't afford health care or child care, women whose lives are threatened by violence, including violence in their own homes.

I want to speak up for mothers who are fighting for good schools, safe neighborhoods, clean air, and clean airwaves; for older women, some of them widows, who find that, after raising their families, their skills and life experiences are not valued in the marketplace; for women who are working all night as nurses, hotel clerks, or fast food chefs so that they can be at home during the day with their children; and for women everywhere who simply don't have time to do everything they are called upon to do each and every day.

Speaking to you today, I speak for them, just as each of us speaks for women around the world who are denied the chance to go to school, or see a doctor, or own property, or have a say about the direction of their lives, simply because they are women. The truth is that most women around the world work both inside and outside the home, usually by necessity.

We need to understand there is no one formula for how women should lead our lives. That is why we must respect the choices that each woman makes for herself and her family. Every woman deserves the chance to realize her own God-given potential. But we must recognize that women will never gain full dignity until their human rights are respected and protected.

Our goals for this conference, to strengthen families and societies by empowering women to take greater control over their own destinies, cannot be fully achieved unless all governments—here and around the world—accept their responsibility to protect and promote internationally recognized human rights. The—The international community has long acknowledged and recently reaffirmed at Vienna that both women and men are entitled to a range of protections and personal freedoms, from the right of personal security to the right to determine freely the number and spacing of the children they bear. No one—No one should be forced to remain silent for fear of religious or political persecution, arrest, abuse, or torture.

Tragically, women are most often the ones whose human rights are violated. Even now, in the late 20th century, the rape of women continues to be used as an instrument of armed conflict. Women and children make up a large majority of the world's refugees. And when women are excluded from the political process, they become even more vulnerable to abuse. I believe that now, on the eve of a new millennium, it is time to break the silence. It is time for us to say here in Beijing, and for the world to hear, that it is no longer acceptable to discuss women's rights as separate from human rights.

These abuses have continued because, for too long, the history of women has been a history of silence. Even today, there are those who are trying to silence our words. But the voices of this conference and of the women at Huairou must be heard loudly and clearly:

It is a violation of human rights when babies are denied food, or drowned, or suffocated, or their spines broken, simply because they are born girls.

It is a violation of human rights when women and girls are sold into the slavery of prostitution for human greed—and the kinds of reasons that are used to justify this practice should no longer be tolerated.

It is a violation of human rights when women are doused with gasoline, set on fire, and burned to death because their marriage dowries are deemed too small.

It is a violation of human rights when individual women are raped in their own communities and when thousands of women are subjected to rape as a tactic or prize of war.

It is a violation of human rights when a leading cause of death worldwide among women ages 14 to 44 is the violence they are subjected to in their own homes by their own relatives.

It is a violation of human rights when young girls are brutalized by the painful and degrading practice of genital mutilation.

It is a violation of human rights when women are denied the right to plan their own families, and that includes being forced to have abortions or being sterilized against their will.

If there is one message that echoes forth from this conference, let it be that human rights are women's rights and women's rights are human rights once and for all. Let us not forget that among those rights are the right to speak freely— and the right to be heard.

Women must enjoy the rights to participate fully in the social and political lives of their countries, if we want freedom and democracy to thrive and endure. It is indefensible that many women in nongovernmental organizations who wished to participate in this conference have not been able to attend—or have been prohibited from fully taking part.

Let me be clear. Freedom means the right of people to assemble, organize, and debate openly. It means respecting the views of those who may disagree with the views of their governments. It means not taking citizens away from their loved ones and jailing them, mistreating them, or denying them their freedom or dignity because of the peaceful expression of their ideas and opinions.

In my country, we recently celebrated the 75th anniversary of Women's Suffrage. It took 150 years after the signing of our Declaration of Independence for women to win the right to vote. It took 72 years of organized struggle, before that happened, on the part of many courageous women and men. It was one of America's most divisive philosophical wars. But it was a bloodless war. Suffrage was achieved without a shot being fired.

But we have also been reminded, in V-J Day observances last weekend, of the good that comes when men and women join together to combat the forces of tyranny and to build a better world. We have seen peace prevail in most places for a half century. We have avoided another world war. But we have not solved older, deeply-rooted problems that continue to diminish the potential of half the world's population.

Now it is the time to act on behalf of women everywhere. If we take bold steps to better the lives of women, we will be taking bold steps to better the lives of children and families too. Families rely on mothers and wives for emotional support and care. Families rely on women for labor in the home. And increasingly, everywhere, families rely on women for income needed to raise healthy children and care for other relatives.

As long as discrimination and inequities remain so commonplace everywhere in the world, as long as girls and women are valued less, fed less, fed last, overworked, underpaid, not schooled, subjected to violence in and outside their homes—the potential of the human family to create a peaceful, prosperous world will not be realized.

Let—Let this conference be our—and the world's—call to action. Let us heed that call so we can create a world in which every woman is treated with respect and dignity, every boy and girl is loved and cared for equally, and every family has the hope of a strong and stable future. That is the work before you. That is the work before all of us who have a vision of the world we want to see—for our children and our grandchildren.

The time is now. We must move beyond rhetoric. We must move beyond recognition of problems to working together, to have the comment efforts to build that common ground we hope to see.

God's blessing on you, your work, and all who will benefit from it.

Godspeed and thank you very much.

Name:

Informative Speech Assignment

This assignment provides you with experience in researching an informative topic, organizing your ideas, and presenting them to an audience.

Be sure to read the chapter on informative speaking before beginning this assignment.

The informative speech is designed to increase the audience's understanding of an idea. In an informative speech, you are educating your audience or sharing information with them on a chosen topic, e.g., a person, event, theory, etc. The speech may be one of description or explanation. Remember: in an informative speech you will not be urging or persuading your audience to adopt certain beliefs or behaviors.

Requirements:

1. Select a topic that you find interesting and that you believe will be of interest to your audience. Be sure the topic is one that you can research at the library. Review the Self-Inventory Questions and Brainstorming Worksheet.

2. This speech should be 4-6 minutes long. Speeches that are under or over the time limit will be penalized.

3. Speeches should be delivered extemporaneously. This means that your speech is delivered from a key word outline (see Chapter 9), is clearly prepared, and well practiced. Speeches that are read word for word will be penalized.

4. Deliver from a key word outline written on index cards.

5. Students must cite at least **four outside sources** as support within the speech. No more than 1 of the 4 sources may be from non print-based Internet sources. **These sources should be explicitly and accurately cited throughout the speech.** Review the Guide to Citing Your Sources.

Formal Outline Format for Informative Speech

Note:
* Use complete sentences.
* Label the parts of the Introduction and Conclusion as shown below.
* Use the notation format shown below (Roman numerals, capital letters, numbers, etc.)
* Your outline may have between 2-4 main points and more or less sub and sub subpoints than the example below.
* Staple your Bibliography to your outline.

Title

Specific Purpose: I want my audience to learn about/understand . . .

Thesis:

Introduction
Attention-Getting Device
[Begin with a story, startling statistic, quote, etc.]

Credibility
[Relate your personal experience with the topic or state that you have done research on the topic.]

Thesis
[A single complete sentence that embodies the idea that you want the audience to understand in order to accomplish your specific purpose.]

Enumerated Preview
[A single, complete sentence that states the 2-4 main points that you will cover in the body.]

Body

I.   First main point

        A. First subpoint (support for I)

             1. First sub-subpoint (support for subpoint A)

                  a. more specific information for sub-subpoint 1

                  b. more specific information for sub-subpoint 1

2. Second sub-subpoint (additional support for subpoint A)

B. Second subpoint

    1. First sub-subpoint (support for subpoint B)

        a. more specific information for sub-subpoint 1

        b. more specific information for sub-subpoint 1

    2. Second sub-subpoint (additional support for subpoint

        B)

        a. more specific information for sub-subpoint 2

        b. more specific information for sub-subpoint 2

Transition: [Write out transition.]

II.   Second main point

       See above under First main point

Transition: [Write out transition.]

III.   Third main point

       Etc.

Transition to conclusion: [Write out transition.]

Conclusion
Summary:
[A single, complete sentence that restates your main points.]

Concluding Remarks:
[Provide creative concluding remarks.]

Bibliography for Informative Speech Outline
[Note: The informative speech should have at least *4 outside sources, no more than 1 non-print based Internet source.* Use the sources you located in the exercise Getting Started on Your Research. Be sure to put the citation information into an accepted citation style, either MLA or APA.]

Sample Student Informative Outline
Contributed by UA student Benita Woollard

Specific Purpose: I want my audience to have a better understanding of fibromyalgia and the struggles that those with the disorder go through on a daily basis.

Thesis: Fibromyalgia is a chronic disorder that, although difficult to diagnose, has symptoms that can be treated.

Introduction:

Attention Getting Device:

> Imagine that every day, 24 hours a day, your body feels like you have the flu. Your body aches from head to toe, you don't sleep well and you feel tired and worn out all the time. On the days when you have pain on top of the aches, you cannot remember a thing and feel that your brain is in a fog. You sometimes go to speak, but your words come out jumbled, as if you are intoxicated. You look fine so people think there is nothing wrong with you.

Credibility:

> I don't have to imagine these symptoms, it is my reality. I was diagnosed with fibromyalgia in 2005 at the Cleveland Clinic. My journey to find out what was wrong with me started back in 1997 after being involved in an automobile accident. I live with pain every minute of every day.

Thesis:

> Fibromyalgia is a chronic disorder that, although difficult to diagnose, has symptoms that can be treated.

Preview:

> I would like to begin by telling you about the symptoms of fibromyalgia. Then I will describe how a diagnosis is made and I will talk about some of the current treatments.

I. Symptoms presented can vary and change with the disorder

    A. The majority of people diagnosed with fibromyalgia experience aches and pains in various degrees.

        1. All those diagnosed with fibromyalgia present symptoms of widespread pain.
        2. It is common for those suffering from fibromyalgia to have pronounced pain in their neck, shoulders and spine.
        3. At times, pain can present itself as stabbing, achy or prickly pain in upper and lower extremities.

    B. Fibromyalgia can affect a person's thought processes and their speech.

        1. Some people, myself included, have experienced what we as suffers term as "fibro fog."

            a. When a person with fibromyalgia experiences "fibro fog," they have difficulty thinking clearly.
            b. A person with the disorder may have short term memory problems as well as problems with their attention span at times.

        2. It is common for people diagnosed with fibromyalgia to also have sleep disturbances. According to "New Hope for People with Fibromyalgia," as many as 75% of people with fibromyalgia have sleep disorders.

            a. Those with sleep disorders have a lack of delta sleep, also known as REM stage sleep.
            b. According to "Fibromyalgia: A Leading Expert's Guide to Understanding and Getting Relief from the Pain that Won't Go Away," 60% of fibromyalgia patients also met criteria for chronic fatigue syndrome.
            c. Depression and anxiety can arise from the vicious cycle of lack of sleep and pain.

    C. Motor skills are also affected by fibromyalgia.

        1. Morning stiffness is common from pain and lack of rest.

2. A person with the disorder may have a difficult time walking short or long distances, depending on their pain and stiffness level at any given day.
3. You would think that sitting would make the person with the disorder feel better since walking can be difficult although actually, sitting can be just as painful.
4. A person's balance can be affected by the disorder.
   a. Shaky legs are a symptom of fibromyalgia causing the person to lose their balance.
   b. Dizziness can occur and can also make a person off balance.

D. People with fibromyalgia can have sensitivity to many sources.

1. A person with the disorder can be sensitive to hot or cold temperatures.
2. Sounds can be distressing to those with the disorder.
3. Some people can experience sensitivity to light.

[Transition: Now that we know some of the symptoms, let's talk about how the condition is diagnosed.]

II. A diagnosis is difficult and may take months or years to find the right physician.

A. Primary care doctors will recommend a rheumatologist to evaluate symptoms.
B. A rheumatologist will utilize different methods to determine a diagnosis of fibromyalgia.

1. A physical exam to determine if 11 or more out of 18 trigger or tender points exist on both sides of the body and both the upper and lower extremities is needed for a diagnosis of fibromyalgia.
2. A physician may also have the patient complete a Symptom Intensity Scale to evaluate and determine if they fit the criteria for a diagnosis of the disorder.
3. Another question the physician will ask is if they have had widespread pain for three or more months.

[Once a patient is diagnosed, their course of treatment can then be determined.]

III. Treatments can be tricky and what works for some does not work for others.

    A. Medication can sometimes be useful for managing fibromyalgia.

        1. Conventional treatments used would include medications for pain, anxiety, sleep disturbances and depression.

            a. A selective serotonin re uptake inhibitor combined with a muscle relaxer can be used for pain and to promote sleep.
            b. SNRI's are the newest drugs that some with the disorder benefit from in reducing pain and helping to fight fatigue and promote better sleep.

        2. Non-conventional supplements are sometimes used to help treat pain and promote sleep.

            a. Melatonin and Hydrotryptophan is used as a supplement for sleep.

    B. There are other options beside medications that can help with the physical and emotional symptoms of fibromyalgia.

        1. Exercise is beneficial to people living with the disorder.

            a. Aerobic exercise benefits heart and lungs and promotes a sense of well-being; it can also help in lessening sleep disturbances.
            b. Yoga, Tai Chi and stretching are good ways to keep the body flexible and toned.

        2. Relaxation techniques can be very beneficial in reducing stress and anxiety.

            a. Meditation and mindfulness are two techniques to help a person with the disorder take their focus off of their pain.
            b. Stress management can be utilized to improve pain, sleep and anxiety.

    C. The goals of the physician and patient after a diagnosis of fibromyalgia has been made would be to treat underlying causes such as depression, anxiety and feelings of helplessness and to manage the specific symptoms of the disorder such as pain, sleep problems and coping skills.

[In conclusion,]

Conclusion:

Review of Main Ideas and Concluding Remarks:

According to *The Complete Idiot's Guide to Fibromyalgia*, more people in the United States have fibromyalgia than lupus, multiple sclerosis and Parkinson's disease combined. With that in mind, it would be beneficial for both those who have the disorder and those who do not to be educated on the symptoms, diagnosis and treatments of fibromyalgia so that with raised awareness it may bring more scientific research to determine better treatments and a possible cure.

References

DiGeronimo, T.F. (M.Ed.). (2001). *New hope for people with fibromyalgia.* Roseville, California: Prima Publishing

Goldenberg, D.L. (M.D.). (2002). *Fibromyalgia: A leading expert's guide to understanding and getting relief from the pain that won't go away.* New York, New York: The Berkley Publishing Group.

Matallana, L. & Bradley, L.A. (Ph.D.). (2009). *The complete idiot's guide to fibromyalgia.* New York, New York: Penguin Group.

Wilke, W. S. (M.D.). (2010). *The Cleveland Clinic guide to fibromyalgia.* New York, New York: Kaplan Publishing.

Sample Student Informative Outline

Specific Purpose: I want my audience to understand the importance of reading to children.

Thesis: Reading to children greatly benefits them.

Introduction

Attention Getter:
> "The more that you read, the more things you will know. The more that you learn, the more places you'll go." This is a quote from the famous Dr. Seuss, which I feel stresses the importance of reading.

Credibility:
> I've been reading to my nephew since the day he was born. When he was in the hospital, the nurses gave us a book to read to him and I haven't stopped reading to him since. He turned two earlier this month and just to let you know how much reading has impacted him, he already can say his ABC's and count to ten. I credit this to him being read to since before he could understand what the words on the page meant.

Thesis:
> His progress along with what I've learned in classes and through studies, provides compelling proof that reading to children greatly benefits them.

Preview:
> Today, I'd like to discuss how important it is to read to the children in your lives, whether they are your own kids, nieces and nephews, or students if you're going to go into the teaching profession. Specifically, I will talk about how reading to children helps to build vocabulary, increases their ability to learn, and leads them to a life-long love of literature while creating a special bond between the adult and child.

> [Transition: Let's begin by looking at how being read to helps a child with language development.]

Body

I.   Reading to children helps to build their vocabulary.

    A.   Children, at a very early age, are primed to learn words and can benefit from the exposure.

        1.   According to the text book, *Children's Literature in the Elementary School*, "at 18 months, the language development is phenomenal; preoccupation with words and sounds of language is characteristic of the very young child. Books help to fulfill this insatiable desire to hear and learn new words. Hearing literature of good quality helps children to develop their full potential."

        2.   From this we can see that when it comes to reading to children we cannot start too soon.

           a.   Children are aware of sounds from birth, which eventually leads to children developing comprehension skills.

           b.   As students we all see how important that skill can be.

        3.   Reading to children can be superior to other exposures they might have.

           a.   According to the article, "The Importance of Reading to your Children for Early Literacy, " by Julie Joy, early literacy expert, "The vocabulary of an average children's picture book is greater than found on prime time television."

           b.   This is one of the many reasons it is so important to read aloud to children every day.

        4.   I've seen the results.

           a.   Reading to my nephew has greatly increased his vocabulary.

              i.   Twenty-four to thirty-six months is the ideal age where children begin talking.

      ii.   My nephew has been talking with a fairly broad vocabulary since he was 18 months old.

      iii.   He talks in full sentences and every day there is at least one new word in his vocabulary from reading to him.

   b.   According to Susan L. Hall and Luisa C. Moats, Doctors of Education, "Young children acquire a big mental dictionary from having books read to them. They also become familiar with language patterns and develop an 'ear' for written English versus spoken English."

   c.   Author/scholar Christine Wilson agrees and also notes the implications for overall mental development, stating: "Children who are introduced to books at an early age are more prone to grasp the variances in phonics, which in turn affects their language skills and cognitive abilities."

[Transition: Reading to children not only impacts their vocabulary, but it also increases their ability to learn, which is my second point and what we'll now examine more closely.]

II.   Reading to children increases their ability to learn and to perform well in school.

   A.   According to the American Association of Pediatrics, "reading is a significant aid in brain development."

      1.   Studies show that children who are read to do better in school than those who are not.

         a.   Many of you may be here because someone read to you.

         b.   Do you remember those first books you loved having read to you over and over?

         c.   You were not just enjoying someone sitting next to you opening that book, but your brain was stimulated and nurtured by those words and pictures.

2.   The American Library Association recognizes this and is a big proponent for reading to children. They submit that, "Reading to children is one – if not the most – important contributions we can make to their ability to learn."

B.   Reading also provides opportunities for physical development.

1.   According to the article, "What Is the Importance of Reading to a Child?" "by simply turning the pages of a book, motor skills are fine tuned."

2.   Also, according to the article, "Reading also stimulates the muscles of the eyes and affects the chemistry of the body by utilizing the brain."

3.   And, "The senses of sight, sound, touch, and smell are also affected."

C.   Socialization skills in the learning environment can also be impacted from reading to children.

1.   The America's Children Report showed that "children's inclinations toward education also affect their ability to learn. By instilling a love for reading and encouraging children to maintain it aids in a stronger desire to resist persuasion of peers in the negative and helps them continue to develop."

2.   For example children who enjoy reading and learning are less likely to drop out of school and get into drugs.

D.   More support for the benefits of reading to children comes from The National Academy on Education Commission on Reading also states that their research shows "that children who have been exposed to reading and other cultural experiences before they begin school have a better chance at success in formal learning."

[Transition: I've talked about the impact that reading to children has on their vocabulary development and how it readies them for the school environment helping them to become better learners. The benefits do not end there, though. Another important reason to read to children is the impact it has on their love of literature, as well as the bond that it creates between adult and child.]

III.   Reading to a child can deepen their appreciation of others.

A.   When adults read aloud to children, it's fun for everyone.

B.   Some of my favorite moments are when I'm reading to my nephew. To see him get excited about hearing a story, gets me more into the story myself.

   1.   According to Penelope Leach, Ph.D., "Once kids are hooked on being read to, they will never be bored if somebody will read, and since there are bound to be times when nobody will read and they are bored, they'll have the best possible reason to learn to read themselves."

      a.   Although children start to read themselves, this is no reason to stop reading to them.

      b.   I can remember being in high school and my college prep writing teacher would read us children's stories. Those were some of my favorite days and I was 17 years old.

   2.   If children are read to and the adult enjoys this, they will enjoy it and view reading as a fun activity.

      a.   According to the article, "Reading to Children is Important," "If a child associates reading with pleasure, they will have a greater desire to learn to read. Get involved and be dramatic and make sure that children see you enjoying reading."

         i.   Children will fall in love with the words on the page
         ii. Children will grow closer to the person reading to them.

      b.   Some of the best words you can hear when reading to a child is "Read it again." I know this because my nephew has said it so many times.

[Transition: As you can clearly see, there is so much to gain and nothing to lose when reading to children. They gain vocabulary, knowledge, a love for literature, and you gain the enjoyment of seeing all this take place.]

Conclusion

Review of Main Ideas:

    Today I have given you the reasons to read to children. We see the knowledge they will gain, the better learners they will be, and the bond they will have to literature and to you.

Creative Concluding Remarks:

    So remember these reasons and read to the various children in your life. Help them grow and help them know what Dr. Seuss knew:

        "The more that you read, the more things you will know.
        The more that you learn, the more places you'll go."

Works Cited

Brennan, Stephanie. "Once Upon A Time: An Internet Webquest on Successful Child Readers." 2002. 10 Feb. 2003. http://www.kn.pacbell.com/wired/fil/pages/webeffects1.html

Force, Pam. "Reading to Children Increases their Ability to Learn." 2000. 10 Feb. 2003. www.geocities.com/prlforce

Hall, Susan L. and Luisa C. Moats, Ed.D. "Reading to Children Is Important," Excerpt from the book *Straight Talk About Reading*. 10 Feb. 2003 http://www.acslp.org/homepages/Siles/september.html

Huck, Charlotte S., Susan Helper, Janet Hickman, and Barbara Z. Kiefer. *Children's Literature in the Elementary School: Seventh Edition*. New York, NY: McGraw-Hill Publishing, 2001.

Joy, Julie. "The Importance of Reading to Children for Early Literacy." 2002. 10 Feb. 2003. http://ma.essortment.com/earlyliteracyp_rxjf.htm

Leach, Penelope, Ph.D. "The Importance of Reading to Children." 1997. 10 Feb. 2003. http://www.amazon.com/exec/obidos/tg/feature/-/145696/103-7842400-6271860

Wilson, Christina. "What is the Importance of Reading to a Child?" 2002. 10 Feb. 2003. http://www.co.essortment.com/childreadingim_rhqw.htm

Persuasive Speech Assignment
Problem-Solution Design

This assignment provides you with experience in researching a persuasive topic, organizing your ideas, and presenting them to an audience.

Be sure to read Chapters 14 and 15 on persuasive speaking before beginning this assignment.

Whereas, in the informative speech you acted as the teacher/educator, in the persuasive speech you will be advocating or urging your audience to believe or act in a particular way. Recall from Chapter 14, persuasive speeches may argue a question of fact (the existence or nonexistence of something), value (the moral worth of something), or policy (a course of action).

In this assignment, you will deliver a persuasion speech of policy following the problem-solution design.

Requirements:

1.   Select a topic that you find interesting and that you believe will be of interest to your audience. Be sure the topic is one that you can research at the library.

      Be sure the topic lends itself to a policy speech based on the problem-solution design. Consider topics that center around a problem—local, national, or international—for which you can propose a solution/course of action/policy.

      Avoid "time-worn" topics. These are topics that, although important, have likely been heard before by your audience. Examples of time-worn topics are drinking and driving, smoking, seat belts, death penalty, abortion. Select a topic that is timely, original, and one of which your audience may not be aware or have knowledge. Review the Self-Inventory Questions and Brainstorming Worksheet. Read the *New York Times* or other credible newspapers or news magazine for recent topics of importance.

2.   This speech should be 5-7 minutes long. Speeches that are under or over the time limit will be penalized.

3. Students are required to use a visual aid during the delivery of this speech. At least one of the persuasive speech presentations should incorporate 3-5 PowerPoint slides designed and constructed by the student. Poster boards, black or dry erase boards, or overhead projectors are not permissible as visual aids.

4. Speeches should be delivered extemporaneously. This means that your speech is delivered from a key word outline (see Chapter 10), is clearly prepared, and well practiced. Speeches that are read word for word will be penalized.

5. Deliver from a key word outline written on index cards.

6. Students must cite at least **six outside sources** as support within the speech. No more than 2 of the 6 sources may be from non print-based Internet sources. **These sources should be explicitly and accurately cited throughout the speech where the speaker provides information from the given source.**

Formal Outline Format for Problem-Solution Speech

Note:
* Use complete sentences.
* Label the parts of the Introduction and Conclusion as shown below.
* Use the notion format shown below (Roman numerals, capital letters, numbers, etc.)
* Your outline will only have 2 main points as shown below.
* Staple your Bibliography to your outline.

Title

Specific Purpose: I want my audience to be persuaded/agree/accept. . . .

Thesis:

Introduction
Attention-Getting Device
[Begin with a story, startling statistic, quote, etc.]

Credibility
[Relate your personal experience with the topic or state that you have done research on the topic.]

Thesis
[A single complete sentence that embodies the idea that you want the audience to accept in order to accomplish your specific purpose.]

Enumerated Preview
[A single, complete sentence that states the problem and solution that you will cover in the body.]

Body

I.   First main idea is your statement of the problem ("The lack of affordable housing near campus is a problem for college students.")
       A. Description of the problem
              1. describe the problem
              2. describe the problem

Transition: Now let me explain why this problem is relevant/important.

      B. Importance of the problem
             1. extent of the problem
             2. who is affected and how

Transition: Now let's talk about what will happen if the problem is not addressed.

      C. Explain what will happen if the problem is not solved
             1.

             2.

Transition to Second main idea, Solution

II.   Second main idea is your statement of solution ("In order to address the lack of affordable housing near campus, I propose that the city of Akron adopt....")
      A. Description of the solution
             1. show how it addresses the problem
             2. describe how it can be implemented

Transition: Now let's see what will happen if we adopt this proposal

      B. Picture the expected results
             1. elaborate
             2. elaborate

Transition to conclusion: [Write out transition.]
Conclusion
Summary:
[A single, complete sentence that restates your main points.]

Appeal:
[Repeat appeal

Concluding Remarks:
[Provide creative concluding remarks.]

Bibliography
[Note: Persuasive speech should have least 6 outside sources, no more than 2 non-print based Internet sources.
Use MLA or APA citation style.]

Sample Student Outline—Problem-Solution

Contributed by UA student Olivia Jerkes

The Importance of School Levies

Specific Purpose: I want my audience to be persuaded to vote for school levies.

Thesis: Public schools are in need of more funding beyond the state aid to achieve greatness and this means asking our communities to pass levies.

Introduction

Attention-getting Device:

Picture the bright lights surrounding the field as the marching band is proudly playing the school fight song at the homecoming football game. The cheerleaders are rooting on the team and encouraging the crowd. The fans are pumped and ready for the big game. Feel the cold air in your face but don't mind because it's high school football season. Parents are in the grandstands proudly supporting their son or daughter. But, if school levies don't pass it's lights out and it's all quiet. Your school sports program has been eliminated and shut down.

Credibility:

This scenario has become a reality for many public school students in the state of Ohio. My 14 year old nephew is a student in the Revere school district. A 2010 pamphlet for the Revere Local School District says that because of the failed levy in November of 2010 all Middle School sports programs and activities will be eliminated. High school students who want to participate in sports will be required to pay $450 per sport, join band or even choir. After school tutoring, elementary librarians and elementary guidance counselors will be completely phased out. The devastated parents, students and staff put forth a passionate effort to pass a special election in February, 2011 and it paid off. As David Gifford, the president of F.A.C.T.S. or Families and Community Together for Schools, states in the letter to the editor in the *West Side Leader* in February 2011 "We have shown that we can pull together as a community and make a statement that continuing to provide excellent schools is important."

Thesis:

Public schools are in need of more funding beyond the state aid to achieve greatness and this means asking our communities to pass levies.

Preview:

Today I will discuss the problems that result when schools are not adequately funded. I will then propose a solution that enables schools to maintain a their extra-curricular programs.

Body

I.   Without funding and support of our community, school districts will struggle to continue to provide our children with a high quality educational experience.

    A.   If levies keep failing we will see fewer opportunities that are currently available for students.

        1.   Course offerings such as foreign language classes, performing arts programs and field trips will be drastically reduced if not completely eliminated.

        2.   Also increased class sizes will not be able to function without a participation fee. John Thompson states in a *USA Today* online article *At Some Schools, Budget Cuts Put the Kibosh on Sports* in 2009 that "one day sports will be out there for people who have money." Where will this leave families who have multiple children or those families who aren't as privileged? Will they miss out on the learning experience of social, personal and behavioral skills that children need?

[Transition: Without extra-curricular activities our children become bored and stagnant.]

    B.   By not providing such opportunities we will see consequences.

        1.   Our youth will miss out on the learning experience of social, personal and behavioral skills they need.

2.   An increase of low self-esteem and a decline in academic performance will be part of the outcome.

3.   Successful employment futures may become bleak due to the lack of technology upgrades. How will future generations compete in a world they don't understand? In an article in U.S. News & World Report published in 2009 First Lady Michelle Obama stated that "children in America will be competing with children around the world for the same jobs, a good education is no longer just one road to opportunity-it's the only road."

[Transition: We still have a chance to make a difference in our children's lives.]

II.   Voting in favor of school levees when they appear on the ballot can ensure that our schools have adequate funding to keep extra-curricular activities in tact.

A.   Extra-curricular programs increase positive attitudes and behavior.

1.   A study by CASEL or the collaborative for Academic, Social, and Emotional Learning in 2007 found that after-school programs improve significantly in feelings, behavioral and school performance.

2.   We can increase the odds that our youth can develop into well rounded, productive individuals who will one day become our leaders, teachers, doctors or our armed forces.

B.   In keeping our schools in excellence standards our community benefits.

1.   When our schools keep high standards and provide quality education our property value goes up.

2.   Also when you have the combination of good schools and increased property value the community grows according to Connie Chung's paper Using Public Schools as Community Development Tools in 2002. This in turn spurs economic growth.

593

Conclusion

Review of Main Ideas and Concluding Remarks:

Let me leave you with the realization that without the help of the community our children will sadly miss out on the good experiences we had that made school so memorable. By reducing the opportunities in advancement and extra-curricular activities we are increasing a troubled outcome of poor social, personal and behavioral skills. I am asking you to please consider voting yes to the levy in May so that we can continue to keep our standards of excellence in education. In my heart, I believe every child deserves a chance and a strong educational base to stand on. People invest in a home with good bones and provide updates to increase its value. Aren't our children worth the investment?

Works Cited

Boroff, Randy S., and Dave Forrest. *Critical Message About Upcoming Levy.*
    Ohio: Revere Local school district, 2010. Print.

Chung, Connie. *Using Public Schools as Community-Development Tools:*
    Strategies for Community-Based Developers. Massachusetts: Neighbor
    Works, 2002. Print.

Durlak, Joseph, and Roger P. Weissberg. *The Impact of After-School Programs*
    That Promote Personal and Social Skills. Illinois: CASEL, 2007. Print

Gifford, David. "FACTS President thanks Revere Community," Letter. *West Side*
    Leader 17 February 2011:2.Print.

Obama, Michelle. "America's Future Lies in its Teachers." *U.S. News & World*
    Report Nov. 2009:36-37. Print.

Thompson, John. "At Some Schools, Budget Cuts Put the Kibosh on Sports."
    USA Today 2 September. 2009. Web. 20 February. 2011.

Peer Evaluation—Problem-Solution Speech

Speaker:_____

Critic:_____**Date:**_____

What seems to be the topic/central idea of this speech?

_____

1. Write a helpful comment about something the speaker did effectively in the *introduction*.

2. Comment helpfully about how the speaker *organized the main points.*

3. Comment helpfully about how the speaker used *supporting material* to help you understand the topic and find it interesting and relevant.

4. Comment helpfully about the *organizational pattern* the speaker used to help the speech flow.

5. Comment helpfully about the speaker's *conclusion:* in terms of summarizing what has been covered, telling you where you could learn more about the topic, and ending memorably.

6. Comment helpfully about how the speaker used *transitions* to let you know where you were in the speech.

7. Comment helpfully about how the speaker used a *presentational aid.* What was it and how effective was it?

8. Comment helpfully about the speaker's *delivery*, which should be well prepared and conversational, expressive, maintaining eye contact, avoiding vocal pauses and verbal clutter.

9. What did you like best about this speech?

10. What do you know now that didn't before?

11. What will you remember in a week?

Persuasive Speech Assignment
Motivated Sequence Design

This assignment provides you with experience in researching a persuasive topic, organizing your ideas, and presenting them to an audience.

Be sure to read Chapters 14 and 15 on persuasive speaking before beginning this assignment.

Whereas, in the informative speech you acted as the teacher/educator, in the persuasive speech you will be advocating or urging your audience to believe or act in a particular way. Recall from Chapter 14, persuasive speeches may argue a question of fact (the existence or nonexistence of something), value (the moral worth of something), or policy (a course of action).

In this assignment, you will deliver a persuasion speech of policy following the motivated sequence design.

Requirements:

1. Select a topic that you find interesting and that you believe will be of interest to your audience. Be sure the topic is one that you can research at the library.

    Be sure the topic lends itself to a policy speech based on the motivated sequence design. Consider topics that center around a need that requires attention and for which you can propose a solution/course of action requiring immediate attention on the part of your audience.

    Avoid "time-worn" topics. These are topics that, although important, have likely been heard before by your audience. Examples of time-worn topics are drinking and driving, smoking, seat belts, death penalty, abortion. Select a topic that is timely, original, and one of which your audience may not be aware or have knowledge. Review the Self-Inventory Questions and Brainstorming Worksheet. Read the *New York Times* or other credible newspapers or news magazine for recent topics of importance.

2. This speech should be 6-8 minutes long. Speeches that are under or over the time limit will be penalized.

3. Students are required to use a visual aid during the delivery of this speech. At least one of the persuasive speech presentations should

incorporate 3-5 PowerPoint slides designed and constructed by the student. Poster boards, black or dry erase boards, or overhead projectors are not permissible as visual aids.

4.   Speeches should be delivered extemporaneously. This means that your speech is delivered from a key word outline (see Chapter 9), is clearly prepared, and well-practiced. Speeches that are read word for word will be penalized.

5.   Deliver from a key word outline written on index cards.

6.   Students must cite at least **six outside sources** as support within the speech. No more than 2 of the 6 sources may be from non print-based Internet sources. **These sources should be explicitly and accurately cited throughout the speech where the speaker provides information from the given source.**

Formal Outline Format for Motivated Sequence Speech

Note:
* Use complete sentences.
* Label the parts of the Introduction and Conclusion as shown below.
* Use the notion format shown below (Roman numerals, capital letters, numbers, etc.)
* Your outline may have between 2-4 main points and more or less sub and sub subpoints than the example below.
* Staple your Bibliography to your outline.

Title

Specific Purpose: I want my audience to be persuaded/agree/accept....

Thesis:

Introduction
Arouse attention:
[Begin with a story, startling statistic, quote, etc. that directs audience attention on the problem.]

Credibility:
[Relate your personal experience with the topic or state that you have done research on the topic.]

Thesis:
[A single, complete sentence that embodies the idea that you want the audience to accept in order to accomplish your specific purpose.]

Enumerated Preview:
[A single, complete sentence that states the problem, solution, and positive results that you will discuss in the body.]

Body

I.   First main idea is your statement of the need that requires attention. ("At-risk teens need after school programs that are affordable and accessible.")
        A. Description of the need
            1. describe the need
            2. describe the need

Transition: Now let me explain why this need requires our attention.

        B. Importance of addressing need
            1. extent of the problem
            2. who is affected and how

Transition to second main idea: Gratification of the need

II.   Second main idea is your statement of solution or how the need can be gratified. ("In order to ensure the accessibility of enriching activities for at-risk teens, I propose....)
        A. Description of the solution
            1. show how it addresses the problem
            2. support
        B. Explain what audience members can do to remedy the situation.

Transition to third main idea: Visualization of the results

III.   Third main idea visualizes the results of adopting the solution
        A. Use vivid language to picture the positive results of enacting the solution.
        B. Elaborate

Transition to conclusion: [Write out transition.]

Conclusion
Summary:
[A single, complete sentence that restates your three main points.]

Appeal:
[Appeal to audience to take a specific action.]

Concluding Remarks:
[Provide creative concluding remarks.]

Bibliography

[Note:
Persuasive speech should have least 6 outside sources, no more than 2 non-print based Internet sources.
Use MLA or APA citation style.]

Sample Student Outline—Motivated Sequence Speech

Overpopulation of Humane Societies and Shelters
Ashley Cosher

Specific Purpose:
I want my audience to learn about the problems Humane Societies are experiencing and persuade them to help out by adopting animals or volunteering.

Introduction:

Attention Getter:
Every day, lives are being taken for no reason. Animals that enter humane societies and shelters do not always make it out and hundreds of thousands of animals do not get a chance at life.

Credibility:
My family has adopted cats from Human Societies three times, and they are truly part of the family. We enjoy being able to give animals a second chance at a better life.

Thesis:
Humane societies are a second chance for animals; however, they are becoming overpopulated and do not have enough help; volunteering and adoption does not only benefit the humane society and animals, it can also benefit you.

Preview:
Today I am going to talk about the overpopulation of animals and lack of help in humane societies and then I will talk about what you can do to help.

Body:

I.   Humane Societies and Shelters are becoming overpopulated with animals at a rapid pace.
    A.   Decreasing the number of animals brought into Humane Societies and Shelters and providing extra help for these shelters is vital.
        1.   According to a 2010 article by Francis Hamilton called, *Leading and Organizing Social Change for Companion Animals,* More than six-million animals enter shelters each year.
            a.   Around 4.2 million will be euthanized (killed).
            b.   This does not include animals that are already in the shelter from previous years.
        2.   There is a lack of suitable homes for these animals.
        3.   There is a lack of people available to help with animals in shelters.

Transition: Now let me explain why this need requires our attention.

B. Without any action, animals will continue overpopulating shelters, resulting in more and more euthanized animals.

  1. In a 2010 article, *Understanding Pet Overpopulation,* Rachael Whitcomb stated that shelters are not required to keep statistics so there is no real known number of how many animals are euthanized each year. It is thought to be around tens of millions of animals.

      a. Francis Hamilton's article stated most animals are killed for non-health reasons and are simply killed to make more room for new animals. Over 50% of animals brought to shelters are completely healthy.

      b. These animals are brought in simply because they have too much energy, keep having litters, their owners are moving and do not want the hassle of bringing them along, etc.

  2. Animals are mainly affected by this; however, we are as well.

      a. Humane Societies struggle to afford food and other supplies to take care of the animals. Those working at the shelters can be overwhelmed with all of the animals that need their care and attention.

      b. By not having pets fixed, people end up with unwanted pets that usually end up in shelters.

          i. In a 2010 USA Today article by Sharon Peters called, *Sterilizing Pets Isn't a Priority for New Owners,* it stated 13% of dog owners and 19% of cat owners end up with litters.

          ii. 38% of 18-34-year-olds do not have their pets spayed or neutered.

      c. Animals are still the main victims.

          i. According to Martha Armstrong's article, *Statistics, Truth, and Action,* about 80% of cats that end up in shelters are euthanized.

          ii. Their lives are cut short because no one can take them in.

          iii. The life they do live is mostly spent in small, crowded cages.

      d. Rachel Whitcomb had another 2010 article called, *Understanding Pet Overpopulation.* In it she interviewed Dr. Lila Miller, a veterinary advisor for *The American Society for the Prevention of Cruelty to Animals.* She stated, "I get distressed when I hear people saying there's no overpopulation here...Tell that to the dogs that are still dying in shelters; that they're in the wrong place at the wrong time."

Transition: Now that you are aware of the needs of Humane Societies and Shelters, I would like to move into the gratification of this need.

II.   In order to decrease the overpopulation of animals in shelters and improve the shelter services, I propose fixing your animals, looking into adoption, and volunteering your time.
    A.   Spaying and neutering your animals limits the number of animals in your area.
        1.   In a 2012 article called, *Take the Bite out of Pet Costs,* by Jessica Anderson, spaying and neutering can cost around $145 for cats and range from $190-$220 for dogs depending on their size.
        2.   You can talk to your local shelters, however, and ask about low-cost or even free services.
    B.   Adopting an animal from a Humane Society or shelter gives that animal a second chance.
    C.   If you are unable to adopt a pet of your own, you can make a difference by volunteering your time at a shelter.
        1.   The Humane Society of Greater Akron states as a volunteer you will help clean cages, help with events and programs, play with the animals, or even something as simple as working with adoption paperwork.
        2.   You can also help advertise for the shelter and participate in adoption fairs to help increase the number of adoptions.

Transition: These three simple gratifications will help tremendously improve Humane Societies and begin visualizing a better future for these animals.

III.   Animals are not the only ones who benefit from these solutions; we benefit as well.
    A.   The animals helped and/or adopted have new homes and better lives.
        1.   They are no longer confined in small cages.
        2.   They have owners to pay direct attention toward them instead of attention spread out to all the animals in the shelter.
    B.   We are benefitted as well.
        1.   By volunteering we get service hours that can be used on resumes.
        2.   By spaying or neutering our pets, fewer litters will be born decreasing the number of stray animals.
        3.   By adopting an animal, we get all of the benefits of a pet.
            a.   Pets are loyal companions.
            b.   Pets are entertaining and loving.
    C.   The shelters are benefitted tremendously.
        1.   The animals will be better taken care of with more help.
        2.   The shelter will not be as crowded, allowing more personal care toward the animals.
        3.   With less crowded shelters, there will be more room for animals that truly need the shelter.

Transition: With a few small actions, we can make a huge difference in the lives of animals.

Conclusion:

Summary:
The overpopulation of animals and lack of assistance in Humane Societies and shelters is a major problem and by spaying and neutering your pets, looking into adopting an animal, or volunteering your time at a shelter, we will see major improvements in the quality of shelters.

Call to Action:
I encourage you all to do what you can to help out animals in these shelters. Even if you do not want a pet of your own, you can still find ways to help out by volunteering your time at a local shelter.

Summary Statement:
With our busy lives, animals tend to be forgotten. With a few small actions we can make a difference in the lives these animals live. Taking care of our pets we already own, making room for new pets, and volunteering are three small steps to we can take today.

Works Cited

Anderson, Jessica. "Take the Bite out of Pet Costs." 66.10 (n.d.): 69-72. *Academic Search Complete.* Oct. 2012. Web. 12 Nov. 2012.

Armstrong, Martha. "Statistics, Truth, and Action." 127.1 (n.d.): 32. *Academic Search Complete.* Jan.-Feb. 1994. Web. 12 Nov. 2012.

Hamilton, Francis E. "Leading and Organizing Social Change for Companion Animals." 23.3 (n.d.): 277-92. *Academic Search Complete.* Sept. 2010. Web. 13 Nov. 2012.

Peters, Sharon L. "Sterilizing Pets Isn't a Priority for New Owners." *USA Today* n.d.: n. pag. 13 Jan. 2010. Web. 13 Nov. 2012.

"Want to Volunteer?" *Humane Society of Greater Akron.* N.p., 2012. Web. 17 Nov. 2012.

Whitcomb, Rachael. "Understanding Pet Overpopulation." 41.4 (n.d.): 30-32. *Academic Search Complete.* Apr. 2010. Web. 13 Nov. 2012.

Sample Student Speech
Giving of Yourself

Specific Purpose: To persuade my audience to volunteer their services to worthy organizations

Thesis: When college students volunteer, both the community and the volunteer benefit.

Introduction

Attention-Arousing material (focuses attention on the problem):

How pressed are you for time? How many hours each day do you go to class? Four? Five? Maybe six if you have a lot of labs. How much time each day do you spend studying or preparing for class? Two hours? Three? This does leave a little bit of time left over. Time you might waste drinking coffee in the student center or just frittering away without accomplishing anything. There is something really constructive you could be doing. You could work as a student volunteer for some local organization that needs your help.

Establish credibility:

Last year I began to work one afternoon a week at the Union Mission's soup kitchen that feeds the homeless. It doesn't take much of my time. I leave campus at about 3:30 and could be back before 6:30 except that many times I stay and eat my own dinner with the people who rely on the Mission to feed them. This experience has been very rewarding for me in many ways. I have a great sense of doing something worthwhile with my time and I've learned and awful lot about people- things I couldn't learn from textbooks in my sociology courses.

Thesis:

When college students volunteer, both the community and the volunteer benefit.

Preview:

Today I'd like to talk with you about the need for volunteers in our community, about how you can become involved, and about what both you and the community can gain from volunteering.

> [transition: I'll begin by telling you about the need for volunteers.]

Body

I. Many worthy organizations in our community need volunteers.

    A. There are many organizations to choose from.

        1. You could pick from the Union Mission, Big Sisters and Big Brothers, AIDS Awareness, shelters for battered or homeless, the Red Cross, museums, religious organizations, nursing homes, or many others.

        2. You can select an organization that interests you or ties in with your studies.

    B. These groups desperately need volunteers.

        1. The public and private funding for these organizations is not sufficient to keep them running.

        2. According to Patsy Vesta, assistant director of student activities, the number of volunteers in Davis has steadily decreased over the last five years.

        3. Without volunteers to keep them going, some of these groups may have to cut back on services or close their doors.

        [transition: I'm sure you see that there is a need for volunteers. But, you may be asking, how can I get involved? Let me tell you.]

II. The state of California has made it easy for us to get involved be passing the Human Corps Bill last year.

    A. The Corps provides funds for volunteer coordinators.

        1. Patsy Vesta is the volunteer coordinator on campus.

            a. She works out of the student's activities office in Maynard Hall.

            b. She will help you find volunteer work that fits your interests and that you can work into your schedule.

        2. Bruce Tsou is the city volunteer coordinator.

            a. He has an office in city hall.

            b. His office hours are from 3 to 9pm weekdays.

B. The Corps helps match volunteers and organizations.

    1. They publish a monthly list of organizations that need volunteers.

    2. They provide weekly updates to local radio and TV stations and to the campus and city newspapers.

    3. Their coordinators screen volunteers before referring them to groups.

    [transition: You see, it's not that hard to get involved. All you really have to do is walk over to Maynard Hall and talk with Patsy. Now let's look at what may happen if you volunteer and what may happen if you don't.]

III. Volunteering benefits both the volunteer and the community.

    A. The personal rewards of volunteering are great.

        1. I feel like I'm doing something that benefits those less fortunate.

        2. I feel like someone really appreciates my efforts (narrative about Laticia M.)

        3. I've learned to work as part of a team.

        4. I've learned that even menial work has its rewards.

        5. I've learned to be more sensitive to others and not prejudge them.

        6. I've learned to appreciate the good things I have.

    B. The benefits to the community are also important.

        1. Without the fourteen volunteers who work at the soup kitchen only half as many people could be fed.

        2. Without the twenty volunteers at the Indian Heritage Museum, it could only be open three days a week.

3. Without a volunteer Big Brother, ten-year-old Kevin might be repeating the third grade this year (tell story).

[transition: summary serves as conclusion]

Conclusion

I.   *Summary Statement*: As you can see, volunteering is very important to our community and has personal rewards as well. It's not hard to get involved. Just go over to the student activities office in Maynard Hall and ask for Patsy Vesta or go down to city hall and ask for Bruce Tsou. Either one will be glad to get you started.

II.   *Concluding remarks*: The soup kitchen, shelters for the battered or homeless, the Red Cross, a church or synagogue, a museum. What's your cup of tea?

III. *Call for action*: Won't you join with me and work to make our community a better place to live. Feel good about yourself. Be a volunteer. Act today.

Reprinted from Public Speaking, Instructor's Resource Manual (1993), by permission of Pearson Education.

Works Cited

Lunsford, Charlotte. "Volunteering in 2001." *Vital Speeches of the Day*, September 15, 1988, 729.

University of California Human Corps Taskforce. "Interim Guidelines for Human Corps Criteria." undated.

Wylie, Frank. "Crisis Time for Non-Profits." *Vital Speeches of the Day*, January 1, 1989, 170.

Interview with Patsy Vesta, Assistant Director of Student Activities and Volunteer Coordinator, September 27, 1990.

Interview with Fredericka Hotchkins, Director, Union Mission's Food Services, September 24, 1990.

Interview with Antonio Valaquez, Director, Big Brothers and Big Sister of Davis, September 26, 1990.

Persuasive Speech Evaluation Form
Motivated Sequence Design

Speaker:

Topic:

Grade:

Evaluation Key:	+ Excellent	✔ Satisfactory
- Needs improvement	0 Failed to complete	

Introduction:

Comments:

Gained attention and focused on the problem ___

Revealed topic and stated central idea ____

Established credibility ___

Previewed main ideas (need, gratification, results) ___

Body:

Stated the need ____

Described need using evidence ____

Explained need using evidence ____

Described solution using evidence ____

Visualized results of acting ____

Use of transitions between main & sub points ___

Used a variety of types of support___

Use of reasoning ___

Cited at least 6 sources smoothly,
   contained necessary information _____

Conclusion:

Transition to closing ___

Summary of main ideas ___

Specific appeal to action ___

Creative concluding remarks ___

Visual Aid:

Incorporated smoothly ___

Neat and professional in appearance ___

Delivery:

Eye contact ___

Extemporaneous delivery ___

Gestures ___

Vocal variety ___

Enthusiasm ___

Rate ___

Volume ___

Articulation ___

Avoided distracting mannerisms, etc ___

Avoided fillers (ya know, um, like) ___

Overall appearance of practice and preparation ___

Speech completed within time limit ___

Comments:

Peer Evaluation—Motivated Sequence Speech

Speaker: _____

Critic: _____ Date: _____

1. Write a helpful comment about something the speaker did effectively in the introduction.

2. Comment helpfully about how the speaker organized the main points.

3. Comment helpfully about how the speaker used supporting material to help you understand the topic and find it interesting and relevant.

4. Comment helpfully about the organizational pattern the speaker used to help the speech flow.

5. Comment helpfully about the speaker's conclusion: in terms of summarizing what has been covered, telling you where you could learn more about the topic, and ending memorably.

6. Comment helpfully about how the speaker used transitions to let you know where you were in the speech.

7. Comment helpfully about how the speaker used a presentational aid. What was it and how effective was it?

8. Comment helpfully about the speaker's delivery, which should be well practiced and conversational, expressive, maintaining eye contact, avoiding vocal pauses and verbal clutter.

9. Has the speaker persuaded you to change or take action?
   (circle one):   yes   somewhat   no
   If so, how will you change? If not, why not?

10. What was most important persuasive in the speech?

11. What was least persuasive in the speech?

12. What will you remember in a week?